THE CLASSICAL TRADITION IN SOCIOLOGY

THE AMERICAN TRADITION

THE CLASSICAL TRADITION IN SOCIOLOGY

THE AMERICAN TRADITION

VOLUME I

EDITED BY
JEFFREY ALEXANDER
RAYMOND BOUDON
MOHAMED CHERKAOUI

SAGE Publications
London • Thousand Oaks • New Delhi

Editorial arrangement © Jeffrey Alexander, Raymond Boudon, Mohamed Cherkaoui, 1997

First published 1997

All rights reserved. No part of this publication may be reproduced, stored in a retrieval system, transmitted or utilized in any form or by any means, electronic, mechanical, photocopying, recording or otherwise, without permission in writing from the Publishers.

Every effort has been made to trace all the copyright holders of the material reprinted herein, but if any have been inadvertently overlooked the publishers will be pleased to make the necessary arrangements at the first opportunity.

SAGE Publications Ltd
6 Bonhill Street
London EC2A 4PU

SAGE Publications Inc
2455 Teller Road
Thousand Oaks, California 91320

SAGE Publications India Pvt Ltd
32, M-Block Market
Greater Kailash
New Delhi 110 048

British Library Cataloguing in Publication Data

A catalogue record for this book is available from the British Library

ISBN 0-7619-5325-6 (set of four volumes)

Library of Congress Cataloging in Publication data has been applied for

Typeset in Berthold Baskerville by The Bardwell Press, Oxford, England
Printed in Great Britain at the Cambridge University Press, Cambridge, England

CONTENTS

VOLUME I

Appendix of Sources
General Introduction   i
Introduction to the Major Sections   xvi

THE EMERGENCE OF AMERICAN SOCIOLOGY: FROM THE ENLIGHTENMENT TO THE FOUNDING FATHERS

1. The Unanimous Declaration of the Thirteen United States of America   1
2. The Union as a Safeguard Against Domestic Faction and Insurrection   *James Madison*   4
3. The Structure of the Government Must Furnish the Proper Checks and Balances Between the Different Departments   *Alexander Hamilton or James Madison*   10
4. The Program in Practice   *Peter Gay*   14
5. Democracy in America: Volume I   *Alexis de Tocqueville*   25
6. Democracy in America: Volume II   *Alexis de Tocqueville*   40
7. The Transcendentalist   *Ralph W. Emerson*   51
8. Where I Lived, and What I Lived For   *Henry David Thoreau*   63
9. William Graham Sumner (1840–1910)   *Daniel W. Rossides*   74
10. Lester F. Ward (1841–1913)   *Daniel W. Rossides*   91
11. W. E. B. Du Bois as a Social Investigator: *The Philadelphia Negro*, 1899   *Martin Bulmer*   108
12. The Causes of Race Superiority   *Edward A. Ross*   127
13. The World of The Academic Quantifiers: The Columbia University Family and its Connections   *Stephen P. Turner*   142

THE EMERGENCE OF AMERICAN SOCIOLOGY: THE CLASSICAL TRADITION

14. The Work of George Mead   *John Dewey*   165
15. The Chicago School of Sociology: What Made it a "School"?   *Martin Bulmer*   168
16. George Herbert Mead and the Chicago Tradition of Sociology   *Berenice M. Fisher and Anselm L. Strauss*   183

17.	The Self as Social Structure *George Herbert Mead*	214
18.	The Self as Sentiment and Reflection *Charles Horton Cooley*	220
19.	Primary Groups *Charles Horton Cooley*	226
20.	*The Polish Peasant in Europe and America*: A Landmark of Empirical Sociology *Martin Bulmer*	231
21.	Situational Analysis: The Behavior Pattern and the Situation *W. I. Thomas*	254
22.	Introduction to *Robert E. Park. On Social Control and Collective Behavior* *Ralph H. Turner*	264
23.	Urbanism as a Way of Life *Louis Wirth*	292
24.	Sociology as a Religious Movement: Thoughts on its Institutionalization in the United States *Russell R. Dynes*	310
25.	Origins of American Sociology: Associationist Social Science *L.L. Bernard and J. Bernard*	321
26.	The Social Construction of Style: Thorstein Veblen's *The Theory of the Leisure Class* as Contested Text *Gary Alan Fine*	341
27.	Introduction to *Middletown: A Study in Modern American Culture* *Robert S. Lynd and Helen Merrell Lynd*	360

VOLUME II

AMERICAN SOCIOLOGY IN THE TWENTIETH CENTURY: FROM PRAGMATISM TO FUNCTIONALISM AND QUANTITATIVE SOCIOLOGY

28.	Elaboration, Revision, Polemic and Progress in the Second Chicago School *Paul Colomy and J. David Brown*	1
29.	Herbert Blumer's Contribution to Twentieth-Century Sociology *Tamotsu Shibutani*	56
30.	The Classic American Pragmatists as Forerunners to Symbolic Interactionism *J. David Lewis*	65
31.	Good People and Dirty Work *Everett Cherrington Hughes*	81
32.	Everett Hughes: Sociology's Mission *Anselm Strauss*	93
33.	Outsiders *Howard S. Becker*	107
34.	Situated Actions and Vocabularies of Motive *C. Wright Mills*	119
35.	The Structure of Social Action *Talcott Parsons*	129
36.	Sociological Aspects of Fascist Movements *Talcott Parsons*	165
37.	The Myth of Functional Analysis as a Special Method in Sociology and Anthropology *Kingsley Davis*	180
38.	The Integration of American Society *Robin M. Williams Jr.*	203

39.	Parsons' "Structure" in American Sociology *Jeffrey C. Alexander*	229
40.	Revolution, Reaction and Reform: The Change Theory of Parsons's Middle Period *Jeffrey C. Alexander*	240
41.	Out of Utopia: Toward a Reorientation of Sociological Analysis *Ralf Dahrendorf*	255
42.	Some Remarks on "The Social System" *David Lockwood*	272
43.	The Functions of Social Conflict *Lewis Coser*	285
44.	Robert K. Merton: The Scholar *Piotr Sztompka*	309
45.	Introduction to Social Theory and Social Structure *Robert K. Merton*	335
46.	The Bearing of Sociological Theory on Empirical Research *Robert K. Merton*	349
47.	The Americanization of Anomie at Harvard *Philippe Besnard*	368
48.	Functionalism and the Survey: The Relation of Theory and Method *Jennifer Platt*	378

VOLUME III

AMERICAN SOCIOLOGY IN THE TWENTIETH CENTURY: FROM PRAGMATISM TO FUNCTIONALISM AND QUANTITATIVE SOCIOLOGY
(continued)

49.	Small-Group Theory and Research *Robert F. Bales*	1
50.	Bringing Men Back In *George C. Homans*	11
51.	The Oversocialized Conception of Man in Modern Sociology *Dennis H. Wrong*	25
52.	Deviant Behavior and Social Structure: Continuities in Social Theory *Robert Dubin*	40
53.	The Curious Importance of Small Groups in American Sociology *Allan Silver*	66
54.	The Authoritarian Personality *T. W. Adorno, Else Frankel-Brunswik, Daniel J. Levinson and R. Nevitt Sanford*	78
55.	Some Types of Character and Society *David Riesman*	104
56.	Contributions to the Theory of Reference Group Behavior *Robert K. Merton and Alice S. Kitt*	129
57.	TVA and the Grassroots *Philip Selznick*	154
58.	Democracy and Oligarchy in Trade Unions *Seymour Martin Lipset, Martin A. Trow and James S. Coleman*	176

59.	The Dynamics of Bureaucracy *Peter Blau*	189
60.	The Organization Man *William H. Whyte*	213
61.	The Power Elite *C. Wright Mills*	248
62.	C. Wright Mills *Ralph Miliband*	272
63.	The Sociology of C. Wright Mills *Eugene V. Schneider*	278
64.	The End of Ideology in the West *Daniel Bell*	285
65.	Two Views of Mass Society *William Kornhauser*	298

AMERICAN SOCIOLOGY IN THE TWENTIETH CENTURY:
RECENT TRENDS IN SOCIOLOGICAL THEORY

66.	Social Differentiation and Organic Solidarity: *The Division of Labor* Revisited *Hans-Peter Müller*	313
67.	Social Theory and Talcott Parsons in the 1980s *David Sciulli and Dean Gerstein*	326
68.	The Role of Efficiency and Power in Explanations of Division of Labour *Dietrich Rueschemeyer*	345
69.	Evaluating the Model of Structural Differentiation in Relation to Educational Change in the Nineteenth Century *Neil J. Smelser*	363
70.	Against Nostalgia: Talcott Parsons and a Sociology for the Modern World *Robert J. Holton and Bryan S. Turner*	377

VOLUME IV

AMERICAN SOCIOLOGY IN THE TWENTIETH CENTURY:
RECENT TRENDS IN SOCIOLOGICAL THEORY
(continued)

71.	Neofunctionalism Today: Reconstructing a Theoretical Tradition *Jeffrey C. Alexander and Paul Colomy*	1
72.	The Post-Industrial Society *Malcolm Waters*	33
73.	The Iron Cage Revisited: Institutional Isomorphism and Collective Rationality in Organizational Fields *Paul J. DiMaggio and Walter W. Powell*	50
74.	Toward a Critique of Sociology *Alvin W. Gouldner*	73
75.	Individualism *Robert N. Bellah, Richard Madsden, William M. Sullivan, Ann Swindler and Steven M. Tipton*	87
76.	The New Forms of Control *Herbert Marcuse*	108
77.	Sociology's Historical Imagination *Theda Skocpol*	120

78.	The Rise and Future Demise of the World Capitalist System: Concepts for Comparative Analysis *Immanuel Wallerstein*	138
79.	The Peasants and Revolution *Barrington Moore Jr.*	149
80.	Sociology, Meet History *Charles Tilly*	172
81.	Introduction to *Frame Analysis* *Erving Goffman*	221
83.	Doing 'Being Ordinary' *Harvey Sacks*	263
84.	Treating Method and Form as Phenomena: An Appreciation of Garfinkel's Phenomenology of Social Action *Lenore Langsdorf*	270
85.	Drama as Life: The Significance of Goffman's Changing Use of the Theatrical Metaphor *Phil Manning*	281
86.	Rational Choice Theory in Sociology *Robert J. Holton*	302
87.	Feminism, Essentialism, and Historical Context *Rosaria Champagne*	317
88.	"I Can't Even Think Straight:" "Queer" Theory and the Missing Sexual Revolution in Sociology *Arlene Stein and Ken Plummer*	330
89.	Social Postmodernism: Beyond Identity Politics *Linda Nicholson and Steven Seidman*	344
90.	The Promise of a Cultural Sociology: Technological Discourse and the Sacred and Profane Information Machine *Jeffrey C. Alexander*	375

APPENDIX OF SOURCES

1. "The Unanimous Declaration of the Thirteen United States of America,"
   Public Domain

2. "The Union as a Safeguard Against Domestic Faction and Insurrection,"
   James Madison
   Public Domain

3. "The Structure of the Government Must Furnish the Proper Checks and Balances Between the Different Departments,"
   Alexander Hamilton or James Madison
   Public Domain

4. "The Program in Practice," *Peter Gay*
   Peter Gay, *The Enlightenment: An Interpretation*, vol. II, *The Science of Freedom*, (New York: Alfred A. Knopf, 1968)

5. "Democracy in America: Volume I," *Alexis de Tocqueville*
   Alexis de Tocqueville, *Democracy in America*, volume I, (New York: Longmans, Green & Co., 1889)

6. "Democracy in America: Volume II," *Alexis de Tocqueville*
   Alexis de Tocqueville, *Democracy in America*, volume II, (New York: Harper & Row, 1966)

7. "The Transcendentalist," *Ralph W. Emerson*
   Ralph W. Emerson, *English Traits and Representative Men*, (London & Toronto: J. M. Dent and Sons, 1908)

8. "Where I Lived, and What I Lived For," *Henry David Thoreau*
   Henry David Thoreau, *Walden*, (London: Walter Scott, 1886)

9. "William Graham Sumner (1840–1910)," *Daniel W. Rossides*
   Daniel W. Rossides, *The History and Nature of Sociological Theory*, (New York: Houghton Mifflin, 1978)

10. "Lester F. Ward (1841–1913)," *Daniel W. Rossides*
    Daniel W. Rossides, *The History and Nature of Sociological Theory*, (New York: Houghton Mifflin, 1978)

11. "W. E. B. Du Bois as a Social Investigator: *The Philadelphia Negro*, 1899," *Martin Bulmer*
    Martin Bulmer, Kevin Bales and Kathryn K. Sklar (eds.), *The Social Survey in Historical Perspective, 1880–1940*, (Cambridge: Cambridge University Press, 1991)

12. "The Causes of Race Superiority," *Edward A. Ross*
    Annals of the American Academy of Political and Social Science, 1901, pp. 67–89

APPENDIX OF SOURCES

13. "The World of The Academic Quantifiers: The Columbia University Family and its Connections," *Stephen P. Turner*
    Martin Bulmer, Kevin Bales & Kathryn K. Sklar (eds.), *The Social Survey in Historical Perspective, 1880-1940*, (Cambridge: Cambridge University Press, 1991)

14. "The Work of George Mead," *John Dewey*
    The New Republic, 1936, July 22, pp. 329-330

15. "The Chicago School of Sociology: What Made it a 'School'?," *Martin Bulmer*
    History of Sociology, 1985, vol. 5, no. 2, pp. 61-77

16. "George Herbert Mead and the Chicago Tradition of Sociology," *Berenice M. Fisher and Anselm L. Strauss*
    Symbolic Interaction, 1979, vol. 2, no. 1, pp. 9-26, no. 2, pp. 9-20

17. "The Self as Social Structure," *George Herbert Mead*
    Spencer Cahill, (ed.) *Inside Social Life*, (Los Angeles: Roxbury Publishing, 1994)

18. "The Self as Sentiment and Reflection," *Charles Horton Cooley*
    Spencer Cahill, (ed.) *Inside Social Life*, (Los Angeles: Roxbury Publishing, 1994)

19. "Primary Groups," *Charles Horton Cooley*
    Charles Horton Cooley, *Social Organization*, (New York: Charles Scribner's Sons, 1909)

20. "*The Polish Peasant in Europe and America*: A Landmark of Empirical Sociology," *Martin Bulmer*
    Martin Bulmer, *The Chicago School of Sociology* (Chicago: University of Chicago Press, 1984)

21. "Situational Analysis: The Behavior Pattern and the Situation," *W. I. Thomas*
    Morris Janowitz (ed.), *W. I. Thomas. On Social Organization and Social Personality*, (Chicago: Chicago University Press, 1966)

22. "Introduction to *Robert E. Park. On Social Control and Collective Behavior*," *Ralph H. Turner*
    Ralph H. Turner (ed.), *Robert E. Park. On Social Control and Collective Behavior*, (Chicago: Chicago University Press, 1967)

23. "Urbanism as a Way of Life," *Louis Wirth*
    American Journal of Sociology, 1938, vol. 44, pp. 1-24

24. "Sociology as a Religious Movement: Thoughts on its Institutionalization in the United States," *Russell R. Dynes*
    American Sociologist, 1974, vol. 9, pp. 169-176

25. "Origins of American Sociology: Associationist Social Science," *L.L. Bernard and J. Bernard*
    L. L. Bernard and J. Bernard, *Origins of American Sociology, The Social Science Movement in the United States*, (New York: Crowell, 1943)

APPENDIX OF SOURCES

26. "The Social Construction of Style: Thorstein Veblen's *The Theory of the Leisure Class* as Contested Text," *Gary Alan Fine*
    Sociological Quarterly, 1994, vol. 35, no. 3, pp. 457–472

27. "Introduction to *Middletown: A Study in Modern American Culture*," *Robert S. Lynd and Helen Merrell Lynd*
    Robert S. Lynd and Helen Merrell Lynd, *Middletown: A Study in Modern American Culture* (New York: Harcourt, Brace & World, 1929)

28. "Elaboration, Revision, Polemic and Progress in the Second Chicago School," *Paul Colomy and J. David Brown*
    Gary Alan Fine (ed.), *A Second Chicago School?*, (Chicago: University of Chicago Press, 1995)

29. "Herbert Blumer's Contribution to Twentieth-Century Sociology," *Tamotsu Shibutani*
    Symbolic Interaction, 1988, vol. 11, pp. 23–31

30. "The Classic American Pragmatists as Forerunners to Symbolic Interactionism," *J. David Lewis*
    Sociological Quarterly, 1976, vol. 17, pp. 347–359

31. "Good People and Dirty Work," *Everett Cherrington Hughes*
    Everett C. Hughes, *The Sociological Eye*, (Chicago: Aldine–Atherton, 1971)

32. "Everett Hughes: Sociology's Mission," *Anselm Strauss*
    Symbolic Interaction, 1996, vol. 19, pp. 271–284

33. "Outsiders," *Howard S. Becker*
    Howard Becker, *Outsiders*, (New York: Free Press, 1966 [1963])

34. "Situated Actions and Vocabularies of Motive," *C. Wright Mills*
    Irving Louis Horowitz (ed.), *Power, Politics and People: The Collected Essays of C. Wright Mills*, (New York: Oxford University Press, 1963)

35. "The Structure of Social Action," *Talcott Parsons*
    Talcott Parsons, *The Structure of Social Action*, (New York: The Free Press, 1949)

36. "Sociological Aspects of Fascist Movements," *Talcott Parsons*
    Talcott Parsons, *Essays in Sociological Theory* (New York: The Free Press, 1954)

37. "The Myth of Functional Analysis as a Special Method in Sociology and Anthropology," *Kingsley Davis*
    American Sociological Review, 1959, vol. 24, pp. 757–772

38. "The Integration of American Society," *Robin M. Williams Jr.*
    Robin M. Williams Jr., *American Society: A Sociological Interpretation*, (New York: Alfred A. Kopf, 1960)

39. "Parsons' 'Structure' in American Sociology," *Jeffrey C. Alexander*
    Sociological Theory, 1988, vol. 6, no. 1, pp. 96–102

APPENDIX OF SOURCES

40. "Revolution, Reaction and Reform: The Change Theory of Parsons's Middle Period," *Jeffrey C. Alexander*
    American Sociological Review, 1978, vol. 43, pp. 177–198

41. "Out of Utopia: Toward a Reorientation of Sociological Analysis," *Ralf Dahrendorf*
    American Journal of Sociology, 1958, vol. 64, pp. 115–127

42. "Some Remarks on 'The Social System'," *David Lockwood*
    British Journal of Sociology, 1956, vol. 7, pp. 134–146

43. "The Functions of Social Conflict," *Lewis Coser*
    Lewis Coser, *The Functions of Social Conflict*, (London: Routledge & Kegan Paul, 1956)

44. "Robert K. Merton: The Scholar," *Piotr Sztompka*
    Piotr Sztompka, *Robert K Merton: An Intellectual Profile*, (London: Macmillan, 1986)

45. "Introduction to Social Theory and Social Structure," *Robert K. Merton*
    Robert K. Merton, *Social Theory and Social Structure*, (New York: The Free Press, 1957)

46. "The Bearing of Sociological Theory on Empirical Research," *Robert K. Merton*
    Robert K. Merton, *Social Theory and Social Structure*, (New York: The Free Press, 1957)

47. "The Americanization of Anomie at Harvard," *Philippe Besnard*
    Knowledge and Society, 1986, vol. 6, pp. 41–53

48. "Functionalism and the Survey: The Relation of Theory and Method," *Jennifer Platt*
    Sociological Review, 1986, vol. 34, pp. 501–536

49. "Small-Group Theory and Research," *Robert F. Bales*
    Leonard Broom, Leonard S. Cottrell and Robert K. Merton, *Sociology Today: Problems and Prospects*, (New York: Basic Books, 1959)

50. "Bringing Men Back In," *George C. Homans*
    American Sociological Review, 1964, vol. 20, pp. 809–818

51. "The Oversocialized Conception of Man in Modern Sociology," *Dennis H. Wrong*
    American Sociological Review, 1961, vol. 26, 184–193

52. "Deviant Behavior and Social Structure: Continuities in Social Theory," *Robert Dubin*
    American Sociological Review, 1959, vol. 24, pp. 147–164

53. "The Curious Importance of Small Groups in American Sociology," *Allan Silver*
    H. J. Gans, (ed.), *Sociology in America*, (Newbury Park: Sage, 1990)

APPENDIX OF SOURCES

54. "The Authoritarian Personality,"
    T. W. Adorno, Else Frankel-Brunswik, Daniel J. Levinson and R. Nevitt Sanford
    T. W. Adorno, Else Frankel-Brunswik, Daniel J. Levinson and R. Nevitt Sanford, *The Authoritarian Personality*, (New York: Harper & Row, 1950)

55. "Some Types of Character and Society," *David Riesman*
    David Riesman, *The Lonely Crowd*, (New Haven: Yale University Press, 1961)

56. "Contributions to the Theory of Reference Group Behavior,"
    Robert K. Merton and Alice S. Kitt
    Robert K. Merton and Paul F. Lazarsfeld, (eds.), *Continuities in Social Research*, (Glencoe, Ill.: The Free Press, 1950)

57. "TVA and the Grassroots," *Philip Selznick*
    Philip Selznick, *TVA and the Grassroots*, (New York: Harper & Row, 1966 [Los Angeles: University of California Press, 1949])

58. "Democracy and Oligarchy in Trade Unions,"
    Seymour Martin Lipset, Martin A. Trow and James S. Coleman
    Seymour Martin Lipset, Martin A. Trow and James S. Coleman, *Union Democracy: The Internal Politics of the International Typographical Union*, (New York: Free Press: 1959)

59. "The Dynamics of Bureaucracy," *Peter Blau*
    Peter Blau, *The Dynamics of Bureaucracy*, (Chcago: University of Chicago Press, 1963)

60. "The Organization Man," *William H. Whyte*
    William Whyte, *The Organization Man*, (Harmondsworth: Penguin, 1965)

61. "The Power Elite," *C. Wright Mills*
    C. Wright Mills, *The Power Elite*, (New York: Oxford University Press, 1959)

62. "C. Wright Mills," *Ralph Miliband*
    G. William Domhoff and Hoyt B. Ballard (eds.), *C. Wright Mills and the Power Elite*, (Boston: Beacon Press, 1968)

63. "The Sociology of C. Wright Mill," *Eugene V. Schneider*
    G. William Domhoff and Hoyt B. Ballard (eds.), *C. Wright Mills and the Power Elite*, (Boston: Beacon Press, 1968)

64. "The End of Ideology in the West," *Daniel Bell*
    Daniel Bell, *The End of Ideology: On the Exhaustion of Political Ideas in the Fifties*, (Glencoe, Ill.: Free Press, 1960)

65. "Two Views of Mass Society," *William Kornhauser*
    William Kornhauser, *The Politics of Mass Society*, (London: Routledge & Kegan Paul, 1960)

66. "Social Differentiation and Organic Solidarity: *The Division of Labor* Revisited," *Hans-Peter Müller*
    Sociological Forum, 1994, vol. 9, no. 1, pp. 73–86

APPENDIX OF SOURCES

67. "Social Theory and Talcott Parsons in the 1980s,"
    David Sciulli and Dean Gerstein
    Annual Review of Sociology, 1985, vol. 11, pp. 369–387

68. "The Role of Efficiency and Power in Explanations of Division of Labour," *Dietrich Rueschemeyer*
    Dietrich Rueschemeyer, *Power and the Division of Labor* (Cambridge: Polity Press, 1986)

69. "Evaluating the Model of Structural Differentiation in Relation to Educational Change in the Nineteenth Century," *Neil J. Smelser*
    Jeffrey C. Alexander (ed.), *Neofunctionalism*, (Beverly Hills: Sage, 1985)

70. "Against Nostalgia: Talcott Parsons and a Sociology for the Modern World," *Robert J. Holton and Bryan S. Turner*
    Robert J. Holton and Bryan S. Turner, *Talcott Parsons on Economy and Society*, (London: Routledge & Kegan Paul, 1986)

71. "Neofunctionalism Today: Reconstructing a Theoretical Tradition," *Jeffrey C. Alexander and Paul Colomy*
    George Ritzer (ed.), *Frontier of Socioglogical Theory*, (New York: Columbia University Press, 1990)

72. "The Post-Industrial Society," *Malcolm Waters*
    Malcolm Waters, *Daniel Bell*, (London: Routledge, 1995)

73. "The Iron Cage Revisited: Institutional Isomorphism and Collective Rationality in Organizational Fields," *Paul J. DiMaggio and Walter W. Powell*
    American Sociological Review, 1983, vol. 48, no. 2, pp. 147–160

74. "Toward a Critique of Sociology," *Alvin W. Gouldner*
    Alvin W. Gouldner, *The Coming Crisis of Western Sociology*, (London: Heinemann, 1971)

75. "Individualism," *Robert N. Bellah, Richard Madsden, William M. Sullivan, Ann Swindler and Steven M. Tipton*
    Robert N. Bellah et al., *Habits of the Heart: Individualism and Commitment in American Life*, (Berkeley: University of California Press, 1996)

76. "The New Forms of Control," *Herbert Marcuse*
    Herbert Marcuse, *One Dimensional Man*, (London: Routledge and Kegan Paul, 1964)

77. "Sociology's Historical Imagination," *Theda Skocpol*
    Theda Skocpol (ed.), *Vision and Method in Historical Sociology*, (Cambridge: Cambridge University Press, 1984)

78. "The Rise and Future Demise of the World Capitalist System: Concepts for Comparative Analysis," *Immanuel Wallerstein*
    Comparative Studies in Society and History, 1974, vol. 16, no. 4, pp. 387–415

79. "The Peasants and Revolution," *Barrington Moore Jr.*
    Barrington Moore, Jr., *Social Origins of Dictatorship and Democracy* (London: Peregrine Books, 1969)

APPENDIX OF SOURCES

80. "Sociology, Meet History," *Charles Tilly*
    Charles Tilly, *As Sociology Meets History: Studies in Social Discontinuity*, (New York: Academic Press, 1981)

81. "Introduction to *Frame Analysis*," *Erving Goffman*
    Erving Goffman, *Frame Analysis*, (Harmondsworth: Penguin Press, 1975)

83. "Doing 'Being Ordinary'," *Harvey Sacks*
    Gail Jefferson (ed.), *Lectures on Conversation*, vol. II, (Oxford: Blackwell, 1992)

84. "Treating Method and Form as Phenomena: An Appreciation of Garfinkel's Phenomenology of Social Action," *Lenore Langsdorf*
    Human Studies, 1995, vol. 18, no. 2-3, pp. 177-188

85. "Drama as Life: The Significance of Goffman's Changing Use of the Theatrical Metaphor," *Phil Manning*
    Sociological Theory, 1990, vol. 9, no. 1, pp. 70-86

86. "Rational Choice Theory in Sociology," *Robert J. Holton*
    Critical Review, 1995, vol. 9, no. 4, pp. 519-537

87. "Feminism, Essentialism, and Historical Context," *Rosaria Champagne*
    Women's Studies, 1995, vol. 25, no. 1, pp. 95-108

88. "'I Can't Even Think Straight:' 'Queer' Theory and the Missing Sexual Revolution in Sociology," *Arlene Stein and Ken Plummer*
    Sociological Theory, 1994, vol. 12, no. 2, pp. 178-187

89. "Social Postmodernism: Beyond Identity Politics,"
    Linda Nicholson and Steven Seidman
    Linda Nicholson and Steven Seidman, *Social Postmodernism: Beyond Identity Politics*, (Cambridge: Cambridge University Press, 1995)

90. "The Promise of a Cultural Sociology: Technological Discourse and the Sacred and Profane Information Machine," *Jeffrey C. Alexander*
    Jeffrey C. Alexander (ed.), *Theory of Culture*, (Berkeley, CA.: University of California Press, 1992)

General Introduction

The Paradoxical Relations of Self and Society in American Sociological Thought

Jeffrey C. Alexander

> What are called new views . . . are not new, but the very oldest of thoughts cast into the mould of these new times. The light is always identical in its composition, but it falls on a great variety of objects . . . In like manner, thought only appears in the objects it classifies. (Emerson, 1842)

The American tradition of sociology can be understood as the "secularization" into scientific language of two utopian movements of social reform. Sectarian Protestantism and anti-authoritarian democracy sought to gain salvation by making practical utopias here on earth. For American sociology the ultimate goal can still be called social salvation. This is pursued, however, not by perfecting the soul or the polity but by reconstructing the civil society. Responding to the crises of industrialization and ethnic heterogeneity, the goal of American sociology has been, as Russell Dynes (1974) once put it, "to create a massive urban renewal project which would build the kingdom of man to replace the lost Kingdom of God." The means for achieving this goal are neither faith nor virtue, but rational, scientific knowledge of society, whether defined in the positivist and quantitative or hermeneutic and qualitative sense.

These roots and ambitions distinguish the American sociological tradition from the European, despite their shared disciplinary matrices and continuous cross-Atlantic interpenetrations.[1] Developed in the context of church religion and collective projects for democratic revolution, European sociology emphasized state organization and the constraints imposed by actors' external environments. By contrast, American ideology has focused, often myopically, on the individual self. What has marked American sociology is its preoccupation with the individual above all else, thus its extraordinary concern with the *motives* of individuals ("action" in sociological terms) and their mutual *relations* ("interaction"). Even when the focus of American sociology has shifted to *institutions*, its concern has been to understand how these collective forces provide either a supportive arena for the realization of individual interactions or block their realization.

European sociology has viewed society as external and dominating, whether in the reformist terms of Durkheim, the radicalism of Marx, or the agnosticism of Weber and Simmel. The perspective of American sociology, even when it is highly critical, has been quite the opposite. The emphasis in studying ordered patterns and structures has been on how they structure individual motivations and on how these "social selves," as Cooley called them, actively orient to patterns and structures in turn. Interactions are viewed less as the deposits of social structure than as patterns emergent from actors' intentions. Institutions, in turn, are linked in a very pronounced way to the interactions of individuals and the groups they form.

The specificity of the American approach to the central topics of sociology can be seen in this comparative light. *Social movements* are viewed, not as systemically generated confrontations or adaptations, but more as communicatively generated and cooperative group activities. *Organizations* are seen less as inherently constraining hierarchies than as networks of collective purpose which may become objectified through individual inattention and conflicting practical goals. *Economic sociology* focuses, not on abstract market requirements, but on commitments between local actors. *Political sociology* is less concerned with class linkages and party oligarchies than with plurality, voter choices, and interest coalitions. *Stratification studies* reveal less about the macrostructuring of unequal opportunities than the opportunities for mobility provided by individual achievement. *Social systems theory*, rather than seeing systems as autonomous and self-referential, examines how systems facilitate voluntarism. *Cultural sociology* focuses on interpretations and social movements, on beliefs rather than on ideologies promoted by elites. Decidedly optimistic, American *postmodernism* proclaims, not the alienating separation of society from individuals, but the liberating connections made possible by recent transformations in gender, race, ethnicity, and sexuality.

All this does not mean that American sociology is oblivious to power and domination or that it lacks a critical tradition. It means, rather, that conflict is often viewed as another form of emancipation, and that instrumental motives and coercive actions are studied as patterned departures, as deviations from the more communicative and cooperative norm. Conflicts are understood as being generated by cynical motives more than by normalizing social structures, by social relationships that have gone awry, and by institutions and organizations from which human attention and purpose have slipped away. If American sociology is the home of voluntaristic systems theory and interactionally-rooted microsociology, its critical macrosociology is triggered by outrage at the failure to sustain connections between interactions and institutions, a breakdown created by the failure of political virtue and the decline of idealistic faith.

The origins of this deeply paradoxical understanding of the fate of the "self" in modern society can be traced back to fundamental dualities in the culture of American civil society. In American ideology, the relation of actors to civil society has been problematized precisely in terms of the motives of individuals, their interrelations, and the institutions these form.[2] An optimistic "discourse of liberty" demarcates the qualities that legitimate inclusion and participation. In terms of their motives, civil actors are idealized as independent, honest, self-controlled; their relations are held to be cooperative and trusting; their institutions are described as responsive, open, and egalitarian. In tension with this idealizing discourse, Americans also have imagined motives, relations, and institutions in a starkly contrasting manner, employing an ideological language that has justified excluding individuals and groups from civil society. According to this anti-democratic "discourse of repression," actors are dependent, deceptive, and impulsive; they enter into relations that are aggressive, distrustful, and conflictual; they form institutions that are unresponsive, closed, and hierarchical.

Insofar as American sociology has secularized and scientized these broader cultural traditions, it is not surprising that sociological thinking has been bifurcated in a very similar way. In one line of sociological observation, the fundamental social processes of modernity – industrialization, plurality, secularization, science – are viewed optimistically. Thinkers explain how these processes emerge from and contribute to creative and cooperative social action, how they restructure but still complement group sentiment and cohesion, how they lead to increasingly open and democratic institutions. According to this sociological version of the discourse of liberty, which cuts across a wide range of empirical and theoretical variations, social scientific findings confirm the strength of modern civil societies.

It is precisely the solidary sentiments underlying this stability that are questioned by the alternative, and typically subordinated, line of sociological thinking informed by the discourse of repression. Modernizing processes are understood as threatening the requirements of civil society, as making actors less, not more fit for the challenge of democratic participation and fraternal support. Industrialization, now understood as capitalism, turns potentially trusting humans into things, making motivation calculating, devious, instrumental. Secularization and plurality are found to create antagonistic social relations in which trust has dissolved. Science has led not to greater clarity and truthfulness but to obfuscation and objectification. Bureaucracy and other hierarchical systems permeate modern societies precisely because only these kinds of institutions can order such dangerously centrifugal force.

While sharply contrasting in ideal-typical terms, in terms of the actual patterns and dynamics of American social thought, these theoretical visions have been empirically intertwined. Consider, for example, the founding documents of American civil society itself, *The Declaration of Independence* (1776) and the *Constitution* (1789). Reflecting Locke's optimism about rationality and cooperative human nature, Thomas Jefferson's radically democratic *Declaration* is a humanistic appeal for individual freedom against collective force. Assuming actors' inherent common sense and good will – the existence of "native justice and magnanimity" – Jefferson suggests that actors are guided by self-generating norms, by ideals that reflect the "inherent rights of individuals."[3] It is this optimism about the reasonableness of actors that justifies direct, democratic self-government, which is instituted only "to secure these rights" of a "free people." Indeed, it is because people are basically cooperative and rational that repressive and authoritarian institutions not only are unnecessary, but often pernicious. Good government can be based only on the "consent" of the individuals who created it. Bad government is authority that disregards voluntary compliance. In response to this disregard, rational individuals will exercise their natural rights, presenting "self-evident truths" to a "candid world." By making such public "petition," political actors will be demonstrating "a decent respect to the opinions of mankind." Right motives and communicative action are at the heart of political conflict. Legitimation depends on "the rectitude of . . . intentions," not on the power of resources.

In sharp contrast, it is Hobbes, rather than Locke, that informs James Madison's defense of the American constitution in his famous contributions (numbers 10 and 51) to the *Federalist Papers*. Madison writes as a self-confessed realist, asserting that, "if men were angels, no government would be necessary." Pointing to a "deficit of better motives" – to a motivational structure that threatens the very existence of liberty – he warns about "zeal," "ambition," and, above all, the "common impulse of passion." These motives, Madison warns, tend to undermine cooperative social relations, creating "mutual animosity" and the "violence of faction." Left to their own devices, as they are in a participatory democracy, such motives and relations create the "instability, injustice, and confusion" that facilitate institutions of domination, for in these kinds of situations actors are "more disposed to vex and oppress each other than to cooperate for their common good." In order to protect liberty, therefore, "neither moral nor religious motives can be relied on," and spontaneous "communication" will only make things worse. Only carefully constructed "powers of government" can control these "dangerous" tendencies. These powers can be found only in the Republican form of government. The indirect representative character of Republican, as compared to direct democracy, allows "the government to control the governed"; the division of powers in Republicanism, moreover, guarantees that there will be "no communication whatever" between plural institutions and contending interest groups.

If Madison's classical formulation of democratic theory adumbrated what later came to be called (Coser 1956) the conflict tradition in American sociology, the writings of the American Transcendentalists, appearing fifty years later, presaged the more optimistic Chicago school of sociology inspired by Pragmatism. In his philosophical transformation of the discourse of liberty, Ralph Waldo Emerson criticized as "materialist" precisely the kind of pessimism about the self and emphasis on restrictive social institutions manifest in

Madison's founding treatise. "The materialist insists on facts, on history, on the force of circumstances, and the animal wants of man," Emerson wrote in 1842. "The idealist," by contrast, insists on "the power of Thought and of Will, on inspiration, [and] on individual culture." Demanding that the individual be more positively evaluated, Emerson firmly places himself, and what he regards as by far the most valuable strand in American thought, in the idealist camp. In praise of subjectivity, he points to the social significance of ideas and motives, and establishes what will eventually come to be regarded as a specifically American social-cum-individual conception of the "me."

> You think me the child of my circumstances: I make my circumstance. Let any thought of mine be different from that they are, the difference will transform my condition and economy. I – this thought which is called I – is the mould into which the world is poured like melted wax. The mould is invisible, but the world betrays the shape of the mould. You call it the power of circumstance, but it is the power of me.

A century after Emerson wrote these words, and in implicit reference to them, John Dewey, in his famous eulogy to George Herbert Mead, suggested that "the emphasis of the Romantic philosophers upon individual consciousness makes explicit the earlier religious idea that nature is but a theatre in which is enacted the drama of the human soul" (1936). In so doing, Dewey connected the philosophical foundations of the Chicago school of sociology to Transcendentalism and to the radical Protestantism which inspired it. Before considering this link, however, we must take up the actual origins of American sociology itself.

European sociology first developed in reaction to the French Revolution, and the first sociology of America, written by the Frenchman Alexis de Tocqueville, considers American social structure and culture in light of this world-historical event. It was the industrial revolution, however, that gave birth to the first American sociology. Like Herbert Spencer, the British sociologist who served as their role model, William Graham Sumner and Lester Ward, the founding figures of the American discipline, wrote in the shadow of the positivist social philosopher Auguste Comte, who gave to sociology its name. Yet the substantive ideas of these Americans were much more deeply influenced, as indeed were Spencer's, by the social facts of the industrial revolution and by the intellectual traditions of political economy and Darwinism. Defiantly "realistic" in the tradition of Madison, Sumner and Ward understood sociology as the definitive rejoinder to idealism in its religious and secular form, displacing ideas of good will, cooperation, reciprocity, and normatively regulated mutual interpretation with hard-edged, materialistic, and scientific conceptions of social force.

While disagreeing profoundly in their ideological reactions to the laissez-faire market economy, both American thinkers agreed that idealism had been destroyed by industrial capitalism. The solidarity underlying civil society had disappeared, the economic and demographic were triumphant. Nature, not other individuals and groups, was the determining environment of human action. Describing the subordination of human subjectivity to natural force, Sumner insisted (quotes in Rossides 1978: 193-211) that there is "no disposition at all in nature to conform her operations to man's standards." Human motives, in his view, were far from the civil and cooperative ones that idealists believe. Defining these as "hunger, sex passion, vanity, and fear," Sumner argued that "under each of these motives are interests," and concluded that "life consists in satisfying interests." The method of sociology should mirror the naturalism and objectivism of its subject matter; only the completely dispassionate, scientific approach of this new discipline could provide insight into the objective and dominating powers that now controlled human life. "Social phenomena are subject to law," Sumner wrote, and "the natural laws of the social order are in their entire character like the laws of physics." In his causal theory, Sumner singled out such factors as population-land ratios and capital formation, deriding the voluntarism and idealism of American ideology in its Jeffersonian form.

> The dogmatic or philosophical theorems, instead of being the cause of our social arrangements, are only the metaphysical dress which we have amused ourselves by imagining upon them. We are not free and equal because Jefferson put it into the Declaration of Independence that we are born so; but Jefferson could put it into the Declaration of Independence that all men are born free and equal because the economic relations existing in America made the members of society to all intents and purposes free and equal.

Cultural ideals, identified by Sumner as "folkways" and "mores," could be studied only as reflections of material structures; norms represent an "adaptation of means to ends."

While the other American sociological pioneer, Lester Ward, was much more critical of industrial capitalism than Sumner, his theoretical framework did not differ in fundamental ways. He described the natural universe as ruled by the principle of "collision" (quotes in Rossides 1978: 212-230), and he defined basic human motives as hunger and sex. While acknowledging that cognition and intention were basic human faculties, and that in the future a more egalitarian and responsive social order would be possible, Ward argued that the subordination of intelligence to animalistic sentiment had created a human history marked by "dark deeds and sinister practices." Deception has been the rule, and social institutions, from economy and politics to religion, had a fundamentally exploitative character. Ward believed that conflict was the master principle defining social life, declaring that humanity's "whole career has been marked by belligerency, internecine strife, and universal rapacity."

The creation of Pragmatic social theory in the turn of the century period, by Charles Sanders Peirce, John Dewey, William James, and George Herbert Mead, provided a philosophical basis for renewing the more optimistic discourse of liberty in American sociology. Because of its emphasis on practical experience and problem-solving, Pragmatism has often been crudely caricatured as anti-idealistic, even materialistic. What really distinguished this quintessentially American approach, however, was its insistence that human experience is mediated by intention and language, that individuals engage in action, rather than mere adaptation, and that this action is directed by a reflexive and intelligent mind. While practical experience triggers action, action itself is subjectively motivated, rooted in interactions with others, and mediated by the continuously emergent and evolving self. Mead rejected the American psychologist Watson's stimulus-response approach, which led, not to action theory, but to a "behaviorism" in line with the pessimistic tradition of American thought. In creating his alternative, "*social* behaviorism," Mead developed the outlines of a sociological theory that emphasized the centrality of the self, its embeddedness in language, and its creativity in response to new situations and tasks. In contrast with the deterministic naturalism of Sumner and Ward, Mead stressed, as Dewey suggests in his above noted eulogy, the "*active* connection between individual organisms and the world," the "part of nature that has become *conscious*, and the "unremitting occurrence of individuality, novelty and the unpredictable" (italics added). The link between the contingency of the developing self and established moral tradition can be found in communication, which must be considered at once as structure (the grounding of contingency in normative control) and as process (the continuous adjustment of self and society to one another).

In the hands of Mead and the sociological generation he critically influenced, then, Pragmatism can be understood as an interactionally generated theory of communication. *Motivated* by the need for reciprocal communication, actors are seen as trusting, truthful, and open in their displays of self. The social *relations* that ensue between such actors are communicative as well, displaying cooperation, mutual adaptation, and exchange. Surrounding and supporting these motives and relations, it is believed, are such communicative *institutions* as the public sphere, mass media, interactional groups, and social movements.

None of Mead's early sociological followers articulated this Pragmatic vision more profoundly than Charles Horton Cooley.[4] Cooley asserted that "where there is no communication there can be no nomenclature and no developed thought," concluding that an egoistic, instrumental approach to the individual was inconceivable: "What we call 'me,' 'mine,' or 'myself' is, then, not something separate from the general life, but the most interesting part of it, a part whose interest arises from the fact that it is both general and individual." The very idea of the "*social* self," in other words, is "drawn from the communicative life": "That the 'I' of common speech has a meaning which includes some sort of reference to other persons is involved in the fact that the word and the ideas it stands for are phenomena of language and the communicative life." Cooley acknowledged that passion is a central human motivation, but, in sharp contrast with Sumner and Ward, he insisted that "passions are socialized by sympathy." Sympathetic motivations lead actors to be centrally concerned with the reactions of others: "The individual will be ambitious, but the chief object of his ambition will be some desired place in the thought of the others." For this reason, actions can be seen as "performances," as symbolic actions aimed at winning the sympathy of an audience. Self-interest and cooperation necessarily coincide, for, in order to gain the sympathy of others, actors must "feel allegiance to common standards of service and fair play."

With his conception of "primary groups," Cooley demonstrated how this communicative approach to motivation and interaction produced solidary bonds of "intimate association and cooperation." He emphasized the importance to society of groups like "the family, the play-group of children, and the neighborhood or community group of elders." Insisting that modernity does not inhibit such solidarizing processes, he called attention to the fact that "in our own society, being little bound by place, people easily form clubs, fraternal societies and the like, based on congeniality, which may give rise to real intimacy." Every "face-to-face" group inspires such mutual sympathy, even economic occupations, e.g., "workmen in the same trade." Viewed from the perspective of the sub-institutional solidarity generated by primary groups, Cooley believed, even the most devastating structural conditions of modern social life can be studied in a more optimistic, individually-affirmative way. "In our own cities the crowded tenements and the general economic and social confusion have sorely wounded the family and the neighborhood, but it is remarkable, in view of these conditions, what vitality they show; and there is nothing upon which the conscience of the time is more determined than upon restoring them to health."

In suggesting the continuing vitality of primary groups despite the urban devastation of his time, Cooley advanced the claim that these "groups . . . are springs of life, not only for the individual but for social institutions." This claim undergirds the research program initiated by such pioneers of Chicago sociology as Robert Park, E. W. Burgess, Louis Wirth, and Willard Waller. This closely connected intergenerational team of researchers and students studied how sympathy and cooperation, and the solidarity they generated, were channelled by the structures and processes of early twentieth century urban life, particularly its ethnic and economic divisions. They described the modern city not as a zone of economic exchange but as an impersonal web of human associations, one which encouraged a dense undergrowth of competitive and accommodative ethnic groups that eventually were assimilated into larger wholes. They studied industrial occupations as arenas for the display of individual learning and identity formation. They approached large, impersonal organizations by constructing their "natural histories." They studied social conflicts as social movements, as clashes between communicatively generated solidarities struggling for moral recognition in the public sphere.

While generally confident about individual and group capacities for social renewal, these early Pragmatic sociologists were also aware that, under the impact of industrialization and mass immigration, the communicative motives and cooperative relations so necessary for civil society could go awry and civil solidarity depleted as a result. Socialist critics like Dewey and Walter Lippman warned that laissez-faire capitalism distorted communicative interaction and solidarity and threatened to put machine-like obedience and domination in their place. Cooley speculated about atomizing and egoistic consequences if the processes threatening primary group adhesion got the upper hand. Robert and Helen Lynd worried about this deterioration in their empirical examinations of "Middletown." In his acerbic observations on the social processes of industrial capitalism, Thorstein Veblen gave up entirely on the optimistic discourse of liberty, suggesting that technological growth had instrumentalized work and that "conspicuous consumption" rested upon animalistic hedonism and egotistical greed.

In decline by the 1930s, the Chicago school of sociology, which had dominated American theory and research from the turn of the century period, was challenged by the emergence of "functionalism," a much more collectively oriented sociological approach formulated by Talcott Parsons. This fiercely contested transition has been subjected to extraordinary misunderstandings. The first is that the sociology of the Chicago school, no longer hegemonic, simply disappeared. In fact, in tense and polemical relationship to the functionalist tradition centered in Harvard and Columbia, Pragmatic sociology continued to develop and evolve in significant ways. The second, much more fundamental misconception is that functionalism itself represented a drastic departure from the American sociological tradition. This second distortion can be traced in the first instance to the polemical manner in which Parsons positioned himself. Despite his familiarity with the "native" American tradition, for personal, institutional, and genuinely theoretical reasons Parsons identified his ideas not with American but with European social thought. In his paradigm-creating *The Structure of Social Action* (1937), Parsons developed a neo-Kantian perspective, dismissing earlier American sociology as thoroughly individualistic and utilitarian in its explanatory scheme and as anti-philosophical and empiricist in its theoretical outlook. He claimed that only upon the European theories of Durkheim and Weber could American sociologists begin to accomplish important work. Needless to say, this "anti-American" orientation called forth indignant and polemical responses from the Chicago sociological school, which had been built upon a philosophical tradition, Pragmatism, that had defined itself in decisive opposition to "European" thought.

More than half a century removed from these polemical misunderstandings, Parsons' brief on behalf of European thinkers can be seen as much as an effort to coopt them as a capitulation to them. What Parsons actually seems to have done is translate their ideas into the idioms of the optimistic line of American thought, which can be understood philosophically just as much in a neo-Kantian as a Pragmatic way. Parsons' functionalism created, in other words, a new, more macrosociological version of the discourse of liberty. Against Durkheim's apparent reification of society and his demands for conformity to the invariant laws of social life, Parsons brought Durkheim's ideas of solidarity and symbolism into the service of his own self-proclaimed "voluntaristic" theory of action. Against Weber's pessimistic political sociology of rationalization, strategic action, group conflict, and domination, Parsons employed key concepts from Weber's own religious sociology to construct an ethically oriented model of modernity that centered on normative action, moral institutions, and the vitality of self-regulating professional groups. It is true that, under the influence of Kant and Dilthey, Parsons insisted on the reality of collective moral values, describing them as "transcendental ends" regulating individual actions. Influenced by the radical Protestant and democratic traditions, however, Parsons also insisted that individuals achieved freedom and autonomy vis-a-vis worldly institutions *precisely because of* their attachment to such values.

It was precisely this orientation to the macrosociological foundations of the discourse of liberty – and not some organicist, conservative bias, as their critics often claimed – that provided the empirical topics for generations of functionalists, from Kingsley Davis, Robin Williams, Bernard Barber, and Robert Merton to Robert Bales, Neil Smelser, Robert Bellah, and Leon Mayhew. Thus, in marked contrast with other macrosociological traditions, they persisted in studying socialization, examining the empirical processes by which individual autonomy is achieved via the internalization of values. Studying such agents of socialization as families and peer groups, they insisted that these primary groups were complementary to such formal institutions as schools and even economic organizations. When functionalists explored the "pattern variables" of culture in every group and institution, they were in search, not of conformity, but of the resources for individuation, autonomy, cooperation, and even emancipation. Deviance emerged when institutional strains severed the connections between individual motives and the values shared by other actors. Intensive social divisions emerged from conflicts between collective values themselves. Social movements were adaptive responses to these fissures, problem-solving developments that produced institutional change and value renewal in an often progressive way.

As the functionalist version of American sociology came into prominence in the 1940s and 1950s, sociologists in the Chicago tradition began to articulate their own approach to the American theoretical tradition in more one-sided, often polemical ways. Against what they conceived to be the mechanistic, collectivist, and anti-individual tendencies of functionalism, the second and third generations of the Chicago school emphasized contingency, self reference, and direct face-to-face interaction *over and against* the influence of more structured cultural patterns, group solidarity, and institutional forms. Even while deepening and elaborating many early Chicago school ideas and themes, these studies narrowed and simplified the scope of Pragmatic sociology in far reaching ways. What emerged between the Pragmatic and functionalist versions of the discourse of liberty was a "dialogue of the deaf," one manifestation of which was the yawning micro-macro split that has continued to bedevil American and, indeed, European sociology until this day. Herbert Blumer, Mead's most influential disciple, made a series of original contributions to conceptualizing the role that individuals play in the construction of social movements and racial solidarities. The impact of these studies was reduced, however, by Blumer's highly polemical claims that collective values are sociologically irrelevant and that the meaning of an individual action is solely determined by another actor's response to it. By so reducing sociology to an exclusive focus on interaction, Blumer truncated the communicative theory of earlier Pragmatic sociology, in effect separating (contra-Wittgenstein) language as a cultural system from language in use.

Even the most distinguished contributions to "symbolic interactionism," the name Blumer gave the Meadian tradition in 1937, suffered from similar limitations. Everett Hughes developed a rich ethnographic approach to work and occupations, but he said precious little about their surrounding cultural and structural environments. While Howard Becker elaborated an original approach to deviance as a "career," describing it as an affirmative and solidaristic response to negative interactional sanctions, he did not explore the institutional strains that produced such sanctions or the consequences for social movements and social change that deviant careers might induce. With his genius for combining close empirical observation with conceptual innovation, Erving Goffman virtually created the contemporary field of "microsociology"; indeed, he and Parsons represent the most original and important American sociological thinkers in the last half century. Yet Goffman's "dramaturgical sociology" was resolute in its insistence that the selves of actors are completely sui generis. In constructing their performances, Goffman's actors pay only lip service to collective values, making strategic and cynical avowals of public fealty in order to gain control over the actions of others.[5] Despite his links with European phenomenology, Harold Garfinkel's "ethnomethodology" can also be seen as a highly original, and highly polemical, continuation of the Pragmatic version of American sociological thought. In the empirical studies produced by Garfinkel and his students, communication is studied not as the expression of sincerely shared values, much less as a trusting effort to gain cooperation; rather, communication is a post-hoc "account" which aims at achieving the veneer of consensus despite practical conflict.

Goffman's profoundly cynical approach to society seems to imply a hardheaded, realistic, and externalist approach that departs from the optimistic presuppositions of the discourse of liberty. Indeed, the exaggerated focus on self-oriented individuals and strategic interaction in the writings of the postwar Chicago school had the paradoxical effect of encouraging an instrumentalist sociology in the Madisonian tradition. In founding "exchange theory," for example, George Homans returned to the laissez-faire liberalism of American sociology's founding figures and to the Watsonian behaviorism that Mead had struggled against. Virtue and normativity were absent from Homansian sociology, which conceived actors as isolated atoms and modelled interaction as an egoistic exchange of positive and negative sanctions. Moving away from Homans' exclusive emphasis on subinstitutional processes, Peter Blau and James Coleman built upon his instrumental, realist theory to create models of binding social structures and institutions.

In this vein of Madisonian realism, there developed, from the 1950s through the 1980s, a wide range of anti-functionalist versions of American sociology. Despite their great differences from one another, these theoretical and empirical studies shared the central proposition that, in modern, democratic, secular, and capitalist societies, actions and institutions can, and perhaps must, be constructed without reference to normativity and subjective good will, without what Locke called a natural identity of interests.

Certainly this was the fundamental claim of the non-Marxist "critical" tradition that emerged in the postwar period of American sociology. In tandem with David Riesman's pessimistic finding that modern individuals were no longer "inner-directed," William H. White discovered that the manipulation of mass values produced the conformity of the "organization man." Disputing Parsons' claim that internalized values allowed individuality, Dennis Wrong claimed, to the contrary, that they created "over-socialization" and repression. In his version of mass society theory, William Kornhauser found that pluralism and individuation smothered autonomy and reason. C. Wright Mills studied how the rise of a national and centralized "power elite" had followed from the destruction of small-town Jeffersonian democracy. Richard Sennett placed the "fall of public man" earlier, tracing it to the rise of capitalism and bureaucracy, as did Robert Bellah – with Amitai Etzioni one of the key figures in American communitarianism – who linked the rise of utilitarian individualism also to the decline of religious values.

While less radical and darkly pessimistic, anti-functionalist approaches to organizations were elaborated in a similarly "Madisonian" way. When Seymour Martin Lipset, James Coleman, and Martin Trow made their pro-democracy arguments against the pessimistic predictions of the Italian sociologist Robert Michels, they suggested that the survival of trade union democracy depended, not on the significance of values or the creative actions of individuals, but on the pluralistic division of social resources. Philip Selznick suggested that, despite the sincerity of human purpose, organizations initially established to realize collective values tend to be "coopted" by their efforts to contain competing social actors; in this way, they become "deflected" from their original purpose, i.e., bureaucratized in the Weberian sense. Reacting against what they regarded as the naiveté of Parsons and even Selznick, "neo-institutionalists" like John Meyer and Paul Dimaggio later developed an even more "realistic" approach to organizations. Building upon Goffman and Garfinkel, they denied the very possibility of cooperative and trusting relations between leaders and followers, declaring every expression of value commitment to be merely an effort at legitimation.

This Madisonian sociological discourse, which is inspired by the omnipresence of repression and domination, also informs the tradition of historical and comparative sociology that, in the 1960s and 1970s, emerged as an American "conflict sociology" in tandem with the recrudescence of European Marxism. Separating themselves from Durkheim and Parsons, and eliding Weber with Marx, such thinkers as Barrington Moore, Immanuel Wallerstein, Charles Tilly, Theda Skocpol, and Randall Collins separated action from subjectively experienced motives. Declaring that values exist only as legitimations for hegemonic institutions, they declared that macrosociology must focus on social structure, conflict, and hierarchy at the expense of action, culture, cooperation, or cross-group solidarity.

In response to these developments, sociological efforts to redeem the discourse of liberty emerged both from within the functionalist tradition and outside it. Distancing themselves from the unreflexive optimism of "American exceptionalism," and incorporating a more realistic understanding of economic and political power, neofunctionalism elaborated a normative vision of society in which individual motives, social groups, and institutions were linked by references to shared ideals. Inspired by the German neo-Kantian philosopher, Jürgen Habermas, who himself had been deeply influenced by Dewey and Mead, neofunctionalism related Parsonian ideas to the more communicative theories of early Pragmatism, acknowledging the importance of Madisonian pluralism but imbedding it in democratic public opinion, critical value commitments, and rational desires. While some of the principal proponents of the new American "sociology of emotions" have elaborated their subdiscipline in the strategic Madisonian vein, others (e.g., Jack Katz) emphasize the spontaneous authenticity of expressive behavior and the solidarities it produces. Similar divisions run through what has been called "the new American cultural sociology."[6] One group of American cultural sociologists, maintaining continuity with the conflict and organizational traditions, analyzes cultural patterns in relation to economic and political constraints. In contrast with this "sociology *of* culture," there has emerged a "cultural *sociology*" that emphasizes the influence of historical traditions rather than purely objective conditions, views symbolic interactions as rituals and not only as conflicts over resources, and pays close attention to how cultural narratives emerge from individual efforts to establish identity. Similarly, while the "resource mobilization" approach to social movements connects closely with conflict theory and neo-institutionalism, the "framing" approach developed by David Snow and his colleagues takes off from the more voluntaristic, communicative, and value-oriented strains of early Pragmatism. While such relatively recent American developments as queer theory, race theory, and feminist sociology certainly display Marxist and

Foucaultian lineages, in the American context these "postmodern" sociologies also reveal a much more optimistic, democratic, and integrative slant.

There are remarkable continuities in the history of American sociological thought, patterns that are obscured by such (all too familiar) juxtapositions as "symbolic interactionism versus functionalism" or "conflict versus order theory." From the historical founding documents of American civil society to contemporary "trends" in the sociological discipline that was established to protect it, one finds an obsessive concern with the vitality of individuals and their scope for free action. One strand of American sociology is relatively pessimistic. Convinced that the independence of the self has been undermined and the human spirit depleted, it has assumed strategic action and explored the threats to civil society that emanate from external, objective social structures. Another strand of American sociology has remained decidedly more optimistic, exploring the creation of individual subjectivity, communicative processes between individuals, and the patterned dynamics of powerful ideals. For this more optimistic and subjectively oriented tradition, the health of civil society rests on the continuing vitality of solidary ties.[7] For the more pessimistic "realist" tradition, protecting civil society depends on preventing the centralization of power and resources. Undoubtedly, civil society depends on both subjective and objective resources. Just as civil society needs both the Jeffersonian and the Madisonian traditions, so does the health of sociology depend on the dialogue between the theoretical and empirical orientations that have translated these traditions in a social scientific way.

Notes

Thanks to Paul Colomy, Stephen Turner and Jack Katz for their assistance in outlining the historical documents of the American sociological tradition. Thanks to Benjamin Alaexander-Bloch for pointing out to me the conflict between Madisonian theory and Transcendentalism.

1. And despite the fact, which cannot too strongly be emphasized, of the manifold internal variations in each of these traditions. These are not only spatial – national and regional – but political, religious, and of course philosophic. Nonetheless, the premise of this essay is that, in terms of their classical and modern exemplars, the historical and geographical referents "European" and "American" can be productively employed to develop contrasting ideal types. As Weber emphasized, ideal types are selectively constructed, highlighting contrasts for specific and delimited heuristic purposes. This stricture raises two important considerations, one methodological, the other normative. First, the sociological traditions that have flourished in Europe and America, and in other regions of the globe, can be parsed in very different ways that can be equally productive for heuristic purposes that cut across national and regional considerations. Second, in presenting a geographically oriented reconstruction of sociology, I am making an empirical, not a normative claim; I am neither advocating community-oriented localism

versus supra-national cosmopolitanism in sociology, nor, much less, am I arguing for the superiority of one community's traditions over another's. To the contrary, ever more intensive and symmetrical communication between Europe and America, among the various Americas and Europes, and between the centers of sociology now proliferating throughout the world is a goal much to be desired. International references have been part of the development of local sociologies from the beginning of the discipline, and the intensity of contemporary "globalization" will continue to counterbalance the regional and civilizational myopias of various sociological traditions.

2. See Jeffrey C. Alexander and Philip Smith, "The Discourse of American Civil Society: A New Proposal for Cultural Studies." *Theory and Society* 22 (2): 1993: 151–207.

3 Unless otherwise indicated, quotations in this essay are drawn from the documents anthologized below. In order to facilitate my editorial narrative, I sometimes refer to the original dates of publication; all other bibliographical information is available in the texts themselves.

4. Quotes are from Cooley's "The Self as Sentiment and Reflection" (in Cahill 1994 [1906]: 16–20) and from his "Primary Groups," in Cooley, *Social Organization* (1909): 23–31.

5. It should be noted, perhaps, that Goffman's emphasis on the separateness and strategizing quality of individuals does not mean that he embraced Blumer's anti-collectivism in every respect. To the contrary, Goffman often juxtaposed the amoral individual with a moralistic and highly constraining social order.

6. Philip Smith, ed., *The New American Cultural Sociology*. New York: Cambridge University Press, 1997.

7. In his recent, avowedly empirical stock-taking of the field, "The Elusive Situation in Social Psychology," Melvin Seeman revealed the moral ambition of sociological work in a manner that demonstrates the extraordinary continuity of the "optimistic tradition" over the course of this century.

> I take my text from the men whose work is truly being honored here: Charles Horton Cooley and George Herbert Mead. For both, the social context of experience – the social situation – served as the basis for the development of the self, *rational* action, and *cohesive* social institutions. These views are expressed in their conviction that *society and the person are complementary*; the social situation is the crucible of interaction in which *reflexive self-consciousness* and *community membership* develop. (*Social Psychology Quarterly* 1997 60 [1]: 4–13, quoting from p. 4, italics added).

In this empirical assessment of a major subdiscipline of contemporary American sociology, we find not only the social scientific translation of the three levels of the discourse of liberty (self, interaction, and institution) but the presuppositions that these levels can be defined and interrelated in a spontaneous, rational, cooperative, and democratic way.

Introduction to the Major Sections

Jeffrey C. Alexander

The Emergence of American Sociology: From the Enlightenment to the Founding Fathers

With less ambivalence than in Europe, sociology in America sprouted directly from the Enlightenment faith that applying scientific reason creates social progress. This belief in a "social" science marked the writings of both Sumner and Ward, which are permeated by naturalism and materialism and leavened with Darwin's emphasis on conflict and evolution; these framing ideas also deeply affected Dubois's pioneering empirical investigations into race. American sociology's eager embrace of quantitative methods was another manifestation of this direct application to sociology of Enlightenment methods and ideals.

Yet it is also important to see that this Enlightenment consensus was marked by theoretical and moral conflict. One strand of American social thought, quintessentially captured by Jefferson's *Declaration of Independence*, was optimistic about the capacity of individual reason to structure human relations and institutions in a cooperative and trusting way. By contrast, the strand of American Enlightenment thought more deeply affected by classical Republicanism evinced more pessimism about reason's triumph, was more inclined to envision unruly conflict, and more sympathetic toward the restrictions imposed by institutions. Madison's contributions to *The Federalist Papers*, the early defense of the American Constitution, crystallized this second strand of American Enlightenment thinking in a fundamental way.

While not an American himself, Tocqueville presented the optimistic confidence in individuality and cooperation in the first volume of *Democracy in America* and the more pessimistic emphasis on conformity and institutional domination in the second volume of that great early work. The major philosophical innovation of this early period, Transcendentalism, articulated the idealism of the Jeffersonian tradition in a manner that was, eventually, to have fundamental repercussions on American sociology. In opposition to this tradition, Sumner and Ward articulated a more materialistic and conflict-oriented approach that was to have far-reaching implications as well.

The Emergence of American Sociology: The Classical Tradition

The origins of what has become known as the most quintessentially "American" form of sociology can be traced to the Pragmatist revolution in philosophy. Against the materialism, pessimism, and scientism of its day, Pragmatism took up the more optimistic, interpretive, and morally-oriented vision earlier proclaimed by Emerson and Thoreau. With such concepts as the generalized other, the I and me, and the significance of gestural communication, Mead translated Pragmatic insights into the framework for sociological theory and research. In Cooley's hands, this general orientation became the basis for a program that focused on the interactional and collective features of social communication: action as dramatic performance, face-to-face interaction, and primary group solidarity. While the "Chicago school" has retrospectively been labelled micro-sociological, the institutional focus of such figures as Park and Wirth belie this narrow focus. What can be said is that the manner in which they approached such institutional phenomena as publics, social movements, and urban social relations reflected their deep concern for individual action and reciprocity, for the social significance of mutual understanding and the social centrality of communication. Similar concerns also informed work outside of the Chicago school, as in the critical perspective on contemporary economic life developed by Veblen and the Lynds.

American Sociology in the Twentieth-Century: From Pragmatism to Functionalism and Quantitative Sociology

During this period the patterns of "modern" American sociology were laid down, establishing the now familiar disciplinary features that were globalized in the postwar period of American sociological expansion.

Central to the formation of this mid-twentieth century discipline was the polarizing confrontation between the emergent, Parsonian functionalism and the version of Pragmatist sociology called symbolic interactionism. In the late 1930s, with the influence of the first Chicago school on the wane, Parsons published a powerful theoretical and programmatic text, *The Structure of Social Action*, which criticized traditional American sociology as individualistic and empiricist and called for a more collective, culturally oriented approach based on theoretical foundations established by Durkheim and Weber, both Europeans. The second generation of the Chicago school, led by Herbert Blumer, denounced this functionalist program as authoritarian, idealist, and empirically irrelevant, initiating a program that focused much more emphatically on face-to-face interactions and local situations than the earlier and broader forms of Pragmatic sociology.

Thus was born the famous split between "macro" and "micro." While certainly an important theoretical topic in its own right, the American form of this confrontation has obscured the fact that functionalism and interactionism are both variations on the optimistic strand of the American sociological tradition. In their approaches to action, both emphasize interpretation and emotion over strategy. In their studies of interaction, both examine trust and mutual understanding. In their conceptualization of institutions and societies, both emphasize solidarity, the public, and communication. It is not surprising, then, that both the functionalist and interactionist traditions developed research programs in the area of small groups.

American Sociology in the Twentieth-Century: Recent Trends in Sociological Theory

One of the paradoxical effects of the narrowing of the Pragmatist tradition was the stimulus it gave to the development of more individualistic and strategic approaches in American sociology. Within interactionism, one can see this development very clearly in the cynical approach to "performance" that inspired Goffman's dramaturgical sociology. Despite its roots in phenomenology and hermeneutic theory, the same tendency increasingly came to dominate Garfinkel's ethnomethodology and conversation analysis. Homans' "exchange" theory, which inspired a wide range of rational choice approaches, is the clearest manifestation of this approach on the micro level. This same pessimistic Madisonianism, however, became even more strongly crystallized in American macro-sociology. Not only in the most influential comparative and historical work, but in organizational studies and "critical" sociology, there emerged an anti-interpretive, anti-cultural framework that paid much less attention to normative solidarity than to conflict over economic and political interest.

In late twentieth century American sociology, there have emerged different kinds of efforts to restore the Jeffersonian tradition. There has been an opening up of the Chicago tradition to more macro concerns, as displayed, for example, in studies of how social movements provide interpretive frames for social problems and in examinations of the "emotion work" upon which institutions depend. Similarly, a "neo" functionalism has broadened traditional Parsonian concerns, connecting it to interaction, interpretation, and communicative forms of solidarity. As Pragmatist inspired communautarianism re-emerged in American philosophy, it began to affect various sociological fields as well. Postmodern studies of gender, ethnicity, and sexuality have emphasized the democratic potentiality of these new forms of differentiating solidarities. The new American cultural sociology has focused on the meaning-making capacities of actors and groups, and the impact that interpretive frameworks have on broader institutions.

THE EMERGENCE OF AMERICAN SOCIOLOGY

FROM THE ENLIGHTENMENT TO THE FOUNDING FATHERS

1

The Unanimous Declaration of the Thirteen United States of America

When, in the course of human events, it becomes necessary for one people to dissolve the political bonds which have connected them with another, and to assume among the powers of the earth, the separate and equal station to which the laws of nature and of nature's God entitle them, a decent respect to the opinions of mankind requires that they should declare the causes which impel them to the separation.

We hold these truths to be self-evident, that all men are created equal, that they are endowed by their Creator with certain unalienable rights, that among these are life, liberty and the pursuit of happiness. That to secure these rights, governments are instituted among men, deriving their just powers from the consent of the governed. That whenever any form of government becomes destructive to these ends, it is the right of the people to alter or to abolish it, and to institute new government, laying its foundation on such principles and organizing its powers in such form, as to them shall seem most likely to effect their safety and happiness. Prudence, indeed, will dictate that governments long established should not be changed for light and transient causes; and accordingly all experience hath shown that mankind are more disposed to suffer, while evils are sufferable, than to right themselves by abolishing the forms to which they are accustomed. But when a long train of abuses and usurpations, pursuing invariably the same object evinces a design to reduce them under absolute despotism, it is their right, it is their duty, to throw off such government, and to provide new guards for their future security. Such has been the patient sufferance of these colonies; and such is now the necessity which constrains them to alter their former systems of government. The history of the present King of Great Britain is a history of repeated injuries and usurpations, all having in direct object the establishment of an absolute tyranny over these states. To prove this, let facts be submitted to a candid world.

He has refused his assent to laws, the most wholesome and necessary for the public good.

He has forbidden his governors to pass laws of immediate and pressing importance, unless suspended in their operation till his assent should be obtained; and when so suspended, he has utterly neglected to attend to them.

He has refused to pass other laws for the accommodation of large districts of people, unless those people would relinquish the right of representation in the legislature, a right inestimable to them and formidable to tyrants only.

He has called together legislative bodies at places unusual, uncomfortable, and distant from the depository of their public records, for the sole purpose of fatiguing them into compliance with his measures.

He has dissolved representative houses repeatedly, for opposing with manly firmness his invasions on the rights of the people.

He has refused for a long time, after such dissolutions, to cause others to be elected; whereby the legislative powers, incapable of annihilation, have returned to the people at large for their exercise; the state remaining in the meantime exposed to all the dangers of invasion from without, and convulsions within.

He has endeavored to prevent the population of these states; for that purpose obstructing the laws for naturalization of foreigners; refusing to pass others to encourage their migration hither, and raising the conditions of new appropriations of lands.

He has obstructed the administration of justice, by refusing his assent to laws for establishing judiciary powers.

He has made judges dependent on his will alone, for the tenure of their offices, and the amount and payment of their salaries.

He has erected a multitude of new offices, and sent hither swarms of officers to harass our people, and eat out their substance.

He has kept among us, in times of peace, standing armies without the consent of our legislature.

He has affected to render the military independent of and superior to civil power.

He has combined with others to subject us to a jurisdiction foreign to our constitution, and unacknowledged by our laws; giving his assent to their acts of pretended legislation:

For quartering large bodies of armed troops among us:

For protecting them, by mock trial, from punishment for any murders which they should commit on the inhabitants of these states:

For cutting off our trade with all parts of the world:

For imposing taxes on us without our consent:

For depriving us in many cases, of the benefits of trial by jury:

For transporting us beyond seas to be tried for pretended offenses:

For abolishing the free system of English laws in a neighboring province, establishing therein an arbitrary government, and enlarging its boundaries so as to render it at once an example and fit instrument for introducing the same absolute rule in these colonies:

For taking away our charters, abolishing our most valuable laws, and altering fundamentally the forms of our governments:

For suspending our own legislatures, and declaring themselves invested with power to legislate for us in all cases whatsoever.

He has abdicated government here, by declaring us out of his protection and waging war against us.

He has plundered our seas, ravaged our coasts, burned our towns, and destroyed the lives of our people.

He is at this time transporting large armies of foreign mercenaries to complete the works of death, desolation and tyranny, already begun with circumstances of cruelty and perfidy scarcely paralleled in the most barbarous ages, and totaly unworth the head of a civilized nation.

He has constrained our fellow citizens taken captive on the high seas to bear arms against their country, to become the executioners of their friends and brethren, or to fall themselves by their hands.

He has excited domestic insurrections amongst us, and has endeavored to bring on the inhabitants of our frontiers, the merciless Indian savages, whose known rule of warfare, is undistinguished destruction of all ages, sexes and conditions.

In every stage of these oppressions we have petitioned for redress in the most humble terms: our repeated petitions have been answered only by repeated injury. A prince, whose character is thus marked by every act which may define a tyrant, is unfit to be the ruler of a free people.

Nor have we been wanting in attention to our British brethren. We have warned them from time to time of attempts by their legislature to extend an unwarrantable jurisdiction over us. We have reminded them of the circumstances of our emigration and settlement here. We have appealed to their native justice and magnanimity, and we have conjured them by the ties of our common kindred to disavow these usurpations, which, would inevitably interrupt our connections and correspondence. We must, therefore, acquiesce in the necessity, which denounces our separation, and hold them, as we hold the rest of mankind, enemies in war, in peace friends.

We, therefore, the representatives of the United States of America, in General Congress, assembled, appealing to the Supreme Judge of the world for the rectitude of our intentions, do, in the name, and by the authority of the good people of these colonies, solemnly publish and declare, that these united colonies are, and of right ought to be free and independent states; that they are absolved from all allegiance to the British Crown, and that all political connection between them and the state of Great Britain, is and ought to be totally dissolved; and that as free and independent states, they have full power to levey war, conclude peace, contract alliances, establish commerce, and to do all other acts and things which independent states may of right do. And for the support of this declaration, with a firm reliance on the protection of Divine Providence, we mutually pledge to each other our lives, our fortunes and our sacred honor.

2

The Union as a Safeguard Against Domestic Faction and Insurrection

James Madison

From the New York Packet.
Friday, November 23, 1787.

To the People of the State of New York:

Among the numerous advantages promised by a wellconstructed Union, none deserves to be more accurately developed than its tendency to break and control the violence of faction. The friend of popular governments never finds himself so much alarmed for their character and fate, as when he contemplates their propensity to this dangerous vice. He will not fail, therefore, to set a due value on any plan which, without violating the principles to which he is attached, provides a proper cure for it. The instability, injustice, and confusion introduced into the public councils, have, in truth, been the mortal diseases under which popular governments have everywhere perished; as they continue to be the favorite and fruitful topics from which the adversaries to liberty derive their most specious declamations. The valuable improvements made by the American constitutions on the popular models, both ancient and modern, cannot certainly be too much admired; but it would be an unwarrantable partiality, to contend that they have as effectually obviated the danger on this side, as was wished and expected. Complaints are everywhere heard from our most considerate and virtuous citizens, equally the friends of public and private faith, and of public and personal liberty, that our governments are too unstable, that the public good is disregarded in the conflicts of rival parties, and that measures are too often decided, not according to the rules of justice and the rights of the minor party, but by the superior force of an interested and overbearing majority.

However anxiously we may wish that these complaints had no foundation, the evidence, of known facts will not permit us to deny that they are in some degree true. It will be found, indeed, on a candid review of our situation, that some of the distresses under which we labor have been erroneously charged on the operation of our governments; but it will be found, at the same time, that other causes will not alone account for many of our heaviest misfortunes; and, particularly, for that prevailing and increasing distrust of public engagements, and alarm for private rights, which are echoed from one end of the continent to the other. These must be chiefly, if not wholly, effects of the unsteadiness and injustice with which a factious spirit has tainted our public administrations.

By a faction, I understand a number of citizens, whether amounting to a majority or a minority of the whole, who are united and actuated by some common impulse of passion, or of interest, adversed to the rights of other citizens, or to the permanent and aggregate interests of the community.

There are two methods of curing the mischiefs of faction: the one, by removing its causes; the other, by controlling its effects.

There are again two methods of removing the causes of faction: the one, by destroying the liberty which is essential to its existence; the other, by giving to every citizen the same opinions, the same passions, and the same interests.

It could never be more truly said than of the first remedy, that it was worse than the disease. Liberty is to faction what air is to fire, an aliment without which it instantly expires. But it could not be less folly to abolish liberty, which is essential to political life, because it nourishes faction, than it would be to wish the annihilation of air, which is essential to animal life, because it imparts to fire its destructive agency.

The second expedient is as impracticable as the first would be unwise. As long as the reason of man continues fallible, and he is at liberty to exercise it, different opinions will be formed. As long as the connection subsists between his reason and his self-love, his opinions and his passions will have a reciprocal influence on each other; and the former will be objects to which the latter will attach themselves. The diversity in the faculties of men, from which the rights of property originate, is not less an insuperable obstacle to a uniformity of interests. The prote ction of these faculties is the first object of government. From the protection of different and unequal faculties of acquiring property, the possession of different degrees and kinds of property immediately results; and from the influence of these on the sentiments and views of the respective proprietors, ensues a division of the society into different interests and parties.

The latent causes of faction are thus sown in the nature of man; and we see them everywhere brought into different degrees of activity, according to the different circumstances of civil society. A zeal for different opinions concerning religion, concerning government, and many other points, as well of speculation as of practice; an attachment to different leaders ambitiously contending for pre-eminence and power; or to persons of other descriptions whose fortunes have been interesting to the human passions, have, in turn, divided mankind into parties, inflamed them with mutual animosity, and rendered them much more disposed to vex and oppress each other than to co-operate for their common good. So strong is this propensity of mankind to fall into mutual animosities, that where no substantial occasion presents itself, the most frivolous and fanciful distinctions have been sufficient to kindle their unfriendly passions and excite their most violent conflicts. But the most common and durable source of factions has been the various and unequal distribution of property. Those who hold and those who are without property have ever formed distinct interests in society. Those who are creditors, and those who are debtors, fall under a like discrimination. A landed interest, a manufacturing interest, a mercantile interest, a moneyed interest, with many lesser interests, grow up of necessity in civilized nations, and divide them into different classes, actuated by different sentiments and views. The regulation of these various and interfering interests forms the principal task of modern legislation, and involves the spirit of party and faction in the necessary and ordinary operations of the government.

No man is allowed to be a judge in his own cause, because his interest would certainly bias his judgment, and, not improbably, corrupt his integrity. With equal, nay with greater reason, a body of men are unfit to be both judges and parties at the same time; yet what are many of the most important acts of legislation, but so many judicial determinations, not indeed concerning the rights of single persons, but concerning the rights of large bodies of citizens? And what are the different classes of legislators but advocates and parties to the causes which they determine? Is a law proposed concerning private debts? It is a question to which the creditors are parties on one side and the debtors on the other. Justice ought to hold the balance between them. Yet the parties are, and must be, themselves the judges; and the most numerous party, or, in other words, the most powerful faction must be expected to prevail. Shall domestic manufactures be encouraged, and in what degree, by restrictions on foreign manufactures? are questions which would be differently decided by the landed and the manufacturing classes, and probably by neither with a sole regard to justice and the public good. The apportionment of taxes on the various descriptions of property is an act which seems to require the most exact impartiality; yet there is, perhaps, no legislative act in which greater opportunity and temptation are given to a predominant party to trample on the rules of justice. Every shilling with which they overburden the inferior number, is a shilling saved to their own pockets.

It is in vain to say that enlightened statesmen will be able to adjust these clashing interests, and render them all subservient to the public good. Enlightened statesmen will not always be at the helm. Nor, in many cases, can such an adjustment be made at all without taking into view indirect and remote considerations, which will rarely prevail over the immediate interest which one party m ay find in disregarding the rights of another or the good of the whole.

The inference to which we are brought is, that the CAUSES of faction cannot be removed, and that relief is only to be sought in the means of controlling its EFFECTS.

If a faction consists of less than a majority, relief is supplied by the republican principle, which enables the majority to defeat its sinister views by regular vote. It may clog the administration, it may convulse the society; but it will be unable to execute and mask its violence under the forms of the Constitution.

When a majority is included in a faction, the form of popular government, on the other hand, enables it to sacrifice to its ruling passion or interest both the public good and the rights of other citizens. To secure the public good and private rights against the danger of such a faction, and at the same time to preserve the spirit and the form of popular government, is then the great object to which our inquiries are directed. Let me add that it is the great desideratum by which this form of government can be rescued from the opprobrium under which it has so long labored, and be recommended to the esteem and adoption of mankind.

By what means is this object attainable? Evidently by one of two only. Either the existence of the same passion or interest in a majority at the same time must be prevented, or the majority, having such coexistent passion or interest, must be rendered, by their number and local situation, unable to concert and carry into effect schemes of oppression. If the impulse and the opportunity be suffered to coincide, we well know that neither moral nor religious motives can be relied on as an adequate control. They are not found to be such on the injustice and violence of individuals, and lose their efficacy in proportion to the number combined together, that is, in proportion as their efficacy becomes needful.

From this view of the subject it may be concluded that a pure democracy, by which I mean a society consisting of a small number of citizens, who assemble and administer the government in person, can admit of no cure for the mischiefs of faction. A common passion or interest will, in almost every case, be felt by a majority of the whole; a communication and concert result from the form of government itself; and there is nothing to check the inducements to sacrifice the weaker party or an obnoxious individual. Hence it is that such democracies have ever been spectacles of turbulence and contention; have ever been found incompatible with personal security or the rights of property; and have in general been as short in their lives as they have been violent in their deaths. Theoretic politicians, who have patronized this species of government, have erroneously supposed that by reducing mankind to a perfect equality in their political rights, they would, at the same time, be perfectly equalized and assimilated in their possessions, their opinions, and their passions.

A republic, by which I mean a government in which the scheme of representation takes place, opens a different prospect, and promises the cure for which we are seeking. Let us examine the points in which it varies from pure democracy, and we shall comprehend both the nature of the cure and the efficacy which it must derive from the Union.

The two great points of difference between a democracy and a republic are: first, the delegation of the government, in the latter, to a small number of citizens elected by the rest; secondly, the greater number of citizens, and greater sphere of country, over which the latter may be extended.

The effect of the first difference is, on the one hand, to refine and enlarge the public views, by passing them through the medium of a chosen body of citizens, whose wisdom may best discern the true interest of their country, and whose patriotism and love of justice will be least likely to sacrifice it to temporary or partial considerations. Under such a regulation, it may well happen that the public voice, pronounced by the representatives of the people, will be more consonant to the public good than if pronounced by the people themselves, convened for the purpose. On the other hand, the effect may be inverted. Men of factious tempers, of local prejudices, or of sinister designs, may, by intrigue, by corruption, or by other means, first obtain the suffrages, and then betray the interests, of the people. The question resulting is, whether small or extensive republics are more favorable to the election of proper guardians of the public weal; and it is clearly decided in favor of the latter by two obvious considerations:

In the first place, it is to be remarked that, however small the republic may be, the representatives must be raised to a certain number, in order to guard against the cabals of a few; and that, however large it may be, they must be limited to a certain number, in order to guard against the confusion of a multitude. Hence, the number of representatives in the two cases not being in proportion to that of the two constituents, and being proportionally greater in the small republic, it follows that, if the proportion of fit characters be not less in the large than in the small republic, the former will present a greater option, and consequently a greater probability of a fit choice.

In the next place, as each representative will be chosen by a greater number of citizens in the large than in the small republic, it will be more difficult for unworthy candidates to practice with success the vicious arts by which elections are too often carried; and the suffrages of the people being more free, will be more likely to centre in men who possess the most attractive merit and the most diffusive and established characters.

It must be confessed that in this, as in most other cases, there is a mean, on both sides of which inconveniences will be found to lie. By enlarging too much the number of electors, you render the representatives too little acquainted with all their local circumstances and lesser interests; as by reducing it too much, you render him unduly attached to these, and too little fit to comprehend and pursue great and national objects. The federal Constitution forms a happy combination in this respect; the great and aggregate interests being referred to the national, the local and particular to the State legislatures.

The other point of difference is, the greater number of citizens and extent of territory which may be brought within the compass of republican than of democratic government; and it is this circumstance principally which renders factious combinations less to be dreaded in the former than in the latter. The smaller the society, the fewer probably will be the distinct parties and interests composing it; the fewer the distinct parties and interests, the more frequently will a majority be found of the same party; and the smaller the number of individuals composing a majority, and the smaller the compass within which they are placed, the more easily will they concert and execute their plans of oppression. Extend the sphere, and you take in a greater variety of parties and interests; you make it less probable that a majority of the whole will have a common motive to invade the rights of other citizens; or if such a common motive exists, it will be more difficult for all who feel it to discover their own strength, and to act in unison with each other. Besides other impediments, it may be remarked that, where there is a consciousness of unjust or dishonorable purposes, communication is always checked by distrust in proportion to the number whose concurrence is necessary.

Hence, it clearly appears, that the same advantage which a republic has over a democracy, in controlling the effects of faction, is enjoyed by a large over a small republic,—is enjoyed by the Union over the States composing it. Does the advantage consist in the substitution of representatives whose enlightened views and virtuous sentiments render them superior to local prejudices and schemes of injustice? It will not be denied that the representation of the Union will be most likely to possess these requisite endowments. Does it consist in the greater security afforded by a greater variety of parties, against the event of any one party being able to outnumber and oppress the rest? In an equal degree does the increased variety of parties comprised within the Union, increase this security. Does it, in fine, consist in the greater obstacles opposed to the concert and accomplishment of the secret wishes of an unjust and interested majority? Here, again, the extent of the Union gives it the most palpable advantage.

The influence of factious leaders may kindle a flame within their particular States, but will be unable to spread a general conflagration through the other States. A religious sect may degenerate into a political faction in a part of the Confederacy; but the variety of sects dispersed over the entire face of it must secure the national councils against any danger from that source. A rage for paper money, for an abolition of debts, for an equal division of property, or for any other improper or wicked project, will be less apt to pervade the whole body of the Union than a particular member of it; in the same proportion as such a malady is more likely to taint a particular county or district, than an entire State.

In the extent and proper structure of the Union, therefore, we behold a republican remedy for the diseases most incident to republican government. And according to the degree of pleasure and pride we feel in being republicans, ought to be our zeal in cherishing the spirit and supporting the character of Federalists.

3

The Structure of the Government Must Furnish the Proper Checks and Balances Between the Different Departments

Alexander Hamilton or James Madison

From the New York Packet.
Friday, February 8, 1788.

To the People of the State of New York:

To what expedient, then, shall we finally resort, for maintaining in practice the necessary partition of power among the several departments, as laid down in the Constitution? The only answer that can be given is, that as all these exterior provisions are found to be inadequate, the defect must be supplied, by so contriving the interior structure of the government as that its several constituent parts may, by their mutual relations, be the means of keeping each other in their proper places. Without presuming to undertake a full development of this important idea, I will hazard a few general observations, which may perhaps place it in a clearer light, and enable us to form a more correct judgment of the principles and structure of the government planned by the convention. In order to lay a due foundation for that separate and distinct exercise of the different powers of government, which to a certain extent is admitted on all hands to be essential to the preservation of liberty, it is evident that each department should have a will of its own; and consequently should be so constituted that the members of each should have as little agency as possible in the appointment of the members of the others. Were this principle rigorously adhered to, it would require that all the appointments for the supreme executive, legislative, and judiciary magistracies should be drawn from the same fountain of authority, the people, through channels having no communication whatever with one another. Perhaps such a plan of constructing the several departments would be less difficult in practice than it may in contemplation appear. Some difficulties, however, and some additional expense would attend the execution of it.

Some deviations, therefore, from the principle must be admitted. In the constitution of the judiciary department in particular, it might be inexpedient to insist rigorously on the principle: first, because peculiar qualifications being essential in the members, the primary consideration ought to be to select that mode of choice which best secures these qualifications; secondly, because the permanent tenure by which the appointments are held in that department, must soon destroy all sense of dependence on the authority conferring them. It is equally evident, that the members of each department should be as little dependent as possible on those of the others, for the emoluments annexed to their offices. Were the executive magistrate, or the judges, not independent of the legislature in this particular, their independence in every other would be merely nominal. But the great security against a gradual concentration of the several powers in the same department, consists in giving to those who administer each department the necessary constitutional means and personal motives to resist encroachments of the others. The provision for defense must in this, as in all other cases, be made commensurate to the danger of attack. Ambition must be made to counteract ambition. The interest of the man must be connected with the constitutional rights of the place. It may be a reflection on human nature, that such devices should be necessary to control the abuses of government. But what is government itself, but the greatest of all reflections on human nature? If men were angels, no government would be necessary. If angels were to govern men, neither external nor internal controls on government would be necessary. In framing a government which is to be administered by men over men, the great difficulty lies in this: you must first enable the government to control the governed; and in the next place oblige it to control itself. A dependence on the people is, no doubt, the primary control on the government; but experience has taught mankind the necessity of auxiliary precautions. This policy of supplying, by opposite and rival interests, the defect of better motives, might be traced through the whole system of human affairs, private as well as public. We see it particularly displayed in all the subordinate distr ibutions of power, where the constant aim is to divide and arrange the several offices in such a manner as that each may be a check on the other that the private interest of every individual may be a sentinel over the public rights. These inventions of prudence cannot be less requisite in the distribution of the supreme powers of the State. But it is not possible to give to each department an equal power of self-defense.

In republican government, the legislative authority necessarily predominates. The remedy for this inconveniency is to divide the legislature into different branches; and to render them, by different modes of election and different principles of action, as little connected with each other as the nature of their common functions and their common dependence on the society will admit. It may even be necessary to guard against dangerous encroachments by still further precautions. As the weight of the legislative authority requires that it should be thus divided, the weakness of the executive may require, on the other hand, that it should be fortified. An absolute negative on the legislature appears, at first view, to be the natural defense with which the executive magistrate should be armed. But perhaps it would be neither altogether safe nor alone sufficient. On ordinary occasions it might not be exerted with the requisite firmness, and on extraordinary occasions it might be perfidiously abused. May not this defect of an absolute negative be supplied by some qualified connection between this weaker department and the weaker branch of the stronger department, by which the latter may be led to support the constitutional rights of the former, without being too much detached from the rights of its own department? If the principles on which these observations are founded be just, as I persuade myself they are, and they be applied as a criterion to the several State constitutions, and to the federal Constitution it will be found that if the latter does not perfectly correspond with them, the former are infinitely less able to bear such a test. There are, moreover, two considerations particularly applicable to the federal system of America, which place that system in a very interesting point of view. First. In a single republic, all the power surrendered by the people is submitted to the administration of a single government; and the usurpations are guarded against by a division of the government into distinct and separate departments. In the compound republic of America, the power surrendered by the people is first divided between two distinct governments, and then the portion allotted to each subdivided among distinct and separate departments. Hence a double security arises to the rights of the people. The different governments will control each other, at the same time that each will be controlled by itself. Second. It is of great importance in a republic not only to guard the society against the oppression of its rulers, but to guard one part of the society against the injustice of the other part.

Different interests necessarily exist in different classes of citizens. If a majority be united by a common interest, the rights of the minority will be insecure. There are but two methods of providing against this evil: the one by creating a will in the community independent of the majority that is, of the society itself; the other, by comprehending in the society so many separate descriptions of citizens as will render an unjust combination of a majority of the whole very improbable, if not impracticable. The first method prevails in all governments possessing an hereditary or self-appointed authority. This, at best, is but a precarious security; because a power independent of the society may as well espouse the unjust views of the major, as the rightful interests of the minor party, and may possibly be turned against both parties. The second method will be exemplified in the federal republic of the United States. Whilst all authority in it will be derived from and dependent on the society, the society i tself will be broken into so many parts, interests, and classes of citizens, that the rights of individuals, or of the minority, will be in little danger from interested combinations of the majority. In a free government the security for civil rights must be the same as that for religious rights. It consists in the one case in the multiplicity of interests, and in the other in the multiplicity of sects. The degree of security in both cases will depend on the number of interests and sects; and this may be presumed to depend on the extent of country and number of people comprehended under the same government. This view of the subject must particularly recommend a proper federal system to all the sincere and considerate friends of republican government, since it shows that in exact proportion as the territory of the Union may be formed into more circumscribed Confederacies, or States oppressive combinations of a majority will be facilitated: the best security, under the republican forms, for the rights of every class of citizens, will be diminished: and consequently the stability and independence of some member of the government, the only other security, must be proportionately increased. Justice is the end of government. It is the end of civil society. It ever has been and ever

4

The Program in Practice

Peter Gay

I

The science of freedom was intended as a practical science, and in the 1770s and early 1780s a series of events in the British colonies of North America roused hopes among the philosophes that this intention might be realized. The Enlightenment was at the height of its influence; its leading ideas had been explored and its great debates had been settled. The Old Guard in the philosophic family was moving from the scene: Hume died in 1776, Rousseau and Voltaire in 1778, Turgot and Lessing in 1781, d'Alembert in 1783, and Diderot in 1784. But the American Revolution brightened the last years of these philosophes; while some of the British brethren were torn between demands of loyalty to empire and devotion to freedom, all the others felt unreserved delight in the events overseas. The splendid conduct of the colonists, their brilliant victory, and their triumphant founding of a republic were convincing evidence, to the philosophes at least, that men had some capacity for self-improvement and self-government, that progress might be a reality instead of a fantasy, and that reason and humanity might become governing rather than merely critical principles.

The philosophes had long taken an interest in the British settlements in America. European ideologues used them for varied, often contradictory purposes: partisans of simplicity and the primitive appealed to them quite as often as partisans of civility and refinement. This is why Benjamin Franklin was such an impressive spokesman for the colonists' cause: his astonished admirers in the European salons found that he embodied the virtues of nature and the triumphs of urbanity at the same time and with equal ease. Franklin greatly enjoyed playing the colonial as philosopher, the sage as backwoodsman. Even the critical minority, who thought the American climate unpropitious to the development of advanced civilizations, were converted by Franklin's imposing performance. Raynal, highly regarded as a specialist in the New World, was one of these converts: after making some derisive remarks about the American

---

Source: Peter Gay, *The Enlightenment: An Interpretation*, vol. II, *The Science of Freedom*, (New York: Alfred A. Knopf, 1968).

colonists, he came to expect great things of them. The Americans, he said, might produce new Homers and new Anacreons, and, even better, "perhaps there will arise another Newton in New England."[1] In the age of the Enlightenment there could be no compliment more trite, or more extravagant, than that.

As the form of Raynal's tribute indicates, European philosophes were regarding British America as a land of potential allies, even of leaders, in the march of human enlightenment. David Hume was among the first to give expression to this view. In 1762, when Benjamin Franklin was making ready to return to America from England, Hume eloquently regretted his imminent departure: "I am very sorry," he wrote to Franklin, "that you intend soon to leave our hemisphere. America has sent us many good things, gold, silver, sugar, tobacco, indigo, etc.; but you are the first philosopher, and indeed the first great man of letters, for whom we are beholden to her."[2] Hume was as ready as anyone in his age to write a graceful letter, but his appreciation of Franklin was authentic enough: he recognized him as a fellow philosophe. In later years, as the troubles with the American colonies became serious, Hume drew the logical consequence: a land of philosophes deserved independence.[3]

The philosophes on the Continent had no doubts – especially by 1778, after the colonists' first impressive victories. America, wrote Turgot in that year, was bound to prosper, for the American people were "the hope of the human race; they may well become its model."[4] About the same time, Diderot interrupted his essay on the reigns of Claudius and Nero with a fervent aside: "After centuries of general oppression," he burst out, "may the revolution which has just occurred across the seas, by offering all the inhabitants of Europe an asylum against fanaticism and tyranny, instruct those who govern men on the legitimate use of their authority! May these brave Americans, who would rather see their wives raped, their children murdered, their dwellings destroyed, their fields ravaged, their villages burned, and rather shed their blood and die than lose the slightest portion of their freedom, prevent the enormous accumulation and unequal distribution of wealth, luxury, effeminacy, and corruption of manners, and may they provide for the maintenance of their freedom and the survival of their government!" In Diderot's frenzied vision, untroubled, it seems, by factual information, rustic American philosophes were facing decadent British barbarians, and enjoying unprecedented opportunities coupled with unprecedented obligations. They must jealously guard their freedom and always remember how they came to be what they now are: "May they defer, at least for a few centuries, the decree pronounced on all the things of this world; the decree that has condemned them to have their birth, their time of vigor, their decrepitude, and their end! May the earth swallow up those of their provinces powerful enough, and mad enough, one day to seek the means of subjugating the others!"[5] A few months before Diderot wrote these words, Voltaire, the arch-philosophe, had come back to Paris to be deified and to die, and among his carefully staged final performances was a highly emotional meeting with Benjamin Franklin in mid-February: twenty spectators, "shedding tender tears," were present to see Voltaire embrace Franklin and bless Franklin's grandson in English with these charged words: "God and liberty."[6] By now God had become the guide to American philosophes, and liberty an American specialty.

The elevation of Benjamin Franklin to mythical status was eminently useful to those who wished the Enlightenment well, for it supported their claim to a practicality that its critics had often refused to grant. It was generally thought one of Franklin's chief virtues that he was an eminently practical man, an experimental scientist, a propagandist in behalf of the dissemination and application of theoretical knowledge through scientific societies, a man of the laboratory who did his duty as a citizen, and a worldly philosopher who brought thinking to bear on action with his collected maxims, which were perhaps as widely read in France as they were back home. After the colonies had won their independence and the colonists had shown their capacity to survive, the myth that Franklin embodied appeared to acquire a good deal of substance. The liberty that the Americans had won and were guarding was not merely an exhilarating performance that delighted European spectators and gave them grounds for optimism about man; it was also proving a realistic ideal worthy of imitation. "Men whom the reading of philosophic books had secretly converted to the love of liberty," Condorcet wrote in his eulogy to Franklin, "became enthusiastic over the liberty of a foreign people while they waited for the moment when they could recover their own, and they seized with joy the opportunity to avow publicly sentiments which prudence had prevented them from expressing."[7] Condorcet composed this tribute in 1790, when the French Revolution was well under way and looked, to all but Burke and émigré nobles, like a blissful dawn. The Americans, it seemed had returned the intellectual investments that Europeans had made in them, with interest.

II

The American Revolution converted America from an importer of ideas into an exporter. What it exported was, of course, mainly itself, but that was a formidable commodity – the program of enlightenment in practice. Before the 1770s, the American colonists had been chiefly consumers: it was significant that Hume should not merely praise Franklin as a philosopher but also implicitly criticize the colonies by calling him the first. In the mid-1760s, when the efflorescence of the American Enlightenment began and came to the attention of Europeans, the intellectual structure of the Enlightenment was practically complete. Not all colonial thought was a mere copy of Europe; like all others, the American philosophes developed their particular intellectual style by responding to domestic developments in Boston or Philadelphia or Richmond or the frontier that lay just beyond. But the substance of their ideas came from a handful of European thinkers.

Traces of this discipleship mark the leading figures in the American Revolution. Benjamin Franklin confessed that he had formed his style on Addison's *Spectator*; he had worked his way into deism by devouring the tracts of English controversialists and perfected his knowledge of modern science by studying the English Newtonians. He greatly admired Voltaire early and late for his good sense, sound reasoning, and amusing wit. Even in his amorous inclination he turned to Europe: in France, he met the widow of Helvétius, and proposed to her what he thought would be a logical match – after all, he said, he and Helvétius had loved the same studies, "the same friends, *and the same wife*."[8] John Adams, though outspoken and ungracious in his contempt for what he was pleased to consider the "naïve optimism" of Helvétius and Rousseau – his own optimism, though less extravagant in expression was quite as strong in substance – made it no secret that his defense of "lawful" revolution owed much to Grotius, Pufendorf, Barbeyrac; his political outlook much to Harrington, Locke, Montesquieu; his view of human nature much to Hutcheson, Ferguson, Bolingbroke. Adams liked to think by fighting opponents, and he freely expressed his distaste for European "dreamers." But if he rejected some European philosophes, he rejected them in the name, and with the aid, of other European philosophes. Even more than Adams, Thomas Jefferson was European to the bone. When Adams still felt malicious about the man who would later become his favorite correspondent, he remarked that Jefferson "drank freely of the French philosophy, in religion, in science, in politics." But this is less than just, and less than complete; Jefferson listened to his Virginian experience quite as much as he did to the writings of French philosophes, and he drank more freely from English than he did from French thought and literary models. Like his British brethren, Jefferson was a Francophile; at the same time, like his French and German brethren, he was an Anglomaniac. He loved the classics but also used them, as the European philosophes had used them, to free himself from the burdens of belief; he worshipped the three giants – Bacon, Newton, and Locke – whom Voltaire, d'Alembert, Hume, Lichtenberg, and Kant also worshipped, as the trinity of the three greatest men the world had ever seen.[9]

James Madison's intellectual development followed similar paths. Madison imitated Addison's style and found Voltaire congenial. Locke and Dubos, Montesquieu and Hume shaped his political thought and, with that, the Constitution of the United States. Finally, whatever the ultimate reasons for Alexander Hamilton's eventual estrangement from this group, it was not caused by any disagreements about the European Enlightenment. True, Hamilton thought better of monarchy and (if we may believe Jefferson) of Julius Caesar than did most of his fellow delegates at the Constitutional Convention or his fellow authors of the *Federalist* papers, but he too had studied the style of *Spectator* to perfect his own, and when as a young revolutionary he debated Samuel Seabury on the merits of the Continental Congress, he showed a thorough grasp of Pufendorf and Burlamaqui, Locke and Montesquieu. His reservations about the masses and advocacy of energetic government are softened by generous and sincere pronouncements in behalf of reason and humanity.

Even George Washington, though less of an intellectual than his colleagues, did not escape, and almost automatically adopted, their enlightened philosophy. When he addressed the governors of the American states in June 1783, shortly after victory, his circular letter breathed pride in his philosophical century: "The foundation of our Empire," he said, "was not laid in the gloomy age of Ignorance and Superstition, but at an Epocha when the rights of mankind were better understood and more clearly defined, than at any former period; the researches of the human mind after social happiness, have been carried to a great extent, the treasures of knowledge, acquired by the labours of Philosophers, Sages, and Legislators, through a long succession of years, are laid open for our use, and their collected wisdom may be happily applied in the Establishment of our forms of Government."[10] Never in the history of man had a statesman so confidently recommended the application of social science to human affairs, or so confidently expected widespread happiness as a consequence of their application. If George Washington thought so well of the Enlightenment, who could deny that the labors of the philosophes had entered the mainstream of eighteenth-century life?

Not unexpectedly, the enlightened, Europe-centered ideology of the Founding Fathers was shared by less celebrated Americans. The radicals who early in the 1760s began to wonder out loud whether the British colonies could continue to live under a monarchy increasingly corrupt and increasingly tyrannical adapted their reading for their own uses, but that reading was European. Whether it was James Otis or Jonathan Mayhew or John Dickinson, the proto-revolutionaries sprinkled their inflammatory writings with ideas, arguments, and phrases – and at times simply plagiarized extensive passages – from Voltaire and Beccaria, Scottish and English moralists, and English common lawyers to whom the Loyalists also turned for comfort and support. The main source of revolutionary logic was the work of English republicans of the late seventeenth and early eighteenth centuries, Milton and Harrington and Sidney, Trenchard and Gordon, and that much maligned, much underestimated Latitudinarian prelate, Bishop Hoadly; these English radicals were to the American rebels the very sum of modern political wisdom.[11] England, it was clear from America, had the best constitution men had ever devised – the mixed constitution – and if it was now becoming necessary to rebel that was only because England was shamefully departing from this glorious invention: England must be rescued from herself, with English and with Continental weapons.

In new hands, and in different circumstances, these weapons acquired new functions. While the formal institutions of the American colonies were all British in origin and management, their political operation was quite distinct from that in Great Britain. In the homeland, noisy opposition orators charged the government with despoiling the magnificent constitution that was the pride and protection of all free Britons, deplored the decay of freedom, painted hideous portraits of corruption, and forecast the collapse of all orderly government in universal tyranny; they aroused fears and suspicions, and could even, at times, thwart the will of ministers. But in the face of this rhetoric the system worked uncommonly well; the bonds of influence and of shared interests held together what the orators and pamphleteers threatened to pull apart. In the colonies, on the other hand, this opposition literature found a wide response even before serious unrest began in the 1760s. The powers of the colonial governors – the executive – were far more extensive in the colonies than those of the crown in Britain; they included the veto, the right to dissolve the legislatures, and control over the judiciary. Yet these "tyrannical" powers were more apparent than real: the supposedly omnipotent governors had little patronage to dispense, faced an uncommonly large body of voters, and were persistently obstructed by orders from overseas. The colonists perceived this incongruity, but far from congratulating themselves on the honesty of their officials, the extent of their franchise, and the impotence of their masters, they looked back to Britain with fears for the future. It was this incongruity between expectations and realities that made them so receptive to the Jeremiads of the British opposition. "Swollen claims and shrunken powers," as Bernard Bailyn has observed, "especially when they occur together, are always sources of trouble, and the malaise that resulted from this combination can be traced through the history of eighteenth-century politics."[12]

This dictum holds true elsewhere in the age of the Enlightenment – it applies aptly to France – but it applies most forcefully to the American colonies, for in true British fashion the colonists were highly articulate, passionately engaged in political arguments, and ready to see the need for change. There might be silence in Prussia or Russia but there was never silence in the colonies. "Whatever deficiencies the leaders of the American Revolution may have had" – to quote Bernard Bailyn once again – "reticence, fortunately, was not one of them."[13] The colonists poured out broadsides, pamphlets, and books by the hundreds; voluble preachers printed sermons touching on high principles of political obligation; ambitious lawyers and aspiring politicians denounced intolerable corruption, confiscatory taxation, oppressive vetoes, tyrannical ministers, and invoked heroes of antique and modern times – Cato, Cicero, Machiavelli, Locke, Trenchard and Gordon, and Montesquieu – with the ease of educated men knowing that they have an educated audience. When the colonists decided, regretfully but irrevocably, that it had become necessary to dissolve their political bonds to the British crown, and to assume, among the powers of the earth, the separate station to which they thought the laws of nature and of nature's God entitled them, they found that the world was listening.

III

As the Revolution took its course and the Founding Fathers established the American Confederation, debate did not slacken. There were new things to talk about in this time of troubles and expectations, and it was in this excited atmosphere that Madison, Hamilton, and Jay wrote the eighty-five articles that were to become *The Federalist*. It was a supremely practical piece of polemics, addressed not to posterity but to the moment, the work of three active politicians with one purpose: to persuade the voters of New York to accept the proposed constitution of the United States. But the *Federalist* has achieved, and fully deserves, immortality as a classic in the art of politics. It is also a classic work of the Enlightenment, a worthy successor to Montesquieu's *De l'esprit des lois* and a worthy companion to Rousseau's *Contrat social.*

The three authors of *The Federalist*, known by their collective signature, "Publius," sound all the great themes of the Enlightenment, if often by implication only: the dialectical movement away from Christianity to modernity; the pessimistic though wholly secular appraisal of human nature coupled with an optimistic confidence in institutional arrangements; the pragmatic reading of history as an aid to political sociology; the humane philosophy underlying their plea for the proposed constitution; the commitment to the critical method and the eloquent advocacy of practicality. The elements of *The Federalist* are thoroughly familiar; it is made of Hobbes and Harrington, Locke and Montesquieu, Hume and the *Encyclopédie*. What is new in the book is its particularly happy fusion of well-worn aspects of enlightened thought – psychology, history, political science, ethics – into a coherent and lucid whole, and its powerful sense that America is somehow different and certainly worth observing. With a certain modest pride, the authors of *The Federalist* accept the invitation to display America as a model for Europe: the Americans are "framing a Government for posterity as well as ourselves,"[14] and for the world as well as for North America "It has been frequently remarked," Hamilton notes in the very first paragraph of the book, "that it seems to have been reserved to the people of this country, by their conduct and example, to decide the important question, whether societies of men are really capable or not, of establishing good government from reflection and choice, or whether they are forever destined to depend, for their political constitutions, on accident and force." The struggle for the union of the American states, Hamilton confidently asserts, involves an empire which is "in many respects, the most interesting in the world."[15] The terms in which Hamilton – and Madison – saw the issue justified their claim: particularly to men of the eighteenth century nothing could be of greater interest than a contest in which, perhaps for the first time in history, reason might triumph over necessity.

In eighty-five papers on a system presumed to be of surpassing importance to all of civilization, the three authors of *The Federalist* drew on the intellectual resources common to educated men in the age of the Enlightenment, referring, freely and familiarly, to the history of Greece, Venice, medieval Europe, and Great Britain, to eighteenth-century struggles, and to colonial experience, and reinforcing these appeals to history, ancient, modern, and contemporary, with attacks on utopian dreamers and arguments from human nature. For them, history is recorded experience, experience material for history, the science of man the systematic explanation of history and experience together, and the science of politics their systematic utilization. The "lessons of history," to which they allude over and over again,[16] are so relevant to the formation of the American Union because they give clear expression to man's essential nature in the remote or the recent past. Like the other philosophes, Madison, Hamilton, and Jay rejoice in the variety of human conduct but insist on the unity of human nature.

The most instructive lesson history has to teach is that men need institutions to master their passions and regulate their conflicts. Man is not all bad, but a mixture of many qualities: "As there is a degree of depravity in mankind which requires a certain degree of circumspection and distrust: So there are other qualities in human nature, which justify a certain portion of esteem and confidence"; in fact the kind of regime Madison is advocating for America, "republican government," is itself an expression of moderate optimism, since it "presupposes the existence of these qualities in a higher degree than any other form."[17] *The Federalist* in its own way, though it persistently employs reasoned argument and addresses the reason of its readers, does not disdain what it regards as the higher passions: pride, humanity, and patriotism. But on balance the passions are anti-social; men, Hamilton writes, are dominated by "ambition, avarice, personal animosity, party opposition," by resentment, vindictiveness, rapacity, and the love of power.[18] The cause of faction, that great enemy of ordered society and rational policy, Madison concurs, is "sown in the nature of man," and the "propensity of mankind to fall into mutual animosities"[19] is overwhelming. And it is because man's vices overbalance his virtues that government is essential. "It may be a reflection on human nature, that such devices should be necessary to controul the abuses of government. But what is government itself but the greatest of all reflections on human nature? If men were angels, no government would be necessary. If angels were to govern men, neither external nor internal controuls on government would be necessary. In framing a government which is to be administered by men over men, the great difficulty lies in this: You must first enable the government to controul the governed; and in the next place, oblige it to controul itself."[20]

The problem that Madison raises here is ancient in lineage: *Sed quis custodiet ipsos custodes?* Juvenal had asked seventeen centuries before. But for the men of the Enlightenment, Juvenal's old question had particular urgency; it was not simply a matter for them of cowing passionate and factious men, for then an oppressive government would have suited them far better than the law-abiding, reasonable, and mild government they were proposing: the authors of *The Federalist* wanted freedom quite as much as they acknowledged the need for order. Like all political theorists in the Enlightenment, therefore, they called for vigorous government not to stifle, but to protect liberty.

Much of this libertarianism is implicit: *The Federalist* does not develop a formal catalogue of values. It does not need to, for values were not a problem;

the kind of qualities necessary to the good society – humanity, public happiness, protection against arbitrary government, popular sovereignty, enlightened policies – seem almost self-evident. But the question of how the government may "controul itself" is more difficult, and this justifies the concentration of *The Federalist* on the institutions proposed for the United States: the bulk of the papers deals with the presidency, Congress, the courts, with foreign and domestic policies and the federal system. The aim of these practical papers is never in doubt: to advocate a government that will guard the passions of individuals for the sake of order and guard the guardians for the sake of freedom.

A political system constructed on distrust of human nature and hostile to utopian optimists is bound to have its conservative side. But this side, though prominent, did not dominate *The Federalist*; the book is a document of the Enlightenment in its hopeful realism. The Founding Fathers, Madison wrote, "accomplished a revolution which has no parallel in the annals of human society: They reared the fabrics of governments which have no model on the face of the globe," and now they were ready to move beyond the achievement of the Confederacy to the still greater achievement of a Union. Again and again "Publius" used the word "experiment" as a word of self-praise: the Americans had made singular and unprecedented experiments, because they had trusted themselves, and experience had proved them to be right. It was Madison's proudest boast that the Americans, though respectful to antiquity, had been pioneers of modernity. Why, he asks, "is the experiment of an extended republic to be rejected merely because it may comprise what is new? Is it not the glory of the people of America, that whilst they have paid a decent regard to the opinions of former times and other nations, they have not suffered a blind veneration for antiquity, for custom, or for names, to overrule the suggestions of their own good sense, the knowledge of their own situation, and the lessons of their own experience? To this manly spirit, posterity will be indebted for the possession, and the world for the example of the numerous innovations displayed on the American theater, in favor of private rights and public happiness."[21] Nothing could epitomize the spirit of the Enlightenment more beautifully than this oratorical flight, with its declared openness to experiment undeterred by its respect for the past, its disdain for authority, and its reliance on autonomous reason, good sense, and experience, all for the sake of freedom and happiness.

The very magnificence of the passage makes it disquieting reading today. This is not a good time to appreciate the claims of enlightened men. Even America, the hope of civilized men everywhere in the eighteenth century, has given and continues to give its most benevolent well-wishers grounds for grave anxiety. If historians have dealt too unkindly with the Enlightenment, history itself has been far from gentle with its hopes and predictions. The world has not turned out the way the philosophes wished and half expected that it would. Old fanaticisms have been more intractable, irrational forces more inventive than the philosophes were ready to conjecture in their darkest moments.

Problems of race, of class, of nationalism, of boredom and despair in the midst of plenty have emerged almost in defiance of the philosophes' philosophy. We have known horrors, and may know horrors, that the men of the Enlightenment did not see in their nightmares. Yet, though few are today inclined to believe it, none of this impairs the permanent value of the Enlightenment's humane and libertarian vision, or the permanent validity of its critical method, any more than the philosophes' failure to live up to their own prescriptions or realize their own ideals compromises the worth of those prescriptions and those ideals. It remains as true today as it was in the eighteenth century: the world needs more light than it has, not less; the cure for the shortcomings of enlightened thought lies not in obscurantism but in further enlightenment. Our recognition of human irrationality, self-centeredness, stupidity beyond the philosophes' most pessimistic appraisals demands not surrender to such forces, but battle against them. In the light of recent history and today's headlines, this may appear to be a truly utopian prescription. It will perhaps appear less quixotic if we recall that there was a time when tough-minded men looked to the young republic in America, saw there with delight the program of the philosophes in practice, and found themselves convinced that the Enlightenment had been a success.

Notes

1. Quoted in Durand Echeverria: *Mirage in the West: A History of the French Image of American Society to 1815* (1957), 31.

2. May 10, 1762. *Letters*, I, 357.

3. In several letters (see for example, Hume to the Earl of Hertford February 27, 1766. *Letters*, II, 18–23; and to William Strahan, October 26, 1775. Ibid., 300–1), Hume expressed his energetic hope for the independence of the colonies, although his reasoning in these letters is normally entirely pragmatic: Britain cannot afford to subjugate the colonies.

4. Quoted in Echeverria: *Mirage in the West*, 69.

5. Denis Diderot: *Œuvres politiques*, ed. Paul Vernière (1963), 491.

6. See Voltaire to the abbé Gaultier, February 20, 1778. *Voltaire's Correspondence*, ed. Theodore Besterman, (1953–86), XCVIII, 110.

7. Quoted in Echeverria: *Mirage in the West*, 42.

8. Alfred Owen Aldridge: "Benjamin Franklin and the Philosophes," *Studies on Voltaire and the Eighteenth Century* ed. Theodore Besterman, XXIV (1963), 44, 58.

9. Dumas Malone: *Jefferson and His Time*, I, *Jefferson the Virginian* (1948), 101.

10. Quoted in Douglass Adair: "'That Politics May Be Reduced to a Science': David Hume, James Madison, and the Tenth *Federalist*," *The Huntington Library Quarterly*, XX, 4 (August 1957), 343.

11. Bernard Bailyn: *The Ideological Origins of the American Revolution* (1967), chap. ii, "Sources and Traditions."

12. Bernard Bailyn: *The Origins of American Politics* (1968), 96.

13. *Ideological Origins*, 1.

14. Alexander Hamilton: *The Federalist*, ed. Jacob E. Cooke (1961), No. 34, 213.
15. Ibid., No. 1, 3.
16. See James Madison: "This melancholy and monitory lesson of history," ibid., No. 20, 128; Hamilton: "History furnishes us with so many mortifying examples," ibid., No. 22, 142. And many other instances.
17. Ibid., No. 55, 378.
18. See ibid., No. 1, 5; the same, ibid., No. 6, 28, and often elsewhere.
19. Ibid., No. 10, 58–9.
20. Probably Madison, ibid., No. 51, 349.
21. Ibid., No. 14, 88–9.

5

Democracy in America: Volume I

Alexis de Tocqueville

Tyranny of the Majority

I hold it to be an impious and an execrable maxim that, politically speaking, a people has a right to do whatsoever it pleases, and yet I have asserted that all authority originates in the will of the majority. Am I then, in contradiction with myself?

A general law – which bears the name of Justice – has been made and sanctioned, not only by a majority of this or that people, but by a majority of mankind. The rights of every people are consequently confined within the limits of what is just. A nation may be considered in the light of a jury which is empowered to represent society at large, and to apply the great and general law of justice. Ought such a jury, which represents society, to have more power than the society in which the laws it applies originate?

When I refuse to obey an unjust law, I do not contest the right which the majority has of commanding, but I simply appeal from the sovereignty of the people to the sovereignty of mankind. It has been asserted that a people can never entirely outstep the boundaries of justice and of reason in those affairs which are more peculiarly its own, and that consequently full power may fearlessly be given to the majority by which it is represented. But this language is that of a slave.

A majority taken collectively may be regarded as a being whose opinions, and most frequently whose interests, are opposed to those of another being, which is styled a minority. If it be admitted that a man, possessing absolute power, may misuse that power by wronging his adversaries, why should a majority not be liable to the same reproach? Men are not apt to change their characters by agglomeration; nor does their patience in the presence of obstacles increase with the consciousness of their strength.[1] And for these reasons I can never willingly invest any number of my fellow-creatures with that unlimited authority which I should refuse to any one of them.

Source: Alexis de Tocqueville, *Democracy in America*, volume I, (New York: Longmans, Green & Co., 1889).

I do not think that it is possible to combine several principles in the same government, so as at the same time to maintain freedom, and really to oppose them to one another. The form of government which is usually termed *mixed* has always appeared to me to be a mere chimera. Accurately speaking there is no such thing as a mixed government (with the meaning usually given to that word), because in all communities some one principle of action may be discovered which preponderates over the others. England in the last century, which has been more especially cited as an example of this form of Government, was in point of fact an essentially aristocratic State, although it comprised very powerful elements of democracy; for the laws and customs of the country were such that the aristocracy could not but preponderate in the end, and subject the direction of public affairs to its own will. The error arose from too much attention being paid to the actual struggle which was going on between the nobles and the people, without considering the probable issue of the contest, which was in reality the important point. When a community really has a mixed government, that is to say, when it is equally divided between two adverse principles, it must either pass through a revolution or fall into complete dissolution.

I am therefore of opinion that some one social power must always be made to predominate over the others; but I think that liberty is endangered when this power is checked by no obstacles which may retard its course, and force it to moderate its own vehemence.

Unlimited power is in itself a bad and dangerous thing; human beings are not competent to exercise it with discretion, and God alone can be omnipotent, because His wisdom and His justice are always equal to His power. But no power upon earth is so worthy of honour for itself, or of reverential obedience to the rights which it represents, that I would consent to admit its uncontrolled and all-predominant authority. When I see that the right and the means of absolute command are conferred on a people or upon a king, upon an aristocracy or a democracy, a monarchy or a republic, I recognize the germ of tyranny, and I journey onwards to a land of more hopeful institutions.

In my opinion the main evil of the present democratic institutions of the United States does not arise, as is often asserted in Europe, from their weakness, but from their overpowering strength; and I am not so much alarmed at the excessive liberty which reigns in that country as at the very inadequate securities which exist against tyranny.

When an individual or a party is wronged in the United States, to whom can he apply for redress? If to public opinion, public opinion constitutes the majority; if to the legislature, it represents the majority, and implicitly obeys its injunctions; if to the executive power, it is appointed by the majority, and remains a passive tool in its hands; the public troops consist of the majority under arms; the jury is the majority invested with the right of hearing judicial cases; and in certain States even the judges are elected by the majority. However iniquitous or absurd the evil of which you complain may be, you must submit to it as well as you can.[2]

If, on the other hand, a legislative power could be so constituted as to represent the majority without necessarily being the slave of its passions; an executive, so as to retain a certain degree of uncontrolled authority; and a judiciary, so as to remain independent of the two other powers; a government would be formed which would still be democratic without incurring any risk of tyrannical abuse.

I do not say that tyrannical abuses frequently occur in America at the present day, but I maintain that no sure barrier is established against them, and that the causes which mitigate the government are to be found in the circumstances and the manners of the country more than in its laws.

Power Exercised by the Majority in America upon Opinion

It is in the examination of the display of public opinion in the United States that we clearly perceive how far the power of the majority surpasses all the powers with which we are acquainted in Europe. Intellectual principles exercise an influence which is so invisible, and often so inappreciable, that they baffle the toils of oppression. At the present time the most absolute monarchs in Europe are unable to prevent certain notions, which are opposed to their authority, from circulating in secret throughout their dominions, and even in their courts. Such is not the case in America; as long as the majority is still undecided, discussion is carried on; but as soon as its decision is irrevocably pronounced, a submissive silence is observed, and the friends, as well as the opponents, of the measure unite in assenting to its propriety. The reason of this is perfectly clear: no monarch is so absolute as to combine all the powers of society in his own hands, and to conquer all opposition with the energy of a majority which is invested with the right of making and of executing the laws.

The authority of a king is purely physical, and it controls the actions of the subject without subduing his private will; but the majority possesses a power which is physical and moral at the same time; it acts upon the will as well as upon the actions of men, and it represses not only all contest, but all controversy.

I know no country in which there is so little true independence of mind and freedom of discussion as in America. In any constitutional state in Europe every sort of religious and political theory may be advocated and propagated abroad; for there is no country in Europe so subdued by any single authority as not to contain citizens who are ready to protect the man who raises his voice in the cause of truth from the consequences of his hardihood. If he is unfortunate enough to live under an absolute government, the people is upon his side; if he inhabits a free country, he may find a shelter behind the authority of the throne, if he require one. The aristocratic part of society supports him in some countries, and the democracy in others. But in a nation where democratic institutions exist, organized like those of the United States, there is but one sole authority, one single element of strength and of success, with nothing beyond it.

In America, the majority raises very formidable barriers to the liberty of opinion: within these barriers an author may write whatever he pleases, but he will repent it if he ever step beyond them. Not that he is exposed to the terrors of an auto-da-fé, but he is tormented by the slights and persecutions of daily obloquy. His political career is closed for ever, since he has offended the only authority which is able to promote his success. Every sort of compensation, even that of celebrity, is refused to him. Before he published his opinions he imagined that he held them in common with many others; but no sooner has he declared them openly than he is loudly censured by his overbearing opponents, whilst those who think without having the courage to speak, like him, abandon him in silence. He yields at length, oppressed by the daily efforts he has been making, and he subsides into silence, as if he was tormented by remorse for having spoken the truth.

Fetters and headsmen were the coarse instruments which tyranny formerly employed; but the civilization of our age has refined the arts of despotism, which seemed, however, to have been sufficiently perfected before. The excesses of monarchical power had devised a variety of physical means of oppression; the democratic republics of the present day have rendered it as entirely an affair of the mind as that will which it is intended to coerce. Under the absolute sway of an individual despot the body was attacked in order to subdue the soul, and the soul escaped the blows which were directed against it and rose superior to the attempt; but such is not the course adopted by tyranny in democratic republics; there the body is left free, and the soul is enslaved. The sovereign can no longer say, 'You shall think as I do on pain of death;' but he says, 'You are free to think differently from me, and to retain your life, your property, and all that you possess; but if such be your determination, you are henceforth an alien among your people. You may retain your civil rights, but they will be useless to you, for you will never be chosen by your fellow-citizens if you solicit their suffrages, and they will affect to scorn you if you solicit their esteem. You will remain among men, but you will be deprived of the rights of mankind. Your fellow-creatures will shun you like an impure being, and those who are most persuaded of your innocence will abandon you too, lest they should he shunned in their turn. Go in peace! I have given you your life, but it is an existence incomparably worse than death.'

Monarchical institutions have thrown an odium upon despotism; let us beware lest democratic republics should restore oppression, and should render it less odious and less degrading in the eyes of the many, by making it still more onerous to the few.

Works have been published in the proudest nations of the Old World expressly intended to censure the vices and deride the follies of the times: Labruyère inhabited the palace of Louis XIV when he composed his chapter upon the Great, and Molière criticized the courtiers in the very pieces which were acted before the Court. But the ruling power in the United States is not to be made game of; the smallest reproach irritates its sensibility, and the slightest joke which has any foundation in truth renders it indignant; from the style of its language to the more solid virtues of its character, everything must be made the subject of encomium. No writer, whatever be his eminence, can escape from this tribute of adulation to his fellow-citizens. The majority lives in the perpetual practice of self-applause, and there are certain truths which the Americans can only learn from strangers or from experience.

If great writers have not at present existed in America, the reason is very simply given in these facts; there can be no literary genius without freedom of opinion, and freedom of opinion does not exist in America. The Inquisition has never been able to prevent a vast number of anti-religious books from circulating in Spain. The empire of the majority succeeds much better in the United States, since it actually removes the wish of publishing them. Unbelievers are to be met with in America, but, to say the truth, there is no public organ of infidelity. Attempts have been made by some governments to protect the morality of nations by prohibiting licentious books. In the United States no one is punished for this sort of works, but no one is induced to write them; not because all the citizens are immaculate in their manners, but because the majority of the community is decent and orderly.

In these cases the advantages derived from the exercise of this power are unquestionable, and I am simply discussing the nature of the power itself. This irresistible authority is a constant fact, and its judicious exercise is an accidental occurrence.

Effects of the Tyranny of the Majority upon the National Character of the Americans

The tendencies which I have just alluded to are as yet very slightly perceptible in political society, but they already begin to exercise an unfavourable influence upon the national character of the Americans. I am inclined to attribute the singular paucity of distinguished political characters to the ever-increasing activity of the despotism of the majority in the United States. When the American Revolution broke out they arose in great numbers, for public opinion then served, not to tyrannize over, but to direct the exertions of individuals. Those celebrated men took a full part in the general agitation of mind common at that period, and they attained a high degree of personal fame, which was reflected back upon the nation, but which was by no means borrowed from it.

In absolute governments the great nobles who are nearest to the throne flatter the passions of the sovereign, and voluntarily truckle to his caprices. But the mass of the nation does not degrade itself by servitude: it often submits from weakness, from habit, or from ignorance, and sometimes from loyalty. Some nations have been known to sacrifice their own desires to those of the sovereign with pleasure and with pride, thus exhibiting a sort of independence in the very act of submission. These peoples are miserable, but they are not degraded. There is a great difference between doing what one does not approve and feigning to approve what one does; the one is the necessary case of a weak person, the other befits the temper of a lacquey.

In free countries, where everyone is more or less called upon to give his opinion in the affairs of state; in democratic republics, where public life is incessantly commingled with domestic affairs, where the sovereign authority is accessible on every side, and where its attention can almost always be attracted by vociferation, more persons are to be met with who speculate upon its foibles and live at the cost of its passions than in absolute monarchies. Not because men are naturally worse in these States than elsewhere, but the temptation is stronger, and of easier access at the same time. The result is a far more extensive debasement of the characters of citizens.

Democratic republics extend the practice of currying favour with the many, and they introduce it into a greater number of classes at once: this is one of the most serious reproaches that can be addressed to them. In democratic States organized on the principles of the American republics, this is more especially the case, where the authority of the majority is so absolute and so irresistible that a man must give up his rights as a citizen, and almost abjure his quality as a human being, if he intends to stray from the track which it lays down.

In that immense crowd which throngs the avenues to power in the United States I found very few men who displayed any of that manly candour and that masculine independence of opinion which frequently distinguished the Americans in former times, and which constitutes the leading feature in distinguished characters, wheresoever they may be found. It seems, at first sight, as if all the minds of the Americans were formed upon one model, so accurately do they correspond in their manner of judging. A stranger does, indeed, sometimes meet with Americans who dissent from these rigorous formularies; with men who deplore the defects of the laws, the mutability and the ignorance of democracy; who even go so far as to observe the evil tendencies which impair the national character, and to point out such remedies as it might be possible to apply; but no one is there to hear these things besides yourself, and you, to whom these secret reflections are confided, are a stranger and a bird of passage. They are very ready to communicate truths which are useless to you, but they continue to hold a different language in public.

If ever these lines are read in America, I am well assured of two things: in the first place, that all who peruse them will raise their voices to condemn me; and in the second place, that very many of them will acquit me at the bottom of their conscience.

I have heard of patriotism in the United States, and it is a virtue which may be found among the people, but never among the leaders of the people. This may be explained by analogy; despotism debases the oppressed much more than the oppressor: in absolute monarchies the king has often great virtues, but the courtiers are invariably servile. It is true that the American courtiers do not say 'Sire,' or 'Your Majesty' – a distinction without a difference. They are for ever talking of the natural intelligence of the populace they serve; they do not debate the question as to which of the virtues of their master is pre-eminently worthy of admiration, for they assure him that he possesses all the virtues under heaven without having acquired them, or without caring to acquire them; they do not give him their daughters and their wives to be raised at his pleasure to the rank of his concubines, but, by sacrificing their opinions, they prostitute themselves. Moralists and philosophers in America are not obliged to conceal their opinions under the veil of allegory; but, before they venture upon a harsh truth, they say, 'We are aware that the people which we are addressing is too superior to all the weaknesses of human nature to lose the command of its temper for an instant; and we should not hold this language if we were not speaking to men whom their virtues and their intelligence render more worthy of freedom than all the rest of the world.' It would have been impossible for the sycophants of Louis XIV to flatter more dexterously. For my part, I am persuaded that in all governments, whatever their nature may be, servility will cower to force, and adulation will cling to power. The only means of preventing men from degrading themselves is to invest no one with that unlimited authority which is the surest method of debasing them.

The Greatest Dangers of the American Republics Proceed from the Unlimited Power of the Majority

Governments usually fall a sacrifice to impotence or to tyranny. In the former case their power escapes from them; it is wrested from their grasp in the latter. Many observers, who have witnessed the anarchy of democratic States, have imagined that the government of those States was naturally weak and impotent. The truth is, that when once hostilities are begun between parties, the government loses its control over society. But I do not think that a democratic power is naturally without force or without resources: say, rather, that it is almost always by the abuse of its force and the misemployment of its resources that a democratic government fails. Anarchy is almost always produced by its tyranny or its mistakes, but not by its want of strength.

It is important not to confound stability with force, or the greatness of a thing with its duration. In democratic republics, the power which directs[3] society is not stable; for it often changes hands and assumes a new direction. But whichever way it turns, its force is almost irresistible. The Governments of the American republics appear to me to be as much centralized as those of the absolute monarchies of Europe, and more energetic than they are. I do not, therefore, imagine that they will perish from weakness.[4]

If ever the free institutions of America are destroyed, that event may be attributed to the unlimited authority of the majority, which may at some future time urge the minorities to desperation, and oblige them to have recourse to physical force. Anarchy will then be the result, but it will have been brought about by despotism.

Mr. Hamilton expresses the same opinion in the 'Federalist,' No. 51. 'It is of great importance in a republic not only to guard the society against the oppression of its rulers, but to guard one part of the society against the injustice of the other part. Justice is the end of government. It is the end of civil society. It ever has been, and ever will be, pursued until it be obtained, or until liberty be lost in the pursuit. In a society, under the forms of which the stronger faction can readily unite and oppress the weaker, anarchy may as truly be said to reign as in a state of nature, where the weaker individual is not secured against the violence of the stronger: and as in the latter state even the stronger individuals are prompted by the uncertainty of their condition to submit to a government which may protect the weak as well as themselves, so in the former state will the more powerful factions be gradually induced by a like motive to wish for a government which will protect all parties, the weaker as well as the more powerful. It can be little doubted that, if the State of Rhode Island was separated from the Confederacy and left to itself, the insecurity of right under the popular form of government within such narrow limits would be displayed by such reiterated oppressions of the factious majorities, that some power altogether independent of the people would soon be called for by the voice of the very factions whose misrule had proved the necessity of it.'

Jefferson has also thus expressed himself in a letter to Madison:[5] 'The executive power in our Government is not the only, perhaps not even the principal, object of my solicitude. The tyranny of the legislature is really the danger most to be feared, and will continue to be so for many years to come. The tyranny of the executive power will come in its turn, but at a more distant period.' I am glad to cite the opinion of Jefferson upon this subject rather than that of another, because I consider him to be the most powerful advocate democracy has ever sent forth.

Religion Considered as a Political Institution, which Powerfully Contributes to the Maintenance of the Democratic Republic Amongst the Americans

Every religion is to be found in juxtaposition to a political opinion which is connected with it by affinity. If the human mind be left to follow its own bent, it will regulate the temporal and spiritual institutions of society upon one uniform principle; and man will endeavour, if I may use the expression, to harmonize the state in which he lives upon earth with the state which he believes to await him in heaven. The greatest part of British America was peopled by men who, after having shaken off the authority of the Pope, acknowledged no other religious supremacy; they brought with them into the New World a form of Christianity which I cannot better describe than by styling it a democratic and republican religion. This sect contributed powerfully to the establishment of a democracy and a republic, and from the earliest settlement of the emigrants politics and religion contracted an alliance which has never been dissolved.

About fifty years ago Ireland began to pour a Catholic population into the United States; on the other hand, the Catholics of America made proselytes, and at the present moment more than a million of Christians professing the truths of the Church of Rome are to be met with in the Union.[6] The Catholics are faithful to the observances of their religion; they are fervent and zealous in the support and belief of their doctrines. Nevertheless they constitute the most republican and the most democratic class of citizens which exists in the United States; and although this fact may surprise the observer at first, the causes by which it is occasioned may easily be discovered upon reflection.

I think that the Catholic religion has erroneously been looked upon as the natural enemy of democracy. Amongst the various sects of Christians, Catholicism seems to me, on the contrary, to be one of those which are most favourable to the equality of conditions. In the Catholic Church, the religious community is composed of only two elements, the priest and the people. The priest alone rises above the rank of his flock, and all below him are equal.

On doctrinal points the Catholic faith places all human capacities upon the same level; it subjects the wise and ignorant, the man of genius and the vulgar crowd, to the details of the same creed; it imposes the same observances upon the rich and needy, it inflicts the same austerities upon the strong and the weak, it listens to no compromise with mortal man, but, reducing all the human race to the same standard, it confounds all the distinctions of society at the foot of the same altar, even as they are confounded in the sight of God. If Catholicism predisposes the faithful to obedience, it certainly does not prepare them for inequality; but the contrary may be said of Protestantism, which generally tends to make men independent, more than to render them equal.

Catholicism is like an absolute monarchy; if the sovereign be removed, all the other classes of society are more equal than they are in republics. It has not unfrequently occurred that the Catholic priest has left the service of the altar to mix with the governing powers of society, and to take his place amongst the civil gradations of men. This religious influence has sometimes been used to secure the interests of that political state of things to which he belonged. At other times Catholics have taken the side of aristocracy from a spirit of religion.

But no sooner is the priesthood entirely separated from the Government, as is the case in the United States, than it is found that no class of men are more naturally disposed than the Catholics to transfuse the doctrine of the equality of conditions into the political world. If, then, the Catholic citizens of the United States are not forcibly led by the nature of their tenets to adopt democratic and republican principles, at least they are not necessarily opposed to them; and their social position, as well as their limited number, obliges them to adopt these opinions. Most of the Catholics are poor, and they have no chance of taking a part in the Government unless it be open to all the citizens. They constitute a minority, and all rights must be respected in order to ensure to them the free exercise of their own privileges. These two causes induce them, unconsciously, to adopt political doctrines which they would perhaps support with less zeal if they were rich and preponderant.

The Catholic clergy of the United States has never attempted to oppose this political tendency, but it seeks rather to justify its results. The priests in America have divided the intellectual world into two parts: in the one they place the doctrines of revealed religion, which command their assent; in the other they leave those truths which they believe to have been freely left open to the researches of political inquiry. Thus the Catholics of the United States are at the same time the most faithful believers and the most zealous citizens.

It may be asserted that in the United States no religious doctrine displays the slightest hostility to democratic and republican institutions. The clergy of all the different sects hold the same language, their opinions are consonant to the laws, and the human intellect flows onwards in one sole current.

I happened to be staying in one of the largest towns in the Union, when I was invited to attend a public meeting which had been called for the purpose of assisting the Poles, and of sending them supplies of arms and money. I found two or three thousand persons collected in a vast hall which had been prepared to receive them. In a short time a priest in his ecclesiastical robes advanced to the front of the hustings: the spectators rose, and stood uncovered, whilst he spoke in the following terms: –

'Almighty God! the God of Armies! Thou who didst strengthen the hearts and guide the arms of our fathers when they were fighting for the sacred rights of national independence! Thou who didst make them triumph over a hateful oppression, and hast granted to our people the benefits of liberty and peace; Turn, O Lord, a favourable eye upon the other hemisphere; pitifully look down upon that heroic nation which is even now struggling as we did in the former time, and for the same rights which we defended with our blood. Thou, who didst create Man in the likeness of the same image, let not tyranny mar Thy work, and establish inequality upon the earth. Almighty God! do Thou watch over the destiny of the Poles, and render them worthy to be free. May Thy wisdom direct their councils, and may Thy strength sustain their arms! Shed forth Thy terror over their enemies, scatter the powers which take counsel against them; and vouchsafe that the injustice which the world has witnessed for fifty years, be not consummated in our time. O Lord, who holdest alike the hearts of nations and of men in Thy powerful hand; raise up allies to the sacred cause of right; arouse the French nation from the apathy in which its rulers retain it, that it go forth again to fight for the liberties of the world.

'Lord, turn not Thou Thy face from us, and grant that we may always be the most religious as well as the freest people of the earth. Almighty God, hear our supplications this day. Save the Poles, we beseech Thee, in the name of Thy well-beloved Son, our Lord Jesus Christ, who died upon the cross for the salvation of men. Amen.'

The whole meeting responded 'Amen!' with devotion.

Indirect Influence of Religious Opinions upon Political Society in the United States

I have just shown what the direct influence of religion upon politics is in the United States, but its indirect influence appears to me to be still more considerable, and it never instructs the Americans more fully in the art of being free than when it says nothing of freedom.

The sects which exist in the United States are innumerable. They all differ in respect to the worship which is due from man to his Creator, but they all agree in respect to the duties which are due from man to man. Each sect adores the Deity in its own peculiar manner, but all the sects preach the same moral law in the name of God. If it be of the highest importance to man, as an individual, that his religion should be true, the case of society is not the same. Society has no future life to hope for or to fear; and provided the citizens profess a religion, the peculiar tenets of that religion are of very little importance to its interests. Moreover, almost all the sects of the United States are comprised within the great unity of Christianity, and Christian morality is everywhere the same.

It may be believed without unfairness that a certain number of Americans pursue a peculiar form of worship, from habit more than from conviction. In the United States the sovereign authority is religious, and consequently hypocrisy must be common; but there is no country in the whole world in which the Christian religion retains a greater influence over the souls of men than in America; and there can be no greater proof of its utility, and of its conformity to human nature, than that its influence is most powerfully felt over the most enlightened and free nation of the earth.

I have remarked that the members of the American clergy in general, without even excepting those who do not admit religious liberty, are all in favour of civil freedom; but they do not support any particular political system. They keep aloof from parties and from public affairs. In the United States religion exercises but little influence upon the laws and upon the details of public opinion, but it directs the manners of the community, and by regulating domestic life it regulates the State.

I do not question that the great austerity of manners which is observable in the United States, arises, in the first instance, from religious faith. Religion is often unable to restrain man from the numberless temptations of fortune; nor can it check that passion for gain which every incident of his life contributes to arouse, but its influence over the mind of woman is supreme, and women are the protectors of morals. There is certainly no country in the world where the tie of marriage is so much respected as in America, or where conjugal happiness is more highly or worthily appreciated. In Europe almost all the disturbances of society arise from the irregularities of domestic life. To despise the natural bonds and legitimate pleasures of home, is to contract a taste for excesses, a restlessness of heart, and the evil of fluctuating desires. Agitated by the tumultuous passions which frequently disturb his dwelling, the European is galled by the obedience which the legislative powers of the State exact. But when the American retires from the turmoil of public life to the bosom of his family, he finds in it the image of order and of peace. There his pleasures are simple and natural, his joys are innocent and calm; and as he finds that an orderly life is the surest path to happiness, he accustoms himself without difficulty to moderate his opinions as well as his tastes. Whilst the European endeavours to forget his domestic troubles by agitating society, the American derives from his own home that love of order which he afterwards carries with him into public affairs.

In the United States the influence of religion is not confined to the manners, but it extends to the intelligence of the people. Amongst the Anglo-Americans, there are some who profess the doctrines of Christianity from a sincere belief in them, and others who do the same because they are afraid to be suspected of unbelief. Christianity, therefore, reigns without any obstacle, by universal consent; the consequence is, as I have before observed, that every principle of the moral world is fixed and determinate, although the political world is abandoned to the debates and the experiments of men. Thus the human mind is never left to wander across a boundless field; and, whatever may be its pretensions, it is checked from time to time by barriers which it cannot surmount. Before it can perpetrate innovation, certain primal and immutable principles are laid down, and the boldest conceptions of human device are subjected to certain forms which retard and stop their completion.

The imagination of the Americans, even in its greatest flights, is circumspect and undecided; its impulses are checked, and its works unfinished. These habits of restraint recur in political society, and are singularly favourable both to the tranquillity of the people and to the durability of the institutions it has established. Nature and circumstances concurred to make the inhabitants of the United States bold men, as is sufficiently attested by the enterprising spirit with which they seek for fortune. If the mind of the Americans were free from all trammels, they would very shortly become the most daring innovators and the most implacable disputants in the world. But the revolutionists of America are obliged to profess an ostensible respect for Christian morality and equity, which does not easily permit them to violate the laws that oppose their designs; nor would they find it easy to surmount the scruples of their partisans, even if they were able to get over their own. Hitherto no one in the United States has dared to advance the maxim, that everything is permissible with a view to the interests of society; an impious adage which seems to have been invented in an age of freedom to shelter all the tyrants of future ages. Thus whilst the law permits the Americans to do what they please, religion prevents them from conceiving, and forbids them to commit, what is rash or unjust.

Religion in America takes no direct part in the government of society, but it must nevertheless be regarded as the foremost of the political institutions of that country; for if it does not impart a taste for freedom, it facilitates the use of free institutions. Indeed, it is in this same point of view that the inhabitants of the United States themselves look upon religious belief. I do not know whether all the Americans have a sincere faith in their religion, for who can search the human heart? but I am certain that they hold it to be indispensable to the maintenance of republican institutions. This opinion is not peculiar to a class of citizens or to a party, but it belongs to the whole nation, and to every rank of society.

In the United States, if a political character attacks a sect, this may not prevent even the partisans of that very sect from supporting him; but if he attacks all the sects together, everyone abandons him, and he remains alone.

Whilst I was in America, a witness, who happened to be called at the assizes of the county of Chester (State of New York), declared that he did not believe in the existence of God, or in the immortality of the soul. The judge refused to admit his evidence, on the ground that the witness had destroyed beforehand all the confidence of the Court in what he was about to say.[7] The newspapers related the fact without any further comment.

The Americans combine the notions of Christianity and of liberty so intimately in their minds, that it is impossible to make them conceive the one without the other; and with them this conviction does not spring from that barren traditionary faith which seems to vegetate in the soul rather than to live.

I have known of societies formed by the Americans to send out ministers of the Gospel into the new Western States to found schools and churches there, lest religion should be suffered to die away in those remote settlements, and the rising States be less fitted to enjoy free institutions than the people from which they emanated. I met with wealthy New Englanders who abandoned the country in which they were born in order to lay the foundations of Christianity and of freedom on the banks of the Missouri, or in the prairies of Illinois. Thus religious zeal is perpetually stimulated in the United States by the duties of patriotism. These men do not act from an exclusive consideration of the promises of a future life; eternity is only one motive of their devotion to the cause; and if you converse with these missionaries of Christian civilization, you will be surprised to find how much value they set upon the goods of this world, and that you meet with a politician where you expected to find a priest. They will tell you that 'all the American Republics are collectively involved with each other; if the republics of the West were to fall into anarchy, or to be mastered by a despot, the republican institutions which now flourish upon the shores of the Atlantic Ocean would be in great peril. It is therefore our interest that the new States should be religious, in order to maintain our liberties.'

Such are the opinions of the Americans, and if any hold that the religious spirit which I admire is the very thing most amiss in America, and that the only element wanting to the freedom and happiness of the human race is to believe in some blind cosmogony, or to assert with Cabanis the secretion of thought by the brain, I can only reply that those who hold this language have never been in America, and that they have never seen a religious or a free nation. When they return from their expedition, we shall hear what they have to say.

There are persons in France who look upon republican institutions as a temporary means of power, of wealth, and distinction; men who are the *condottieri* of liberty, and who fight for their own advantage, whatever be the colours they wear: it is not to these that I address myself. But there are others who look forward to the republican form of government as a tranquil and lasting state, towards which modern society is daily impelled by the ideas and manners of the time, and who sincerely desire to prepare men to be free, When these men attack religious opinions, they obey the dictates of their passions to the prejudice of their interests. Despotism may govern without faith, but liberty cannot. Religion is much more necessary in the republic which they set forth in glowing colours than in the monarchy which they attack; and it is more needed in democratic republics than in any others. How is it possible that society should escape destruction if the moral tie be not strengthened in proportion as the political tie is relaxed? and what can be done with a people which is its own master, if it be not submissive to the Divinity?

Notes

1. No one will assert that a people cannot forcibly wrong another people; but parties may be looked upon as lesser nations within a greater one, and they are aliens to each other: if therefore it be admitted that a nation can act tyrannically toward another nation, it cannot be denied that a party may do the same towards another party.

2. A striking instance of the excesses which may be occasioned by the despotism of the majority occurred at Baltimore in the year 1812. At that time the war was very popular in Baltimore. A journal which had taken the other side of the question excited the indignation of the inhabitants by its opposition. The populace assembled, broke the printing-presses, and attacked the houses of the newspaper editors. The militia was called out, but no one obeyed the call; and the only means of saving the poor wretches who were threatened by the frenzy of the mob was to throw them into prison as common malefactors. But even this precaution was ineffectual; the mob collected again during the night, the magistrates again made a vain attempt to call out the militia, the prison was forced, one of the newspaper editors was killed upon the spot, and the others were left for dead; the guilty parties were acquitted by the jury when they were brought to trial.

I said one day to an inhabitant of Pennsylvania, 'Be so good as to explain to me how it happens that in a State founded by Quakers, and celebrated for its toleration, freed Blacks are not allowed to exercise civil rights. They pay the taxes; is it not fair that they should have a vote?'

'You insult us,' replied my informant, 'if you imagine that our legislators could have committed so gross an act of injustice and intolerance.'

'What! then the Blacks possess the right of voting in this country?'

'Without the smallest doubt.'

'How comes it, then, that at the polling-booth this morning I did not perceive a single Negro in the whole meeting?'

'This is not the fault of the law: the Negroes have an undisputed right of voting, but they voluntarily abstain from making their appearance.'

'A very pretty piece of modesty on their parts!' rejoined I.

'Why, the truth is that they are not disinclined to vote, but they are afraid of being maltreated; in this country the law is sometimes unable to maintain its authority without the support of the majority. But in this case the majority entertains very strong prejudices against the Blacks, and the magistrates are unable to protect them in the exercise of their legal privileges.'

'What! then the majority claims the right not only of making the laws, but of breaking the laws it has made?'

3. This power may be centred in an assembly, in which case it will be strong without being stable; or it may be centred in an individual, in which case it will be less strong, but more stable.

4. I presume that it is scarcely necessary to remind the reader here, as well as throughout the remainder of this chapter, that I am speaking, not of the Federal Government, but of the several Governments of each State which the majority controls at its pleasure.

5. 15th March, 1789.

6. [It is difficult to ascertain with accuracy the amount of the Roman Catholic population of the United States, but in 1868 an able writer in the *Edinburgh Review* (vol. cxxvii. p. 521) affirmed that the whole Catholic population of the United States was then about 4,000,000, divided into 43 dioceses, with 3,795 churches, under the care of 45 bishops and 2,317 clergymen. But this rapid increase is mainly supported by immigration from the Catholic countries of Europe.]

7. The New York *Spectator* of August 23, 1831, relates the fact in the following terms: – 'The Court of Common Pleas of Chester county (New York) a few days since rejected a witness who declared his disbelief in the existence of God. The presiding judge remarked that he had not before been aware that there was a man living who did not believe in the existence of God; that this belief constituted the sanction of all testimony in a court of justice, and that he knew of no cause in a Christian country where a witness had been permitted to testify without such belief.'

6

Democracy in America: Volume II

Alexis de Tocqueville

How Democracy Modifies the Relations Between Master and Servant

An American who had travelled a lot in Europe once said to me: "We find the haughtiness and imperiousness of the English toward their servants astonishing, but on the other hand, the French sometimes treat them with a friendliness and considerate politeness which we cannot understand. One would think they were afraid of giving orders. The position of superior and inferior is ill-maintained."

The observation is fair and I have often noticed it myself.

In the whole world in our time I have always considered England as the country in which the bonds of domestic service are most tight, and France as that in which they are most relaxed. The extremes of haughtiness and humility on the master's part are found in these two countries.

The Americans come somewhere between these two extremes.

Such are the superficial and apparent facts. One has to go a long way back to find their causes.

There has not yet been a society in which conditions were so equal that there was neither rich nor poor, and consequently neither masters nor servants.

Democracy in no way prevents the existence of these two classes, but it changes their attitudes and modifies their relations.

In aristocracies servants are a class apart, which changes no more than that of the masters. A fixed order is soon created; in both classes there is soon a hierarchy, with numerous classifications and defined ranks, and generation succeeds generation without positions changing. There are two societies imposed one on top of the other, always distinct, but with analogous principles.

This aristocratic constitution has as much influence on the opinions and manners of the servants as on those of the masters, and though the effects are different, one can easily see the same cause at work.

Both classes form little nations within the great one, and in the end certain permanent conceptions of right and wrong are established among them. Some

---

Source: Alexis de Tocqueville, *Democracy in America*, volume II, (New York: Harper & Row, 1966).

aspects of human behaviour come to be seen in a quite particular and unchanging light. Within the community of servants, as in that of masters, men exercise great influence over one another. They recognize fixed rules, and in default of law, come up against a directing public opinion; their ways are settled and controlled.

These men whose destiny is to obey certainly do not understand fame, virtue, honesty, and honour in the same way as their masters. But they have devised fame, virtues, and honesty suited to servants, and they conceive, if I may put it so, a sort of servile honour.[1]

Because a class is low, one must not suppose that all its members are mean-spirited; that would be a great mistake. However inferior the class may be, he who is first within it and has no thought of leaving it has an aristocratic position which prompts high thoughts, strong pride, and self-respect and makes him capable of heroism and actions out of the ordinary.

In the service of the great lords of an aristocratic society it was not rare to find men of noble and vigorous character, who did not feel the servitude they bore and submitted to the will of their masters without fearing their wrath.

It has hardly ever been like that in the lower ranks of domestic servants. It may be imagined that he who occupies the lowest step in a hierarchy of valets is low indeed.

The French invented a word especially to designate this lowest of the servants of an aristocracy. They call him the lackey.

The term "lackey" served, when all other words were exhausted, as the ultimate designation of human meanness. Under the old monarchy, when one wanted a single expression to denote a vile and degraded creature, one said he had "the soul of a lackey." That alone was enough. The full meaning was understood.

Permanent inequality not only gives servants certain particular virtues and vices but also places them in a particular position as against their masters.

In aristocratic societies the poor are trained from infancy to thoughts of obedience. All around, wherever they look, they see hierarchies of command.

Hence, in countries where permanent inequality prevails, the master easily obtains from his servants an obedience which is prompt, complete, respectful, and easy, because they honour him not only as the master, but as representing the class of masters. He brings the whole weight of the aristocracy to bear on their wills.

He commands their actions and also to some extent directs their thoughts. In aristocracies the master often exercises, even unconsciously, an immense power over the thoughts, habits, and mores of those who obey him, and his influence extends far beyond even his authority.

In aristocratic societies, not only are there hereditary families of valets, as there are of masters, but the same families of valets are settled for generations with the same families of masters (they are parallel lines which never meet and never separate); and that makes prodigious modifications in the mutual relations between the two orders.

Thus, though under an aristocracy there is no natural resemblance between master and servant, though fortune, education, opinion, and rights set them at great distance apart on the ladder of existence, yet time in the end binds them together. Long-shared memories unite them, and however different they be, yet they grow alike. But in democracies, where by nature they are almost alike, they always remain strangers one to the other.

In aristocracies the master comes to think of his servants as an inferior and secondary part of himself, and he often takes an interest in their fate by the extended scope of his selfishness.

The servants, for their part, see themselves in almost the same way, and they sometimes identify themselves so much with the master personally that they become an appendage to him in their own eyes as well as in his.

In aristocracies the servant occupies a subordinate position from which he cannot escape; close to him stands another man with a higher rank which he cannot lose. On the one side, obscurity, poverty, and obedience for ever; on the other, fame, wealth, and power to command for ever. Their lots are always different and always close, and the link between them is as lasting as life itself.

In this extreme case the servant ends by losing his sense of self-interest; he becomes detached from it; he deserts himself, as it were, or rather he transports the whole of himself into his master's character; he there creates an imaginary personality for himself. He takes pleasure in identifying himself with the wealth of those whom he obeys; he glories in their fame, exalts himself by their nobility, and constantly feeds on borrowed grandeur to which he often attaches more value than do those who possess it fully and in truth.

There is something both touching and ridiculous in this strange medley of two existences.

These emotions of masters, passed into the souls of valets, adopt the size appropriate to the place they *occupy*; they shrink and lower themselves. What had been pride in the former becomes childish vanity and wretched pretension in the latter. The servants of a great man are usually very punctilious about the attentions due to him, and they care more about his smallest privileges than he does himself.

One still sometimes meets among us one of these old servants of the aristocracy; they are survivals from a race which will soon vanish.

In the United States I have not seen anyone at all like them. The Americans not only have no knowledge of the type in question, but are very hard to convince of his existence. It is almost as difficult for them to form an idea thereof as for us to picture a Roman slave or a serf of the Middle Ages. All these men are in fact, though to different degrees, the result of the same cause. They are slipping from our sight and daily merging into the darkness of the past with the social state that bore them.

Equality makes new men of servant and of master and establishes new connections between them.

When conditions are almost equal, men are continually changing places. There is still a class of valets and a class of masters, but they are not for ever composed of the same individuals, and more especially, not of the same families. Those who give the orders are no more permanent than those who obey.

As servants do not form a race apart, they have no customs, prejudices, or mores peculiar to themselves; one does not notice that they have any special ways of thought or modes of feeling; they know nothing of vices or virtues peculiar to their status, but share the education, opinions, feelings, virtues, and vices of their contemporaries; and they are honest or scoundrels in the same style as their masters.

The same equality prevails among servants as among masters.

As no fixed ranks or permanent hierarchies are found among them, one must not expect to find either the meanness or the distinction seen in the aristocracy of valets as in all other aristocracies.

Never in the United States have I seen anything to put one in mind of the trusted retainer whose memory still haunts us in Europe, but neither did I find the conception of the lackey. Both are lost without trace.

In democracies servants are not only equal among themselves, but one can say that in some fashion they are equal to their masters.

That needs some explanation to be fully understood.

The servant may at any time become the master, and he wants to do so. So the servant is not a different type of man from the master.

Why, then, has the latter the right to command, and what makes the former obey? A temporary and freely made agreement. By nature they are not at all inferior one to the other, and they only become so temporarily by contract. Within the terms of the contract, one is servant and the other master; beyond that, they are two citizens, two men.

I would like the reader to understand clearly that this is not just the way in which the servants see their position. The masters see domestic service in the same light, and the precise limits of command and obedience are as firmly fixed in the mind of the one as of the other.

When most of the citizens have long since attained a roughly similar status, and equality is an old and accepted fact, public opinion, which is never influenced by exceptions, broadly speaking, assigns certain limits to a man's worth, and it is difficult for any man long to rise above or fall below this level.

No matter how wealth or poverty, power or obedience, accidentally put great distances between two men, public opinion, based on the normal way of things, puts them near the common level and creates a sort of fancied equality between them, in spite of the actual inequality of their lives.

This all-powerful opinion finally infuses itself into the thoughts even of those whose interest it is to fight against it, it both modifies their judgment and subdues their will.

In the depths of their being neither master nor servant any longer sees a profound difference between them, and they neither hope nor fear ever to find such a difference. Hence they are neither scornful nor angry, and look at each other without pride or humility.

The master considers the contract the sole source of his power, and the servant thinks it the sole reason for his obedience. There is no dispute between them about their reciprocal position; each easily sees what is his and keeps to it.

In our army the soldier comes from much the same class as the officer and may reach the same ranks. In civil life he considers himself completely the equal of his commanders, and in fact is so. But in the army he does not hesitate to obey, and his obedience is no less prompt, precise, and ready for being freely given and defined.

That will give an idea of the relations between master and servant in a democracy.

It would be silly to suppose that there could ever be between these two men such warm and deep emotions as are sometimes kindled in the domestic service of aristocracy, nor should one expect striking examples of self-sacrifice.

In aristocracies servant and master see each other only occasionally, and often they talk only through an intermediary. Yet they usually stand firmly by each other.

In democracies servant and master are very close, their bodies constantly touch, but their souls remain apart; they have occupations together, but they hardly ever have common interests.

Among such peoples the servant always thinks of himself as a temporary inmate in his master's house. He has not known his ancestors and will not see his descendants; he has nothing lasting to expect from them. Why, then, should he identify his life with his master's, and what reason could there be for such a strange sacrifice of himself? The reciprocal position is changed; the relationship must be changed also.

I want to base all I have just said on the example of the Americans, but I cannot do so without making careful distinctions concerning persons and places.

In the South there is slavery, so all I have said cannot apply there.

In the North most of the servants are freed slaves or the sons of these. Such men hold a doubtful position in public esteem. The law brings them up close to their master's level. Mores obstinately push them back. They cannot see their own status clearly and are almost always either insolent or cringing.

But in these northern states, especially in New England, one does find a fairly large number of white men who agree for wages temporarily to perform the wishes of others. I have heard it said that these servants usually carry out the duties of their status accurately and sensibly, and without thinking themselves naturally inferior to those who give the orders, they submit without reluctance to obey them.

It seems to me that such men carry into domestic service some of those manly habits which are born of freedom and equality. Having once chosen a hard lot, they do not strive by indirect means to escape from it, and they have enough self-respect not to refuse their masters the obedience which they have freely promised.

The masters, for their part, do not expect more from their servants than the faithful and strict performance of the contract; they do not ask for marks of respect; they do not claim their love or devotion; it is enough if they are punctual and honest.

It would not therefore be true to say that in a democracy the relationship between master and servant is unorganized; it is organized in another way; the rule is different, but there is a rule.

It is not my business here to discover whether the new state of affairs which I have described is worse than what went before or simply different. It is enough for me that it is fixed and regulated, for what is important to find among men is not any particular order but just order.

But what am I to say of those sad and troubled times when equality comes into its own in the midst of revolutionary tumult, when democracy, after it has been established in the social system, still fights painfully against prejudice and mores?

Already law and, in part, public opinion proclaim that there is no natural and permanent inferiority of servant compared to master. But this new belief has not yet penetrated right to the bottom of the latter's mind, or rather his heart rejects it. In the secret places of his soul the master still considers that he is of a different and superior race; he does not dare to say so, but he shudders at allowing himself to be dragged down to the same level. His commands become at once timid and harsh; already he no longer feels those protective and kindly sentiments toward his servants which are always the fruit of long and uncontested power, and, changed himself, he is surprised to find his servant changed; he wants a man who is, so to say, only passing through a phase of domestic service to contract regular, permanent habits; he wants him to appear satisfied and proud of the servile status from which, sooner or later, he should escape; that he should sacrifice himself for a man who can neither protect nor ruin him; and finally, that he should be attached by an eternal link to beings who are like himself and do not endure longer than he.

In aristocratic societies it often happens that a man's soul is not degraded by the fact that he is a domestic servant, because he neither knows nor thinks of any other status, and the immense inequality between him and his master seems the necessary and inevitable effect of some hidden law of Providence.

In a democracy there is nothing degrading about the status of a domestic servant because it is freely adopted and temporary and because it is not stigmatized by public opinion and creates no permanent inequality between master and servant.

But in the journey from one social condition to the other, there is almost always a moment of hesitation between the aristocratic conception of subjection and the democratic conception of obedience.

Obedience, then, loses its moral basis in the eyes of him who obeys; he no longer considers it as some sort of divinely appointed duty, and he does not yet see its purely human aspect; in his eyes it is neither sacred nor just, and he submits to it as a degrading though useful fact.

It is at this moment that a confused and incomplete picture of equality forms itself in the servants' minds; they do not at once perceive whether this equality to which they have a right is to be found within or outside the scope of domestic service, and from the bottom of their hearts they revolt against an inferiority to which they have themselves submitted and from which they draw the profit. They agree to serve and are ashamed to obey; they are fond of the advantages of service but not of their master, or more accurately, they are not sure that they should not be the masters, and they are inclined to consider the man who gives them orders as an unjust usurper of their rights.

Then, every citizen's house shows the same sad spectacle as can be seen in the world of politics. There is an unspoken intestinal war between permanently suspicious rival powers; the master is malevolent and soft, the servant malevolent and intractable; the former constantly tries by unfair restrictions to evade his duty to protect and remunerate, and the latter shirks his duty to obey. The reins of domestic administration flap between them, each trying to grasp them. The lines between authority and tyranny, liberty and licence, and right and might seem to them so jumbled and confused that no one knows exactly what he is, what he can do, and what he should do.

Such a condition is revolutionary, not democratic.

Influence of Democracy on the Family

I have just been considering how among democratic peoples, particularly America, equality modifies the relation between one citizen and another.

I want to carry the argument further and consider what happens within the family. I am not trying to discover new truths, but to show how known facts have a bearing on my subject.

Everyone has noticed that in our time a new relationship has evolved between the different members of a family, that the distance formerly separating father and son has diminished, and that paternal authority, if not abolished, has at least changed form.

Something analogous, but even more striking, occurs in the United States.

In America the family, if one takes the word in its Roman and aristocratic sense, no longer exists. One only finds scattered traces thereof in the first years following the birth of children. The father then does, without opposition, exercise the domestic dictatorship which his sons' weakness makes necessary and which is justified by both their weakness and his unquestionable superiority.

But as soon as the young American begins to approach man's estate, the reins of filial obedience are daily slackened. Master of his thoughts, he soon becomes responsible for his own behaviour. In America there is in truth no adolescence. At the close of boyhood he is a man and begins to trace out his own path.

It would be wrong to suppose that this results from some sort of domestic struggle, in which, by some kind of moral violence, the son had won the freedom which his father refused. The same habits and principles which lead the former to grasp at independence dispose the latter to consider its enjoyment as an incontestable right.

So in the former one sees none of those hateful, disorderly passions which disturb men long after they have shaken off an established yoke. The latter feels none of those bitter, angry regrets which usually accompany fallen power. The father has long anticipated the moment when his authority must come to an end, and when that time does come near, he abdicates without fuss. The son has known in advance exactly when he will be his own master and wins his liberty without haste or effort, as a possession which is his due and which no one seeks to snatch from him.[2]

Perhaps it is useful to point out how the changes that have taken place within the family are closely connected with the social and political revolution taking place under our eyes.

There are certain great social principles which a people either introduces everywhere or tolerates nowhere.

In countries organized on the basis of an aristocratic hierarchy, authority never addresses the whole of the governed directly. Men are linked one to the other and confine themselves to controlling those next on the chain. The rest follows. This applies to the family as well as to all associations with a leader. In aristocracies society is, in truth, only concerned with the father. It only controls the sons through the father; it rules him, and he rules them. Hence the father has not only his natural right. He is given a political right to command. He is the author and support of the family; he is also its magistrate.

In democracies, where the long arm of government reaches each particular man among the crowd separately to bend him to obedience to the common laws, there is no need for such an intermediary. In the eyes of the law the father is only a citizen older and richer than his sons.

When conditions generally are very unequal and this inequality is permanent, the conception of superiority works on the imagination of men. Even if the law gave no parental prerogatives, custom and public opinion would supply them. But when men are little different from one another and such differences are not permanent, the general conception of superiority becomes weaker and less defined. It would be useless for a legislator to put the man who obeys in a position of great inferiority compared to him who gives the orders; mores bring these two men close to one another, and daily put them more on a level.

So, then, if I do not see any particular privileges accorded to the head of a family in the legislation of an aristocratic people, I can nonetheless rest assured that his power is much respected there and of wider extent than in a democracy, for I know that, whatever the laws may be, the superior will always seem higher and the inferior lower in aristocracies than in democracies.

When men are more concerned with memories of what has been than with what is, and when they are much more anxious to know what their ancestors thought than to think for themselves, the father is the natural and necessary link between the past and the present, the link where these two chains meet and join. In aristocracies, therefore, the father is not only the political head of the family but also the instrument of tradition, the interpreter of custom, and the arbiter of mores. He is heard with deference, he is addressed always with respect, and the affection felt for him is ever mingled with fear.

When the state of society turns to democracy and men adopt the general principle that it is good and right to judge everything for oneself, taking former beliefs as providing information but not rules, paternal opinions come to have less power over the sons, just as his legal power is less too.

Perhaps the division of patrimonies which follows from democracy does more than all the rest to alter the relations between father and children.

When the father of a family has little property, his son and he live constantly in the same place and carry on the same work together. Habit and necessity bring them together and force them all the time to communicate with each other. There is bound, then, to be a sort of intimate familiarity between them which makes power less absolute and goes ill with respectful formalities.

Moreover, in democracies those who possess these small fortunes are the very class which gives ideas their force and sets the tone of mores. Both its will and its thoughts prevail everywhere, and even those who are most disposed to disobey its orders end by being carried along by its example. I have known fiery opponents of democracy who allowed their children to call them "thou."

So at the same time as aristocracy loses its power, all that was austere, conventional, and legal in parental power also disappears and a sort of equality reigns around the domestic hearth.

I am not certain, generally speaking, whether society loses by the change, but I am inclined to think that the individual gains. I think that as mores and laws become more democratic the relations between father and sons become more intimate and gentle; there is less of rule and authority, often more of confidence and affection, and it would seem that the natural bond grows tighter as the social link loosens.

In a democratic family the father scarcely exercises more power than that gladly given to the kindness and experience of an old man. His orders might be ill-received, but his advice is usually weighty. He may not be surrounded with formal marks of respect, but at least his sons address him with confidence. There is no recognized formula of address, but they talk to him constantly and freely consult him every day. The master and magistrate have vanished; the father remains.

A perusal of the family correspondence surviving from aristocratic ages is enough to illustrate the difference between the two social states in this respect.

The style is always correct, ceremonious, rigid, and cold, so that natural warmth of heart can hardly be felt through the words.

But among democratic nations every word a son addresses to his father has a tang of freedom, familiarity, and tenderness all at once, which gives an immediate impression of the new relationship prevailing in the family.

An analogous revolution changes the relations between the children.

As in aristocratic society, so in the aristocratic family, all positions are defined. Not only the father holds a rank apart and enjoys immense privileges; the children too are by no means equal among one another, age and sex irrevocably fix the rank for each and ensure certain prerogatives. Democracy overthrows or lowers all these barriers.

In the aristocratic family the eldest son, who will inherit most of the property and almost all the rights, becomes the chief and to a certain extent the master of his brothers. Greatness and power are his; for them there is mediocrity and dependence. But yet it would be a mistake to suppose that in aristocracies the privileges of the eldest are profitable to him alone and that they excite nothing but jealousy and hatred around him.

The eldest usually takes trouble to procure wealth and power for his brothers, the general reputation of the house reflecting credit on its head. And the younger sons try to help the eldest in all his undertakings, for the greatness and power of the head of the family increase his ability to promote all the branches of the family. So the various members of the aristocratic family are closely linked together; their interests are connected and their minds are in accord, but their hearts are seldom in harmony.

Democracy too draws brothers together, but in a different way.

Under democratic laws the children are perfectly equal, and consequently independent; nothing forcibly brings them together, but also nothing drives them apart. Having a common origin, brought up under the same roof, and treated with the same care, as no peculiar privilege distinguishes or divides them, the affectionate and frank intimacy of childhood easily takes root among them. Scarcely anything can occur to break the bond thus formed at the start of life for brotherhood daily draws them together, and there is no cause for friction.

Not interest, then, but common memories and the unhampered sympathy of thoughts and tastes draw brothers, in a democracy, to one another. Their inheritance is divided, but their hearts are free to unite. This gentleness of democratic manners is such that even the partisans of aristocracy are attracted by it, and when they have tasted it for some time, they are not at all tempted to return to the cold and respectful formalities of the aristocratic family. They gladly keep the family habits of democracy, provided they can reject its social state and laws. But these things hold together, and one cannot enjoy the one without putting up with the others.

What I have said about filial love and fraternal affection applies to all the spontaneous feelings rooted in nature itself.

If a certain way of thinking or feeling is the result of particular conditions of life, when the conditions change, nothing is left. Thus law may make a very close link between two citizens; if the law is repealed, they separate. Nothing could have been tighter than the bond uniting lord and vassal in the feudal world. Now those two men no longer know each other. The fear, gratitude, and affection which once joined them have vanished. One cannot find a trace of them.

But it is not like that with feelings natural to man. Whenever a law attempts to shape such feelings in any particular way, it almost always weakens them. By trying to add something, it almost always takes something away, and they are always stronger if left to themselves.

Democracy, which destroys or obscures almost all old social conventions and which makes it harder for men to establish new ones, leads to the complete disappearance of almost all the feelings originating in such conventions. But it only modifies those of the other sort and often affords them an energy and gentleness which they had not before.

I think that I may be able to sum up in one phrase the whole sense of this chapter and of several others that preceded it. Democracy loosens social ties, but it tightens natural ones. At the same time as it separates citizens, it brings kindred closer together.

Notes

1. If one makes a close and detailed examination of the chief opinions which guide men, the analogy is even more striking. One is astonished to find among them, as among the most highly placed members of the feudal hierarchy, pride of birth, respect for ancestors and descendants, scorn for inferiors, a fear of contact, and a taste for etiquette, precedents, and antiquity.

2. It has, however, never occurred to the Americans to do what we have done in France and take away from fathers one of the chief elements of their power by refusing them the right to dispose of their possessions after their death; in the United States testamentary powers are unlimited. In this as in almost every other case, it is easy to see that while American political legislation is much more democratic than ours, our civil legislation is infinitely more democratic than theirs. That is easily understood. Our civil code was written by a man who saw that it was to his interest to satisfy all the democratic yearnings of his contemporaries in everything that did not immediately and directly threaten his power. He gladly allowed certain popular principles to control property and the management of family affairs, provided there was no pretension to apply them to the management of the state. While the torrent of democracy flooded over civil law, he hoped he could easily keep safe entrenched behind political laws. In this he was both very skilful and very selfish, but such a compromise could not be lasting. For in the long run political society cannot fail to become the expression and mirror of civil society. Indeed, it is in that sense that one can say that there is nothing more political about a people than its civil legislation.

7

The Transcendentalist[1]

Ralph W. Emerson

The first thing we have to say respecting what are called *new views* here in New England, at the present time, is, that they are not new, but the very oldest of thoughts cast into the mould of these new times. The light is always identical in its composition, but it falls on a great variety of objects, and by so falling is first revealed to us, not in its own form, for it is formless, but in theirs; in like manner, thought only appears in the objects it classifies. What is popularly called Transcendentalism among us, is Idealism; Idealism as it appears in 1842. As thinkers, mankind have ever divided into two sects, Materialists and Idealists; the first class founding on experience, the second on consciousness; the first class beginning to think from the data of the senses, the second class perceive that the senses are not final, and say, the senses give us representations of things, but what are the things themselves, they cannot tell. The materialist insists on facts, on history, on the force of circumstances, and the animal wants of man; the idealist on the power of Thought and of Will, on inspiration, on miracle, on individual culture. These two modes of thinking are both natural, but the idealist contends that his way of thinking is in higher nature. He concedes all that the other affirms, admits the impressions of sense, admits their coherency, their use and beauty, and then asks the materialist for his grounds of assurance that things are as his senses represent them. But I, he says, affirm facts not affected by the illusions of sense, facts which are of the same nature as the faculty which reports them, and not liable to doubt; facts which in their first appearance to us assume a native superiority to material facts, degrading these into a language by which the first are to be spoken; facts which it only needs a retirement from the senses to discern. Every materialist will be an idealist; but an idealist can never go backward to be a materialist.

The idealist, in speaking of events, sees them as spirits. He does not deny the sensuous fact: by no means; but he will not see that alone. He does not deny the presence of this table, this chair, and the walls of this room, but he looks at these things as the reverse side of the tapestry, as the *other end*, each

---

Source: Ralph W. Emerson, *English Traits and Representative Men*, (London & Toronto: J. M. Dent and Sons, 1908).

being a sequel or completion of a spiritual fact which nearly concerns him. This manner of looking at things, transfers every object in nature from an independent and anomalous position without there, into the consciousness. Even the materialist Condillac, perhaps the most logical expounder of materialism, was constrained to say, "Though we should soar into the heavens, though we should sink into the abyss, we never go out of ourselves; it is always our own thought that we perceive." What more could an idealist say?

The materialist, secure in the certainty of sensation, mocks at fine-spun theories, at star-gazers and dreamers, and believes that his life is solid, that he at least takes nothing for granted, but knows where he stands, and what he does. Yet how easy it is to show him, that he also is a phantom walking and working amid phantoms, and that he need only ask a question or two beyond his daily questions, to find his solid universe growing dim and impalpable before his sense. The sturdy capitalist, no matter how deep and square on blocks of Quincy granite he lays the foundations of his banking-house, or Exchange, must set it, at last, not on a cube corresponding to the angles of his structure, but on a mass of unknown materials and solidity, red-hot or white-hot, perhaps at the core, which rounds off to an almost perfect sphericity, and lies floating in soft air, and goes spinning away, dragging bank and banker with it at a rate of thousands of miles the hour, he knows not whither – a bit of bullet, now glimmering, now darkling through a small cubic space on the edge of an unimaginable pit of emptiness. And this wild balloon, in which his whole venture is embarked, is a just symbol of his whole state and faculty. One thing, at least, he says is certain, and does not give me the headache, that figures do not lie; the multiplication table has been hitherto found unimpeachable truth; and, moreover, if I put a gold eagle in my safe, I find it again to-morrow; – but for these thoughts, I know not whence they are. They change and pass away. But ask him why he believes that an uniform experience will continue uniform, or on what grounds he founds his faith in his figures, and he will perceive that his mental fabric is built up on just as strange and quaking foundations as his proud edifice of stone.

In the order of thought, the materialist takes his departure from the external world and esteems a man as one product of that. The idealist takes his departure from his consciousness, and reckons the world an appearance. The materialist respects sensible masses, Society, Government, social art, and luxury, every establishment, every mass, whether majority of numbers, or extent of space, or amount of objects, every social action. The idealist has another measure which is metaphysical, namely, the *rank* which things themselves take in his consciousness; not at all, the size or appearance. Mind is the only reality, of which men and all other natures are better or worse reflectors. Nature, literature, history, are only subjective phenomena. Although in his action overpowered by the laws of action, and so, warmly co-operating with men, even preferring them to himself, yet when he speaks scientifically, or after the order of thought, he is constrained to degrade persons into representatives of truths.

He does not respect labour, or the products of labour, namely, property, otherwise than as a manifold symbol, illustrating with wonderful fidelity of details the laws of being; he does not respect government, except as far as it reiterates the law of his mind; nor the church; nor charities; nor arts, for themselves; but hears, as at a vast distance, what they say, as if his consciousness would speak to him through a pantomimic scene. His thought – that is the Universe. His experience inclines him to behold the procession of facts you call the world, as flowing perpetually outward from an invisible, unsounded centre in himself, centre alike of him and of them, and necessitating him to regard all things as having a subjective or relative existence, relative to that aforesaid Unknown Centre of him.

From this transfer of the world into the consciousness, this beholding of all things in the mind, follow easily his whole ethics. It is simpler to be self-dependent. The height, the deity of man is, to be self-sustained, to need no gift, no foreign force. Society is good when it does not violate me; but best when it is likest to solitude. Everything real is self-existent. Everything divine shares the self-existence of Deity. All that you call the world is the shadow of that substance which you are, the perpetual creation of the powers of thought, of those that are dependent and of those that are independent of your will. Do not cumber yourself with fruitless pains to mend and remedy remote effects; let the soul be erect, and all things will go well. You think me the child of my circumstances: I make my circumstance. Let any thought or motive of mine be different from that they are, the difference will transform my condition and economy. I – this thought which is called I – is the mould into which the world is poured like melted wax. The mould is invisible, but the world betrays the shape of the mould. You call it the power of circumstance, but it is the power of me. Am I in harmony with myself? my position will seem to you just and commanding. Am I vicious and insane? my fortunes will seem to you obscure and descending. As I am, so shall I associate, and, so shall I act; Caesar's history will paint out Caesar. Jesus acted so, because he thought so. I do not wish to overlook or to gainsay any reality; I say, I make my circumstance: but if you ask me, Whence am I? I feel like other men my relation to that Fact which cannot be spoken, or defined, nor even thought, but which exists, and will exist.

The Transcendentalist adopts the whole connection of spiritual doctrine. He believes in miracle, in the perpetual openness of the human mind to new influx of light and power; he believes in inspiration, and in ecstasy. He wishes that the spiritual principle should be suffered to demonstrate itself to the end, in all possible applications to the state of man, without the admission of anything unspiritual; that is, anything positive, dogmatic, personal. Thus, the spiritual measure of inspiration is the depth of the thought, and never, who said it? And so he resists all attempts to palm other rules and measures on the spirit than its own.

In action, he easily incurs the charge of antinomianism by his avowal that he, who has the Lawgiver, may with safety not only neglect, but even contravene every written commandment. In the play of "Othello," the expiring Desdemona absolves her husband of the murder, to her attendant Emilia. Afterwards, when Emilia charges him with the crime, Othello exclaims,

"You heard her say herself it was not I."

Emilia replies,

"The more angel she, and thou the blacker devil."

Of this fine incident, Jacobi, the Transcendental moralist, makes use, with other parallel instances, in his reply to Fichte. Jacobi, refusing all measure of right and wrong except the determinations of the private spirit, remarks that there is no crime but has sometimes been a virtue. "I," he says, "am that atheist, that godless person who, in opposition to an imaginary doctrine of calculation, would lie as the dying Desdemona lied; would lie and deceive, as Pylades when he personated Orestes; would assassinate like Timoleon; would perjure myself like Epaminondas, and John de Witt; I would resolve on suicide like Cato; I would commit sacrilege with David; yea, and pluck ears of corn on the Sabbath, for no other reason than that I was fainting for lack of food. For, I have assurance in myself, that, in pardoning these faults according to the letter, man exerts the sovereign right which the majesty of his being confers on him; he sets the seal of his divine nature to the grace he accords."[2]

In like manner, if there is anything grand and daring in human thought or virtue, any reliance on the vast, the unknown; any presentiment; any extravagance of faith, the spiritualist adopts it as most in nature. The oriental mind has always tended to this largeness. Buddhism is an expression of it. The Buddhist who thanks no man, who says, "do not flatter your benefactors," but who, in his conviction that every good deed can by no possibility escape its reward, will not deceive the benefactor by pretending that he has done more than he should, is a Transcendentalist.

You will see by this sketch that there is no such thing as a Transcendental *party*; that there is no pure Transcendentalist; that we know of none but prophets and heralds of such a philosophy; that all who by strong bias of nature have leaned to the spiritual side in doctrine, have stopped short of their goal. We have had many harbingers and forerunners; but of a purely spiritual life, history has afforded no example. I mean, we have yet no man who has leaned entirely on his character, and eaten angels' food; who, trusting to his sentiments, found life made of miracles; who, working for universal aims, found himself fed, he knew not how; clothed, sheltered, and weaponed, he knew not how, and yet it was done by his own hands. Only in the instinct of the lower animals, we find the suggestion of the methods of it, and something higher than our understanding. The squirrel hoards nuts, and the bee gathers honey, without knowing what they do, and they are thus provided for without selfishness or disgrace.

Shall we say, then, that Transcendentalism is the Saturnalia or excess of Faith; the presentiment of a faith proper to man in his integrity, excessive only when his imperfect obedience hinders the satisfaction of his wish. Nature is transcendental, exists primarily, necessarily, ever works and advances, yet takes no thought for to-morrow. Man owns the dignity of the life which throbs around him in chemistry, and tree, and animal, and in the involuntary functions of his own body; yet he is balked when he tries to fling himself into this enchanted circle, where all is done without degradation. Yet genius and virtue predict in man the same absence of private ends, and of condescension to circumstances, united with every trait and talent of beauty and power.

This way of thinking, falling on Roman times, made Stoic philosophers; falling on despotic times, made patriot Catos and Brutuses; falling on superstitious times, made prophets and apostles; on popish times, made protestants and ascetic monks, preachers of Faith against the preachers of Works; on prelatical times, made Puritans and Quakers; and falling on Unitarian and commercial times, makes the peculiar shades of Idealism which we know.

It is well known to most of my audience, that the Idealism of the present day acquired the name of Transcendental, from the use of that term by Immanuel Kant, of Konigsberg, who replied to the sceptical philosophy of Locke, which insisted that there was nothing in the intellect which was not previously in the experience of the senses, by showing that there was a very important class of ideas, or imperative forms, which did not come by experience, but through which experience was acquired; that these were intuitions of the mind itself; and he denominated them *Transcendental* forms. The extraordinary profoundness and precision of that man's thinking have given vogue to his nomenclature, in Europe and America, to that extent, that whatever belongs to the class of intuitive thought, is popularly called at the present day *Transcendental.*

Although as we have said, there is no pure Transcendentalist, yet the tendency to respect the intuitions, and to give them, at least in our creed, all authority over our experience, has deeply coloured the conversation and poetry of the present day: and the history of genius and of religion in these times, though impure, and as yet not incarnated in any powerful individual, will be the history of this tendency.

It is a sign of our times, conspicuous to the coarsest observer, that many intelligent and religious persons withdraw themselves from the common labours and competitions of the market and the caucus, and betake themselves to a certain solitary and critical way of living, from which no solid fruit has yet appeared to justify their separation. They hold themselves aloof; they feel the disproportion between their faculties and the work offered them, and they prefer to ramble in the country and perish of *ennui,* to the degradation of such charities and such ambitions as the city can propose to them. They are striking work, and crying out for somewhat worthy to do! What they do, is done only because they are overpowered by the humanities that speak on all sides;

and they consent to such labour as is open to them, though to their lofty dream the writing of Iliads or Hamlets, or the building of cities or empires seems drudgery.

Now every one must do after his kind, be he asp or angel, and these must. The question, which a wise man and a student of modern history will ask, is, what that kind is? And truly, as in ecclesiastical history we take so much pains to know what the Gnostics, what the Essenes, what the Manichees, and what the Reformers believed, it would not misbecome us to inquire nearer home, what these companions and contemporaries of ours think and do, at least so far as these thoughts and actions appear to be not accidental and personal, but common to many, and the inevitable flower of the Tree of Time. Our American literature and spiritual history are, we confess, in the optative mood; but whoso knows these seething brains, these admirable radicals, these unsocial worshippers, these talkers who talk the sun and moon away, will believe that this heresy cannot pass away without leaving its mark.

They are lonely; the spirit of their writing and conversation is lonely; they repel influences; they shun general society; they incline to shut themselves in their chamber in the house, to live in the country rather than in the town, and to find their tasks and amusements in solitude. Society, to be sure, does not like this very well; it saith, Whoso goes to walk alone, accuses the whole world; he declareth all to be unfit to be his companions; it is very uncivil, nay, insulting; Society will retaliate. Meantime, this retirement does not proceed from any whim on the part of these separators; but if any one will take pains to talk with them, he will find that this part is chosen both from temperament and from principle: with some unwillingness, too, and as a choice of the less of two evils; for these persons are not by nature melancholy, sour, and unsocial – they are not stockish or brute – but joyous; susceptible, affectionate; they have even more than others a great wish to be loved. Like the young Mozart, they are rather ready to cry ten times a day, "But are you sure you love me?" Nay, if they tell you their whole thought, they will own that love seems to them the last and highest gift of nature; that there are persons whom in their hearts they daily thank for existing – persons whose faces are perhaps unknown to them, but whose fame and spirit have penetrated their solitude – and for whose sake they wish to exist. To behold the beauty of another character, which inspires a new interest in our own; to behold the beauty lodged in a human being, with such vivacity of apprehension, that I am instantly forced home to inquire if I am not deformity itself: to behold in another the expression of a love so high that it assures itself – assures itself also to me against every possible casualty except my unworthiness: – these are degrees on the scale of human happiness, to which they have ascended; and it is a fidelity to this sentiment which has made common association distasteful to them. They wish a just and even fellowship, or none. They cannot gossip with you, and they do not wish, as they are sincere and religious, to gratify any mere curiosity which you may entertain. Like fairies, they do not wish to be spoken of. Love me, they say, but do not ask who is my cousin and my uncle. If you do not need to hear my thought, because you can read it in my face and behaviour, then I will tell it you from sunrise to sunset. If you cannot divine it, you would not understand what I say. I will not molest myself for you. I do not wish to be profaned.

And yet, it seems as if this loneliness, and not this love, would prevail in their circumstances, because of the extravagant demand they make on human nature. That, indeed, constitutes a new feature in their portrait, that they are the most exacting and extortionate critics. Their quarrel with every man they meet, is not with his kind, but with his degree. There is not enough of him – that is the only fault. They prolong their privilege of childhood in this wise, of doing nothing – but making immense demands on all the gladiators in the lists of action and fame. They make us feel the strange disappointment which overcasts every human youth. So many promising youths, and never a finished man! The profound nature will have a savage rudeness; the delicate one will be shallow, or the victim of sensibility; the richly accomplished will have some capital absurdity; and so every piece has a crack. 'Tis strange, but this masterpiece is the result of such an extreme delicacy, that the most unobserved flaw in the boy will neutralise the most aspiring genius, and spoil the work. Talk with a seaman of the hazards to life in his profession, and he will ask you, "Where are the old sailors? do you not see that all are young men?" And we, on this sea of human thought, in like manner inquire, Where are the old idealists? where are they who represented to the last generation that extravagant hope, which a few happy aspirants suggest to ours? In looking at the class of counsel, and power, and wealth, and at the matronage of the land, amidst all the prudence and all the triviality, one asks, Where are they who represented genius, virtue, the invisible and heavenly world, to these? Are they dead – taken in early ripeness to the gods – as ancient wisdom foretold their fate? Or did the high idea die out of them and leave their unperfumed body as its tomb and tablet, announcing to all that the celestial inhabitant, who once gave them beauty, had departed? Will it be better with the new generation? We easily predict a fair future to each new candidate who enters the lists, but we are frivolous and volatile, and by low aims and ill example do what we can to defeat this hope. Then these youths bring us a rough but effectual aid. By their unconcealed dissatisfaction, they expose our poverty, and the insignificance of man to man. A man is a poor limitary benefactor. He ought to be a shower of benefits – a great influence, which should never let his brother go, but should refresh old merits continually with new ones; so that, though absent, he should never be out of my mind, his name never far from my lips; but if the earth should open at my side, or my last hour were come, his name should be the prayer I should utter to the Universe. But in our experience, man is cheap, and friendship wants its deep sense. We affect to dwell with our friends in their absence, but we do not; when deed, word, or letter comes not, they let us go. These exacting children advertise us of our wants.

There is no compliment, no smooth speech with them; they pay you only this one compliment, of insatiable expectation; they aspire, they severely exact, and if they only stand fast in this watch-tower, and persist in demanding unto the end, and without end, then are they terrible friends, whereof poet and priest cannot choose but stand in awe; and what if they eat clouds, and drink wind, they have not been without service to the race of man.

With this passion for what is great and extraordinary, it cannot be wondered at, that they are repelled by vulgarity and frivolity in people. They say to themselves, It is better to be alone than in bad company. And it is really a wish to be met – the wish to find society for their hope and religion – which prompts them to shun what is called society. They feel that they are never so fit for friendship, as when they have quitted mankind, and taken themselves to friend. A picture, a book, a favourite spot in the hills or the woods, which they can people with the fair and worthy creation of the fancy, can give them often forms so vivid, that these for the time shall seem real, and society the illusion.

But their solitary and fastidious manners not only withdraw them from the conversation, but from the labours of the world; they are not good citizens, not good members of society; unwillingly they bear their part of the public and private burdens; they do not willingly share in the public charities, in the public religious rites, in the enterprises of education, of missions foreign and domestic, in the abolition of the slave-trade, or in the temperance society. They do not even like to vote. The philanthropists inquire whether Transcendentalism does not mean sloth: they had as lief hear that their friend is dead, as that he is a Transcendentalist; for then is he paralysed, and can never do anything for humanity. What right, cries the good world, has the man of genius to retreat from work, and indulge himself? The popular literary creed seems to be, "I am a sublime genius; I ought not therefore to labour." But genius is the power to labour better and more availably. Deserve thy genius: exalt it. The good, the illuminated, sit apart from the rest, censuring their dulness and vices, as if they thought that, by sitting very grand in their chairs, the very brokers, attorneys, and congressmen would see the error of their ways, and flock to them. But the good and wise must learn to act, and carry salvation to the combatants and demagogues in the dusty arena below.

On the part of these children, it is replied, that life and their faculty seem to them gifts too rich to be squandered on such trifles as you propose to them. What you call your fundamental institutions, your great and holy causes, seem to them great abuses, and, when nearly seen, paltry matters. Each "Cause," as it is called – say Abolition, Temperance, say Calvinism, or Unitarianism – becomes speedily a little shop, where the article, let it have been at first never so subtle and ethereal, is now made up into portable and convenient cakes, and retailed in small quantities to suit purchasers. You make very free use of these words "great" and "holy," but few things appear to them such. Few persons have any magnificence of nature to inspire enthusiasm, and the philanthropies and charities have a certain air of quackery. As to the general course of living, and the daily employments of men, they cannot see much virtue in these, since they are parts of this vicious circle; and, as no great ends are answered by the men, there is nothing noble in the arts by which they are maintained. Nay, they have made the experiment, and found that, from the liberal professions to the coarsest manual labour, and from the courtesies of the academy and the college to the conventions of the cotillon-room and the morning call, there is a spirit of cowardly compromise and seeming, which intimates a frightful scepticism, a life without love, and an activity without an aim.

Unless the action is necessary, unless it is adequate, I do not wish to perform it. I do not wish to do one thing but once. I do not love routine. Once possessed of the principle, it is equally easy to make four or forty thousand applications of it. A great man will be content to have indicated in any the slightest manner his perception of the reigning Idea of his time, and will leave to those who like it the multiplication of examples. When he has hit the white, the rest may shatter the target. Everything admonishes us how needlessly long life is. Every moment of a hero so raises and cheers us, that a twelvemonth is an age. All that the brave Xanthus brings home from his wars, is the recollection that, at the storming of Samos, "in the heat of the battle, Pericles smiled on me, and passed on to another detachment." It is the quality of the moment, not the number of days, of events, or of actors, that imports.

New, we confess, and by no means happy, is our condition: if you want the aid of our labour, we ourselves stand in greater want of the labour. We are miserable with inaction. We perish of rest and rust: but we do not like your work.

"Then," says the world, "show me your own."

"We have none."

"What will you do, then?" cries the world.

"We will wait."

"How long?"

"Until the Universe rises up and calls us to work."

"But whilst you wait, you grow old and useless."

"Be it so: I can sit in a corner and *perish* (as you call it), but I will not move until I have the highest command. If no call should come for years, for centuries, then I know that the want of the Universe is the attestation of faith by my abstinence. Your virtuous projects, so called, do not cheer me. I know that which shall come will cheer me. If I cannot work, at least I need not lie. All that is clearly due to-day is not to lie. In other places, other men have encountered sharp trials, and have behaved themselves well. The martyrs were sawn asunder, or hung alive on meat-hooks. Cannot we screw our courage to patience and truth, and without complaint, or even with good-humour, await our turn of action in the Infinite Counsels?"

But, to come a little closer to the secret of these persons, we must say, that to them it seems a very easy matter to answer the objections of the man of the world, but not so easy to dispose of the doubts and objections that occur to themselves. They are exercised in their own spirit with queries, which acquaint them with all adversity, and with the trials of the bravest heroes. When I asked them concerning their private experience, they answered somewhat in this wise: It is not to be denied that there must be some wide difference between my faith and other faith; and mine is a certain brief experience, which surprised me in the highway or in the market, in some place, at some time – whether in the body or out of the body, God knoweth – and made me aware that I had played the fool with fools all this time, but that law existed for me and for all; that to me belonged trust, a child's trust and obedience, and the worship of ideas, and I should never be fool more. Well, in the space of an hour, probably, I was let down from this height; I was at my old tricks, the selfish member of a selfish society. My life is superficial, takes no root in the deep world; I ask, When shall I die, and be relieved of the responsibility of seeing an Universe which I do not use? I wish to exchange this flash-of-lightning faith for continuous daylight, this feverglow for a benign climate.

These two states of thought diverge every moment, and stand in wild contrast. To him who looks at his life from these moments of illumination, it will seem that he skulks and plays, a mean, shiftless, and subaltern part in the world. That is to be done which he has not skill to do, or to be said which others can say better, and he lies by, or occupies his hands with some plaything, until his hour comes again. Much of our reading, much of our labour, seems here waiting; it was not that we were born for. Any other could do it as well, or better. So little skill enters into these works, so little do they mix with the divine life, that it really signifies little what we do, whether we turn a grindstone, or ride, or run, or make fortunes, or govern the state. The worst feature of this double consciousness is, that the two lives, of the understanding and of the soul, which we lead, really show very little relation to each other, never meet and measure each other: one prevails now, all buzz and din; and the other prevails then, all infinitude and paradise; and, with the progress of life, the two discover no greater disposition to reconcile themselves. Yet, what is my faith? What am I? What but a thought of serenity and independence, an abode in the deep blue sky? Presently the clouds shut down again; yet we retain the belief that this pretty web we weave will at last be overshot and reticulated with veins of the blue, and that the moments will characterise the days. Patience, then, is for us, is it not? Patience, and still patience. When we pass, as presently we shall, into some new infinitude, out of this Iceland of negations, it will please us to reflect that, though we had few virtues or consolations, we bore with our indigence, nor once strove to repair it with hypocrisy or false heat of any kind.

But this class are not sufficiently characterised, if we omit to add that they are lovers and worshippers of Beauty. In the eternal trinity of Truth, Goodness, and Beauty, each in its perfection including the three, they prefer to make Beauty the sign and head. Something of the same taste is observable in all the moral movements of the time, in the religious and benevolent enterprises. They have a liberal, even an aesthetic spirit. A reference to Beauty in action sounds, to be sure, a little hollow and ridiculous, in the ears of the old church.

In politics, it has often sufficed, when they treated of justice, if they kept the bounds of selfish calculation. If they granted restitution, it was prudence which granted it. But the justice which is now claimed for the black, and the pauper, and the drunkard is for Beauty – is for a necessity to the soul of the agent, not of the beneficiary. I say, this is the tendency, not yet the realisation. Our virtue totters and trips, does not yet walk firmly. Its representatives are austere; they preach and denounce; their rectitude is not yet a grace. They are still liable to that slight taint of burlesque which, in our strange world, attaches to the zealot. A saint should be as dear as the apple of the eye. Yet we are tempted to smile, and we flee from the working to the speculative reformer, to escape that same slight ridicule. Alas for these days of derision and criticism! We call the Beautiful the highest, because it appears to us the golden mean, escaping the dowdiness of the good, and the heartlessness of the true. – They are lovers of nature also, and find an indemnity in the inviolable order of the world for the violated order and grace of man.

There is, no doubt, a great deal of well-founded objection to be spoken or felt against the sayings and doings of this class, some of whose traits we have selected; no doubt, they will lay themselves open to criticism and to lampoons, and as ridiculous stories will be to be told of them as of any. There will be cant and pretension; there will be subtilty and moonshine. These persons are of unequal strength, and do not all prosper. They complain that everything around them must be denied; and if feeble, it takes all their strength to deny, before they can begin to lead their own life. Grave seniors insist on their respect to this institution, and that usage; to an obsolete history; to some vocation, or college, or etiquette, or beneficiary, or charity, or morning or evening call, which they resist, as what does not concern them. But it costs such sleepless nights, alienations, and misgivings – they have so many moods about it; – these old guardians never change *their* minds; they have but one mood on the subject, namely, that Antony is very perverse – that it is quite as much as Antony can do, to assert his rights, abstain from what he thinks foolish, and keep his temper. He cannot help the reaction of this injustice in his own mind. He is braced-up and stilted; all freedom and flowing genius, all sallies of wit and frolic nature are quite out of the question; it is well if he can keep from lying, injustice, and suicide. This is no time for gaiety and grace. His strength and spirits are wasted in rejection. But the strong spirits overpower those around them without effort. Their thought and emotion comes in like a flood, quite withdraws them from all notice of these carping critics; they surrender themselves with glad heart to the heavenly guide, and only by implication reject the clamorous nonsense of the hour. Grave seniors talk to the deaf – church and old book mumble and ritualise to an unheeding, pre-occupied, and advancing mind, and thus they by happiness of greater momentum lose no time, but take the right road at first.

But all these of whom I speak are not proficients; they are novices; they only show the road in which man should travel, when the soul has greater health and prowess. Yet let them feel the dignity of their charge, and deserve a larger power. Their heart is the ark in which the fire is concealed, which shall burn in a broader and universal flame. Let them obey the Genius then most when his impulse is wildest; then most when he seems to lead to uninhabitable deserts of thought and life; for the path which the hero travels alone is the highway of health and benefit to mankind. What is the privilege and nobility of our nature, but its persistency, through its power to attach itself to what is permanent?

Society also has its duties in reference to this class, and must behold them with what charity it can. Possibly some benefit may yet accrue from them to the state. In our Mechanics' Fair, there must be not only bridges, ploughs, carpenters' planes, and baking troughs, but also some few finer instruments – rain gauges, thermometers, and telescopes; and in society, besides farmers, sailors, and weavers, there must be a few persons of purer fire kept specially as gauges and meters of character; persons of a fine, detecting instinct, who betray the smallest accumulations of wit and feeling in the bystander. Perhaps too there might be room for the exciters and monitors; collectors of the heavenly spark with power to convey the electricity to others. Or, as the storm-tossed vessel at sea speaks the frigate or "line packet" to learn its longitude, so it may not be without its advantage that we should now and then encounter rare and gifted men, to compare the points of our spiritual compass, and verify our bearings from superior chronometers.

Amidst the downward tendency and proneness of things, when every voice is raised for a new road or another statute, or a subscription of stock, for an improvement in dress, or in dentistry, for a new house or a larger business, for a political party, or the division of an estate – will you not tolerate one or two solitary voices in the land, speaking for thoughts and principles not marketable or perishable? Soon these improvements and mechanical inventions will be superseded; these modes of living lost out of memory; these cities rotted, ruined by war, by new inventions, by new seats of trade, or the geologic changes: – all gone, like the shells which sprinkle the sea-beach with a white colony to-day, for ever renewed to be for ever destroyed. But the thought which these few hermits strove to proclaim by silence, as well as by speech, not only by what they did, but by what they forebore to do, shall abide in beauty and strength, to re-organise themselves in nature, to invest themselves anew in other, perhaps higher endowed and happier mixed clay than ours, in fuller union with the surrounding system.

Notes

1. Lecture read in The Masonic Temple, Boston, January, 1842.
2. Coleridge's Translation.

8

Where I Lived, and What I Lived For

Henry David Thoreau

At a certain season of our life we are accustomed to consider every spot as the possible site of a house. I have thus surveyed the country on every side within a dozen miles of where I live. In imagination I have bought all the farms in succession, for all were to be bought, and I knew their price. I walked over each farmer's premises, tasted his wild apples, discoursed on husbandry with him, took his farm at his price, at any price, mortgaging it to him in my mind; even put a higher price on it, – took everything but a deed of it, – took his word for his deed, for I dearly love to talk, – cultivated it, and him too to some extent, I trust, and withdrew when I had enjoyed it long enough, leaving him to carry it on. This experience entitled me to be regarded as a sort of real estate broker by my friends. Wherever I sat, there I might live, and the landscape radiated from me accordingly. What is a house but a *sedes*, a seat? – better if a country seat. I discovered many a site for a house not likely to be soon improved, which some might have thought too far from the village, but to my eyes the village was too far from it. Well, there I might live, I said; and there I did live, for an hour, a summer and a winter life; saw how I could let the years run off, buffet the winter through, and see the spring come in. The future inhabitants of this region, wherever they may place their houses, may be sure that they have been anticipated. An afternoon sufficed to lay out the land into orchard, woodlot, and pasture, and to decide what fine oaks or pines should be left to stand before the door, and whence each blasted tree could be seen to the best advantage; and then I let it lie, fallow perchance, for a man is rich in proportion to the number of things which he can afford to let alone.

My imagination carried me so far that I even had the refusal of several farms, – the refusal was all I wanted, – but I never got my fingers burned by actual possession. The nearest that I came to actual possession was when I bought the Hollowell place, and had begun to sort my seeds, and collected materials with which to make a wheelbarrow to carry it on or off with; but before the owner gave me a deed of it, his wife – every man has such a wife –

Source: Henry David Thoreau, *Walden*, (London: Walter Scott, 1886).

changed her mind and wished to keep it, and he offered me ten dollars to release him. Now, to speak the truth, I had but ten cents in the world, and it surpassed my arithmetic to tell, if I was that man who had ten cents, or who had a farm, or ten dollars, or all together. However, I let him keep the ten dollars and the farm too, for I had carried it far enough; or rather, to be generous, I sold him the farm for just what I gave for it, and, as he was not a rich man, made him a present of ten dollars, and still had my ten cents, and seeds, and materials for a wheelbarrow left. I found thus that I had been a rich man without any damage to my poverty. But I retained the landscape, and have since annually carried off what it yielded without a wheelbarrow. With respect to landscapes, –

"I am monarch of all I *survey*,
   My right there is none to dispute."

I have frequently seen a poet withdraw, having enjoyed the most valuable part of a farm, while the crusty farmer supposed that he had got a few wild apples only. Why, the owner does not know it for many years when a poet has put his farm in rhyme, the most admirable kind of invisible fence, has fairly impounded it, milked it, skimmed it, and got all the cream, and left the farmer only the skimmed milk.

The real attractions of the Hollowell farm, to me, were: its complete retirement, being about two miles from the village, half-a-mile from the nearest neighbour, and separated from the highway by a broad field; its bounding on the river, which the owner said protected it by its fogs from frosts in the spring, though that was nothing to me; the grey colour and ruinous state of the house and barn, and the dilapidated fences, which put such an interval between me and the last occupant; the hollow and lichen-covered apple trees, gnawed by rabbits, showing what kind of neighbours I should have; but above all, the recollection I had of it from my earliest voyages up the river, when the house was concealed behind a dense grove of red maples, through which I heard the house-dog bark. I was in haste to buy it, before the proprietor finished getting out some rocks, cutting down the hollow apple trees, and grubbing up some young birches which had sprung up in the pasture, or, in short, had made any more of his improvements. To enjoy these advantages I was ready to carry it on; like Atlas, to take the world on my shoulders, – I have never heard what compensation he received for that, – and do all those things which had no other motive or excuse, but that I might pay for it and be unmolested in my possession of it; for I knew all the while that it would yield the most abundant crop of the kind I wanted if I could only afford to let it alone. But it turned out as I have said.

All that I could say, then, with respect to farming on a large scale (I have always cultivated a garden), was, that I had had my seeds ready. Many think that seeds improve with age. I have no doubt that time discriminates between the good and the bad; and when at last I shall plant, I shall be less likely to be disappointed. But I would say to my fellows, once for all, as long as possible live free and uncommitted. It makes but little difference whether you are committed to a farm or the county jail.

Old Cato, whose "De Re Rusticâ" is my "Cultivator," says, and the only translation I have seen makes sheer nonsense of the passage, "When you think of getting a farm, turn it thus in your mind, not to buy greedily, nor spare your pains to look at it, and do not think it enough to go round it once. The oftener you go there the more it will please you, if it is good." I think I shall not buy greedily, but go round and round it as long as I live, and be buried in it first, that it may please me the more at last.

The present was my next experiment of this kind, which I purpose to describe more at length; for convenience, putting the experience of two years into one. As I have said, I do not propose to write an ode to dejection, but to brag as lustily as Chanticleer in the morning, standing on his roost, if only to wake my neighbours up.

When first I took up my abode in the woods, that is, began to spend my nights as well as days there, which, by accident, was on Independence Day, on the 4th of July, 1845, my house was not finished for winter, but was merely a defence against the rain, without plastering or chimney, the walls being of rough weather-stained boards, with wide chinks, which made it cool at night. The upright white hewn studs and freshly planed door and window-casings gave it a clean and airy look, especially in the morning, when its timbers were saturated with dew, so that I fancied that by noon some sweet gum would exude from them. To my imagination it retained throughout the day more or less of this auroral character, reminding me of a certain house on a mountain which I had visited the year before. This was an airy, an unplastered cabin, fit to entertain a travelling god, and where a goddess might trail her garments. The winds which passed over my dwelling were such as sweep over the ridges of mountains, bearing the broken strains, or celestial parts only, of terrestrial music. The morning wind forever blows, the poem of creation is uninterrupted; but few are the ears that hear it. Olympus is but the outside of the earth everywhere.

The only house I had been the owner of before, if I except a boat, was a tent, which I used occasionally when making excursions in the summer, and this is still rolled up in my garret; but the boat, after passing from hand to hand, has gone down the stream of time. With this more substantial shelter about me, I had made some progress toward settling in the world. This frame, so slightly clad, was a sort of crystallisation around me, and reacted on the builder. It was suggestive somewhat as a picture in outlines. I did not need to go out doors to take the air, for the atmosphere within had lost none of its freshness. It was not so much within doors as behind a door where I sat, even in the rainiest weather. The Harivansa says, "An abode without birds is like a meat without seasoning." Such was not my abode, for I found myself suddenly neighbour to the birds; not by having imprisoned one, but having caged myself near them. I was not only nearer to some of those which commonly frequent the garden and the orchard, but to those wilder and more thrilling songsters of the forest which never, or rarely, serenade a villager, – the woodthrush, the veery, the scarlet tanager, the field-sparrow, the whippoorwill, and many others.

I was seated by the shore of a small pond, about a mile and a half south of the village of Concord and somewhat higher than it, in the midst of an extensive wood between that town and Lincoln, and about two miles south of that our only field known to fame, Concord battle ground; but I was so low in the woods that the opposite shore, half-a-mile off, like the rest, covered with wood, was my most distant horizon. For the first week, whenever I looked out on the pond, it impressed me like a tarn high up on the one side of a mountain, its bottom far above the surface of other lakes, and, as the sun arose, I saw it throwing off its nightly clothing of mist, and here and there, by degrees, its soft ripples or its smooth reflecting surface was revealed, while the mists, like ghosts, were stealthily withdrawing in every direction into the woods, as at the breaking up of some nocturnal conventicle. The very dew seemed to hang upon the trees later into the day than usual, as on the sides of mountains.

This small lake was of most value as a neighbour in the intervals of a gentle rain-storm in August, when, both air and water being perfectly still, but the sky overcast, mid-afternoon had all the serenity of evening, and the woodthrush sang around, and was heard from shore to shore. A lake like this is never smoother than at such a time; and the clear portion of the air above it being shallow and darkened by clouds, the water, full of light and reflections, becomes a lower heaven itself so much the more important. From a hilltop near by, where the wood had been recently cut off, there was a pleasing vista southward across the pond, through a wide indentation in the hills which form the shore there, where their opposite sides sloping toward each other suggested a stream flowing out in that direction through a wooded valley, but stream there was none. That way I looked between and over the near green hills to some distant and higher ones in the horizon, tinged with blue. Indeed, by standing on tip-toe I could catch a glimpse of some of the peaks of the still bluer and more distant mountain ranges in the north-west, those true-blue coins from heaven's own mint, and also of some portion of the village. But in other directions, even from this point, I could not see over or beyond the woods which surrounded me. It is well to have some water in your neighbourhood, to give buoyancy to and float the earth. One value even of the smallest well is, that when you look into it you see that earth is not continent but insular. This is as important as that it keeps butter cool. When I looked across the pond from this peak toward the Sudbury meadows, which in time of flood I distinguished elevated perhaps by a mirage in their seething valley, like a coin in a basin, all the earth beyond the pond appeared like a thin crust insulated and floated even by this small sheet of intervening water, and I was reminded that this on which I dwelt was but *dry land.*

Though the view from my door was still more contracted, I did not feel crowded or confined in the least. There was pasture enough for my imagination. The low shrub-oak plateau to which the opposite shore arose, stretched away toward the prairies of the West and the steppes of Tartary, affording ample room for all the roving families of men. "There are none happy in the world but beings who enjoy freely a vast horizon," said Damodara, when his herds required new and larger pastures.

Both place and time were changed, and I dwelt nearer to those parts of the universe and to those eras in history which had most attracted me. Where I lived was as far off as many a region viewed nightly by astronomers. We are wont to imagine rare and delectable places in some remote and more celestial corner of the system, behind the constellation of Cassiopeia's Chair, far from noise and disturbance. I discovered that my house actually had its site in such a withdrawn, but for ever new and unprofaned, part of the universe. If it were worth the while to settle in those parts near to the Pleiades or the Hyades, to Aldebaran or Altair, then I was really there, or at an equal remoteness from the life which I had left behind, dwindled and twinkling with as fine a ray to my nearest neighbour, and to be seen only in moonless nights by him. Such was that part of creation where I had squatted –

> "There was a shepherd that did live,
>   And held his thoughts as high
> As were the mounts whereon his flocks
>   Did hourly feed him by,"

What should we think of the shepherd's life if his flocks always wandered to higher pastures than his thoughts?

Every morning was a cheerful invitation to make my life of equal simplicity, and I may say innocence, with Nature herself. I have been as sincere a worshipper of Aurora as the Greeks. I got up early and bathed in the pond: that was a religious exercise, and one of the best things which I did. They say that characters were engraven on the bathing tub of king Tching-thang to this effect: "Renew thyself completely each day; do it again, and again, and forever again." I can understand that. Morning brings back the heroic ages. I was as much affected by the faint hum of a mosquito making its invisible and unimaginable tour through my apartment at earliest dawn, when I was sitting with door and windows open, as I could be by any trumpet that ever sang of fame. It was Homer's requiem; itself an Iliad and Odyssey in the air, singing its own wrath and wanderings. There was something cosmical about it; a standing advertisement, till forbidden, of the everlasting vigour and fertility of the world. The morning, which is the most memorable season of the day, is the awakening hour. Then there is least somnolence in us; and for an hour, at least, some part of us awakes which slumbers all the rest of the day and night. Little is to be expected of that day, if it can be called a day, to which we are not awakened by our Genius, but by the mechanical nudgings of some servitor, are not awakened by our own newly acquired force and aspirations from within, accompanied by the undulations of celestial music, instead of factory bells, and a fragrance filling the air – to a higher life than we fell asleep from; and thus the darkness bear its fruit, and prove itself to be good, no less than the light. That man who does not believe that each day contains an earlier, more sacred, and auroral hour than he has yet profaned, has despaired of life, and is pursuing a descending and darkening way. After a partial cessation of his sensuous life, the soul of man, or its organs rather, are reinvigorated each day, and his Genius tries again what noble life it can make. All memorable events, I should say, transpire in morning time and in a morning atmosphere. The Vedas say, "All intelligences awake with the morning." Poetry and art, and the fairest and most memorable of the actions of men, date from such an hour. All poets and heroes, like Memnon, are the children of Aurora, and emit their music at sunrise. To him whose elastic and vigorous thought keeps pace with the sun, the day is a perpetual morning. It matters not what the clocks say or the attitudes and labours of men. Morning is when I am awake and there is a dawn in me. Moral reform is the effort to throw off sleep. Why is it that men give so poor an account of their day if they have not been slumbering. They are not such poor calculators. If they had not been overcome with drowsiness they would have performed something. The millions are awake enough for physical labour; but only one in a million is awake enough for effective intellectual exertion, only one in a hundred millions to a poetic or divine life. To be awake is to be alive. I have never yet met a man who was quite awake. How could I have looked him in the face?

We must learn to reawaken and keep ourselves awake, not by mechanical aids, but by an infinite expectation of the dawn, which does not forsake us in our soundest sleep. I know of no more encouraging fact than the unquestionable ability of man to elevate his life by a conscious endeavour. It is something to be able to paint a particular picture, or to carve a statue, and so to make a few objects beautiful; but it is far more glorious to carve and paint the very atmosphere and medium through which we look, which morally we can do. To affect the quality of the day, that is the highest of arts. Every man is tasked to make his life, even in its details, worthy of the contemplation of his most elevated and critical hour. If we refused, or rather used up, such paltry information as we get, the oracles would distinctly inform us how this might be done.

I went to the woods because I wished to live deliberately to front only the essential facts of life, and see if I could not learn what it had to teach, and not, when I came to die, discover that I had not lived. I did not wish to live what was not life, living is so dear; nor did I wish to practise resignation, unless it was quite necessary. I wanted to live deep and suck out all the marrow of life, to live so sturdily and Spartan-like as to put to rout all that was not life, to cut a broad swath and shave close, to drive life into a corner, and reduce it to its lowest terms, and, if it proved to be mean, why then to get the whole and genuine meanness of it, and publish its meanness to the world; or if it were sublime, to know it by experience, and be able to give a true account of it in my next excursion. For most men, it appears to me, are in a strange uncertainty about it, whether it is of the devil or of God, and have *somewhat hastily* concluded that it is the chief end of man here to "glorify God and enjoy Him forever."

Still we live meanly, like ants; though the fable tells us that we were long ago changed into men; like pygmies we fight with cranes; it is error upon error, and clout upon clout, and our best virtue has for its occasion a superfluous and evitable wretchedness. Our life is frittered away by detail. An honest man has hardly need to count more than his ten fingers, or in extreme cases he may add his ten toes, and lump the rest. Simplicity, simplicity, simplicity! I say, let your affairs be as two or three, and not a hundred or a thousand; instead of a million count half-a-dozen, and keep your accounts on your thumb-nail. In the midst of this chopping sea of civilised life, such are the clouds and storms and quicksands and thousand-and-one items to be allowed for, that a man has to live, if he would not founder and go the bottom and not make his port at all, by dead reckoning, and he must be a great calculator indeed who succeeds. Simplify, simplify. Instead of three meals a-day, if it be necessary eat but one; instead of a hundred dishes, five; and reduce other things in proportion. Our life is like a German Confederacy, made up of petty states, with its boundary forever fluctuating, so that even a German cannot tell you how it is bounded at any moment. The nation itself, with all its so-called internal improvements, which, by the way, are all external and superficial, is just such an unwieldy and overgrown establishment, cluttered with furniture and tripped up by its own traps, ruined by luxury and heedless expense, by want of calculation and a worthy aim, as the million households in the land; and the only cure for it as for them is in a rigid economy, a stern and more than Spartan simplicity of life and elevation of purpose. It lives too fast. Men think that it is essential that the *Nation* have commerce, and export ice, and talk through a telegraph, and ride thirty miles an hour, without a doubt, whether *they* do or not; but whether we should live like baboons or like men, is a little uncertain. If we do not get out sleepers, and forge rails, and devote days and nights to the work, but go to tinkering upon our *lives* to improve *them*, who will build railroads? And if railroads are not built, how shall we get to heaven in season? But if we stay at home and mind our business, who will want railroads? We do not ride on the railroad; it rides upon us. Did you ever think what those sleepers are that underlie the railroad? Each one is a man, an Irishman, or a Yankee man. The rails are laid on them, and they are covered with sand, and the cars run smoothly over them. They are sound sleepers, I assure you. And every few years a new lot is laid down and run over; so that, if some have the pleasure of riding on a rail, others have the misfortune to be ridden upon. And when they run over a man that is walking in his sleep, a supernumerary sleeper in the wrong position, and wake him up, they suddenly stop the cars, and make a hue and cry about it, as if this were an exception. I am glad to know that it takes a gang of men for every five miles to keep the sleepers down and level in their beds as it is, for this is a sign that they may sometime get up again.

Why should we live with such hurry and waste of life? We are determined to be starved before we are hungry. Men say that a stitch in time saves nine, and so they take a thousand stitches to-day to save nine to-morrow. As for *work*, we haven't any of any consequence. We have the Saint Vitus' dance, and cannot possibly keep our heads still. If I should only give a few pulls at the parish bell-rope, as for a fire, that is, without setting the bell, there is hardly a man on his farm in the outskirts of Concord, notwithstanding that press of engagements which was his excuse so many times this morning, nor a boy, nor a woman, I might almost say, but would forsake all and follow that sound, not mainly to save property from the flames, but, if we will confess the truth, much more to see it burn, since burn it must, and we, be it known, did not set it on fire, – or to see it put out, and have a hand in it, if that is done as handsomely; yes, even if it were the parish church itself. Hardly a man takes a half-hour's nap after dinner, but when he wakes he holds up his head and asks, "What's the news?" as if the rest of mankind had stood his sentinels. Some give directions to be waked every half-hour, doubtless for no other purpose; and then to pay for it, they tell what they have dreamed. After a night's sleep the news is as indispensable as the breakfast. "Pray, tell me anything new that has happened to a man anywhere on this globe," – and he reads it over his coffee and rolls, that a man has had his eyes gouged out this morning on the Wachito River; never dreaming the while that he lives in the dark unfathomed mammoth cave of this world, and has but the rudiment of an eye himself.

For my part, I could easily do without the post office. I think that there are very few important communications made through it. To speak critically, I never received more than one or two letters in my life – I wrote this some years ago – that were worth the postage. The penny-post is commonly, an institution through which you seriously offer a man that penny for his thoughts which is so often safely offered in jest. And I am sure that I never read any memorable news in a newspaper. If we read of one man robbed, or murdered, or killed by accident, or one house burned, or one vessel wrecked, or one steamboat blown-up, or one cow run over on the Western Railroad, or one mad dog killed, or one lot of grasshoppers in the winter, – we never need read of another. One is enough. If you are acquainted with the principle, what do you care for a myriad instances and applications? To a philosopher all *news*, as it is called, is gossip, and they who edit and read it are old women over their tea. Yet not a few are greedy after this gossip. There was such a rush, as I hear, the other day at one of the offices to learn the foreign news by the last arrival, that several large squares of plate glass belonging to the establishment were broken by the pressure, – news which I seriously think a ready wit might write a twelvemonth or twelve years beforehand with sufficient accuracy. As for

Spain, for instance, if you know how to throw in Don Carlos and the Infanta, and Don Pedro and Seville and Granada, from time to time in the right proportions, – they may have changed the names a little since I saw the papers, – and serve up a bull-fight when other entertainments fail, it will be true to the letter, and give us as good an idea of the exact state or ruin of things in Spain as the most succinct and lucid reports under this head in the newspapers: and as for England, almost the last significant scrap of news from that quarter was the Revolution of 1649; and if you have learned the history of her crops for an average year, you never need attend to that thing again, unless your speculations are of a merely pecuniary character. If one may judge who rarely looks into the newspapers, nothing new does ever happen in foreign parts, a French revolution not excepted.

What news! how much more important to know what that is which was never old! "Kieou-he-yu" (great dignitary of the state of Wei) sent a man to Khoung-tseu to know his news. Khoung-tseu caused the messenger to be seated near him, and questioned him in these terms: What is your master doing? The messenger answered with respect: My master desires to diminish the number of his faults, but he cannot come to the end of them. The messenger being gone, the philosopher remarked: What a worthy messenger! What a worthy messenger!" The preacher, instead of vexing the ears of drowsy farmers on their day of rest at the end of the week, – for Sunday is the fit conclusion of an ill-spent week, and not the fresh and brave beginning of a new one, – with this one other draggle-tail of a sermon, should shout with thundering voice, – "Pause! Avast! Why so seeming fast, but deadly slow?"

Shams and delusions are esteemed for soundest truths, while reality is fabulous. If men would steadily observe realities only, and not allow themselves to be deluded, life, to compare it with such things as we know, would be like a fairy tale and the Arabian Nights' Entertainments. If we respected only what is inevitable and has a right to be, music and poetry would resound along the streets. When we are unhurried and wise, we perceive that only great and worthy things have any permanent and absolute existence, – that petty fears and petty pleasures are but the shadow of the reality. This is always exhilarating and sublime. By closing the eyes and slumbering, and consenting to be deceived by shows, men establish and confirm their daily life of routine and habit everywhere, which still is built on purely illusory foundations. Children, who play life, discern its true law and relations more clearly than men, who fail to live it worthily, but who think that they are wiser by experience, that is, by failure. I have read in a Hindoo book, that "there was a king's son, who, being expelled in infancy from his native city, was brought up by a forester, and, growing up to maturity in that state, imagined himself to belong to the barbarous race with which he lived. One of his father's ministers having discovered him, revealed to him what he was, and the misconception of his character was removed, and he knew himself to be a prince. So soul," continues the Hindoo philosopher, "from the circumstances in which it is placed, mistakes its own character, until the truth is revealed to it by some holy teacher, and then it knows itself to be *Brahme*." I perceive that we inhabitants of New England live this mean life that we do because our vision does not penetrate the surface of things. We think that that *is* which *appears* to be. If a man should walk through this town and see only the reality, where, think you, would the "Mill-dam" go to? If he should give us an account of the realities he beheld there, we should not recognise the place in his description. Look at a meeting-house, or a court-house, or a jail, or a shop, or a dwelling-house, and say what that thing really is before a true gaze, and they would all go to pieces in your account of them. Men esteem truth remote, in the outskirts of the system, behind the farthest star, before Adam and after the last man. In eternity there is indeed something true and sublime. But all these times and places and occasions are now and here. God himself culminates in the present moment, and will never be more divine in the lapse of all the ages. And we are enabled to apprehend at all what is sublime and noble only by the perpetual instilling and drenching of the reality that surrounds us. The universe constantly and obediently answers to our conceptions; whether we travel fast or slow, the track is laid for us. Let us spend our lives in conceiving then. The poet or the artist never yet had so fair and noble a design but some of his posterity at least could accomplish it.

Let us spend one day as deliberately as Nature, and not be thrown off the track by every nutshell and mosquito's wing that falls on the rails. Let us rise early and fast, or break fast, gently and without perturbation; let company come and let company go, let the bells ring and the children cry, – determined to make a day of it. Why should we knock under and go with the stream? Let us not be upset and overwhelmed in that terrible rapid and whirlpool called a dinner, situated in the meridian shallows. Weather this danger and you are safe, for the rest of the way is down hill. With unrelated nerves, with morning vigour, sail by it, looking another way, tied to the mast like Ulysses. If the engine whistles, let it whistle till it is hoarse for its pains. If the bell rings, why should we run? We will consider what kind of music they are like. Let us settle ourselves, and work and wedge our feet downward through the mud and slush of opinion, and prejudice, and tradition, and delusion, and appearance, that alluvion which covers the globe, through Paris and London, through New York and Boston and Concord, through church and state, through poetry and philosophy and religion, till we come to a hard bottom and rocks in place, which we can call *reality*, and say, This is, and no mistake; and then begin, having a *point d'appui*, below freshet and frost and fire, a place where you might found a wall or a state, or set a lamp-post safely, or perhaps a gauge, not a Nilometer, but a Realometer, that future ages might know how deep a freshet of shams and appearances had gathered from time to time. If you stand right fronting and face to face to a fact, you will see the sun glimmer on both its surfaces, as if it were a cimeter, and feel its sweet edge dividing you through the heart and marrow, and so you will happily conclude your mortal career. Be it life or death, we crave only reality. If we are really dying, let us hear the rattle in our throats and feel cold in the extremities; if we are alive, let us go about our business.

Time is but the stream I go a-fishing in. I drink at it; but while I drink I see the sandy bottom and detect how shallow it is. Its thin current slides away, but eternity remains. I would drink deeper; fish in the sky, whose bottom is pebbly with stars. I cannot count one. I know not the first letter of the alphabet. I have always been regretting that I was not as wise as the day I was born. The intellect is a cleaver; it discerns and rifts its way into the secret of things. I do not wish to be any more busy with my hands than is necessary. My head is hands and feet. I feel all my best faculties concentrated in it. My instinct tells me that my head is an organ for burrowing, as some creatures use their snout and fore-paws, and with it I would mine and burrow my way through these hills. I think that the richest vein is somewhere hereabouts; so by the divining rod and thin rising vapours I judge; and here I will begin to mine.

9

William Graham Sumner (1840–1910)

Daniel W. Rossides

The establishment of sociology as an independent discipline in the United States is due in no small measure to the work of William Graham Sumner. A good part of Sumner's success is explained by the fact that his work took place within the setting of a university – Yale – something that was to become increasingly characteristic of sociologists. Sociology did not find immediate acceptance, however, either inside or outside the academic world. Of course, Sumner's attitude toward the conventional disciplines, expressed in barbs and taunts about the unscientific and useless character of much of what passed for intellectual activity, was not calculated to endear him to the academic community.

Unlike his predecessors in sociology, Sumner saw no need to construct a philosophy of positivism. He once made a serious proposal that the teaching of philosophy be abolished at Yale. His objection to philosophy stemmed from a deep-rooted nominalism that made him suspicious of all formal intellectual activity. Sumner's deep distrust of abstract thought, which he shared with American pragmatism, did not mean that he made any significant alteration in the tradition of monistic naturalistic positivism. Despite his avowed nominalism and well-known contribution to cultural analysis, Sumner's work never veered from the basic goal of early sociology, the search for the truth about human nature and society in terms of natural, physical–psychological causation.

Philosophy and Method

Characteristically, Sumner wrote no formal treatise on the logic of social science. Nevertheless, his work provides significant insights into the nature and development of positivism and the logic of scientific method.[1] Much of the world's mischief, Sumner argued, can be laid at the door of those who explain things by reference to ideas or ethics. In one of his few philosophical essays, "Purposes and Consequences," he distinguished between those who rely on ideas and ethics, or purposes, and those who rely on science and facts, or

---

Source: Daniel W. Rossides, *The History and Nature of Sociological Theory*, (New York: Houghton Mifflin, 1978).

consequences. Any attempt to impose ethical considerations on the world of fact, he argued, is unacceptable to the scientific spirit. "In fact, the judgment of probable consequences is the only real and sound ground of action."[2] The world is in an age of transition, he concluded, between a period when purposes and consequences have been united and a period when they will be divorced and metaphysics left behind.

Sumner's bias against metaphysics was not directed only against medieval survivals. He was if anything even more intent on assailing the metaphysics of the Enlightenment and what he felt was its grossly unscientific concept of natural rights. Eschewing any recourse to formal philosophical analysis, he peremptorily dismissed the idea of natural rights as unworthy of scientific belief. In such essays as "Rights," "Equality," and "Liberty" he rejected all efforts to establish absolute standards prior to social life. It is clear that Sumner was protesting not so much against the idea of individual rights as against the natural-law basis on which theorists had sought to establish them.

The rejection of natural rights is not new to sociological theory; Saint-Simon, Comte, and Spencer, for example, also saw them as relics of a prescientific age. Saint-Simon and Comte had ignored individual rights altogether. Sumner, like Spencer, accepted them but on different grounds; both theorists were inclined to think of individual rights in utilitarian terms, as both the product of human adjustment to nature in the past, and the means for waging a more successful struggle for existence in the future. Sumner, however, was too unphilosophical to attempt, as Spencer had done, a cosmic philosophy of evolution in which human beings are simply one aspect of an evolving nature. He was content to say simply that individual rights come from experience.

Underlying the entire range of Sumner's thinking is the crucial assumption of the struggle for existence, an assumption that the source of knowledge about human beings was their relations with nature. As philosophical nominalism, this assumption expressed Sumner's belief that these relations are unalterably empirical rather than rational since there is "no disposition at all in nature to conform her operations to man's standards." It was a philosophical position, in short, that had abandoned the Enlightenment's belief in the corresponding structures of the human mind and of nature. For Sumner, population–land ratios and capital formation were the primary determinants of intellectual life and of all social relations. His economic determinism is most clearly expressed in such essays as "Power and Progress," "Consequences of Increased Social Power," "The Absurd Effort to Make the World Over," and "Earth Hunger or the Philosophy of Land Grabbing." In the second of these essays he stated flatly that individualism developed in the United States not because of metaphysical discourse but because of economic conditions.

> Is not this the correct interpretation of what has happened in America? If it is, then the dogmatic or philosophical theorems, instead of being the cause of our social arrangements, are only the metaphysical dress

which we have amused ourselves by imagining upon them. We are not free and equal because Jefferson put it into the Declaration of Independence that we were born so; but Jefferson could put it into the Declaration of Independence that all men are born free and equal because the economic relations existing in America made the members of society to all intents and purposes free and equal. It makes some difference to him who desires to attain to a correct social philosophy which of these ways of looking at the matter is true to the facts.[3]

The facts of human behavior are not too various and unstable to admit of generalization. On the contrary, Sumner was convinced "that social phenomena are subject to law, and that the natural laws of the social order are in their entire character like the laws of physics".[4] Even though he sharply denied that the mind can find moral law in nature – a position that in its Humian rigor is unprecedented in sociological theory – he did feel that science can provide a guide for action:

The moral deductions as to what one ought to do are to be drawn by the reason and conscience of the individual man who is instructed by science. Let him take note of the force of gravity, and see to it that he does not walk off a precipice or get in the way of a falling body.[5]

Sumner's identification of morality with the factual world amounted to an almost fatalistic acceptance of social and historical structures, a conscious equation of might with right. Sumner's concern for facts led him, like Spencer, into a massive exploration of ethnography. Sumner's conviction that the data of behavior and belief can be traced to the conditions of existence is central to his best-known work, the loosely structured *Folkways*, and his fundamental nominalism is clearly evident in the structure of *The Science of Society*. The latter contains no methodological analysis; it simply states some starting points, or self-evident propositions about the relationship of human beings to nature. Significantly, Sumner relegated the discussion of scientific social thought to the end of the last volume of text. Basically, science consists of "trained and organized common sense," and its mode of procedure is to plunge into the realm of facts in order to obtain the generalizations necessary to intelligent adjustment. Once obtained, these generalizations will effectively separate sociology from metaphysics as well as from history.

Sumner shared many philosophical assumptions with his predecessors in sociology. Like them, he articulated a positivism that was avowedly anti-metaphysical. Distinctive in his philosophy and method was his rejection of what he felt were the exaggerated claims that had been made on behalf of reason. He was unique in his definition of reason as an instrument of adjustment. In this respect his antimetaphysical bias allowed him to go even further than Spencer in transforming mind into function. However, Sumner also believed that the mind as science was somehow capable of unearthing the underlying pattern that controls the destiny of human beings, a pattern that he identified as the law of evolutionary adjustment.

Substantive Work

Population–Land Ratios

The relationship between human beings and nature, which for Sumner constituted the starting point of all social science, was stated more precisely as the relation between population and land.

> How much land there is to how many men is the fundamental consideration in the life of any society. The ratio between these two factors means the ratio of numbers to sustenance, or of mouths to food; for the fact that all food comes in the last analysis from the earth should not be let slip because it is obvious. This relation of numbers to sustenance affords a firm, unspeculative, unselected footing for a science of society. It is a matter of observation and of recorded experience. It is also determinative for organic life in general. Where Mother Earth has more children than she can nourish, they die or exist in misery; where beasts or men are fewer, they get more nourishment and may live on in comfort. This simple and objective relation furnishes, we say, a firm footing for a science of society; we start with an incontrovertible and, indeed, implacable fact of life, and not with any speculative considerations.[6]

In addition to his "economic" determinism, Sumner believed that there were elemental motives or interests behind the struggle for adjustment.

> There are four great motives of human action which come into play when some number of human beings are in juxtaposition under the same life conditions. These are hunger, sex passion, vanity, and fear (of ghosts and spirits). Under each of these motives are interests. Life consists in satisfying interests, for "life," in a society, is a career of action and effort expended on both the material and social environment. However great the errors and misconceptions may be which are included in the efforts, the purpose always is advantage and expedience.[7]

Sumner never formulated an explicit biopsychological theory of society; that is, he never said that elemental human needs are directly translatable into human behavior. In the passage just quoted, for example, the fact that human beings must be in "juxtaposition" suggests that interaction is necessary before the four motives become operative. Furthermore, his "economic" determinism, together with his cultural approach, by illustrating the variegated forms that these elemental urges could take, contained the broad suggestion that social existence makes possible a wide transcendence of biology and psychology. Though Sumner never satisfactorily defined the role of biopsychological forces in human behavior, he tended to limit them as explanatory factors, suggesting that human nature is a set of indefinite promptings upon which society builds.

Folkways and Mores

Perhaps the best known aspect of Sumner's work is his contribution to the understanding of social values and norms – in his own terms, *folkways* and *mores*. The belief that the values and norms by which human beings live can be understood scientifically, and not in terms of revelation, authority, reason, or specially endowed human beings, is implicit in the entire tradition of sociological theory. All the sociological theorists whose work has been examined attempted, at least in some way, to explain the origin and nature of social norms. Sumner's careful choice of the terms *folkways* and *mores* indicates his desire to make a fresh start in this area. He signaled this approach by insisting that the most important thing about social norms is that they arise "without rational reflection or purpose" from the struggle of the human animal to cope with the pitiless forces of nature.

The folkways arise from pleasure–pain responses. The mechanism of pleasure–pain produces, first, a "strain of improvement toward better adaptation of means to ends"; next, there develops "a strain of consistency" to bring norms into line with each other. Groups characteristically elaborate sentiments of solidarity, ethnocentric emotions that differentiate in-group from out-group and serve to strengthen the rest of the folkways. Relative to time and place, the folkways prescribe the good and the true. When they involve the welfare of society itself – that is, when they involve such things as property, sex, and power – they become mores – that is, they become deeply lodged in the personality.

Two themes emerged in Sumner's analysis of folkways and mores. The first received the most attention and constitutes Sumner's contribution to the concept of culture. Like Spencer, Sumner was greatly influenced by the ripening discipline of cultural anthropology. However, Sumner went beyond Spencer and revived the cultural emphasis that figured so heavily in the work of Vico and Montesquieu. The second theme, which Sumner never developed adequately, grew from his insight into the cultural sources of behavior. If social existence takes place through the medium of culture and is not directly derived from natural forces, then it follows that folkways and mores can be discussed in terms of the relations of human beings to each other, that is, in terms of interaction or social process.

Types of Social Process

Sumner's main concern was to show that norms originate in the relationship between human beings and nature. However, he was aware that relationships among human beings also affected the nature of norms and the functioning of society. In his discussion of the four motives, Sumner was careful to add that these motives come into play only when individuals are in juxtaposition. His awareness of social interaction as a sociologically important variable is apparent in such phrases as "near each other," "mutual reactions," "methods of interaction," and "adjustment of adjacent interests." Sumner also developed, at least embryonically, the related idea of social status or "fixed positions," and the idea that the totality of relations and positions connected to social functions can be conceived as a structure. Sumner's interest in interaction also led him to accept the idea of "suggestion" as the origin of norms. In the same connection, he made fleeting references to the importance of subgroup membership, references that suggest a crude awareness of what has come to be known as reference-group theory.

Though Sumner's insight into the importance of interaction was deeper than that of Spencer, his contribution in this area was minimal. His ideas about interaction were incidental to other concerns, and he never focused on social relationships as the core of sociological analysis as did, say, Durkheim and Simmel. He was far more disposed to regard norms as arising from human beings' relation to nature than as a product of interaction. His failure to identify interaction as an important sociological variable is one of emphasis rather than of omission, and he managed to say a number of interesting things about the causes and types of social process. He was aware that population density influences the quality of social relationships, as does the growth of what he called the "industrial organization." This development, which stems from human efforts to cope more efficiently with the forces of nature, affects social relationships by disciplining individuals and by restricting both liberty and equality – a price, Sumner said, not too high for the benefits organization brings.

Sumner's awareness of the increasing complexity of society, especially in the economic sphere, links him with Saint-Simon, Comte, Spencer, and the entire sociological tradition. Though some sociologists, such as Comte, Durkheim, and Max Weber, were concerned about the stability of a complex society, almost all felt that the increased division of labor was ultimately functional. Basically, Sumner was disposed not to worry about this question; indeed, he developed a number of ideas to show that the grand idea of automatic evolutionary adjustment through specialization posed no problem for social unity and stability. *Antagonistic cooperation*, for example, which is unconscious and basically akin to the processes of the natural world, reconciles antagonistic interests so that common purposes can be achieved. Though Sumner failed to develop the idea in his later work, he nevertheless maintained that antagonistic cooperation was the primary mechanism by which society benefits by the division of labor and competition and by which society insures its own integration.[8]

Also relevant to the explanation of social stability and integrity is Sumner's concept of *conventionalization*. This is the process whereby certain standards and practices are placed in a special category by convention, thus preventing a clash with the general body of mores. These socially acceptable inconsistencies contribute to the richness and diversity of social unity, often acting to reconcile nonrational remnants with the growth of new mores and rationality.

Society as an Evolutionary Functional Structure

Underlying Sumner's discussion of folkways and mores is the idea of functional adjustment to life conditions, an idea that bound together the whole range of Sumner's thought. Again and again he affirmed his belief that norms do not emerge from the ruminations of philosophers, but as solutions to the problems of existence. They are relative to life conditions and survive only to the extent that they satisfy human needs. The only criterion for judging mores, therefore, is by their utility for social existence; mores are "bad" only when they outlive their historical usefulness. Despite their deep "inertia and rigidity," the mores nonetheless exhibit "changeableness and variation." As new conditions arise, the mores either assume new forms or are discarded. The entire process is natural, though great societal crises or revolutions are often necessary to cleanse society of its backlog of outmoded mores. Finally, Sumner concluded, little can be done to modify this process through artificial human effort. "There is logic in the folkways, but never rationality." The logic presumably emerges from the workings of the automatic strains toward improvement and consistency that are natural to society.

Sumner also had faith in the inherent rationality of interaction. When human beings come together in the struggle for existence, their interaction seems to have an inherent capacity for producing both functional mores and functional patterns of behavior. If the *Folkways* has any theme apart from the emphasis on the cultural sources of behavior, it is that social norms are explicable only insofar as they can be related to environmental conditions and to social purposes. Despite the fact that, on the whole, the *Folkways* is heavily deficient in causal theory, Sumner insisted that norms and practices be viewed in terms of time, place, and need. For example, such practices as slavery, cannibalism, abortion, infanticide, killing the old, polygamy, and polyandry are products of economic necessity. Such practices, Sumner argued, may be quite functional to one society and should not be judged by the standards of another.

Sumner's realistic appraisal of culture and social life held forth the possibility that his sociology would fulfill the promise of Spencer's work, but neither the *Folkways* nor *The Science of Society* went beyond Spencer in any significant way. It is true that the overall framework of *The Science of Society* is stated in functional terms. The institutions of society are described in terms of how well they fulfill the four human motives, and society is repeatedly defined as an interdependent survival unit that gradually builds institutions around these motives or interests. Unfortunately the promise in this vague but genuinely scientific approach never bore fruit. In regard to how human beings cope with nature, Sumner made little theoretical advance beyond the *Folkways*. He made a small effort to identify evolutionary stages and to correlate them with economic systems. There are also some scattered references to the economic basis of such phenomena as slavery and family forms, but these merely repeat insights in the *Folkways*. In truth, Sumner made no serious effort to tackle empirically the problem of causation. He was content to reiterate his vague assertion that adjustments to natural conditions determine the structure of both culture and society. Similarly he made no theoretical advance in regard to a second type of environment, relations among human beings. All in all, Sumner's faith in the automatic nature of evolution made it unnecessary for him to take the question of causation seriously.

However, Sumner's treatment of a third type of environment, the world of ghosts and spirits, holds considerable interest for the historian of sociology. Sumner regarded religion as part of the human attempt to adjust to a hostile world, in this case the world of the unknown. Religion, along with the rest of the mores, is therefore subject to the law of evolution and the "strain toward consistency." Arising as a naive anthropomorphism and evolving through definite stages, religion gradually developed an awareness of First Cause. Historically, said Sumner, religion has often retarded social evolution. It adjusts less slowly to new situations and in many cases blocks required adjustments by insisting on beliefs and practices that are detrimental to economic progress. Sumner's interesting and rather unexpected conclusion to all this is that while religion often obstructs rational solutions to human problems, on the whole it plays a positive role in the "strain toward improvement." Indeed, Sumner went on to argue that religion is indispensable not only to the formation of social order, but to economic and scientific progress as well. It contributes to evolutionary adjustment in many ways; it disciplines individuals, provides the sanctions for nonreligious mores, causes labor to be performed, and settles disputes between contending factions. Finally, its intuitive statements about the forces of the universe are the crude but necessary beginnings of the long self-correcting intellectual process known as science.

Sumner's evaluation of the nature and function of religion was not an isolated feature of his sociology. On the contrary, his proclivity for finding utility in beliefs and practices that violate the canons of science, already pronounced in the *Folkways*, became an important unifying thread in *The Science of Society*. His emphasis on the social value of error was matched by an emphasis on the social value of evil. One practice after another – coercion, inequality, injustice, slavery, war, infanticide, killing the old, human sacrifice, polygamy, monarchical absolutism, monasticism, feudalism – is cited and justified in terms of historic utility. Behind this approach is a genuinely functional spirit, which Sumner stated in more theoretical terms: a given cause may have different consequences depending on time and place, while different causes may have the same consequence. The motives of any actor may have no relation to consequences – that is, a given purpose may have consequences quite at variance with a person's intentions. Sumner even recognized that the distinction between intentions and consequences implied a rejection of psychology as the basis for social science.

Sumner's functionalism stemmed from his assumption that science can never establish the intrinsic worth of any objective or subjective fact. Like Montesquieu and Spencer, the two most consciously functional thinkers before him, Sumner sought knowledge about human behavior by relating given practices to given contexts. However, Sumner had a deeper intellectual kinship with Spencer than with Montesquieu. Like Spencer, he employed a relational approach to knowledge without becoming a relativist. For Sumner, science is not defeated by the multiplicity and contradictoriness of human affairs; the phenomena of the social realm are ultimately lawful. He admitted that Spencer's biological analogy had been misused and that organic and societal evolution cannot be equated, but he said that this does not mean cultural and social structures are not natural. The science of society must still model itself after the natural sciences and conduct an unremitting search for law. Thanks largely to the work of Herbert Spencer, the science of society

> ... has worked out a conception of society as a unified whole – as a great entity, self-maintaining and self-perpetuating, something more and greater than the sum of its parts, whose evolution and life are susceptible of investigation, whose forms pass from phase to phase, from the most primitive up to the most sophisticated, remaining yet constantly interdependent in the most intimate and intricate of relations.[9]

Sumner felt that the ability of social science to find law in facts – to generalize – separates it from the art of history and gives it its supreme generalization, the law of evolution. Society does not dissolve into a series of unrelated and disparate historical complexes. Society is a natural structure having a natural sequence and thus is as immune to political control as it is to ethical criticism. Whatever exists at any given time is necessary, expedient, true, and good; the only standards by which to judge the workings of society are its own needs and its responses to these needs.

Despite Sumner's nominalism and emphasis on culture, therefore, his thought is more in keeping with the tradition of monistic naturalistic positivism stemming from the work of Condorcet, Saint-Simon, Comte, and Spencer than it is with the sociocultural positivism of Vico and Montesquieu. Though his profound nominalism disposed him toward an acceptance of the given, and was therefore conservative, it was not traditionalistic. While his work lacks the glowing optimism and commitment to science that informs the work of his predecessors in naturalistic positivism, Sumner firmly believed that the evolutionary development of society stemmed from the rise of science, especially as it translated itself into economic efficacy. Though never stated in systematic terms, there is throughout Sumner an undercurrent of tension between the mores and science. While the mores are always functional for their time, they are also always under attack by new and better ways of coping with the problems of existence. Sumner expressed this contrast between the "rational" and the "more rational" in a number of ways, most frequently by posing the mores against science. However, he also made the contrast by posing folkways and mores against such things as interests, rational reflection, legislative action, and positive law.

The tension between mores and science also emerged in Sumner's efforts to understand the phenomenon of social stratification. His theory of stratification was based largely on Galton's (1822–1911) psychology. Society, Sumner argued, tends to select those who are best equipped to serve social interests. Fundamental to all societies is a division between the masses and the classes; the former embody the mores and resist change, and the latter introduce variation and change. As the conditions of life change, a new elite arises to realize the new possibilities for satisfying interests. In a manner reminiscent of Saint-Simon, Sumner argued that very often there are unexpected consequences, good and bad, that flow from the selfish actions of classes. The historical trend has been to place the direction of the masses in the hands of the sober and responsible middle class. Any action by the working masses on their own would be disastrous to society. At the apex of society are the few individuals of genius and talent; at its base are the defective and delinquent.

Sumner's theory of social stratification in *Folkways* differed little from the ideas in his famous essay, "What Social Classes Owe to Each Other," published more than twenty years earlier, though the Darwinian emphasis is perhaps more strongly and callously expressed in the earlier work. Modern society, Sumner argued, has evolved from a system based on customary status to one based on rational contract, and it now provides individuals with the opportunity to prove themselves. Merit is inherent in the individual; society merely brings it out through the processes of education and competition. The muddle-headed talk of the reformers notwithstanding, liberty and equality are intrinsically opposed to each other. All schemes to help the weak are wrong-headed interferences with nature's stern commandment that survival depends on "labor and self-denial." Such schemes are doubly injurious because they also penalize the diligent and resourceful individual, an allusion to the middle-class individual, or "forgotten man," that Sumner defended throughout his career. Just as nature owes an individual nothing, so classes owe each other nothing except for the mutual recognition that individuals are obligated to help only themselves.

Sumner's wide acquaintance with ethnographic data allowed him to see the multiple bases on which inequality can rest. Though he failed to use the term *class* with any precision, he distinguished between inequality based on birth, whose extreme form is caste, and inequality based on wealth, whose extreme form is plutocracy. The crucial insight is that "among primitive peoples wealth is perhaps more likely to be a result of power than power of wealth."

All history, Sumner went on, is primarily a struggle between classes, especially in regard to living standards. In this struggle, classes use both ideas and political power to bend society to their own interests. The historical trend is toward inequality based on economic performance. Citing two of his favorite authors, Lippert (1839–1909) and Gumplowicz (1838–1909), and again referring to Galton, Sumner concluded that inequality and struggle are intrinsic to human nature and social evolution. The process of evolution creates new and unequal rights by giving power to those best equipped to carry on the struggle for survival. The corollary of this process is the weeding out of the unfit. Any attempt to protect the weak through ethical doctrines or through state action can lead only to social stagnation and destruction.

Though this is never stated systematically, Sumner's theory of social stratification is organically connected with his belief in a pattern of emerging rationality in history. Social strata are the embodiment of the differences and tensions that exist between the mores and science, between "rational" and "more rational" beliefs and values. Sumner's equation of social adjustment with inequality again connects his thought with that of Saint-Simon and Comte and, for that matter, with much of later sociological theory. His beliefs that conflicting views of social welfare and adjustment are embodied in specific social classes and that these classes, often unwittingly, serve as the agents of social change are similar to ideas in Saint-Simon and, of course, in Marx. However, whereas Saint-Simon saw the climax of history in the triumph of a scientific and industrial elite and Marx saw it in the victory of the proletariat, Sumner, who was almost as critical of the plutocracy as he was of the proletariat, felt that history had ordained the dominance of the individualistic middle class.

Though Sumner never openly embraced a doctrine of progress, it is clearly implicit in his work and therefore raises the liberal dilemma. His efforts to overcome the liberal dilemma are characteristically his own, despite the fact that like some of his predecessors he eventually resorted to the idea of a hidden logic to pull together the loose ends of his thought. He avoided first of all an explicit contrast between evil and good and between error and science. Evil, for Sumner, often contributes to the adjustment of society and can therefore be a source of good. As for error, it also contributes to rational adjustment and can therefore be "scientific." For from envisioning a sudden and miraculous enlightenment that enables human beings to transcend experience, Sumner saw human progress as a piecemeal, fitful process completely confined to historical experience. In one place he even went so far as to say that human beings have "stumbled upon" science.

The rise of science and the evolution of society, however, are not haphazard, accidental occurrences. Individuals may be caught in the grip of an irrational culture with no metaphysical standards to which to appeal, error and evil may tenaciously obstruct adjustment, the interests of individuals may be deeply antagonistic to each other; but underneath humanity's blind strivings a hidden logic meshes these feeble efforts into a unified structure of evolution.

The antipathies among the interests of individuals are harmonized by the automatic process of antagonistic cooperation. Even when the interests of a group seem in fundamental conflict with the interests of humankind, evolution insures rational adjustment.

Conclusion

Sumner's Radical Nominalism

Sumner is the most consistently antimetaphysical of the theorists whose work I have examined. Taking his cue from Spencer but eschewing Spencer's belief that the science of society should be based on a formally constructed cosmic philosophy, Sumner based his thought on a frankly stated naturalistic nominalism. Like Spencer he was greatly interested in ethnographic and ecological data, but whereas Spencer was avowedly metaphysical, so great was Sumner's nominalism that one even hesitates to classify him as a monistic positivist. However, Sumner's monistic temperament is unmistakable. The distinction between the monists and pluralists rests not so much upon the amount of data contained in their work as upon their basic orientation toward and appraisal of social facts. The monists are interested, of course, in facts, but the pluralists tend to be far more concerned with the adequacy of their methodology and far more cautious and tentative in their conclusions. Sumner never particularly concerned himself with the methodology of social science for the simple reason that he considered all such discussion to be philosophy and thus futile. It was self-evident that one had to be "tough-minded," that facts are facts, and that a few patent assumptions were all one needed to uncover the empirical realm. Sumner's genuine awareness of the historical and cultural sources of behavior did not extend far enough to force him to re-evaluate the methods and assumptions of earlier positivism. Like his predecessors, he remained a naturalist in that he defined the data of social behavior in terms of experience and in that he believed human behavior contains the same unalterable kind of law as physical nature. His reliance on psychology illustrates the fact that he was ultimately a naturalistic, not a sociocultural positivist.

Sumner never sensed the dangers of assuming that generalizations about physical nature can be stretched to cover human behavior. His awareness of cultural causation did not alert him to the inescapable role of ideas in empirical research – not ideas in the sense of logic but ideas as derivatives of the social scientist's own experience. One need only compare Sumner's nominalism with the equally radical nominalism of his contemporary Pareto to see that similar methodologies can lead to appreciably different overall theories. Sumner's and Pareto's conclusions contained a host of assumptions and values derived from different cultural experiences – in Sumner, the social perspectives of an Anglo-Saxon Protestant culture aware of its progress; in Pareto, the frustrations of Italian and French society. Neither thinker ever developed an acute historical–cultural perspective and neither realized the complications of assuming that since physical and human nature are both lawful, the same laws must obtain in each.

The shortcomings of Sumner's nominalism can also be seen as a deficiency in causal analysis. Though he sometimes suggested a multicausal analysis – at one point making a rather interesting, almost Marxian distinction between economy and superstructure, even indicating that the superstructure of society can affect the maintenance structure[10] – he was content to reiterate his belief in the causal efficacy and logic of population–land ratios. He seemed completely unaware that his treatment of religion amounted to a contribution to causal theory and gave his work a strong flavor of ideological determinism.

In effect, Sumner's deficiency in causal analysis was enough to vitiate his nominalism and transform it into metaphysics. By assuming that social facts, no matter how unscientific, are self-explanatory and always rational and functional to social existence, he was propounding an ill-disguised substantialism. Despite the elaborate structure and carefully delineated subdivisions of *The Science of Society*, it remains a strangely shapeless book displaying little theoretical advance over the *Folkways*. Like the *Folkways*, it is a vast catalog of customs that substitutes description for explanation and fact for theory. Its only unifying thread is Sumner's faith that ideas and practices emerge automatically to further the evolutionary adjustment of the race. His deep antipathy to abstraction prevented him from unifying his data in terms of causation or social-system types. Like the mores themselves, Sumner's thought contains a logic that is not always rational – nor for that matter is it always logical. Judged by his own criterion of rationality, his thought is not rational because he failed to judge modern mores by their efficacy, and he is not logical because he used efficacy to judge only primitive mores. Though he hinted that contemporary institutions might someday be superseded, the day he had in mind is very vague and distant. Underlying and ordering his material is the assumption that the institutions of liberal society are products of an automatic, natural evolutionary process and that they thereby possess an efficacy for human welfare that renders them inviolate from criticism or reform.

The Commitment to Liberalism

Sumner's deep commitment to liberalism is apparent on almost every page of his writings. With the possible exceptions of the works of Condorcet and Saint-Simon, and perhaps of Ward, there is no greater attempt in the annals of bourgeois social thought to define human nature and society strictly in terms of the mastery of nature. It is axiomatic for Sumner that since the relationship of human beings to nature not only defines their moral nature but determines the structure of society as well, this relationship will be the subject matter of sociology. His view that the human struggle to achieve a more rational control of nature has led to an ever-more complex division of labor is a standard feature of sociological thought in particular and of liberalism in general. Though his thought lacked an explicit doctrine of progress, he suggested this idea when he said that the trend of history was toward an ever-more satisfactory adjustment to nature. Since satisfactory adjustment in Sumner's thought meant science, the destiny of society was ultimately dependent on the success of science.

Sumner's eagerness to subordinate philosophical, political, moral, and ethical values to economic need identifies his thought in a more general way with the main trend of bourgeois civilization. In some ways his thought is part of the late-liberal current in that it recognized the social and historical roots of individual rights. However, the current of late liberalism used this perspective to justify reform proposals to achieve a more adequate social adjustment and to insure the spread of social benefits; Sumner used it to reject reform proposals and to insist on the historic necessity of inequality. His deep suspicion of government and his belief that governmental acts are always less rational than economic acts is also characteristic of early liberal thought. Human beings, he felt, had to fight for rights because they lived in a world of scarcity. Accordingly, Sumner chose the free competitive economy as the best mechanism for distributing rights and integrating and directing society. Thus did Sumner wed the sociological insights of late-liberal thought to the laissez faire metaphysics of early liberalism.

Sumner's liberalism can be seen most simply in his belief that society is fundamentally composed of autonomous beings. Although he hedged on psychological explanations, there is no mistaking the affinity between his idea of the four motives and the social-contract theory of early liberalism. Sumner's individualism, which he made no attempt to disguise, is the social counterpart to his philosophical nominalism. His nominalism is related to liberalism in yet another way. His definition of reason as a means–ends relationship and his denunciation of those who seek to define reason in terms of purposes rather than consequences coincided perfectly with the pragmatism inherent in the needs of an advanced business civilization.

However, Sumner's liberalism was not so utilitarian and historically pragmatic as the foregoing might suggest. For one thing, he never abandoned the belief that the data of social behavior are reducible to general laws analogous to those in physics. Despite his cultural approach, he never discarded psychology as a permanent variable in the drama of evolution. Like some of his predecessors in sociology, Sumner explained social inequality as a derivative of the innate inequality of individuals. He based his theory of class largely on Galton's psychology, just as Saint-Simon and Comte had used the similar theory of Bichat. The thought of Sumner, like much of sociology, sought to base the historical need of an expanding, industrial capitalism for social specialization in human nature itself.

Sumner's belief that the multifariousness of human history can be reduced to a determinate pattern of evolution is unabashed liberal substantialism. If this belief was inconsistent with his deeply held nominalism, so was his attempt to specify the institutional structure that he regarded as the climax to the pattern of evolution. Though his sarcastic critique of metaphysics did not spare the liberal metaphysics of the Enlightenment, Sumner was not averse to accepting the ironclad economic laws of Thomas Malthus (1766–1834) and David Ricardo (1772–1823); nor did he hesitate to adapt the older idea of natural harmony and adjustment through laissez faire to the newer idea of harmony and adjustment through natural selection and antagonistic cooperation. His theory, in short, was based on the monistic conclusion that the empirically given always contains the necessary elements of social adjustment, that the process of adjustment is comprehensible as a law of rational evolution even though its elements are often nonrational and exceedingly complex, and that the given is always moral because it stems from the iron necessities of the struggle for survival.

All this suggests that the empirical functionalism of Sumner's thought, which foreshadowed the dominant intellectual mood of twentieth-century sociology, was historically determined, and that the scientific method itself must always be judged by the context in which it is used. Montesquieu's functionalism, for example, was innovational in that it was directed against natural law, but at the same time it was heavily conservative – something that did not escape the notice of the philosophes who shared many of Montesquieu's assumptions. So, too, Spencer's functionalism was innovational and dynamic in that it showed the superiority of the Industrial to the Military society, but it was also conservative in that it was identified with laissez faire economics during a period when laissez faire was itself the chief obstacle to social adjustment.

In much the same way, Sumner's functionalism and the overall theory in which it was embedded served a number of different and contradictory functions. It is generally overlooked, for example, that his ideas were quite dynamic and progressive, especially if contrasted with the Populist reform proposals inspired by the agrarian–humanitarian ideals of the eighteenth and early nineteenth centuries. From the standpoint of the sociology of knowledge, one can identify Hamilton as the progressive figure in American life and Jefferson as the conservative. Sumner's position, in effect, was in direct harmony with the dynamic world-mastery orientation of the middle-class civilization that had shattered and replaced the static world-accommodation orientation of the medieval world. This cultural and social revolution raised economic ideas and values from their traditional subordination to moral and social values. Thus, Sumner in effect upheld the authentic liberal perspective during the post-Civil War period of American industrial expansion and defended it against reform proposals that threatened to blunt the capacity of the American people to achieve a new plateau of mastery over nature. By combining the classical economics of Malthus and Ricardo with the nominalism and morality of science and Protestantism, within a framework inspired by the Darwinian theory of natural selection, Sumner led the struggle of American capitalism to update an earlier liberalism based on the agrarian–commercial economy of the pre-Civil War period. Earlier liberalism had not only an outmoded economic theory, but dangerously high and rigid moral and political standards. Sumner had an instinctive distrust of attempts to subordinate the workings of a free, individualistic market economy to ethical and moral judgments. This distrust stemmed from a belief that stagnation and disaster await those who deviate from the real world of competition, "labor," and "self-denial." No other sociologist, with the exception of Max Weber, saw so clearly the sharp antagonism between the demands of a "rational" economy and ethical and moral values.

In another sense Sumner was a conservative, a right-wing liberal. Much of the reform movement he opposed was perfectly compatible with the needs of an expanding industrial society and posed little threat to the core norms of liberalism. Indeed, even in his own day his ideas had become outmoded; their very success had transformed the United States from a nation of scarcity to one of relative plenty, from a nation of small economic units to one of large-scale, even monopolistic structures, and from a nation with a clear sense of direction to one beset by a growing sense of anxiety about the cosmic processes that were supposed to harmonize disputes and reward sacrifice and effort. Of course, Sumner's rejection of natural rights separated him from the main stream of late-nineteenth-century American conservatism (or right-wing liberalism). Regardless of differences, however, right-wing liberals aggravated the problems of advanced industrialization by defining social advance and adjustment as a natural process. It is ironic that in derogating rational adjustment through human effort and foresight, right-wing liberals were sharply limiting the sovereign goal of bourgeois civilization, the mastery of human destiny. To some extent, Sumner could not envisage this goal more broadly because his thought was an ideological reflection of a given stage of economic development. This is again ironic, for the intellectual tools with which this indictment can be made were forged by his own strenuous efforts to show that ideas, including those of early liberalism, are valid only insofar as they reflect economic conditions.

Notes

1. Sumner devoted his early career mostly to economics and topical political issues, and with the exception of a few articles, his early work contains little of interest to the historian of sociology. As sociology came to dominate Sumner's intellectual interests, he undertook a large-scale treatise on the science of society that was never finished. Sumner's reputation rests mostly on a portion of this work, *Folkways* (1906; reprint ed., Boston: Ginn and Company, 1940), available as a New American Library paperback. The larger treatise was completed by Sumner's disciple Albert G. Keller, under joint authorship, as *The Science of Society*, 4 vols. (New Haven, Conn.: Yale University Press, 1927). Since its spirit and content do not differ from the main bent of Sumner's mind, it will be considered an organic part of his work. A running commentary with a liberal sprinkling of quotations from Sumner's writings, especially from *Folkways*, is

provided by Maurice R. Davie, *William Graham Sumner* (New York: Thomas Y. Crowell, 1963).

2. William Graham Sumner, *Selected Essays* (New Haven, Conn.: Yale University Press, 1924), p. 5.

3. Ibid., p. 149.

4. *War and Other Essays*, p. 191.

5. William Graham Sumner, *What Social Classes Owe to Each Other* (Caldwell, Idaho: The Caxton Printers, 1952), p. 137f.

6. *Science of Society*, 1:4.

7. *Folkways*, p. 18f.

8. *Science of Society*, 1:28f; 3:2231–2237.

9. *Science of Society*, 3:2194; for a further depiction of society as a functional system, see 3:2220.

10. Ibid., 3:2239.

10

Lester F. Ward (1841–1913)

Daniel W. Rossides

The discipline of sociology in the United States is no less indebted to Lester Ward for its inception and furtherance than it is to Sumner. Like most of the theorists' work I have discussed, Ward's was heavily influenced by the natural sciences. Though Ward was not unique in this respect, he also had personal experience in the natural sciences as a practicing botanist and geologist. Unlike Sumner, who had no such experience, Ward explicitly modeled his thought on natural science. Again unlike Sumner, his thought was deliberately speculative after the manner of Comte and Spencer. Indeed, Ward's work bears a deeper relationship to Comte and Spencer than is apparent, being in effect an attempt to combine the distinctive insights of these earlier theorists.

Philosophy and Method

Ward's commitment to monistic positivism was deep and explicit. At the base of his thought[1] is the assumption that human nature and nature are one and that both are subject to the universal principle of evolution, a principle that produces not only knowledge but virtue (or "utility") as well.

The Evolutionary Levels of Nature

Ward gave credit to Spencer for having laid down the fundamental ideas in the theory of evolution, although he said he preferred the term *aggregation* to evolution. He distinguished three levels of evolutionary phenomena: matter, life, and society. Basic to all levels is the law of material aggregation, which is guided in its choice of products by the principle of adaptation. It is apparent that Ward's thought lies within the genuine tradition of evolution (qualitative changes occur in phenomena), that it is a monistic theory (all phenomena are subject to its workings), and that it belongs to the tradition of naturalistic positivism. In all these respects his theory is much closer to Spencer's view of

---

Source: Daniel W. Rossides, *The History and Nature of Sociological Theory*, (New York: Houghton Mifflin, 1978).

evolution than to Comte's. However, Ward did not discard the distinctive aspect of Comte's view of evolution, the belief that the fundamental result of nature's itinerary through time is the acquisition by humanity of full knowledge about the laws of nature.

Methodology

Though Ward repeatedly referred to the philosophical assumptions behind science, he wrote little about methodology, engaged in no social research of his own, and made little use of the research of others.[2] Actually, his approach to knowledge was highly deductive, reminding one more of Comte than of Spencer – though even Comte had more to say about methodology than Ward. Ward's lack of interest in the data of human behavior is also more like Comte than like Spencer, though Comte was far more inclined to use historical data than Ward. Ward was content to make extensive analyses in the field he knew best, natural science, and then to apply his findings to social behavior. As such, his basic methodological tool was logic with a heavy emphasis on homological and teleological reasoning. In the single chapter in the whole of his work devoted to methodology, Ward's approach was stated in philosophical rather than scientific language. "The basis of method," he said, "is logic, and the basis of logic is the sufficient reason or law of causation."[3]

Though Ward paid special attention to efficient causation, criticizing Comte severely for failing to distinguish between efficient and final causation, his emphasis on the need for a viable theory of causation should not be misinterpreted. He never questioned the assumption that the logical structure of the mind is identical with the structure of phenomena. His fundamental philosophical and methodological orientation, therefore, was continuous with the basic orientation of the Enlightenment, which itself was continuous with the basic orientation of Western idealism or rationalism. Like his predecessors in monistic positivism, Ward continued the prescientific acceptance of a great chain of being, assuming like them that humanity's place in the hierarchy of being can be established only through the rigorous pursuit of science. Since human beings form part of an ultimately unitary structure of being, what holds for some parts of nature must hold for other parts, and logic is therefore a reliable tool in establishing the unity that obtains among nature's various parts. In other words, Ward began his work with the conclusion that a monistic principle governs the universe.

In defending his view that sociology is a science, Ward was answering two sets of critics, those who claimed that sociology can arrive only at "probability or moral certainty" and those who would deny it the status of a science because human phenomena cannot be known with mathematical precision. It is a mistake, Ward said, to think that even natural science is based only on mathematics. Its basic task, like that of social science, is to establish the uniformities in phenomena, something that has been done successfully in many areas without the aid of mathematics. The basic method of science, Ward insisted, is generalization, and exactness in the complex sciences is possible only at the upper levels of abstraction. As the most complex of sciences, Ward went on, sociology searches for the generalizations in phenomena, using details only as aids in finding law. It does not even establish its own data, which are supplied by the special social and natural sciences. Its basic task is to coordinate data until unity has been found.

Given this orientation, it is not surprising that Ward had little to say about methodology and that his thought succumbed to homological and teleological reasoning. Such an orientation also prevented him from suspecting that there might be a deep and unbridgeable gap between human and physical nature and from ever wondering whether or not a great chain of being really existed.

Substantive Work

Creative Synthesis

In his later work, *Pure Sociology*, Ward tightened his theory of evolution under the general concept of *creative synthesis* and tried to specify the concrete mechanism of evolutionary development and the causal links between natural and social evolution. Nature, he claimed, is everywhere characterized by struggle and striving, an "eternal pelting of atoms," a restless surging. In short, the main cause at work in the universe is not matter but "collision." Though there is a monistic principle unifying all existence, there is also a dualism or polarity in nature that produces conflict. The process that mediates this conflict and produces new evolutionary products is *synergy*. Essentially a process of equilibration, synergy explains the existence of structure at every level of nature. However, the overall process of creative synthesis is not yet explained. Ward, who had a penchant for establishing and then qualifying universal principles, introduced a distinction between social statics and social dynamics, a distinction that required a further set of principles: *difference of potential, innovation,* and *conation,* all unconscious agencies of social progress.

Such is the general scheme of evolution. Nature in its struggle to achieve ever-higher forms of organization finally produces human beings and thus society The general process is unconscious and wasteful, marked by conflict and crisis, yet somehow functional and progressive. At the highest level of organic development stand human beings, who emerge out of the lower levels as sentient beings capable of ever-more-complex behavior. Within the general history and constitution of humanity are two fundamentally different agencies or causal processes. The first, *genesis*, is an unconscious process and its history is the history of all nature. The second process, *telesis*, is marked by consciousness, and while it has existed from the beginning of time, its real history lies in the future.

The Social Forces

The distinction between conative (or efficient) cause and intellectual (or final) cause is central to Ward's thought. These two causes form what he called the *social forces*, the special class of variables that make up the domain of social science. The social forces fall into two general categories: the physical forces, hunger and sex, and the spiritual or moral, aesthetic, and intellectual forces. Out of these forces come the institutional structures of society.

The division of the social forces into physical and spiritual – or biological and psychic – also contains, implicitly at least, Ward's distinction between conative cause and intellectual cause, or, more simply, genesis and telesis. The truly dynamic or efficient cause in human affairs is the conative, or what Ward also called feeling or desire or the subjective aspect of mind. The basic desires, hunger and sex, are the source of a host of derivative desires. All desires express themselves in obedience to pleasure and pain, and "all social progress, in the proper sense of the phrase, is a movement from a pain economy toward a pleasure economy, or at least a movement in the direction of the satisfaction of a greater and greater proportion of the desires of men." At work in human affairs, in other words, is the law of parsimony, or marginal utility, which is conative and therefore unconscious.

At the beginning, said Ward, the ends of nature and of humanity were identical, and human feelings were merely means to secure the functional needs of nature, basically the need to perpetuate and increase life. Since evolution had special plans for humanity, the feelings developed and awareness or *interest* began. The individual became an actor in the drama of evolution. Henceforth, a conflict of interests developed between the creature and nature and between the individual and the race. This development, said Ward,

> ... was nothing less than the dawn of mind in the world. Before its appearance all nature had been mindless and soulless. Henceforth there was to be *animated nature* with all that the phrase carries with it. In it were contained the psychic world and the moral world. With it came pleasure and pain with all their momentous import, and out of it ultimately grew thought and intelligence. Nature cared nothing for any of these. They were unnecessary to her general scheme, and not at all ends of being. Mind was therefore an accident, an incidental consequence of other necessities – an *epiphenomenon*.[4]

Though the self has emerged and individuals have become conscious of themselves, they are not yet aware of the direction of nature or of the fact that it is under rational, efficient direction. Evolution throughout its history has been under the control of genesis – impelled by blind, natural, subjective forces. Evolution has achieved its purposes unconsciously through trial and error, evolving products at "enormous expense and involving infinite sacrifice of life and energy."

It has produced egoism to satisfy desire, and it has constructed vast systems of religion to counteract selfishness, often leading to "extravagant follies and shocking practices."

Full consciousness and economy of effort, said Ward, will come only when evolution is placed under the direction of telesis. Under telesis, evolution will operate according to the dictates of humanity's objective faculties, which will bring "knowledge" about the workings of nature and will enable human beings to make "artificial" and economical adjustments of means to ends with the grand object of reducing nature to human service.

However, the human telic capacity, which has existed from the beginning of time and is itself an accidental and unintended product of genesis, has so far been unable to impose its husbandry on nature. On the contrary, it has been subservient to feeling and thus has helped to perpetrate "dark deeds and sinister practices." This is because the telic faculty always proceeds through indirection. When one human being uses it against another, it takes the form of "deception" and is fundamentally immoral. Deception and its various forms, ruse, cunning, shrewdness, strategy, and diplomacy, are the basis throughout history of the fundamentally exploitative character of religion, the economy, politics, and law. However, when the telic agent is directed against nature, it results not in deception but in "ingenuity."[5]

Ironically, the chief beneficiary of deception is telesis itself. Deception produces inequality, inequality produces leisure, and the surplus intellectual energy that leisure makes available is used by the telic faculty in a "nonadvantageous" manner – that is, in a manner that is not concerned with satisfying immediate and direct needs. The Greeks, Ward continued, developed marvels of telic speculation, though their use of mind alone resulted in a fruitless anthropomorphism in which human beings projected their own intelligence into nature. However, the Greek philosophers who speculated about matter made a great contribution to knowledge even though they were seriously handicapped by an insufficiency of facts. With the slow accumulation of facts in the postmedieval world, the same speculative genius that the Greeks had displayed produced a vast expansion of knowledge. Telesis has begun at last to free itself from its bondage to genesis. Beginning with astronomy in the fifteenth century and climaxed by the greatest generalization of all, the law of evolution, telesis has achieved nothing less than the conquest of nature, a conquest that includes knowledge about human as well as physical nature.

The Origin and Nature of Social Structures

Ward's theory of society was based explicitly on biology and psychology, and therefore his explanation of the origin of society requires only a brief treatment. His explanation of how biopsychic traits are translated into social institutions is the weakest and least credible part of his work. Indeed, his explanation of the origin and nature of society is everywhere vitiated by vagueness and excessive reliance on logic. In Ward, the general process of evolution emerges out of material relationships and ascends from the inorganic to the organic levels of nature. From organic nature there emerges mind or reason, which is a combination of feeling and intellect – two aspects of mind that can also be described as psychic factors, social energy, or social forces. At first, feeling dominates intellect and is in perfect harmony with the general aim of nature that the race should multiply and survive; or, as Ward also stated it, the structure of human instinctual nature is in harmony with its function. All this changes as time passes, for with the growth of feeling there also grows an antagonism between the psychic structure of the individual and the function of individual and racial survival.

The idea of conflict became quite important in Ward's later work. In *Pure Sociology* he elevated the idea into an evolutionary principle of considerable importance, especially in explaining the origin and nature of society. He was prepared, for example, to accept Gumplowicz's and Ratzenhofer's (1842–1904) theory that the origin of society arises from racial struggle. In Ward's own language, the social forces (physiological–psychological desires) are mutually antagonistic and threaten the survival of the race. Thanks to the process of social synergy, however, these destructive forces are transformed into social structures that perform social functions. The struggle for greater efficiency is the struggle for structure. Human institutions emerge to control and use social energy. The essence of social energy, "the primordial, homogeneous, undifferentiated social plasma" out of which institutions develop, can also be called the "group sentiment of safety." Out of this social energy (or psychic energy) develops religion and then morals, law, politics, and all other institutions. In short, the social forces, which by themselves are destructive and constitute a menace to human existence, are transmuted by social synergy, or conflict, into beneficial, functional institutions.

Each of the social forces leads to the formation of a social structure. The physical or essential forces, hunger and sex, lead to economic and family institutions; the spiritual or nonessential forces lead to moral, aesthetic, and intellectual structures. Ward's account of how the biopsychological forces become social institutions is unconvincing, not clearly saying where political and religious institutions come from. While social institutions must certainly be lodged in biotic and psychic structures, it is quite another thing to say that society is unilaterally derived from these structures.

The Network of Causation

If one of the measures of a theorist's contribution to sociology and to social science is his insight into causation, Ward's work did little to advance humanity's knowledge of itself. Actually, his causal theory was retrogressive. Despite his wide familiarity with the work of other sociologists, Ward failed to advance or even to absorb their insights into social causation, largely because he had made up his mind from the beginning that social phenomena could be explained exclusively in terms of biology and psychology. Like many naturalistic positivists, Ward assumed that the social realm is part of a unitary natural structure accessible to scientific method. Like his predecessors in monistic positivism, he also assumed that all effects have antecedent causes and that these causes are reducible to the one cause that informs all phenomena. However, Ward's predecessors, while searching for a unified theory of causation, managed to identify a variety of causes such as climate, soil, population, interaction, invention, and norms. Ward was content from the beginning to stake his entire system on a single cause, the effects of biotic and psychic evolution. Committing himself to this idea confronted Ward with an insurmountable difficulty. It is one thing to trace the development of the human organism as it makes its way from primordial slime into biopsychic time, but in attempting to equate this process of biopsychic time with social time, one encounters the fact that human beings had fully evolved long before the start of significant social evolution. In other words, one cannot use a constant (human nature, biology, psychology) to explain change.

To circumvent this difficulty Ward was forced to rely on the very type of thinking that science had struggled so mightily to supplant – philosophical discourse. He constantly fell back on the assumption of a great chain of being that is self-sufficient and continuous. While Ward defined being in naturalistic terms, he also carried forward the prescientific faith that being is replete with all its necessaries and contains no radical breaks or gaps. Under this assumption the avenue to knowledge is logic, and since being or nature is a unity, it is quite permissible to use homologous reasoning. In point of fact, Ward made extensive use of this type of logical explanation, especially when trying to explain the translation of psychic factors into social effects.

Ward's use of homologous arguments, however, is only one aspect of his overall acceptance of logic as a legitimate avenue to truth. He also indulged in an extensive use of teleological explanation. Just as logic presupposes a unitary structure of being connected by a single cause, which once identified in one area can be used homologously to explain behavior in another, so too it presupposes that any given effect, however far removed from an important cause in another area, must somehow be related to that cause. In other words, because of his underlying conviction that nature is a unitary structure, Ward simply assumed that social phenomena are part of the process of evolution. He simply assumed that the tremendously important process of evolution that had been identified in geology and biology must somehow be related to sociology. Further, since the same assumption cannot permit irrationality in nature, the process of evolution must be purposeful. Thus does teleological reasoning short-circuit science to produce two corollaries: the belief that all effects or historical manifestations have been for the best, and the belief that it is scientifically respectable to use the device of a hidden logic to explain the intermediate steps between ultimate principle and remote effect.

Ward's work is no exception to this pattern of quasi-scientific reasoning. Logic superseded science at every vital juncture in his thought, as, for example, when he attempted to justify the ultimate worth of all historical events and practices and when he used explanations based on hidden logic. From the flux of matter come inorganic and organic forms. With the development of life emerge feeling and intellect to form mind. Even within the purely biological–psychological sequence of development, Ward abandoned causation when he attributed the development of feeling and intellect to accident. His explanation of the origin and development of society is no less unscientific. The flux of human passions, he argued, is transmuted into social structures by the static or constructive principle of synergy and by the dynamic principles of difference of potential, innovation, and conation. In explaining the transition of mind to society, he again abandoned causation in favor of homologues and attributed social effects to a blind, wasteful, but ultimately functional set of processes called synergy and dynamic principles. The entire process called genesis everywhere simulates telesis despite its basically unconscious, accidental, and wasteful mode of operation.

Framed in terms of the liberal dilemma, the breakdown of Ward's causal theory becomes even more evident. Why is it that a rational universe has produced waste and pain or error and evil, and that human beings, who possess the telic capacity to see the lawfulness of nature, have failed to do so, except in a sporadic and error-filled way? The liberal dilemma posed no problem for Ward to the extent that he adopted a Spencerian naturalism in which there is no separate order of truth and error or good and evil but only an empirical "is" that absorbs both the true and the good. However, Ward also accepted the distinctive feature of Comte's view of evolution, that the main purpose of evolution is to supply human beings with a hierarchy of truth and goodness that is ultimately realized in the social life of humanity. Fundamentally, Comte's theory of evolution was based on the view that the universe, including humankind, is static but that somehow human beings obtain progressively more knowledge about first physical and then human nature. By accepting Comte's belief that truth and goodness are the terminuses of evolution, Ward's theory floundered on the liberal dilemma. Though evolution manifests itself in ways that seem to be erroneous and evil, Ward was convinced that it is basically orderly and progressive. Appearances to the contrary, he asserted, those things that philosophers have characterized as error and evil are in reality rational and moral.

The philosophical assumption underlying Ward's attempt to explain away error and evil is that conflict between particulars is not a barrier to law, but its essence – conflict is how nature works to produce law. The mixture of unlikes is a principle at work within sexual forces as well as within society. When conflict manifests itself as war and imperialism, it is really leading to progress because these social manifestations increase social activity. When the forces of nature take social shape as inequality, caste, slavery, exploitation, elitism, or deception, they are progressive because they discipline human beings and release the "surplus social energy" that is eventually used to direct the telic power of individuals away from themselves and toward nature.

Religion also participates in this process. Religion is unscientific, but because it stems from nature it can be thought of scientifically as the "instinct of group safety." Religion could not have come into existence, Ward argued, if it were not basically advantageous to the human race. The clergy has been among the elites who have benefited humanity through their possession of "surplus social energy."

As an evolutionary monist, therefore, Ward was ultimately forced to argue that everything is for the best and that error and evil disappear when placed in an evolutionary frame. Thus, in a way that we have encountered from Condorcet on, Ward was saying that everything in society works for the conservation of the group; that the proper attitude toward any institution is not to condemn it out of hand but to examine it to see what stage of evolution it is in; and that the majority of customs around the world are conducive to race safety.

Ward's fatalistic optimism was matched by a faith in hidden logic. Even the crowning glory of evolution, the modification of nature by human beings, is an accident. Science, knowledge, and invention, like the mind, are the results of haphazard processes. Egoistic telic action by the individual is the cause of that wasteful and pernicious but ultimately functional and progressive process known as social genesis. Even though humanity's "whole career has been marked by belligerency, internecine strife, and universal rapacity," the ultimate evolutionary effect of nature's forces is to produce social telesis, the stage of evolution in which human beings will have knowledge of themselves and can thus consciously control their own destiny. The beginnings of this terminal stage in the history of humankind can already be seen in the growth of collectivism, which is an outgrowth of natural evolution. However, knowledge about human nature is merely a higher stage of knowledge about physical nature, and it too must presumably emerge from accident. Thus social telesis, the apex of social evolution, the period in which human beings will run their affairs with full knowledge and full consciousness, is a social state that emerges from a magically efficacious process beyond human ken.

Social Evolution

Though Ward's sociological thought was permeated by the idea of evolution, he said surprisingly little about the various stages of social evolution. While constantly referring to the genetic and telic stages of social development, he rarely described them in terms of their characteristic institutions. His few references to concrete stages of social evolution were not developed systematically, nor did he place any great emphasis on them. In *Dynamic Sociology* he briefly referred to a fourfold pattern of social aggregation: the solitary or autarchic, the constrained aggregate or anarchic, the national or politarchic, and the cosmopolitan or pantarchic stages. However, having mentioned them, he never referred to them again. In another place he referred casually to the hunting, agricultural, and pastoral stages of development, and after a crude attempt to identify the psychic traits appropriate to each stage, he dropped the matter.[6] In his last work, there is a brief but unexplored allusion to "national freedom, political freedom, and social freedom" as stages within the process of evolutionary development.[7]

Ward's only real effort to identify stages of social development is found in *Pure Sociology*, but even here he showed no great interest in the problem. He expressed his general agreement with Gumplowicz and Ratzenhofer that the origin of society is to be found in racial struggle. Again displaying his penchant for analogues, he likened social development to the biological process called *karyokinesis*. Both here and elsewhere, however, he never explicitly defined in terms of concrete stages the struggle between genesis and telesis, the essence of cosmic evolution. Ward's work contains neither a definite philosophical nor a social series, nor does it make any attempt to correlate the development of thought with the development of society. The process of evolution, it would seem, grinds out its qualitative changes so gradually that no discernible divisions can be found.

In marking the divisions in intellectual history, Ward used a simple distinction between theological, dualistic and scientific, monistic explanations of phenomena, or, as he also called them, *theo-teleological* and *anthro-teleological* explanations. The primary distinction in intellectual history is between those who view the antecedents of phenomena as "arbitrary and independent" of phenomena and those who view them as "constant and connected necessarily" with phenomena. The theological stage, said Ward, is anthropomorphic in origin. In it, individuals impute to nature or to deities characteristics derived from an awareness of their own willful, purposeful behavior. When individuals direct their attention to theology, spiritual things, or pure thought, stagnation results; only when they direct their attention to matter does their thought become dynamic.

Ward was slightly more informative about social evolution. The displacement of theo-teleological explanations by anthro-teleological explanations in the natural sciences will eventually find its counterpart in social science, and human beings will be in a position to install a true system of society, one based on knowledge of human nature and devoted to human betterment. Ward's depiction of the terminal stage of social evolution, however, is no more carefully delineated than the previous stage. Of all the monistic naturalistic positivists that I have discussed, only Comte was willing to give a detailed picture of the scientific society. Ward's picture of the final society, however, is unmistakable in its general outlines. It rests on the assumption that science is inherently serviceable to human beings. On the assumption that all individuals are educable, he predicted that scientific legislation would translate social knowledge into social practice. The essential equality of human beings, a belief Ward held throughout his life, rests on a distinction between intellect, the untrustworthy source of the theo-teleological world view, and intelligence, the intellect infused and disciplined by knowledge. Ward argued that intellect is equal in all human beings but that intelligence differs because of faulty social organization. Therefore, society has always been divided into two classes, the informed exploiters and the uninformed exploited. However, history shows that the informed class has been infused steadily by new blood; it now remains only for the masses to be uplifted. If this is true, Ward concluded, the Helvetian doctrine of intellectual equalitarianism, which assumes an equal capacity for achievement, means that no individual can be excluded from eventual membership in society's highest class.

After a careful scrutiny of existing research, Ward became convinced that his intuitive belief in the essential equality of human beings was supported by facts. The new society, therefore, must and will eliminate the causes of unequal intelligence. The main fault in the organization of society is the system for distributing knowledge. The avenue to economic equality, and to the achievement of happiness in general, lies in the systematic and intensive education of all individuals. No other problem can be solved until inequality in education has been eliminated.

Ward concluded his final book by spelling out the principle of attraction that underlies applied sociology. It is fundamental to social science, he insisted, that the laws of mind and thus of human behavior obey the same Newtonian laws that govern nature. Once the law of parsimony is united with the principle of attraction, the prospects for scientific legislation will be almost boundless.[8] Scientific legislation may also be called *attractive legislation* as opposed to prescientific *compulsory legislation.* The forces of human nature can be steered in directions that are beneficial to both the individual and society, and the traditional repression of these forces can be discarded. Though Ward stated that his discussion of the Telic society in *Applied Sociology* superseded previous discussions, he was still vague about the institutional structure of the new society.

The fundamental condition for scientific legislation is an educated people guided by sociologists. In the Telic society all aspects of social life will awaken to the touch of enlightened legislation. In particular, economic production will be facilitated, not through public control or ownership of industry but by making labor attractive. Giving credit to Charles Fourier (1772–1837) for first propounding the principle of attractive labor, and agreeing with Veblen (1857–1929) and Ratzenhofer that the distaste for work is due to caste traditions, Ward gave a high priority to the problem of making labor satisfying in his schedule of reform. According to Ward, once labor is attractive, there will be a vast increase in social efficiency and improvement.

The Telic society is also characterized by the absence of social opposition to the individual; it is a social state in which one can "conceive of the final disappearance of all restrictive laws and of government as a controlling agency."

This view, of course, is similar to Saint-Simon's image of the Positive society, to Marx's picture of the classless society, and to Spencer's Ethical society. Though Ward used organic analogies more sparingly and less rigorously than Spencer, he did use one to envisage the future society. In animals and human beings, he noted, the brain as it has grown has steadily taken over the body's unconsciously performed functions, and social development can be seen in analogous terms. As the homologue to the brain, the state will see to it that an ever-more-perfect coordination of parts and functions takes place socially. However, Ward cautioned, Spencer was correct in not carrying the analogy too far. Unlike in the organic world, the perfection of the social whole will be for the benefit of its parts. The superior achievement of the Anglo-Saxon race up to now has been because it has been able "to see and act upon the principle that while individual initiative can alone accomplish great results, *it must be free*, and that, under the influence of the normal and natural forces of society, and taking the whole of human nature into account, it cannot be free unless the avenues for its activity be kept open by the power of society at large."[9]

In short, society, guided by the knowledge that there can be a full congruity between its own self-consciousness and that of the individual, will set itself to realizing a full measure of liberty, equality, and happiness for all – a goal that is possible only through the accumulation and distribution of knowledge.

Conclusion

Ward and the Positive Tradition

Ward's general theory of society is an amalgam of the distinctive features in the evolutionary theories of Comte and Spencer. To the extent that he framed his theory of evolution in terms of material relationships and insisted that all aspects of nature undergo qualitative changes, his thought was in line with Spencer's and with the authentic scientific view of evolution. As a consequence, Ward placed human beings themselves in a natural setting and then sought to explain their psychic attributes as products of a process of natural evolution. However, in making an explicit identification between the growth of biopsychic traits and the structure and development of society, Ward parted company with Spencer. Whereas Spencer had sensed the difficulty in equating biology and psychology with social behavior, Ward felt no such qualm and adopted a thoroughgoing doctrine of biopsychological evolutionism. Furthermore, Spencer was somewhat aware that an evolutionary point of view precluded a terminal point, especially one in which conflict, the very stuff of evolution, was eliminated simply because science emerged in full possession of the uniformities of nature; Ward, however, believed that the conflict-ridden process of evolution would end when human beings obtained total knowledge about their universe. To the extent that he adopted this view, his thought is similar to the pseudo-evolutionary theory of Auguste Comte.

The similarity between Ward's work and Comte's can be seen in a number of other ways. Both believed that evolution must eventually produce a society that would embrace humanity; that the growth of human knowledge and consciousness comes from teleological causation; and that the terminal social system would be superintended by sociologists. Even Ward's notion of scientific legislation based on the principle of attraction is a curious throwback to the static cosmology of Newtonian physics and thus also Comtean in outlook. Ward, who wrote long summaries of the theories of both Comte and Spencer in *Dynamic Sociology*, never noticed Comte's failure to develop a genuine evolutionary view and never recognized the contradiction entailed in his own acceptance of Comte's ideological evolutionism. Of course, Ward's equalitarianism separated him from Comte, and from his contemporary Sumner. Finally, Ward's emphasis on an interventionist state separated him from both Spencer and Sumner, though Spencer, like Ward, was more disposed to think of the future society as a realization of individual equality.

Ward and Late Liberalism

Like his predecessors in both naturalistic and sociocultural positivism Ward is easily identified with liberal civilization. His thought represents the equalitarian strand of the Enlightenment far more than the thought of any of his predecessors in sociology with the exception of Condorcet. Whereas Comte had found in evolution the justification for hierarchical industrial society, and Spencer and Sumner had found a justification for atomistic individualism (or early Anglo-American liberalism), Ward found a justification for the late-liberal belief that society should liberate the individual by perfecting its institutional structures.

Ward's liberalism is apparent throughout his work. Informing his entire point of view was the belief that egoism is the fundamental feature of human nature. Throughout his writings egoism appeared again and again in various guises. Egoism is lawful in that it proceeds according to pleasure and pain as measured by the principle of parsimony or marginal utility. Ward's use of a term from liberal economic theory was not coincidental. His entire attitude toward human nature, especially toward the passions, was authentically liberal. Gone are the theological and the rationalist distrust and fear of human passions. In a straightforward, hedonistic fashion, the conventional terms of moral philosophy are given a naturalistic basis. Happiness and the good are the same as pleasure, while evil comes from pain. Virtue is merely the performance of the necessary functions that make for individual and racial adjustment and survival.

Gone too is the traditional definition of human passions as too empirical to be known. It was axiomatic for Ward that human passions are structured and therefore knowable. Furthermore, the passions are good: they serve useful purposes as means toward other ends as well as being ends in themselves.

It is not surprising that with such an orientation, Ward, an authentic son of the Enlightenment, looked upon history as a process that produces secular happiness; nor is it surprising that he thought of the conquest of nature, or more exactly of the intellectual conquest of nature, as the key to happiness. Intellectual progress, which human beings translate into the economic conquest of nature, stems from the organism's struggle to adjust itself to its environment. The more successfully individuals adjust themselves to the forces of nature, the more they will have conquered ignorance and evil. The struggle to conquer nature, however, is not a conventional or haphazard process; it emerges from within nature itself – that is, from human nature defined in terms of egoism or self-interest. It is individual rationality (individual telesis), spurred on by hunger and sex, that is the driving force behind the patterned process of scientific and economic achievement. Ward assumed throughout his work that while the use of human reason against other human beings is immoral, its use against nature is inherently beneficial. The net effect of these views was to provide a metaphysical basis for the ideas and values of an expanding industrial capitalism.

Ward is a late liberal in that the forces of egoism do not lead directly or automatically to social harmony and welfare. A tension emerges early in the evolutionary process between the individual and the group. Individuals are creative actors, but their creativity poses a danger to society and it is necessary to curb them. Social control, however, is not a product of random conventionalization or the outcome of political struggle and compromise; it is a natural outgrowth of natural processes. The structures of control, at first centered mainly in religion and then the state, are natural evolutionary products. The nation-state is the highest product of the process of social *karyokinesis*.

Ward's definitions of property and the state are further clues to his late liberal orientation. Property, he insisted, is private and individual, not because of an abstract doctrine of natural rights but because of law and the state. Indeed, there are no rights at all except in and through the state. The state is the prime mechanism for controlling unbridled egoism, and without the state there can be neither unity nor individualism. However, the individual and the state are not in permanent opposition. Once the Telic society has emerged, social control will achieve its ends through the release of the socially beneficial capacities of individuals. Since the exercise of these capacities is beneficial to the individual as well, the individual and society are reconciled. They are in opposition only because of the faulty organization of society. However, in pointing out the defects in society, Ward did not question liberalism's basic institution, the market economy. For him, the main institutional defect in liberal society was its failure to distribute knowledge properly. Once this defect is corrected, social efficiency and social improvement will be powerfully augmented, since an educated population is more productive and supportive of scientific legislation.

Ward's immersion in the thought structure of liberalism is evident in yet another way. He thought of evolution as a process in which the continuous manifestation of egoism and its continuous reconciliation with society resulted in progressively better adaptation to nature. The defective nature of Ward's theory was pointed out in the discussion of his causal theory. His explanation can now be seen as a naive attempt to place the natural-law theory of liberal society on a scientific basis. Ward merely restated the Anglo-American commitment to laissez faire, in which self and society are in a continuous process of equilibration, in naturalistic, evolutionary terms, with the novel addition that the reconciliation must be made more consciously by public agencies. Nature was still basically orderly in Ward's theory, except that it now decreed a greater role for human beings in establishing social order than could be found in earlier liberal thought.

Ward, who criticized anthropomorphism in prescientific thought, is himself subject to analysis in terms of the sociology of knowledge. As a naturalist who believed in the automatic emergence of a mind destined to have full knowledge of the universe at large, he was ultimately a substantialistic idealist. Had Ward maintained that the growth of truth was a consequence of the biological growth of mind, he would have been wrong but consistent, and he would have avoided the liberal dilemma. However, to maintain that the telic capacity of human beings emerged before the dawn of science and that it was once used to produce false and immoral doctrines is to espouse a theory that pins him to the horns of the liberal dilemma.

Ward's theory can be thought of as a reflection of American society in the late nineteenth century. Industrial conflict and economic concentration required a rethinking of traditional American assumptions about society. Sumner used science to explain and justify the conflicts and hardships of industrialization in terms of the Darwinian struggle for existence. Ward, however, used science to show that the struggle for existence in nature and society, while purposeful, is extremely wasteful, and that just as individuals can bring nature under control through knowledge, they can also control society. Human beings who are natural creatures, are somehow miraculously able to separate themselves from nature and to rise above its dictates. Nowhere is Ward's commitment to Western idealism more apparent than his belief that mind, though subject to the compulsions of nature, is able ultimately to transcend nature's deceptive and destructive ways.

Ward, experiencing the growing conflicts of post-Civil War American society, read this experience into all human history. His experience with economic conflict and economic concentration, combined with his deep commitment to equality (and his origins in the American Midwest), gave him a fresh perspective on society. However, in formulating his concern for American society and his reform proposals, Ward went far beyond what was warranted by either his experience or his scholarship. He read his ideas into the cosmos at large. The ideological nature of his analysis and main reform proposal should not go unnoticed. Ward was aware that human history up to his own day was a vast catalog of misery and blindness, and he could not have been unaware that a rampant capitalism was increasingly identified as a major cause of instability and exploitative inequality. However, despite his awareness of waste, conflict, and injustice and his deep sensitivity to human suffering, Ward placed the main cause of social insufficiency in education.

Looking back, one is struck by the unreality of much of what Ward had to say about social behavior. Admirably equipped as a natural scientist, Ward was out of touch with the complexities of human behavior. The root trouble lay not only in his belief in a unified theory of human nature based on biopsychic forces, but also in his lack of historical and social knowledge. Of all the monists whose work I have covered, Ward was the most lacking in any real insight or knowledge about human behavior. He had no qualms or inhibitions about indiscriminately applying the substantive concepts of natural science to human behavior. His predecessors in monistic positivism all had in their thought secondary strands based on a wider knowledge of the empirical data of human behavior. They were thus able to discern social and cultural processes and causes and to avoid a total interpretation of human behavior in terms of physics, psychology, or biology.

Little schooled in history, Ward perceived all social data in natural-science terms. No insight into the cultural and social sources of behavior could penetrate the fine mesh of his positivism, which assumed that human behavior was reducible to naturalistic, biopsychological processes. In this sense, Ward's early career in natural science and his late entry into sociology explain and somewhat excuse his inability to question the literal identification of human beings with nature. Even his wide acquaintance with the literature of sociology never freed him from his single-minded emphasis on biopsychological evolutionism.

Ward deserves a place within the maturing tradition of sociology for a number of reasons. Like Spencer and Sumner, he frankly accepted a naturalistic approach to human behavior and thus helped to establish the respectability of a scientific study of society. Like Spencer, Ward made a literal identification of human nature and nature and thereby made the negative contribution of showing the limits of a biopsychologically based social science. Ward's naturalism included an open acceptance of the passions as the avenue to human welfare and a rejection of transcendental moral and rational approaches to human behavior. However, though his thought is everywhere marked by a suspicion of reason and a commitment to empirical investigation, Ward, like so many of his predecessors, succumbed to the temptations of both overt and hidden logic, and in this way he smuggled prescientific thought forms into the structure of sociology.

Notes

1. Ward's first major work (1883) was *Dynamic Sociology*, 2 vols. (New York: Appleton, 1902). Later major works include *Pure Sociology* (New York: Macmillan, 1925), originally

published in 1903, and *Applied Sociology* (Boston: Ginn 1906). In addition, Ward wrote two other works: *The Psychic Factors of Civilization* (Boston Ginn, 1906), originally published in 1892; and *Outlines of Sociology* (New York: Macmillan, 1897). A selection from Ward's works is available in Israel Gerver, ed., *Lester Frank Ward* (New York: Thomas Y. Crowell paperback 1963). For a collection of Ward's writings that focus on his promotion of the late liberal interventionist state, see Henry Steele Commager, ed., *Lester Ward and the Welfare State* (Indianapolis: Bobbs-Merrill, 1967).

2. The one exception is Ward's last work, *Applied Sociology*, where he made extensive use of the research data of other social scientists to support his contention that human beings could be educated into equality.

3. *Pure Sociology*, p. 45.

4. Ibid., p. 128.

5. An almost identical emphasis, it will be remembered, is found in Saint-Simon's work.

6. *The Psychic Factors of Civilization*, 2nd ed. (Boston: Ginn, 1906), p. 186.

7. *Applied Sociology* (Boston: Ginn, 1906), p. 26.

8. Ibid., pp. 331–334.

9. *Pure Sociology*, p. 567f.

11

W. E. B. Du Bois as a Social Investigator: *The Philadelphia Negro*, 1899

Martin Bulmer

The present period in the development of sociological study is a trying one; it is the period of observation, research and comparison – work always wearisome, often aimless without well settled principles and guiding lines, and subject always to the persistent criticism: What, after all, has been accomplished? To this the most positive answer which years of research and speculation have been able to return is that the phenomena of society are worth the most careful and systematic study, and whether or not this study may eventually lead to a systematic body of knowledge deserving the name of science, it cannot in any case fail to give the world a mass of truth worth the knowing.

Being then in a period of observation and comparison, we must confess to ourselves that the sociologists of few nations have so good an opportunity for observing the growth and evolution of society as those in the United States. The rapid rise of a young country, the vast social changes, the wonderful economic development, the bold political experiments, and the contact of varying moral standards – all these make the American students crucial tests of social action, microcosmic reproductions of long centuries of world history and rapid – even violent – repetitions of great social problems. Here is a field for the sociologists – a field rich, but little worked, and full of great possibilities. European scholars envy our opportunities and it must be said to our credit that great interest in the observation of social phenomena has been aroused in the last decade – an interest of which much is ephemeral and superficial, but which opens the way for broad scholarship and scientific effort.

In one field, however – and a field perhaps larger than any other domain of social phenomena, there does not seem to have been awakened as yet a fitting realization of the opportunities for scientific inquiry.

Source: Martin Bulmer, Kevin Bales and Kathryn K. Sklar (eds.), *The Social Survey in Historical Perspective, 1880–1940*, (Cambridge: Cambridge University Press, 1991).

> This is the group of social phenomena arising from the presence in this land of eight million persons of African descent.[1]

The writer was W. E. B. Du Bois, the year 1898. The tone of his remarks have a remarkably modern ring to them, and suggest a sophisticated understanding of the possible contribution of empirical social science before that contribution was well established. He had just completed the field work for his study *The Philadelphia Negro*, published in 1899. Yet Du Bois' work in Philadelphia and his subsequent attempts to develop a research programme at Atlanta University failed to have significant impact, and twelve years later, in 1910, he himself abandoned empirical social science for political activism and journalism. This episode forms part of the American social survey tradition, and is instructive both in its own right and by comparison with the position of women discussed by Kathryn Sklar in relation to Florence Kelley.

William Edward Burghardt Du Bois was born in Great Barrington, Massachusetts in 1868, into a free black family. He was descended through his mother's side from an African slave, Tom Burghardt, who had been brought to New England early in the eighteenth century by a Dutch family. His father's family was of mixed white and black descent; his father abandoned his mother when he was small, and he – an only child – was brought up by her, who worked as a maid. Growing up in Great Barrington in a community where the colour line was not rigidly enforced, the young Du Bois learnt protestant, Yankee, values and to look down on ethnic immigrants from Central and Eastern Europe. Du Bois, however, was one of very few black people in a predominantly white community, which had a determining influence on his education. When he graduated from the local high school, he was the first black student to do so. Shortly thereafter his mother died. Four members of the white elite of the town stepped in, and arranged for Du Bois' study at college to be financially supported. Du Bois himself hoped to attend Harvard, but they arranged for him to be admitted to Fisk University in Nashville, the leading black college in the South, which he entered in 1885 and graduated from in 1888, having studied classics and liberal arts and edited the college newspaper. During the summer vacations he taught in black schools in the rural south.

In 1888 Du Bois achieved his ambition of being admitted to Harvard, financing his studies with a mixture of scholarships and vacation earnings. There he took undergraduate courses for two years, graduating with honours in philosophy and giving the class oration in 1890. This was followed by two years of graduate study working towards the PhD, taking courses in history and political science and starting work on a dissertation on the African slave trade which he submitted in 1895.[2] Although he took a course in sociology at Harvard from Edward Cummings, a professor of ethics with interests in this subject, it apparently made little impression. His dissertation is much more a straight historical monograph. A far more formative influence was the two years which Du Bois spent studying in Germany between 1892 and 1894, financed by the

Slater Fund for the Education of Negroes, chaired by former President Rutherford B. Hayes.

At the University of Berlin, he took courses in economic history and sociology, including a course by the young Max Weber, and was particularly influenced by Gustav Schmoller. With Schmoller, Du Bois did research on the pattern of plantation economics and peonage in the South. Schmoller favoured the use of induction to accumulate historical and descriptive material. Social scientific facts, accumulated by careful inductive analysis, could produce systematic causal explanations of social phenomena. Schmoller, however, was also deeply involved in issues of social policy through the *Verein für Sozialpolitik* and believed that social science could contribute to social intervention. He insisted, however, on the distinction between fact and value, and instilled this in his students. Du Bois quoted his mentor as having said in a seminar: 'My school tries as far as possible to leave the *Sollen* [should be] for a later stage and study the *Geschehen* [is] as other sciences have done'.[3]

Du Bois' early studies, up to 1910, bear the influence of Schmoller: the careful attention to empirical detail as a means of making inductive generalisations, the use of empirical inquiry to illuminate issues of social policy, an underlying interest in social justice and an historical approach. 'Schmoller . . . drew Du Bois away from history into a type of political economy which could easily be converted into sociology, and, at a more general level, encouraged him to a career devoted to scholarship.'[4] As Du Bois himself later recalled, he reacted against grand theories and appeals to abstract principles. 'I determined to put science into sociology through a study of the condition and problems of my own group. I was going to study the facts, any and all the facts, concerning the American Negro and his plight, and by measurement and comparison and research, work up to any valid generalization which I could.'[5]

These details about Du Bois' early development are more relevant to understanding his pioneering use of the social survey method than in the case of, say, residents at the Hull-House, because as a scholar Du Bois lacked the support of those around him and was essentially solitary, working on his own and relying almost entirely upon his own resources. To some extent this was a matter of temperament, but it mainly reflected the social isolation which he experienced after 1888 as a black student in a white world. At Harvard he mixed little with his white peers and experienced loneliness. He found more congenial social contacts while in Germany but still relied to a great extent upon his own resources. A diary entry on his twenty-fifth birthday found him singing 'Jesus, Lover of my Soul' and 'America' alone in his Berlin room and ruminating about his future responsibility to advance the scientific study of the black race, the search for scientific truth, the 'cold and indisputable' research that was necessary to advance the interests of all black people. 'These are my plans: to make a name in science, to make a name in literature and thus to raise my race.'[6]

The Trustees of the Slater Fund would not extend Du Bois' award to remain in Berlin for the third year necessary to obtain the PhD degree there. Schmoller petitioned for Du Bois to be admitted to the degree with less than the requisite number of semesters of study, but was not successful. Du Bois returned to the United States to work on completing his PhD for Harvard. Immediately he began teaching at Wilberforce University, an African Methodist church school in Ohio, where he stayed for two years, wrote up his PhD for publication, married and clashed with the school authorities over various matters. An approach in 1896 to conduct a study of the black community in Philadelphia was therefore welcome and one which he accepted with alacrity.

The offer came from the Provost of the University of Pennsylvania, Charles C. Harrison, who wrote that the aim was to conduct an extensive study 'of the social condition of the Coloured People in the Seventh Ward of Philadelphia . . . We want to know precisely how this class of people live; what occupations they follow; from what occupations they are excluded; how many of their children go to school; and to ascertain every fact which will throw light on this social problem'.[7] The instigator of the idea of the study was Susan P. Wharton, a member of the family which established the Wharton School and a Quaker member of the executive committee of the Philadelphia College Settlement, long interested in philanthropy for the black population. Wharton herself, Harrison and many of Philadelphia's wealthier families themselves lived in the Seventh Ward and had had an opportunity to observe social conditions at first hand. The meeting to plan the idea of the study took place at Wharton's house, only a few blocks from the black ghetto and the College Settlement House.[8] She asked the provost 'for the cooperation of the University in a plan for the better understanding of the coloured people, especially of their position in the city . . . [we] are interested in a plan to obtain a body of reliable information as to the obstacles to be encountered by the coloured people in their endeavour to be self-supporting'.[9] One may speculate that the influence of the *Hull-House Maps and Papers* may not have been inconsiderable in suggesting a model for such a study.

Du Bois' name as a possible scholar to undertake the task was apparently suggested by Pennsylvania sociology professor Samuel McCune Lindsay. Du Bois was offered and accepted the one-year appointment at a salary of US $800 and moved with his young wife to the city in the summer of 1896, living in a one-room apartment above a cafeteria run by the College Settlement. Du Bois later described its location as 'in the worst part of the Seventh Ward. We lived there a year,[10] in the midst of an atmosphere of dirt, drunkenness, poverty and crime. Murder sat on our doorsteps, police were our government and philanthropy dropped in with periodic advice.'[11]

For fifteen months, Du Bois immersed himself in the detailed empirical study of the Seventh Ward, the largest concentration of black people in a city which at that time had a black population of 45,000, the largest anywhere in the North. His experience of carrying out the study was different from that of

Charles Booth or Florence Kelley, for he worked on his own with little support from others. Although nominally attached to the university with the position of 'Assistant Instructor', he had a one-year appointment which was not renewed, no office there, his name did not appear in the university catalogue, he taught no students, and he had only peripheral contact with members of the sociology department. His time was spent entirely in the black district, his principal social contacts, perforce, were with black rather than white Philadelphians. Colour distanced him too from the white philanthropists who had initiated the study, and meant that his contact with them was not on a regular basis. (A decade later Du Bois was in regular collaboration with Mary White Ovington, a white New York social worker with Settlement House connections and strong interests in the condition of black people. They both helped to establish the National Association for the Advancement of Coloured People in 1909, an organisation in which both white women and black men were prominent.[12]) The contrast between the Seventh Ward study and Hull House was marked. Florence Kelley was a resident of Hull House and full participant, W. E. B. Du Bois resided above a cafeteria belonging to the Philadelphia Settlement and was not a participant in the work of the Settlement.

This, it is true, was partly a matter of his own choice. Du Bois' study was a study of the *black* community and for many years his main social contacts, out of necessity and to some extent out of choice, were with other black people.[13] More important, his conception of science was a more rigorous one than that of Florence Kelley, and it precluded too close identification with philanthropy and social intervention. His task was to carry out the study. That task he fulfilled, and the empirical research required he did himself without the assistance of settlement house residents or a recruited research team.

The resulting monograph, a classic of American social science, was more limited in scale than the studies of Booth or Kelley, but gained in scope and penetration what it lost in extensiveness. *The Philadelphia Negro* was a study in depth of the social conditions of the 4,000 black people living in the Seventh Ward. After a historical introduction, it described their geographical distribution in the ward, the demographic, occupational and family structure, educational and housing conditions, and relations between the black and the white communities. Social and political organisation, the incidence of crime and the causes of pauperism and alcoholism were also examined. The emphasis upon social problems, however, was considerably less than in either *Life and Labour* or the *Hull-House Maps and Papers*, reflecting the fact that *The Philadelphia Negro* was a sociological community study as much as an examination of a social problem, or rather an approach to the latter through the former. It was intended to be a work of social science as well as an examination of social conditions. Indeed one of W. E. B. Du Bois' aims was to provide a detailed portrayal of life for black people in the Seventh Ward, and to show that black Philadelphians were a product of their social environment.

The design and execution of *The Philadelphia Negro* was clearly influenced by recent social surveys which had been carried out in Britain and the United States, particularly by Booth's London survey. Although there are a few references to Booth in the monograph, in general there is very little in the way of citation of other literature, so one's inferences are necessarily somewhat speculative. The short bibliography (pp. 419–23) is mainly devoted to material about and by black Philadelphians, but there are twenty-eight more general references. Three of these are to publications of Du Bois himself, thirteen are historical works about slavery or the history of Pennsylvania, five are publications of the Society of Friends (Quakers) about slavery, only seven are contemporary data sources or studies relevant to his subject. They include the US Census as a source of data, Richmond Mayo Smith's *Statistics and Sociology*, Carroll D. Wrights's 1894 report *Slums of Great Cities*, three Atlanta University monographs from 1896-8 on the condition of the black population, and only three monographs. These are the *First and Second Sociological Canvasses* of the Federation of Churches and Christian Workers in New York City, edited by Walter Laidlaw, from 1896-7, the *Hull-House Maps and Papers* from 1895, and Booth's *Life and Labour* in the 1892 edition. This list points to Carroll Wright and Richmond Mayo-Smith as influences on the statistical side, and the Booth and Hull House studies as models for the investigations as a whole.

This conclusion is supported by Du Bois' use of maps. The colour map appears to be closely modelled upon those in the *Hull-House Maps and Papers*. Part of the household map of 'The Distribution of the Negro Inhabitants throughout the Ward, and their social condition'[14] is reproduced in plate 4. It shows the black population of the ward classified house by house into one of four social classes in a manner combining the mapping techniques of Booth and Hull House. Du Bois' use of maps was sparing, but it was clear what were his contemporary models.

In his *Autobiography*, Du Bois recalled that he produced a clear plan of research when initially approach by the university, but that he had no particular methodological predilections:

> I started with no 'research methods' and I asked little advice as to procedure. The problem lay before me. Study it. I studied it personally and not by proxy. I sent out no canvassers. I went myself. Personally I visited and talked with 5,000 persons. What I could, I set down in orderly sequence on schedules which I made out and submitted to the University for criticism. Other information I stored in my memory or wrote out as memoranda. I went through the Philadelphia libraries for data, and gained access in many instances to private libraries of coloured folk and got individual information. I mapped the district, classifying it by conditions; I compiled two centuries of the history of the negro in Philadelphia and in the Seventh Ward.[15]

This account owes something to hindsight, for Du Bois clearly did have ideas about how to collect data which were not simply derived from his studies in Berlin nor constructed from common sense.

Two features of the study were particularly important. A systematic attempt was made to gather and collate data about the black population of the Seventh Ward from various sources. A principal source was a house-to-house canvas carried out by Du Bois himself throughout the ward, using schedules that he filled in. He constructed a family schedule and an individual schedule with questions about age, sex, conjugal condition, birthplace, literacy, occupation, earnings, ill health and association membership. The schedules contained simple questions about particular topics, but with explanatory notes which indicated a considerable degree of thought had gone into their preparation. For example, the family schedule included the questions 14 and 15: Occupations since 1 October 1891? *and* Present occupation? The rubric accompanying these two questions was as follows:

> This is an important inquiry. Simple as it appears, it is always difficult in census work to get satisfactory replies to the question. Inaccuracy and insufficiency of statement are the most prominent evils to be avoided;
>
> For instance, *remember*: We want to know not what a man 'works in' but what he does. We want to *distinguish between*: the owner or director of a business and one who works at it; between waiters and head waiters; between cooks in private families and in hotels; between coachmen, hackmen and draymen; between merchants and pedlers and those who keep stands.[16]

These detailed guidelines for the inquiry in the Seventh Ward read as if they may have been derived from the practice of the United States Census.

The second innovation was in conducting personal interviews himself with the black inhabitants of the Seventh Ward. Like Rowntree, Du Bois concluded that there was no substitute for direct questioning of the population to gather social data, using a systematic method of recording data. Like Rowntree, he carried out a complete enumeration of all households. Unlike Rowntree, he did all the interviewing himself. He described it in his monograph:

> [i]n the fall of 1896 a house-to-house visitation was made of all the Negro families of this ward. The visitor went in person to each residence and called for the head of the family. The housewife usually responded, the husband now and then, and sometimes an older daughter or other member of the family. The fact that the University was making an investigation of this character was known and discussed in the ward, but its exact scope and character was not known. The mere announcement of the purpose secured, in all but about twelve cases, immediate

admission. Seated then in the parlor, kitchen or living room, the visitor began the questioning, using his discretion as to the order in which they were put, and omitting or adding questions as the circumstances suggested. Now and then the purpose of a particular query was explained, and usually the object of the whole inquiry indicated. General discussion often arose as to the condition of the Negroes, which were instructive. For ten minutes to an hour was spent in each home, the average time being fifteen to twenty-five minutes.[17]

Du Bois was aware of the limitations of the study. Non-response was a problem in only a few cases. Of the twelve cases where no data was obtained, the majority were brothels but a few were 'homes of respectable people who resented the investigation as unwarranted and unnecessary'.[18] To assuage concern, the Family Schedule ended with the following caveat, which has a curiously modern ring to it:

> Finally, remember that the information given is confidential; the University of Pennsylvania will strictly guard it as such, and allow no-one to have access to the schedules for other than scientific purposes. We ask, under these conditions, careful, accurate and truthful answers.[19]

But the reception that he received was not always of the warmest. As he recalled in his autobiography, his respondents did not receive him with open arms, and had a natural dislike of being studied as a 'stranger species'. It was a learning experience for the intellectual Du Bois. 'They set me groping. I concluded that I did not know so much as I might about my own people . . . I became painfully aware that merely being born in a group, does not necessarily make one possessed of complete knowledge concerning it'.[20] One may surmise that the social distance between Du Bois and some of his respondents was considerable. Only two years before, colleagues at Wilberforce University in Ohio has been disconcerted by Du Bois appearing in high silk hat, gloves and walking stick, which combined with his dapper Vandyke beard, created a distinctive impression.[21] No doubt his dress was adjusted for the Seventh Ward, but this distinguished young member of the 'talented tenth' did not fit naturally into the milieu which he was studying. This made what he achieved all the more remarkable.

He himself recognised in the monograph that the quality of the data collected in the household interviews might have been contaminated by various factors, and he attempted to compensate for it.

> Usually the answers [to the visitor's questions] were prompt and candid, and gave no suspicion of previous preparation. In some cases there was evident falsification or evasion. In such cases the visitor made free use of his best judgement and either inserted no answer at all, or one which

seemed approximately true. In some cases the families visited were not at home, and a second or third visit was paid. In other cases, and especially in the case of the large class of lodgers, the testimony of landlords and neighbours often had to be taken. No one can make an inquiry of this sort and not be painfully conscious of a large margin of error from omissions, errors of judgement and deliberate deception. Of such errors this study has, without doubt, its full share. Only one fact was particularly favourable and that is the proverbial good nature and candour of the Negro. With a more cautious and suspicious people, much less could have been obtained. Naturally some questions were answered better than others; the chief difficulty arising in regard to the questions of age and income. The ages given for people forty and over [born prior to the abolition of slavery – MB] have a large margin of error, owing to ignorance of the real birthday. The question of income was naturally a delicate one, and often had to be gotten at indirectly.[22]

The methods of research used attempted to take account of the imperfections of the various sources, but placed particular weight upon the information gathered by Du Bois himself from a complete enumeration of black families in the Seventh District. Du Bois also made brief comparative studies of black Philadelphians in other parts of the city to compare his results with those that might be obtained in other areas. His empirical methods thus proceeded along careful lines which anticipated several standard features of twentieth-century social research. What is remarkable is how well worked-out they were at this period, when systematic social investigation using the survey method was in its infancy. Nor was the study purely descriptive, incorporating analyses of family structure, social stratification within the black community, the causation of crime and the effects of colour prejudice. Many of the black residents of the Seventh Ward came from rural Virginia, and at the same time as researching the monograph, Du Bois carried out a study of the skills, attitudes and habits which they brought with them to the North, which was published in 1898.[23]

The book begins with a clear statement of why the Negro problem in Philadelphia is of interest,

> Here is a large group of people . . . who do not form part of the larger social group. This is not altogether unusual; there are other unassimilated groups: Jews, Italians, even Americans; and yet in the case of the Negroes, the segregation is more conspicuous, patent to the eye, and so intertwined with a long historical evolution, with peculiarly pressing social problems of poverty, ignorance, crime and labour, that the Negro problem far surpasses in scientific interest and social gravity most of the other race and class questions.'[24]

Two chapters provide an historical introduction about black people in Philadelphia but the study is not primarily historical. Six chapters describe the characteristics of the black population of the Seventh Ward demographically, in terms of conjugal condition, birthplace, education and illiteracy, occupation and health. There then follow several chapters on Philadelphia Negroes as a social group, dealing with the negro family, black churches and other social organisations, the negro criminal and pauperism and alcoholism as problems in the community. A final group of chapters consider the physical and social environment, including housing and social stratification within the black community (on which Du Bois laid considerable emphasis in his introduction), race contacts and negro suffrage. In the final chapter, 'a word of general advice in the line of social reform is added',[25] though it is notable for the detached tone in which policy issues were addressed.

Instances only of the analysis offered may be given here. The chapter on the family presented data on black family structure in the Seventh Ward derived from Du Bois' survey. He had data on 2,441 families, containing 7,751 members; in addition, 1,924 lodgers lived in these families, a total population of 9,675. He analysed family incomes, some data on property ownership, and commented on the social disorganisation of family life consequent upon the experience of slavery, low incomes and high rents. Among the poor, temporary cohabitation was not uncommon; among the families with comfortable incomes, taking in of lodgers was common as means of meeting the rent. The analysis is a mixture of descriptive sociology and identification of social problems – for example the presence of adult strangers as lodgers in households with unsupervised young children – with an emphasis upon the former.

In the chapter on contact between the races, Du Bois provided an analysis of the effects of colour prejudice upon black Philadelphians, observing that while it did not account for the greater part of Negro problems, it was a far more powerful social force than most Philadelphians realised. He distinguished its effects upon ability to secure and to keep work, upon income and expenditure, upon children, and upon social intercourse with other racial groups. The effects of prejudice in each of these areas were illustrated with detailed cases collected during field work. This chapter was more analytical than several of the more descriptive ones, pointing out the obstacles under which black Americans laboured, and the role of white public opinion in maintaining this state of affairs.

Du Bois' capacity for analysis of a problem in the light of his data is evident in his discussion of stratification within the black community. Du Bois paid explicit attention to this, as he did in his rural study of Farmville, Virginia, within the framework of a sociological rather than a social policy problematic.

> There is always a strong tendency on the part of the community to consider the Negroes as composing one practically homogeneous mass. This view has of course a certain justification: the people of Negro

descent in this land have had a common history, suffer today common disabilities, and contribute to one general set of social problems. And yet if the foregoing statistics have emphasized any one fact it is that wide variation in antecedents, wealth, intelligence and general efficiency have already been differentiated within this group. These differences are not, to be sure, so great or so patent as those among the whites today, and yet they undoubtedly equal the difference among the masses of the people in certain sections of the land fifty or one hundred years ago; and there is no surer way of misunderstanding the Negro or being misunderstood by him than by ignoring manifest differences of condition and power in the 40,000 black people in Philadelphia.

And yet well-meaning people continually do this. They regale the thugs and whoremongers and gamblers of Seventh and Lombard streets with congratulations on what the Negroes have done in a quarter century and pity for their disabilities; and they scold the caterers of Addison Street for the pickpockets and paupers of the race. A judge of the city courts, who for years had daily met a throng of lazy and debased Negro criminals, comes from the bench to talk to the Negroes about their criminals; he warns them first of all to leave the slums and either forgets or does not know that the fathers of the audience he is speaking to, left the slums when he was a boy and the people before him are as distinctly differentiated from the criminals he has met, as honest laborers anywhere differ from thieves. Nothing more exasperates the better class of Negroes than this tendency to ignore utterly their existence.[26]

Du Bois was not just making a point about the treatment of black Philadelphians, for he immediately followed with an analysis of the social structure of the black community. He distinguished four groups within the black people of the seventh ward. The first were 'families of undoubted respectability earning sufficient income to live well; not engaged in menial service of any kind'. These were 'the aristocracy of the Negro population in education, wealth and general social efficiency'. He estimated that they comprised about 11 per cent of the black population of the Seventh Ward. He emphasised that this group kept to itself socially, and it would be almost impossible for a white person to meet members of the class. The second were 'the respectable working class', in comfortable circumstances in a good home with steady work. These were the mass of the servant class, the porters and waiters, and the 'best of labourers'. He estimated from his survey data that they comprised 56 per cent of the black population of the ward.

The third were the poor, persons not earning enough to keep them at all times above want. They were honest, though not always energetic or thrifty. According to his survey, just over 30 per cent of families fell into this category of the poor or very poor. The fourth were the lowest class of criminals, prostitutes and loafers, the 'submerged tenth'. Du Bois estimated that on the basis of his canvas about 6 per cent of the population of the ward fell into this category; the proportion might rise slightly if one made allowance for defective data.[27] Du Bois also made a separate classification of his data in terms of income, and compared the incidence of poverty in black Philadelphia with its distribution in London according to Booth. Figure 6.1 shows the results presented, which as Du Bois observes, depend heavily upon how the 'comfortable' are treated. The line between that group and the 'poor' is less stable than in London because their economic status is less fixed.

> In good times perhaps 50 percent of the Negroes could well be designated comfortable but in times of financial stress vast numbers of this class fall below the line into the poor and go to swell the number of paupers, and in many cases criminals. Indeed, this whole division of incomes of different classes is, among the Negroes, much less stable than among the whites, just as it used to be less stable among the whites of fifty years ago than it is among those of today.[28]

How is one to assess the contribution of *The Philadelphia Negro*? It made no conceptual breakthrough comparable to Booth's or Rowntree's conceptualisation of poverty. It was not a study of a whole city or town, but of the black population of one section of a city; in that respect it was less comprehensive in its coverage than Booth or Rowntree. The monograph was, however, a pioneering social survey which studied that black population comprehensively and systematically. It was unique in its intensity of study, and there was nothing comparable being produced at the time from Columbia under Giddings or Chicago under Small. It was one of the first sociological urban community studies, employing a conception of social structure and addressing a wide range of sociological issues both descriptively and analytically. The description is more apparent, but underlying the description were theoretical notions which informed the analysis, ideas about the role of social environment in the determination of social outcomes which were quite novel for the period.[29] For example, in his analysis of the causes of crime in the black community, he suggested a connection between the experience of racial prejudice and involvement in crime. But the connection was not simple or direct.

> The boy who is refused promotion in his job as porter does not go out and snatch somebody's pocketbook. Conversely the loafers at Twelfth and Kater streets, and the thugs in the county prison are not usually graduates of high schools who have been refused work. The connections are much more subtle and dangerous; it is the atmosphere of rebellion and discontent that unrewarded merit and reasonable but unsatisfied ambition make. The social environment of excuse, listless despair, careless indulgence and lack of inspiration to work is the growing force that turns black boys and girls into gamblers, prostitutes and rascals. And this

social environment has been built up slowly out of the disappointments of deserving men and the sloth of the unawakened.[30]

Average earnings per wk	No. of families		%	Comparison	
$5 & less	420	192	8.9	Very poor	
		228	9.6	Poor	
$5–10		1088	47.8	Fair	
$10–15		581	25.5	Comfortable	
$15–20		91	4.0	Good circumstances	
$20 & over		96	4.2	Well-to-do	
TOTAL		2276	100%		

It is difficult to compare this with other groups because of the varying meaning of the terms poor, well-to-do, and the like. Nevertheless, a comparison with Booth's diagram of London will, if not carried too far, be interesting:

Figure 1: Poverty among negroes in Philadelphia, 1896, and a comparison with Booth's findings in London.
From W. E. B. Du Bois, *The Philadelphia Negro*, p. 171.
The Booth data is taken from *Life and Labour of the People*, II, p. 21.

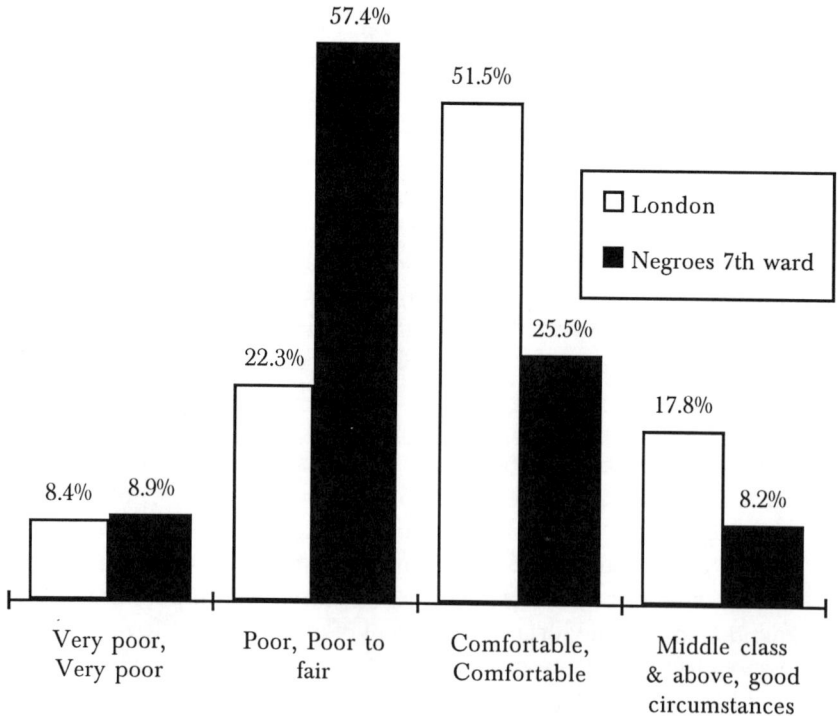

The extent to which Du Bois' study was a pioneering one has not been recognised to the extent that it should be. The omissions are of two kinds. On the one hand the sheer failure to mention *The Philadelphia Negro* in discussions of the history of the early social survey is remarkable. Out of eleven publications between 1911 and 1952 which reviewed the use of the social survey in sociology, only one mentions Du Bois.[31] One is struck by the lack of impact which the study had at the time and its lack of emulators. It is extraordinary, for example, that even in the city in which it was carried out, it was 'the one important study of lower-class life in Philadelphia done before the 1960's ... it did not stimulate further analysis along similar lines, at least not in Philadelphia'.[32] This neglect of a classic study owed a great deal to the fact that Du Bois was black, and that American sociologists in the period between 1890 and 1910 were not particularly interested in studying black America.[33] Robert Park did not begin teaching at the University of Chicago until 1913.

Yet contemporary evidence of Du Bois' stature is provided by his contacts with Max Weber. On his visit to the United States in 1904[34], to attend the St Louis Congress of Arts and Sciences, where he presented a paper on German social structure, Weber met Du Bois in Atlanta; he had either known Du Bois in Berlin or heard of him from Schmoller[35] and had been in correspondence with him.[36] He arranged for Du Bois to contribute an article on the situation of the negro in the United States to the *Archiv*, which was published in 1906.[37] The preceding article to that by Du Bois in the journal was by Georg Simmel, the article immediately following by Robert Michels. He was in good company.

Du Bois' race meant that when the study was completed, he had no chance of an appointment at one of the leading American universities, all of which were all-white.[38] Baltzell observes that had the monograph been published in the 1960s, Du Bois would have been besieged with job offers from leading departments. This was not so in the 1890s. In his presentation to the American Academy of Arts and Sciences in 1898, shortly after research for *The Philadelphia Negro* was finished but before it was published, he called for a research programme located in a black college 'which is not merely a teaching body, but a centre of sociological research, in close connection and cooperation with Harvard, Columbia, Johns Hopkins and the University of Pennsylvania'.[39] There was no response. After the completion of the study Du Bois moved to Atlanta University, a black university, where he continued a research programme on black Americans over the next decade, with creditable results considering the lack of resources from which he suffered there.

The Philadelphia Negro was reviewed in a number of magazines and in the *American Historical Journal*.[40] It was not reviewed in the *American Journal of Sociology*. Du Bois received almost no acknowledgement among (white) sociologists. The sociology of race relations, when it first became substantially established, developed at the University of Chicago a decade later under W. I. Thomas and Robert Park, assisted by black sociologist Charles S. Johnson.[41]

Du Bois struggled purposefully at Atlanta University to develop a research programme, but with relatively little success. He observed in 1904:

> We can go to the South Sea Islands half way around the world and beat and shoot a weak people longing for freedom into the slavery of American colour prejudice at the cost of hundreds of millions, and yet at Atlanta University we beg annually and beg in vain for the paltry sum of $500 simply to aid us in replacing gross and vindictive ignorance of race conditions with enlightening knowledge and systematic observation.[42]

Despite these obstacles, he organised a programme of research, enlisted the help of part-time, unpaid assistants throughout the South, and published sixteen monographs between 1898 and 1914.[43] Their quality, however, was not as high as that of *The Philadelphia Negro*, inevitably given the demands on Du Bois' time from teaching. This also reflected the funding difficulties.

> The total cost of the thirteen publications [published in the Atlanta series up to that date, he wrote in 1909] has been about $14,000 or a little over $1,000 a year. The growing demands of the work, the vast field to be covered and the delicacy and equipment needed in such work call for far greater resources. We need, for workers, laboratory and publications, a fund of $6,000 a year, if this work is going to adequately fulfil its promise. Last year a small temporary grant from the Carnegie Institution in Washington greatly helped us, and this year our work was saved from suspension by an appropriation from the John F. Slater Fund.[44]

For a decade following 1898, Du Bois was a most serious scholar, with an excellent scientific understanding and first-class academic credentials, intensely committed to academic work, establishing the first major black department of sociology in the country. He was also an essayist and commentator on the position of black people in the United States, a member of the 'talented tenth' and antagonist of Booker Washington in arguments over the best strategy for black people to follow. His public clashes with Washington no doubt contributed to his inability to secure research funding, since white philanthropists supporting black Americans relied heavily upon Washington for advice.[45] During the first decade of the century, these political interests became more salient and Du Bois' concerns shifted.[46] In 1909 Du Bois was one of the founders of the National Association for the Advancement of Coloured People (NAACP), and in 1910 he left academic life permanently to become editor of the NAACP magazine, *The Crisis*. He did not leave his academic interests entirely behind. In *The Crisis* he used facts, observation and historical material in articles where appropriate, but the magazine was aimed at a mass audience in political and emotional terms as well as providing analysis of the social situation of black people. For Du Bois it was a marked change of direction. This abandonment of a scholarly career at the age of forty-two was a response to the isolation and neglect from which Du Bois' work suffered, and his feeling that it was very difficult to make a significant impact upon American race relations as a black academic.

'Two considerations', he wrote in old age, 'broke in upon my academic work and eventually disrupted it: First, one could not be a calm, cool and detached scientist while Negroes were lynched, murdered and starved; and secondly, there was no such definite demand for scientific work of the sort that I was doing as I had confidently assumed would be easily forthcoming'.[47] Among these experiences was the writing of a pioneering monograph which was almost completely ignored by his academic peers, yet which we can now recognise as an important part of the social survey tradition and a classical sociological monograph.

It is necessary to keep this phase of Du Bois' career in perspective. In his later writings, particularly his autobiographies, Du Bois had become somewhat disenchanted not only with academic social science but even with many aspects of American society, and the past was reinterpreted through presentist concerns. Du Bois' career as a writer and propagandist after 1910, moreover, meant also that he tended to be seen in the 1920s and 1930s by social scientists more in that role as political activist than as the historian and social scientist he had been between the ages of twenty-two and forty-two. Nevertheless, there can be little doubt that one important factor in Du Bois' abandonment of social science was the indifference with which his work was received in the white scholarly world. It is this experience which sets him apart from other early survey researchers, for although their findings by no means commanded universal assent, they did command attention and publicity when they were published. Du Bois was denied that attention, because he was black, because the condition of black Americans was not a matter of major political or scholarly concern around 1898, and because a racially stratified system of higher education gave him no significant opportunities for sustained interaction with his white peers in the academic community.

Notes

1. W. E. B. Du Bois, 'The Study of the Negro Problems', *Annals of the American Academy of Political and Social Science*, 9 (January, 1898), 1–2.

2. W. E. B. Du Bois, *The Suppression of the African Slave Trade to the United States of America 1638-1870* (New York: Longmans Green, 1896), the first monograph in the Harvard Historical Studies series, based on his Harvard PhD thesis submitted in 1895.

3. Quoted in D. S. Green and E. D. Driver, 'Introduction', in Green and Driver (eds.), *W. E. B. Du Bois on Sociology and the Black Community* (Chicago: University of Chicago Press, 1978), p. 7.

4. F. L. Broderick, *W. E. B. Du Bois: Negro Leader in a Time of Crisis* (Stanford: Stanford University Press, 1959), p. 27.

5. W. E. B. Du Bois, *Dusk of Dawn* (New York: Harcourt, Brace, 1940), p. 51.

6. W. E. B. Du Bois writing in his diary, quoted in M. Marable, *W. E. B. Du Bois: Black Radical Democrat* (Boston: Twayne, 1986), p. 19.

7. Quoted in Marable, *Du Bois*, p. 25.

8. E. Digby Baltzell, 'Introduction', to W. E. B. Du Bois, *The Philadelphia Negro; A Social Study* (first published by the University of Pennsylvania 1899; New York: Schocken, 1967), p. xviii.

9. Quoted in E. M. Rudwick, *W. E. B. Du Bois: Voice of the Black Protest Movement* (Philadelphia: University of Pennsylvania Press, 1960), p. 30.

10. In fact, for a total of fifteen months, from the beginning of August 1896 until the end of December 1897, with a break of two months in the summer of 1897 when he was carrying out for the US Commissioner of Labor the study of Farmville, Virginia, cited in n. 23.

11. W. E. B. Du Bois, 'My Evolving Program for Negro Freedom', in Rayford W. Logan (ed.), *What the Negro Wants* (Chapel Hill: University of North Carolina Press, 1944), p.38.

12. See Nancy J. Weiss, *The National Urban League, 1910–1940* (New York: Oxford University Press, 1974), pp. 20–8, 48–60. In 1911 Ovington published a study, *Half a Man: The Status of the Negro in New York* (New York: 1911) which followed the example of *The Philadelphia Negro*. She and Du Bois apparently first met in 1903, when Miss Ovington became interested in the condition of black Americans, as a result of the reputation which he established with *The Philadelphia Negro* and by his essays *The Souls of Black Folk* (Chicago: A. C. McClurg, 1903). See 'Introduction' by Charles Flint Kellogg to the 1969 edition of *Half A Man* (New York: Hill and Wang), p. xiv.

13. 'These efforts to withdraw from almost all contacts with white people he used to consolidate an identity for himself. He wanted to know and to embrace who and what he was and what his own life and society were. Most of all, however, he had, in order to save and use his talent, to learn and think of himself as a gifted scholar, writer and social scientist.' Allison Davis, 'Du Bois and the Problem of the Black Masses' (W. E. B. Du Bois Institute for the Study of the American Black, mimeo, n.d.).

14. *The Philadelphia Negro*, between pages 60 and 61. (page 1 in 1899 edition).

15. W. E. B. Du Bois, The *Autobiography of W. E. B. Du Bois* (New York: International Publishers, 1968), p. 198.

16. Du Bois, *The Philadelphia Negro*, p. 402.

17. *The Philadelphia Negro*, pp. 62–3.

18. *The Philadelphia Negro*, p. 62, note 12.

19. *The Philadelphia Negro*, p. 403.

20. Du Bois, *Autobiography*, p. 198.

21. Marable, *Du Bois*, p. 22.

22. Du Bois, *The Philadelphia Negro*, p. 63.

23. W. E. B. Du Bois, 'The Negroes of Farmville, Virginia: a Social Study', *Bulletin of the Department of Labor*, 3 (January, 1898), 1–38, reprinted in abridged form in D. S. Green and E. D. Driver (eds.), *W. E. B. Du Bois on Sociology and the Black Community* (Chicago: University of Chicago Press, 1978), pp. 165–95.

24. 'The Negroes of Farmville, Virginia', p. 5.

25. 'The Negroes of Farmville, Virginia', p. 9

26. 'The Negroes of Farmville, Virginia', p. 310.
27. 'The Negroes of Farmville, Virginia', pp. 309–19.
28. 'The Negroes of Farmville, Virginia', p. 172.
29. Baltzell, 'Introduction', p. xxiv–xxv. Du Bois explicitly referred in his introduction to the need to study the environment in which black people lived, including the physical environment and 'the far mightier social environment – the surrounding world of custom, wish, whim and thought which envelops the group and powerfully influences its social development' (*The Philadelphia Negro*, p. 5).
30. Du Bois, *The Philadelphia Negro*, p. 351.
31. D. S. Green and E. D. Driver, 'W. E. B. Du Bois: A Case in the Sociology of Sociological Negation', *Phylon*, 37, 4 (December, 1976), 322. See also E. M. Rudwick, 'Note on a Forgotten Black Sociologist: W. E. B. Du Bois and the Sociological Profession', *The American Sociologist*, 4 (November, 1969), 303–6. The monograph is not mentioned, for example, in Park and Burgess' *Introduction to the Science of Sociology* of 1921.
32. Allen F. Davis, 'Introduction', in A. F. Davis and M. H. Haller (eds.), *The Peoples of Philadelphia: A History of Ethnic Groups and Lower Class Life 1790-1940* (Philadelphia: Temple University Press, 1973), p. 4.
33. In contrast to studies of white ethnic minorities. For an example, see Peter Roberts, *Anthracite Coal Communities* (New York, 1904), a study of coal-mining settlements in western Pennsylvania. Roberts was a student of W. G. Sumner at Yale, and addresses ethnic differences in the villages. The book is permeated with explicit assertions about the superiority of Anglo-Saxons and the inferiority of Slavic immigrants to the United States.
34. On Weber's American visit see Marianne Weber, *Max Weber: A Biography* (English translation, New York: Wiley, 1975), pp. 279–304. On Weber's interest in race and nationality, see E. M. Manasse, 'Max Weber on Race', *Social Research*, 14, 2 (1947), 191–221, and John Stone, 'Race Relations and the Sociological Tradition', in J. Stone (ed.), *Race, Ethnicity and Social Change* (North Scituate, Mass.: Duxbury Press, 1977), pp. 67–8.
35. Manasse, 'Max Weber on Race', p. 197, n. 15.
36. Du Bois, *Dusk of Dawn* (New York: Harcourt Brace and Co., 1940), p. 67.
37. W. E. B. Du Bois, 'Die Negerfrage in den Vereinigten Staaten', *Archiv für Sozialwissenschaft und Sozialpolitik*, 22 (1906), 31–79.
38. See M. Weinberg, *A Chance to Learn: A History of Race and Education in the United States* (Cambridge: Cambridge University Press, 1977), pp. 263–336.
39. Du Bois, 'The Study of the Negro Problems', p. 20,
40. Rudwick, *W. E. B. Du Bois*, pp. 33–4.
41. W. I. Thomas was writing earlier about race and ethnic differences and their explanation, but the work on race did not really take off until Park's arrival in 1913. The first major piece of research on black Americans, as distinct from white European immigrants, was the research for the Chicago Commission on Race Relations, *The Negro in Chicago* (Chicago: University of Chicago Press 1923). For more details, see M. Bulmer, 'Charles S. Johnson, Robert E. Park and the Research Methods of the Chicago Commission of Race Relations 1920-1922: An Early Experiment in Applied Social Research', *Ethnic and Racial Studies*, 4 (July, 1981), 289–306.
42. W. E. B. Du Bois, 'The Atlanta Conferences', *Voice of the Negro*, 1 (March, 1904), 86.
43. The Atlanta studies of which Du Bois was the principal author were: *Some Efforts of Negroes for Social Betterment* (1898); *The Negro in Business* (1899); *The College-Bred Negro*

(1900); *The Negro Common School* (1901); *The Negro Artisan* (1902); *The Negro Church* (1903); *Some Notes on Negro Crime, Particularly in Georgia* (1904); *A Select Bibliography of the American Negro* (1905); *Health and Physique of the Negro American* (1906); *Economic Cooperation among Negro Americans* (1907); *The Negro American Family* (1909); *Efforts for Social Betterment among Negro Americans* (1909); *The College-Bred Negro American* (1910); *The Common School and the Negro American* (1911); *The Negro American Artisan* (1912); *Morals and Manners among Negro Americans* (1914), all published by the Atlanta University Press.

44. W. E. B. Du Bois, preface to *The Negro American Family* (Atlanta: Atlanta University Press, 1909), p. 5.

45. The course of their conflict, which first became apparent in 1902 and 1903 when Du Bois published a critical review of *Up From Slavery* and his chapter 'On Mr Booker T. Washington and Others', in *The Souls of Black Folk*, which contained measured criticism of Washington's strategy for black advancement, is described in Louis R. Harlan, *Booker T. Washington: The Wizard of Tuskegee, 1900–1915* (New York: Oxford University Press, 1983), esp. pp. 50–1. Before 1902 they appear to have maintained mutually respectful relations, Washington indeed attempting to bring Du Bois to Tuskegee to direct research with a job offer around 1900.

46. See Arnold Ramapersad, *The Art and Imagination of W. E. B. Du Bois* (Cambridge, MA: Harvard University Press, 1976).

47. Du Bois, *Autobiography*, p. 222.

12

The Causes of Race Superiority

Edward A. Ross

The superiorities that, at a given time, one people may display over other peoples, are not necessarily racial. Physical inferiorities that disappear as the peoples are equalized in diet and dwelling; mental inferiorities that disappear when the peoples are levelled up in respect to culture and means of education, are due not to race but to condition, not to blood but to surroundings. In accounting for disparities among peoples there are, in fact, two opposite errors into which we may fall. There is the equality fallacy inherited from the earlier thought of the last century, which belittles race differences and has a robust faith in the power of intercourse and school instruction to lift up a backward folk to the level of the best. Then there is the counter fallacy, grown up since Darwin, which exaggerates the race factor and regards the actual differences of peoples as hereditary and fixed.

Just now the latter error is, perhaps, the more besetting. At a time when race is the watchword of the vulgar and when sciolists are pinning their faith to breed, we of all men ought to beware of it. We Americans who have so often seen the children of underfed, stunted, scrub immigrants match the native American in brain and brawn, in wit and grit, ought to realize how much the superior effectiveness of the latter is due to social conditions. Keleti, from his investigations in Hungary, has come to the conclusion that in most of the communes there the people have less to eat than is necessary to live and work, the result being alcoholism, weakness, disease and early death. Atwater, on the other hand, has found that the average wage-worker in New England consumes more food than health requires.

What a host of consequences issue from this one primary contrast!

A generation ago, in the first enthusiasm over the marvels of heredity, we were taught that one race is monotheistic, another has an affinity for polytheism. One race is temperamentally aristocratic, while another is by instinct democratic. One race is innovating and radical, another is by nature conservative. But it is impossible to characterize races in respect to such large complex traits. A keener analysis connects these great historical contrasts with a number

Source: *Annals of the American Academy of Political and Social Science*, 1901, pp. 67–89.

of slight specific differences in body or temperament. For example, four diverse traits of the greatest social importance, namely, progressiveness, the spirit of adventure, migrancy and the disposition to flock to cities, can be traced to a courageous confidence in the unknown coupled with the high physical tone that calls for action. Similarly, if we may believe Signor Ferrero, of two equally gifted races the one that is the less sensual will be inferior in aesthetic output, less apt to cross with lower types, more loyal to the idea of duty, better adapted to monotonous factory labor, and more inclined to the Protestant form of religion. It is only by establishing fixed, specific differences of this kind that we can hope to explain those grand race contrasts that enchant the historian.

The first cause of race superiority to which I invite your attention is a physiological trait, namely, *climatic adaptability*. Just now it is a grave question whether the flourishing and teeming peoples of the North Temperate zone can provide outlets for their surplus population in the rich but undeveloped lands of the tropics. Their superiority, economic and military, over the peoples under the vertical sun is beyond cavil. But can they assert and profit by this superiority save by imposing on the natives of the tropics the odious and demoralizing servile relation? Can the white man work and multiply in the tropics, or will his role be limited to commercial and industrial exploitation at a safe distance by means of a changing, male contingent of soldiers, officials, business agents, planters and overseers?

The answer is not yet sure, but the facts bearing on acclimatization are not comforting to our race. Immunity from the fevers that waste men in hot, humid climates seems to be in inverse ratio to energy. The French are more successful in tropical settlement than the Germans or the English. The Spanish, Portuguese and Italians surpass the French in almost equal measure. When it comes to *settling* Africa, instead of merely exploring or subduing it, the peoples may unexpectedly change their roles. With all their energy and their numbers the Anglo-Saxons appear to be physiologically inelastic, and incapable of making of Guiana or the Philippines a home such as they have made in New Zealand or Minnesota. In the tropics their very virtues – their push, their uncompromising standards, their aversion to intermarriage with the natives – are their destruction.

Ominous, on the other hand, is the extraordinary power of accommodation enjoyed by the Mongolians. Says Professor Ripley: The Chinese succeed in Guiana where the white man cannot live; and they thrive from Siberia where the mean temperature is below freezing, to Singapore on the equator. There are even some who believe that the Chinaman is destined to dispossess the Malay in southwestern Asia and the islands of the Pacific, and the Indian in the tropical parts of South America.

There is, indeed, such a thing as acclimatization; but this is virtually the creation at a frightful cost of a new race variety by climatic selection. We may therefore regard his lack of adaptability as a handicap which the white man must ever bear in competing with black, yellow, or brown men. His sciences and his inventions give him only a temporary advantage, for, as the facilities for diffusion increase, they must pass to all. Even his educational and political institutions will spread wherever they are suitable. All precedence founded on the possession of magazine rifles, or steam, or the press, or the Christian religion, must end as these elements merge into one all-embracing, everywhere disused, cosmopolitan culture. Even the advantage conferred upon a race by closer political cohesion, or earlier development of the state, cannot last. Could we run the coming centuries through a kinetoscope, we should see all these things as mere *clothes*. For, in the last analysis, it is solely on its persistent physiological and psychological qualities that the ultimate destinies of a race depend.

The next truth to which I invite our attention is, that one race may surpass another in *energy*. The average of individual energy is not a fixed race attribute, for new varieties are constantly being created by migration. The voluntary, unassisted migration of individuals to lands of opportunity tends always to the upbuilding of highly energetic communities and peoples. To the wilderness go, not the brainiest or noblest or highest bred, but certainly the strongest and the most enterprising. The weakling and the sluggard stay at home, or, if they are launched into the new conditions, they soon go under. The Boers are reputed to be of finer physique than their Dutch congeners. In America, before the days of exaggerated immigration, the immigrants were physically taller than the people from which they sprang, the difference amounting in some instances to an average of more than an inch. By measurements taken during the Civil War the Scotch in America were found to exceed their countrymen by two inches. Moreover, the recruits hailing from other states than those in which they had been born were generally taller than those who had not changed their residence. The Kentuckians and the Texans have become proverbial for stature, while the surprising tallness of the ladies who will be found shopping, of an afternoon, on Kearney street in San Francisco testifies to the bigness of the "forty-niners." Comparative weights tell the same tale. Of the recruits in our Civil War, the New Englanders weighed 140 pounds, the Middle State men 141 pounds, the Ohians and Indianans 145 pounds, and the Kentuckians 150. Conversely, where, as in Sardinia, the population is the leavings of continued emigration, the stature is extraordinarily low.

This principle that repeated migrations tend to the creation of energetic races of men, opens up enchanting vistas of explanation in the jungle of history. Successive waves of conquest breaking over a land like Sicily or India may signify that a race, once keyed up to a high pitch of energy by gradual migration from its ancient seats, tends to run down as soon as such beneficent selections are interrupted by success, and settlement in a new home. Cankered by a long quiet it falls a prey in a few centuries to some other people that has likewise been keyed up by migration.

Again, this principle may account for the fact that those branches of a race achieve the most brilliant success which have wandered the farthest from their ancestral home. Of the Mongols that borrowed the old Babylonian culture, those who pushed across Asia to the Yellow Sea, have risen the highest. The Arabs and Moors that skirted Africa and won a home in far-away Spain, developed the most brilliant of the Saracenic civilizations. Hebrews, Dorians, Quirites, Rajputs, Hovas were far invaders. No communities in classic times flourished like the cities in Asia created by the overflow from Greece. Nowhere under the Czar are there such vigorous, progressive communities as in Siberia. By the middle of this century, perhaps, the Russian on the Yenesei or the Amur will be known for his "push" and "hustle" as is today the American on Lake Michigan or Puget Sound. It is perhaps on this principle that the men who made their way to the British Isles have shown themselves the most masterful and achieving of the Germanic race; while their offshoots in America and Australia, in spite of some mixture, show the highest level of individual efficiency found in any people of the Anglo-Saxon breed. Even in America there is a difference between the East and the West. The listlessness and social decay noticeable in many of the rural communities and old historic towns on the Atlantic slope, are due, no doubt, to the loss of their more energetic members to the rising cities and to the West.

There is no doubt that the form of society which a race adopts is potent to paralyze or to release its energy. In this respect Americans are especially fortunate, for their energies are stimulated to the utmost by democracy. I refer not to popular government, but to the fact that with us social status depends little on birth and much on personal success. I will not deny that money, not merit, is frequently the test of social standing, and that Titania is often found kissing "the fair long ears" of some Bottom; but the commercial spirit, even if it cannot lend society nobility or worth, certainly encourages men to strive.

Where there is no rank or title or monarch to consecrate the hereditary principle, the capillarity of society is great, and ambition is whetted to its keenest edge. For it is hope not need that animates men. Set ladders before them and they will climb until their heart-strings snap.

Without a social ladder, without infection from a leisure class that keys up its standard of comfort, a body of yeomen settling in a new and fertile land will be content with simplicity and rude plenty. A certain sluggishness prevails now among the Boers, as it prevailed among the first settlers beyond the Alleghenies. If, on the other hand, there is a social ladder, but it is occupied by those of a military or hereditary position, as in the Spanish communities of the southwest, there is likewise no stimulus to energy. But if vigorous men form new communities in close enough touch with rich and old communities to accept their exacting standards of comfort, without at the same time accepting their social ranking, each man has the greatest possible incentive to improve his condition. Such has been the relation of America to England, and of the West to the East.

This is why America spells Opportunity. Inspired by hope and ambition the last two generations of Americans have amazed the world by the breathless speed with which they have subdued the western half of the continent, and filled the wilderness with homes and cities. Never has the world seen such prodigies of labor, such miracles of enterprise, as the creation within a single lifetime of a vast ordered, civilized life between the Mississippi and the Pacific. Witnessing such lavished expenditures of human force, can we wonder at American "rush," American nervousness and heart failure, at grey hairs in the thirties and old age in the fifties, at our proverb "Time is money!" and at the ubiquitous American rocking chair or hammock which enables a tired man to rest very quickly!

Closely related to energy is the virtue of *self-reliance*. There is a boldness which rises at the elbow touch of one's fellows, and there is a stout-heartedness which inspires a man when he is alone. There is a courage which confronts resolutely a known danger, and a courage which faces perils unknown or vague. Now, it is this latter quality – self-reliance – which characterizes those who have migrated the oftenest and have migrated as individuals. On our frontier has always been found the Daniel Boone type, who cared little for the support of his kind and loved danger and adventure for its own sake. The American's faith in himself and confidence in the friendliness of the unknown may be due to his enlightenment, but it is more likely the unapprehensiveness that runs in the blood of a pioneering breed. Sometimes, as in the successive trekkings of the Boers from Cape Town to the Limpopo, the trait most intensified is independence and self-reliance. Sometimes, as in the settling of the Trans-Mississippi region, the premium is put on energy and push. But in any case voluntary migration demands *men*.

Even in an old country, that element of the population is destined to riches and power which excels in self-reliance and enterprise. Cities are now the places of opportunity and of prosperity, and it has been shown conclusively that, in the urban upbuilding now going on in Central Europe, where long-skull Teutons and broad-skull Celto-Slavs are mingled, the cities are more Teutonic than the rural districts from which their population is recruited. The city is a magnet for the more venturesome, and it draws to it more of the long-skulled race than of the broad-skulled race. In spite of the fact that he has no greater wit and capacity than the Celt, the Teuton's superior migrancy takes him to the foci of prosperity, and procures him a higher reward and a superior social status.

Wherever there is pioneering or settlement to do, self-reliance is a supreme advantage. The expansion of the English-speaking peoples in the nineteenth century – the English in building their Empire, the Americans in subduing the West – seems to be due to this trait. Self-reliance is, in fact, a sovereign virtue in times of ferment or displacement. In static times, however, other qualities outweigh it, and the victory may fall to those who are patient, obedient, and quick-witted, rather than to the independent in spirit. If this be so, then the great question of the hour: What is to be the near destiny of the Anglo-Saxon race? invokes the question whether we stand on the threshold of a dynamic, or a static epoch. If the former, well for the Anglo-Saxon, if the latter, it may be the Latins who, renewing their faith in themselves, will forge ahead.

I think there can be no doubt that we are entering a tumultuously dynamic epoch. Science, machinery and steam – our heritage from the past century – together constitute a new economic civilization which is destined to work in the world a transformation such as the plow works among nomads. Two centuries ago Europe had little to offer Asia in an industrial way. Now, in western Europe and in America, there exists an industrial technique which alters the face of society wherever it goes. The exploitation of nature and man by steam and machinery directed by technical knowledge, has the strongest of human forces behind it, and nothing can check its triumphant expansion over the planet. The Arab spreads the religion of Mahomet with the Koran in one hand and the sword in the other. The white man of to-day spreads his economic gospel, one hand on a Gatling, the other on a locomotive.

It will take at least two or three generations to level up the industrial methods of continents like South America or Africa or Asia, as a Jamaica, a Martinique, or a Hawaii have been levelled up; and all this time that race which excels in energy, self-reliance and education will have the advantage. When this furiously dynamic epoch closes, when the world becomes more static, and uniformism recurs, self-reliance will be at a discount, and the conditions will again favor the race that is patient, laborious, frugal, intelligent and apt in consolidation. Then, perhaps, the Celtic and Mediterranean races will score against the Anglo-Saxon.

For economic greatness perhaps no quality is more important than *foresight*. To live from hand to mouth taking no thought of the morrow, is the trait of primitive man generally, and especially of the races in the tropical lands where nature is bounteous, and the strenuous races have not yet made their competition felt. From the Rio Grande to the Rio de la Plata, the laboring masses, largely of Indian breed, are without a compelling vision of the future. The Mexicans, our consuls write us, are "occupied in obtaining food and amusement for the passing hour without either hope or desire for a better future." They are always in debt, and the workman hired for a job asks something in advance to buy materials or to get something to eat. "Slaves of local attachments" they will not migrate in order to get higher wages. In Ecuador the laborer lets tomorrow take care of itself and makes no effort to accumulate. In Guiana, where Hindoos, Chinese, Portuguese, and Creoles labor side by side, the latter squander their earnings while the immigrants from the old economic civilizations all lay by in order to return home and enjoy. In Colombia the natives will not save, nor will they work in order to supply themselves with comforts. In British Honduras the natives are happy-go-lucky negroes who rarely save and who spend their earnings on festivals and extravagances, rather than on comforts and decencies. In Venezuela the laborers live for to-day and all their week's earnings are gone by Monday morning. The Brazilians work as little as they can and live, and save no money; are satisfied so long as they have a place to sleep and enough to eat.

Since, under modern conditions, abundant production is bound up, not so much with patient toil, as with the possession of ample capital, it is evident that, in the economic rivalry of races, the palm goes to the race that discounts the future least and is willing to exchange present pleasures for future gratifications most nearly at par. The power to do this depends partly on a lively imagination of remote experiences to come, partly on the self-control that can deny present cravings, or resist temptation in favor of the thrifty course recommended by reason. We may, in fact, distinguish two types of men, the sensori-motor moved by sense-impressions and by sensory images, and the ideo-motor moved by ideas. For it is probable that the provident races do not accumulate simply from the liveliness of their anticipation of future wants or gratifications, but from the domination of certain ideas. The tenant who is saving to build a cottage of his own is not animated simply by a picture of coming satisfactions. All his teaching, all his contact with his fellows, conspire to make home the goal of his hopes, to fill his horizon with that one radiant idea. So in the renter who is scrimping in order to get himself a farm as in the immigrant who is laying by to go back and "be somebody" in the old country, the attraction of a thousand vaguely imagined pleasures is concentrated in one irresistible idea. The race that can make *ideas* the lodestars of life is certain to supplant a race of impulsivists absorbed in sensations, and recollections or anticipations of sensations.

It is certain that races differ in their attitude toward past and future. M. Lapie has drawn a contrast between the Arab and the Jew. The Arab *remembers*, he is mindful of past favors and past injuries. He harbors his vengeance and cherishes his gratitude. He accepts everything on the authority of tradition, loves the ways of his ancestors, forms strong local attachments, and migrates little. The Jew, on the other hand, turns his face toward the future. He is thrifty and always ready for a good stroke of business, will, indeed, join with his worst enemy if it pays. He is calculating, enterprising, migrant and ambitious.

An economic quality quite distinct from foresight is *the value sense*. By this I mean that facility of abstraction and calculation which enables a man to fix his interest on the value in goods rather than on the goods themselves. The mere husbandman is a utility perceiver. He knows the power of objects to keep human beings alive and happy, and has no difficulty in recognizing what is good and what is not. But the trader is a value perceiver. Not what a thing is good for, but what it will fetch, engages his attention. Generic utilities are relatively stable, for wine and oil and cloth are always and everywhere fit to meet human wants; but value is a chameleon-like thing, varying greatly from time to time and place to place and person to person. The successful trader dares form no fixed ideas with regard to his wares. He must pursue the elusive value that hovers now here and now there, and be ready at any moment to readjust his notions. He must be a calculator. He must train himself to recognize the abstract in the concrete and to distill the abstract out of the concrete. Economically, then, the trader is to the husbandman what the husbandman is to the hunter. The appearance of cities, money, and commerce puts a premium on the man who can perceive value. He accumulates property and founds a house, while his less skillful rival sinks and is devoured by war and by labor.

All through that ancient world which produced the Phoenician, the Jew, the Greek and the Roman, the acquisition of property made a difference in survival we can hardly understand to-day. Our per capita production is probably three or four times as great as theirs was, and hence the grain-handlers of Buffalo are vastly more able to maintain a family than were the grain-handlers of old Carthage or Alexandria. All around the Mediterranean trade prospered the value perceivers, and that type tended to multiply and tinge more and more the psychology and ideals of the classic world. In ancient society the difference in death rates and in family-supporting power of the various industrial grades exceeded anything we are familiar with, and hence those who were steady and thrifty in labor or shrewd and prudent in trade vastly improved their chances of survival. Thus the economic man multiplied, and commercial, money-making Byzantium rose on the ruins of the old races. "Long before the seat of empire was moved to Constantinople," says Mr. Freeman, "the name of Roman had ceased to imply even a presumption of descent from the old patricians and plebeians." "The Julius, the Claudius, the Cornelius of those days was for the most part no Roman by lineal descent, but a Greek, a Gaul, a Spaniard or an Illyrian."

Between the economic type and the military type there is abrupt contrast, and the social situation cannot well favor them both at the same time. The warrior shows passional courage and the sway of impulse and imagination. The trader is calculating, counts the cost, and prizes a whole skin. From the second century B.C. the substitution of this type for the old, heroic, Cincinnatus type went on so rapidly that a recent writer finds congenital cowardice to be the mark of the Roman Senate and nobility during the empire. We all know the brilliant picture that Mr. Brooks Adams, in his "Law of Civilization and Decay," has given of the replacement of the military by the economic type in western Europe since the Crusades.

If this hypothesis be sound, the value perceiving sense is to be looked for in old races that have long known cities, money and trade. The Jew came under these influences at least twelve centuries earlier than did our Teutonic ancestors and has therefore had about forty or fifty generations the start of us in becoming economic. Equal or even greater is the lead of the Chinaman. It is, then, no wonder that the Jews and the Chinese are the two most formidable mercantile races in the world today, just as, in the Middle Ages, the Greeks and the Italians were the most redoubtable traffickers and money-makers in Europe. The Scotchman, the Fleming, and the Yankee, minor and later economic varieties developed in the West, can, indeed, exist alongside the Jew. The less mercantile German, however, fails to hold his own, and vents his wrath in Anti-Semitism. The Slav, unsophisticated and rural, loses invariably in his dealings with the Jew, and so harshly drives him out in vast numbers.

May we not, then, conveniently recognize two stages in the development away from the barbarian? Hindoos, Japanese, North Africans and Europeans, in their capacity for steady labor, their foresight, and their power to save, constitute what I will call *the domesticated races.* But the Jews, the Chinese, the Parsees, the Armenians, and in general the peoples about the Mediterranean constitute *the economic races.* The expurgated and deleted Teuton of the West, on the other hand, is more recently from the woods, and remains something of the barbarian after all. We see it in his migratoriness, his spirit of adventure, his love of dangerous sports, his gambling propensities, his craving for strong drink, his living up to his standard of comfort whether he can afford it or not. In quest of excitement he betakes himself to the Far West or the Klondike, whereas the Jew betakes himself to the Board of Trade or the Bourse. In direct competition with the more economic type the Anglo-Saxon is handicapped by lack of patience and financial acumen, but still his virtues insure him a rich portion. His energy and self reliance locate him in cities and in the spacious, thriving parts of the earth where the economic reward is highest. Born pioneer, he prospects the wilderness, pre-empting the richest deposits of the precious metals and skimming the cream from the resources of nature. Strong in war and in government, he jealously guards his own from the economic races, and meets finesse with force; so that despite his less developed value sense, more and more the choice lands and the riches of the earth come into his possession and support his brilliant yet solid civilization.

It is through no inadvertence that I have not brought forward *the martial traits* as a cause of race superiority. I do not believe that the martial traits apart from economic prowess are likely in the future to procure success to any race. When men kill one another by arms of precision instead of by stabbing and hacking, the knell is sounded for purely warelike races like the Vandals, the Huns and the Turks. Invention has so completely transformed warfare that it has become virtually an extra-hazardous branch of engineering. The factory system receives its latest and supreme application in the killing of men. Against an intelligent force equipped with the modern specialized appliances of slaughter no amount of mere warlike manhood can prevail. The fate of the Dervishes is typical of what must more and more often occur when *men* are pitted against properly operated lethal *machinery.*

Now, the war factory is as expensive as it is effective. None but the economic races, up to their eyes in capital and expert in managing machinery, can keep it running long. Warfare is becoming a costly form of competition in which the belligerents shed each other's treasure rather than each other's blood. A nation loses, not when it is denuded of men, but when it is at the end of its financial resources. War is, in fact, coming to be the supreme, economic touchstone, testing systems of cultivation and transportation and banking, as well as personal courage and military organization.

At the same time that war is growing more expensive it is becoming less profitable. The fruits of victory are often mere apples of Sodom. A decent respect for the opinion of mankind debars a civilized people from massacring the conquered in order to plant its own colonists on their land, from enslaving them, from bleeding them with heavy and perpetual tribute. Fortunate, indeed, is the victor if he can extort enough to indemnify him for his outlay. Therefore, at the very moment that the cost of war increases, the declining profits of war stamp it as an industry of decreasing returns. Wealth is a means of procuring victory, but victory is no longer a means of procuring wealth. A non-martial race may easily become victorious by means of its prosperity, but it will be harder and harder for a non-economic race to become prosperous by means of its victories. Even now the Turks in Europe are declining in numbers, and in spite of Armenian massacres the industrial races of the empire are growing up through the top-dressing of oppressors. It would seem safe to say that the purely war-like traits no longer insure race survival and expansion, and that in the competitions of the future the traits which enhance economic efficiency are likely to be most decisive.

In the dim past when cultures were sporadic, each developing apart in some island or river delta or valley closet, no race could progress unless it bore its crop of inventive genius. A high average of capacity was not so important as a few Gutenbergs and Faradays in each generation to make lasting additions to the national culture. If fruitful initiatives were forthcoming, imitation and education could be trusted to make them soon the common possession of all.

But when culture becomes cosmopolitan, as it is to-day, the success of a race turns much more on the efficiency of its average units than on the inventions and discoveries of its geniuses. The heaven-sent man who invents the locomotive, or the dynamo, or the germ theory, confers thereby no exclusive advantage on his people or his race. So perfect is intellectual commerce, so complete is the organization of science, that almost at once the whole civilized world knows and profits by his achievements. Nowadays the pioneering genius belongs to mankind, and however patriotic he may be he aids most the race that is most prompt and able to exploit his intention. Parasitism of this kind, therefore, tends to annul genius as a factor in race survival. During the century just closed the French intellect has stood supreme in its contributions to civilization; yet France has derived no exclusive advantage from her men of genius. It is differences in the qualities of the common men of the rival peoples that explains why France has not doubled its population in a century, while the English stock in the meantime has peopled some of the choicest parts of the world and more than quadrupled its numbers.

Henceforth this principle of cosmopolitanism must be reckoned with. Even if the Chinese have not yet vanquished the armies of the West with Mauser rifles supplied from Belgium, there is no reason why that mediocre and intellectually sterile race may not yet defeat us industrially by the aid of machines and processes conceived in the fertile brains of our Edisons and Marconis. Organizing talent, of course, – industrial, administrative, military, – each race must, in the long run, produce from its own loins; but in the industrial

Armageddon to come it may be that the laurels will be won by a mediocre type of humanity equipped with the science and the appliances of the more brilliant and brain-fertile peoples. Not preponderance of genius will be decisive, but more and more the energy, self-reliance, fecundity, and acquired skill of the average man; and the nation will do most for itself that knows how best to foster these winning qualities by means of education and wise social institutions.

How far does moral excellence profit a race? Those who hold that *Die Weltgeschichte ist das Weltgericht* tell us that the weal or woe of nations depends upon morals. Indeed, every flourishing people lays its prosperity first to its religion, and then to its moral code. Climatic adaptation or economic capacity is the last thing to be thought of as a cause of superiority.

The chief moral trait of a winning race is *stability of character*. Primitive peoples are usually over-emotional and poised unstably between smiles and tears. They act quickly if at all, and according to the impulse of the moment. The Abyssinian, for example, is fickle, fleeting and perjured, the Kirghiz "fickle and uncertain," the Bedouin "loves and honors violent acts." The courage of the Mongol is "a sudden blaze of pugnacity" rather than a cool intrepidity. We recall Carlyle's comparing Gallic fire which is "as the crackling of dry thorns under a pot," with the Teutonic fire which rises slowly but will smelt iron. In private endeavor perseverance, in the social economy the keeping of promises, and in the state steadfastness – these are the requisites of success, and they all depend on stability of character. Reliability in business engagements and settled reverence for law are indispensable in higher social development. The great economic characteristics of this age are the tendency to association, the growth of exchange, the increasing use of capital and the greater elaborateness of organization. They all imply the spreading of business over more persons, more space, and more time, and the increasing dependence of every enterprise upon what certain persons have been appointed to do or have engaged to do. Unreliable persons who fail to do their duty or keep their promises are quickly extruded from the economic organization. Industrial evolution, therefore, places a rising premium on reflection and self-control, the foundations of character. More and more it penalizes the childishness or frivolousness of the cheaply-gotten-up, *mañana* races.

As regards the altruistic virtues, they are too common to confer a special advantage. Honesty, docility, faithfulness and other virtues that lessen social friction abound at every stage of culture and in almost every breed. The economic virtues are a function of *race*; but the moral virtues seem rather to be a function of *association*. They do not make society; society makes them. Just as the joint secretes the lubricating synovial fluid so every settled community, if undisturbed, secretes in time the standards, ideals and imperatives which are needed to lessen friction. Good order is, in fact, so little a monopoly of the higher races that the attainment of it is more difficult among Americans at Dutch Flat or Skagway than it is among Eskimos or Indians. Sociability and sympathy are, indeed, serviceable in promoting cohesion among natural men; but they are of little account in the higher social architecture. The great races have been stern and grasping, with a strong property sense. More and more the purposive triumphs over the spontaneous association; so that the great historic social edifices are built on concurrence of aims, on custom or religion or law, never on mere brotherly feeling.

Indeed, the primary social sentiments are at variance with that sturdy self-reliance which, as we have seen, enables a race to overrun the earth. It was observed even in the California gold diggings that the French miners stayed together, while the solitary American or Briton serenely roamed the wilderness with his outfit on a burro, and made the richest "strikes." To-day a French railway builder in Tonkin says of the young French engineers in his employ: "They sicken, morally and physically, these fellows. They need papa and mamma! I had good results from bringing them together once or twice a week, keeping them laughing, making them amuse themselves and each other, in spite of lack of amusement. Then all would go well." It is perhaps this cruel homesickness which induces the French to restrict their numbers rather than expatriate themselves to over-sea colonies. Latin sociability is the fountain of many of the graces that make life worth living, but it is certainly a handicap in just this critical epoch when the apportionment of the earth among the races depends so much on a readiness to fight, trade, prospect or colonize thousands of miles from home.

The superiority of a race cannot be preserved without *pride of blood* and an uncompromising attitude toward the lower races. In Spanish America the easy going and unfastidious Spaniard peopled the continent with half-breeds and met the natives half way in respect to religious and political institutions. In East Africa and Brazil the Portuguese showed toward the natives even less of that race aversion which is so characteristic of the Dutch and the English. In North America, on the other hand, the white men have rarely mingled their blood with that of the Indian or toned down their civilization to meet his capacities. The Spaniard absorbed the Indians, the English exterminated them by fair means or foul. Whatever may be thought of the latter policy, the net result is that North America from the Behring Sea to the Rio Grande is dedicated to the highest type of civilization; while for centuries the rest of our hemisphere will drag the ball and chain of hybridism.

Since the higher culture should be kept pure as well as the higher blood, that race is stronger which, down to the cultivator or the artisan, has *a strong sense of its superiority*. When peoples and races meet there is a silent struggle to determine which shall do the assimilating. The issue of this grapple turns not wholly on the relative excellence of their civilizations, but partly on the degree of faith each has in itself and its ideals. The Greeks assimilated to themselves all the peoples about the Mediterranean save the Jew, partly because the humblest wandering Greek despised "the barbarians," and looked upon himself as a missionary to the heathen. The absorbent energy of the United States probably surpasses that of any mere colony because of the stimulus given us by an independent national existence. America is a psychic maelstrom that has sucked in and swallowed up hosts or aliens. Five millions of Germans, for instance, have joined us, and yet how little has our institutional development been deflected by them! I dare say the few thousand university-trained Germans, and Americans educated in Heidelberg or Göttingen, have injected more German culture into our veins than all the immigrants that ever passed through Castle Garden. There is no doubt that the triumph of Americanism over these heterogeneous elements, far more decisive now than eighty years ago, has been hastened by the vast contempt that even the native farm-hand or mechanic feels for the unassimilated immigrant. Had be been less sure of himself, had he felt less pride in American ideals and institutions, the tale might have been different.

One question remains. Is the Superior Race as we have portrayed it, able to survive all competitions and expand under all circumstances? There is, I am convinced, one respect in which very foresight and will power that mark the higher race dig a pit beneath its feet.

In the presence of the plenty produced by its triumphant energy the superior race forms what the economists call "a Standard of Comfort," and refuses to multiply save upon this plane. With his native ambition stimulated by the opportunity to rise and his natural foresight reinforced by education, the American, for example, overrules his strongest instincts and refrains from marrying or from increasing his family until he can realize his subjective standard of comfort or decency. The power to form and cling to such a standard is not only one of the noblest triumphs of reason over passion, but is, in sooth, the only sure hope for the elevation of the mass of men from the abyss of want and struggle. The progress of invention held out such a hope but it has proven a mockery. Steam and machinery, it is true, ease for a little the strain of population on resources; but if the birth-rate starts forward and the slack is soon taken up by the increase of mouths, the final result is simply more people living on the old plane. The rosy glow thrown upon the future by progress in the industrial arts proves but a false dawn unless the common people acquire new wants and raise the plane upon which they multiply.

Now this rising standard, which alone can pilot us toward the Golden Age, is a fatal weakness when a race comes to compete industrially with a capable race that multiplies on a lower plane. Suppose, for example, Asiatics flock to this country and, enjoying equal opportunities under our laws, learn our methods and compete actively with Americans. They may be able to produce and therefore earn in the ordinary occupations, say three-fourths as much as Americans; but if their standard of life is only half as high, the Asiatic will marry before the American feels able to marry. The Asiatic will rear two children while his competitor feels able to rear but one. The Asiatic will increase his children to six under conditions that will not encourage the American to raise more than four. Both, perhaps, are forward-looking and influenced by the worldly prospects of their children; but where the Oriental is satisfied with the outlook the American, who expects to school his children longer and place them better, shakes his head.

Now, to such a competition there are three possible results. First, the American, becoming discouraged, may relinquish his exacting standard of decency and begin to multiply as freely as the Asiatic. This, however, is likely to occur only among the more reckless and worthless elements of our population. Second, the Asiatic may catch up our wants as well as our arts, and acquire the higher standard and lower rate of increase of the American. This is just what contact and education are doing for the French Canadians in New England, for the immigrants in the West, and for the negro in some parts of the South; but the members of a great culture race like the Chinese show no disposition, even when scattered sparsely among us, to assimilate to us or to adopt our standards. Not until their self-complacency has been undermined at home and an extensive intellectual ferment has taken place in China itself will the Chinese become assimilable elements. Thirdly, the standards may remain distinct, the rates of increase unequal, and the silent replacement of Americans by Asiatics go on unopposed until the latter monopolize all industrial occupations, and the Americans shrink to a superior caste able perhaps by virtue of its genius, its organization, and its vantage of position to retain for a while its hold on government, education, finance, and the direction of industry, but hopelessly beaten and displaced as a race. In other words, the American farm hand, mechanic and operative might wither away before the heavy influx of a prolific race from the Orient, just as in classic times the Latin husbandman vanished before the endless stream of slaves poured into Italy by her triumphant generals.

For a case like this I can find no words so apt as "race suicide." There is no bloodshed, no violence, no assault of the race that waxes upon the race that wanes. The higher race quietly and unmurmuringly eliminates itself rather than endure individually the bitter competition it has failed to ward off from itself by collective action. The working classes gradually delay marriage and restrict the size of the family as the opportunities hitherto reserved for their children are eagerly snapped up by the numerous progeny of the foreigner. The prudent, self-respecting natives first cease to expand, and then, as the struggle for existence grows sterner and the outlook for their children darker, they fail even to recruit their own numbers. It is probably the visible narrowing of the circle of opportunity through the infiltration of Irish and French Canadians that has brought so low the native birth-rate in New England.

However this may be, it is certain that if we venture to apply to the American people of today the series of tests of superiority I have set forth to you at such length, the result is most gratifying to our pride. It is true that our average of energy and character is lowered by the presence in the South of several millions of an inferior race. It is true that the last twenty years have diluted us with masses of fecund but beaten humanity from the hovels of far Lombardy and Galicia. It is true that our free land is gone and our opportunities will henceforth attract immigrants chiefly from the humbler strata of East European peoples. Yet, while there are here problems that only high statesmanship can solve, I believe there is at the present moment no people in the world that is, man for man, equal to the Americans in capacity and efficiency. We stand now at the moment when the gradual westward migration has done its work. The tonic selections of the frontier have brought us as far as they can bring us. The testing individualizing struggle with the wilderness has developed in us what it would of body, brain and character.

Moreover, free institutions and universal education have keyed to the highest tension the ambitions of the American. He has been chiefly farmer and is only beginning to expose himself to the deteriorating influences of city and factory. He is now probably at the climax of his energy and everything promises that in the centuries to come he is destined to play a brilliant and leading role on the stage of history.

13

The World of The Academic Quantifiers: The Columbia University Family and its Connections

Stephen P. Turner

By 1900, Columbia University was the leading center of academic statistical social science in the United States, a position of dominance it held until the twenties. The two figures who had positions of intellectual leadership in the 'Social Science' programme, Richmond Mayo-Smith and Franklin H. Giddings, were part of the same network of personal relationships and memberships in voluntary associations as the figures who were most closely identified with the idea of the social survey, such as Paul Kellogg. Many of the figures in the movement were trained at Columbia or had ties to the university. Columbia research often served as methodological inspiration for later social survey work or was inspired by the defects of the knowledge available to such organisations as the Charity Organisation Societies, the settlement houses, and other such organisations. In this process of intellectual exchange, the early elements of a distinctively 'sociological' conception of surveys and community studies emerged, as did a distinctive philosophical rationale for quantification in sociology. Several of the surveys of small communities that were exemplary for the emerging field of Rural Sociology, for example, were Columbia dissertations.

There is an unsurprising tendency on the part of anyone writing on the history of the social survey in the United States to think of the social survey movement itself, retrospectively, in terms of the definitions, claims of originality, and models developed by Paul Kellogg and Russell Sage Foundation, one of the major backers of community surveys. Kellogg, in his enthusiasm for the programme that emerged around the Pittsburgh survey, tended to fail to acknowledge the antecedents of the survey, especially in the doomed European tradition of Moral Statistics, of which Mayo-Smith was in a sense the last

Source: Martin Bulmer, Kevin Bales & Kathryn K. Sklar (eds.), *The Social Survey in Historical Perspective, 1880–1940*, (Cambridge: Cambridge University Press, 1991).

representative, and in the collection of statistics by State and subsequently national bureaux of 'Labor Statistics' after the civil war, and in the expansion of the collection of federal social statistics under the auspices of the census, which repeatedly expanded the range of its questions, and various federal commissions, such as the Tenement study, sponsored by the leading figure in the Labor Statistics movement, Carroll Wright, which was the original source of data for the Hull House maps.

Columbia's early and intense commitment to quantitative social research reflected the broader appreciation of these roots that one would expect to find in an academic institution, and this is evident in the dissertations done by the students in the department who were to go on to become academic sociologists. As we shall see, the topics selected by Columbia sociologists for their own surveys reproduced the canon of reform topics established by the 1880s by the Massachusetts Bureau of Labor Statistics. Columbia's distinctive contribution, which is evident in the transition from the statistical thinking of Mayo-Smith to that of Giddings, was to define this work in terms of an explicit philosophy of science, derived from Karl Pearson, which was the basis for the distinctive strain of social research that became 'mainstream sociology' and came to be supported by the Social Science Research Council in the twenties and thirties. This new style of survey was in a certain sense the successor of the Kellogg-style survey supported by the Russell Sage Foundation. But there was no 'discontinuity'. If we consider the diversity of the research activities of the sociologists who were part of the larger Columbia family, of its graduates and their students in the interwar years, the picture is rather one of close personal patronage, and professional connections between a relatively small group of researchers whose careers and interests spanned a broad range, in which the Kelloggian social survey had an important, but subordinate place. Some of the research topics and styles that fell in this range, perhaps most of them, had an afterlife in academic sociology; but the Kelloggian survey, poorly adapted to the rhythms and constraints of academic life and part time, individualistic research, and orphaned as a result of the declining financial fortunes and changed interests of its main financial supporter, did not, though its variants were to be found as late as the fifties, for example in the Kansas City survey performed in connection with the University of Chicago.

This chapter will tell the story of the Columbia family and its connections in the milieu shared by Columbia social science and New York philanthropy, the source of much of the survey work done in the period 1905–25 and of course subsequently the source of much of the funding for later 'academic' survey research done under the auspices of the SSRC. The members of this 'family' had a role in settlement houses, reform survey work, foundations, the government, reform politics, and of course the emerging discipline of academic sociology. Because this story is largely a story of networks and connections and their intellectual consequences, and because the number of connections is large, it is necessary to limit the discussion to a few exemplary situations and relationships, and a few strands in the fabric of connections between academic social science and the movements of institutionalised reform.

The Background: Reform Statistics and Reformist Associations

In the disciplines of both statistics and sociology, American universities took over topics that had a long prehistory in public discourse, a discourse that took place in part in the intellectual journals of the period after the Civil War, such as *The North America Review* and the *Century*, but which was sustained by a large set of interested organisations, both governmental and private, and a relatively well-defined set of public issues toward which these organisations were oriented. Typically these organisations, several of which were under the umbrella of the American Social Science Association, had an explicitly reformist character, and were organised around specific topics, such as prison reform. They generally took the form of a 'council' of some sort that included reformist luminaries, but the main work of the organisation, to hold meetings and often to produce a publication, was usually in the hands of a small number of activists. In time, the universities contributed to the leadership of these organisations, and overlapping membership on these boards constituted a kind of web that tied together a large number of intellectual activists, reformers, university professors and presidents, and governmental officials. The development of social science in the university for the most part followed the establishment of these organisations, so the original flow of personnel was from the organisations to the university.

The character of this network, which reached its peak in the early nineties, may be seen in the careers of its ubiquitous members. The 'statisticians' most frequently represented in this network of boards of directors were Carroll D. Wright and Francis Amasa Walker, each of whom rose through the ranks in the Union army, and ultimately became professors, civil servants, and college presidents.[1] Wright rose to the rank of colonel in the war, and became a state senator in 1871. In 1873 he took over the Massachusetts Bureau of Labor Statistics, which had been founded in 1869, and became US Commissioner of Labor in 1888, honorary professor of political science at Catholic University in 1895, president of Clark College and professor of Applied Sociology in 1902. He served as the original director of the Carnegie Institute's programmes on economics and sociology, in 1902.[2] Walker, son of an Amherst economist, had a similar career, playing a large role in the development of the census, ending as President of MIT.

Wright's great success was the Massachusetts Bureau, which became an international model of research and a pioneer both in methods and in the topics addressed. It was in the work of this bureau that the characteristically modern methods of survey analysis — machine tabulation, individual data cards, interviews based on printed schedules or questionnaires, concerns with sampling, the use of index numbers, and large numbers of respondents (sometimes in the tens of thousands) – were first combined. Under Wright and his predecessors, who controlled the bureau for the first four years after its founding in 1869, a wide range of reform topics was addressed. These went far beyond the census and far beyond the narrower questions of the economics of labor to an extensive examination of a wide range of topics relating to the life of workers. In the first report of the Massachusetts Bureau in 1869, the following 'very important subjects' were cited as matters for inquiry: 'the hours of labor, the wages, the savings, the manner of life at home and from home, the recreations, the culture, moral and mental, of the laborers, and the influence of the several kinds of labor upon their health and body and brain, not ignoring the subjects of cooperation strikes, trades-unions, and the general relations of capital and labor, with such matter relating to the history of labor and labor legislation, here and abroad, as we might be able to gather'.[3] By 1870, this list had expanded to include research on housing, intemperance, and child labour, by 1871, poverty, Boston tenements, domestic and women's work, and so on. In the 1870s, pauperism, crime, the 'afflicted classes', the cost of living, nativity, convict labour, and other topics had been added.[4] Later, indeed by the 1890s, the work of these bureaus had largely narrowed to the economic and demographic interests of the present day employment surveys, with some interesting exceptions, such as the concern with child labour. As we shall see, the range of these early studies, and the topics themselves, were taken up again under academic auspices at Columbia.

Like Major John Wesley Powell, who created and headed the Bureau of Indian Ethnology and the US Geological Survey and who, like Walker, was politically sponsored by Garfield,[5] Wright and Walker were largely autodidacts, rather than university scholars. Both Wright and Walker were active participants in the reform movements and pre-academic social science of their time: each served as an officer or board member of the American Social Science Association, the American Statistical Association, the Association for the Promotion of Profit-Sharing, and each of them participated in the American Economic Association. The pattern was not uncommon. Giddings was one of those who followed this path.

Giddings, born in 1855, had been forced to leave Union College for financial reasons in 1875, after completing two years of study. He became a newspaperman in Springfield, Massachusetts, an area which was a hotbed of organisations of this sort. Giddings was soon part of the discussions of the problems of employment, inflation, and monetary policy: among his earliest writings was a proposal for price-indexing contracts. By the close of his career as a newsman he was delivering papers to the meetings of economics societies and editing movement journals. The character of this milieu is difficult to recapture. The sheer number and variety of the organisations that were founded in the late nineteenth century is itself astonishing. They ranged from various anti-vice leagues and prohibitionist organisations to associations for 'scientific' exchange, such as the Connecticut Valley Economic Association, one of Giddings' first arenas.

The reform organisations served as the framework for a porous and absorptive intellectual community which was not dependent, at first, on the university or on any specific European inspirations: the community was an analogue to the socialist left in Europe, in that it provided an audience for the ideas of the day, a source of non-academic intellectual recruits, and a great deal of intellectual work, in the form of editing and writing, as well as a degree of practical engagement and experience that prevented the rise of doctrinaires. American sectionalism and federalism, especially the fact that the states, and in the case of poor relief, the counties, still possessed the bulk of legal and regulatory power over social and economic questions, meant that the focus of these organisations was localistic, and that national organisations served as means for sharing local experiences rather than as bearers of national programme. The experience of participation in these organisations left a mark on what was to follow, both at Columbia and at Chicago, where Robert Park had undergone a similar education. Giddings, like Park, was organisationally adept, talented at communicating ideas to a wider public, both journalistically and as a public speaker, and somewhat cynical about what Park called do-gooders. Having been raised as a child of a particularly strict congregationalist minister of the Christian reformist type that flourished after the success of the abolitionist movement, Giddings was also explicitly sceptical about many of the manifestations of these movements, including those that flourished under the leadership of the main competitor to Columbia social science, the Johns Hopkins University family, of which Richard T. Ely was the personal and spiritual leader, and to whom such Chicago personalities as Small were devoted.[6] In the case of Giddings, this cynicism sometimes extended to aspects of the survey movement itself, as it did for Park. In time, these differences in temperament led to, or supported, other differences that separated Giddings from the survey movement. But the differences took the form they did in part because of the manner in which the academic environment at Columbia itself developed. This is a complex story, much of which precedes Giddings' entry onto the Columbia scene in the early nineties.

The Columbia Idea

When John Burgess returned from Germany to Amherst College in 1874 as a professor, he sought to recreate on the American soil something analogous to the schooling in social science he had received in Europe. This experience, and the model of learning and especially *Forschung* that Burgess and many other Americans acquired, was the inspiration for the creation of programmes of graduate education in the expanding American universities of the post-Civil War era. Part of Burgess' German experience was with the statistics of Wappaus, a Göttingen Professor. Statistics was thus an essential element of Burgess' image of the social sciences from the start. When he was called to Columbia, he took with him an Amherst student who was to become a leader in statistics,

Richmond Mayo-Smith, to be one of the four original members of the faculty of political science. By 1890 Mayo-Smith accounted for the largest body of statistical course work in the United States: four courses, all designed for the graduate social science students at Columbia.

In 1877, Mayo-Smith was twenty-four years old, a newly appointed assistant to Burgess. In 1888 he was appointed full professor of political economy. He began the teaching of statistics in 1883, with a course attended by three students.[7] His rationale for the course was fitted to Burgess's aim of producing civil servants, and to the Cameralism that Burgess espoused: statistical method, Mayo-Smith said, 'gives us a picture of actually existing society and is thus more fitted for guiding state action'.[8] The statistics in question were those collected by the government, and it was simply assumed in the discussions of statistics of the era that the employer of statisticians would be the government and that the government would collect the statistics.

Mayo-Smith had an interesting and complex relation to governmental statistics, reform and social science. On the one hand, the American statistical community in the United States was small, and he was quickly absorbed into the networks of reformers and reform intellectuals of which Burgess was already a part. Mayo-Smith was active in the American Statistical Association and the Charity Organisation Society of New York. Within these diverse movements and organisations there was a great deal of room for disagreement over such questions as immigration (one of Mayo-Smith's specialities), the trend of wages (a concern of his student Charles Spahr), as well as divorce, the topic of Willcox's dissertation of 1892, the first American statistical dissertation on a recognisably 'sociological' topic. Yet these communities were sufficiently small that the kinds of intellectual conflicts that inevitably arose could be managed personally, especially by a person like Mayo-Smith, an inveterate Club man at a time when such clubs as the Century in New York, of which he was a member, were foci of scientific and literary life. Mayo-Smith and Wright were on friendly terms, and Mayo-Smith was evidently well-liked in the Massachusetts Bureau: in 1887, Pidgin, one of the pioneers of machine tabulation, proposed that Mayo-Smith spend the summer with him at one of the Boston beaches to work with him on a book of practical statistics.[9]

Academic-Philanthropic Relations in New York

In 1891, Burgess and Mayo-Smith raised the subject of the need for a chair of sociology, meaning ethnology, penology, charity, and poor-relief – subjects that Burgess' friend Sanborn had taught at Cornell in the late eighties as a special lecturer.[10] Seth Low, who had been a reform mayor of Brooklyn, persuaded the board to appoint Giddings, then thirty-six, who had in 1888 been appointed at Bryn Mawr as professor of political science (the position held previously by Woodrow Wilson), to commute to Columbia on Friday to give a joint seminar with Mayo-Smith. In 1894, Low offered to pay the salary of a professor of sociology, and Giddings was appointed. Giddings soon made his mark, and a programme in sociology developed quickly. Giddings himself exerted his influence in a special way. He ran a kind of beer-and-pretzels salon known as the FHG Club, to which his best students and a few others, such as Arthur and Paul Kellogg (editor of *The Survey*) and Charles Beard, were invited. Invitations were an honour for the students, and the experience was formative for many of those who participated: they acquired a common set of ideas about the prospects of sociology as a science, and a strong core of personal relationships to peers.[11]

The slogan 'the city is the laboratory of the social sciences', variously attributed to Mayo-Smith and Giddings, appeared in the earliest announcements of the new programme in sociology,[12] and both Giddings and Mayo-Smith put the idea into effect by initiating research projects using available data. In 1894, Mayo-Smith secured authorisation to use COS case records as research material.[13] Mayo-Smith and Giddings themselves served on a three-person committee that statistically examined 500 records, examining 'causes' of distress and tabulating methods of treatment. They recognised the inadequacies of the records for statistical purposes, 'and confessed that the benefit of such an investigation as they had made came principally to the students who had engaged in it'.[14] But the studies had some consequences: for example, they contributed in succeeding years to reforms of case record keeping and an attack on the doctrine of causality implicit in the old standard COS blank, which was replaced in 1907.[15]

The studies grew out of a complex body of personal relations to the wider philanthropic scene. In this respect, Giddings continued the practices of Mayo-Smith, whose primary 'public service' contribution had been to serve as a district officer of the Charity Organization Society in New York. Giddings' student Tenney recounts that Giddings

> found that one of the expectations connected with the chair of Sociology was that the occupant should serve on the councils of the University Settlement and the Charity Organization Society. For many years, therefore, after coming to Columbia, Professor Giddings was one of the directing minds guiding the policies of these institutions . . . In part because of these connections, the lectures and seminars in Sociology and in Statistics from their inception were attended by many persons interested in what is now known as social work.[16]

Giddings eventually served not only on the COS and University Settlement House boards, but as President of Richmond Hill House, on the board of the State Charities Aid Association and even on the New York City Board of Education.[17]

The COS network was an incubator of the survey movement in that these networks provided the structure of patronage and community of intellect that made possible the enormous infusion of funds for surveys in the period after

1905. The Russell Sage Foundation was created as a direct outgrowth of the network established by the New York COS and the attitude toward research that flourished there. At the death of Russell Sage, a financier of enormous wealth and exceeding personal unsavouriness, his widow, on the advice of her attorneys, Robert W. de Forest and his brother Henry, and with the encouragement of other trusted persons, including Johns Hopkins President Daniel Coit Gilman, himself a Baltimore COS leader, established the foundation bearing Sage's name.[18] De Forest suggested modelling the finances of the organisation on the (Rockefeller) General Education Board, Carnegie Institute, and Borke Foundation, and to aspire to become for the nation such a 'center of charitable and philanthropic information as the Charity Organization Society makes for the city', stressing 'research, study, teaching, publication', but not excluding other kinds of aid to activities leading to 'the permanent improvement of social conditions'.[19] Yet the contribution of Mayo-Smith and of Giddings (who was favourably inclined to the reformist aims, but suspicious of the foundations[20]) to the creation of the intellectual climate which made possible this channelling of funds into surveys is difficult to specify precisely. Personal ties, however, are quite readily traced. Mayo-Smith's student Spahr edited the reformist *Outlook*; and Giddings' students, as we shall see, were distributed widely around the foundations and the surveys themselves. The COS created in 1898 a tenement house commission, which included the architect and philanthropist I. N. Phelps Stokes, who was later to head a race-relations foundation, endowed by a relative, to which one of Giddings' students, T. J. Jones, was appointed as an executive.[21]

Giddings and His Students

Giddings had, by 1901, developed a complex conception of sociology as a quantifiable subject, and this conception was impressed relentlessly on his students. Giddings, as Sims recalled, 'had developed a true scientific approach . . . [which] he communicated to his students. He was definitely trying to develop a quantitative instead of a purely qualitative sociology . . . To find ways of measuring and weighing sociological data was his chief interest.'[22] But though the researches of Giddings' students reflected Giddings' theoretical ideas and the current state of his methodological thinking, the content of the research reflected the standard topics of the reform catalog, and these were the topics of research done by the MBLS as early as its first few years. Thus the research agenda itself directly reflected the reform agenda that grew up and gained coherence in the period 1866–1905.

The topics of the Columbia dissertations before World War I were strikingly similar to those done by the MBLS, including among others, studies of *The Enforcement of the Statutes of Laborers* (Putnam, 1908), *A History of California Labor Legislation* (Eaves, 1910), *Factory Legislation in Maine* (Whiting, 1908), *The Employment of Women in the Clothing Trade* (Willett, 1903), *The Negro at Work in*

New York City (Haynes, 1912), *Minimum Wage Legislation in Australia* (Collier, 1915), and *Dressmaking as a Trade for Women in Massachusetts* (Allison, 1916), which, like Parmelee's *Inebriety in Boston* (1909), even shared the locale; Ogburn's dissertation on the emergence of consistency between the states with respect to child labour legislation was based on material of a kind collected routinely as part of Labor Statistics reports under the heading of surveys of legislation; Chapin's study of the emergence of certain common education practices was analogous; T. J. Jones' study of a New York City block of tenements was a Giddingsonian approach to this topic. Giddings himself planned a study of workingmen's leisure in 1912–13, using the same kinds of questions asked by the MBLS studies of the same topics, and Gillin later published 'Wholesome Citizens and Spare Time'.[23]

But there was a distinctive intellectual orientation to this new research. Jones' study of a block of tenements, published in 1904, but based on field research that began in 1897, is illustrative of several features of this new model of sociological scholarship. Jones begins the study by observing that 'the rural character of the people swarming in our tenements' is largely unknown, and that 'even the missionary, the pastor, and the settlement worker have but an inadequate and erroneous idea of the peoples around them'.[24] Jones spoke from experience: he had 'at different times been engaged as a visitor for a church, for a settlement, and for an organization that searched independently for facts concerning life in the tenement districts, and . . . found that the information gained in the first two instances too often contradicted that gained in the third'.[25] In fact, he had matriculated at Union Theological Seminary and Columbia, receiving an MA in sociology in 1899, the BD in 1900. He served as acting headworker of the University Settlement of New York City, editing its annual report of 1902, a collection of studies of urban conditions. He was also briefly employed by the Charity Organization Society, the Federation of Churches of New York City, and by the Census Bureau.[26] He was thus well aware of the status of knowledge of the tenement dwellers, and Giddings' views were persuasive to him. The flaw in past research, he believed was 'a lack of unity of conception in regard to the matters to be learned'.[27] His own study, in contrast, he described as a self-conscious

> attempt to study a New York city street according to a complete system of social principles. Even if the system were proved to be arbitrary, the work would be more valuable, the writer believes, than an unsystematic attempt, however long continued, for the reasons that the investigator has a basis for search and an order for arranging in his mind the innumerable impressions made by the unit considered. Without a system the study of a people is but a wild-goose chase, and this, indeed, is the nature of too many of the so-called sociological investigations now carried on. Read the results of these investigations and you feel that you have been through a mine more or less rich in information. You are possibly

stirred to pity or to blame by the conditions described, and you may give your help accordingly; but when this task is accomplished the outcome of the investigation is simply a conglomerate mass of facts, practically useless for the future. According to the system used in this dissertation we shall gather facts which may be expected to substantiate or to overthrow certain theories as to the manner in which well-known social forces work themselves out. Thus we may hope for results of permanent value.[28]

This is of course the voice of Giddings as well.[29] Jones concerned himself with one of Giddings' pet, indeed primary, ideas, that 'concerted volition' took place differently among groups of different kinds, particularly groups of different ethnicities. This was tied in part to an anxiety that immigrants could not be assimilated into the kinds of social relations characteristic of American democracy. The Jews and Italians who predominated in Jones's block were particular objects of concern.

Jones described in great detail, in terms of Giddings' categories, the development and occurrence of 'like behavior,' 'motives of conduct' according to Giddings' categories of ideo-motor, ideo-emotional, dogmatic. emotional (Giddings' term for the puritanism he grew up with) and critically intellectual (of which no instances could be found in the block), and forms of 'concerted volition' or association. His 'method' was to perform a 'sociological census', to visit each family in the block, on Saturday morning. 'No more than twenty families were visited in a day, so as not to overburden the mind with facts'. Basic demographic data was collected on a blank; the observational results would be classified in a day or two in the next week: necessary because the system of classification was a system of ratings by the observer. 'Provided with blanks used by the Federation of Churches the investigator knocked at the door of a tenement. Generally a voice from within would call out, "Come in." Quite often a voice would ask, "What do you want?" And the visitor would answer, "I want to know how many persons are in this family," or in more difficult cases the answer was "I am taking a sociological census," with emphasis on the last word. The door opened in all but one case out of the two hundred and eleven'.[30] Jones was following in the footsteps of others. Indeed, he wrote 'These people have been visited by so many officers and agents that they have grown indifferent to all investigations. They take it as a matter of course'. But his own investigation 'was a surprise to them, and many were curious about it. The curiosity was soon lost, in the great majority of the cases, in the friendly relations that arose between the visitor and the family'.[31] Jones, a Welshman by birth, looked enough like a Jew to pass as one.

> From the Hebrews a hearty welcome was gained by the ability to pronounce the Talmud in the original. The visitor's corrupt German and dark complexion were often taken by the Jew as a guarantee that he was one of their race.[32]

The Italians were more difficult, but his appearance helped there as well, and in 'one instance he was asked if he was an Italian priest'. To the Irish, 'he could claim to be a brother Celt', but the Irish did 'not care who knows about them'.[33] Knowledge of German and 'an admiration for the German character' sufficed in the case of the Germans.

In a typical case, the Cohens, Jones visited the family on a Saturday morning. The father, a tailor born in New York City, was not home, but his wife and two young children, and mother-in-law, were home. The motherin-law had been born in Russia, married a Jew in Portugal, moved to England and then to 'America with a number of children, who', Jones wrote, 'are now well situated, one daughter being married to a fairly well-to-do Jew and living comfortably on Long Island'. Jones learned all this 'in an interesting conversation about' such topics as 'the progress of the Hebrew people', the movement from the lower to the upper East side, 'where the block was located, to the West side', the comparative morality of the ethnic groups, and the observations of the two women that the Irish were 'very thriftless and careless, spending much of their money in drink' but their observation that some of the children nevertheless 'grew up to be fine men and women'.[34] They also discussed their own religious practices: the mother tried to keep the Sabbath; the daughter 'no longer cared for Jewish customs . . . [and] ate what she wanted, . . . checked only by her mother's wishes'. The daughter took herself not to look like a Jew, and believed that *her* daughter was 'not anything like a Jew'.[35] These were, in short, Americanisation stories.

Jones, however, was concerned to classify the families in terms of his 'scheme of mental and moral types', so these discussions were the basis of ratings, which he explains, in this specimen case. The family was not 'impulsive', because the mother-in-law showed self-restraint on an occasion 'when the landlord abused her people'. Intellectually, the family had left the 'credulous' stage, as shown by the daughter's attitude toward 'Hebrew customs'. The mother's 'credulousness' in this instance was overweighed by her tolerance of her daughter and the acuteness of her own observations on this and other subjects. Unlike most of the residents of this block, this family did 'think for themselves'. Of the four types of character identified by Giddings, Jones thought it evident that the family had passed the threshold of the 'rationally conscientious' type, though 'not a high example'.[36] In addition, Jones recorded the various traits of character that were associated with social life, ascribing to this family compassion and generosity, and such traits as truthfulness, industriousness, frugality, cleanliness, and orderliness.[37] These classifications were applied to each family in the block, and the numbers in each of these categories and other Giddingsonian categories, leading to such results as

> In 21 families mere persistence was found to be the dominant method of accommodation, and in 121 more families a subordinate method. In 149 families accommodation was the dominant, and in 51 families a

subordinate method. In 27 families self-control was the dominant, and in 22 families a subordinate method.[38]

No cross tabulations were performed, but for each category the ethnic distribution was discussed.

One aim of the discussion was obviously to account for the susceptibility of each group to machine politics, and the distance of each group from full participation in 'Anglo-Saxon' political culture. As Jones put it, 'A dictator seems to be necessary to every successful organization on the upper East side'. Jewish 'individualism' was least susceptible to this pattern. Jewish organisations 'are not large; leadership is not strongly emphasized; argument, discussion, and disagreement are matters of course. The Irish, with their qualities of leadership and their strong social instincts, form societies in which the "machine system" is always to be observed'.[39] Jones, like Giddings, saw as a danger 'the infusion' into American life 'of foreign ideas and manners, and its tendency thereby to modify Anglo-Saxon habits'.[40]

Giddings as a Methodologist

Giddings of course did not invent community studies. In Small and Vincent's Chautauqua text of 1894, *An Introduction to the Science of Society*, the topic of variant forms of community life and various kinds of social relations within communities was the core of the book, which had a full complement of exemplary maps and discussions of the kinds of group life that are to be found in rural, small town, and urban society.[41] Many of the kinds of strategies that interested Giddings, such as grouping persons by dominant motives, were part of Small and Vincent's book. What Giddings added was a complex methodological rationale and an argument for the preferability of certain kinds of social knowledge, or more precisely an image of the evolution of social knowledge. The effects of this conception are evident only in modest ways in Jones' dissertation, and in fact Giddings seems to have been, in practice, rather tolerant of different methods. The community studies done under his influence tended to be descriptive, as Jones' was, rather than quantitative. But they shared with Jones' the use of his distinctive theoretical terminology.

The primary source of the methodological considerations that marked out Giddings from such contemporaries as Small and Vincent and from the social surveyors outside academia, was Karl Pearson's philosophy of science text, *The Grammar of Science*. What Giddings took from Pearson were two closely connected thoughts: first, that the stages which a body of thought passed through to become a science were the ideological, the observational, and the metrical;[42] second, that the highest metrical form which sociology was able to attain would be correlational analysis. Thus the business of sociology, for Giddings, was precisely the transformation of speculations tied together by a logical bond, such as his own sociological theory, which was a theory of forms of association, *into* a set of correlations. Giddings regarded this methodological work as his primary contribution. *Inductive Sociology*, published in 1901, was not, however, a critical success. Yet he stuck to the basic ideas in it, and improved them to fit with new developments in statistics.

In *Inductive Sociology* Giddings gives an example of what he takes to be a paradigmatic scientific demonstration of sociology – he generates, on speculative and logical grounds, the following proposition; only the population that has many, varied, and harmoniously combined interests is consistently progressive in its choices.[43] He metricises this by constructing an index number of heterogeneity (based on distributions of blacks and foreign-born in state populations, something easily derived from census data) and producing a categorisation of states based on this number. The distribution of the states indeed corresponds to our intuitive sense of the progressiveness of their politics.[44] He does not create an index number for this. Had he done so, he could have calculated a Pearsonian correlation.

The problem Giddings faced in actualising this model of scientific development, and to which he devoted an extraordinary amount of effort, was in creating 'indices'. The efforts are retrospectively quite odd. At first, Giddings produced long lists of things that are countable, that correspond to theoretical concepts, or which sort objects into categories that correspond to the kinds of categories used in nineteenth-century social theory and in public discourse about social questions. A glance at Giddings' early lists shows how difficult this problem in fact was. In *Inductive Sociology*, he tried to come up with indices for the following classificatory categories, among many others: 'emotional types', including 'choleric', 'sanguine', 'melancholic' and 'phlegmatic',[45] 'state of political cooperation' including under the subheading 'public' from 'Activity Violent, Military, Coercive' to 'Activity Peaceful, Legislative, and Administrative, but Dogmatic and Coercive' or 'Peaceful, Legislative, and Administrative, Deliberative, Reasonable, Educative'.[46] Most of these distinctions, he thought, could be made by observers, and as we have seen his students, such as T. J. Jones, reported systematic classifications of individuals into similar categories on the basis of 'observation'. F. Stuart Chapin later recalled that 'Giddings in his treatment of method in connection with seminars and in conferences with students was all for clarification of social observations'. But what he arrived at was 'more of a rating system'.[47] The drive to construct 'behavioural indices' was in any event already present in 1901; its roots were deeper.

The development of Giddings' methodological thinking is visible in the gradual evolution of the form of the empirical dissertations done under him. The earliest are 'observational' as T. J. Jones' tenement study had been; J. M. Williams (1906) simply returned to the small New York town in which he had grown up and performed a 'census', and examined the social and economic relations that bound the town to its countryside, a hop-producing region. This book, *An American Town* (1906), Giddings regarded as the 'best approximation' to a 'comprehensive sociological survey of a community'.[48] This general topic was the theme of a series of dissertations which took the form of community studies focused on the same 'theoretical' theme, the interlayering of various forms of association (which itself built on the topic of cooperation, especially as it had become extended in the 1890s to the notion of 'socialisation', by which Giddings meant the development of social ties and associations, of which cooperative associations were a particular type).[49] There were many studies of this same general type performed at Columbia, including Warren Wilson's *Quaker Hill* (1907), E. S. Todd's *A Social Study of Clark County, Ohio* (1904), F. V. Soule's *An American Village Community* (1909), and Newell Sims' *A Hoosier Village* (1911), and others. J. L. Gillins' *The Dunkers* (1906) was concerned with a form of community association; Chaddock's *Ohio Before 1850* with the problem of individualism and the role of different groups in the westward migration to the creation of community institutions and frontier democracy.

In the twenties, these slowly gave way, proportionally at least, to correlational studies: T. J. Woofter's *Negro Migration* (1920) was the first to use multiple regression techniques; Luther Fry's *Diagnosing the Rural Church*, an ISRR study, and F. A. Ross' *School Attendance in 1920*, both published in 1924, represented the most complete realisations of Giddings' methodological ideas. In Ross one finds the regression equations familiar to readers of present structural equations modelling, and the same reasoning. But studies of small communities and their 'associations' remained a staple product of Columbia sociology throughout this period. These evolved as well. Chaddock's study of Ohio before 1850 was perhaps the most Giddingsonian of the early community studies, and pioneered the metricisation of his concerns. Wilson, who became the Presbyterians' researcher on country churches, produced sixteen 'community and church' studies, usually with the county as the unit of analysis. As early as Odum's dissertation, which involved fifty southern communities, the community had been used as the unit for aggregated data analysis. The fullest development of this came in the work of the Institute for Social and Religious Research, which published many volumes of correlational analyses, including a great deal of partialling, using 'indices' relating to community and church life.[50]

Contemporaries regarded all such studies as 'social surveys'. The ISRR evolved out of the failure of an attempt to perform a world religious survey, and is thus a lineal product of the 'survey' movement. Lynd's *Middletown* was done under ISRR auspices and with ISRR financing. Lynd's career, which included a BD from Union Seminary, home mission work in the west, Rockefeller patronage, and extensive foundation work in the inner circles of New York philanthropy and the SSRC, reads very much like the careers of various earlier Columbia students, with a few differences: Lynd was an old Princetonian and socially connected to New York philanthropy and Club life to a greater extent than any of them had been prior to becoming a 'social researcher.' Where *Middletown* differed from its predecessors was in the fact that the dissertations were one-person efforts, while Lynd, with the backing of the ISRR, had a staff of helpers, and in the fact that the guiding sociological hypothesis being examined – which was initially, and not surprisingly given the dominance of the ISRR by Giddings' students, a concern with the social correlates of religious life – disappeared in Lynd's write up, which was rejected by the ISRR and ultimately published through other Lynd connections. Its 'methods' were those of the earlier studies, and the academic sociologists who performed these studies were enraged by Lynd's claims of methodological priority, which were quite false.

The Survey Movement and the Academic Quantifiers

The later work of these students developed the ideas and practices they had learned at Columbia: Woofter on Blacks and migration, Woolston on prostitution, Gillin on criminology and penology, Gehlke on delinquency – it is a list which could be easily extended. Many other sociology departments produced survey researchers and statisticians; but the Columbia contribution was ubiquitous and relatively uniform. With these later studies, the methodological impulses that the movement for a scientific sociology had shared with the social survey movement took on new aims. Giddings' students in academic positions generally turned away from community studies, though these survived as a genre in rural sociology for much longer, and toward such topics as the measurement of social status, Chapin's concern. His students also continued to develop his methodological conception and revised his theoretical ideas, which often appeared without full acknowledgement in their writings.

The separation of academic sociology and its quantitative work from the Kelloggian model of the social survey was thus a gradual affair. The changes and the close connections between the various spheres of activity that contributed to the social survey may be seen in some of the careers of the members of the Columbia family. Ogburn, who was at the University of Washington before going to the National War Labor Board during the First World War, wrote the following in a 1919 letter of recommendation for Howard P. Woolston's career:

> He has a good record of substantial achievement. His four-volume survey for the Factory Investigating Commission of New York is quite a splendid piece of work. He also drove home a [sic] excellent year's work with the Social Hygiene Society – making a survey of the whole U.S. He is now head of department of social, economic, and political science at the College of the City of New York, taking Clark's place who left to become president of some western state university. He studied under Tarde and Durkheim in France. Is thought highly of at the Univ. of Chicago as well as Columbia, having studied at both places. He was head worker in earlier years at Greenwich Settlement House. Is thought well of by the *Survey* group in New York, Paul Kellogg and others.[52]

Woolston had his first contact with sociology as a Divinity Student at Chicago, where he was briefly employed by Small. In his student years he worked at Harvard on a scheme to create a 'social museum' as part of the Peabody, and studied in Germany with Simmel. He spent the bulk of his academic career at Washington, which was the largest and most successful sociology department in the West in the interwar years, with a large faculty. In the twenties he chaired a multidisciplinary Committee on Community Research at the University, and proposed a civic centre for Seattle designed to help serve to interpret the City to its citizens and others, with a 'sociological department' which would contain educational exhibits on such things as death rates sociologically subcategorised – a permanent form of the kind of exhibits that were part of the Springfield and Pittsburgh survey models.

This range of experiences was not atypical. A similar list of activities could be drawn up for the others in Woolston's cohort, such as Odum, Chapin, or Ogburn. The transitions from one employer to another were not absolute passages from one sphere to another. Connections were kept up, consulting work performed, and advisory roles continued to be played.[53] The range of activities of the members of the Columbia family expanded over time. T. J. Jones became a major figure in the promotion of practical education for Blacks in the South, and the strategies he promoted there were adopted by the British Colonial authorities in Africa, after a survey by the Phelps-Stokes African Education Commission.[54] Yet the topics as well as the focus on the community that were central concerns for the survey movement as it developed from the time of the Pittsburgh Survey to *Middletown* remained basic topics of concern to most of Giddings' students throughout their careers, which in several cases reached into the fifties. What was the relationship between the two bodies of work? What changed?

The students of Giddings prospered in academic sociology, and with the rise to prosperity of academic sociology, to an extent not generally recognised by historians of sociology, for whom the rise and fall of Chicago is the simpler and more dramatic story. There were six Columbia presidents of the American Sociological Society in the interwar era, Lichtenberger, Gillin, Ogburn, Odum, Chapin, and Hankins. They were each, in the language of the day, 'Giddings men', who shared a coherent methodological vision, and shared a great deal of Giddings' own theoretical vision and conception of the field. Odum edited *Social Forces*, and Hankins became the first *ASR* editor. The group almost totally controlled the sociology funded through the SSRC in its first five, and most successful, years. The Columbian group had an exceptional degree of social coherence. Giddings' FHG Club held reunion dinners at least into the twenties, and students would be recommended from one generation of Columbians to another as having been FHG Club members.[55] The ties were profitable in many ways. When Odum needed information on the situation in New York foundations, he could and did call on his graduate school peers, such as Ogburn, or even receive grants from those who had become foundation executives, such as T. J. Jones, who helped fund the Sea Islands research while at the Phelps Stokes foundation.[56] In short, the academic quantifiers in the Columbia family had the same roots as the survey movement, but they were broadly enough trained, and their methodological vision was sufficiently strong that they adapted – for example, to the changes in sources of funding and to the rise of quantitative psychology.

The survey movement represented by Kellogg, in contrast, could not adapt to the changed political climate of the twenties. The early survey model depended heavily on civic support and especially on voluntary participation. In the twenties, the simplicities of the pre-war reform idea no longer attracted the support of the professional classes, at least to the extent they had before. The paradoxes of patronage and dependence,[57] and the financial weakness of the Russell Sage Foundation, conspired against the survey idea. In his 1909 dissertation, Woolston wrote that his study was 'but a fragment of a complete investigation of neighborhood life' by which he meant one which dealt 'with housing conditions and home life, with business interests, social activities, political organization and general ethical tendencies'.[58] The study of fragments survived the ideal of comprehensiveness and the Behemoth efforts they entailed.

When the depression shifted power from the states to the federal government, academic sociology, with its broader methodological remit, particularly its capacity to deal with demographic change and with psychological aspects of social life, was better (though only slightly better) able to respond. Such pressing regional problems as the race problems of the south, the national problem of the migration of rural blacks to the urban north, and the general problem of the response to the newly visible Black presence, became central to the SSRC agenda. These topics were largely beyond the power of the local 'survey' to illuminate, and typically beyond the capacity of local establishments to face.

Notes

1. Walker's father had himself been a member of a board which produced a survey-like study for Massachusetts (Charles F. Pidgin, *History of the Bureau of Statistics of Labor of Massachusetts and of Labor Legislation in that State from 1833 to 1876* (Boston: Wright & Potter, State Printers, 1876), p. 16).

2. Carroll Davison Wright: His Life and Statistical Works, L. L. Bernard Papers, Chicago, University of Chicago Library.

3. Quoted in Pidgin, *History of the Bureau of Statistics*, pp. 54–5.

4. Some of these researches were narrowly statistical. Most of them, however, included and sometimes consisted of, what we would now call 'qualitative' material, including testimony by participants, folk-theorising by physicians and other persons with expertise, and the reproduction of responses to open-ended questions.

5. On Powell and the patronage of science in Washington in this period, see Stephen P. Turner, 'The Survey in Nineteenth-Century American Geology: The Evolution of a Form of Patronage', *Minerva*, 25, 3 (1987), 282–330.

6. Giddings' contempt for Chicago sociology in general and Small in particular was intense, and this was communicated to and shared by his students. Yet Giddings himself remained personally on good terms with many of the sociologists who came out of the Chicago tradition. Even C. A. Ellwood, a Small student who often wrote for a liberal Protestant audience, had one of his explicitly religiously oriented books of the early twenties endorsed by Giddings.

7. Joseph Dorfman, 'The Department of Economics', in Gordon Hoxie, Sally F. Moore, Joseph Dorfman et al. (eds.), *A History of the Faculty of Political Science Columbia University* (Morningside Heights, NY: Columbia University Press, 1955), pp. 161–206; p. 173.

8. Dorfman, 'Department of Economics', p. 173.

9. Mayo-Smith to Mrs Mayo-Smith, 22 May, 1887, Mayo-Smith Papers.

10. The Teaching of Sociology at Cornell University, L. L. Bernard Papers, p. 2.

11. Charles Elmer Gehlke, L. L. Bernard Papers, p. 4.

12. Robert E. Chaddock, 'Social Statistics in the Faculty of Political Science', *Columbia University Quarterly*, 24 (1932), 431; Howard W. Odum, *American Sociology: The Story of Sociology in the United States through 1950* (New York: Greenwood Press, 1951), p. 61.

13. Kellogg facilitated the use of the records J. S. Lowell and C. R. Lowell to Mayo-Smith, 22 March, 1894, Mayo-Smith Papers).

14. E. T. Devine, *When Social Work Was Young* (New York: Macmillan, 1939), p. 35. One of the students who studied COS records was the author of one of the first Masters' theses done under Giddings, Elsie Clews Parsons, later to become famous as an anthropologist.

15. Gustav Kleene, 'The Statistical Study of Causes of Destitution', *Journal of the American Statistical Association*, 11 (1908), 284.

16. A. A. Tenney, Sociology at Columbia University, L. L. Bernard Papers, p. 7.

17. See Giddings to Odum, 11 Dec., 1924, Howard W. Odum Papers, Southern Historical Collection, Chapel Hill, University of North Carolina Library. Hankins even suggests 'that Giddings thought of himself as a potential Mayor of New York' (Frank H. Hankins, Oral History Collection, Columbia University).

18. John M. Glenn, Lillian Brandt and F. Emerson Andrews, *Russell Sage Foundation, 1907–1946*, vol. I (New York: Russell Sage Foundation, 1947), pp. 4–5.

19. Glenn et al., *Russell Sage Foundation*, p. 8.

20. Giddings simply did not find the idea that the wealthy would serve the cause of genuine reform credible. He expressed his reservations on the subject in a paper, 'The Dangers of Charitable Trusts', published shortly after the establishment of the Russell Sage Foundation, at a time when his academic peers were applauding the prospective contributions of the fund to social change (Glenn et al., *Russell Sage Foundation*, p. 17). The foundations were equally suspicious of Giddings; Lawrence Frank, an ISRR and Rockefeller insider, at the time of the negotiations for the Chicago Local Community Research Grant, insisted that they take care to avoid drilling 'their ideas into their students' heads' in the fashion of Giddings (quoted in Martin Bulmer, *The Chicago School of Sociology: Institutionalization, Diversity, and the Rise of Sociological Research* (Chicago: University of Chicago Press, 1984), p. 142).

21. Devine, *When Social Work Was Young*, p. 73.

22. Quoted in Lowry Nelson, *Rural Sociology: Its Origins and Growth in the United States* (Minneapolis: University of Minnesota Press, 1969), p. 29.

23. The labour problem and its various solutions, such as profit-sharing, trade-unionism, and syndicalism, were interests of Giddings to the end of his life. (See 'An

Intensive Sociology: A Project', *American Journal of Sociology*, 36 (1930), 13). One of the few dissertations to which Giddings wrote an introduction was Louis Levine's *Syndicalism in France*, which had a high reputation among Giddings' students (Ogburn to Odum, 17 April, 1923, Odum Papers).

24. Thomas Jesse Jones, *The Sociology of a New York City Block* (New York: AMS Press, 1968), p. 7.

25. Jones, *City Block*, p. 7.

26. Jones, *City Block*, p. 135.

27. Jones, *City Block*, p. 7.

28. Jones, *City Block*, p. 8.

29. Virtually the same sequence from settlement canvassing to more 'scientific' description is found in H. B. Woolston's *A Study of the Population of Manhattanville* (Studies in History, Economics and Public Law 93 (1909), who cites Jones, Booth, Rowntree, and the Hull House and (Boston) South End House studies. Woolston's approach is more exclusively demographic than Jones', but he treats this as a flaw, and embraces both the ideal of a comprehensive survey and the idea that the aim of the survey is to aid in the creation of a 'comprehensive scheme of betterment' (p. 5) which he thought would best be pursued through socialisation and the schools, but with an eye to local variation in neighbourhood communities. This enterprise is described in the theoretical vocabulary of Giddings as a product of like response to like stimuli (pp. 7–8).

30. Jones, *City Block*, p. 10.

31. Jones, *City Block*, p. 10.

32. Jones, *City Block*, p. 10.

33. Jones, *City Block*, p. 11.

34. Jones, *City Block*, p. 12.

35. Jones, *City Block*, p. 12.

36. Jones, *City Block*, pp. 14–15.

37. Somes of this was based on observation of the house and its contents. Thus drinking habits were indicated by the 'vichy bottle' in the houses of the Jews, the beer-bucket in that of the Irish. Jones, *City Block*, p. 15.

38. Jones, *City Block*, p. 60.

39. Jones, *City Block*, p. 129.

40. Jones, *City Block*, p. 129.

41. Albion Small and George E. Vincent, *An Introduction to the Science of Society* (New York: American Book Co., 1894).

42. An idea with obvious Comtean origins. As a Cambridge student, Pearson had come under the influence of a Comtean librarian.

43. Franklin Henry Giddings, *Inductive Sociology: A Syllabus of Methods, Analyses and Classifications, and Provisionally Formulated Laws* (New York: Macmillan, 1901), p. 181.

44. Giddings, *Inductive Sociology*, pp. 286–90.

45. Giddings, *Inductive Sociology*, p. 75.

46. Giddings, *Inductive Sociology*, p. 175.

47. P. W. Althouse, *The Intellectual Career of F. Stuart Chapin* (New York: Columbia University Press, 1980), p. 228. These systems, on which Chapin himself was put to work, were not so far removed, conceptually, from Chapin's own living-room scale of the late twenties. Some of the examples in *Field Work and Social Research* (New York: Century, 1920), may be seen as an intermediate step (e.g. pp. 148–9). For other historically proximate sources, see Jean Converse, *Survey Research in the United States* (Berkeley: University

of California Press, 1987, pp. 34, 426). It may be noted that Chapin was himself the product of a reform-oriented Brooklyn family which included a former mayor.

48. Franklin H. Giddings, 'Exploration and Survey', *Journal of Social Forces*, 3 (1925), 206.

49. 'Socialisation' in this sense is the theme of the classical studies in rural sociology by Charles J. Galpin. See his *Rural Life* (New York: Century, 1920).

50. Giddings wrote the introduction to the 'methodological' volume in the series, Luther Fry's Columbia dissertation (*Diagnosing the Rural Church: A Study in Method* (New York: George H. Doran, 1924)). In the thirties and later this kind of work was subject to severe criticism on much-overstated grounds as the problem of ecological correlation. The strategy has since revived. The Columbia people were well aware of the difficulties with interpreting partials, as is evident in the volume produced by Stuart Rice's Committee on Social Statistics of the American Statistical Association. See Ogburn, 'Statistical Studies of Marriage and the Family', in Stuart Rice (ed.), *Statistics in Social Studies* (Philadelphia: University of Pennsylvania Press, 1930), p. 29. Nor were they unaware of the problems with what was to be claimed as the solution, the elaboration model. See F. A. Ross, 'The Use of Statistical Data and Techniques in Sociology', in L. L. Bernard (ed.), *The Fields and Methods of Sociology* (New York: Ray Long & Richard R. Smith, 1934), pp. 458–75; p. 469.

51. Suzzalo was himself an educationalist who had taught the first course in Educational Sociology at Columbia, and a prominent figure in foundation circles, especially the Carnegie Foundation.

52. Ogburn to Suzzalo, 10 April, 1919, Presidential Papers, University of Washington Archives, Seattle, Washington.

53. Odum, for example, had at the beginning of his career a position with a municipal bureau in Philadelphia, and continued his relationship with Philadelphia reform groups long after going to North Carolina. This was quite common.

54. The later part of the Jones story is told in Edward H. Berman, 'Educational Colonialism in Africa: the Role of American Foundations, 1910–1945', in Robert F. Amove (ed.), *Philanthropy and Cultural Imperialism* (Boston: G. K. Hall, 1980), pp. 179–201.

55. Ogburn to Odum, 3 May, 1922. Odum Papers.

56. E.g. Ogburn to Odum, 18 January, 1924, Guy B. Johnson and Guion G. Johnson, *Research in Service to Society: The First Fifty Years of the Institute for Research in Social Science at the University of North Carolina* (Chapel Hill: University of North Carolina Press, 1980), pp. 50–1.

57. In a sense, surveys of the Kelloggian sort, which relied very heavily on local professionals for advice and participation, were in effect consensus building devices. The full realisation of the survey as a means of reforms required the support of the leading business and professional classes to make the survey relevant to the community and of course to carry the reforms out. The interests of these groups were ultimately in conflict with the ideas of movement figures like Kellogg, or at least potentially so.

58. Woolston, *Manhattanville*, p. 6.

THE EMERGENCE OF AMERICAN SOCIOLOGY

THE CLASSICAL TRADITION

14

The Work of George Mead

John Dewey

George Mead held while he lived and taught a peculiar position among American teachers of philosophy. He published but little, and that little was of a comparatively scattered and almost fragmentary character. Yet his intellectual influence upon associates and the students in his classes was so profound as to be revolutionary. Moreover, there is something paradoxical as well as peculiar about his work. For his mind, in contrast to his published writings, was of the unifying and systematizing type to an unusual degree. The materials he strove to synthesize were of a remarkable wide range. They extended from the technicalities of physical and biological science to the phenomena of human life, historical, political, economic and cultural. More than any recent thinker whom I can call to mind, he felt that no philosophy can satisfy the demands of the present that does not bring these two seemingly opposed things into a just relation with one another – just, because not permitting one to swallow the other, but allowing each to express itself in its own terms.

Thus the problem that he set himself, unconsciously rather than deliberately, is the most difficult that any thinker can face. He was too well aware of the new conceptions and method of science and the new movements in social life to take the short-cut method of adherence to some one of the types of philosophy that had already been formulated. He thus denied himself the relatively easy recognition that can be obtained by developing further some already established point of view. Yet he was not animated by any zeal for novelty and originality. On the contrary, he was personally given to attributing ideas that he undoubtedly originated to authors from who he had derived suggestions. He was original because of unusual sensitiveness to underlying problems that most philosophers do not feel. This sensitiveness took him into new fields in which absence of established formulas, and of vocabularies made familiar by prior use, made expression difficult. The very scope of his knowledge increased rather than lessened his difficulties. Judicious ignorance is always an aid to simplification. The period in which he taught was one of revolutionary change

---

Source: *The New Republic*, 1936, July 22, pp. 329–330.

in science and one of great social change. Mead was keenly sensitive to these changes, and so aware of their quality that he was not tempted to fit them mechanically into preconceptions, no matter how current and influential the latter had become.

One cannot read any of the volumes[1] now being edited and published by a group of his former students and colleagues without being struck by the central importance he attached to the idea of reconstruction as something continuously going on in nature, in human institutions and in ideas. This idea, as developed in the first published volume, "Mind, Self and Society," exemplifies Mead's sense of the basic problem every significant present philosophy must face: How are we to unite in a coherent way the presence of those relatively settled orders to which the name of all uniformities, laws, universals is given, with the unremitting occurrence of individuality, novelty and the unpredictable? The idea of continuity, of remaking, of reconstruction, was with Mr. Mead more than an idea in any abstract sense of the word; it was an immediate and living feeling. As such it provided the binding thread by which he interpreted the great variety and seeming disparity presented by the movements of nineteenth-century thought.

In one sense, the use he made of this conception allies him closely with that conception of evolution and development which is probably the most characteristic contribution of the period dealt with by "Movements of Thought in the Nineteenth Century." But in another sense, his identification of the process of evolution with that of continuous reconstruction by which nature and man (as a part of nature that has become conscious) solve the problem of the relations of the universal and individual, the regular and the novel – this identification is his own outstanding contribution to philosophy. Mead's sensitiveness – not just in general but in extensive detail – to both sides of the problem explains, I think, the seeming contradiction between the systematizing character of his mind and the systematic nature of his public actions. He was continually engaged in the reconstructive development of his own ideas.

It is impossible for me to give here even a bare outline of the various topics treated by Mead in "Currents of Thought in the Nineteenth Century." Mr. Moore, in the introduction prefixed to the work, has provided its readers with an excellent guide to understanding. There are, however, three general points, all of them connected with what I have just said, to which I would call special attention. One of them is the demonstration of how nineteenth century thought was in continuity with the whole intellectual European tradition, including not merely the ideas of the Renaissance and of the seventeenth century, but those of medieval theologians. The first chapter shows clearly the connection of the scientific postulate as to the intelligibility of nature with earlier theological notions, and brings out the otherwise surprising fact that the emphasis of the Romantic philosophers upon individual consciousness makes explicit the earlier religious idea that nature is but a theatre in which is enacted the drama of the human soul. At the same time, there are clearly portrayed the reconstructive forces that changed dependence upon the authority of the institutional church to dependence on the authority of human reason in knowledge and of the secular community in politics. In the second place, throughout the whole discussion there is exhibited constant correlation between changes in science and those in social institutions and philosophy – two things usually kept in separate compartments.

The third point concerns the main original contribution of Mead's constructive philosophy. He recognizes, with no attempt to explain them away, the facts that have led so much of modern philosophy into subjectivism, but shows that these facts are to be explained in terms of active connection between individual organisms and the world, not in terms of "consciousness," while he shows the importance of the social nature of selves in making possible a common and universal point of view. The concluding chapter, "Individuality in the Nineteenth Century," is worth the most careful study. It alone more than justifies the publication of the volume. I do not know its equal in anything like similar compass for far-reaching suggestiveness.

As the reader will infer from what has been said, the second volume, like its predecessor, does not come directly from the hand of Mead, but is the result of editing, from stenographic reports, lectures given by him at Chicago. As the editor indicates in his preface, there is no guarantee that the text states exactly what Mead would have said if he had himself given the volume its final form. While doubtless the work suffers from some defects on this account, nevertheless there are compensations. The lecture is more conducive to excursions and side-remarks than is the studied form of the published book. The variety of Mead's interests and the range of his knowledge were so great that there is hardly a page not enriched by some suggestion, comparison or comment that might not have found its way into a more formal treatment. Everyone interested in philosophic thought that is profoundly original and productive of creative thought in others, as well as grounded in genuine scholarship, cannot be too grateful for the intellectual piety that has made available to a wider public the wealth of ideas and of knowledge that Mead conveyed to his own students. It would be difficult to find a work that displays such constant respect for scientific method and for human values as do these books, and that connects them together so integrally without either apologetics, forced sacrifice or sentimentality.

Note

1. *Mind, Self and Society*, by George H. Mead. The University of Chicago Press. 439 pages. $5. *Movements of Thought in the Nineteenth Century*, by George H. Mead. The University of Chicago Press. 558 pages. $5.

15

The Chicago School of Sociology: What Made it a "School"?

Martin Bulmer

Why, during the 1920s, was the University of Chicago such a creative center for the growth of the Chicago School of Sociology? How and why, between 1915 and 1935, did sociology flourish so notably on the Midway at a university which, since its foundation in 1892, had exercised a quite disproportionate influence upon the development of the social sciences in the United States? Not only was Chicago the leading center of sociology in the world at this period, but the hallmark of the department's approach was one of broad, collective intellectual endeavor. Nor was sociology unique. The Chicago school of philosophy, founded by John Dewey, was at the height of its influence. The Chicago school of political science was gaining in strength and reputation. The Chicago school of economics was over the horizon.

Schools of social science, particularly those committed to systematic empirical inquiry, are sufficiently unusual to merit some consideration. Most university departments of sociology are an assemblage of more or less independent scholars, pursuing diverse interests either individually or in small groups. They cooperate for purposes of teaching and administration, but in research go their own way. Any suggestion that there should be an integrated research program across a department, or that individuals should orient their research to certain central themes, ideas or problems, would be regarded by most academic sociologists as anathema. Yet such a collective enterprise was the Durkheim school (Besnard, 1983). In social anthropology, the "schools" associated with Bronislaw Malinowski at the London School of Economics in the 1920s and 1930s, and with Max Gluckman at the Rhodes–Livingstone Institute in Northern Rhodesia and the University of Manchester in the 1940s and 1950s produced much significant work (Kuper, 1983: 1–35, 142–155). Although this paper is primarily concerned with Chicago sociology, it casts glances at these other "schools."

A "school" in the social sciences may be thought of as akin to the term used in art history to designate a group of contemporaries sharing a certain style,

Source: *History of Sociology*, 1985, vol. 5, no. 2, pp. 61–77.

technique or set of symbolic expressions, and having at some point or other in time or space a high degree of interaction (e.g., the Impressionists, the Bauhaus School, etc.). A local example would be the Chicago School of Architecture, centered on Louis Sullivan and Frank Lloyd Wright (Condit, 1964; Duncan, 1965; Siegel, 1969: 3–26).

Several ideal-typical characteristics may be seen to distinguish a school of social science. It has a founder-leader and his/her followers, usually ranging in size from one to three dozen members. This leader has a relatively dominating personality. Its members are usually drawn together by a set of ideas, beliefs and normative dispositions, articulated by the founder-leader, which are somewhat at odds with those prevailing in the discipline at the time. A school typically seeks to modernize or renovate the discipline. It consists of

> a scientific community integrated around a central figure, an intellectual charismatic leader, and a paradigm of empirical reality which is subject to investigation. The paradigm's core formulations are those of the founder-leader, but the full-blown paradigm is typically a collective enterprise, fashioned by the founder-leader and his immediate entourage (Tiryakian, 1979: 218–219).

Schools flourish in settings with an institutional affiliation, typically an academic site of general excellence in a great metropolitan area. A journal, review or other means of regularly publishing research is required to communicate with a wider scholarly public, as well as to integrate the activities of dispersed members of the school. A school is thus considerably more than a collection of distinguished individual scholars working in a leading department. It implies the existence of collaborative scholarly activity integrated through the work of one or more leading figures in the school.

The term "school" is not used in this paper in two other senses, to refer to schools of thought or to posthumous followers of a particular sociologist. Sorokin, for example, in *Contemporary Sociological Theories* (1928) treated as belonging to a school of thought social scientists who might be separated in time and/or space but shared a recognizably common approach, theory or method, even if they never had contact with one another. This is quite different usage, which stretches the term to the point of credibility. A different usage is the "Le Play School" of Patrick Geddes and Victor Branford in Britain in the early years of the twentieth century (Silver, 1982: 123–124; Abrams, 1968: 101–120; Kitchen, 1975; Boardman 1978; Mumford, 1982; Bulmer, 1984b). Starting long after Le Play's death Geddes and Branford believed that they were creating a group, centered eventually at Le Play House in London, which would carry forward his ideas. The usage of "school" in this paper refers to a collectivity existing at the same time and place as the dominant figure, usually involving a high degree of face to face contact and personal ties between members of the group.

The earliest use of the term "Chicago school" appears to be by L.L. Bernard (1930: 133) though the term was not in use at the University of Chicago in the 1920s (Cavan, 1983: 408). The existence of the Chicago school is documented in a number of standard histories, such as Faris (1970), Carey (1975) and Raushenbush (1979), many of the volumes of the Heritage series (particularly Short, 1971), and in Fred Matthews' illuminating biography of Robert Park (1977) which includes the term in its subtitle. Shils (1970, 1980) discusses this among the other characteristics of Chicago sociology, but from the slightly different perspective of the academic institutionalization of the discipline, which does not require the formation of schools to be effective. Tiryakian (1979: 226–228) makes some brief suggestive comments, while Wiley (1979) takes the integration of the school for granted and compares it to other leading departments of the period.

Nine features can be identified as contributing to the creation and sustenance of the Chicago school of sociology. Some of these have been identified by previous writers on the subject, others have not. The focus of this discussion is upon the conditions leading to the formation of a school, not to other aspects of Chicago sociology (as, for example, in Lewis & Smith, 1980; Bennett, 1981; or Thomas, 1983).

A school requires a central figure around whom it is organized. Durkheim, Malinowski, and Gluckman were individuals by whom their research group was led and which gave it its identity. Yet the ideal type does not allow for joint leadership. This was the case in the Chicago school. The time period with which we are concerned is loosely thought of as the 1920s, but may in fact be extended back to 1913, when Robert Park joined W.I. Thomas in the Chicago department and worked with him until Thomas' dismissal in 1918 (Janowitz, 1966:xiv–xvi). Thomas was the intellectual progenitor of empirical inquiry in the Chicago department, an important theorist, and one whose mark both through his association with Park and through the influence of his writings carried through into the 1920s. The research interests of Thomas and Park overlapped particularly closely in the fields of race and ethnicity, and after 1918 they completed together, as part of the Carnegie Americanization project, the monograph *Old World Traits Transplanted* (Park & Miller, 1921), though Thomas' collaboration could not be acknowledged on publication and was only revealed thirty years later. Robert Park was the central and leading figure of the Chicago school but these early fruitful years in harness with Thomas are often overlooked. Park himself was quite clear about their importance, as he acknowledged explicitly in 1939 to the Society for Social Research (Kurtz, 1982; Bulmer, 1983).

After 1918, Park and Ernest Burgess were closely identified, sharing an office in the east tower of the Harper Library and planning together the program of urban studies which is one of the school's hallmarks (Burgess, 1964; Cottrell, 1973). The particular contribution Burgess made was as mainstay and facilitator of the empirical research. Without him, Park's ideas would probably not have been transformed into research of substance (Bulmer, 1984a). Leadership of the school was thus shared, first between Thomas and Park, then between Park and Burgess. Park's was the dominant contribution and intellect, but the case is a reminder that there may be one or two key figures at the head of a school. The genesis of the Chicago school of economics during the 1930s under Frank Knight and Jacob Viner is another interesting case of a school with dual leadership.

Schools of sociology are phenomena of the academic world. They exist in universities and require students as a necessary and integral part of their activity. The second characteristic of the Chicago school was that its university location was particularly propitious for the fostering of serious intellectual activity. From its foundation in 1892, the University of Chicago placed particular emphasis upon the performance of research and standards of scholarship. Significant research was expected from its faculty and publication was fostered. Greater importance was attached to training graduates in research than to undergraduate teaching than was common in universities in the English-speaking world. At the outset, and even in the 1920s, it faced little competition from the reformed colleges of Oxford and Cambridge, the numerous undergraduate colleges across North America, or even the colleges of distinguished universities such as Yale and Harvard. Sociology, for example, was only established at Harvard in 1930, and languished at Yale under Sumner's successor, who only taught undergraduates. The ecology of scholarship at Chicago was also of significance and fostered intellectual exchange (Shils, 1970). Most members of the university lived on or near the campus. The sociologists shared buildings for teaching and research, and after 1929 a single building (1126) which housed all the social sciences.

The tendency of Chicago to produce schools – academically of sociology, political science and economics, culturally of architecture and literature – may also be accounted for in terms of the distinguishing qualities of the city and the university's relation to it. The university was not isolated from the city in which it was located. Members of the university staff were heavily involved in local affairs from the beginning, providing an orientation and a set of connections which helped stimulate local research (Diner, 1980; Carey, 1975; Hunter, 1980). Park's involvement in the Chicago Urban League, for example, led directly to the appointment of Charles Johnson as research director for the riot commission, and his collaboration with Park that produced *The Negro in Chicago* (Chicago Commission, 1922; Bulmer, 1981a).

The local community was the focus of almost all research in sociology and political science during the 1920s. This gave those involved a delimited frame within which to work. Park and Burgess' program of urban research, in many ways rather diffuse and unfocused, gained coherence and importance from being carried out within a specific local setting. Similarly, Merriam's pioneering political science surveys were made manageable (and to some extent sidestepped sampling problems) by being studies of political behavior within the city (Karl, 1974: 140–156).

It has also been suggested that as a city Chicago has been more tolerant of intellectual diversity than New York City.

> The great good fortune of our university was that it was not established on the East Coast. . . . Fortunately we were established in Chicago, a new, raw city, bursting with energy, far less sophisticated than New York, but for that very reason far more tolerant of diversity, of heterodox ideas. . . . Chicago [was] characterized by diversity in every dimension, by a willingness to experiment, to judge people by their performance rather than their origins, to judge ideas by their consequences rather than their antecedents (Friedman, 1974: 7).

Thus it could foster at a later period a school of economics whose major tenets were at variance with those of major universities on the east coast. Certainly the Chicago base seemed to stimulate W.I. Thomas to heights he never achieved after 1918 when living in New York. Willard Waller, at a later period, dissipated most of his scholarly energies when he moved to New York City (Goode, 1970:viii–ix). Lasswell never subsequently achieved the heights he reached at Chicago after he departed in 1938 (Shils, 1981).

These general qualities of university and city could only be necessary, not sufficient, conditions. A fourth characteristic of the Chicago school, as of other schools, was the dominating personality of its key figure, Robert Park. Thomas alone would not have created the Chicago school, and after Park's retirement in 1934, Burgess alone could not sustain it. One of the common characteristics of the leaders of schools of social science in Chicago was inspiring and effective teachers. Park aroused the curiosity of his students, built on their capacities, and pushed them toward the empirical study of phenomena in which he was interested, complemented by Burgess' more practical skills. Charles Merriam in political science did not have Park's intellectual curiosity or sharp insight. At the core of his thought, there was a rhetorical element which diminished its impact. But he was able to seek that quality of curiosity in others such as Harold Lasswell and Harold Gosnell, and foster it. Coupled with his vision of a quantitative, scientific, political science, and his administrative and organizational capability (which was far superior to Park), he created single-handed the school of political science. "It was the *department* which engaged in research and the projects announced to the profession at various times were referred to as departmental enterprises. Junior members were not distinguished from senior members in such announcements, and joint citations were the custom. The Chicago department was conceived of by Merriam as a community of research" (Karl, 1974: 145). In economics slightly later, Frank Knight gathered about him an informal group of students and protegés, including Henry Simons, Milton Friedman, Aaron Director, George Stigler and Allen Wallis, which in time came to constitute a school (Reder, 1982: 5–6).

Academic leaders such as Park commanded personal loyalty and admiration of their colleagues and students. They maintained integration within the department and prevented fission. They looked for talented collaborators to participate in the research they conducted. Dominance, however, did not mean at all that students were expected to reproduce the views of their teacher. There was a degree of openness about the Chicago schools of sociology and political science which in part explains their success. Park provided a loose framework for research in his essay on "The City" in 1915 which Burgess developed with the theory of concentric zones (Park & Burgess, 1925). Within this, students were encouraged to investigate undogmatically. Merriam's framework was more in the nature of a general methodological orientation, but with this same quality of openness. The contrast could not be greater with those who were not successful in promoting sociology, such as Franklin Giddings, head until 1927 of the sociology department at Columbia, which rivalled Chicago in the early years of the century, but which by the 1920s was but a pale shadow.

> His personal dogmatism, conceit and prejudices alienated many prominent and influential members of the Columbia faculty, who saw to it that sociology would not be expanded there before Giddings retired. Giddings himself contributed to it by surrounding himself with second-rate men who were no threat to his leadership. According to those who knew him personally, he was anti-Semitic and had poor relations with outstanding Columbia social scientists like Boas and Seligman because they were Jewish (Oberschall, 1972: 226).

Park, by contrast, was infinitely curious about the relevance of ideas from other disciplines for sociology, on cordial personal relations with colleagues in other departments, and through his interest in ethnic groups was free from many of the conventional prejudices of the time. It was no accident that two of the most outstanding early black sociologists, Charles S. Johnson and E. Franklin Frazier, were his students. The contrast between Park and Giddings exemplifies the point that the leader of a school must command respect and affection without stamping out intellectual originality and creativity in his students and protegés.

The most important characteristic of the leader or leaders of a school is that they should possess a clear intellectual vision and missionary drive. That it comes fifth does not diminish its overriding importance. A school requires a coherent and distinguishable intellectual framework at its core which may be provided by a new theory or theories, and/or new methods of research and/or a strong commitment to a particular type of empirical inquiry. At the heart of any academic school are one or two individuals with a body of ideas or a compelling vision which attracts others, binds the group together, and gives it a greater degree of intellectual cohesion than is usual among colleagues in academic social science departments. A school is ultimately the product of that personal quality of intellectual passion or self-confidence which emanates from one or two individuals who stand out at some distance from their colleagues. The dependence of schools upon their leading figures is very striking. Albion Small created the conditions after 1892, but it was not until Thomas brought Park to Chicago in 1913 that the Chicago school began to develop. In Merriam's case the start was even less propitious, due to an antagonism with the university president (who was also head of the political science department), until 1923.

Intellectual dominance could take various forms. Later schools such as those of Malinowski and Gluckman had a more explicit theory at their center than in the case of those around Park and around Merriam. Chicago sociology and political science had nevertheless an implicit general theory and a clear intellectual vision. In sociology several elements were distinctive. Park's general ideas about social process and social control were linked with ecological theory to focus upon the city. The processes of competition, conflict accommodation and assimilation were of central concern, and could be used to explain the "natural history" of particular groups (Turner, 1967; Coser, 1978). Burgess' formulation of the concentric zones hypothesis, and classification of the metropolis into 75 natural areas, identified the milieux in which studies could be conducted (Hunter, 1974). The metaphor of the city as a social laboratory provided the methodological rationale for a series of intensive field studies. Chicago sociology bore the marks of Park's origins as a newspaperman – Park sought no Malinowskian theoretical synthesis, for example – but nevertheless there were quite strong theoretical elements implicit in his approach.

The term "school" sometimes has connotations of a clique or a cult. Certainly it usually involves the members' acceptance of the central ideas of the leading figure(s), which are usually distinct from those prevailing in the discipline at the time. A school must therefore lay claim to originality in the ideas or approach it adopts. A certain passion is also necessary, a belief that prevailing ideas or approaches lack the purchase upon the social world that the school's approach embodies. Yet a breadth of vision, rather than narrowness, is also a prerequisite, and this the groups of scholars around Park and Merriam possessed. In the case of Chicago sociology, some of the lack of constraint was due to the looseness of Park's theory and the freedom of students to investigate widely varying types of urban life in very different milieux, as extreme as the Gold Coast and the slum.

Next in importance to intellectual vision is a sixth characteristic, the gravity, seriousness and intensity of the intellectual exchanges between the leader and other members of the group, whether these are colleagues or graduate students. Such scholarly networks are more closely-knit than is usual in academic departments or disciplines. In relation to graduate students, the leader may display a caring attitude such as that displayed by Frank Knight to Chicago economists, Malinowski and Gluckman to their anthropology students. The qualities to be developed in students are the ability to understand, apply and develop further the central tenets of the school in an original way. This does not entail parrotting the ideas of a leader but developing them creatively and moving beyond some initial formulation. Lasswell did this in relation to Merriam, Mauss and Halbwachs in relation to Durkheim. The process, however, is one which involves intense and serious discussion carried out over a long period of time.

The institutional arrangements by which this is achieved vary somewhat, but two elements are of major importance: the existence of seminars where ideas and approaches are developed and applied, and the availability of avenues for the publication of the work of the school. The most famous seminar was perhaps that of Malinowski, described by one of its participants, Audrey Richards:

> These weekly discussions became famous, and attracted students of the most different types. Colonial officials on leave valued his live approach, if they were not too much alarmed by his question-and-answer method of teaching. Senior research students came from many parts of the world, and Malinowski would often flash retorts in four or five different languages. University lecturers sat side-by-side with the veriest amateurs. These seminars varied, but at their best they were brilliant performances. Malinowski was a man of wide culture and great personal charm. He could be provocative and prejudiced, but he could also be profound, penetrating and constructive. His wit was proverbial. There was a curious kindling touch in all that he did, and a rare power of evoking ideas in others. His directness forced students to get to the bottom of a problem and express its essentials simply (1943: 3).

For Chicago economists, the crucible in which graduate students in the 1930s received their professional induction was Jacob Viner's tough, demanding and rigorous graduate course 301 on economic principles (Reder, 1982: 8–9). In sociology, Park and Burgess' seminar on Field Studies from 1918 onwards played a similar role (Bulmer, 1984a).

Formal seminars were not the only setting however. The importance of the Society for Social Research in fostering links between staff and students and – through its Summer Institute – with former students, has recently become apparent (Bulmer, 1983). Local Community Research seminars (Bulmer, 1980), the Greek letter societies, the Sociology Club, and involvement in first-hand empirical research also reinforced these ties between teachers and students. This contributed to the sense of intellectual seriousness among the student body. Sociology graduate students of the period have testified to the extent to which they "lived sociology" and were preoccupied with their studies much of the time (Carey, 1975: 153–159). The small size of the teaching staff made contact with teachers straightforward. Park in particular was always conferring with students. It is not generally appreciated what an inordinate amount of time Park spent with his students advising them how to write and helping them to rewrite and polish their work. Indeed one reason he wrote so little himself was the time he spent doing this.

> Park saw himself as a captain of inquiry with a company of men and women who must be directed to a worthwhile topic. . . . [His] involvement with his students was unsystematic but often extensive, and contributed much to the great admiration with which many of them recalled him. If a student or a topic seemed promising, Park arranged long interviews in which the subject was defined, methods were discussed, and the student's own experience and concerns were integrated with his research topic. . . . Some students were treated to field trips, strolls through Chicago on which Park mused on the significance of what they saw; others recalled casual encounters in the street which became long discussions of the student's work. . . . Colleagues as well as students recalled the long conversations, sometimes continued from one day to another, in which Park, pacing the floor, tried to clarify his or their ideas. His assistant often listened to these talks, noting down the more promising ideas for further development. These conversations, or monologues, roved over concrete categories of investigations and the lives, interests and peculiarities of people; but they also tried to connect the concrete data with coherent social theory. . . .
>
> While Park gave his time lavishly, not only in interviews and tours of exploration but in dinners for students and extensive loan of books, his principal concern was the project and not the student. Although many students seem to have adopted him as Honorable Ancestor, his attitude was more that of the city editor – pushing, suggesting, inquiring, needling, rewriting, scolding – than that of a father or guidance counselor (Matthews, 1977: 107–109).

Publication of the work of the school is the other means by which intense intellectual interchange is achieved. The prime example of this, indeed the means by which his school was created, is the role played by Durkheim's journal *L'Année Sociologique*. The process of contributing to and editing this publication, in which book reviews of other sociological work were a very major feature, was the chief means by which Durkheim built up a scholarly network (Besnard, 1983: 11–39). The members of the group scarcely ever met together. Drawn from a variety of disciplines, some seemed to be unaware of each other's existence. This reliance on publication as a means of integrating the school is unusual.

More common is the role of publication, first, in providing a focus for guidance on the completion of work, and, second, guaranteeing its dissemination to a wider scholarly audience. The second point is most usually seized upon. Chicago enjoyed advantages in that the *American Journal of Sociology* was edited there and the University of Chicago Sociological Series provided an outlet for the best Ph.D.s to be published. Park and Burgess' textbook (1921), the "green bible" was its first title, is generally credited with spreading the Chicago approach to other departments across the country. The first point, however, is much the more interesting. Nels Anderson, for example, has described (1975) how Burgess and Park gave him detailed advice upon how to revise and rewrite the manuscript which was published as *The Hobo* (Anderson, 1923), the first monograph in the series. Park and Burgess were unstinting in their help to students to fashion their ideas and results into publishable form, often pushing them beyond what they might have accomplished otherwise (Matthews, 1977: 109).

Publication arrangements provide a reminder of the seventh characteristic of schools which engage in empirical research, that they require an adequate infrastructure. This infrastructure is composed of several elements of rather different kinds. A common characteristic of the schools of Park, Merriam, Malinowski and Gluckman was that they made considerable advances in research method. Park's students pioneered the multi-method study of small social milieux, Merriam's the modern political science survey, Malinowski's ethnographic involvement in a strange society and Gluckman's the extended case method and situational analysis. The advancement of an empirical school of social science depends upon effective methods of research as well as good ideas, and a pioneering role as a consequence. The variety of methods used at Chicago in the 1920s has been obscured by the assimilation of Chicago sociology to symbolic interactionism (Rock, 1979). In fact, quantitative methods were also used (Bulmer, 1981b) and the belief in them embodied on the exterior of the Social Science Building opened in 1929:

"When you cannot measure * your knowledge * is * meagre * and * unsatisfactory * Lord Kelvin."

Certain institutional links were also of considerable significance. The existence of publication outlets has already been mentioned. Albion Small founded the *American Journal of Sociology* and it continued to be run by the department. The existence of the University of Chicago Press, with which Park and Burgess initiated a publication program, was also important. Association with adjunct institutions, such as the Institute for Juvenile Research, the Juvenile Protective Association and the Chicago Crime Commission, to which students could be attached, provided valuable outside contacts. In Malinowski's case the International African Institute and in Gluckman's the Rhodes-Livingstone Institute in Northern Rhodesia provided a more embracing structure for the promotion of empirical inquiry (Kuper, 1983: 32; Brown, 1979). In Chicago the Local Community Research Committee funded a considerable proportion of the sociological research (Bulmer, 1980).

This directs attention to the important role played by outside financial support in making schools of empirical social science possible. In the case of

Chicago the Laura Spelman Rockefeller Memorial was of pre-eminent importance (Bulmer & Bulmer, 1981), though other sources also contributed (Smith & White, 1929: 33–46). To what extent did such support nurture the Chicago schools? Lack of support could clearly be a decisive obstacle, as DuBois' earlier attempts at Atlanta to initiate serious research on black Americans showed. Malinowski in the 1930s obtained support from the Rockefeller Foundation for the International African Institute and used it as a means of supporting his students in the field. Gluckman's students shared in the awards of the Colonial Social Science Research Council, and at Manchester had access to special funds in the form of Simon Fellowships.

Such outside funds could be used to provide student's grants, meet fieldwork expenses, and pay for writing up after withdrawal from the field. At Chicago they were also used to provide replacement teaching to release staff for full-time research, the employment of research assistants, provision of clerical and statistical help, and subsidy of publication (Bulmer, 1980). Controversy will continue to rage over the social role of philanthropic foundations in social science in the twentieth century, but it is clear that their support was a necessary condition for the flowering of empirical research in the 1920s and 1930s under the direction of Robert Park in sociology, Charles Merriam in political science and Bronislaw Malinowski in anthropology.

Schools do not last beyond the generation of their founders. This is their eighth characteristic. Several of the reasons for their existence ensure that after their leader or leaders decline, retire or die, the school is unlikely to continue long on its former path. At Chicago, the decline of sociology began in the early 1930s, and within a decade both Harvard (where Parsons was increasingly influential) and Columbia (where Lazarsfeld and Merton were in partnership) rivaled Chicago as leading departments (Kuklick, 1973; Wiley, 1979). The controversy over the American Sociological Society and the founding of the *American Sociological Review* in 1936 (Lengermann, 1979) signaled the change, but it began earlier even before Park retired in 1934 and went to live at Fisk.

The Chicago school was built around Park, but he did little to ensure its survival. Most of his students moved on to teaching positions elsewhere. Chicago sociology was influential throughout the mid-west and the rest of the United States, but the originality of its perspective was waning. The department failed to maintain its cohesion, and failed to recruit sociologists familiar with European social theory or new fields such as organizational sociology or media research where Harvard and Columbia were strong. Burgess was occupied with the sociology of the family, Ogburn with *Recent Social Trends* and (slightly later) Stouffer with methodology and migration. They were not able to provide departmental leadership. The mantle of Park passed to Everett Hughes, who returned from McGill in 1938, but by then the original Chicago school had had its day.

So too in other cases: Charles Merriam's group of political scientists had its heyday in the 1930s, but university president Robert M. Hutchins, by denying them promotion, encouraged Harold Lasswell and Harold Gosnell to leave Chicago for the east coast. The school did not survive Merriam's retirement. Malinowski's group at the London School of Economics broke up in 1939 when Malinowski left for Mexico, not to return, partly due to internal disagreements. The local influence of other dominant social scientists – for example Lazarsfeld at Columbia, Max Gluckman at Manchester – was dissipated almost immediately after their deaths. An interesting exception to this generalization is the Chicago school of economics, which has endured over a longer period. Although it did not really come into existence until the 1940s and 1950s, it was never so dependent as sociology and political science on one or two individuals throughout. It had more of a collective leadership (Reder, 1982; Patinkin, 1981, ch. 1).

One must distinguish clearly between the survival of a school and the survival of a particular sociologist's ideas and approach. The former is extremely rare, the latter more common. The institutional arrangements centered on one or two individuals do not have an infinite existence because of the limited reach of innovatory ideas, the inability of a single approach to regenerate itself from within, and generational change in academic life which ensures that the successors to powerful elderly professors do not aspire to fashion the department in their predecessor's image. The very rarity of schools of social science, moreover, suggests their relative fragility. The preservation of a close-knit group of like-minded scholars within a single department for more than fifteen to twenty years is altogether exceptional.

A final characteristic of schools in social sciences, other than economics, is their openness to ideas and influences from other disciplines. There is an institutional danger in exaggerating the closure achieved by a school. As a structure, it is an informal group based on intellectual affinity reinforced by particularistic and affective ties. Unlike a university faculty or department, it has no legally constituted continuing existence, no offices to be filled, no clearly defined roles (particularly when succession is at issue). Successful schools of empirical social science have been remarkably open to the stimulus of cross-fertilization from other disciplines. As leaders of schools, Park, Merriam, Malinowski and Gluckman all maintained extensive interdisciplinary contacts. The Durkheimians, for all the image of their leader as the prophet of sociologism, constituted a veritable interdisciplinary program (Besnard, 1983: 27). Park drew particularly on ideas from biology, literature and anthropology; Merriam from psychology and statistics; Malinowski from biology and economics; and Gluckman from law and sociology. Academic disciplines have tendencies to be inward looking. It is an hypothesis that the fertility of certain schools owed to their ability to overcome this tendency.

The search for common elements should not be pushed too far. There are also important differences between them: in intellectual content; in the personalities of the leading figures; in the way in which the school is institutionalized and the means by which intensity is sustained; in the extent of its domination within a particular discipline; and the standing, nationally or internationally, of the university at which the school is located. The comparison made here between the Chicago school of sociology and certain other schools of social science nevertheless suggests certain hypotheses for further examination. There are also pointers to some of the roots of the creativity of the Chicago school of sociology itself. Like a rare and fragile plant, it emerged, grew to full strength and then wasted away. What is certain is that such unusual occurrences are spontaneous events, which cannot be planned for or anticipated.

References

Otherwise unsubstantiated statements about the Chicago school in this paper are documented in Bulmer (1984a).

Abrams, P. 1968 *The Origins of British Sociology 1834–1914.* Chicago: University of Chicago Press.

Anderson, N. 1923 *The Hobo: The Sociology of the Homeless Man.* Chicago: University of Chicago Press.

Anderson, N. 1975 *The American Hobo: An Autobiography.* Leiden: E.J. Brill.

Bennett, J. 1981 *Oral History and Delinquency: The Rhetoric of Criminology.* Chicago: University of Chicago Press.

Bernard, L.L. 1930 "Schools of Sociology." *Southwestern Political & Social Science Quarterly* 11 (September).

Besnard, P. (ed.) no date *The Sociological Domain: The Durkheimians and the Founding of French Sociology.* Cambridge: Cambridge University Press.

Boardman, P. 1978 *The Words of Patrick Geddes: Biologist, Town Planner, Re-educator, Peace-warrior.* London: Routledge & Kegan Paul.

Brown, R. 1979 "Passages in the Life of a White Anthropologist: Max Gluckman in Northern Rhodesia." *Journal of African History* 20: 525–541.

Bulmer, M. 1980 "The Early Institutionalization of Social Science Research: The Local Community Research Committee at the University of Chicago 1923–30." *Minerva* 18: 51–110.

Bulmer, M. 1981a "Charles S. Johnson, Robert E. Park and the Research Methods of the Chicago Commission on Race Relations, 1920–1922: An Early Experiment in Applied Social Research." *Ethnic and Racial Studies* 4: 289–306.

Bulmer, M. 1981b "Quantification and Chicago Social Science in the 1920s: A Neglected Tradition." *Journal of the History of the Behavioral Sciences* 17: 312–331.

Bulmer, M. 1983a "The Society for Social Research: An Institutional Underpinning to the Chicago School of Sociology." *Urban Life* 11: 421–439.

Bulmer, M. 1983b "Chicago Sociology and the Society for Social Research: A Comment." *Journal of the History of the Behavioral Sciences* 19: 353–356.

Bulmer, M. 1984a *The Chicago School of Sociology: Institutionalization, Diversity and the Rise of Sociological Research.* Chicago: University of Chicago Press.

Bulmer, M. (ed.) 1984b *Essays on the History of British Sociological Research.* Cambridge: Cambridge University Press.

Bulmer, M. and J. Bulmer 1981 "Philanthropy and Social Science in the 1920s: The case of Beardsley Ruml and the Laura Spelman Rockefeller Memorial 1922-1929." *Minerva* 19: 347-407.
Burgess, E.W. 1964 "Research in Urban Society: A Long View." Pp. 2-13 in E.W. Burgess and D.J. Bogue (eds.), *Urban Sociology.* Chicago: University of Chicago Press.
Carey, J.T. 1975 *Sociology and Public Affairs: The Chicago School.* Beverly Hills: Sage.
Cavan, R.S. 1983 "The Chicago School of Sociology, 1918-1933." *Urban Life* 11: 406-420.
Chicago Commission on Race Relations 1922 *The Negro in Chicago.* Chicago: University of Chicago Press.
Condit, C.W. 1964 *The Chicago School of Architecture.* Chicago: University of Chicago Press.
Coser, L.A. 1978 "American Trends." Pp. 287-320 in T.B. Bottomore and R. Nisbet (eds.), *A History of Sociological Analysis.* London: Heinemann.
Cottrell, L.S., Jr., A. Hunter and J.F. Short, Jr. (eds.) 1973 *Ernest W. Burgess on Community, Family and Delinquency.* Chicago: University of Chicago Press.
Diner, S.J. 1980 *A City and its Universities: Public Policy in Chicago 1892-1919.* Chapel Hill: University of North Carolina Press.
Duncan, H.D. 1965 *Culture and Democracy: The Struggle for Form in Society and Architecture in Chicago and the Middle West During the Life and Times of Louis H. Sullivan.* Totowa, NJ: The Bedminster Press.
Faris, R.E.L. 1970 *Chicago Sociology, 1920-1932.* Chicago: University of Chicago Press.
Friedman, M. 1974 "Remarks at the 54th Annual Board of Trustees' Dinner for the Faculty." *University of Chicago Record* 8 (1): 3-7.
Goode, W.J., F. Furstenberg, Jr, and L.R. Mitchell (eds.) 1973 *Willard W. Waller on the Family, Education and War: Selected Writings.* Chicago: University of Chicago Press.
Hunter, A. 1974 *Symbolic Communities: The Persistence and Change of Chicago's Local Communities.* Chicago: University of Chicago Press.
Hunter, A. 1980 "Why Chicago? The Rise of the Chicago School of Urban Social Science." *American Behavioral Scientist* 24: 215-227.
Janowitz, M. (ed.) 1966 *William I. Thomas on Social Organization and Social Personality.* Chicago: University of Chicago Press.
Karl, B.D. 1974 *Charles E. Merriam and the Study of Politics.* Chicago: University of Chicago Press.
Kitchen, P. 1975 *A Most Unsettling Person: An Introduction to the Ideas and Life of Patrick Geddes.* London: Gollancz.
Kuklick, H. 1973 "A 'Scientific Revolution': Sociological Theory in the United States, 1930-1945." *Sociological Inquiry* 43: 3-22.
Kuper, A. 1983 *Anthropology and Anthropologists: The British School.* London: Routledge & Kegan Paul.
Kurtz, L.R. 1982 "Robert E. Park's 'Notes on the Origin of the Society for Social Research.'" *Journal of the History of the Behavioral Sciences* 18: 332-340.
Lengermann, P. 1979 "The Founding of the *American Sociological Review:* The Anatomy of a Rebellion." *American Sociological Review* 44: 185-198.
Lewis, J.D. and R.L. Smith 1980 *American Sociology and Pragmatism: Mead, Chicago Sociology and Symbolic Interaction.* Chicago: University of Chicago Press.
Matthews, F.H. 1977 *Quest for an American Sociology: Robert E. Park and the Chicago School,* Montreal: McGill-Queens University Press.

Mumford, L. 1982 *Sketches From Life: The Autobiography of Lewis Mumford – The Early Years.* New York: Dial Press.
Oberschall. A. 1972 "The Institutionalization of American Sociology." Pp. 187–251 in A. Oberschall (ed.), *The Establishment of Empirical Sociology.* New York: Harper & Row.
Park, R.E. and E.W. Burgess 1921 *Introduction to the Science of Sociology.* Chicago: University of Chicago Press.
Park, R.E. and E.W. Burgess 1925 *The City.* Chicago: University of Chicago Press.
Park, R.E. and H.A. Miller 1921 *Old World Traits Transplanted.* New York: Harper.
Patinkin, D. 1981 *Essays On and In the Chicago Tradition.* Durham, NC: Duke University Press.
Raushenbush, W. 1979 *Robert E. Park: Biography of a Sociologist.* Durham, NC: Duke University Press.
Reder, M.W. 1982 "Chicago Economics: Permanence and Change." *Journal of Economic Literature* 20: 1–38.
Richards, A. 1943 "Bronislaw Kaspar Malinowski, 1884–1942." *Man* 43: 1–4.
Rock, P. 1979 *The Making of Symbolic Interactionism.* London: Macmillan.
Shils, E. 1970 "Tradition, Ecology and Institution in the History of Sociology." *Daedalus* 99: 760–825.
Shils, E. 1980 *The Calling of Sociology and Other Essays on the Pursuit of Learning.* Chicago: University of Chicago Press.
Shils, E. 1981 "Some Academics – Mainly in Chicago." *The American Scholar.* Spring, pp.179–196.
Short, J,F., Jr, (ed.) 1971 *The Social Fabric of the Metropolis: Contributions of the Chicago School of Urban Sociology.* Chicago: University of Chicago Press.
Siegel, A. (ed.) 1969 *Chicago's Famous Buildings.* Chicago: University of Chicago Press.
Silver, C.B. 1982 *Frederic Le Play on Family, Work and Social Change.* Chicago: University of Chicago Press.
Sorokin, P.A. 1928 *Contemporary Sociological Theories.* New York: Harper.
Smith, T.V. and L.D. White (eds.) 1929 *Chicago: An Experiment in Social Science Research.* Chicago: University of Chicago Press.
Thomas, J. (ed.) 1983 "The Chicago School: The Tradition and the Legacy." Special issue of *Urban Life* 11 (4) : 387–527.
Tiryakian, E.A. 1979 "The Significance of Schools in the Development of Sociology." In W.E. Snizek, E.R. Fuhrman and M.K. Miller (eds.), *Contemporary Issues in Theory and Research: A Metasociological Perspective.* Westport, CT: Greenwood Press.
Turner, R. (ed.) 1967 (ed.) *Robert E. Park on Social Control and Collective Behavior.* Chicago: University of Chicago Press.
Wiley, N. 1979 "The Rise and Fall of Dominating Theories in American Sociology." Pp. 47–79 in W.E. Snizek, E.R. Fuhrman and M.K. Miller (eds.), *Contemporary Issues in Theory and Research: A Metasociological Perspective.* Westport, CT: Greenwood Press.

16

George Herbert Mead and the Chicago Tradition of Sociology

Berenice M. Fisher and Anselm L. Strauss

One of the major ironies of the Chicago tradition of sociology is its association with the name of George Herbert Mead. Despite his symbolic importance to the tradition developed at the University of Chicago, Mead's thought had only a partial and indirect impact on how Chicago sociology was actually done. Neither Mead's theory of society nor his theory of social psychology were incorporated, in his own terms, into the mainstream of Chicago research. In making this point, we have no interest in debunking Mead as a 'founding father.' Rather, an examination of Mead's thought in relation to the Chicago tradition of doing sociology should shed light on both that body of work and the nature of intellectual traditions themselves.

We propose to indicate how Mead shared the same general problem with the actual founders of Chicago sociology, how his particular approach and conclusions differed from theirs and how these differences ramified his view of social science. We also shall suggest how Mead's basic argument was picked up in fragmentary form by the sociologists themselves, and what neglected aspects of Mead's arguments might still be of value to the Chicago sociological tradition, or at least help those interested in its potentials to raise leading questions about its basic arguments (Fisher and Strauss, 1978). In the concluding section of this paper, we suggest a number of questions which our interpretation of Mead's social theory raises for sociology.

In years, Mead was a close contemporary of William I. Thomas and Robert Park the two Chicago sociologists who established how sociology, as they saw it, was to be "done." Mead was also born in the 1860s, and although he began life in Massachusetts, he too was a product of the American Midwest (Reck, 1964). His humanistic, educational background was that of both Thomas and Park. His educational career took him to the liberal college at Oberlin, to Harvard's philosophy department (like Park), and to Germany (like Park, Thomas, and numbers of other pioneer academics). In the early 1890s, Mead returned to begin teaching in the philosophy department at the University of Michigan, and shortly after, he followed his colleague, John Dewey, to the University of Chicago's department of philosophy, where he remained until his death in 1931.

During that entire period – in which Thomas began teaching in the new sociology department, worked on the *Polish Peasant*, brought Park, the journalist–investigator, to teach in the department (from which Thomas himself was fired while Park remained to build up the Chicago department into a famous center for sociological research) – Mead gave courses in philosophy. He gave courses on the Greeks, Descartes and Kant and Hegel, on ethics, logic and the philosophy of science. While his students loyally recorded his lectures (many of which remain unpublished), Mead himself published one or more papers virtually every year of his professional life. Mead was, in fact, a professional academic philosopher, and his career followed the common pattern being established for that area of work.

The fact that Mead made his career as a professional philosopher leads toward the core of the differences between his work and that of the sociologists. Before we turn to those differences, it is worthwhile to point to further experiences and qualities he shared with the sociologists. In addition to those already mentioned, Mead shared the experience of being brought up in a world of progressive social reform. That is, they all came of age in a world of expanding immigrant population, rising labor agitation, giant business expansion, and a variety of voluntary reform efforts aimed at controlling or integrating diverse or troublesome elements of the population into a more cooperative and cohesive society.

Mead, like many progressives, including both Thomas and Park, viewed the problem of progressive reform as the problem of building up a new, and complex, nation. Like them, his assumptions were inclusionary and reformistic rather than exclusionary or revolutionary. Unlike the outright conservatives, he sought to include all incoming elements of the population in the process of building up American life. Unlike revolutionaries, or other groups he would label "utopian," he denied that society could be built anew. Rather, the problem was how to move from the current capitalist order toward a cooperative, democratic, inclusive society. Mead, in his way, was even more deeply convinced than Thomas or Park that this could and would be done. Moreover, he was convinced such reform would take place through nondestructive means: by way of the rational reconstruction of aims by conflicting social groups, and the democratic participation of citizens in the setting of public policy. Consequently, Mead was a longtime, active participant in progressive associations and progressive social causes (Petras, 1968). He attended meetings, wrote articles relevant to current issues, and gave speeches to interested groups. Unlike Thomas and Park, he did not participate in such projects as an academic expert – indeed, what kind of expertise in social reform could a professional philosopher provide? Rather, Mead makes clear his own participation was part and parcel of the kind of progressive participation in social reform and government which citizenship itself, in the highest manifestation, required. Mead the philosopher paralleled Mead the citizen and, in a sense, it was the question of the relation between these roles that deeply informed his social philosophy. How these roles were related also had crucial bearing on the implications of his work for sociology, both as he himself saw it and as it was viewed by the successive generations in the Chicago sociological tradition.

Mead's Concept of Progress

In developing an interpretation of Mead's social thought as it relates to the development of Chicago sociology, we have been struck by how differently, from Thomas and Park, Mead approached the problem of the relation of social science to social action, and how the differences were grounded in his entire approach to the meaning of social change. Although there are evident similarities between Mead and Thomas/Park in this respect (each was, in his way, a part of the American pragmatic movement – Thomas, apparently in his bones; Park via the acknowledged influence of Dewey and James), Mead's interpretation of the nature of social progress, the role of science, the possibilities of social leadership, and the most promising arenas and mechanisms of social reform differed in significant ways from those of both Thomas and Park. Since, elsewhere (Fisher and Strauss, 1978), we have analyzed the thought of the latter in terms of these same four categories (progress, science, leadership, and the arenas and mechanisms of change), we shall continue the analysis here of Mead, using the same dimensions. In Mead's own writing, these questions are given different weight than by either Thomas or Park.

Mead's concept of social progress was marked by two distinguishing features. His view of social change was fundamentally species – related, or civilizational, his notion of the basic precondition of social change was psychological or social-psychological. Mead's concept of social progress was far broader and more directly linked to the social version of Darwinian evolutionism than either Thomas' concept of social stages or Park's contradictory notions of ceaseless but generally upward change. Moreover, Mead specifically connected the problems of how social change could be rationally directed with the problem of what kind of human consciousness made such direction possible. Although Thomas clearly acknowledged the importance of this latter question, his own efforts to provide a model of human nature adequate to his sociology were limited to his famous, but rudimentary, "four wishes" and the "the definition of the situation." Park did not even directly cope with the problem of human nature. He settled for a compound image of motivation, drawing heavily on James' notion of the real self behind the mask, and a general image of an impulsive human nature which drove us forward.

Mead's notion of social progress as the history of the human species and human civilization emerges *throughout* his work, from his earliest reformist pieces, his early social psychological lectures, to those later well known lectures that were finally published posthumously, as *Mind, Self, and Society* (Reck, 1964; Mead, 1912 ms.; 1934). As in the original Darwinian concept of evolution, this notion stressed the continuities between our animal origins and our human struggle to survive. For Mead, that struggle had little flavor of the survival of the fittest: on the contrary, the basic struggle from the point at which human life emerged was simply the struggle to make a better and better place for itself on earth. From our emergence out of animal origins, we were always "at home" on earth (Mead, 1923). The problem was to make that home an increasingly rich and comfortable one for more and more of the human species.

Although making a home on earth (i.e., the entire project of developing human civilization) was clearly an inevitable process for Mead, it was not an easy one. On one hand, the march of human development was irreversible, but it did not unroll in predictable chapters. Progress was problematic, in the sense that the species could stumble and falter in attempting to grapple with the problems it encountered. This *stalling* of progress was the most crucial feature of civilizational history, because the stalling meant human suffering. To the extent to which people were slow in grasping the problems they faced and working out solutions for them, the suffering of those who had not fully reaped the benefit of current development – those left out or exploited – would have their suffering prolonged. The problem of human progress was to increase the *rate* at which we gained control over the conditions that limited or furthered happiness. Suffering was an inevitable part of the animal condition which man had inherited; but such suffering could be justified only to the extent to which humans made fullest use of their capacities to shape the world, to learn from such suffering how to control the conditions that produced it. In this sense, the history of the species implied the justification of suffering through intellectual works (Mead, 1923, 1934).

The obligation to gain control over the conditions of human life was tantamount to the obligation to be free, and in this sense the history of the species was the history of its gaining its freedom. Mead's account of that possibility focused on both the objects of control and the mechanisms by which they could be controlled. The objects were both external and internal. But he spent relatively little time in his writing on the problem of conquering the external world: natural science had done and was doing this job. The problem of contemporary world was to develop the struggle with our own impulsive inheritance, those attributes of our biologic selves which continued to stall the development of the species.

Mead was not moralistic in his account of this inheritance. On the contrary, his argument stressed the fundamentally amoral nature of our biologic grounding. Impulses as part of animal life were evaluated naturally in their application to the problems of survival, but the criterion of mere survival was insufficient for humans. Humans were able and willing to ask themselves what various impulsive reactions contributed to their own progress. The basic impulses, hostility and friendliness, then would have to be evaluated in terms of their consequences under given sets of conditions. Each basic impulse produced consequences that were both constructive and destructive to the further development of the species. War, for example, was the joining together of hostile (toward the enemy) and friendly (toward one's allies) impulses in a way that developed the unity of part of the species at the expense of others. Social reform, in contrast, could make use of the differentiating effects of hostility – it taught us how to differentiate ourselves and hence become individuals – as well as the beneficent effects of friendliness – its fostering of helping relationships (Mead, 1917–1918; 1929).

The mechanisms of control were as universal as the objects of control. For Mead (in contrast with Thomas' and Park's emphases on the conflict between social groups), the emergence of mechanisms by which the species could direct its progress represented crucial steps by which all mankind moved forward. In a sense, the history of civilization was the history of the emergence of these mechanisms. The advance from purely instinctual animal life to rational human life was, of course, the critical first step – handedness and language development providing the mechanisms. The emergence of modern natural science represented another crucial juncture, in which rationality was enlarged to include the process of assimilating experience and testing ideas concerning it. Modern social knowledge was developing as the most recent mechanism of gaining control over constraining conditions. What had been an unconscious social adjustment would become conscious and more efficient, with respect to the elimination of suffering. This last mechanism was already in use, in the crude form of social reform movements and tentative but developing social science. The problem was now to refine such social understanding in relation to action.

In many ways, of course, Mead's account of progress and its reformist direction echoed the general "reform evolutionism" of the period. Yet, from the standpoint of the relation between Mead and Chicago sociology, the most interesting dimension of his argument about progress concerns how he differed from both Thomas and Park, and how his posing of the question sent him in other intellectual directions. Whereas Thomas' notion of social change came out of the problem of the rate and path of national development, Mead's concept of national development came out of his image of general social progress. Whereas Park's contradictory notion of social change resulted from his idea of the inevitable contract, conflict, and accommodation of groups, Mead's notion of the conflict of social groups presupposed a general path down which the human species was already travelling. Equally important, Mead differed from Thomas and Park in his approach to the status of the mechanisms by which society would progress. Whereas Thomas and Park assumed the efficacy of those mechanisms which they trusted (although Park was not very trusting with regard to progress), Mead could not take such efficacy for granted.

As a philosopher, the possibility of rational problem-solving, of natural science, and of a grasp of the social world, constituted problematics for his own intellectual career. Overall, he could not argue the possibility of progress without establishing the possibility of a human species capable of both looking back at itself and forward in the direction it wished to struggle. That is, if the history of the species was the history of the development of mechanisms of gaining control over the conditions of life, it would also have to be the history of the development and growth of human consciousness: the process by which evolving consciousness had become reflective and could thus identify itself with the process of evolution (Mead, 1899; Petras, 1968).

Mead's interest in the problem of consciousness was, of course, firmly rooted in the problems faced by contemporary philosophy itself: the challenge to it by the growing laboratory research in psychology and the theories of behavior that such research was generating (Rucker, 1969; Reck, 1968; Hall, 1924; Miller, 1973; Metraux, ms). For Mead, the challenge of the new experimental psychology was to find a way of explaining how the human species could both be shaped by the world, the world in which it was at home, and shape that world. The theories forwarded by the influential German physiological psychologist, Wilhelm Wundt, had propounded a kind of "parallelism" in which people were seen as basically responding to their world (Mead, 1929–30; 1909). Socially conscious American theorists, like Charles Cooley, had answered such parallelistic arguments by postulating a basically idealistic notion of human intelligence in which humankind became essentially the maker of its own social reality (Mead, 1912 ms; 1929–1930b). Mead himself struggled for a solution that simultaneously would take account of the kind of human response which laboratory psychology was investigating and the kinds of constructive human activities in which social reformers were engaging. In seeking his answer, he leaned heavily – although not exclusively – on the work of the philosophers Royce, James and Dewey.

Mead's account of how the thought of these three figures related to the problem of consciousness is more immediately relevant to our discussion of his notion of progress than his more technical writings on the problem of consciousness. Moreover, Mead's account of the development of Royce's, James' and Dewey's thought reveals the degree to which Mead's concern about consciousness was deeply rooted in his image of American society and its fit with the progress of civilization as a whole Mead begins his analysis of the three philosophers by discussing the split in American life between economic and political activity on the one hand, and cultural life on the other. Despite the wide scope and successful pursuit of entrepreneurial activity in the United States, there had been little pressure to develop self-conscious political life or the ideational foundations on which political activity usually rested. In contrast to Europe, where organization along class lines has forced societies to revolutionize or reconstruct their institutions and to state their ideals for change in terms of political programs, the American system had continued to stress economic development with minimal, democratic governmental control, leaving the work of developing our cultural foundations to European intellectuals or their disciples on the American East coast. This dichotomy between economics and culture had both advantageous and disadvantageous consequences. On the one hand, it had pointed American intelligence toward an interest in process rather than ends, and in so doing freed that intelligence from the numerous traps into which static, idealistic thought had led. On the other hand, the neglect of culture and the role of intellect in economics and political life permitted a continuation of the kind of *laissez faire*, middle class view of social life which – despite its former vigor and usefulness in building the country – no longer could offer guidance in coping with social problems.

Royce, James and Dewey had each attempted to develop concepts of human nature and human actions better fitted to the changed realities of American life. In philosophic terms, the problems of the relation of individual to society and of cultural to economic and political life, took the form of determining how human will and intellect could affect social conditions. The starting point was the 18th Century revolution in science and the corresponding notion that science could discover laws of society, to be applied by the rising European monarchs in shaping their societies. Such a notion of social planning (continued, as Mead often pointed out, to the present day) conceived of both laws of change and individual efforts toward social reform as prior to society itself. It ignored the sense in which the individual was also shaped by the society. The romantic movement in philosophy represented an advance over this position, stressing the development of self and placing that self in the context of a larger transcendental realm. But the notion of transcendence, or the concept of an overarching Absolute, gave little guidance to the concrete difficulties that people faced in the world of social action. Although it laid the ground for making society prior to the individual, it could not develop the relations between them.

Royce's effort to attack this question had failed because he clung to the very same tradition of European idealism. Despite his attempt to translate the Absolute into terms consonant with his experience with American community life, his concept of moral knowledge and action still appealed to a disembodied a priori. The "Blessed Community," in which the self and social understanding was to be based, had nothing in common with the American tradition of economic liberalism, democratic politics, and anti-clerical religious sentiment. James' effort to solve the problem of consciousness had also resulted in noble failure. For while James abandoned transcendence for physiology, and developed the notion of the perceiving, attending, and selecting individual with a "will to live," that individual was still basically isolated from society. James' "satisfaction" criterion for the truth reflected that isolation. James' image of human nature, while better corresponding with the individualistic dimension of the American experience, contained no clue of how to go beyond it.

This is where Dewey's answer to the problem fitted, and why Mead saw Dewey as such a leading figure in American intellectual life. Rather than making either knowledge or will prior to action, Dewey placed knowledge, will and their consequences within the act itself – making moral action the context in which human knowledge and effort must be evaluated and making human action itself profoundly social. This linkage was accomplished not only by connecting thought with its evolutionary and practical base, but by simultaneously freeing thought, so that consciousness could analyze reality and find better solutions to social problems, rather than being merely determined by the social world. However, such freeing did not free the individual from society. The act itself was preeminently social, because it was rooted in communication. It was communication which gave meaning to the very objects with which consciousness concerned itself, and made the social character of individual life the precondition of intellectual activity.

Mead's own development of the pragmatic argument followed Dewey's closely in its insistence that the notion of an active, creative, and socially grounded individual established the possibility of knowledge about and activity geared toward society. On the other hand, the necessity of such knowledge and action flowed from the evolutionary argument, and Mead's conviction that the human species faced a crisis in its forward march.

This conception of evolutionary crisis might well be compared to the conception of crisis as it appears in the work of Thomas and Park. Although both Mead and the sociologists shared the evolutionary assumption that society would move forward through meeting and facing critical problems, each differed in their images of the rhythm of such crisis and with what social processes they were connected. For Thomas, the basic pattern of crisis, disorganizations and reorganization, was linked to the rise and fall of societies – eventually, national societies. This crisis pattern was a regular occurrence, not in the sense that all societies went through the same process, at the same pace, but in the sense that progress consisted of the fact that societies continued to fall apart and reintegrate, and their reintegration was always progressive. Park's image of group contact, conflict, and accommodation also stressed the inevitable and promising character of conflict. But Park's image of the clash of group was tinged with a deep, psychologically based pessimism about what people could and often would accept as satisfactory forms of reintegration. Their needs for stability and a focus for their sentiments could easily lead to the support of nonprogressive, perhaps even vicious leadership, so that crisis in and of itself gave no promise of progressive outcomes.

For Mead, the then current societal crisis was neither merely one of many such crises nor a cause for pessimism. It was unique in the history of civilization, and it was bound to result in progress – although the particular solutions to the current social crisis remained to be discovered. The crisis resulted from the confluence of two major and multifaceted processes in the development of human life: the process by which human experience was universalized, and the process by which human life was concretized (Mead, 1908a, 1912 ms, 1934). Although, in a sense, history proceeded by way of a dialectical relationship between these two – both were necessary to the progress of humankind – they could, and had, gotten seriously out of gear with each other. The process of universalizing was fostered by two central institutions: religion and economic exchange. Through these institutions, people learned to see each other as human, both as sharing sentiments and as capable of holding different (exchange) values. It was through these institutions that humankind learned respectively to recognize commonalities and to take-the-role-of-the-other. The result, in the positive sense, was the possibility of sharing in relationships of wider and wider scope: all the world could be included in the True Church, and trade could be conducted with virtually anyone. On the other hand, this very same process of universalizing led to at least three destructive and related consequences: the undercutting of intimacy, the concentration of hostility, and the increasingly abstract image of fellow humans. Broadening the scope of relationships was bound to lessen the intimacy that living and working together supported. Moreover, despite the bonds of friendliness and the intelligent recognition of differences that religion and commerce inspired, each type of activity allowed the expression of deeply hostile impulses – toward the enemy or toward one's trading adversary. Such impulses were finally finding expression in both the sphere of politics, where the building of nation states had led toward greater and greater national wars, and in the area of economics, where the division of labor in terms of its abstract characteristics – as "economic man" – had led to the vicious exploitation that the current capitalist order displayed.

The basic problem, then, was to preserve the positive consequences of the universalizing process, while reintegrating it with a concrete conception and a concretizing process of joint human activity. Such a synthesis had been found originally in American smalltown life: people had both recognized their commonality in community membership and respected (and self-respected) their different functional roles in keeping the community going. Such an experience, however, only pointed to the possibility of combining universality with concreteness in human activity. It did not, for Mead, imply any romantic return to smalltown roots. On the contrary, Mead was highly critical of any form of primitivism or romanticism. Primitive simplicity (for example, in Cooley's image of the community) was a questionable description of reality, while the actual smalltown life that characterized the American scene had also entailed an endemic anti-intellectualism which could only harm attempts to solve the current social crisis (Mead, 1912 ms, 1934).

Mead's solution, in contrast, attempted to reconcile the bigness which the universalizing process inevitably produced with the concretizing effect that a functional division of labor would bring about (by requiring individuals to understand not only their own activities but, in order to coordinate their efforts, the activities of others). In this respect, industrial democracy provided a unique solution to the unique historical crisis which the human species was confronting. Unfortunately, the notion of industrial democracy had its difficulties too. Mead faced a social situation in which the drive for purely technocratic social management – experts shaping a division of labor that would lead to the greatest "efficiency" – was rampant. Mead, like Dewey and Thomas and other pragmatic progressives, deplored the path of social technocracy because it violated the country's basically democratic tradition. On the other hand, Mead ran into problems defining precisely what the "democratic" component of industrial democracy would be.

His concept of democracy drew on two basic images: the American small town and the modern scientific community. Both relied heavily on a basis of consensus which the recognition of commonalities made possible. In the small town, it was possible to reconcile this democratic base with the division of labor because – as in both the family and the species itself – the experience of commonality, the common struggle to make a home on earth, was clearly prior. But science, although itself an extension of that struggle, entailed the kind of abstractness of social relationship that led to precisely the forms of hostility and exploitation against which Mead was reacting. That is, if science were to be used as even a partial model for social democracy, Mead would have to develop a notion of science which required a concretizing dimension to activity while involving a division of labor which expressed that commitment to the concrete.

Science, Social Science and Social Psychology

Like many late 19th and early 20th Century philosophers and social theorists Mead deeply admired the work of natural science. Galileo and his period represented a major transition point in the history of civilization. The nub of this scientific revolution, for Mead, was the shift from an essentialist interpretation of reality (in which the scientist was held to discover the essence of an object by way of showing its correspondence to a prior idea or ideal) to an experiential attitude toward reality (in which those aspects of reality which cannot be explained by prior theory are nevertheless, "tolerated" as a part of that reality) (Mead, 1917). As a result of the change to this latter approach, scientists were able to locate the conflict between accepted theories and their perceptions of reality. Such contradictions became the core of scientific problems. The change to an experiential approach also had important consequences for the character of the investigator. The scientist was no longer prior to and outside the problem. The very formulation of the problem not only arose out of experience, but demanded a reconstruction of prior theory that would change the scientist's own understanding of that experience. The scientist had no choice but to engage in intellectual struggle toward finding such a theory – to resolve the "logical contradictions" encountered in the attempt to understand the world. Such a struggle was rewarded by a higher, or rather broader, degree of intellectual control over that world – a more adequate kind of control inasmuch as it spoke to more of the world's reality.

The nature of this intellectual struggle was crucial to Mead's argument and of particular relevance to the possibility of social science. As with thought in general, the process by which scientific thinking placed objects in the context of ongoing experience resulted, for Mead, in a challenge to the established meanings of objects, without guaranteeing that new meanings could be found or would emerge. More exactly, the process of scientific thought involved denuding objects of a critical dimension of their meaning, namely propositions concerning their status as universals. As a result, the scientist grappling with objects whose relation to reality had been rendered problematic was free to attempt the reconstruction of those objects, unencumbered by past meanings or previous status. This process of free, "irresponsible" creativity could not, itself, be easily explained; but there was nothing anarchic about the procedure. Scientists not only grasped problems in the context of past, shared meanings, but were obliged to cast their solutions in universally comprehensible terms and to submit their proferred explanations to the community of their peers for testing and judgment on shared standards.

There were, then, three main points characterizing the knowledge and conduct of natural science which could, in turn, serve as a guide for social knowledge and activity. First, natural science concerned itself with facts which contradicted accepted theories. In the social world, the main facts which concerned Mead as unexplained by dominant social theories were those relating to human suffering – that is, those realities indicated a stalling of civilizational progress. Thus, the facts of unemployment or hunger contradicted the predominant *laissez faire* theory of economics, the theory that argued pursuit of self-interest as the best route to human wellbeing (Mead, 1923, 1930).

Second, natural science required a free scope for creativity or "genius," the opportunity for the individual to struggle towards a reconstruction of accepted doctrine precisely because it conflicted with individual experience. This gave individual experience a special status. While on one hand it did not compete with theory (because the experience had not yet been incorporated into a universal formulation), on the other hand it permitted such experience to mandate new explanations of reality.

The application of this second feature of natural science was especially important, but ambiguous, for the realm of society. In one way, it implied that grasping what was "wrong" with society was basically a matter of individual consciousness. This accorded with Mead's emphasis on the power of personal encounters (imaginative but realistic literature could have the same effect) in driving reflective individuals toward an attempt to reconstruct society – to eliminate the contradictions. The idea, however, was less easily applied to the experience of group conflict. Social contradictions were often called to public attention through the agitation of exploited members of society or excluded minority groups. The "public" to which such attention was drawn did not possess individual consciousness, and indeed it often seemed to display little consciousness at all. In reality, only certain members of the public perceived these deep, social contradictions. Of those who did perceive them, not everyone moved to alleviate them. And of the activist members of the society, not all were busy developing creative responses to persisting contradictions. The ideal applications of the natural science model would make every citizen a perceiver of social contradictions, who pursued the problems that they presented to some creative solution.

This is precisely what industrial democracy involved for Mead: each, knowing how his or her work fit in with the whole and was related to the work of every member would perceive contradictions in functioning and be able to present creative alternatives. Yet, several obvious facts stood in the way of realizing such a situation. People at large neither related to each other functionally nor saw the world in terms of functionality. Basic structural changes and education were needed to create such a situation. Those who perceived social contradictions needed to discover the conditions under which social contradictions could be eliminated and the possibility of everyone participating in developing creative solutions to social problems realized.

This ideal underlines the great strain in Mead's argument when it came to applying the third characteristic of the natural science model: the notion that the scientist must bring his or her potential contribution back to the community for judgment. Among natural scientists, the community was a pure democracy, moreover, one in which the standards of judgment were virtually identical. (Mead's account of natural science stressed only agreement on rules, not the actual conflicts that have always taken place within the various scientific worlds). In society, even American society, nothing approaching real democracy had been achieved. The great majority had neither the education not understanding to see how the small minority made decisions affecting themselves. At the same time, however, Mead was unwilling to abandon the ideal of democracy. Ideals were those hopes and values which had not yet been incorporated into institutions, and yet, purely as human values, had a claim on social reform effort. The problem was to be willing to reconstruct the ideal of democracy itself, to find a form for its realization which would enable every member of the society to judge whether proposed social solutions were adequate; that is, whether they resolved the contradictions that individual conscience perceived.

The most striking thing about Mead's attempt to apply the natural science model to the solution of current social problems is that, in contrast to many if not most of his social science contemporaries, he applied the model of natural science to society as a *whole* – rather than merely to the social sciences. The implications of his argument can be seen by contrasting his notions of the specific tasks of social science with those of Thomas and Park (Fisher and Strauss, 1978). The thrust of Thomas' argument concerning science was to establish what social scientists could accomplish over and against the work of practical reformers, and what sociologists in particular could discover in contrast to other social scientists. Despite Thomas' following the pragmatic argument concerning education, and promoting the ideal of a cooperative society in which expertise would be replaced by something similar to Mead's industrial democracy, Thomas faced the problem of establishing sociology as a profession, *as* a kind of expertise. Park, in contrast, came to the Chicago department when Thomas' professional ideal had started to become a reality: not only did Chicago's reform elites seek the help of sociologists (putting them on boards and commissions and funding their research), but sociologists were training and influencing the first generations of social service experts, the professional practitioners, who were becoming the direct agents of social reform, (Carey, 1975). In this context, Park could afford to pay as little attention to scientific legitimacy as he did (afford it, at least, in the short run). He could hedge his scientific claims by stressing the problematic nature of social reform, dwelling instead on the more human and communal values of "bringing in the news." Like Thomas, his argument about science was of less importance than his practice. By "doing" sociology and teaching students how to become sociologists, they established the discipline in fact, with or without theoretical justification.

Mead's problem was neither to establish the possibility of a social science discipline nor to provide the model for sociological activity. Indeed, his image of the role of social science in promoting social progress was quite vaguely suggested. The social scientists were to discover the social conditions under which society could be reconstructed. This was not, however, the exclusive province of social science. Perceptive and committed reformers like Jane Addams were just as helpful in calling attention to the contradictions under which society labored, the conditions that produced these contradictions, and how the society needed to move in order to resolve them (Mead, 1907). Moreover, just as all those who sensed social contradictions did not plunge ahead to explore and attempt to resolve them, all those who studied social conditions did not connect their studies with the actual problems of suffering and the contradictions they implied. The product of this latter pattern was social technocracy and technocratic social science – both permeated with the assumption that social problems could be solved without active, democratic participation. The only way to insure that professional social scientists would grasp the real social questions of the day was through their own active participation, by their actually experiencing (as individuals and/or as participants in reform activities) the contradictions which they were required to resolve.

Yet, participation alone did not guarantee good social science, and Mead, generally quite contained in his criticisms, made it clear he thought there was bad social science. Gustave Le Bon's work on crowds and on the nature of socialist movements was bad social science, because it reduced human activity and striving to a set of psychocultural impulses which merely expressed themselves in the world rather than changing it (Mead, 1899b). Good social science required a theory of human nature that could show why people responded to the conditions shaping human life as they did. Good social science required good social psychology. Contemporary social psychology was not adequate because it was mired in the kinds of parallelistic dichotomies which it inherited from theories of individual psychology, as the latter discipline sought to define itself over and against philosophy. Thus, the problem of social psychology – its penchant for dividing subjective response from objective reality, of perception from intelligence, of self from society – were themselves rooted in the struggle between philosophy and psychology over the nature of knowledge and action. In short, the only path to an adequate theoretical base for social science lay *through a philosophical critique of social psychology* – one which could show the possibility of relating the parts of the dichotomized world to each other, in such a way that reflective consciousness could forward human progress.

This intellectual program was simply the logical culmination of Mead's own dual career. As a philosopher speaking to philosophers, he saw an important part of his professional work in the context of completing the "Hegelian program of giving reality and creative import to individual experience" (Mead, 1917). As a socially conscious citizen, he saw himself obliged to talk and to join with others who had sensed society's deep contradictions. In both capacities, as a friend of the social sciences, he offered a new theoretical base. But he left the problems of its application up to them.

The Practice of Social Reform: Agents, Arenas and Mechanisms

Although as a philosopher giving aid to social scientists Mead could neglect the problem of application, his own activities as a citizen could not be pursed without facing the problem of how to apply social knowledge to social reality. For this reason, Mead's reform articles have a special importance for his theory of social change. Significantly, these articles have been virtually ignored by the Chicago sociologists who claimed Mead as a founding figure.

In general terms, Mead's notions of who should engage in social reform (the agents), where reforms were most needed (the arenas), and how reforms should be carried out (the mechanisms of social change) follow from his general image of progress and how social knowledge could forward it. The proper arenas for reform were those places in which the progressive movement of civilization had gotten stalled: that is, where the dominant theory and practice could no longer justify the degree of suffering that people had to endure, and where therefore a reconstruction of ideas and institutions was required. The natural agents for such reform efforts were the people who could perceive this situation and who were able and willing to search out its remedy. The mechanisms for social reconstruction were determined by the character of progress in general: the necessity for reflective consciousness to overcome inadequate theories by finding new ones, and the necessity to ground these new ideas in agreement so that reconstruction could begin.

Labor was the first and perhaps (together with war) the most important arena for social change. Labor had posed the key social question of the era raising the issue of socialism (Mead, 1899a, 1908a, 1908–1909). The question, which Mead had first encountered in his student days in Germany and later found "the social question" with which Americans were struggling, could be simply put: Could the current order justify the extent of suffering it imposed? The clear answer was no. Labor's demands – for everything from moderate reform to revolutionary overthrow of the ruling class – followed quite naturally from this answer. Mead's quarrel with labor was not with its motives, but with its choice of methods. Too many participants in the labor movement (revisionists as well as revolutionaries) considered it possible to realize a socialist ideal either by legislative fiat or by force. The prior point was not that legislation was preferable to force, but that no ideal could be realized by direct translation into reality. Progress and the social understanding on which it needed to be based were achieved through discovering the contradictions between established ideas and experience, not by bringing about conformity between them. Businessmen often suffered from the same problem, only from a different angle: that is, in clinging to the old ideals which had served their interest, they refused to recognize the depth of the contradictions they encountered. They ignored the contradiction between poverty and the industrial system, defending themselves with oldfashioned individual charity or vicious industrial practices. In this respect, their motives were inferior to those of labor – which at least pressed toward the necessity for change – while their methods were no less advanced than those of the "utopians" who tried to realize their ideals without recognizing history (Mead, 1930).

In these terms, Mead's image of the path to reform follows the well known pragmatic model: to bring together those progressive leaders of labor and capital in order to search for a common program of social reconstruction. The fact that such leaders had become leaders through their capacity to generalize the attitudes of members of their groups, implied their potential for taking the role of the other groups within such forums (Mead, 1912 ms, 1934). Such a capacity, together with an understanding of the nature of reconstructive thought, provided the preconditions for joint reconstruction. Mead-as-citizen could only act as a midwife with respect to such capacities, pointing out the contradictions that the various group members perceived and suffered, showing how the inherent logic of the social situation led to the need for reconstruction, reminding that reconstruction required a tentative and open attitude toward received truths. This was precisely the role that his writing when addressed to business and labor leaders reflected, as did his actual reform activities. If he saw his role as a teaching one, it was teacher as a kind of dialectician, helping unfold the dialectical interplay between the history of human effort and the history of consciousness. Unlike Thomas, he did not argue that the social scientist (or philosopher) occupied an advanced position with respect to such questions, or that, like Park, he was particularly skilled at offering useful theories for interpretation or bringing back the news. The philosopher as citizen, the labor leader, and the businessman alike stood at the cutting edge of history. Rather than teach each other, they stood in the relation of fellow scientists, searching together for common answers.

Mead's treatment of the labor question suggest the sense in which he muted the question of mechanisms for social change. The issue for him was method, rather than mechanisms (so much so that he paid far less attention than Dewey, for example, to the great impact of technological change on communication). In contrast to Park, he did not display a great deal of interest in the newspaper. Even his treatment of education – though clearly a central institution – was qualified by his conviction that some of the most important lessons could not be taught in schools. Institutions, including educational institutions, were merely common responses to problems jointly faced (Mead, 1915, 1934). One of the main functions of educational institutions was to present and help children internalize the best and broadest of these solutions – the norms of the current society. Beyond this, the school could merely help people to learn how to take theoretical advantage of their experience. The school could not substitute for experience. (The only mechanism that could pretend to do this was realistic literature, which gave us unique access to the roles of others.) Nor could it provide a scientific method apart from experience. Although thinking at its best was profoundly scientific and logical, these were outcomes of intellectual struggle rather than static models (Mead, 1917).

Mead's muting of the role of mechanisms for social change fit neatly with his attempt to make institutional life ultimately subservient to the efforts of creative individuals, working together. This argument could be applied quite persuasively to an area like penal reform, in which Mead showed a continuing interest (Mead, 1917–1918). As long as legal and penal institutions merely expressed the natural hostility of a community towards those who violated its laws or stood outside its norms, crime would be perpetuated. Criminal acts themselves were simply responses to the defensive aspect of community life: excluded members sought to define themselves over and against the community by themselves engaging in hostile acts. The only way to break the cycle was to bring the individual into the community (by making him or her a functional part of it) and to bring the community inside the individual (by internalizing, through education, its broadest norms). This solution clearly involved a reconstruction of institutions, an abandonment of revenge in favor of joint responsibility in solving a common social problem.

The benefits of such a solution seemed evident, and the gratification involved in merely punishing one's enemy seemed to involve the sacrifice of a relatively minor and atavistic tendency in contemporary human life. In the case of war, the applicability of this line of reasoning was more questionable. Mead's attitude toward war also derived fairly directly from his progressive stance. As with many progressives, war posed a profound problem in its full contradictory reality. For Mead, war would exist as long as it had an evolutionary function. The function of war had always been to unite community members against their common enemy (Mead, 1929). The only further justification of war – which Mead had employed in his support of Wilson's war effort – had to derive from the same notion of progress: namely, that war was justifiable as a mode of eliminating those institutions (militaristic governments) which threatened to abolish the very bulwarks of progress (democratic governments) (Mead, " Democracy's Issues. . . .", "America's Ideal. . . ."; Lasch, 1962). On the same grounds, however, Mead was profoundly distressed by the technological implications of this same war to end all war. The instruments of war had become so powerful that war itself must be held to be inadmissible mechanism of progress. At an earlier stage of evolution, war had led to progress by uniting peoples and gradually, in combination with the institution of property, replacing annihilation by conquest and administration. Now war, in combination with technological innovation, threatened to replace conquest and administration by annihilation.

Mead's mentor, James, had suggested that sports be developed as a "moral equivalent to war," but Mead was not sanguine about such a possibility. People continued to go to war because of the sense of unity it gave them and in that common identity, a sense of worth. This demand for a sense of worth was no more than our primary selves asserting the value of our existence and, as such, of our evolutionary development. As long as societies failed to develop social structural arrangements in which people could affirm their self-worth – i.e., functional arrangements such as industrial democracy – they would be prone to solving their problems through military means. Moreover, the existence of armies also encouraged societies to solve their internal problems by way of force. If statesmen managed to reach international agreements by which force itself was outlawed, the countries would be forced to solve their labor questions and crime problems without benefit of coercive means.

By such an argument, Mead strained his optimism regarding civilizational progress to its utmost, but also revealed deep cleavages within the argument. The dialectical process by which political and economic development were to converge in democratic government (and even an international order) seemed to have fallen apart. Politics had not moved toward more inclusive and less coercive forms of government, while economics – through producing great skill in bargaining, even on the international scale – had not evolved into a process of taking-the-role-of-the-other for mutual benefit. This meant that although statesmen might take the role of other countries, they had not yet been able to take the role of their own people. This default, in turn, was due to the lack of common values among people achieved by means other than mutual hostility toward enemies. Mead was hard pressed to explain why people in general, or at least leaders, did not follow this logic to its inevitable reform conclusions.

In a sense, he did not try to explain it. He continually held out hope that civilizational progress, though slow, was still on the way. If one or another particular focus of reform seemed to be lagging, nevertheless the overall picture of human progress showed constant improvement. One of our basic problems, said Mead, was we tend to lose sight of the fact that we are part of a human species – and that had involved a long struggle upward and promised a shared, common reward. The fundamental insight into the nature of this reward was part of the reward itself: that is, the development of a reflective consciousness that could see the self as part of human history – in short, grasp the fundamental worth of the self in the context of purposeful social change.

Mead's deep hopefulness suggested basic differences from his sociological colleagues, despite many similarities in their ideas of progress. When the world did not seem to be going well, Thomas fell back on the need for more education: followers must teach leaders their real needs; leaders would have to teach followers the balanced way to social change; sociologists would have to teach leaders how to understand their followers and relate this understanding to social progress. When Park's pessimistic streak emerged, he could always point to the seemingly ceaseless pattern of conflict and accommodation, and the abiding needs for security and integrity that human nature demanded, and that leadership and individual mobility provided Mead's fallback position did not abandon dialectics for pedagogics, nor split social needs from individual ones. To that extent, he succeeded in accomplishing his task of finding a relationship between the active, individual self and the moving, determining environment. On the other hand, by responding to the evident stalling of progress by simply reiterating the process by which progress was inevitably achieved Mead avoided the entire problem of application. With it he sidestepped one of the central issues of social science.

The Use Of Mead In The Chicago Tradition

The Problem of how to apply Mead's ideas in the realm of sociology fell to the sociologists themselves – to the extent they cared to address that problem. The relation between Mead's thought and the ongoing work of the Chicago sociology department was affected by several key factors. Perhaps the most important was that Mead did not have direct successors in the sociology department because Mead was a philosopher. For the sociologists to develop his arguments as a philosopher would have required not only philosophic training but a range of theoretical interests and a type of theoretical focus quite different than those involved in the Chicago idea of "doing" sociology. Of course, aspects of Mead's social theory could have been developed outside the setting of philosophic activity. However, *which* aspects of his theory would be so developed and how they would be developed were shaped by considerations other than those tending to shape the careers and work of professional philosophers.

In discussing Chicago sociology, we have likened such an intellectual tradition to an auction house, in which a wide variety of items are offered for sale and picked according to the needs and resources of various customers (Fisher and Strauss 1978). Extending the metaphor to include a figure like Mead, we note that material for sale can come to the auction house from quite unrelated sources and be dispersed in ways having little to do with the material's original organization. In Mead's case, although he had some important intellectual ties to the founding figures of Chicago sociology – all had been touched by the pioneers of pragmatic philosophy, more or less directly – his intellectual career was relatively unrelated to theirs. The importation of his work into Chicago sociology took place because: (1) students were sent to "take" Mead's course in social psychology; (2) Chicago sociologists, like Ellsworth Faris and Herbert Blumer, gave courses in social psychology which cited and developed Mead's arguments; and (3) succeeding generations of students picked out ideas from these courses and their reading of Mead, and variously attempted to "apply" Mead to their particular sociological projects (cf., Faris, 1967). Their notions of doing sociology itself did not and – as we would argue on the basis of our preceding discussion – could not have stemmed from Mead himself. The students learned to do sociology from Thomas, Park, their students, and others whose work was combined with or (as in the case of William Ogburn) posed against that of the main figures in the tradition. Mead's ideas were slotted in where they seemed to be helpful for doing sociology.

From the standpoint of understanding this tradition, therefore, our question is not that of who the legitimate successors to Mead have been, or which sociological interpretation has captured the "real" Mead, but rather to what uses Mead's ideas have been put. The answer seems to be that Mead's work was used relatively *little* within the Chicago tradition of doing sociology and the uses to which it was put were quite *diverse*.

The most conspicuous use was not directly related to doing sociology at all: Mead was used as an intellectual resource for the teaching of social psychology, but social psychology was primarily a teaching rather than a research subject. In connection with such teaching, several Chicago sociologists developed theoretical work in social psychology (Faris, 1937; Blumer 1969) and wrote textbooks used for teaching (Lindesmith, Strauss, & Denzin 1975; Shibutani 1961). This work was not directly tied to sociological research. Quite the contrary, the work of someone like Blumer, who has been so closely associated with Mead's ideas, suggests a virtually complete bifurcation between the theoretical discussions of Mead and the doing of Chicago sociology, In Blumer's frequent discussions of social psychology, he writes as an explicator and developer of Mead's idea of the "self". When Blumer writes on substantive matters (industrial relations or race or public opinion), he makes virtually no use – at least not explicitly – of Mead's social psychology.

To the extent that Mead was used in such sociological enterprises, his ideas provided philosophical justification for the general "anti-determinist" thrust of such sociology. Indeed, aside from its use in teaching and textbooks, the main function of Meadian social psychology for the tradition seemed to be to support its fight against a series of competing positions which the Chicago sociologists continually characterized as "deterministic": the behaviorism of the 1920s and 1930s, the Freudian and neo-Freudianism, the biological determinism which continued to crop up, the Marxism of the old and new left. This commitment to an anti-determinist posture stemmed primarily from the Thomas–Park tradition of doing sociology – with its complex and contradictory interest in showing the relation between individual and society – rather than directly from Mead's social psychology, let alone his social theory. Chicago sociologists drew relatively little from Mead's theory of consciousness as it related to the classic problem of freedom. In fact, that would have been relatively difficult for them to do, because they did not address Mead in the context of his theory of social change. Nor did they need to do so. By and large, they had already acquired one or another theory of social change from the mainstream of Chicago thinking. Since, for reasons we suggest elsewhere (Fisher and Strauss, 1978), that mainstream itself began to pay less and less attention to the very theories of social change that were actually inherited, the question of how Mead's theory related to Thomas' or Park's was not likely to be raised.

This pattern is very clear in the work of a number of well-known Chicago sociologists who, although they have utilized a variety of concepts drawn from Mead's work, neither have located these ideas in the theoretical context out of which Mead's own argument was developed nor have raised some of the basic sociological questions that might have followed from an awareness of that context. In pointing to particular examples of research done by these sociologists we wish only to point out how their work relates to Mead's general argument concerning social change, *not* to characterize their work as a whole nor to question its merit as sociological research.

One of the most revealing documents concerning how Mead has been merged with the working, researching side of Chicago sociology is *Boys In White*, a study of "student culture in medical schools," done largely by Howard Becker and Blanche Geer (Becker, *et al*, 1961). This monograph self-consciously utilizes one of Mead's central concepts – "perspective" – to organize its sociological approach. The book itself explicitly acknowledges the debt of its authors to the "symbolic interactionist" tradition founded by Cooley, Dewey, and Mead, expanded by others including Park. The debt to Mead is underscored by prefatory quotes concerning perspectives and embodying several familiar Meadian themes: (1) reflective experience *vis-à-vis* "situations;" (2) the relationship between the individual and the environment; and (3) individual mentality as arising out of the social process.

What the researchers actually undertook was a study of the experiences of students as they progress through their medical education. Being Chicago sociologists, they went into the field with a focus on careers, work, occupations–professions as well as organizational considerations. They also had a keen eye for the encounters between groups, especially those engendering or flowing from conflict. Not unexpectedly, they employed fieldwork to get at what was important to the respective actors, which, in turn, was used to interpret the observed interaction and the social organization. These authors' interest, however, was particularly focused on the collective fate of students as a group. In this context, the Meadian concept of perspective is applied primarily to the ideas and actions of the students and how they develop a definition of the situation (Thomas' phrase, not Mead's). From the researchers' own standpoint, such group perspectives are important because they show the customary ways by which groups deal with problematic situations; how, in fact, a collective student culture had been evolved to cope with constraints on autonomy, level, and direction of effort which the faculty in particular had imposed.

The problem of this monograph derives from the concerns of the mainstream of Chicago sociology, rather than the work of Mead. It reflects Thomas' concern with what more powerful and "advanced" groups can learn from those beneath them (if the faculty only better understood the students' needs and struggles, perhaps they could improve the education), and the Parkian interest in the continual struggle and accommodation of groups (reform as we may, the Sumnerian pattern of precipitating group culture out of group encounters can be expected to go on and on). Moreover, as both Thomas and Park, each in his own way, emphasized, the study of student culture suggests the limits on the degree to which any situation is "compelling": counter-definitions and actions are bound to emerge in the attempt to reshape the situation in terms of the actors' collective needs. Inasmuch as such a process affirms the possibility of a creative response to social constraint, this Thomas–Park orientation overlaps Mead's own theory of social change. But, outside of the general conviction that reflective experience can result in a creative response to the environment, Mead's argument about the nature of reflective experience *vis-à-vis* social understanding and social progress is in little evidence. How perspectives operate in Mead's thinking as a bridge on the organism-reality issue, or in relation to the long road from primitive beginnings to the most complexly functioning and hopefully ideal universal society, is either excess baggage or not actively noted. The monograph has little relation to civilizational history, even in the short term sense: students, faculty and medical school are essentially studied in a flat, ahistorical manner, without attention to the contemporary movements in medicine, medical education, or America of the 1950s. Any of these movements might have been relevant in terms of Mead's theory of social change. The questions directed to them would have come from Mead's concern for their relations to the general course of progress, and how their conflict and mutual reconstruction of social conditions might contribute to that progress.

Essentially, the same, point can be made concerning a number of other well-regarded studies in the Chicago tradition. Tamotsu Shibutani's *Improvised News* (1966) draws explicitly on the writings of Dewey, Wirth, Park and Mead in order to develop a sociological theory to account for rumor. His use of Mead is particularly focused on how "concerted action" is made possible because each individual is able to exert self-control, and self-control "can lead to a co-ordination because each approaches his world from the standpoint of a common definition of the situation". This interest in the possibility of coordinated action is, in turn, linked to Shibutani's conviction that public discussion and role-taking are crucial mechanisms for developing consensus within the community – the kind of Deweyan consensus which he finds essential to the conduct of community life. Rumor plays its role when the normal channels of communication are not adequate; the community in a sense seeks to correct this situation by searching out the best ideas by which it can keep itself going. Self-control plays a special part because, while it permits individuals to see how their behavior will fit into the proposed behavior of others, it provides an internal standard (based on past community agreements) by which the individual's own participation can be judged. In this way, the Meadian reflective consciousness becomes, for Shibutani, a mechanism for furthering society's cohesion and continuity. Very little room is left for the innovative role of individual consciousness in promoting social progress. The basic image of the social context is derived from Park rather than Mead: a world "in the state of continuous flux . . ." in which social clashes continually threaten to dissolve sociality into its underlying, psychological chaos.

Fred Davis' monograph, *Passage Through Crisis* (1963) suggests a use of Mead which, while while equally prone to ignore the larger social theoretical context of its Meadian concepts, nevertheless touches on several important dimensions of Mead's view of history. Subtitled, "Polio victims and Their Families," this study essentially traces the sequential stages from the onset of symptoms through the months after a stricken child is on the road to recovery. The three major themes of the monograph are: emergence, continuation of identity, and clash between hospital and home. Emergence pertains to the pacing, quality, and development of the family's reactions to "the many novel conditions and events occasioned by the child's illness." Continuity pertains to how the family members were, nevertheless, "to maintain some sense of stability and sameness in their lives," while the clash between hospital and home results from the difference between professional and lay conceptions of illness. One important aspect of the family's struggle to face the emerging series of problematic situations is through its "unwitting reevaluations of relevant past and impending situations." (Here, Davis refers to Mead's *Philosophy of the Present*.) The family is seen as a unit moving through history and seeing itself, though perhaps unwittingly, as an historical entity. Again (although Davis does not look toward the broader historical setting and ask where is the family moving in relation to the movement of other groups toward some kind of mutually determined improvement), the monograph does deal with the problem of gaining more rational control over the irrational facts of suffering and thus reflects, or parallels, a basic thrust of Mead's theory of history.

Rather than slotting Mead into sociological work in the form of useful concepts, some Chicagoans have confronted his arguments more directly. A well-known paper by Gregory Stone, "Appearance and the Self" (1962), exemplifies that approach. Its opening lines state that: "A primary tenet of all symbolic interaction theory holds that the self is established, maintained, and altered in and through communication." Most investigators, Stone points out, have confined their notion of communication to discourse, while he proposes to extend the perspective of symbolic interaction by including the dimension of "appearance." Thus, Stone's criticism of Mead and the beginning point of his own work is the need to extend the analysis of social transactions to cover the importance of appearance in establishing and maintaining the self, and particularly in the process of the self's early development. It is this latter aspect of Stone's discussion which reveals the relation of his argument – and lack of relation of his argument – to Mead's notion of civilizational progress. Although Stone's account sensitively traces how the gaining of access to clothing as communication equipment can play a crucial role in "growing up" he does not raise the equally Meadian question of growing up into what? That is, society itself is taken as a given, and the direction in which society might be moving, and how that would relate not only to the mores of appearance but innovation in the realm of appearance, is not explored.

Finally, in our brief sketches of the use of Meadian concepts and problems in the Chicago tradition, we should point to the small but distinct group of its practitioners, who have interpreted Mead's work as a series of social psychological hypotheses to be tested and evaluated in terms of their scientific validity. There are several such verificatory studies, the authors of each assuming that Meadian ideas may be true, but arguing it is about time for interactionists to stop assuming that they are true. Typical among these studies is "Self-Conceptions and Others – A Further Test of Meadian Hypotheses," by Enrico Quarantelli and Joseph Cooper (1966). The authors conceive of symbolic interactionism's "central thesis" as "the view that the self is social in that it is derived from responses of other persons." They wish to replicate and improve previous studies as well as to add a temporal dimension missing in them. Specific hypotheses include: "The mean of the perceived responses by others is higher for those persons with high self-rating than for those with low-rating," an hypothesis which the researchers checked out by their specific questioning of subjects. Such a procedure, according to the researchers, contributes to the systematizing and rigorizing of Mead's ideas, and the possibility, therefore, of evaluating Mead's actual contribution to social science: "After all, whether in the course of the development of sociology Mead is to be eventually ranked with the alchemists or as a Lavoisier is yet to be decided." Presumably, since most of their hypotheses tended to be true, Mead would fall on the Lavoisier side. His theory, having become the simple object of scientific study rather than part of its moral context, would be redeemed: the researchers, like keen-eyed placer miners panning for gold, have discovered the nuggets in the Meadian stream while throwing back the dirt and dross within which the treasures were embedded.

Mead's Social Theory as Problems for Sociology

While our examples of sociological work should not be read as an account of the total Meadian impact on the Chicago tradition, neither do we propose to offer a Meadian "program" for renovation of that tradition. We are inclined to doubt whether Mead himself would have envisioned or even desired such a program. The problem, from his standpoint, was for social science researchers to get an adequate social psychology, and to pursue the study of relevant social conditions in the moral and intellectual context imposed by science and progressive citizenship. There is far less in Mead's work to suggest a highly structured program of such activities (which, indeed, would have run counter to his argument about "programs" in general), than there is to suggest his concern that social science not turn in certain directions. In this respect, it is more Meadian in spirit to ask what problems Mead's theory of social progress raises for sociologists than to outline a Meadian discipline.

Mead's social theory raises four problems which we think are of particular importance to contemporary sociology: (1) the problem of *progress*; (2) the problem of the relation of *universals*; (3) the problem of a *social psychology*; and (4) the problem of *ethics* for social scientists. We emphasize these, not because of their exclusive importance with respect to the implications of Mead's work, but because they are directly related to the relatively neglected dimensions of Mead's social theory. The concepts which sociologists recognize most immediately (taking-the-role-of-the-other, the "I" and the "me," the generalized other, the conversation of gestures) and even the more general outlooks that have been drawn from Mead (the importance of perspectives, the dimension of temporality) should be related to this theoretical context.

Given the complexity of Mead's argument, our treatment must be as superficial as it is brief. The problem of progress, of course, has haunted modern social theory since at least the 18th Century, and permeated the work of sociologists who were Mead's contemporaries. Moreover, how Thomas and Park respectively viewed progress had definite implications for how they did – and expected others to do – sociological work. Thomas' view of progress as taking place through the ability of more advanced groups to help less advanced, through the intelligent and understanding interaction of leadership, led to the need for sociological research about the less advanced groups for the sake of teaching the leadership of the more advanced group how the power to lead could be effectively exercised. Park's image of progress was more contradictory but it also directed attention to the study of group life, both to understand why groups were responding to conflict as they did and to bring back the news of group life to a democratic public – presumably in the process of formation and avid interest to understand the conditions of its own development. Because of their conceptions of progress, both Thomas' and Park's sociologies concentrated on the study of group life from the perspectives of its membership; that is, how people as group members attempt to solve the objective problems of their lives. Mead's social theory is quite consistent with this general approach (undoubtedly part of the implicit reason the Chicago sociologists were comfortable with his ideas), but his treatment of progress actually requires him to go further and in a somewhat different direction.

Whereas both Thomas and Park were inclined to assume that groups would develop solutions to their social problems – the more advanced, the more advanced the solutions – Mead was far less sanguine. Although his evolutionary argument assumed a general onward and upward movement of civilization, Mead was deeply concerned with the problem of the consequences of stalled progress for human suffering. This turned his attention, not only to the problematic character of particular reform solutions (a view he shared with Thomas and Park and which clearly make his ideas attractive to their students), but to the problematic quality of the intellectual process by which solutions were sought. Mead was not always consistent on this point, for he was inclined to treat scientific method itself as a solved problem, and therefore its application to the social world as automatically producing adequate answers and full agreement. On the other hand, the thrust of his thinking about society was to establish the possibility of applying scientific thinking to the moral realm, to both the ends and means of moral activity.

In this sense, his argument for such a possibility raises a series of questions: whether the conditions for recognizing social problems are the same for social scientists as for "ordinary" citizens? How and under what conditions an innovative social science could be developed and encouraged (the questions of education for and the institutionalization of, and how these differ from other forms of education and other modes of institutionalization)? Whether social scientists need their own community, and if so, how it should differ from the general community? Under what conditions, if at all, is it possible to develop a public capable of judging social science results? Or in turn, what kind of social science (if any) would such a public require?

The whole question of the possibility of a public for sociological research is closely tied with Mead's argument about universality and the development of universes of discourse. Here again, certain difficulties crop up in Mead's own argument, but they are difficulties that lead to useful questions. Like both Thomas and Park (and reflecting the common, pragmatic thread in all three thinkers), Mead paid special attention to the problem of communication and its relevance for the formation of a democratic public. Mead's argument again went farther, making history itself the history of an expanding universe of discourse. In viewing social change in this light, Mead pointed to a series of universalizing processes through which people could not only come into new relationships with each other but, through the convergence of such processes, build a more universal society. The differentiating but universalizing process of economics would converge with the binding and universalizing processes of religion and nationalism to produce the possibility of a non-exploitative and democratic political life. This two-pronged movement was a far cry from the kind of emancipation involved in the peasant–entrepreneur or rural–urban shifts which so interested Thomas and Park. Rather than pointing to the conditions of emancipation from customary thought, Mead's theory raised questions of what kinds of social relationships could be universally extended, how these processes related to each other, and what were the consequences of their extension and convergence?

It is clear that any sociological questioning which took Mead's argument as a beginning point in this respect, would have to go farther than Mead himself: first, because his own argument assumed which were the universal processes, without establishing (in contrast to Marx) why these were the only universalizing processes; and second, because he assumed their convergence and did not entertain the possibility of their interfering with each other. This problem became particularly clear with respect to the relationship between economics and politics – Mead's conviction that their universalizing trends would be mutually reinforcing. This, he argued, would result in a kind of consciousness which could direct the further development of history toward rectification of the consequences of abstraction itself; that is, could direct society towards the kind of industrial democracy that would counterbalance the hostile (exploitative and domineering) dimensions of the universalizing processes. If Mead did not show that these processes reinforced each other and were capable of producing the results he desired, then the question of universalizing processes and their relations becomes an open one for sociologists who are interested in Mead's general argument.

At the same time, his argument concerning social psychology implies that the question of which kinds of social relationships extend a given universe of discourse is not entirely open. Social psychological needs and capacities limit how and with whom people are able to communicate, and to a certain extent affect the consequences of that communication. Thus, any study of the potentials and consequences of extending any universe of discourse, as well as the potential relation between such universalizing processes, raised both a sociological and social psychological question: the objective and subjective conditions for seeing a given social world in the same way as others.

The fact that Mead attempted to solve the problem of social psychology on a fundamental level sets his work apart from the mainstream of Chicago sociology, although the problem was also a crucial one for some of the sociologists themselves – e.g., Albion Small and, to some extent, Thomas. Small put the question in explicitly historical terms: is it possible to explain historical change until we are able to explain why people are willing to cut loose from established institutions and customary behavior and launch into new ways of behaving? (Small, 1910). Thomas' answer to this question is revealing, because it was very influential for Chicago sociology and because, although it resembles Mead's own answer in many ways, it suggests how Mead was required to go beyond it.

For Thomas, the problem of motivation was to find a new balance between competing, basic desires (the four wishes) whose habitual balance had been disturbed by the introduction of new social conditions (the growth of urban life stimulates the curiosity of village youth, etc.). The problem of social psychology was what kind of balance would take into account pressing needs while yet contributing to the development of the social order that was coming into being. This was the problem which more advanced groups struggled to solve – groups for whom rationality played a greater part in determining the optimum balance, and whose members (at least some of those members) were more inclined to attack problems because of the spontaneous benevolence made possible by their greater security. Thus, in the study of motivation, the sociologists could take for granted the rational and charitable potentials of more advanced groups. The task of social psychology was to help shape that rationality and benevolence by showing progressive leaders how the struggles of the less advanced were rooted in their attempts to balance their various desires with mastery of a new environment. Progressive leadership would assist this natural struggle rather than fruitlessly attempt to stop it.

Mead shared key elements in this account with Thomas: first, the idea that value was rooted in human nature and its attempt to realize its potentials within a social context; and second, the conception that the development of reason has yielded increased control. Mead's social psychology, however, like his social theory, could not take the emergence of rationality and benevolence for granted. The difficulty for Mead was posed by the fact that the attempt to realize the values of the "biologic individual" led to certain intrinsically based conflicts – not merely because, in Thomas' sense, human desires conflicted with each other, but because the attempt to realize human desire led to dialectical contradiction within human effort itself: the realization of common interest through friendly association which itself was based on hostility to others; the development of human individuality through learning how others differed led to the potential for exploiting them by means of their differences.

Because of such inherent human contradictions, the role of reason, for Mead, could not be merely that of balancing desires with each other or with reality. There was no way in which reason, through an inspection of relevant factors, could determine what balance actually was. Reflective consciousness differed from *a priori* rationality and the notion that social groups could be based on such rationality precisely because it implied a reason embedded in the process of history, a reason that could look back on the role of values in history and ask what they might contribute to further progress.

To pose such a question, however, reflective consciousness also required a community over and against which such questions could be posed and to which such answers could be proffered. In social psychological language, this meant that every new expression of human desires implied a challenge to accepted theories of society (of the "I" to the "me"), while the possibility of finding a way to incorporate those desires into ongoing group action implied a norm-sharing community (the "generalized other") to which such solutions were brought back. From the standpoint of Mead's own image of history, however, members of the community could only share standards of judgment to the degree that the community itself had reconciled the conflicts inherent in the processes of universalizing, had developed a universal outlook that could be genuinely universal because it had also succeeded in concretizing these processes in joint activity. But as Mead the social reformer readily admitted, even the leading democratic society (his own) had not begun to realize such a possibility. Thus, in reality, only partial and inherently contradictory resolutions of values were possible: the individual consciousness would be split in much the same way the society itself was split, and would have to struggle to gain greater reflective control through such contradictions.

Thus, when Mead's argument regarding social psychology is seen in the context of his social theory, it actually leads to a quite different series of questions than asked by most researchers operating under his banner: not, how, when, etc., the individual internalizes the role of the community, the "generalized other," but: To what degree is it possible to internalize conflicting values? To what extent can the individual, in relation to society, affect a greater integration of such values? How does his/her success or lack of success relate to the possibility of developing those social conditions under which a greater integration of values would be possible?

Mead, of course, looked forward to the possibility of a full integration of human values and correspondingly to a society that would make such integration possible. Tellingly, while such a society had not come into being, Mead pointed to his mentor, William James, as an example of the complete human being, someone who "lived freely and thought freely," actualizing every aspect of his being without apparent contradiction (Mead, 1929–1930a). The example is telling precisely because Mead had criticized James' solution of the problem of consciousness as itself being far too individualistic in its premises. Moreover, James represented another weakness in American thought: the lack of full integration of cultural with economic and political life. James, in fact, represented a culturally privileged strata, which had not been able to fulfill the deeper sense of culture, because it could not feed that culture back into the realities of American experience. However, the example of James – both as realization and failure – went far beyond James himself and the isolation of the New England intelligentsia. It is clear that, for Mead, the problem applied to intellectuals in general.

The problem of justifying the condition of cultural privilege into which some are born or have relatively easy access was the counterpart of the problem of justifying the inevitable fact of suffering. In the end, argued Mead, it was the monopoly over cultural wealth that constituted the greatest injustice in the relations between the classes. Yet the remedy could not be a simple redistribution of culture any more than giving one's goods to the poor would remedy economic injustice. The problem was to reconstruct social relations in such a way that culture was not the privilege of the few. The obligation to so reconstruct society flowed not merely from the "generous" impulses of members of the privileged classes, but from the logical necessity for change implicit in the recognition of suffering. More pointedly, the fact of suffering, in its contradiction to accepted morality and scientific theory, gave the fundamental perspective to the problem of knowledge – not vice-versa. Thus, whether as citizen or scientist, the confrontation between the reflective individual and any given group is informed by the relative cultural privilege of the former and the degree of suffering of the latter. The suffering at issue is not only the primary suffering of biological beings, but the additional suffering they endure as members of a species trying to gain control, over its own destiny. Being stalled in the morass of dogmatism, false science, or irrationality just as surely constitutes a form of suffering as hunger or injury. Anyone who is stalled is, in essence, precluded from participation in the project of constructing the species' future. The compassionate and thinking individual, facing such a group of sufferers is forced to ask: What are the sources of its suffering? To what extent is this moral suffering shaped by its practical disadvantages, the education of Its members, its own institutionalization of values which it fears to abandon and which prevents its participating in a wider universe of discourse?

For the social scientist as reflective person, then, there can be nothing random in the decision to study certain groups and nothing relativistic in one's relationship to them. The groups most in need of understanding and help – not sentimental empathy and social tutelage, but compassion and help in searching out the conditions for their reentrance into the stream of common history – are the groups least connected with that history. These include the exploited who have not begun to insist on their own entrance, the narrow-minded, the vicious, the technocratic, the conservative. If the history of civilization is the history of an expanding and humanizing universe, the ethical social scientist must act to realize that universe – not by imposing a preconceived outline on the present, but by discerning its potentials in the humblest and most benighted of its would-be participants.

References

Becker, Howard, *et al.* 1961. *Boys in White.* Chicago: University of Chicago Press.
Blumer, Herbert. 1969. *Symbolic Interactionism.* Englewood Cliffs, N.J.: Prentice-Hall.
Carey, James. 1975. *Sociology and Public Affairs: The Chicago School.* Beverly Hills, Cal: Sage Publications, vol. 16, Sage Library of Sociological Research.
Davis, Fred. 1963. *Passage Through Crisis.* Indianapolis, Ind.: Bobbs-Merrill.
Faris, Ellsworth. 1937. *The Nature of Human Nature.* New York: McGraw-Hill.
Faris, Robert. 1967. *Chicago Sociology, 1920–1932.* Chicago: University of Chicago Press.
Fisher, Berenice and Strauss, Anselm. 1976. "Dilemmas of Social Change: Chicago Sociology." Unpubl. ms.
Fisher, Berenice and Strauss, Anselm. 1978. "The Chicago Tradition: Thomas, Park and Their Successors." *Symbolic Interaction,* Vol. 1 (12).
Fisher, Berenice and Strauss, Anselm. 1978. "The Chicago Tradition: Thomas, Park and Their Successors." *Symbolic Interaction,"* Vol. 1.
Hall, G. Stanley. 1924. *Founders of Modern Psychology.* New York: Appleton. (Orig. pub. 1912)

Lasch, Christopher. 1962. *The American Liberal and the Russian Revolution.* New York: Columbia University Press.

Lindesmith, Alfred, Strauss, Anselm, and Denzin, Norman. 1975. *Social Psychology.* Hinsdale, Ill.: Dryden Press, 4th edition.

Mead, George Herbert. 1899a. "The Working Hypothesis in Social Reform." *Am. J. Soc.*, 3, 369–71. (Petras, 125–129).

Mead, George Herbert. 1899b. "Le Bon, The Psychology of Socialism," reviewed in *Am. J. Soc.*, 5, 404–412.

Mead, George Herbert. 1907. "Jane Addams, The Newer Ideals of Peace." Reviewed in *Am. J. Soc.*, 13, 121–128.

Mead, George Herbert. 1908. "The Philosophical Basis of Ethics." *Int. J. Ethics*, 18, 311–323. (Reck, pp. 82–93).

Mead, George Herbert. 1908–1909. "Industrial Education, the Working Man and the School," *Elementary School Teacher*, 369–383. (Petras, pp. 50–62).

Mead, George Herbert. 1909. "Social Psychology as Counterpart to Physiological Psychology." *Psych. Bull.*, 6, 401–408. (Reck, pp. 94–104).

Mead, George Herbert. 1915. "Democracy's Issues in the World War." Also, "America's Ideals and the War." Dates not known, but about 1916–1917 probably: copies of newspaper clippings in the Univ. Chicago Library Archives).

Mead, George Herbert. 1915. "Natural Rights and the Theory of the Political Institution." *J. Phil., Psych., and Scientific Methods*, 12, 141–155. (Reck, pp. 150–170).

Mead, George Herbert. 1915. "Social Psychology: Course by George Herbert Mead." (Student notes taken about 1912, Univ. Chicago Library Archives).

Mead, George Herbert. 1917. "Scientific Method and the Individual Thinker." In, John Dewey and others (eds.), *Creative Intelligence: Essays in the Pragmatic Attitude.* New York: Holt, 176–227. (Reck, pp.171–211).

Mead, George Herbert. 1917–1918. "The Psychology of Punitive Justice," *Am. J. Soc.*, 223, 557–602. (Reck, pp. 212–239).

Mead, George Herbert. 1923. "Scientific Method and the Moral Sciences." *Int. J. Ethics*, 32, 229–247. (Reck, pp. 248–266; Petras, pp. 83–96).

Mead, George Herbert. 1929. "National-Mindedness and International Mindedness." *Int. J. Ethics*, 39, 392–407. (Reck, pp. 355–370).

Mead, George Herbert. 1929–1930. "The Philosophies of Royce, James, and Dewey in Their American Setting." *Int. J. Ethics*, 40: 211–231. (Reck, pp. 371–391; Petras, pp. 97–108.)

Mead, George Herbert. 1929–1930a. "The Philosophies of Royce, James, and Dewey, in their American Setting." *Int. J. Ethics*, 40, 211–231. (Reck, pp. 371–391; Petras, pp. 97–108).

Mead, George Herbert. 1929–1930b. "Cooley's Contribution to American Thought." *Am. J. Soc.*, 35, 693–706. (Strauss, pp. 293–307).

Mead, George Herbert. 1930. "Philanthropy from the Point of View of Ethics." In E. Faris, (ed.) *Intelligent Philanthropy.* Chicago: University of Chicago Press, 133–148. (Reck, pp. 392–407; Petras, pp. 97–108).

Mead, George Herbert. 1934. *Mind, Self, and Society.* Chicago: University of Chicago Press.

Metraux, Alexandre. Unpub. ms. on Wundt.

Miller, David. 1973. *George Herbert Mead: Self, Language, and the World.* Austin, Texas: University of Texas Press.

Petras, John (ed.). 1968. *George Herbert Mead: Essays on his Social Philosophy*. New York: Teachers College Press.

Quarantelli, Enrico and Cooper, Joseph. 1966. "Self-conceptions and others – A Further test of Meadian Hypotheses." *The Sociological Quarterly* (Summer): 281–297.

Reck, Andrew (ed.). 1964. *George Herbert Mead: Selected Writings*. Indianapolis, Ind.: Library of Liberal Arts.

Rucker, Darnell. 1969. *The Chicago Pragmatists*. Minneapolis: University of Minnesota Press.

Shibutani, Tamotsu. 1961. *Society and Personality*. Englewood Cliffs, N.J.: Prentice-Hall.

Shibutani, Tamotsu. 1966. *Improvised News*. Indianapolis: Bobbs-Merrill.

Small, Albion. 1910. *The Meaning of Social Science*. Chicago: University of Chicago Press.

Stone, Gregory. 1962. "Appearance and the Self." Pp. 86–118. In, A. Rose (ed.), *Human Behavior and Social Processes*. Boston: Houghton-Mifflin.

17

The Self as Social Structure†

George Herbert Mead

The self has the characteristic that it is an object to itself, and that characteristic distinguishes it from other objects and from the body. It is perfectly true that the eye can see the foot, but it does not see the body as a whole. We cannot see our backs; we can feel certain portions of them, if we are agile, but we cannot get an experience of our whole body. There are, of course, experiences which are somewhat vague and difficult of location, but the bodily experiences are for us organized about a self. The foot and hand belong to the self. We can see our feet, especially if we look at them from the wrong end of an opera glass, as strange things which we have difficulty in recognizing as our own. The parts of the body are quite distinguishable from the self. We can lose parts of the body without any serious invasion of the self. The mere ability to experience different parts of the body is not different from the experience of a table. The table presents a different feel from what the hand does when one hand feels another, but it is an experience of something with which we come definitely into contact. The body does not experience itself as a whole, in the sense in which the self in some way enters into the experience of the self.

It is the characteristic of the self as an object to itself that I want to bring out. This characteristic is represented in the word "self," which is a reflexive, and indicates that which can be both subject and object. This type of object is essentially different from other objects. . . .

The self, as that which can be an object to itself, is essentially a social structure, and it arises in social experience. . . . The individual experiences himself as such, not directly, but only indirectly, from the particular standpoint of other individual members of the same social group, or from the generalized standpoint of the social group as a whole to which he belongs. For he enters his own experience as a self or individual, not directly or immediately, not by becoming a subject to himself, but only insofar as he first becomes an object to himself, just as other individuals are objects to him or in his experience, and he becomes an object to himself only by taking the attitudes of other individuals toward

---

Source: Spencer Cahill, (ed.) *Inside Social Life*, (Los Angeles: Roxbury Publishing, 1994).

himself within a social environment or context of experience and behavior in which both he and they are involved.

After a self has arisen, it in a certain sense provides for itself its social experiences, and so we can conceive of an absolutely solitary self. But it is impossible to conceive of a self arising outside of social experience. When it has arisen, we can think of a person in solitary confinement for the rest of his life, but who still has himself as a companion, and is able to think and to converse with himself as he had communicated with others. . . . We are continually following up our own address to other persons by an understanding of what we are saying, and using that understanding in the direction of our continued speech. We are finding out what we are going to say, what we are going to do, by trolling the process itself. In the conversation of gestures, what we say calls out a certain response in another and that in turn changes our own action, so that we shift from what we started to do because of the reply the other makes. The conversation of gestures is the beginning of communication. The individual comes to carry on a conversation of gestures with himself. He says something, and that calls out a certain reply in himself which makes him change what he was going to say. One starts to say something, we will presume an unpleasant something, but when he starts to say it, he realizes it is cruel. The effect on himself of what he is saying checks him; there is here a conversation of gestures between the individual and himself. We mean by significant speech that the action is one that affects the individual himself, and that the effect upon the individual himself is part of the intelligent carrying out of the conversation with others. Now we, so to speak, amputate that social phase and dispense with it for the time being so that one is talking to one's self as one would talk to another person. . . .

We have discussed the social foundations of the self. . . . We may now explicitly raise the question as to the nature of the "I" which is aware of the social "me". . . . The "I" reacts to the self which arises through taking the attitudes of others. Through taking those attitudes, we have introduced the "me" and we react to it as an "I."

The "I" is the response of the individual to the attitude of the community as this appears in his own experience. His response to that organized attitude in turn changes it. . . . [T]his is a change which is not present in his own experience until after it takes place. The "I" appears in our experience in memory. It is only after we have acted that we know what we have done; it is only after we have spoken that we know what we have said. The adjustment to that organized world which is present in our own nature is one that represents the "me" and is constantly there. But if the response to it is a response which is of the nature of the conversation of gestures, if it creates a situation which is in some sense novel, if one puts up his side of the case, asserts himself over against others and insists that they take a different attitude toward himself, then there is something important occurring that is not previously present in experience. . . . Such a novel reply to the social situation . . . constitutes the "I" as over against the "me". . . .

The problem now presents itself as to how, in detail, a self arises. We have to note something of the background of its genesis. . . . We have seen . . . that there are certain gestures that affect the organism as they affect other organisms and may, therefore, arouse in the organism responses of the same character as aroused in the other. Here, then, we have a situation in which the individual may at least arouse responses in himself and reply to these responses, the condition being that the social stimuli have an effect on the individual which is like that which they have on the other. That, for example, is what is implied in language; otherwise, language as significant symbol would disappear, since the individual would not get the meaning of that which he says. . . . It is out of that sort of language that the mind of Helen Keller was built up. As she has recognized, it was not until she could get into communication with other persons through symbols which could arouse in herself the responses they arouse in other people that she could get what we term a mental content, or a self.

Another set of background factors in the genesis of the self is represented in the activities of play and the game.

We find [among] children . . . invisible, imaginary companions. . . . [Children] organize in this way the responses which they call out in other persons and call out also in themselves. Of course, this playing with an imaginary companion is only a peculiarly interesting phase of ordinary play. Play in this sense, especially the stage which precedes the organized games, is a play at something. A child plays at being a mother, at being a teacher, at being a policeman; that is, he is taking different roles, as we say. We have something that suggests this in what we call the play of animals: a cat will play with her kittens, and dogs play with each other. Two dogs playing with each other will attack and defend, in a process which if carried through would amount to an actual fight. There is a combination of responses which checks the depth of the bite. But we do not have in such a situation the dogs taking a definite role in the sense that a child deliberately takes the role of another. This tendency on the part of the children is what we are working with in the kindergarten where the roles which the children assume are made the basis for training. When a child does assume a role he has in himself the stimuli which call out that particular response or group of responses. He may, of course, run away when he is chased, as the dog does, or he may turn around and strike back just as the dog does in his play. But that is not the same as playing at something. Children get together to "play Indian." This means that the child has a certain set of stimuli which call out in itself the responses that they would call out in others, and which answer to an Indian. In the play period the child utilizes his own responses to these stimuli which he makes use of in building a self. The response which he has a tendency to make to these stimuli organizes them. He plays that he is, for instance, offering himself something, and he buys it; he gives a letter to himself and takes it away; he addresses himself as a parent, as a teacher; he arrests himself as a policeman. He has a set of stimuli which call out in himself the sort of responses they call out in others. He takes this group of responses and organizes them into a certain whole. Such is the simplest form of being another to one's self. It involves a temporal situation. The child says something in one character and responds in another character, and then his responding in another character is a stimulus to himself in the first character, and so the conversation goes on. A certain organized structure arises in him and in his other which replies to it, and these carry on the conversation of gestures between themselves.

If we contrast play with the situation in an organized game, we note the essential difference that the child who plays in a game must be ready to take the attitude of everyone else involved in that game, and that these different roles must have a definite relationship to each other. Taking a very simple game such as hide-and-seek, everyone, with the exception of the one who is hiding, is a person who is hunting. A child does not require more than the person who is hunted and the one who is hunting. If a child is playing in the first sense he just goes on playing, but there is no basic organization gained. In that early stage he passes from one role to another just as a whim takes him. But in a game where a number of individuals are involved, then the child taking one role must be ready to take the role of everyone else. If he gets in a ball nine, he must have the responses of each position involved in his own position. He must know what everyone else is going to do in order to carry out his own play. He has to take all of these roles. They do not all have to be present in consciousness at the same time, but at some moments he has to have three or four individuals present in his own attitude, such as the one who is going to throw the ball, the one who is going to catch it, and so on. These responses must be, in some degree, present in his own make-up. In the game, then, there is a set of responses of such others so organized that the attitude of one calls out the appropriate attitudes of the other.

This organization is put in the form of the rules of the game. Children take a great interest in rules. They make rules on the spot in order to help themselves out of difficulties. Part of the enjoyment of the game is to get these rules. Now, the rules are the set of responses which a particular attitude calls out. You can demand a certain response in others if you take a certain attitude. These responses are all in yourself as well. There you get an organized set of such responses as that to which I have referred, which is something more elaborate than the roles found in play. Here there is just a set of responses that follow on each other indefinitely. At such a stage we speak of a child as not yet having a fully developed self. The child responds in a fairly intelligent fashion to the immediate stimuli that come to him, but they are not organized. He does not organize his life as we would like to have him do, namely, as a whole. There is just a set of responses of the type of play. The child reacts to a certain stimulus, and the reaction is in himself that is called out in others, but he is not a whole self. In his game he has to have an organization of these roles; otherwise, he cannot play the game. The game represents the passage in the life of the child from taking the role of others in play to the organized part that is essential to self-consciousness in the full sense of the term.

The fundamental difference between the game and play is that in the latter the child must have the attitude of all the others involved in that game. The attitudes of the other players which the participant assumes organize into a sort of unit, and it is that organization which controls the response of the individual. The illustration used was of a person playing baseball. Each one of his own acts is determined by his assumption of the action of the others who are playing the game. What he does is controlled by his being everyone else on that team, at least in so far as those attitudes affect his own particular response. We get then an "other" which is an organization of the attitudes of those involved in the same process.

A multiple personality is in a certain sense normal. . . . There is usually an organization of the whole self with reference to the community to which we belong, and the situation in which we find ourselves. What the society is, whether we are living with people of the present, people of our own imaginations, people of the past, varies, of course, with different individuals. Normally, within the sort of community as a whole to which we belong, there is a unified self, but that may be broken up. To a person who is somewhat unstable and in whom there is a line of cleavage, certain activities become impossible, and that set of activities may separate and evolve into another self. Two separate "me's" and "I's," two different selves result, and that is the condition under which there is a tendency to break up the personality. There is an account of a professor of education who disappeared, was lost to the community, and later turned up in a logging camp in the West. He freed himself of his occupation and turned to the woods where he felt, if you like, more at home. The pathological side of it was the forgetting, the leaving out of the rest of the self. This result involved getting rid of certain bodily memories which would identify the individual to himself. We often recognize the lines of cleavage that run through us. We would be glad to forget certain things, get rid of things the self is bound up with in past experiences. What we have here is a situation in which there can be different selves, and it is dependent upon the set of social reactions that is involved as to which self we are going to be.

The unity and structure of the complete self reflects the unity and structure of the social process as a whole; and each of the elementary selves of which it is composed reflects the unity and structure of one of the various aspects of that process in which the individual is implicated. In other words, the various elementary selves which constitute, or are organized into, a complete self are the various aspects of the structure of that complete self answering to the various aspects of the structure of the social process as a whole; the structure of the complete self is thus a reflection of the complete social process. The organization and unification of a social group is identical with the organization and unification of any one of the selves arising within the social process in which that group is engaged, or which it is carrying on.

The organized community or social group which gives to the individual his unity of self may be called "the generalized other." The attitude of the generalized other is the attitude of the whole community.

I have emphasized what I have called the structures upon which the self is constructed, the framework of the self, as it were. . . . We cannot be ourselves unless we are also members in whom there is a community of attitudes which control the attitudes of all. We cannot have rights unless we have common attitudes. That which we have acquired as self-conscious persons makes us such members of society and gives us selves. Selves can only exist in definite relationships to other selves. No hard-and-fast line can be drawn between our own selves and the selves of others, since our own selves exist and enter as such into our experience only insofar as the selves of others exist and enter as such into our experience also. The individual possesses a self only in relation to the selves of the other members of his social group; and the structure of his self expresses or reflects the general behavior pattern of this social group to which he belongs; just as does the structure of the self of every other individual belonging to this social group.

Note

†. Extracted from George Herbert Mead, *Mind, Self, Society*, (Chicago: University of Chicago Press, 1962), pp. 136–7, 140–141, 138, 144–145, 149–154, 142–3, 173–174, 196, 163–4.

18

The Self as Sentiment and Reflection†

Charles Horton Cooley

It is well to say at the outset that by the word "self" in this discussion is meant simply that which is designated in common speech by the pronouns of the first person singular, "I," "me," "my," "mine," and "myself." "Self" and "ego" are used by metaphysicians and moralists in many other senses, more or less remote from the "I" of daily speech and thought, and with these I wish to have as little to do as possible. What is here discussed is what psychologists call the empirical self, the self that can be apprehended or verified by ordinary observation. I qualify it by the word social not as implying the existence of a self that is not social — for I think that the "I" of common language always has more or less distinct reference to other people as well as the speaker — but because I wish to emphasize and dwell upon the social aspect of it.

The distinctive thing in the idea, for which the pronouns of the first person are names, is apparently a characteristic kind of feeling which may be called the my-feeling or sense of appropriation. Almost any sort of ideas may be associated with this feeling, and that alone, it would seem, is the determining factor in the matter. As Professor James says in his admirable discussion of the self, the words "me" and "self" designate "all the things which have the power to produce in a stream of consciousness excitement of a certain peculiar sort. . . ." The social self is simply any idea, or system of ideas, drawn from the communicative life that the mind cherishes as its own. Self-feeling has its chief scope within the general life, not outside of it. . . .

That the "I" of common speech has a meaning which includes some sort of reference to other persons is involved in the very fact that the word and the ideas it stands for are phenomena of language and the communicative life. It is doubtful whether it is possible to use language at all without thinking more or less distinctly of someone else, and certainly the things to which we give names, and which have a large place in reflective thought, are almost always those which are impressed upon us by our contact with other people. Where there is no communication there can be no nomenclature and no developed thought. What we call "me," "mine," or "myself' is, then, not something separate from

---

Source: Spencer Cahill, (ed.) *Inside Social Life*, (Los Angeles: Roxbury Publishing, 1994).

the general life, but the most interesting part of it, a part whose interest arises from the very fact that it is both general and individual. That is, we care for it just because it is that phase of the mind that is living and striving in the common life, trying to impress itself upon the minds of others. "I" is a militant social tendency, working to hold and enlarge its place in the general current of tendencies. So far as it can it waxes, as all life does. To think of it as apart from society is a palpable absurdity of which no one could be guilty who really saw it as a fact of life. . . .

If a thing has no relation to others of which one is conscious, he is unlikely to think of it at all and if he does think of it he cannot, it seems to me, regard it as emphatically *his*. The appropriative sense is always the shadow, as it were, of the common life; and when we have it, we have a sense of the latter in connection with it. Thus, if we think of a secluded part of the woods as "ours," it is because we think also, that others do not go there. . . .

The reference to other persons involved in the sense of self may be distinct and particular, as when a boy is ashamed to have his mother catch him at something she has forbidden; or it may be vague and general, as when one is ashamed to do something which only his conscience, expressing his sense of social responsibility, detects and disapproves; but it is always there. There is no sense of "I," as in pride or shame, without its correlative sense of you, or he, or they. Even the miser gloating over his hidden gold can feel the "mine" only as he is aware of the world of men over whom he has secret power; and the case is very similar with all kinds of hidden treasure. Many painters, sculptors, and writers have loved to withhold their work from the world, fondling it in seclusion until they were quite done with it; but the delight in this, as in all secrets, depends upon a sense of the value of what is concealed.

In a very large and interesting class of cases, the social reference takes the form of a somewhat definite imagination of how one's self – that is, any idea he appropriates – appears in a particular mind, and the kind of self-feeling one has is determined by the attitude toward this attributed to that other mind. A social self of this sort might be called the reflected or looking-glass self:

"Each to each a looking-glass
    Reflects the other that doth pass."

As we see our face, figure, and dress in the glass, and are interested in them because they are ours, and pleased or otherwise with them according as they do or do not answer to what we should like them to be; so in imagination we perceive in another's mind some thought of our appearance, manners, aims, deeds, character, friends, and so on, and are variously affected by it.

A self-idea of this sort seems to have three principal elements: the imagination of our appearance to the other person; the imagination of his judgment of that appearance; and some sort of self-feeling, such as pride or mortification. The comparison with a looking glass hardly suggests the second element, the imagined judgment, which is quite essential. The thing that moves us to pride or shame is not the mere mechanical reflection of ourselves, but an imputed sentiment, the imagined effect of this reflection upon another's mind. This is evident from the fact that the character and weight of that other, in whose mind we see ourselves, makes all the difference with our feeling. We are ashamed to seem evasive in the presence of a straightforward man, cowardly in the presence of a brave one, gross in the eyes of a refined one, and so on. We always imagine, and in imagining share, the judgments of the other mind. A man will boast to one person of an action – say some sharp transaction in trade – which he would be ashamed to own to another. . . .

[This] view [of] "self" and the pronouns of the first person . . . was impressed on me by observing my child M. at the time when she was learning to use these pronouns. When she was two years and two weeks old, I was surprised to discover that she had a clear notion of the first and second persons when used possessively. When asked, "Where is your nose?" she would put her hand upon it and say "my." She also understood that when someone else said "my" and touched an object, it meant something opposite to what was meant when she touched the same object and used the same word. Now, anyone who will exercise his imagination upon the question of how this matter must appear to a mind having no means of knowing anything about "I" and "my," except what it learns by hearing them used, will see that it should be very puzzling. Unlike other words, the personal pronouns have apparently no uniform meaning, but convey different and even opposite ideas when employed by different persons. It seems remarkable that children should master the problem before they arrive at the considerable power of abstract reasoning. How should a little girl of two, not particularly reflective, have discovered that "my" was not the sign of a definite object like other words, but meant something different with each person who used it? And, still more surprising, how should she have achieved the correct use of it with reference to herself which, it would seem, *could not be copied from anyone else,* simply because no one else used it to describe what belonged to her? The meaning of words is learned by associating them with other phenomena. But how is it possible to learn the meaning of one which, as used by others, is never associated with the same phenomenon as when properly used by one's self? Watching her use of the first person, I was at once struck with the fact that she employed it almost wholly in a possessive sense, and that, too, when in an aggressive, self-assertive mood. It was extremely common to see R. tugging at one end of a plaything and M. at the other, screaming, "My, my." "Me" was sometimes nearly equivalent to "my" and was also employed to call attention to herself when she wanted something done for her. Another common use of "my" was to demand something she did not have at all. Thus, if R. had something the like of which she wanted, say a cart, she would exclaim, "Where's *my* cart?"

It seemed to me that she might have learned the use of these pronouns as follows. The self-feeling had always been there. From the first week she had wanted things and cried and fought for them. She had also become familiar by observation and opposition with similar appropriative activities on the part of R. Thus, she not only had the feeling herself, but by associating it with its visible expression had probably defined it, sympathized with it, resented it, in others. Grasping, tugging, and screaming would be associated with the feeling in her own case and would recall the feeling when observed in others. They would constitute a language, precedent to the use of first-person pronouns, to express the self-idea. All was ready, then, for the word to name this experience. She now observed that R., when contentiously appropriating something, frequently exclaimed, "*my*," "*mine*," "give it to *me*," "*I* want it," and the like. Nothing more natural, then, than that she should adopt these words as names for a frequent and vivid experience with which she was already familiar in her own case and had learned to attribute to others. Accordingly, it appeared to me, as I recorded in my notes at the time, that "'my' and 'mine' are simply names for concrete images of appropriativeness," embracing both the appropriative feeling and its manifestation. If this is true, the child does not at first work out the I-and-you idea in an abstract form. The first-person pronoun is a sign of a concrete thing, after all, but that thing is not primarily the child's body, or his muscular sensations as such, but the phenomenon of aggressive appropriation, practiced by himself, witnessed in others, and incited and interpreted by a hereditary instinct. This seems to get over the difficulty mentioned above, namely, the seeming lack of a common content between the meaning of "my" when used by another and when used by one's self. This common content is found in the appropriative feeling and the visible and audible signs of that feeling. An element of difference and strife comes in, of course, in the opposite actions or purposes which the "my" of another and one's own "my" are likely to stand for. When another person says "mine" regarding something which I claim, I sympathize with him enough to understand what he means, but it is a hostile sympathy, overpowered by another and more vivid "mine" connected with the idea of drawing the object my way.

In other words, the meaning of "I" and "mine" is learned in the same way that the meanings of hope, regret, chagrin, disgust, and thousands of other words of emotion and sentiment are learned: that is, by having the feeling, imputing it to others in connection with some kind of expression, and hearing the word along with it. As to its communication and growth, the self-idea is in no way peculiar that I see, but essentially like other ideas. In its more complex forms, such as are expressed by "I" in conversation and literature, it is a social sentiment, or type of sentiments, defined and developed by intercourse. . . .

I imagine, then, that as a rule the child associates "I" and "me" at first only with those ideas regarding which his appropriative feeling is aroused and defined by opposition. He appropriates his nose, eye, or foot in very much the same way as a plaything – by antithesis to other noses, eyes, and feet, which he cannot control. It is not uncommon to tease little children by proposing to take away one of these organs, and they behave precisely as if the "mine" threatened were a separable object – which it might be for all they know. And, as I have suggested, even in adult life, "I," "me," and "mine" are applied with a strong sense of their meaning only to things distinguished as peculiar to us by some sort of opposition or contrast. They always imply social life and relation to other persons. That which is most distinctively mine is very private, it is true, but it is that part of the private which I am cherishing in antithesis to the rest of the world, not the separate but the special. The aggressive self is essentially a militant phase of the mind, having for its apparent function the energizing of peculiar activities, and, although the militancy may not go on in an obvious, external manner, it always exists as a mental attitude. . . .

The process by which self-feeling of the looking-glass sort develops in children may be followed without much difficulty. Studying the movements of others as closely as they do, they soon see a connection between their own acts and changes in those movements; that is, they perceive their own influence or power over persons. The child appropriates the visible actions of his parent or nurse, over which he finds he has some control, in quite the same way as he appropriates one of his own members or a plaything; and he will try to do things with this new possession, just as he will with his hand or his rattle. A girl six months old will attempt in the most evident and deliberate manner to attract attention to herself, to set going by her actions some of those movements of other persons that she has appropriated. She has tasted the joy of being a cause, of exerting social power, and wishes more of it. She will tug at her mother's skirts, wriggle, gurgle, stretch out her arms, etc., all the time watching for the hoped-for effect. . . .

The young performer soon learns to be different things to different people, showing that he begins to apprehend personality and to foresee its operation. If the mother or nurse is more tender than just, she will almost certainly be "worked" by systematic weeping. It is a matter of common observation that children often behave worse with their mother than with other and less sympathetic people. Of the new persons that a child sees, it is evident that some make a strong impression and awaken a desire to interest and please them, while others are indifferent or repugnant. Sometimes the reason can be perceived or guessed, sometimes not; but the fact of selective interest, admiration, and prestige is obvious before the end of the second year. By that time a child already cares much for the reflection of himself upon one personality and little for that upon another. Moreover, he soon claims intimate and tractable persons as *mine*, classes them among his other possessions, and maintains his ownership against all comers. M., at three years of age, vigorously resented R.'s claim upon their mother. The latter was "*my* mamma," whenever the point was raised.

Strong joy and grief depend upon the treatment this rudimentary social self receives. . . . At about fifteen months old [M.] had become "a perfect little actress," seeming to live largely in imaginations of her effect upon other people. She constantly and obviously laid traps for attention, and looked abashed or wept at any signs of disapproval or indifference. At times it would seem as if she could not get over these repulses, but would cry long in a grieved way, refusing to be comforted. If she hit upon any little trick that made people laugh, she would be sure to repeat it, laughing loudly and affectedly in imitation. She had quite a repertory of these small performances, which she would display to a sympathetic audience, or even try upon strangers. I have seen her at sixteen months, when R. refused to give her the scissors, sit down, and make-believe cry, putting up her underlip and sniffling, meanwhile looking up now and then to see what effect she was producing. . . .

Progress from this point is chiefly in the way of a greater definiteness, fullness, and inwardness in the imagination of the other's state of mind. A little child thinks of and tries to elicit certain visible or audible phenomena, and does not go beyond them; but what a grown-up person desires to produce in others is an internal, invisible condition which his own richer experience enables him to imagine, and of which expression is only the sign. Even adults, however, make no separation between what other people think and the visible expression of that thought. They imagine the whole thing at once, and their idea differs from that of a child chiefly in the comparative richness and complexity of the elements that accompany and interpret the visible or audible sign. There is also a progress from the naive to the subtle in socially self-assertive action. A child obviously and simply, at first, does things for effect. Later there is an endeavor to suppress the appearance of doing so; affection, indifference, contempt, etc., are simulated to hide the real wish to affect the self-image. . . .

Note

†. Extracted from Charles Horton Cooley, *Human Nature and the Social Order*, (New Brunswick: Transaction Publishers, 1983 [1906]), pp. 168–170, 179–184, 189–194, 196–199.

19

Primary Groups

Charles Horton Cooley

By primary groups I mean those characterized by intimate face-to-face association and coöperation. They are primary in several senses, but chiefly in that they are fundamental in forming the social nature and ideals of the individual. The result of intimate association, psychologically, is a certain fusion of individualities in a common whole, so that one's very self, for many purposes at least, is the common life and purpose of the group. Perhaps the simplest way of describing this wholeness is by saying that it is a "we"; it involves the sort of sympathy and mutual identification for which "we" is the natural expression. One lives in the feeling of the whole and finds the chief aims of his will in that feeling.

It is not to be supposed that the unity of the primary group is one of mere harmony and love. It is always a differentiated and usually a competitive unity, admitting of self-assertion and various appropriative passions; but these passions are socialized by sympathy, and come, or tend to come, under the discipline of a common spirit. The individual will be ambitious, but the chief object of his ambition will be some desired place in the thought of the others, and he will feel allegiance to common standards of service and fair play. So the boy will dispute with his fellows a place on the team, but above such disputes will place the common glory of his class and school.

The most important spheres of this intimate association and coöperation – though by no means the only ones – are the family, the play-group of children, and the neighborhood or community group of elders. These are practically universal, belonging to all times and all stages of development; and are accordingly a chief basis of what is universal in human nature and human ideals. The best comparative studies of the family, such as those of Westermarck[1] or Howard,[2] show it to us as not only a universal institution, but as more alike the world over than the exaggeration of exceptional customs by an earlier school had led us to suppose. Nor can any one doubt the general prevalence of play-groups among children or of informal assemblies of various kinds

---

Source: Charles Horton Cooley, *Social Organization*, (New York: Charles Scribner's Sons, 1909).

among their elders. Such association is clearly the nursery of human nature in the world about us, and there is no apparent reason to suppose that the case has anywhere or at any time been essentially different.

As regards play, I might, were it not a matter of common observation, multiply illustrations of the universality and spontaneity of the group discussion and coöperation to which it gives rise. The general fact is that children, especially boys after about their twelfth year, live in fellowships in which their sympathy, ambition and honor are engaged even more, often, than they are in the family. Most of us can recall examples of the endurance by boys of injustice and even cruelty, rather than appeal from their fellows to parents or teachers – as, for instance, in the hazing so prevalent at schools, and so difficult, for this very reason, to repress. And how elaborate the discussion, how cogent the public opinion, how hot the ambitions in these fellowships.

Nor is this facility of juvenile association, as is sometimes supposed, a trait peculiar to English and American boys; since experience among our immigrant population seems to show that the offspring of the more restrictive civilizations of the continent of Europe form self-governing play-groups with almost equal readiness. Thus Miss Jane Addams, after pointing out that the "gang" is almost universal, speaks of the interminable discussion which every detail of the gang's activity receives, remarking that "in these social folk-motes, so to speak, the young citizen learns to act upon his own determination."[3]

Of the neighborhood group it may be said, in general, that from the time men formed permanent settlements upon the land, down, at least, to the rise of modern industrial cities, it has played a main part in the primary, heart-to-heart life of the people. Among our Teutonic forefathers the village community was apparently the chief sphere of sympathy and mutual aid for the commons all through the "dark" and middle ages, and for many purposes it remains so in rural districts at the present day. In some countries we still find it with all its ancient vitality, notably in Russia, where the mir, or self-governing village group, is the main theatre of life, along with the family, for perhaps fifty millions of peasants.

In our own life the intimacy of the neighborhood has been broken up by the growth of an intricate mesh of wider contacts which leaves us strangers to people who live in the same house. And even in the country the same principle is at work, though less obviously, diminishing our economic and spiritual community with our neighbors. How far this change is a healthy development, and how far a disease, is perhaps still uncertain.

Besides these almost universal kinds of primary association, there are many others whose form depends upon the particular state of civilization; the only essential thing, as I have said, being a certain intimacy and fusion of personalities. In our own society, being little bound by place, people easily form clubs, fraternal societies and the like, based on congeniality, which may give rise to real intimacy. Many such relations are formed at school and college, and among men and women brought together in the first instance by their occupations –

as workmen in the same trade, or the like. Where there is a little common interest and activity, kindness grows like weeds by the roadside.

But the fact that the family and neighborhood groups are ascendant in the open and plastic time of childhood makes them even now incomparably more influential than all the rest.

Primary groups are primary in the sense that they give the individual his earliest and completest experience of social unity, and also in the sense that they do not change in the same degree as more elaborate relations, but form a comparatively permanent source out of which the latter are ever springing. Of course they are not independent of the larger society, but to some extent reflect its spirit; as the German family and the German school bear somewhat distinctly the print of German militarism. But this, after all, is like the tide setting back into creeks, and does not commonly go very far. Among the German, and still more among the Russian, peasantry are found habits of free coöperation and discussion almost uninfluenced by the character of the state; and it is a familiar and well-supported view that the village commune, self-governing as regards local affairs and habituated to discussion, is a very widespread institution in settled communities, and the continuator of a similar autonomy previously existing in the clan. "It is man who makes monarchies and establishes republics, but the commune seems to come directly from the hand of God."[4]

In our own cities the crowded tenements and the general economic and social confusion have sorely wounded the family and the neighborhood, but it is remarkable, in view of these conditions, what vitality they show; and there is nothing upon which the conscience of the time is more determined than upon restoring them to health.

These groups, then, are springs of life, not only for the individual but for social institutions. They are only in part moulded by special traditions, and, in larger degree, express a universal nature. The religion or government of other civilizations may seem alien to us, but the children or the family group wear the common life, and with them we can always make ourselves at home.

By human nature, I suppose, we may understand those sentiments and impulses that are human in being superior to those of lower animals, and also in the sense that they belong to mankind at large, and not to any particular race or time. It means, particularly, sympathy and the innumerable sentiments into which sympathy enters, such as love, resentment, ambition, vanity, hero-worship, and the feeling of social right and wrong.[5]

Human nature in this sense is justly regarded as a comparatively permanent element in society. Always and everywhere men seek honor and dread ridicule, defer to public opinion, cherish their goods and their children, and admire courage, generosity, and success. It is always safe to assume that people are and have been human.

It is true, no doubt, that there are differences of race capacity, so great that a large part of mankind are possibly incapable of any high kind of social organization. But these differences, like those among individuals of the same race, are subtle, depending upon some obscure intellectual deficiency, some want of vigor, or slackness of moral fibre, and do not involve unlikeness in the generic impulses of human nature. In these all races are very much alike. The more insight one gets into the life of savages, even those that are reckoned the lowest, the more human, the more like ourselves, they appear. Take for instance the natives of Central Australia, as described by Spencer and Gillen,[6] tribes having no definite government or worship and scarcely able to count to five. They are generous to one another, emulous of virtue as they understand it, kind to their children and to the aged, and by no means harsh to women. Their faces as shown in the photographs are wholly human and many of them attractive.

And when we come to a comparison between different stages in the development of the same race, between ourselves, for instance, and the Teutonic tribes of the time of Caesar, the difference is neither in human nature nor in capacity, but in organization, in the range and complexity of relations, in the diverse expression of powers and passions essentially much the same.

There is no better proof of this generic likeness of human nature than in the ease and joy with which the modern man makes himself at home in literature depicting the most remote and varied phases of life – in Homer, in the Nibelung tales, in the Hebrew Scriptures, in the legends of the American Indians, in stories of frontier life, of soldiers and sailors, of criminals and tramps, and so on. The more penetratingly any phase of human life is studied the more an essential likeness to ourselves is revealed.

To return to primary groups: the view here maintained is that human nature is not something existing separately in the individual, but a *group-nature or primary phase of society*, a relatively simple and general condition of the social mind. It is something more, on the one hand, than the mere instinct that is born in us – though that enters into it – and something less, on the other, than the more elaborate development of ideas and sentiments that makes up institutions. It is the nature which is developed and expressed in those simple, face-to-face groups that are somewhat alike in all societies; groups of the family, the playground, and the neighborhood. In the essential similarity of these is to be found the basis, in experience, for similar ideas and sentiments in the human mind. In these, everywhere, human nature comes into existence. Man does not have it at birth; he cannot acquire it except through fellowship, and it decays in isolation.

If this view does not recommend itself to common-sense I do not know that elaboration will be of much avail. It simply means the application at this point of the idea that society and individuals are inseparable phases of a common whole, so that wherever we find an individual fact we may look for a social fact to go with it. If there is a universal nature in persons there must be something universal in association to correspond to it.

What else can human nature be than a trait of primary groups? Surely not an attribute of the separate individual – supposing there were any such thing – since its typical characteristics, such as affection, ambition, vanity, and resentment, are inconceivable apart from society. If it belongs, then, to man in association, what kind or degree of association is required to develop it ? Evidently nothing elaborate, because elaborate phases of society are transient and diverse, while human nature is comparatively stable and universal. In short the family and neighborhood life is essential to its genesis and nothing more is.

Here as everywhere in the study of society we must learn to see mankind in psychical wholes, rather than in artificial separation. We must see and feel the communal life of family and local groups as immediate facts, not as combinations of something else. And perhaps we shall do this best by recalling our own experience and extending it through sympathetic observation. What, in our life, is the family and the fellowship; what do we know of the we-feeling? Thought of this kind may help us to get a concrete perception of that primary group-nature of which everything social is the outgrowth.

Notes

1. *The History of Human Marriage.*
2. *A History of Matrimonial Institutions.*
3. *Newer Ideals of Peace,* 177.
4. De Tocqueville, *Democracy in America,* vol. i, chap. 5.
5. These matters are expounded at some length in the writer's *Human Nature and the Social Order.*
6. *The Native Tribes of Central Australia.* Compare also Darwin's views and examples given in chap. 7 of his *Descent of Man.*

20

The Polish Peasant in Europe and America: A Landmark of Empirical Sociology

Martin Bulmer

The beginnings of the Chicago school are usually identified with the urban research of Robert Park and Ernest Burgess and their students, which began around 1920. The influence of W. I. Thomas, however, was of great significance, particularly through his massive study with Florian Znaniecki, *The Polish Peasant in Europe and America*,[1] published between 1918 and 1920. The significance of the publication of *The Polish Peasant* can hardly be exaggerated. Though it has been something of a neglected classic in the literature, referred to far more often than it has been read, it is a classic nevertheless. It was not the first American sociological monograph, but it was a landmark because it attempted to integrate theory and data in a way no American study had done before. It had, moreover, a major impact upon future developments. It is "the first great classic in American empirical sociology,"[2] "one of the half dozen most influential books in the history of social psychology."[3] Edward Shils has compared W. I. Thomas with his other great contemporaries, "Durkheim, Weber, and Pareto, in whose class he surely belongs."[4]

The Polish Peasant marked a shift in sociology away from abstract theory and library research toward a more intimate acquaintance with the empirical world, studied nevertheless in terms of a theoretical frame. Of the Big Four of the sociology department, it was only Thomas who became wholeheartedly committed to empirical research. At first, Thomas worked from documentary sources and did not do firsthand research. But in the first decade of the century his orientation changed, and as he later recalled:

> I explored the city. This last was also a matter of curiosity. I remember that Professor Henderson of sainted memory, once requested me to get him a bit of information from the saloons. He said that he himself had never entered a saloon or tasted beer.[5]

Source: Martin Bulmer, *The Chicago School of Sociology* (Chicago: University of Chicago Press, 1984).

From the time of his earlier work on *Social Origins*,⁶ Thomas had stressed the necessity of having concrete, objective detailed studies of social behavior and attitudes. The common element in the Chicago school of sociology, commitment to empirical research,⁷ owed an enormous amount to the example set by Thomas.

The Polish Peasant had a triple importance as an empirical monograph. By using personal documents, it employed novel methods of empirical research and suggested directions in which empirical sociology could develop distinct from historical and comparative methods in the manner of Sumner or the social survey movement. By blending theory and data, it provided a basis for generalization and the forward movement both of sociology and social psychology. And by focusing upon the immigrant as the subject of study, it helped to strengthen sociology as an autonomous academic discipline. The subject became institutionalized in America in separate departments in part because no other social science dealt with the problems created by immigration.⁸

Thomas's interest in European immigration developed in the context described (in the previous chapter). The reform orientation, the interest in the city, the concern in the sociology department with social problems, all had their effect on him, as did outside influences such as Upton Sinclair's muckraking novel about East European immigrants in the Chicago stockyards, *The Jungle*.⁹ Thomas's approach, however, was detached, unemotional, and scientific,¹⁰ marked by penetrating curiosity and the desire to understand human behavior rather than moral fervour and the desire to change society. In his theory of social disorganization, for example, Thomas attempted to interpret deviance from social norms or rules as culturally patterned behavior, not an adaptation to strain, in contrast to Durkheim's theory of anomie. This theoretical statement was an attempt to give a more scholarly form to concerns that had infused the beginnings of sociology in America and to make the study of social problems more scientific.

The decision to study an immigrant group reflected Thomas's Chicago location:

> Immigration was a burning question. About a million immigrants were coming here annually, and this was mainly the newer immigration, from southern and eastern Europe. The larger groups were Poles, Italians, and Jews. When I became a member of the faculty of Chicago, I gave, among other courses, one on immigration and one on social attitudes, and eventually I decided to study an immigrant group in Europe and America to determine as far as possible what relation their home mores and norms had to their adjustment and maladjustment in America.¹¹

Immediately after gaining his Ph.D. in 1896, Thomas had visited Europe, on what he later described as a "sort of vagabonding trip."

> I reached the coronation of the czar the day after it was over, circulated among the peasants of several countries, and visited an exposition in Budapest where there were a lot of peasants. While looking at a group of these, I said to myself: "It would be very interesting to study a European group from which immigration is heavy and then study the representatives of the same group in America and see to what degree and in what respects their behavior in America is related to the habits of their home situation." That was the origin of *The Polish Peasant* but I did not get around to undertaking it until 1908.[12]

Thomas's work on *The Polish Peasant* was pathbreaking in another respect. To carry out the study, he received very substantial outside funding. In 1908 he obtained from Helen Culver, heiress of the Hull of Hull-House (who in all gave the university about one million dollars),[13] the then enormous sum of $50,000 with which to carry out research on immigrant problems.

> I was now in a rather alarming situation. I had made positive representations, I had got a lot of money, I had promised a great (also big) work, and what was I going to do about it? I first of all went over to Europe to locate a suitable group, where good materials were available. The choice was between the Italians, the Jews, and the Poles. The Poles are very repulsive people on the whole, but there had been a movement for "enlightenment" and freedom that had developed many documents and masses of material on the peasant, so I decided to bore in there.[14]

Between 1908 and 1913 Thomas spent a considerable time – about eight months a year – in Europe. The grant from Miss Culver paid for replacement teaching at the university in his absence, a policy Harper had encouraged to allow teachers time for their own research and another innovation for research in sociology. Thomas visited Warsaw, Cracow, and Poznan about six times each, and "travelled extensively among the peasants."[15] He learned enough Polish to make selections of materials and in these five years "accumulated materials equalling in volume the *Encyclopaedia Britannica*" from the three parts of the country.[16] During this time he also employed a Polish research assistant. "After about eight experiments with translators, I found a superior man, with university training, name Kulikowski."[17]

Thomas had plans for an even more ambitious study, most of which did not materialize, although he did later publish some of the comparative materials he had collected on other immigrant groups in *Old World Traits Transplanted*.[18] In June 1912, for example, Thomas wrote from Berlin to Samuel Harper, son of the president and a Russian specialist at the university, about enlisting his help in a study of Russian peasants. He expected to remain in Berlin until August, then visit Posnan and Cracow for six weeks, then go to Hungary "where I have some work underway" and on to Italy until December or January. He would then travel to Liverpool (where Harper was spending a year) to discuss the Russian research, taking a month to do so if necessary. He would return via Ireland to the United States, where he was due on 1 April.[19] This extensive itinerary was in aid of a projected comparative study of the "mental and social life of the European peasant." Thomas planned to edit a number of "source books" – one each devoted to the Poles, Russians, Magyars, Slovaks, Rumanians, Italians, Irish, and East European Jews. (He was attempting to enlist Harper's assistance with the Russian volume.) The aim of the volumes would be to describe the life of each group, to provide the basis for a comparative study of the Negro in America, and "to furnish a body of facts which will be of general service in the interpretation of racial and sociological problems."[20] Thomas's work on the European peasantry was conceived on a large scale. In this, in the funding of the project, and in the time he was able to devote to it, he was the prototype of the modern sociologist with large-scale external support.

In 1913, on his last visit to Warsaw, Thomas called on the Bureau for the Protection of Immigrants, where he met "a very charming and superior man who was in charge,"[21] Florian Znaniecki. This was his introduction to his future collaborator. Florian Znaniecki (1882–1958) was the son of a Polish landed family, a philosopher by training who had studied at Geneva, Zurich, and Paris, where he came under the influence of Henri Bergson. He also spent a brief period in the French Foreign Legion. He published in Polish *The Problem of Values in Philosophy* (1910), *Humanism and Knowledge* (1912), and an annotated translation of Bergson's *Creative Evolution* (1913).[22] Though he had on his return received the Ph.D. degree from the University of Cracow in 1909, Znaniecki was barred for political reasons from holding an appointment at a Polish university, then under Russian control. He therefore took the post as head of the Polish Emigrants' Protective Association.[23]

There is some uncertainty about whether Thomas did or did not invite Znaniecki to come to the United States to work with him.[24] When Thomas met him in 1913

> the function of this bureau, as I appreciated it at least, was to facilitate the emigration of undesirable citizens and to hinder the emigration of the desirable. At any rate the bureau had important records . . . Znaniecki agreed to copy some of his records for me, and I left $200 or $300 for that purpose. During this conversation Znaniecki said that he might possibly visit America to promote the publication of translations of certain Polish scientific works and that a learned society was promoting the undertaking, but might not be able to finance the trip completely. I said that if he came to America at any time I would give him as much work as he wanted to do, if that would help any.[25]

In 1914, Znaniecki came to the United States just before war broke out and called on Thomas in Chicago. As he could not return to Poland because of the war, Thomas employed him to work on his project – at first hourly and then on a salary – and a most fruitful collaboration ensued.[26] Their relative contributions to the work over the next four years, which culminated in the publication of *The Polish Peasant* in 1918, is a matter of some controversy. Some consider that Znaniecki was "the junior partner" and that Thomas had formulated the plan of the research and his main ideas before Znaniecki arrived in Chicago.[27] Others point out that although Znaniecki was relatively unschooled in empirical sociology on arriving in Chicago in 1914 and learned the tools of the trade from Thomas, he was well-read in the works of European sociologists and his theoretical knowledge was at least as extensive as that of Thomas.[28] He had also done some research on the sociology of emigration. It is quite clear that to regard Znaniecki as merely Thomas's assistant is incorrect, although Thomas was the more experienced researcher and it was he who provided the strong commitment to empirical inquiry.

Indeed, at the outset, according to Thomas in 1935, Znaniecki "was opposed to the documentation" by means of empirical materials and "did not hesitate to say so. He strongly urged a 'treatise,'"[29] but adapted to Thomas's conception of how the work would be shaped. Once he did so, he took a most active part. Paradoxically, while Thomas and a Polish research assistant had collected all the materials used on the peasant in Poland, Znaniecki collected all the materials on the Poles in America – from the records of Polish-American societies, juvenile court and social work records, and the like. Znaniecki collated the letters of Polish families in America and dealt with Wladek while he was writing his life history. He took a major part in drafting the book. "It would be true that he wrote more than I did, but also true that little stands as he wrote it,"[30] as Thomas revised, rejected, or rewrote.

Looking back, Thomas thought that "it would be quite impossible to establish who wrote what."[31] The two were true collaborators, for Znaniecki's interest in philosophy and methodology and his intimate knowledge of Polish society complemented Thomas's interest in sociology and social psychology and his detailed knowledge of the Chicago of the day. Moreover, it was Znaniecki who suggested that the authors add the "Methodological Note." On the other hand, it was Thomas who persuaded Znaniecki to become a sociologist, so that at the time of their collaboration Znaniecki's contribution was more in the spheres of concrete knowledge about Polish society and of general methodology. In the last analysis, Thomas's was the preeminent part, for he pioneered empirical sociological research in a way that Znaniecki by himself would have been unlikely to do.[32] Znaniecki's book *Cultural Reality*, written in Chicago and published in 1919,[33] was primarily philosophical. *The Polish Peasant*, nonetheless, was their joint work, a work greater for being so than had either man produced the work alone.

The Polish Peasant, all 2,232 pages of it, is a work more revered or referred to than read. Its substance was the empirical study of Polish peasant life.

> Our object-matter is one class of a modern society in the whole concrete complexity of its life.... The Polish peasant finds himself now in a period of transition from the old forms of social organization that had been in force, with only insignificant changes for many centuries, to a modern form of life. He has preserved enough of the old attitudes to make their sociological reconstruction possible, and he is sufficiently advanced upon the new way to make a study of the development of modern attitudes particularly fruitful.[34]

The scale of Polish migration to the United States was very large. Between 1899 and 1910, Poles accounted for one-quarter of all immigrants to the United States, and they tended to settle in urban areas, particularly in large cities such as Chicago, Pittsburgh, Buffalo, Cleveland, and Detroit. Whereas immigration into America up to 1890 was very largely from northwestern Europe, between 1890 and 1914 immigrants were drawn largely from southern and eastern Europe.[35] At the late peak of immigration in 1907, for instance, 1.28 million people migrated to America, including 338,000 from Austria-Hungary and 258,000 from Russia. Chicago with its 360,000 Poles ranked after Warsaw and Lodz as the third largest Polish center in the world.[36]

There were several reasons for this changed pattern of migration. The replacement of sail by steam meant that as many people could come in one year at the turn of the century as came in one decade fifty years previous. Awareness of the possibility of migration spread slowly, too, as the process of movement was cumulative. There were significant relaxations in several southern and eastern European countries toward the end of the century in the laws relating to migration. Much immigration was due to political, religious, and cultural persecution in Eastern Europe. Anti-Semitism intensified after 1880, and Poles in particular were subject to political persecution. Though bound together by linguistic and cultural ties, Poland did not exist as a political entity between 1789 and 1918. Economic factors, however, were the principal reason for migration from Poland to America at this period. Emigration was not a once-for-all process. As *The Polish Peasant* demonstrated, it was part of wider social changes, and the decision to leave the country for America was only the last of a whole series of moves that Poles were making during this period. Return migration across the Atlantic was, moreover, not insignificant.

The Polish Peasant is a massive work that defies adequate treatment as a whole in a short space. Since excellent summaries and overviews are already available, the discussion here concentrates upon the research methods used to gather empirical data, the work's theoretical significance, and the work's wider impact.[37] It is necessarily selective, highlighting in particular its contribution to research methods. A summary of the substantive concerns and research techniques appears in figure 1.

Thomas's approach involved moving out of the library into the field, but he did not use the firsthand methods of the early social survey or participant

Figure 1: Summary of the Substantive Concerns and Research Techniques of *The Polish Peasant in Europe and America*

Substantive concern	Research Techniques
I. The organization of the peasant primary group (family and community) and the partial evolution of this system of organization under the influence of industrialization and migration.	By means of private letters (written entirely in the first person and without a view to publication) between immigrants in America and their families in Poland.
Subjects covered include the peasant family, marriage, the class system, the social and economic environment, religious and magical attitudes, and the theoretic and aesthetic interests of the peasant.	There are 762 letters in all, arranged into 50 series by family.
The letters are published more or less verbatim, and the authors make generalizations on the basis of their content.	
II. The life record of an immigrant. The autobiography of Wladek, an immigrant of peasant origins now in an occupation "of the lower city class" in Chicago, who "illustrates the tendency to disorganization of the individual under the conditions involved in a rapid transition from one type of social organization to another."	By means of a life history, a lengthy and detailed account by one individual of his life experience, given verbatim in 312 pages.
The authors claim that the document is representative of the experience of many individuals. The authors add interpretive notes.	
III. The strains and tensions within the primary group in Poland and its social and political reorganization on modern rather than traditional lines. Five problems are discussed: (1) leadership, (2) education of the peasants, (3) the press, (4) cooperative organizations, (5) role of the peasant class in the nation.	By means of third-person accounts of Polish life, from the files and archives of Polish newspapers, and from the Bureau for the Protection of Immigrants.
IV. The extent and kinds of social disorganization experienced by the peasant in America – demoralization, economic dependency, break-up of the conjugal relation, crime, etc.	By means of third-person reports from social work agency and court records, and records of Polish-American organizations.
The beginnings of self-help as a community, e.g., the formation of Polish-American organizations.	

observation. His main method of research was to gather what he called "documentary materials." As he wrote in 1912,

> I am especially interested in securing what I have called "undesigned records," that is, letters, data from newspapers, records of court trials, sermons, pamphlets issued by the clergy and by political parties, the records of peasant agricultural societies and any materials reflecting the mental, social, and economic life of the peasant and the Jew.[38]

One factor influencing Thomas to undertake the study originally had been the availability of certain types of document. He first looked at journals of folklore that discussed peasant life, but "they dealt with things such as the coloring of Easter eggs, figures in weaving, hedges, plows, outhouses, magical practices, etc."[39] He then discovered that in 1863 a weekly journal, published in Warsaw, the *Gazeta Swiateczna* had been established for the benefit of Polish peasants, as part of the general movement of enlightenment arising out of resistance to Russian rule. Peasants began to write to the newspaper on all sorts of topics. In 1909–10 Thomas purchased the files of the journal covering the last twenty years, which provided "the most important of all my sources"[40] gathered in Europe for the study. But this was only part of the material he gathered. In all, during eight periods of residence in Poland, Thomas collected about eight thousand documents or items.[41]

Thomas faced familiar methodological problems of gaining the trust and securing the cooperation of those whom he was studying and, more unusually, suffered from the impact of war.

> I was viewed with a great deal of suspicion by prominent Poles, because, while they claimed to be, and were, an oppressed minority, their oppression of the Ruthenians in Austrian Poland was more ferocious than their own oppression in Russian Poland. In this connection, a good many important documents, especially manuscripts, were withheld from me.[42]

The editor of the *Gazeta Swiateczna* refused to let Thomas copy eight thousand letters that the paper had received from Poles in America or to buy one of the only two complete sets of the *Gazeta* from 1863 in existence. After Thomas's last visit, the editor had a change of heart, and Thomas sent his research assistant to collect the material, which he did. At this point in 1914, however, war broke out, and Kulikowski, fleeing the country to avoid conscription, lost all this new material in Vilna.[43] The loss of about one-third of the materials gathered in Poland was a great grief to Thomas, but he treated it philosophically and thought it made little difference to the final result.[44]

The main sources used for the material published verbatim in *The Polish Peasant* were in fact Poles who had come to America. The use of series of letters in the analysis seems to have had a pragmatic origin. Thomas is supposed to have decided to use them when walking one day down the back alley behind his house, he had to leap aside to avoid rubbish being thrown from an upper window. Among the rubbish was a long letter, which he picked up, took home, and discovered was written in Polish by a girl taking a training course in a hospital, to her father discussing family matters. It then occurred to Thomas that such letters could be used as research material.[45] The letters used in the research were obtained by advertising in newspapers in Poland and in America. "We advertised in the Chicago Polish newspapers that we would pay ten cents each for every letter from a family member or friend submitted for us to read, and would return the letter. The idea was mainly to find here and there a big bunch of letters extending over a period of years from the same person, showing changes of attitudes over time. This turned out alright and it seemed we could have got a million letters. These persons brought the letters to Znaniecki in the office."[46] The series of letters were primarily to or from emigrants from Poland to America, drawn from different levels of society and parts of Poland, and representing all sections of peasant life.

The letters were published in family series with relatively little selection.[47] Each of the fifty series of letters had a theoretical introduction, there were numerous theoretical comments in the footnotes, and a two-hundred-page introduction characterizing Polish peasant society. The approach was inductive, and the materials were presented verbatim.

The use of letters as sociological data was original. So, too, was the second type of personal document in *The Polish Peasant*, the life history of Wladek Wiszniewski. Its use may quite possibly have had a theoretical origin. Dilthey, for instance, thought highly of such material: "Autobiography is the highest and most instructive form in which the understanding of life comes before us."[48] Thomas and Znaniecki were originally in touch with Wladek through their advertisement for letter series. They were able to check the reliability of his account against the evidence in his series of family letters and found no major discrepancies. Although they paid the author to write the life history, from their own observations they thought that ambition, literary interest, and interest in his own life were his main motives in writing it. Thomas and Znaniecki reduced the original by half by summarizing events[49] described there and putting them in brackets in the account. The life history of Wladek occupied 312 pages, was extensively footnoted, and was followed by a short general analysis in which the authors characterized the personality of Wladek and traced its formation in different social settings.

The reliance on personal documents marked out *The Polish Peasant* as a new departure. The subsequent use in sociological research of personal documents, such as life histories, letters, diaries, and other first-person material, may in large measure be traced back to the influence of *The Polish Peasant*.[50] The life history of Wladek was the first systematically collected sociological life history. At the same time, Thomas and Znaniecki emphasized that the underlying aim was scientific generalization. The subjective point of view was being caught as part of a scientific enterprise. The use of personal documents aided the construction of social types. It was claimed, without clear support, that Wladek was a representative case.[51]

In addition to personal documents, Thomas and Znaniecki also used more conventional third-person documents including the Polish newspaper materials already mentioned, records from Polish-American organizations and churches, files of social agencies, and court records. The use made of these records and documents and their analysis was rather different from that made of personal documents. There was much more selection and a more analytical presentation.[52] Though less original, this was one of the earliest systematic uses of newspapers as a source of data.[53]

The contribution that Thomas and Znaniecki made to the development of methods of empirical social research did not extend to face-to-face observation and interviewing. Indeed, Thomas was pointedly critical of the interview, which he felt manipulated the respondent excessively. It was not a neutral instrument, but itself a social process. In 1912 he wrote: "interviews in the main may be treated as a body of error to be used for purposes of comparison in future observation."[54] On the other hand, he conceded that middle-class informants such as social workers, editors, teachers, and doctors could provide reliable information and were interested in doing so.

Such reliance on *Sachverständige* was also characteristic of the early stages of anthropological fieldwork. Informants who had firsthand contact with the subjects of research were used to provide reports on those subjects. Max Weber used such methods in his studies of Prussian agriculture.[55] Thomas did not take the step Park urged his students to take of going out to talk to and observe the subjects at firsthand. Thomas's approach, however, did not rely only upon secondhand reports. He attached such importance to the *Gazeta* materials because they included firsthand written communications from peasants to the newspaper. Indeed, the main methodological innovation of *The Polish Peasant* was in the use of firsthand documentary materials that Thomas and Znaniecki believed could constitute the basis of a generalizing social science.

> We are safe in saying that personal life records, as complete as possible, constitute the perfect type of sociological material, and if social science has to use other materials at all it is only because of the practical difficulty of obtaining at the moment a sufficient number of such records to cover the totality of sociological problems, and of the enormous amount of work demanded for an adequate analysis of all the personal materials necessary to characterize the life of a social group.[56]

This very strong claim was not borne out by subsequent developments, and within two decades the use of such methods had gone into a sharp decline, because of the greater efficiency of observational methods and the rise of the social survey. Nevertheless, at the time the claim was made, *The Polish Peasant* did change the direction of empirical methods of sociological research in the United States and influence some of the methods used by the students of Park and Burgess in the 1920s.

The importance of personal documents lay in the opportunity they provided to study the world from the point of view of the subject and this general methodological influence has been much more enduring. Indeed, for all the recent emphasis on the Meadian "I" and "me" in the history of Chicago sociology, Thomas and Znaniecki were more important antecedents of contemporary versions of social action theory through the example of their empirical research, than was Mead in the seminar room.

One of Thomas's original reasons for choosing the Poles as an immigrant group to study was their behavior in America, which often seemed incomprehensible. They vacillated between two extreme attitudes to authority, either passively accepting it, like peasants accepting their landlord, or behaving as if there were no limits to the boasted American "freedom," for instance, in what the American police called "Polish warfare."[57] Personal documents such as life histories and letters were used to try to understand why immigrants acted in the way they did. This involved studying their objective conditions, their pre-existing attitudes, and their "definition of the situation."[58] Social change was to be understood as the product of continual interaction between individual consciousness and objective social reality.[59] Interpreting social behavior necessarily required knowledge of the subjective meaning that individuals attached to their action.[60]

> We must put ourselves in the position of the subject who tries to find his way in the world, and we must remember, first of all that the environment by which he is influenced and to which he adapts himself is *his* world, not the objective world of science– is nature and society as he sees them, not as the scientist sees them.[61]

Their general methodological ideas were set out in an 86–page "Methodological Note" at the beginning of the book. This was written after the research was completed at the instance of Znaniecki.[62] Though similar in form to Durkheim's *Rules of Sociological Method*, which Znaniecki probably knew from his years studying in France, its content was different and, indeed, seemed designed to refute *The Rules*. Moreover, it bore distinct traces of pragmatism in the centrality given to activity.[63]

To be adequate, social theory must include both "the objective cultural elements of social life" or *social values*, and the subjective characteristics of the members of the social group or *attitudes*. A social value was defined as

> any datum having an empirical content accessible to the members of some social group and a meaning with regard to which it is or may be

an object of activity. Thus a foodstuff, an instrument, a coin, a piece of poetry, a university, a myth, a scientific theory, are social values.[64]

An attitude was defined as

> a process of individual consciousness which determines real or possible activity of the individual in the social world. . . . The attitude is thus the individual counterpart of the social value; activity, in whatever form, is the bond between them. . . . By its reference to activity and thereby to the social world the attitude is distinguished from the psychical state.[65]

The authors stressed the combined social and individual components of social behavior, summed up in the principle that "The cause of a value or an attitude is never an attitude or a value alone, but always a combination of an attitude and a value." The authors specifically criticized Durkheim's formula that the cause of a social phenomenon must be sought, not at an individual level, but exclusively in another social phenomenon, for they argued that a fact in social theory must include both an attitude and a value, and "a succession of values alone cannot constitute a fact."[66]

External or objective factors played upon individuals, and through the subjective experiences of these individuals, led to certain forms of activity:

> Activity is the link between attitude and value: Indeed, every manifestation of conscious life . . . can be treated as an attitude, because everyone involves a tendency to action, whether this action is a process of mechanical activity producing physical changes in the material world, or an attempt to influence the attitudes of others by speech and gesture, or a mental activity which does not at the given moment find a social expression.[67]

It was in the relation between objective factors and subjective dispositions that causal explanations were to be sought.

The link between the individual and the social was found partly through their theory of social personality and Thomas's "four wishes." These were the wish for (a) new experience, (b) security, (c) response, and (d) recognition. The process by which the "temperamental attitudes" derived from the four wishes were transferred into character attitudes which formed the basis of the individual's social personality was through the interaction between the individual and the group. Such a process involved the individual "defining his situation."[68]

Social psychology was defined as the "science of attitudes," but was extended beyond individual psychology to be "the general science of the subjective side of social culture." Sociology, on the other hand, involved the study of social values, particularly those embodied in rules of behavior:

> The rules of behavior, and the actions viewed as conforming or not conforming with those rules, constitute with regard to their objective significance a certain number of more or less connected and harmonious systems which can be generally called *social institutions*, and the totality of institutions found in a concrete social group constitutes the *social organization* of the group.[69]

Sociology was the theory of social organization. *Social theory* embraced both sociology and social psychology, being concerned with the relationship between the individual and the social from the two different standpoints.

The Chicago school produced very few published statements of methodology in either its more general or more specific senses. The "Methodological Note" stood alone in this respect as a general statement, and its standpoint – particularly the emphasis upon the subjective dimension of social action – had considerable impact in the 1920s.[70] The influence of *The Polish Peasant* as an exemplary work of sociology lay not only in the "Methodological Note," however, for it was programmatic and contained only a set of general sociological orientations rather than a theory. The discussion bore little relation to the substantive analysis that followed.[71] The concept of values drew too heavily on idealism, while the most precisely specified concepts – Thomas's "four wishes" – lacked social anchoring. The authors were correct in saying that *"The Polish Peasant* claims to be, not mere sociography, but at least a fragmentary and tentative contribution to sociology, viewed as an inductive, analytic, classificatory, and nomothetic science,"[72] but this contribution was found in the introductions and footnotes to the empirical analysis rather than in the "Methodological Note."

For *The Polish Peasant* was a major macrosociological study of the interdependence of institutions, in the context of the social changes precipitated by urbanization and industrialization. Far from being mere description, though the data were woefully underanalyzed, a careful institutional analysis was made of the basic units of the primary group, then of the community, and then of certain larger entities such as the press, voluntary associations, and educational institutions. For each institution, the authors sought to define its formal properties. This analysis was linked to the theory of social disorganization. This was seen as originating precisely in the absence of mediating community institutions among Poles in the United States. At the societal level, the analysis of the role of the press was particularly incisive, though politics was entirely neglected and the role of tradition in Poland in explaining differences within the United States was underplayed.[73] This analysis was grounded in empirical materials to such an extent that the theory was understated and often implicit. But it provided a model for the Chicago tradition of research, blending empirical data and generalization as a contribution to theory-building.

The Polish Peasant was also one of the most important methodological contributions to the establishment through empirical research of *the social* as a distinct and legitimate area of inquiry. This was a particularly important point to establish in the study of immigration, where biological theories of ethnic and racial difference had a powerful influence. Thomas and Znaniecki rejected entirely any element of biological reductionism and sought to explain social behavior in terms of sociological and social psychological categories. The concept of "attitude" was the key to this change, which can be followed in the development of Thomas's ideas over time; some of his earliest writings still retained elements of instinct theory.[74] The concept of "attitude" embodied an intellectual revolution, referring to a mental state with no intrinsic physiological content. *The Polish Peasant* made the excision of reductionism stick.[75] In his ideas on race, Thomas was influenced by Franz Boas[76] and was hardly a highly original thinker. The synthesis and reformulation he and Znaniecki provided, however, was a notable step along the road to an autonomous empirical sociology of race and ethnic relations[77] and thereby to the secure establishment of an autonomous discipline.

Publication of the first two volumes of *The Polish Peasant* by the University of Chicago Press in 1918 was a landmark overshadowed for Thomas personally by his almost immediate departure from the university. The great tragedy that struck his career when he was fifty-five was not made public knowledge until Morris Janowitz published an account in 1966.[78] In recent years a good deal of attention has been focused on cases of academic freedom in the late nineteenth and early twentieth centuries, whenever American university presidents treated political dissidents harshly.[79] Moral lapses were treated even more harshly, and without apparent controversy. Thomas was an outgoing man, enjoying company, good living, and a wide range of acquaintance. The subject-matter of some of his researches, for example, sexual behavior,[80] was daring for the time. Addressing the National American Woman Suffrage Association in Chicago in 1917, Thomas urged the granting of legitimate status to illegitimate children and better efforts for providing information about birth control. He was misquoted in the press,[81] which brought the wrath of President Judson down upon him, through his head of department, Small. Thomas was obliged to apologize in an abject manner.[82] The matter blew over, but it reinforced the view of Thomas as a controversial figure, a view clearly held by some members of the university. In October 1917, for example, Thomas clashed with Professor Shailer Mathews in the Divinity School, who had strenuously criticized Thomas's teaching in his course Social Origins.[83]

Thomas's connection with the University of Chicago ended in April 1918. In that month he was arrested at a Chicago hotel in company with a Mrs. Granger and charged with violation of the Mann Act and with false hotel registration. Mrs. Thomas was active in Henry Ford's peace movement, and it has been suggested that Thomas's arrest was a means of embarrassing and discrediting her. Though the charges were thrown out of court (where Thomas was represented by Clarence Darrow), there was extensive press coverage, partly because Mrs. Granger was the wife of an army officer serving in Europe.

President Judson, supported by the trustees, moved directly to dismiss Thomas.[84]

Albion Small reportedly burst into tears upon hearing the news of Thomas's dismissal, but appeared to be convinced that he must depart. Robert Park attempted to defend him, but he then held only a marginal position in the university.[85] Charles Merriam brought Thomas from his home, where he had closeted himself away, to lunch in the faculty club, but it could only be a gesture.[86] There was no protest from the faculty, and at the time right to academic tenure did not exist. The matter might be dealt with in different ways, but universities of the period were wholly intolerant of what they judged moral laxity. Thorstein Veblen's career was blighted by the conflicts he provoked with university administrations through his sexual behavior. The psychologist Mark Baldwin was dismissed from Johns Hopkins in 1908 after being discovered in a Negro brothel.[87] John B. Watson ended his academic career in 1920 by announcing his intention to divorce (on leaving Johns Hopkins, Watson went to stay in New York with Thomas).[88] And in the 1920s, a president of the University of Chicago left office very suddenly for similar reasons. Thomas was thus not alone in his misfortune, for the moral climate of the period was chilly.

His dismissal was nonetheless a cruel and considered blow, which was pushed through with thoroughness. The University of Chicago Press, which had published the first two volumes of *The Polish Peasant*, was ordered by the president to terminate the contract and cease distribution of the volumes published. They and the plates were handed over to the author, who arranged for publication by Richard Badger of Boston.[89] Thomas's name was to be expunged from the university. On assuming the presidency over a decade later, it was suggested to Robert M. Hutchins in late 1929 by Edwin Wilson, president of the SSRC, that Chicago might make amends by reappointing W. I. Thomas. Hutchins replied sympathetically that "I have known and admired the gentleman for many years. I suppose he is still the leading sociologist in the United States."[90] Hutchins pressed the proposal with Harold Swift, chairman of the trustees of the university, who replied that he thought it neither feasible nor desirable to bring Thomas back to the university. "We deliberately chose as to whether we wanted him at the time and I, personally, see no reason to change the judgement."[91] When Hutchins pressed the point again, Swift replied that Thomas, at sixty-seven, was too old and that "the knowledge of his presence would do us more harm than his presence would do good."[92] He also implied that some members of the faculty – naming James Tufts and Shailer Mathews – would be implacably opposed. So there the matter rested, and the wrong was not undone.

Thomas's subsequent career was spent as a freelance research worker. He moved initially to New York, where he worked on the Carnegie Americanization study, then on *The Unadjusted Girl*, and later in the 1920s, with Dorothy Swaine Thomas, on *The Child in America*.[93] He did some teaching at the New School for Social Research and in the 1930s spent one year as a visiting lecturer at Harvard, at Sorokin's invitation. The most productive and fruitful years of his work as a sociologist ended with his departure from Chicago. The institutional base that Chicago provided was more steady than the uncertainties of freelancing and the intellectual milieu more nurturing. After he left Chicago, Thomas's psychological orientation grew stronger and the sociological and anthropological elements in his work weaker, probably because of this loss of an institutional anchor.

Like J. B. Watson, Thomas found research outside the university less productive, though he did not capitulate to commercialism as Watson did. Like Harold Lasswell[94] and Willard Waller,[95] in different ways, Thomas seemed to find less stimulus once he moved away from Chicago, and it is likely that there were particular features of the interdisciplinary atmosphere in the social sciences at Chicago that encouraged scholars like Thomas and Lasswell to produce of their best.

What the Chicago Department of Sociology might have achieved in the 1920s, had Thomas not been dismissed from the university, is one of the fascinating counterfactuals of academic intellectual history. As it was, the influence of Thomas was felt in part through the use of *The Polish Peasant* in teaching and the model it provided of an empirical monograph exemplifying the use of personal documents. The theory of social disorganization developed there was influential in several studies published in the 1920s. Social disorganization was defined as a decrease in the influence of existing social rules of behavior upon a group. The theory sought to explain how, in certain circumstances, social rules lose their effectiveness.[96] Harvey Zorbaugh, for example, wrote in *The Gold Coast and the Slum* that "the best analysis of the community and its control has been given us by W. I. Thomas in *The Polish Peasant* and in *The Unadjusted Girl*."[97] Ernest Mowrer in *Family Disorganization* drew directly upon both Thomas and Znaniecki's theory of social disorganization and their attitude–value distinction.[98] Frederic Thrasher in *The Gang* employed Thomas's concept of the "four wishes."[99] More diffusely, the repertoire of methods used by Park and Burgess's students was considerably influenced by the example of Thomas and Znaniecki. The collection of life histories, for instance, was used for studies such as Nels Anderson's *The Hobo*[100] and Paul G. Cressey's *The Taxi-Dance Hall*.[101]

Their influence was also felt more directly, through the close affinity between Thomas and Robert Park. In 1912, Park was still working as Booker T. Washington's secretary at Tuskegee and had organized the International Conference on the Negro, planned to bring together blacks from the United States, the West Indies, and Africa, in part in response to the Universal Races Conference in London the previous year.[102] W. I. Thomas was one of the invited speakers, and at this conference the two men first met. That a close intellectual relationship sprang up between them is apparent from correspondence between Thomas and Park in the following months. Thomas wrote to Park: "I am amazed to find how ignorant I was before I met you and how wise I seem to be now. Truly it was a great experience to meet you, greater than to meet all the other colored persons present."[103] Park reciprocated. "I found in Thomas, almost for the first time, a man who seemed to speak the same language as myself."[104] They immediately began comparing the situation of the Negro with that of the peasant and making plans for future joint publications and research visits together to the West Indies and possibly Africa. Thomas enthused: "Up to this point, golf has been my main interest, but I think I shall be pleased to work now in our vineyard."[105] They met in New York in June while Thomas was en route to Europe, and he wrote to Park from Berlin in July 1912: "I got a lot out of our visit and confirmed in my alliance with you."[106] Meanwhile, Thomas had raised with Small the possibility of appointing Park to a post teaching at Chicago. Small was very interested. Thomas suggested to Park the possibility of a part-time appointment for two quarters (as he himself currently had), so that they could go into the field together the other six months of the year.[107]

As a result, Park began teaching sociology at Chicago, initially in the fall quarter 1913, the next and subsequent years in the summer quarter, for a stipend of $500. The first course that he taught was "The Negro in America." From 1913 to 1918, Park and Thomas worked side by side in the department, and their collaboration continued after Thomas's dismissal, when he worked with Park on the Americanization studies for the Carnegie Corporation.[108] Later in the 1920s, Park organized a group of Chicago sociologists to nominate Thomas, successfully, for the presidency of the American Sociological Society and thus restore him to professional respectability.[109]

It is clear that Thomas exercised a powerful intellectual influence upon Robert Park and helped to shape his conception of empirical sociology. He helped him develop some of the theoretical insights he had derived from Simmel[110] and gave Park an appreciation of the relationship between sociological ideas and social research. Their five years together in the department coincided with Park's easing himself into the academic role.

When Thomas moved to New York, Park kept in close touch with him and stayed with him or visited when in the city. According to Park, Thomas's apartment smelled of Thomas – his pipe, his dusty books, and endless piles of papers – "as a lion's den smells of the lion."[111] Park was considerably influenced by Thomas in developing his conception of the sociological task, and this tie was not completely broken by Thomas's departure from the university, though contact became less frequent.

In later years, Park paid tribute to that influence. In 1939, he wrote an account in the *Bulletin of the Society for Social Research* of the origins of the society. The short article was in fact mainly a tribute to the influence W. I. Thomas had had on sociological research at Chicago:

> It is in the work of W. I. Thomas, I believe, that the present tradition of research at Chicago was established. . . . In [his] earlier writings . . .

we ... find the first positive expression of a point of view which has found a consistent expression in most, if not all, of the subsequent published studies of the students and instructors in sociology at Chicago.[112]

Starting with the *Source Book for Social Origins*, Thomas developed "the disinterested investigation of the origin and function of social institutions,"[113] emancipating sociology from its preoccupations with becoming a science of social reform or social welfare. Thomas helped sociologists to develop "that intellectual interest and natural curiosity which has been so largely responsible for the growth of science in other fields (social anthropology, for instance) which have not been dominated by practical and ethnocentric interests to the same extent that is true of sociology in the United States."[114] Thomas succeeded in imparting this interest and curiosity about human beings, particularly about their intimate thoughts and feelings, to his students.[115] Work like Thrasher's study of the gang or Shaw's life histories of delinquents enlarged our knowledge of the subjective aspects of life in the tradition of Thomas.

> Thomas's interest was always, it seems, that of a poet (although he never, so far as I know, wrote poetry) and of a literary man in the reportorial sense, and not that of a politician or of a practical man. He wanted to see, to know, and to report, disinterestedly and without respect to anyone's policies or program, the world of men and things as he experienced it.[116]

The influence of Thomas carried forward through the work of Park and Burgess by encouraging the empirical study of individual human beings rather than using informants or simply official data. The importance of the actor's "definition of the situation" was highlighted. And the potential for theoretically informed empirical work was classically demonstrated.

Notes

1. William Isaac Thomas and Florian Znaniecki, *The Polish Peasant in Europe and America*. The five-volume edition was published in 1918–20, the first two volumes by the University of Chicago Press and then (after Thomas's dismissal by the University of Chicago), the whole five volumes by Richard Badger, a Boston publishing house, after the University of Chicago Press broke the contract on the instructions of the president of the university. In 1926 Alfred Knopf of New York purchased the plates and copyright and brought out in 1927 a two-volume edition, an unabridged version of the first edition with slight transposition of material, repagination, and the addition of an index. This was reprinted by Dover in New York in 1958. All references in this chapter are to this two-volume edition. At the time of writing (1983), *The Polish Peasant in Europe and America* is out of print.

2. Lewis Coser, *Masters of Sociological Thought* (New York: Harcourt Brace Jovanovich, 1977), p. 381. See also Robert K. Merton, *Social Theory and Social Structure* (2d ed.; New York: Free Press, 1957), p. 62, note 69.

3. Donald Fleming, "Attitude: The History of a Concept in America," *Perspectives in American History* 1 (1967):325.

4. Edward Shils, *The Present State of American Sociology* (Glencoe, Ill.: Free Press, 1948), p. 26, note 33.

5. W. I. Thomas, "Life History," *American Journal of Sociology* 79 (1973):248 (written in 1928).

6. W. I. Thomas, ed., *Sourcebook for Social Origins* (Chicago: University of Chicago Press, 1909).

7. Morris Janowitz, Introduction to *W. I. Thomas on Social Organization and Social Personality* (Chicago: University of Chicago Press, 1966), p. viii.

8. See Shils, *The Present State of American Sociology*, p. 25.

9. Upton Sinclair, *The Jungle* (New York: Jungle Publishing Co., 1906).

10. Ellsworth Faris, "W. I. Thomas, 1863-1947," *Sociology and Social Research* 32 (March-April 1948):757.

11. W. I. Thomas, speaking on 10 December 1938, quoted in Herbert Blumer, *Critiques of Research in the Social Sciences, vol. 1: An Appraisal of Thomas and Znaniecki's "The Polish Peasant"* (New York: Social Science Research Council, 1939), p. 103.

12. William Isaac Thomas to Dorothy Swaine Thomas, January 1935 memorandum "How *The Polish Peasant* came about," Dorothy S. Thomas correspondence, University of Chicago Archives, p. 1.

13. Thomas W. Goodspeed, *A History of the University of Chicago: The First Quarter Century* (Chicago: University of Chicago Press, 1916), p. 273. Helen Culver's interests in race and ethnic relations went back to her Civil War work with the Sanitary Commission and post-Civil War experiences with blacks in the South. See Rudolf K. Haerle, Jr. "William Isaac Thomas and the Helen Culver Fund for Race Psychology: Foundation for *The Polish Peasant*" (Middlebury College, Vermont, 1984).

14. W. I. Thomas, "How *The Polish Peasant* came about," pp. 1-2.

15. Ibid., pp. 2-3.

16. Ibid., p. 3.

17. Ibid.

18. Robert E. Park and Herbert A. Miller, *Old World Traits Transplanted* (New York: Harper, 1921).

19. W. I. Thomas to Samuel N. Harper from Berlin, 30 June 1912, Samuel N. Harper Papers, University of Chicago Archives, Box 1, Folder 15.

20. Ibid., outline of projected study attached to letter.

21. Thomas, "How *The Polish Peasant* came about," p. 1.

22. A full bibliography of the published works of Florian Znaniecki in both Polish and English is to be found in the Introduction (by Helen Znaniecki Lopata) to F. Znaniecki, *Social Relations and Social Roles: The Unfinished "Systematic Sociology"* (San Francisco: Chandler, 1965).

23. These and other biographical details of Florian Znaniecki are drawn principally from Robert Bierstedt, ed., *Florian Znaniecki on Humanistic Sociology* (Chicago: University of Chicago Press, 1969), pp. 1-5; Lewis A. Coser, *Masters of Sociological Thought* (2d ed.; New York: Harcourt Brace Jovanovich, 1977), pp. 511-59; and Helena Znaniecki Lopata,

"Florian Znaniecki: Creative Evolution of a Sociologist," *Journal of the History of Behavioral Sciences* 12 (1976):203–15.

24. Contrast Janowitz, *W. I. Thomas*, p. xxv, and Bierstedt, *Znaniecki*, p. 2.
25. Thomas, "How *The Polish Peasant* came about," p. 2.
26. Ibid., p. 3.
27. Janowitz, *W. I. Thomas*, p. xxv.
28. Coser, *Masters of Sociological Thought*, p. 539.
29. Thomas, "How *The Polish Peasant* came about," p. 4.
30. Ibid.
31. Ibid.
32. In part the explanation for the greater credit which tends to have been given to Thomas lies in his much greater visibility in American sociology. While Znaniecki returned to Poland and remained there until 1939 (apart from a visiting appointment at Columbia in 1931–33), Thomas continued to be active in America and was president of the American Sociological Society in 1927. His social psychological writings were widely read in the 1920s, particularly in Chicago, and the tendency to attribute the principal authorship of *The Polish Peasant* to him may have stemmed partly from this greater influence. In addition, the history of American sociology has been written principally by American sociologists, some of whom were ardent admirers of Thomas. The most extreme example of favoring Thomas is to be found in Edmund H. Volkart's edition of Thomas's papers, *Social Behaviour and Personality* (New York: Social Science Research Council, 1951), which reprints twenty pages of the "Methodological Note" as if it were exclusively the work of Thomas. More justly, Bierstedt, *Florian Znaniecki*, includes the whole of the "Methodological Note." For a discussion of rival interpretations of the relative influence of Thomas and of Znaniecki, see Konstantin Symmons-Symondewicz, "*The Polish Peasant in Europe and America*: Its First Half-Century of Intellectual History, 1918–68," *Polish Review* 13, no. 2 (1968):14–27.
33. Florian Znaniecki, *Cultural Reality* (Chicago: University of Chicago Press, 1919). For a critical view of the relationship between sociology and philosophy in Znaniecki's work, see Z. A. Jordan, *Philosophy and Ideology* (Dordrecht, Holland: D. Reidel, 1963), pp. 63–68.
34. *The Polish Peasant* 1:74–75. All references are to the two-volume edition published in New York by Knopf in 1927 and reprinted by Dover in 1958.
35. Maldwyn A. Jones, *American Immigration* (Chicago: University of Chicago Press, 1960).
36. *The Polish Peasant* 2:1511.
37. For an excellent summary of the book, see John Madge, *The Origins of Scientific Sociology* (London: Tavistock, 1963), pp. 52–87. Coser, *Masters of Sociological Thought*, pp. 511–59, provides a sympathetic critical assessment. Janowitz, *Thomas*, and Bierstedt, *Znaniecki*, are companion volumes in this series.
38. Thomas to S. N. Harper, 30 June 1912, Outline of Projected Study.
39. Thomas, quoted in Blumer, *An Appraisal*, p. 104.
40. Thomas, "How *The Polish Peasant* came about," p. 3.
41. Thomas, in Blumer, *An Appraisal*, p. 104.
42. Ibid., p. 105.
43. Ibid., and Thomas, "How *The Polish Peasant* came about," p. 3.
44. Thomas, in Blumer, *An Appraisal*, p. 105.
45. Coser, *Masters of Sociological Thought*, p. 533.

46. Thomas, "How *The Polish Peasant* came about," p. 4.
47. *The Polish Peasant* 1:76.
48. Herbert A. Hodges, *William Dilthey: An Introduction* (London: Routledge, 1944), p. 29. See also Kenneth Plummer, *Documents of Life* (London: Allen & Unwin, 1983), p.52.
49. Thomas, "How *The Polish Peasant* came about," p. 4.
50. For further discussion, see James Bennett, *Oral History and Delinquency: The Rhetoric of Criminology* (Chicago: University of Chicago Press, 1981), pp. 123-50; Plummer, *Documents of Life*, esp. pp. 39-63.
51. *The Polish Peasant*, 2:1852, 1834-35.
52. Ibid., pp. 1122-23.
53. This use was later extended in the work that Thomas and Robert Park conducted for the Carnegie project on Americanization; see p. 93.
54. W. I. Thomas, "Race Psychology: Standpoint and Questionnaire with Particular Reference to the Immigrant and the Negro," *American Journal of Sociology* 17 (May 1912):771.
55. Max Weber, "Die Verhältnisse der Landarbeiter im ostelbischen Deutschland," *Schriften des Vereins für Sozialpolitik*, vol. 55 (Berlin, 1892). See also Reinhard Bendix, *Max Weber* (New York, 1959), chap. 2, and Anthony Oberschall, *Empirical Social Research in Germany, 1848-1914* (The Hague: Mouton, 1965), pp. 21-27. Weber was concerned, at a slightly earlier period, with a phenomenon studied by Thomas and Znaniecki, the very large-scale seasonal migration of agricultural workers from Poland to Prussia, which reached a peak of 600,000 per year in 1913.
56. *The Polish Peasant* 2:1832-33.
57. Thomas, in Blumer, *An Appraisal*, p. 107.
58. *The Polish Peasant* 1:68.
59. Ibid., 2:1831.
60. Ibid., 1:38.
61. Ibid., 2:1846-47.
62. Bierstedt, *Florian Znaniecki*, p. 11; Coser, *Masters of Sociological Thought*, p. 539.
63. In *Cultural Reality*, published in 1919, Znaniecki wrote: "Of all my later debts, none is as great as the one I owe to pragmatism, of which, in fact, I am inclined to consider myself a disciple"; pp. iii-iv.
64. *The Polish Peasant* 1:21.
65. Ibid., p. 22.
66. Ibid., p. 44.
67. Ibid., p. 27-28.
68. The idea was developed further in W. I. Thomas, *The Unadjusted Girl: With Cases and Standpoint for Behavior Analysis* (Boston: Little, Brown, 1923), and in W.I. Thomas and Dorothy Swaine Thomas, *The Child in America: Behavior Problems, and Programs* (New York: Alfred A. Knopf, 1928).
69. *The Polish Peasant* 1:32-33.
70. See p. 61.
71. This was demonstrated most convincingly in Blumer, *An Appraisal*, in 1939. See also Blumer's Introduction to the reprint of *An Appraisal* (New Brunswick, N.J.: Transaction Books, 1979), pp. v-xxxviii.
72. Florian Znaniecki, in Blumer, *An Appraisal*, p. 90.
73. Janowitz, *W. I. Thomas*, pp. xxxiv-xxxviii.

74. See William I. Thomas, "The Psychology of Race Prejudice," *American Journal of Sociology* 9 (1904):593–611.

75. Fleming, "Attitude," pp. 326–27.

76. George W. Stocking, Jr., *Race, Culture, and Evolution: Essays on the History of Anthropology* (New York: Free Press, 1968), pp. 258–64.

77. Edward B. Reuter, "Racial Theory", *American Journal of Sociology* 50 (1945):456, and Hamilton Cravens, *The Triumph of Evolution* (Philadelphia: University of Pennsylvania Press, 1978), p. 181.

78. Janowitz, *W. I. Thomas*, pp. xiv–xx.

79. See Mary O. Furner, *Advocacy and Objectivity: A Crisis in the Professionalization of American Social Science, 1865–1905* (Lexington: University of Kentucky Press, 1975).

80. See W. I. Thomas, *Sex and Society: Studies in the Social Psychology of Sex* (Chicago: University of Chicago Press, 1907).

81. *Chicago Examiner*, 10 June 1915; *Chicago Tribune*, 12 June 1915.

82. Thomas to Small, 17 June 1915, 23 June 1915, 5 July 1915, and Small to Judson, 21 June 1915, 6 July 1916, Papers of the Presidents of the University, 1889–1925, University of Chicago Archives, Box 64, Folder 4.

83. Thomas to Dean Shailer Mathews, 5 October 1917, Divinity School Papers, University of Chicago Archives, Box 17, Folder 1.

84. Janowitz, *W. I. Thomas*, pp. xiv–xv.

85. Fred H. Matthews, *Quest for an American Sociology: Robert E Park and the Chicago School* (Montreal: McGill–Queens University Press, 1977), pp. 102–3.

86. Barry D. Karl, *Charles E. Merriam and the Study of Politics* (Chicago: University of Chicago Press), p. 87.

87. David Cohen, *J. B. Watson: The Founder of Behaviorism* (London: Routledge & Kegan Paul, 1980), pp. 53–54.

88. Ibid., p. 159.

89. Karl, *Charles E. Merriam*, p. 87.

90. Robert M. Hutchins to Edwin B. Wilson, 4 January 1930, Harold H. Swift Papers, University of Chicago Archives, Box 135, Folder 20.

91. Harold H. Swift to Robert M. Hutchins, 11 January 1930, Swift Papers, Box 135, Folder 20.

92. Swift to Hutchins, 17 January 1930, Swift Papers, Box 135, Folder 20.

93. Robert E. Park and Herbert A. Miller, *Old World Traits Transplanted* (New York: Harper, 1921). The book was actually written by Thomas but could not be published in his name because of the controversy surrounding his dismissal. W. I. Thomas, *The Unadjusted Girl* (Boston: Little, Brown, 1923); W. I. Thomas and D. S. Thomas, *The Child in America* (New York: Knopf, 1928).

94. See Dwaine Marvick, *Harold D. Lasswell on Political Sociology* (Chicago: University of Chicago Press, 1977), pp. 32–34; Edward Shils, "Some Academics, Mainly at Chicago," *American Scholar* 50 (Spring 1981):195.

95. William J. Goode, Frank Furstenberg, Jr., and Larry R. Mitchell, eds., *Willard W. Waller on the Family, Education, and War* (Chicago: University of Chicago Press, 1970), pp. 72–79.

96. See Earl Rubington and Martin S. Weinberg, *The Study of Social Problems: Five Perspectives* (New York: Oxford University Press, 1971), pp. 47–79.

97. Harvey Zorbaugh, *The Gold Coast and the Slum* (Chicago: University of Chicago Press, 1929), p. 223.

98. Ernest Mowrer, *Family Disorganization* (Chicago: University of Chicago Press, 1927), pp. 188–93, 256–57.

99. Frederic Thrasher, *The Gang* (Chicago: University of Chicago Press, 1927), p. 68.

100. Nels Anderson, *The Hobo* (Chicago: University of Chicago Press, 1923).

101. Paul G. Cressey, *The Taxi-Dance Hall* (Chicago: University of Chicago Press, 1932).

102. Fred H. Matthews, *Quest for an American Sociology*, p. 1.

103. Winifred Raushenbush, *Robert E. Park: Biography of a Sociologist* (Durham, N.C.: Duke University Press, 1979), p. 68.

104. Ibid., p. 74.

105. Ibid., p. 69.

106. W. I. Thomas to R. E. Park from Berlin, 3 July 1912, in Robert E. Park Papers, University of Chicago, Additional Papers II, Box 1, Folder 3.

107. Raushenbush, *Robert E. Park*, p. 69.

108. Park and Miller [Thomas], *Old World Traits*.

109. Janowitz, *W. I. Thomas*, p. xvii.

110. See Matthews, *Quest for an American Sociology*, pp. 97–103.

111. Quoted in Helen Snick Perry, *Psychiatrist of America: The Life of Harry Stack Sullivan* (Cambridge, Mass.: Belknap Press, Harvard University Press, 1982), pp. 255–56.

112. Robert E. Park, "Notes on the Origin of the Society for Social Research," *Bulletin of the Society for Social Research*, August 1939, pp. 3–5, at p. 3. It has been published with an introduction by Lester R. Kurtz, "Robert E. Park's 'Notes on the Origin of the Society for Social Research,'" *Journal of the History of the Behavioral Sciences* 18 (October 1982):332–40. See also Martin Bulmer, "Chicago Sociology and the Society for Social Research: A Comment," *Journal of the History of the Behavioral Sciences* 19 (October 1983):35–56. The *Bulletin* was a quarterly mimeographed newsletter distributed to members of the society (see chap. 7).

113. Ibid., p. 3.

114. Ibid.

115. See Robert E. Park, "The Sociological Methods of William Graham Sumner and of William I. Thomas and Florian Znaniecki," in Stuart A. Rice, ed., *Methods in Social Science: A Casebook* (Chicago: University of Chicago Press, 1931), pp. 154–75, reprinted in Robert E. Park, *Society* (Glencoe, Ill.: Free Press, 1955), pp. 243–66.

116. Park, "Notes on the Origins of the Society for Social Research," p. 4.

21

Situational Analysis: The Behavior Pattern and the Situation

W. I. Thomas

The lines of social research have largely converged on the question of behavior reactions and the processes involved in their formation and modification. It appears that the particular behavior patterns and the total personality are overwhelmingly conditioned by the types of situations and trains of experience encountered by the individual in the course of his life. The question of heredity remains a factor, but this is also being studied in terms of behavior; it is, in fact, defined as the phylogenetic memory of experience – memory organically incorporated.

In approaching problems of behavior it is possible to emphasize – to have in the focus of attention for working purposes – either the attitude, the value, or the situation. The attitude is the tendency to act, representing the drive, the affective states, the wishes. The value represents the object or goal desired, and the situation represents the configuration of the factors conditioning the behavior reaction. It is also possible to work from the standpoint of adaptation – that is, how are attitudes and values modified according to the demands of given situations.

Any one of these standpoints will involve all the others, since they together constitute a process. But I wish to speak at present of the situational procedure as having certain experimental, objective, and comparative possibilities and as deserving of further attention and elaboration. As I have said, the emphasis of this standpoint by no means obscures the other factors; on the contrary, it reveals them. The situations which the individual encounters, into which he is forced, or which he creates, disclose the character of his adaptive strivings, positive or negative, progressive or regressive, his claims, attainments, renunciations, and compromises. For the human personality also the most important content of situations is the attitudes and values of other persons with which his own come into conflict and co-operation, and I have thus in mind the study

---

Source: Morris Janowitz (ed.), *W. I. Thomas. On Social Organization and Social Personality*, (Chicago: Chicago University Press, 1966).

of types of situation which reveal the role of attitudes and values in the process of behavior adaptation.

The situational method is the one in use by the experimental physiologist and psychologist who prepare situations, introduce the subject into the situation, observe the behavior reactions, change the situation, and observe the changes in the reactions. Child rendered one point in the situation more stimulating than others by applying an electric needle or other stimulus and made heads grow where tails would otherwise have grown. The situational character of the animal experimentation of the psychologists is well known. The rat, for example, in order to open a door, must not only stand on a platform placed in a certain position, but at the same time pull a string. A complete study of situations would give a complete account of the rat's attitudes, values, and intelligence.

The study of behavior with reference to situations which was begun by Vervorn, Pfeffer, Loeb, Jennings, and other physiologists and was concerned with the so-called "tropisms" or the reaction of the small organism to light, electricity, heat, gravity, hard substances, etc., was continued, or paralleled, by the experiments of Thorndike, Yerkes, Pavlov, Watson, Köhler, and others with rats, dogs, monkeys, and babies as subjects, but until quite recently no systematic work from this standpoint has involved the reactions of the individual to other persons or groups of persons. That is to say, the work has not been sociological, but physiological or psychological.

Recently, however, there have developed certain directly sociological studies of behavior based on the situation. These are either experimental in the sense that the situations are planned and the behavior reactions observed, or advantage is taken of existing situations to study the reactions of individuals comparatively.

We may notice first the significant work of Bühler, Hetzer, and Tudor-Hart[1] upon the earliest social reactions of the child. Working in the Vienna clinics they divided 126 children into 9 groups of 14 each, the first group containing children 3 days old and under, and the last group containing those 4–5 months old, and experimenting with sound-stimuli they observed the rate at which the child learns to separate out and give attention to the human voice among other sounds. All the children noticed all the sounds (striking a porcelain plate with a spoon, rattling a piece of paper, and the human voice) sometimes, but the reaction of the newborn to noises in the first weeks is far more positive than the reaction to the voice, even to loud and noisy conversation: 92 per cent of frequency to the noises and 25 per cent to the voice. But in the third week the proportion is about the same, and in the fourth week the reaction is more frequent to the voice. The first positive reaction to the voice, other than listening, is a puckering of the lips, a sucking movement. The quality of the voice or the person speaking is at first of no significance. A child of three months when scolded angrily laughed gleefully. As yet angry tones had not been associated with punishment. A voice of any kind meant feeding.

Working with another group of 114 children, not newborn but borrowed from nursing mothers at a milk depot, placing them together in groups of two or more, and giving them toys, the most various reactions were disclosed in the unfamiliar situation. Some were embarrassed and inactive; others were openly delighted; some pounced upon the toys and paid no attention to the children; others explored the general environment; some robbed their companions of all the toys; others proffered, exchanged, or exhibited them; some were furious in the new situation, already, in the first year, positively negativistic. It is impossible to say to what degree these children had been conditioned by association with their mothers and how far the reactions were dispositional. But it is plain that by the end of the first year the most positive personality trends had been established. At this early age the experimenters think they distinguish three main personality types: the dominant, the amiable or humanitarian, and the exhibitionist, or producer.

Situational work of this type is now being carried on in several child-study institutes in the United States, and is foundational for the work in which we are more directly interested. Anderson and Goodenough, for example, and their associates, working in Minneapolis and observing the reactions of children among themselves in spontaneous play, found that a given child participating in play actively with all the other members of the group successively might be found leading or dominating in 95 per cent of the situations, whereas another child, under the same conditions, was found to be in the leading position only 5 per cent of the time. That is, within a constant period one child is getting twenty times as much practice in meeting social situations in a given way as a second child. We have here a type of organization of behavior where not only the lack of practice but the habit of subordination will have the most far-reaching consequences in the development of efficiency and personality. Observations will now be undertaken by the same observers on the effect of the alteration of the composition of groups with the object of giving the less dominant children opportunity to assume more important roles.[2]

Another item in the program of this institute is the study of habit formation in connection with games of skill. It has appeared that the children develop idiosyncrasies in their technique of throwing a ring at a peg. If an effort, however awkward, happens to be successful, the child tends to adopt and perseverate in this method, regardless of his later insuccesses.[3] Evidently the fixation of many undesirable social habits has this origin. Whimpering, crying, lying, vomiting, bed-wetting have had an initial success in dominating the mother, and may become a part of the child's behavior repertory. It is to be remembered also that the initiation of one mode of reaction to a situation tends to block the emergence of other types of reaction. Moreover, it appears from other sources that children are capable of developing dual and contrasting behavior reactions in different types of situations. Miss Caldwell, in Boston, working mainly with Italian children, has astonishing records showing consistently defiant, destructive, negativistic behavior in the home and relatively orderly behavior in the nursery school. And this duality of behavior is carried on for years – bad in one situation, good in another.

Freeman and his associates in Chicago are now publishing a situational study of the greatest importance based on the placing of about six hundred children in foster homes, in response, apparently, to the following challenge by Terman: "A crucial experiment," Terman says, "would be to take a large number of very young children from the lower classes and after placing them in the most favorable environment obtainable compare their later mental development with that of the children born into the best homes." In this experiment comparisons were made between results on intelligence tests which had been given before adoption, in the case of one group, and the results after they had been in the foster home a number of years. Another comparison was made between children of the same family who had been placed in different homes, the home being rated on a scheme which took into consideration the material environment, evidence of culture, occupation of foster father, education and social activity of foster parents. Both of these comparisons had held heredity constant, letting the situation vary. A third comparison held environment constant, letting heredity vary, that is, concerning itself with a comparison of the intelligence of the own children of the foster parents and of the foster children. The results, stated in a word, show that when two unrelated children are reared in the same home, differences in their intelligences tend to decrease, and that residence in different homes tends to make siblings differ from one another in intelligence. This study is limited to the question of intelligence, but it is obvious that a fundamental study of behavior could be made by the same method.

Esther Richards, of the Phipps Psychiatric Clinic in Baltimore, has been experimenting with psychopathic children by placing them in homes and on farms and moving them about until a place is found in which they are adjusted. She discovered that there were whole families of hypochondriacs showing no symptoms of organic deficiency. To be "ailing, and never so well" had become a sort of fashion in families, owing, perhaps, to the hysterical manifestations of the mother. These attempts are rather uniformly successful as long as the parents remain away from the child. One boy had been manifesting perfect health and robust activity on a farm, but conceived a stomach ache on the appearance of his mother, which disappeared with her departure. And it is the prevailing psychiatric standpoint that the psychoneuroses – the hysterias, hypochondrias, schizophrenias, war neuroses, etc., are forms of adaptations to situations.

Dr. Harry Stack Sullivan and his associates, working at the Sheppard and Enoch Pratt Hospital, Baltimore, are experimenting with a small group of persons now or recently actively disordered, from the situational standpoint, and among other results this study reveals the fact that these persons tend to make successful adjustments in groupwise association between themselves.

The sociologist has found the behavior document, the life-record, a very useful aid in exploring the situation and determining the sources of maladjustment. It is true that this introspective method has the disadvantages encountered in the taking of legal testimony. It has been shown by students of testimony that in case of false testimony the witness frequently brings a preconception, a behavior schema, to the situation, that he testifies egocentrically, overweighting certain aspects and adding perceptual elements and interpretations as a result of his own memories and experiences; his perceptions of the events of which he testifies are thus anticipatory and reminiscent. And he has also excluded from perception factors which he did not anticipate. The same holds in varying degrees of the human document. Shaw, working with the Institute of Juvenile Research in Chicago, has pointed out that some of his subjects prepare dry and objective chronicles while others are mainly self-justificatory and exculpatory. A document prepared by one compensating for a feeling of inferiority or elaborating a delusion of persecution is certainly as far as possible from objective reality. On the other hand, this definition of the situation is from one standpoint quite as good as if it were true. It is a representation of the situation as appreciated by the subject, "as if" it were so, and this is for behavior study a most important phase of reality.

The psychologists and social workers connected with the juvenile courts and child clinics, the visiting teachers, and other organizations are now preparing extensive records tending to take the behavior of the child in connection with all the contacts and experiences which may have influenced the particular delinquency or maladjustment. And finally the regional and ecological behavior surveys with which Park, Burgess, Thrasher, Shaw, Zorbaugh, and others are identified attempt to measure the totality of influence in a community, the configuration and disposition of social stimuli, as represented by institutions, localities, social groups, and individual personalities, as these contribute to the formation of behavior patterns.

The merit of all these exploratory approaches is that they tend to bring out causative factors previously neglected and to change the character of the problem. Thrasher's study of 1,313 gangs in Chicago changes the character of the crime problem, and this study merely opens up a new situation. Other researchers, not yet published, will show that, recruited from the gangs, criminal life is as definitely organized in Chicago as the public school system or any other department of life, the criminals working behind an organization of "irreproachable" citizens. Shaw has studied the cases of boys brought before the juvenile court in Chicago for stealing with reference to the number of boys participating, and finds that in 80 per cent of the cases two or more boys were involved. It is certain that many of the boys concerned were not caught, and that the percentage of groupwise stealing is therefore greater than 90 per cent. This again throws a new light on the nature of the problem of crime. Again, Burgess and Shaw have studied the incidence of delinquency for different neighborhoods and find that in the so-called "interstitial zones," lying along the railroad tracks and between the better neighborhoods, the boys are almost 100 per cent delinquent, while in other neighborhoods there is almost no delinquency. Burgess found one ward in a city of 12,000 population with about eight times as many cases of juvenile delinquency as in any of the other wards.[4]

These are examples of factors of delinquency which turn up or come to the front in the course of the exploration of situations. But with reference to the relationship of the factors, their distribution in the ratio of delinquency, or even the certitude that we are aware of all the factors, we are in one respect in the position of the person who gives false testimony in court. We overweight the standpoint acquired by our particular experience and our preconceived line of approach. In the literature of delinquency we find under the heading "causative factors" such items as the following: Early sex experience, 18 per cent for boys and 25 per cent for girls; bad companionship, 62 per cent for both sexes; school dissatisfaction, 9 per cent for boys and 2 per cent for girls; mental defect, 14 per cent; premature puberty, 3 per cent; psychopathic personality, 14 per cent; mental conflict, 6.5 per cent; motion pictures, 1 per cent, etc. Now it is evident that many young persons have had some of these experiences without becoming delinquent, and that many mentally defective persons and psychopathic personalities are living at large somewhat successfully without any record of delinquency; some of them are keeping small shops; others are producing literature and art. How can we call certain experiences "causative factors" in a delinquent group when we do not know the frequency of the same factors in a non-delinquent group? In order to determine the relation of a given experience to delinquency it would be necessary to compare the frequency of the same experience in the delinquent group and in a group representing the general non-delinquent population. It is now well known that the findings of Lombroso in his search for a criminal type went completely to pieces when Goring and others compared a series of criminals with a series taken from otherwise comparable non-delinquents. Lombroso's "criminal stigmata" are simply physical marks of the human species distributed pretty uniformly through the general population. Similarly, it is obviously absurd to claim that feeblemindedness or psychopathic disposition is the *cause* of crime so long as we have no idea of the prevalence of these traits in the general population. No subject is perhaps in so naïve and grotesque a position in this respect as psychoanalysis. The "Oedipus complex" and the "Electra complex" – the "fixation" of son on mother and daughter on father – are discovered and weighted by Freudians and made prominent sources of the psychoneuroses and of delinquency, whereas the clinical records show a multitude of cases where children with behavior disturbances are either indifferent to the parents or directly hate them. Again, with regard to economic factors as cause of crime, we find, for example, in the records of the White-Williams Foundation of Philadelphia (an organization dealing primarily with non-delinquent children) the same unfavorable economic conditions, broken homes, etc., which are usually assigned as "causative factors" in the studies of delinquency, but in this case without delinquency.

The psychiatrist Kempf, speaking of the diagnosis and classification of nervous diseases, has given the opinion that if twenty cases were given to twenty psychiatrists separately for diagnosis and their findings were sealed and given to a committee for a comparison of the results the whole system of diagnosis would blow up. And something of this kind would happen if students of delinquency, under the same conditions, attempted to name the causative factors in a crime wave or in the heavy incidence of delinquency in a given locality. The answers would certainly be weighted on the side of bad heredity, gang life, poverty, commercialized pleasure, decline of the church, post-encephalitic behavior disturbances, etc., according to the different standpoints represented.

Since the establishment of the first juvenile court in 1899 there has been a very careful elaboration of procedure with reference to the treatment of the young delinquent – systematic study of the case, oversight in the home or in a detention home, placing in good families, psychiatric social workers, visiting teachers, attempts to improve the attitudes of parents toward children, recreation facilities, children's villages and farm schools – and there is, I think, a general impression that there is a steady improvement, an evolution of method, and a gradual approach to a solution of the problem of delinquency. But there is no evidence that juvenile-court procedure or any procedure tends to reduce the large volume of juvenile delinquency. This is not surprising in view of the present rapid unstabilization of society connected with the urbanization of the population, the breakdown of kinship groups, the circulation of news, the commercialization of pleasure, etc. But it is more significant that the methods of the juvenile courts, when applied by their best representatives and in the most painstaking way, cannot be called successful in arresting the career of children who once appear in court, that so many first offenders become recidivists and eventually criminals. Healy and Bronner, who were the first court psychologists, and whose work commands the highest respect in the world, have recently reviewed this point on the basis of the records of their cases during the past twenty years in Chicago and Boston. They say:

> Tracing the lives of several hundred youthful repeated offenders studied long ago by us and treated by ordinary so-called correctional methods reveals much repetition of offense. This is represented by the astonishing figures of 61 per cent failure for males (15 per cent being professional criminals and 5 per cent having committed homicide), and 46 per cent failure for girls (19 per cent being prostitutes). Thus in over one-half the cases in this particular series juvenile delinquency has continued into careers of vice and crime.... This is an immense proportion to be coming from any series of consecutive cases studied merely because they were repeated offenders in a juvenile court. It represents a most disconcerting measure of failure.[5]

They mention that no less than 209 of the 420 boys whom they knew when they appeared in the Chicago juvenile court had later appeared in adult courts, and of these 157 had received commitment to adult correctional institutions 272 times. The first court appearance is thus not to be regarded as the initiation of a reform, but in many youthful offenders it appears as a sort of confirmation or commencement ceremony initiating a criminal way of life. There are, indeed, many records of positive successes under juvenile court treatment, especially among the cases of Healy and Bronner, but the most successful workers confess that they do not know how they obtained their successes, whether through their own efforts or through spontaneous changes in the child.

Now there is reason to believe that we are deluded or not properly informed as to the efficiency of other behavior-forming situations and agencies on which we are confidently relying for the control of behavior and the development of normal personality. We assume that good families produce good children, but certain of the experimental nursery schools, selecting their children carefully in order to avoid material already spoiled, find nevertheless that they have drawn from the best families a large percentage of problem children. Our school curricula, based on reading ability and lesson-transfer, drive many children gifted along perceptual-motor lines into truancy and delinquency. It would be possible to show by cases that the home and the school are hardly less unsuccessful behavior-forming situations than the juvenile court.

Naturally the greatest amount of attention, up to the present, has been given to the study of abnormal behavior in the forms which come to public attention, become a nuisance; but behavior difficulties are widespread in the whole population, and it is certain that we can understand the abnormal only in connection with the normal, in relation to the whole social process to which they are both reactions. The same situation or experience in the case of one person may lead this person to another type of adjustment; in another it may lead to crime; in another, to insanity, the result depending on whether previous experiences have formed this or that constellation of attitudes.

The answer is, we must have more thoroughgoing explorations of situations. In our planning we should include studies and surveys of behavior-forming situations, measurements of social influences which will enable us to observe the operation of these situations in the formation of delinquent, emotionally maladjusted, and stable personalities and determine the ratios. A plan of this kind, which has been discussed by some of the sociologists present, proposes to take selected localities or neighborhoods in given cities, including, for example, the interstitial zones where delinquency is highest and the good neighborhoods where delinquency is lowest, and study all the factors containing social influence.

A survey of this kind would involve a study of all the institutions – family, gang, social agencies, recreations, juvenile courts, the daily press, commercialized pleasure, etc. – by all the available techniques, including life-records of all the delinquent children and an equal number of non-delinquent children, for the purpose of tracing the effects of the behavior-forming situations on the particular personalities.

It is known also that cities and other localities differ greatly as total behavior-forming situations. Healy and Bronner estimated, for example, that their failures in Chicago were 50 per cent and in Boston only 21 per cent. The difference is certainly not due in the main to differences in juvenile-court procedure, but to differences in the attitudes of the population, and this in turn to differences in the configurations of social influence. The juvenile court of Cincinnati has excited interest by the fact that it institutionalizes very few children, uses foster homes rarely, has only a nominal probation system, and is thought nevertheless to have greater success than other cities. The court procedure in Cincinnati is not elaborate; the co-operative agencies are not well organized. Nearly all the youthful offenders are simply turned back into the community. Is the relative success in this situation due to lack of too much zeal, to a refusal to treat and classify the child too promptly as delinquent? Is the large and stable element of German and German-Jewish population a factor in the situation? Rochester, New York, is the only city in the country where the visiting teacher organization is incorporated in the public school system. What is the efficiency of this effort to treat the child in the predelinquent stages of his behavior difficulties? An inventory and measure of the social influences of selected cultural centers taken comparatively is thus very desirable.

There is a type of behavior reaction going on every day before our eyes which has to do with the participation of masses of the population, often whole populations, in common sentiments and actions. It is represented by fashions of dress, mob action, war hysteria, the gang spirit, mafia, omertà, fascism, popularity of this or that cigarette or tooth paste, the quick fame and quick infamy of political personalities. It uses language – spoken, written, and gesture. It is emotional, imitative, largely irrational and unconscious, weighted with symbols, and sometimes violent. It is capable of manipulation and propagation by leading personalities and the public print. Its result is commonly and publicly accepted definitions of situations. Its historical residuum constitutes the distinctive character of races, nationalities, and communities. This is the psychology of the evolution of public opinion and of social norms. As long as the definitions of situations remain constant and common we may anticipate orderly behavior reactions. When rival definitions arise (as between the wets and drys at the present moment) we may anticipate social disorganization and personal demoralization. There are always constitutional inferiors and divergent personalities in any society who do not adjust, but the mass of delinquency, crime, and emotional instability is the result of conflicting definitions. When, as Justice McAdoo says, a large number of young men in New York City have made up their minds that they will live without working, this is a new definition of the situation and the formation of a criminal policy.

Now these expressions of public opinion, the rise of common attitudes, the establishment of a group morale, the culmination of emotional outbursts, and the formulation of more deliberate policies have also a situational origin – one in which the situation is weighted with pre-established attitudes, with conflicts arising over definitions of situations and influenced by the propaganda of word, print, and gesture, and it is desirable that selected types of behavior-forming situations should be studied along these lines.

And, finally, I will not here emphasize the point which I have attempted to exemplify in a particular study, that it is desirable to extend our studies of this situational character to the large cultural areas, to the races and nationalities, in order to understand the formation of behavior patterns comparatively, in their most general and particular expressions.

Notes

1. Charlotte Bühler, Hildegard Hetzer, and Beatrix Tudor-Hart. *Soziologische und psychologische Studien über das erste Lebensjahr* (Quellen und Studien zur Jugendkunde), Jena, 1927.

2. John E. Anderson, "The Genesis of Social Reactions in the Young Child," in *The Unconscious: A Symposium*, pp. 69–90.

3. *Ibid.*

4. E. W. Burgess, "Juvenile Delinquency in a Small City," *Journal of Criminal Law and Criminology*, 6: 726–28.

5. Healy and Bronner, *Delinquents and Criminals: Their Making and Unmaking*, pp. 201–2.

22

Introduction to *Robert E. Park. On Social Control and Collective Behavior*

Ralph H. Turner

Probably no other man has so deeply influenced the direction taken by American empirical sociology as Robert Ezra Park. His students, inspired by his teaching and impressed with the serious task of finding out what actually went on about them, carried out much of the early empirical research in sociology and established a pattern for the work of others. Perhaps it is because of Park's intense personal impact on his students that rather less attention has been devoted to the system of sociology that is conveyed in his own writings. In this brief essay we hope to recall attention to some of Park's own major ideas, selecting especially those which have applicability to current sociological preoccupations.

Like any seminal thinker, Park put forth some incompletely digested ideas, revised his thinking in the course of his intellectual career, and suffered from some of the limitations of the era in which he worked. To call attention to these features of his thought is not to detract from his stature. His was "an exceedingly vigorous, searching mind. His thought was continually roving around, ever on the alert to new leads and ever searching for new insights and perspectives."[1] Many of his characteristically dynamic ideas were rendered static in the hands of his followers. Renewed attention to Park's own writings may help to restore some of the lost vitality.

The only comprehensive account we have of Park's view of sociology is to be found in the *Introduction to the Science of Sociology*,[2] a collaborative work. Although Burgess was admittedly a junior author, and Park himself wrote the chapter on the nature of sociology and either wrote or outlined the content of the initial essays in the remaining chapters, the collaboration was lively.

The Nature and Tasks of Sociology

In the *Introduction*, Park traces the development of the idea of sociology since Comte's initial statement, stressing the distinctions from history, from the special

---

Source: Ralph H. Turner (ed.), *Robert E. Park. On Social Control and Collective Behavior*, (Chicago: Chicago University Press, 1967).

social sciences, and from the applied sciences. The pivotal idea is Simmel's distinction between the concrete, factual character of history, and the abstract, generalizing nature of sociology. Education and social service apply principles which sociology and psychology deal with explicitly.

That Park today is best known for his contributions to such concrete areas as urban sociology and race relations seems to belie this formal conception of an abstract science. But the impression is not altogether just. The tendency to generalize to process rather than structure – to be remarked at greater length – turned his attention toward a different kind of generalization than came to dominate a subsequent generation of sociologists. A reading of his papers shows a characteristic approach in which he moves from the close examination of some restricted datum to explore parallels in a wide range of phenomena. His overarching concern with abstraction and generalization becomes clear as the reader discovers that a very few facts about the press are used again and again to support a constant search for the general conditions affecting consensus in society, and that a relatively small amount of objectifiable information about race relations serves to launch Park into broad exploration of the accommodations among groups or the relationship between individual and society.

Park's definition of sociology as "the science of collective behavior"[3] suggests at once the study of a fluid congeries rather than a stable structure. The import of the definition can best be grasped by considering the tasks which are assigned to the discipline. In tracing the historical conceptions of sociology, Park takes up the "social organism" issue, the reality of society apart from the individuals who make it up. He concludes that society is more than a body of like-minded individuals "because of the existence (1) of a social process and (2) of a body of tradition and opinion – the products of this process – which has a relatively objective character and imposes itself upon the individual as a form of control, social control."[4] Accordingly, social control becomes the "central fact and the central problem of society."[5]

> Society is everywhere a control organization. Its function is to organize, integrate, and direct the energies resident in the individuals of which it is composed.[6]

Social control as the central problem. Social control has had several meanings in sociological usage. It has commonly meant the constraint or organization of human impulses by some system of mores, folkways, laws, collective representations, culture – that is, the imposition of impersonal patterns on individual behavior. Students divide into those who, like Sumner, assume a simple opposition between individual impulse and culture, and those who, like Durkheim, see culture as supplying avenues for the crystallization and productive expression of impulse. On another axis, students divide between those who see a relatively fixed pattern that is acquired by internalization or habituation and those who see control as situational – as the constantly changing requirements for collaboration within sets of relationships. Park's views are clearly stated, and fall closer to the second alternative in each case, although he occasionally lapses into an opposite stance.

From Herbert Spencer, Park takes the question, "How does a mere collection of individuals succeed in acting in a corporate and consistent way?"[7] Giddings' "like-mindedness" and Tarde's "imitation" supply one kind of answer: "men act together because they act alike."[8] Durkheim on the other hand answers that a *common purpose* "imposes itself upon the individual members of a society at the same time as an ideal, a wish and an obligation."[9] After acknowledging some virtue in both sides of the Giddings–Tarde versus Durkheim controversy, he opts for the latter, saying, "the thing that distinguishes a mere collection of individuals from a society is not like-mindedness, but corporate action."[10]

Differences are often as necessary as likenesses for society to operate. Accordingly, sociology is "a point of view and method for investigating the processes by which individuals are inducted into and induced to cooperate in some sort of permanent corporate existence we call society."[11] The imposition of fixed behavior patterns is but one phase of the larger problem of human collaboration, which Park identifies as social control.

This view of social control is underlined by the close identification Park makes between social control and collective behavior. The two terms apply to the same phenomena, except that social control refers to *mechanism* and collective behavior to *process*. Since collective behavior describes the forming and re-forming of society, social control concerns not only the mechanisms underlying traditional continuity but also the means through which the coordination involved in change is achieved. The most elementary form of control is the rapport among crowd members, entirely without tradition; but even such highly rationalized forms of control as law and public opinion arise out of efforts to compromise conflict. Although the force of the mores is acknowledged, they are merely the residuals of earlier public opinion, with the issues forgotten. In the formal discussion of social control, Park even leaves the impression that an aroused public opinion might readily overwhelm the mores.

Likewise, as Park deals with social control in the abstract, he finds little occasion to stress opposition between human impulses and societal demands. Public opinion and the mores are collective responses to changing situations and are based on fundamental human nature. They are "forms of behavior which spring directly and spontaneously out of the innate and instinctive responses of the individual to a social situation."[12] At one point Park seems to presage that type of social psychological functionalism which sees human impulse as fully harnessed to the requirements of society. Thus, "as members of society, men act as they do elsewhere from motives they do not fully comprehend, in order to fulfill aims of which they are only dimly or not at all conscious."[13]

But as Park leaves the abstract treatment of social control to examine concrete problems, his words are occasionally different. The family is singled out as a vestige from an earlier "authoritative and sacred society in which everyone has duties and no one has rights,"[14] and in which personal interests are invariably subject to communal authority. At a still earlier date, in connection with his one brief foray into the problem of juvenile delinquency, Park had written bitterly of a much more ubiquitous opposition.

> So ill-adapted is the natural, undomesticated man to the social order into which he is born, so out of harmony are all the native impulses of the ordinary healthy human with the demands which society imposes, that it is hardly an exaggeration to say that if his childhood is spent mainly in learning what he must not do, his youth will be devoted mainly to rebellion. As to the remainder of his life, his recreations will very likely turn out to be some sort of vacation and escape from this same social order to which he has finally learned to accommodate, but not wholly reconcile, himself....
>
> One reason why human beings, in contrast with the lower animals, seem to be so ill-adapted to the world in which they are born is that the environment in which human beings live is so largely made up of the experience and memories and the acquired habits of the people who have preceded them.[15]

In spite of these early jeremiads, Park never supported an anarchistic fantasy of society, nor did he ever incline toward a utopia in which the oppositions might be engineered away. Perhaps his closest approach to utopianism is found in an observation that the best integrated society is one in which there are the fewest enacted laws – an assumption which is contradicted by a large body of his thinking regarding *civilization* as contrasted with *culture*. His last writings contain frequent assertions of the necessity for a universe of discourse, including shared and understandable personal loyalties. In a mood which contrasts sharply with his earlier protest, Park at one point argues even that a system of magical belief is essential to social order. But the balanced view, that social control involves the creation of enthusiasms as well as negative restraints, is perhaps best exemplified in the culminating chapter of the *Introduction*, where progress is interpreted as a vital myth.

> The conception that man's fate lies somehow in his own hands, if it gains general acceptance, will still be, so far as it inspires men to work and strive, an article of faith, and the image in which he pictures the future of mankind, toward which he directs his efforts, will still have the character of myth. That is the function of myths. It is this that lends an interest to those ideal states in which men at different times have sought to visualize the world of their hopes and dreams.[16]

Selection of social control, and the problem of the relationship of the individual to the group, as a central concern for sociology, suggests an approach that is social psychological in emphasis. The impression is reinforced in a chapter dealing with the "social forces" in the *Introduction*. The unexpected obstacles to social reform which can be traced to influential persons and powerful groups suggest that community life should be conceived as a *constellation of social forces*. But instead of offering a discussion of the distribution and exercise of power, Park carries the reader by steps back to a sort of social atom, which is the individual attitude, and is in turn constituted from the four wishes of W. I. Thomas. The task of resolving attitudes into finer elements Park assigns to psychology, but the sociologist locates the dynamic element shaping the accommodations of society in the individual attitude. In a subsequent chapter of the book we read that "It is with social forces and human nature that sociology is mainly concerned."[17]

Although social control is the central problem of sociology, there is a sharp contrast to the thoroughly socio-psychological concern of E. A. Ross and others with the dynamics of particular control mechanisms. The materials deal rather with the historical and situational evolution and use of the various means of control. If control mechanisms intervene between society and the individual, Park is less interested in the link between mechanism and individual than he is in the link between society and mechanism.

Park did indeed have a deep concern for human nature, and his conception of society seldom moves far from the patterned collaboration and accommodation among persons. His most important contributions include *social role*, the *self conception*, and the *marginal man* – all concepts dealing with the relationship between individual and society. But seldom did his attention turn to the psychological makeup of the individual, or even to microsociology. Although he did not describe "structures" in the sense in which sociologists have come to use the term, the patterns of interaction he describes generally take place on a large scale, or in organized community and institutional settings, or between groups rather than individuals. Park's reference to the social forces can perhaps be dismissed as a concession to completeness which he never followed up in his own work. His emphasis upon social control directs more attention to the individual than approaches that center on institutions, culture, or organization structures, but he uses a conception of the individual that depends very little upon the discipline of psychology. It is not then a psychological bias but his conception of a fluid social order that requires constant attention to individual attitudes as phases of societal process.

Uses of sociology. Although Park adopted an abstract formal conception of sociology from Simmel, he nevertheless saw sociology as ultimately useful and practical. Social problems are the natural focus for sociological research, and the pursuit of sociology appears to be inseparable from the point of view of Graham Wallas' "Great Society" and the liberal tradition. It is largely, but not exclusively, this orientation that leads Park to concern himself disproportionately with what some call the pathologies of society. But Park is satisfied to take for granted that the inequities of race relations, the corruption of political machines, criminality, and vice are problems, and proceed directly to their examination without stopping to moralize in the fashion so common during his era. Park endorses W. I. Thomas' repudiation of "ordering–forbidding" as an approach to social reform, and explicitly defers the practical contribution until the problem area has been studied in breadth and depth. Burgess points out how Park dealt with students who were predisposed to fight for Negro rights.

> Park told them flatly that the world was full of crusaders. Their role instead was to be that of the calm, detached scientist who investigates race relations with the same objectivity and detachment with which the zoologist dissects the potato bug.[18]

Park acknowledges that administrative problems offer a legitimate focus for sociological research but passes quickly to the more fundamental problems of policy, which have to do with the character of social institutions and of human nature. Applied sociology is not concerned with uncovering mechanisms and devices for reform, but with exposing the broad setting of social organization and human nature which policy-makers must take into account. Park's few attempts to offer specific advice to social workers, educators, and others must have been disappointing to the practitioners, for this very reason.

Foremost among the guiding values for his approach to applied sociology is the counterpart to his theoretical emphasis upon social control: a concern with reconciling or balancing the requirements of human collaboration against the goal of individual freedom. Coupled with this concern is the goal of rationality in human society, but not so much in the individual as in the collective sense. Park plainly approved of the historical shift from a society in which men are governed by sentiment to a society which takes account, through public opinion, of the divergent interests intrinsic to a heterogeneous social structure.

For all of his concern with race relations, it is striking that the achievement of social and economic equality never emerges as a dominant goal in Park's thought. He toyed with ideas of racial temperament, and never wholly rejected the idea of a biological basis for racial inequality. The problems he examined are not those that would have preoccupied an investigator convinced that reduction of inequalities was the most urgent agendum. Perhaps it is for this reason that Park took no substantial steps toward developing a theory of stratification.

The Method of Sociology

Park continued the work of W. I. Thomas in turning the attention of sociologists away from speculation over vast evolutionary fictions, away from moralization, and toward the development of a body of knowledge firmly based upon those phenomena that were close enough and concrete enough to be examined reliably. But he also came to be identified popularly with an atheoretical and undisciplined empirical approach, personifying a stereotype of the dominant trend in American sociology during the interwar period. His reluctance to engage in formalization, his avoidance of the language of deductive inquiry or hypothesis-testing, his tendency to generalize from anecdotes, all suggest a wholly inductive approach, guided by intuition rather than systematic concerns. But a fuller account of Park's methodological concerns will show the popular version to be a badly distorted picture.

Scientific sociology. In spite of strong views regarding the essentially empirical character of sociology and the importance of working with facts rather than suppositions, Park concerned himself very little with details of data collection and analysis. An essay entitled "The Sociological Methods of William Graham Sumner, and of William I. Thomas and Florian Znaniecki"[19] turns out to be an exposition of their conceptual apparatus, without serious consideration of the means employed in data gathering and data analysis. The exposition contains the justification for this emphasis. The chief contribution of the *Polish Peasant*, we are told, "is not a body of fact, but a system of concepts." Sumner started with an interest rather than a problem, and then defined the problem only after he had learned a good deal about his subject. Only after problem formulation is it appropriate to speak of methods. Concepts and frame of reference are the most important part of method, but are usually the by-products of research, rather than antecedent to it.

Without formalizing it, Park adumbrates a sophisticated conception in which the method of social science supplies a frame of reference through which it is possible to observe significant regularities. Without a conceptual apparatus, useful observation is impossible; with such an apparatus, the specific data-gathering procedures are of lesser moment. But not *any* conceptual apparatus will do, for what one can see is dependent upon the concepts employed. Hence there must be a continuous interplay between observation and conceptualization. He repudiates the practice by which an investigator takes a full-blown theory into the field with him, and seeks to confirm or refute it. In one of his most bitter attacks upon quantification, Park stresses the deficiency of "a purely scholastic exercise in which the answers to all the questions are already implicit in the conceptions and assumptions with which the inquiry started."[20] At the same time, Park could not have commended Lundberg's "social bookkeeping." His method was deeply committed to theory and intertwined with theory.

Although all of Park's own work follows the same pattern, seeking creative conceptualizations that will informally illumine empirical observation and then using the concepts to shed light on a wider range of observations, his early writings advocate enhanced methodological rigor. "Facts have not been collected to check social theories. Social problems have been defined in terms of common sense . . ."[21] "Sociology seems now, however, in a way to become, in some fashion or other, an experimental science."[22] Although his conception of an experiment was perhaps closer to common sense than to current scientific usage, the student was being encouraged explicitly to follow the lead of experimental psychology and medicine.

Park gave impetus to quantification through his formulation of the idea of *social distance* and of the *ecological* approach to community study. The concept of social distance does two things to the ideas of prejudice and antagonism. It directs attention beneath the overt manifestations of intergroup relations to the stable terms of their accommodation, and it formulates the latter as a readily quantifiable phenomenon. "The point is that we are clearly conscious, in all our personal relationships, of degree of intimacy. A is closer to B than C and the degree of this intimacy measures the influence which each has over the other."[23] E. S. Bogardus credits Park with the suggestion that he develop a generally applicable device for the measurement of social distance – a suggestion which resulted in the widely used social distance scale.[24]

One aspect of the ecological approach in sociology was the use of the more tangible and hence measurable phenomena as indexes for the more strictly social processes. Land values are prime indicators of social forces. Social metabolism, measured through such indexes as mobility rates, indicates in quantitative terms the intensity of the social process. "In so far as social structure can be defined in terms of position, social changes may be defined in terms of movement; and society exhibits, in one of its aspects, characters that can be measured and described in mathematical formulas."[25]

Perhaps it is unfair to employ a paper that Park never chose to publish to exemplify his later thoughts. Yet Thorndike's attempt to measure the "goodness of life" in American cities brought forth pungent comments on the misuse of quantification. After berating Thorndike for reducing a complex set of processes to oversimplified perspective, and overlooking the difference among communities in the relationship of the incorporated city to the daily round of life among its inhabitants, Park speaks in more general terms. "The manipulation of statistical data by which such scales are contrived and applied has always impressed me a good deal like parlor magic. One is frequently startled by the results but is mainly interested to discover by what sleight of hand the trick was turned."[26] Although Park did not actively repudiate his earlier views, he did not employ the newer quantitative procedures, and made less and less use of quantitative materials of any sort in his later writings.

More characteristic, then, than Park's advocacy of a rigorously scientific approach to sociology are his endorsement of the "methods of anthropologists" and his insistence on the crucial place of history. After his review of devices for quantifying the objects of study, Park asserts that "History alone can, it would seem, make these different meanings intelligible to us . . . . Just because it has been a *record of events* rather than a *description of things*, history has given sociology much, if not most, of its subject matter."[27] Park's own most serious excursion into empirical research, reported in *The Immigrant Press and its*

Control,[28] is fundamentally like the work of a historian who writes topically rather than chronologically. The methodological problems are chiefly those of ferreting out the many obscure records, and employing letters and similar documents as a guide to commonsense interpretations of the record.

Meaning and process. A scholar's choice of methods depends upon the character of findings and conclusions that he finds most useful or intuitively most satisfying. The crucial emphasis upon history, the reliance on life histories and the procedures of participant observation, and the reaction against trends in quantification are understandable in light of the two prime objectives that governed Park's work. His conclusions were characteristically the description of a *process* and the specification of the *meaning* of an individual or collective action.

Park insisted that we search for causes rather than correlations, and that we concern ourselves with the meanings of acts, rather than with behavior in a limited sense. Park sometimes used William James' essay, "A Certain Blindness in Human Beings,"[29] as the springboard for exposition of the preferred method in sociology. Before one can begin to make sociological sense of any group, the investigator must overcome the normal "blindness to the feelings of creatures and people other than ourselves." If anything customary seems shocking or quaint, it is because the custom is not quite intelligible to the observer. The difficulties in sociological investigation do not lie in describing external forms, but in discovering the meaning and function of usages and institutions. The investigator must involve himself until he uncovers the basis of the zest for life in a particular culture. "This zest for life is just that personal and vital secret which, for each one of us, gives meaning and significance not merely to the life of the individual but of the society, of whatever sort it be, of which he is a member and a part."[30]

The influence of W. I. Thomas upon Park – or the similarity of their outlooks – is clearest in this respect. Human documents are the foremost media for achieving sympathetic identification.

Not only the ability to predict the course of action, but the investigator's intuitive sense of being at home in the culture, feeling the depression and elation of a member of the society, is the criterion of successful investigation. Thus while Park is on the side of *verstehen* sociology as opposed to positivistic approaches, his goals are not to be confused with the primarily cognitive and formalistic typologies of action which come out of the work of Max Weber.

If the central concern with affective meanings, approached through sympathetic identification, limits the usefulness of most objective procedures to supplying quite indirect indexes of sociology's main concerns, the emphasis upon process renders the easy formalizations and the simple correlational models so characteristic of structural analysis of equally limited value. Society is in constant flux, and Park is more interested in the past and future of events than he is in their momentary interrelationships.

Contemporary debate concerns the usefulness of equilibrium models of society. Park's view might be labeled a dynamic disequilibrium model. Implicit in his formulations are potential states of equilibrium – the end points of his idealized natural histories – and the constant pull in the direction of these states keeps the system changing. An idealized state of assimilation stands at the end of conflict, institutionalization is the end product of collective behavior; public opinion process rigidifies into the mores. But either these states are never reached or the approach to one equilibrium creates another disequilibrium that starts a second sequence before the first is finished.

Unlike equilibrium theorists, Park tells us little about the hypothetical states of equilibrium. He seems to be little interested in the characteristics of states of assimilation and institutionalization, and when he does take time to describe them, his characterizations are contradictory and sound more like states of disequilibrium. These states merely serve as points of reference, and his preoccupation is with the movements, the sequences, that take place. But his concern with patterned sequences of change likewise distinguishes him from the most articulate opponents of equilibrium theory in sociology today.

Nowhere more than in ecology did Park develop the idea of process. While Burgess elaborated his concept of natural areas into zones, Park dwelt more on the processes of invasion and succession – the sequence of events through which natural areas were constantly being transformed. The principal tool, and probably the most important concept in Park's methodology, is the natural history. The natural history is typically described as a series of stages that are set in motion by some disequilibrating event and lead toward the hypothetical state of equilibrium. Under Park's influence Lyford Edwards uncovered a set of stages that applied equally to several revolutions in history. Bogardus developed an informative "race relations cycle" based on West Coast experience, expressing the tendency for both conflict and accommodation in the economic sphere to precede and bring about changes in the social area. Stonequist applied the approach to identifying the crucial process through which an individual becomes a marginal man.

At different places Park reveals what he regards as essential elements in a natural history, although he offers neither formal definition nor careful prescription. A natural history is, first, a typical or collective account, the sequence leading to establishment of a form rather than a specific instance. "What is needed, however, is not so much a history as a natural history of the press – not a record of the fortunes of individual newspapers, but an account of the evolution of the newspaper as a social institution."[31] Second, a natural history is a cycle produced by natural forces, rather than by human planning.

> The newspaper has a history; but it has, likewise, a natural history. The press, as it exists, is not, as our moralists sometimes seem to assume, the willful product of any little group of living men. On the contrary, it is the outcome of an historic process in which many individuals

participated without foreseeing what the ultimate product of their labors was to be.[32]

Third, in the natural history each stage inevitably triggers the next. And finally, the natural history is not foreign to the natural order but is part and mechanism in the functioning of a social order.

> Race relations . . . can best be interpreted if what they seem to be at any time and place is regarded merely as a phase in a cycle of change which, once initiated, inevitably continues until it terminates in some predestined racial configuration and one consistent with an established order of which it is a part.[33]

The natural history approach fell into gradual disrepute in sociology after the initial period of vital use, chiefly because neither Park nor its other adherents elaborated it from common sense into a sophisticated method. Inevitable stages were seldom inevitable; the statistically typical series had little meaning in Park's own frame of reference; the prediction that cycles should ultimately be measurable temporally came to naught; stages were often – like Hiller's – no more than logical dissections of a definition; what to do with the stages after they were identified other than to classify phenomena was often unclear; and frequently the natural history became, instead of a phase of inevitable disequilibrium, a series of steps toward a utopian equilibrium. Even Park fell into the latter error, contributing to the paradisiacal fantasy about Hawaii with his observation that "Race relations in Hawaii today seem to be approaching the terminus of such a cycle as here described."[34] But a refined natural history approach, allowing for branching, and specifying the different contingencies which determine progression between each pair of stages, may still be a vital alternative to static, relational formulations.

City as laboratory. One final feature of Park's methodology deserves to be stressed. All of Park's interests found their focus in the city, a world which he often romanticized, and which he urged on other sociologists as a "laboratory" for the study of human society. One of his earliest papers was a lengthy catalog of suggestions for investigating human behavior in the urban environment, and Park's name has come to be identified with the monographic studies of city life, such as *The Gold Coast and the Slum, The Ghetto, The Gang,* conducted by his students. Although there is nothing in the logic of Park's ecological theory which restricts its applications to cities, the ideas have taken concrete form almost exclusively with reference to the metropolis.

It is characteristic of Park's generalizing propensity that he was not satisfied to concentrate on the city merely because he found it interesting, but that he should justify his work as shedding light on issues that transcended the city. The city is a convenient locus for investigation because every human impulse finds expression somewhere in a relatively small area, and because institutions grow more rapidly there. It is also a more relevant environment than small towns and primitive societies because the city is par excellence the world that man has made for himself.

But there is a very special sense in which Park sees the city as a microcosm in which are exposed and magnified, as under a microscope, the processes taking place in the larger society.

> Our political system is founded upon the conviction that people who live in the same locality have common interests, and that they can therefore be relied upon to act together for the common welfare. This assumption, as it turns out, is not valid for large cities. The difficulty of maintaining in the city intimate contacts which in the small town insured the existence of a common purpose and made concerted action possible is certainly very great.[35]

The processes of establishing concerted action are in continuous operation everywhere. But just because they function smoothly, it is difficult to detect their operation in the small town. When the processes are blocked, their operation is exposed to public view. In this special sense the city is a laboratory in which the investigator can see what he may only infer elsewhere. Here as elsewhere it is Park's interest in process rather than factual description or static relationship that turns him toward purposive observation rather than representative sampling.

Symbiosis and Socialization

Because it gave rise to a "school," Park's most conspicuous contribution to sociology was the distinction between two orders, governed by somewhat different principles, yet constantly interacting upon one another. Park adumbrated the distinction in his earliest writings, and continued to rework the fomulation until his death. In the *Introduction to the Science of Sociology* they are not yet presented as separate orders, but the idea is implicit in the separate treatment of competition and conflict processes. The orders are best known as the ecological and the social, and the distinction gave rise to the distinctively American sociological specialty known as ecology. But Park also spoke of community and society, of the biotic and the moral orders, and later of two contrasting processes, symbiosis and socialization. A distinction between civilization and culture seems to be related to these distinctions, although it does not carry the same implications.

The ecological order. There were at least two stages in the development of Park's formulation of ecology. In the first stage the specification of separate orders had not yet appeared or did not receive primary emphasis. Park was still concerned with making sociology scientific, although he was convinced that the social phenomena in which he was most interested were not directly measurable. The social tends to be projected into a spatial realm, social groups finding their habitats in natural areas, and social change being reflected in spatial mobility. The distribution and movement of populations in space can be precisely quantified, and thus they supply useful indexes for the social realm. At this stage, Park did not stress an autonomous ecological order, nor did he suggest the study of spatial patterns as a field of investigation in its own right. Some of the misunderstanding of Park's sociology stems from the fact that many investigators have used these early formulations without taking account of the subsequent probing efforts to develop a more vital and fundamental set of ideas.

The formulation of a distinctive ecological order appears in the second phase. "Symbiosis" and "socialization" come closest to capturing the main impetus of Park's repeated discussions. If Park first discovered the spatial order by approaching sociology from geography, his more characteristic and enduring outlook derived from the biological or organismic approach. The organismic approach had been brought from Europe and given its fullest development in American sociology by Lester F. Ward, who extended the biological idea of symbiosis into a universal principle of *synergy*, "the systematic and organic working together of the antithetical forces of nature."[36]

The recognition of a biological and a social order in human life was not uncommon, but followers of the organismic school often simply derived the categories and principles for analysis of the social order from the biological. Park recognized that the two orders were governed by different principles but interacted. The clue to the symbiotic (or ecological) order was to be found in the impersonal struggle for existence among animals and plants, and its imperfect analogy in economic competition among men. A different set of principles was required, however, to deal with man's capacity to create a *moral* order and to engage in communication. Park contrasts Spencer's view of society, founded upon the division of labor, to Comte's idea of society as consensus.

> Now, it is an indubitable fact that societies do have this double aspect. They are composed of individuals who act independently of one another, who compete and struggle with one another for mere existence, and treat one another, as far as possible, as utilities. On the other hand, it is quite as true that men and women are bound together by affections and common purposes; they do cherish traditions, ambitions, and ideals that are not all their own, and they maintain, in spite of natural impulses to the contrary, a discipline and a moral order that enables them to transcend what we ordinarily call nature, and through their collective action, recreate the world in the image of their collective aspirations and their common will.[37]

If the central problem of sociology is social control, the most important difference lies in the mechanism through which the two orders are regulated.

Competition governs the ecological order, not merely as a divisive and selective principle, but as a bonding process through the interdependencies it produces. The social order is governed by communication, directed by the conceptions of *self* and *other* which the members develop as social beings. The peculiar significance of communication is that it makes *collective* action possible. There is no collective action in the ecological order: individuals constitute a mass, and their actions are patterned because similar interests respond similarly to similar situations. Demographic methods are best suited for the study of parallel individual behavior but not for the distinctively collective behavior in society.

Some of the confusion regarding the essential nature of ecology emerges from Park's effort to integrate his earlier concern with a spatial realm into an order in which the assignment of position and change depend upon the operation of the impersonal process of competition. Park effects the integration by locating these processes in the *community*, which is

> (1) a population, territorially organized, (2) more or less completely rooted in the soil it occupies, (3) its individual units living in a relationship of mutual interdependence that is symbiotic rather than societal, in the sense in which that term applies to human beings.[38]

The division of labor, which reflects specialized competence and competitive advantage, sorts people into *natural areas*. Certain of these areas exhibit dominance, meaning that they are most responsive to external influence, and they control the competitive struggle in other areas. There is a tendency toward equilibrium, in which competition is regularized and its intensity reduced to a moderate level. When the equilibrium is disturbed by an external event which alters the "balance of nature," competition is intensified, setting in motion a process of *succession* in which the division of labor and the distribution in space are readjusted until once more a less intense competition serves merely to maintain the existing patterns of dominance and dispersion.

Nowhere else are the dynamic interrelations between the ecological order and the social (or moral) order systematically described, but they are mentioned in scattered contexts. Occasionally Park followed the earlier organismic theorists who derived social processes from the biotic, when he attempted to describe dominance and succession as processes manifested at every level. Typically, however, he saw the social order as restricting the intensity and softening the impact of the struggle for existence, by the operation of custom and sentiment. On the other hand, through technological innovation, the social order might disrupt the biotic equilibrium and intensify competition. Influence from the biotic to the social order is simpler, as social definitions tend to arise to express and reinforce the interpersonal order which has been produced by competition. Competition tends to become conflict, and such vital social facts as racial prejudice are ultimately social expressions of an impersonal division of labor. On those frequent occasions when the biotic order is grossly disrupted, competition is greatly intensified and society (in the narrow sense) ceases to function until biotic equilibrium has been approached closely enough so that competition subsides to a normal pace. There is also a more complex kind of influence, as when high density of population brings about individuation, partly through the necessarily more complex division of labor and partly because the absence of natural barriers to social intercourse forces the individual to erect social walls.

It is unfortunate that the study of urban spatial patterns is sometimes identified as ecology. The effect of spatial distribution on social life is one among many problems for ecological analysis, and propinquity in mate selection and de facto segregation in race relations are elementary ecological concerns. But Park's ecology refers to a set of processes that cannot be observed except in conjunction with social processes. Spatial patterns may be a direct indication of the biotic order among animals and plants, but among humans they reflect the joint operation of the two orders. Empirically the ecological order is an inference that supplies the explanation for many failures in control at the social level, and for innovations and deviations from the patterns of human collaboration embodied in the strictly social order. If the system of values and norms that men erect is conservatizing, the ecological order is like the unconscious realm in the individual, constantly unsettling the stable order and precipitating change.

Because of the emphasis on competition there is sometimes a mistaken tendency to identify the ecological order with economic processes and to equate Park's thought with a type of economic determinism. But Park reminds us that commercial bargaining is a highly evolved social transaction, and thus different in kind from the biotic competition that underlies social life. Nevertheless, when Park sought to specify just what constitutes the ecological order among human beings, he sometimes referred to impersonal and utilitarian dealings as contrasted to relationships governed by positive sentiment and obligation. Furthermore, the emergence of Marxian class consciousness through a group's discovery of their true interests supplies an excellent instance of the translation of ecological competition into social conflict. Here, as elsewhere, Park suggests an approach rather than developing a scheme in sufficient detail to yield researchable hypotheses. But in light of the constant failure of our expressed ideals to shape the functioning social order about us, renewed attention might profitably be devoted to the idea of a biotic order constantly interacting with the moral, the political, and the economic orders.

Civilization. Oddly, the idea of civilization, so inextricably linked to the metropolis and formulated from many of the same ideas that directed Park's thinking about the ecological order, is broached chiefly in another context. It is when Park seeks to account for race relations that he resorts to the idea of civilization, as a recent principle of social organization vaster than those that characterize the less developed world.

The focal point of a civilization is the marketplace. Its boundaries are the limits of the market, and the key to the growth of civilization has been expansion of the market. People come together in the market, not because of shared sentiments or any desire to participate in a common life, but because they are useful to each other. People of diverse races and cultures come together. Although tradition and sentiment develop, the sense of solidarity characteristic of simpler societies is lacking. On the other hand, trading requires a special skill – to know both one's own and the other's mind at a single instant.

Civilization has distinctive organizational characteristics. There is an inherent opposition between the unity of the whole and the closed sentiments of we-groups. Like W. I. Thomas, Park sometimes sees primary groups and the family in particular as incongruous survivals of an earlier era, although one senses that the struggle between we-groups and civilization will not soon end. The once autonomous territorial societies are brought under common domination, and superordination-subordination replaces territoriality as a principle of organization. Nationalistic movements are the natural reaction to the new principle. But people move about, territorial integrity is diluted, and race becomes temporarily a major criterion for stratification, only to be replaced eventually by caste and class. Class consciousness replaces ethnic and racial consciousness, since it expresses more faithfully the pattern of relationships to the market.

Once again Park owes much to German scholars, such as Simmel, Tönnies, and Oswald Spengler. But the relation of this idea, which is especially prominent in his later writings, to the ecological and social orders is not made explicit. Certain features of civilization suggest the interpretation that intensified ecological competition undermines the strictly social order and reinstates an order resembling the plant and animal world in the minimal effectiveness of social norms and primary group sentiments. But social contact and communication are of central importance, civilization is plainly not territorial and precultural but multicultural, and the capability for collective behavior is high. Thus the distinction between culture and civilization refers to the social and ecological systems together and does not rely upon the one or the other.

It is illuminating to contrast civilization to ecology as a basis for understanding the distinctive features of cities. The ecological approach as developed by Park's students stressed demographic criteria in defining the urban community. But this view has been called into question because of evidence that the way of life in cities outside the Western world often fails to fit theories derived from the study of American communities. But Park's conception of civilization distinguishes modern cities, which grew up about the international marketplaces, from the older cities, which grew up as fortresses. Not simply density of population and similar demographic considerations give the modern city its characteristic tendencies (such as weakening kinship ties), but the fact that people with diverse cultures are permanently brought together to carry on a distinctive type of social relationship. Here Park's wide knowledge of history led him to a more viable conception of urbanism than was possible for students who knew only the modern Western city.

The Social Order as Accommodation

If there is one aspect of Park's work that was ahead of its time, it is the conception of the social order as a pattern maintained by accommodation. If the central problem of sociology is to account for human collaboration, Park describes this collaboration as the continual accommodation necessary to carry on a collective life in the presence of competition and conflict. The formal treatment of conflict in the *Introduction* and the central place it occupies in his thought are notable reflections of his studies under Georg Simmel. But sociologists were unready to make constructive use of such an approach, and so for two decades the followers dutifully mentioned competition, conflict, accommodation, and assimilation in their introductory courses, without going much beyond taxonomy and illustration. After World War II equilibrium theory found little need for these concepts, and it was only as a reaction set in that scholars began to ask why there was no American sociology of conflict and to urge a conflict model of society as a corrective to equilibrium theory.

The "natural" state of society is not one of peace derived from unanimity, but a working adjustment to differences.

> Every society represents an organization of elements more or less antagonistic to each other but united for the moment, at least, by an arrangement which defines the reciprocal relations and respective spheres of action of each. This accommodation, this *modus vivendi* may be relatively permanent as in a society constituted by castes, or quite transitory as in societies made up of open classes.[39]

Conflict remains latent although antagonisms are regulated. Any change in the situation may upset the accommodation and nullify control over the antagonistic forces. Although tradition, the mores, and collective representations constitute consensus, this very consensus represents a set of social accommodations.

If accommodation is the normal state of society, it is reached through a series of stages that Park described first in completely general form and later rediscovered in the natural history of race relations in Hawaii. *Competition* comes first, as "interaction without contact," meaning that the individual is unaware of his competitors or is impersonal in his relations with them. Competition is universal and continuous, and normally proceeds unobserved. But in a crisis, when the circumstances of competition are altered, it is converted into conflict. *Conflict* is intermittent, is personal and conscious, and aims at control. If competition dictates the division of labor, conflict fixes the individual's place in society. *Accommodation* is a cessation of overt conflict, an agreement to disagree, which comes about when the systems of superordination–subordination and control which have developed in conflict become fixed and established in custom and the mores. Once an accommodation is reached, the slower process of *assimilation* sets in. The absorption of a cultural heritage and a thoroughgoing transformation of personality take place under the influence of intimate and concrete contacts.

The concept of assimilation is one of the more difficult of Park's terms to define precisely. Writers who like neat schemes often identify it as a process of losing separate group identity by adopting the host culture. One might then interpret the natural history as movement to a quiescent state founded on unanimity. But Park explicitly repudiates the view that assimilation means becoming alike. In national groups, likeness is superficial, and individual differences are considerable. But the superficial similarity is important because it nullifies the taboos against free movement and enables the individual to move into strange groups. It is in spite of individual differences that a unity of experience and of orientation permits development of a "community of purpose and action."

The nature of assimilation as the ultimate resolution of conflict relates to another large problem, the basis for solidarity in society. Giddings' *consciousness of kind* had considerable currency as an explanation for intergroup prejudices, and as a positive principle relating bondedness to likeness. Park rejected the concept in no uncertain terms while making clear what he regarded as the nature of social ties.

> Likeness is, after all, a purely formal concept which of itself cannot hold anything together.
>
> In the last analysis social solidarity is based on sentiment and habit. It is the sentiment of loyalty and the habit of what Sumner calls "concurrent action" that gives substance and insures unity to the state, as to every other type of social group. This sentiment of loyalty has its basis in a *modus vivendi*, a working relation and mutual understanding, of the members of the group. Social institutions are not founded in similarities any more than they are founded in differences, but in relations, and in the mutual interdependence of parts. When these relations have the sanction of custom and are fixed in individual habit, so that the activities of the group are running smoothly, personal attitudes and sentiments, which are the only forms in which individual minds collide and clash with one another, easily accommodate themselves to the existing situation.[40]

The immigrant does not become assimilated simply by adopting American ways. He first forms an immigrant group, which helps him find a place and make his way in American society. By arousing nationalistic feelings and a concern for the reputation of his first country among Americans, he breaks down the provincial loyalties he brought with him.

Although Park looked at race relations over the long run in terms of assimilation in this untidy sense, his chief preoccupation lay in the movements between accommodation and conflict. He saw a stable accommodation under slavery, made possible by the intimate relations between master and slave and the observance of well-understood patterns of social distance. Reduction of interracial intimacy led to mobilization of the racial minority, increasing contact within the race, and the development of common interest and sense of solidarity among Negroes. The result was movement toward a new basis for accommodation, a biracial organization of society with parallel class structures. In the simplest of terms, accommodation prevails when social distances are known and every man is in his place; conflict breaks out when the distances are ill defined or people abandon their assigned stations. Racial conflict is not so much the relationship among individuals as it is among persons conscious of their racial identities. The upshot of racial conflict is readjustment in the distribution of status and power between the races, which is translated into accommodation temporarily by devices such as accepting an "etiquette" of race relations.

The Person in Society

In spite of the social psychological tenor of his approach and his explicit concern with human nature, Park is seldom singled out for his contributions to this area. He was indeed overshadowed at Chicago by Thomas, Mead, and Faris, and in much that he wrote he was merely an able disciple of Thomas. But his concentration upon the person coping with the dynamic features of urban civilization, as the focus of the conflict and accommodation between races led him to certain profound and influential formulations. These have principally to do with race prejudice, self-conception and role, and the marginal man.
Race prejudice. Park was concerned with the dynamics of race prejudice throughout his career. At least three features of his approach were unchanged during this time. First, he approached prejudice as he did everything else, as merely a special case of a universal phenomenon. Men are practical creatures, and their attitudes and their knowledge are relative to their purposes. Race prejudice is no different from any other attitude in this respect. Second, race prejudice is an aspect of an intergroup process rather than a product of personal peculiarities. "Prejudice, in this broad conception of the term, seems to be an incident of group consciousness just as reserve seems to be an incident of self-consciousness."[41]

Races and ethnic groups meet as strangers, and as strangers people see a type rather than an individual.

Third, it is only when relationships are established on a personal rather than group basis that prejudices are undermined. But Park did not seem, here, to be referring to the reduction of prejudice in occasional individuals. His discussion and examples refer to the system of relations between the groups. Park often noted that nothing like the personal relationship of master and slave had arisen to take its place, and that the Negro's position as a stranger in the North made his position there, though more egalitarian, especially precarious. It is not that personal relations destroy the attitudes that foster an established system of racial superordination–subordination; these are changed only as the actual relations between groups change. But the attitudes of compassion and acceptance of the other as human develop in these settings.

Park's treatment of race prejudice evolved in his successive writings. In 1917 he laid the foundation, with a thoroughly economic interpretation. Prejudice is not dispelled by knowledge or acquaintanceship. Rather, we hate because we fear. We fear because of economic competition, and especially because the competitor has the advantage of a lower standard of living.

In 1924 the conception that forms the basis for his chief contribution to the understanding of race prejudice took form when he advanced the idea of social distance. Social distance does not imply ill feeling, antagonism, or conflict, but merely a degree of intimacy. "Everyone, it seems, is capable of getting on with everyone else, providing each preserves his proper distances."[42] To explain the rise of prejudice, we look at the analogy of individual self-consciousness, which develops from personal conflict. Prejudice, then, is manifested when social status is threatened.

> Prejudice and race prejudice are by no means to be identified by social distance, but arise when our personal and racial reserves are, or seem to be, invaded. Prejudice is not on the whole an aggressive but a conservative force; a sort of spontaneous conservation which tends to preserve the social order and the social distances upon which that order rests."[43]

Later, Park altered the terms by which he referred to these phenomena. Prejudice came to be equated more nearly with social distance, and contrasted with racial antagonism. Antagonisms are found where there is conflict between the races. "There is probably less racial prejudice in America than elsewhere, but there is more racial conflict and more racial antagonism. There is more conflict because there is more change, more progress."[44] Prejudice and antagonism must be clearly separated in the student's thinking. Both are group phenomena. The former refers merely to the normal process of categorizing individuals according to the positions they are assigned in the traditional order. Race antagonism is often a sign that the traditional order is weakening, that the customary accommodations are no longer effective, and thus may be taken as an encouraging sign of change.

In his later writing Park further extended his thinking to observe that a fundamental cause of prejudice is the insecurity of relations with a stranger. Thus he recognized predictability as an essential condition to human interaction. As the sense of insecurity becomes an attitude, the racial mark becomes a symbol of that insecurity, and the initial relationship of stranger is kept in effect. The explanation of prejudice is a historical event whose initial character is perpetuated in time through embedding a symbol and its associated sentiments into an ideology. Thus, while emergence of race prejudice as a phase in intergroup process is a constant throughout Park's thought, he progressed from identifying a rather direct response to economic competition to describing a complex attitude preserved through ideology and conservative of the social structure.

Role and self. A constant theme in Park's treatment of human nature is self-consciousness, developed in a manner which probably owes most to William James. Self-consciousness is rooted in the moral order rather than the ecological. In Park's efforts to deal with the continuous dialectic between the two orders, an idea such as the self, which can view itself as an object, becomes a crucial link in the social process. Unlike social psychologists who based their theories of human nature on the primary group, Park's treatment was centered in civilization, marked by the constant challenge to tradition through the medium of collective behavior, and by the pervasive clash of divergent cultures. Mead's self-process was formulated in complete generality, Cooley insisted upon the key place of primary groups even in the most secular society, and Thomas leaned toward a frustration theory. But Park saw more clearly a self-consciousness specifically charged with coming to terms with civilization.

As compared with animals, man lives in a world with a temporal dimension. "The fact that men can look back with regret to their past, and forward with lively expectation to their future, suggests that there is, ordinarily, in the lives of human beings, an amount of tension and sustained suspense which tends to break up established habits and to hold those habits not yet established in solution."[45] Because our actions cover a long period and many objects, man's life is a series of episodes and adventures. "These episodes in so far as they are integrated in some general scheme or life program, represent a career. It is characteristic of man that he has a career."[46] The career, like the life history, is one of the foundation concepts in Park's analysis of human nature.

A crucial feature of the social order for the individual is the division of labor. Each part in the division of labor is a role. The social order exists only insofar as there is a capacity for concerted action, which in turn depends upon the division of labor. This capacity becomes less fragile only as roles are fixed in habit and regularized in custom and tradition. But habit is not sufficient to insure a functioning social order, and we must look toward social control. Human control revolves about the capacity of individuals for conscious participation in a common purpose, and the tendency of every action to become a gesture that is observed by one's fellows as an indication of one's intentions. The word "person" in its first meaning is "mask." "Everyone is always and everywhere, more or less consciously, playing a role . . . . It is in these roles that we know each other; it is in these roles that we know ourselves."[47] It is this conception of social role, subsequently expanded by Ralph Linton, upon which the modern burgeoning of role theory was built.

It was but a step from this conception of role to formulation of the crucial idea of *self-conception*. As early as 1921 Park and Burgess had used the title, "The Self as the Individual's Conception of his Role," to designate a selection from Alfred Binet dealing with transformations in personality under the influence of suggestion in hypnosis.[48] Thomas and Znaniecki had spoken of "life organization" as bringing unity into the individual's perspective. Park borrowed their concept, but renamed it to reflect more fully the process which was involved. Man forms a conception of self, through which he gets and maintains control over his impulses. But the self-conception is rooted in the division of labor.

> The conceptions which men form of themselves seem to depend upon their vocations, and in general upon the role that they seek to play in the communities and social groups in which they live, as well as upon the recognition and status which society accords them in these roles.[49]

In this way the perspectives of Thomas and Znaniecki were united with those of Mead and Cooley to produce a concept which is perhaps especially applicable to civilization, in which conflict and change of cultures make habit alone an ineffective basis for social control.

Marginal Man. The idea of the marginal man is in one sense the application of role and self-conception to the situation of unusually intense culture clash. Certain groups of people, such as the American mulattoes, European Jews, Asiatic mixed bloods, and the Chinese traders of south-east Asia, have become deeply enough involved in two distinct societies that they cannot wholly accept the one, or be wholly accepted into the other. Confronted with the necessity to strive toward an internally consistent self conception, these people develop distinctive personal characteristics. Building upon Simmel's analysis of the stranger, Park observes that it is not his mixed blood but the fact that he "lives in two worlds, in both of which he is more or less of a stranger,"[50] which accounts for the marginal man's distinctive characteristics.

That the marginal man experiences stress, uncertain self-conception, depression, and other symptoms was not the most important part of Park's observation. "Inevitably he becomes, relatively to his cultural milieu, the individual with the wider horizon, the keener intelligence, the more detached and rational viewpoint. The marginal man is always relatively the more civilized human being."[51] As compared with other Negroes, the mulatto is more enterprising, restless, aggressive, and ambitious. "He is more intelligent because, for one thing, he is more stimulated, and, for another, takes himself more seriously."[52]

Aside from the continuing intrinsic utility of the concept of marginal man, two aspects of the idea have grown in importance since Park wrote. The idea that a man's attitudes reflect the group with which he identifies, and that this need not be the group in which he has recognized membership and active participation, underlies the modern concept of reference group behavior. And although Park's influence was neither first nor greatest, the wide circulation given his comments on the social determination of intelligence undoubtedly contributed to the more sophisticated understanding of the nature of intelligence which is now general.

Collective Behavior

Park named the field of study and identified the major forms and processes of collective behavior in much the fashion that prevails today. Although he accepted the substance of LeBon's description of crowd behavior, he appraised its relation to social order differently. The crowd, to Park, was merely the most intense example of social control, upon which social order depends, and a special form of the recurrent collaborative efforts to bring about change in society. Dramatic forms of collective behavior develop because custom and the mores (that is, society) impede continuous adjustments in social structure, and the natural end product of collective behavior is a new or modified institution.

It is characteristic of Park that he presented collective behavior more as an approach to the study of social order than as a distinctive field of investigation. Although he focused on distinctive phenomena such as social unrest and social movements, which have become staples of the field, collective behavior was identified as the group in action. A formal definition of collective behavior has broad applicability; "Collective behavior, then, is the behavior of individuals under the influence of an impulse that is common and collective, an impulse, in other words, that is the result of social interaction."[53] Although he advanced the principle of *circular interaction*, which Blumer then refined as the central concept in crowd analysis, he found it equally characteristic of both crowds and publics and went further to offer it as a generally applicable historical principle.

In firmly identifying collective behavior as a normal operation of society, Park was in tune with trends which developed much later. His cautious observation that the students of crowd behavior had failed to distinguish clearly between the psychological crowd and other similar types of social groups was echoed more loudly four decades later than it was when he wrote it. Of many continuities in Park's writing about collective behavior, three will serve to illustrate the social order in process.

Process of societal change. It is well to recall the special meaning Park gave to "society" as the traditional and rigidified patterns of collaboration. The central problem of collective behavior is to identify the processes by which society is formed and reformed. Park's most general answer was a three-stage sequence or "natural history," beginning with social unrest, leading to mass movements, and ending in the formation or modification of institutions. Social unrest "represents at once a breaking up of the established routine and a preparation for new collective action."[54] It often develops from discovery that an individual or family problem requires modification of the social order. Riots – an intense form of social unrest – stem from desperation over the group's declining capacity for collective action, in the face of rapid social change.

Under appropriate circumstances the crowd excitement and rapport supply the basis for collaboration of a different sort. "The crowd has no tradition .... It has therefore neither symbols, ceremonies, rites, nor ritual; it imposes no obligations and creates no loyalties."[55] Individual unrest becomes social unrest when it is transmitted through milling. "The effect of this circular form of interaction is to increase the tensions in the group and, by creating a state of expectancy, to mobilize its members for collective action."[56] Religious sects and social movements have their origins in this crowd excitement.

Park noted that scholars had generally concentrated on the characteristics of crowds as if they were transitory disruptions in the social order. He urged that more attention be given to the manner and course of change from ephemeral actions to permanent organization. The strike, for example, is not to be viewed as an isolated incident, but as part of a social movement of which the members are only dimly conscious. The enduring effects of social unrest depend upon the imposition of stable control over its vital energies. Because the crowd lacks tradition and the movement repudiates tradition, leaders must develop techniques for exercising discipline over the membership. When tradition as the basis for human collaboration is weakened, its place is necessarily taken by authority if the group is still to act. This general principle took on further significance in Park's later writing. During World War II, without direct reference to totalitarianisms of the right or the left, Park pointed to a danger from too rapid social change. Through the effects of collective behavior in undermining tradition, reformers might inadvertently deliver the community into the hands of irresponsible and intractable authority during the period when needed reforms were being consolidated.[57]

The sect was singled out for special attention, although Park seemed undecided whether it was a deviant terminus to the collective behavior sequence, an alternative line of development to more active movements, or a stage in the mobilization and discipline of members for extreme action. The sect develops out of a crowd: Park endorses Sighele's view that a sect is a chronic sort of crowd, with established membership. The thoroughly intransigent posture of the sect and its demand for absolute unanimity distinguish the sect from other groups. Every thoroughgoing revolution has its origin in a sect, for the internal ferment and fervor of the sect is necessary for new and daring ideas to be made articulate. Why some sects turn outward to political action and others turn inward as religious communities is unanswered, except that they have their origins respectively in acting and expressive crowds. Additionally, in order to explain the otherwise incomprehensible behavior in religious sects we must recognize that they have at some time been individually or collectively frustrated in their efforts to act.

The view that from expressive crowd to religious sect is an altogether separate line of development is compromised when Park examines nationalistic movements. He did not have the advantage of the more recent studies that have shown the interrelationship and sequence between millennial and political movements in underdeveloped areas of the world; yet he seemed aware that nationalistic movements have at successive stages the attributes of religious sect and of political movements. Like a religious sect, a nationalistic movement arises in response to culture conflict, to save the individual from personal disorganization. But the sectarian life then arouses a lively sense of common purpose and the inspiration of a common cause, which may permit the group to develop a political aim and become a power to be reckoned with.

Public and the News. In the *Introduction*, the public receives only the briefest attention but appears as a repeated and central concern in Park's essays dealing with news and the workings of democratic society. Unlike the crowd, interaction in the public "takes the form of discussion. Individuals tend to act upon one another critically; issues are raised and parties form. Opinions clash and thus modify and moderate one another."[58] Park takes the crucial importance of the public as the mechanism for democratic decision-making and its function of facilitating change without disruption so entirely for granted that he does not deal with these matters explicitly.

It is perhaps obvious that the public thrives in a free society and that the people must have access to knowledge of what is going on. But the essential mechanism of the public is discussion that centers on the news. And here we find requirements both of uniformity and of diversity. It is only because the news is capable of more than one interpretation that we discuss it. Yet, "there can be no such thing as news, in so far as concerns politics, except in a community in which there is a body of tradition and common understanding in terms of which events are ordinarily interpreted."[59] For news to circulate there must be both a degree of rapport in the community and a degree of inner tension.

The impact of the press in this process drew Park's special attention. He frequently observed that it was the historic shift from the journal filled primarily with editorial views to the paper dispensing news that gave the press its mass appeal. Editorial views in an earlier era had considerable influence because each locality and occupation had its intellectual leaders who read the journals and relayed the opinions. While thus adumbrating the theory of a two-step communication flow, Park deemphasized its application to modern mass communication. Perhaps in retrospect he overstressed the rapidity with which happenings cease to be news and attention shifts. His discussions likewise give us no basis for anticipating the vital place of syndicated columnists and other media commentators in recent years.

Park explicitly denied that it was the function of the news to shape public opinion. It is the role of the press to facilitate the emergence of a collective will *after* a sequence of agitation and unrest. By dispersing and distracting attention, news decreases tension, and by keeping people in touch with a larger world than the immediate publics, encourages them to break out of these limited circles and act on their own. Although he addressed himself to the problem of propaganda on one occasion one may feel that he never threw off his identity as a reporter sufficiently to distinguish consistently between the news as it ought to be and the news as it is.

In spite of his devotion to the public, Park did not share the utopian conception of consensus through discussion. He noted that at certain times excitement rises, and when this happens interest narrows and discussion ceases and the demand for immediate action strengthens the hands of the dominant community leaders. But more particularly, the product of discussion of public issues is not agreement but heightened dissension. The superficial consensus grounded in tradition gives the impression of an agreement, which sanctions the acts of officials. But through discussion people penetrate this surface consensus, lay bare hidden disagreements, and find the reconciliation of their views more difficult than heretofore. The result, therefore, is not to facilitate change and bring about constructive solutions to problems. Most reform measures are placed on the books when the public is at a low ebb. It is not the function of publics to make peace, and war is often the natural continuation of discussion. His observation concerning the exposure and magnification of latent disagreement through discussion deserves greater attention than it has received. It is consistent with Park's views in another area that the relinquishment of disagreement in discussion is more a matter of accommodation than of the discovery of similar values and viewpoints.

Morale. Unlike writers who have treated morale as a sort of personal attribute and attitude, Park viewed it plainly as an aspect of collective behavior. Although Park concerned himself explicitly about morale only when World War II brought it to the forefront of attention, the idea of a quality related to the ability of a society (in the more common sense) to maintain tension over time and carry an enterprise to completion appears often in his writing. When individuals are in sufficient rapport, "a diffuse social excitement tends to envelop, like an atmosphere, all participants in the common life and to give direction and tendency to their interests and attitudes."[60] In intimate groups morale is esprit de corps; in religious sects it is founded on dogma. The idea of morale is inapplicable to the crowd, because its actions are unpremeditated. In the larger unit morale is itself the product of involvement in collective action. "There is probably no other social process, no form of interaction, by which the individual components of a society are so effectively or so completely integrated, if not fused, as they are by participation in some form of collective action."[61] The will to carry a collective action to completion is developed in the course of that very collective action. Like his mentor, Simmel, Park observes that conflict with another nation, or a minority group's identification of a supposed oppressor, is often the most effective way to morale.

Notes

1. Herbert Blumer, in personal communication.
2. *Introduction to the Science of Sociology*, with Ernest W. Burgess (Chicago: University of Chicago Press, 1921; 2d ed. 1924). Hereafter referred to as *Introduction*. All citations refer to the second edition.
3. *Ibid.*, p. 42.
4. *Ibid.*, p. 39.
5. *Ibid.*, p. 42.
6. "Human Ecology," *American Journal of Sociology*, 42 (July, 1936): 14.
7. *Introduction*, p. 27.
8. *Ibid.*, p. 33.
9. *Ibid.*
10. *Ibid.*, p. 42.
11. *Ibid.*
12. *Ibid.*, p. 787.
13. *Ibid.*, p. 30.
14. "Personality and Cultural Conflict," *Publications of the American Sociological Society*, 25 (May, 1931): 101.
15. "Community Organization and Juvenile Delinquency," in *The City*, by Park, Ernest W. Burgess, and R. D. McKenzie (Chicago: University of Chicago Press, 1925; reissued 1966), pp. 99–100.
16. *Introduction*, p. 692.
17. *Ibid.*, p. 785.
18. Ernest W. Burgess, "Social Planning and Race Relations," in *Race Relations: Problems and Theory: Essays in Honor of Robert E. Park*, ed. Jitsuiki Masuoka and Preston Valien (Chapel Hill: University of North Carolina Press, 1961), p. 17.
19. *Methods in Social Science: A Case Book*, ed. Stuart A. Rice (Chicago: University of Chicago Press, 1931), pp. 154–75
20. "The City as a Natural Phenomenon," in *Human Communities* (Glencoe, Ill.: Free Press, 1952), p. 125.
21. *Introduction*, p. 44.
22. *Ibid.*, p. 45.
23. "The Concept of Social Distance: As Applied to the Study of Racial Attitudes and Racial Relations," *Journal of Applied Sociology*, 8 (July, 1924): 339.
24. E. S. Bogardus, *Social Distance* (Los Angeles: 1959), p. 5.
25. "The Urban Community as a Spatial Pattern and a Moral Order," in *The Urban Community*, ed. Ernest W. Burgess (Chicago: University of Chicago Press, 1926), p. 4.
26. "The City as a Natural Phenomenon" (1952), pp. 123–24.
27. "Sociology," in *Research in the Social Sciences*, ed. Wilson Gee (New York: Macmillan, 1929), p. 38.
28. Chicago: University of Chicago Press, 1922.
29. William James, *Talks to Teachers on Psychology, and to Students on Some of Life's Ideals* (New York: Henry Holt, 1901).
30. Introduction to *Shadow of the Plantation* by Charles S. Johnson (Chicago: University of Chicago Press, 1934; reissued 1966), p. xvi.
31. "The American Newspaper," *American Journal of Sociology* (March, 1927): 806.

32. "The Natural History of the Newspaper," *American Journal of Sociology*, 29 (November, 1923): 273.

33. Introduction to *Interracial Marriage in Hawaii* by Romanzo Adams (New York: Macmillan, 1937), p. xiv.

34. *Ibid.*

35. Introduction to *The Gold Coast and the Slum* by Harvey W. Zorbaugh (Chicago: University of Chicago Press, 1929), p. ix.

36. Lester F. Ward, *Pure Sociology*, 2d ed. (New York: Macmillan, 1908), p. 171.

37. "Sociology" (1929), p. 6.

38. "Human Ecology" (1936), p. 4.

39. *Introduction*, p. 665.

40. "Racial Assimilation in Secondary Groups: With Particular Reference to the Negro," *American Journal of Sociology*, 19 (March, 1914): 609.

41. "The Concept of Social Distance: As Applied to the Study of Racial Attitudes and Race Relations" (1924), p. 343.

42. *Ibid.*, p. 341.

43. *Ibid.*, p. 344.

44. "The Bases of Race Prejudice," *Annals of the American Academy of Political and Social Science*, 140 (November, 1928): 13.

45. "Human Nature, Attitudes, and the Mores," in *Social Attitudes*, ed. Kimball Young (New York: Henry Holt, 1931), p. 25.

46. *Ibid.*, p. 27.

47. "Behind Our Masks," *Survey Graphic*, May 1, 1926, p. 137.

48. *Introduction*, pp. 116–20.

49. "Human Nature, Attitudes, and the Mores" (1931), p. 37.

50. "Human Migration and the Marginal Man," *American Journal of Sociology*, 33 (May, 1928): 893.

51. Introduction to *The Marginal Man* by Everett V. Stonequist (New York: Charles Scribner's Sons, 1937), p. xviii.

52. "Mentality of Racial Hybrids," *American Journal of Sociology*, 36 (January, 1931): 545.

53. *Introduction*, p. 865.

54. *Ibid.*, p. 866.

55. *Ibid.*, p. 790

56. *Ibid.*, p. 789.

57. "Social Planning and Human Nature," *Publications of the American Sociological Society* (August, 1935), pp. 19–28.

58. *Introduction*, p. 869.

59. "News and the Power of the Press," *American Journal of Sociology*, 47 (July, 1941): 1–11.

60. "News as a Form of Knowledge," *American Journal of Sociology*, 45 (March, 1940): 683.

61. "Morale and the News," American *Journal of Sociology*, 47 (November, 1941): 361–2.

Urbanism as a Way of Life

Louis Wirth

I. The City and Contemporary Civilization

Just as the beginning of Western civilization is marked by the permanent settlement of formerly nomadic peoples in the Mediterranean basin, so the beginning of what is distinctively modern in our civilization is best signalized by the growth of great cities. Nowhere has mankind been farther removed from organic nature than under the conditions of life characteristic of great cities. The contemporary world no longer presents a picture of small isolated groups of human beings scattered over a vast territory, as Sumner described primitive society.[1] The distinctive feature of the mode of living of man in the modern age is his concentration into gigantic aggregations around which cluster lesser centers and from which radiate the ideas and practices that we call civilization.

The degree to which the contemporary world may be said to be "urban" is not fully or accurately measured by the proportion of the total population living in cities. The influences which cities exert upon the social life of man are greater than the ratio of the urban population would indicate, for the city is not only in ever larger degrees the dwelling-place and the workshop of modern man, but it is the initiating and controlling center of economic, political, and cultural life that has drawn the most remote parts of the world into its orbit and woven diverse areas, peoples, and activities into a cosmos.

The growth of cities and the urbanization of the world is one of the most impressive facts of modern times. Although it is impossible to state precisely what proportion of the estimated total world population of approximately 1,800,000,000 is urban, 69.2 per cent of the total population of those countries that do distinguish between urban and rural areas is urban.[2] Considering the fact, moreover, that the world's population is very unevenly distributed and that the growth of cities is not very far advanced in some of the countries that have only recently been touched by industrialism, this average understates the extent to which urban concentration has proceeded in those countries where the impact of the industrial revolution has been more forceful and of less recent date. This shift from a rural to a predominantly urban society, which has taken place within the span of a single generation in such industrialized areas as the United States and Japan, has been accompanied by profound changes in virtually every phase of social life. It is these changes and their ramifications that invite the attention of the sociologist to the study of the differences between the rural and the urban mode of living. The pursuit of this interest is an indispensable prerequisite for the comprehension and possible mastery of some of the most crucial contemporary problems of social life since it is likely to furnish one of the most revealing perspectives for the understanding of the ongoing changes in human nature and the social order.[3]

Since the city is the product of growth rather than of instantaneous creation, it is to be expected that the influences which it exerts upon the modes of life should not be able to wipe out completely the previously dominant modes of human association. To a greater or lesser degree, therefore, our social life bears the imprint of an earlier folk society, the characteristic modes of settlement of which were the farm, the manor, and the village. This historic influence is reinforced by the circumstance that the population of the city itself is in large measure recruited from the countryside, where a mode of life reminiscent of this earlier form of existence persists. Hence we should not expect to find abrupt and discontinuous variation between urban and rural types of personality. The city and the country may be regarded as two poles in reference to one or the other of which all human settlements tend to arrange themselves. In viewing urban–industrial and rural–folk society as ideal types of communities, we may obtain a perspective for the analysis of the basic models of human association as they appear in contemporary civilization.

II. A Sociological Definition of the City

Despite the preponderant significance of the city in our civilization, however, our knowledge of the nature of urbanism and the process of urbanization is meager. Many attempts have indeed been made to isolate the distinguishing characteristics of urban life. Geographers, historians, economists, and political scientists have incorporated the points of view of their respective disciplines into diverse definitions of the city. While in no sense intended to supersede these, the formulation of a sociological approach to the city may incidentally serve to call attention to the interrelations between them by emphasizing the peculiar characteristics of the city as a particular form of human association. A sociologically significant definition of the city seeks to select those elements of urbanism which mark it as a distinctive mode of human group life.

The characterization of a community as urban on the basis of size alone is obviously arbitrary. It is difficult to defend the present census definition which designates a community of 2,500 and above as urban and all others as rural. The situation would be the same if the criterion were 4,000, 5,000, 10,000,

25,000, or 100,000 population, for although in the latter case we might feel that we were more nearly dealing with an urban aggregate than would be the case in communities of lesser size, no definition of urbanism can hope to be completely satisfying as long as numbers are regarded as the sole criterion. Moreover, it is not difficult to demonstrate that communities of less than the arbitrarily set number of inhabitants lying within the range of influence of metropolitan centers have greater claim to recognition as urban communities than do larger ones leading a more isolated existence in a predominantly rural area. Finally, it should be recognized that census definitions are unduly influenced by the fact that the city, statistically speaking, is always an administrative concept in that the corporate limits play a decisive role in delineating the urban area. Nowhere is this more clearly apparent than in the concentrations of population on the peripheries of great metropolitan centers which cross arbitrary administrative boundaries of city, county, state, and nation.

As long as we identify urbanism with the physical entity of the city, viewing it merely as rigidly delimited in space, and proceed as if urban attributes abruptly ceased to be manifested beyond an arbitrary boundary line, we are not likely to arrive at any adequate conception of urbanism as a mode of life. The technological developments in transportation and communication which virtually mark a new epoch in human history have accentuated the role of cities as dominant elements in our civilization and have enormously extended the urban mode of living beyond the confines of the city itself. The dominance of the city, especially of the great city, may be regarded as a consequence of the concentration in cities of industrial and commercial, financial and administrative facilities and activities, transportation and communication lines, and cultural and recreational equipment such as the press, radio stations, theaters, libraries, museums, concert halls, operas, hospitals, higher educational institutions, research and publishing centers, professional organizations, and religious and welfare institutions. Were it not for the attraction and suggestions that the city exerts through these instrumentalities upon the rural population, the differences between the rural and the urban modes of life would be even greater than they are. Urbanization no longer denotes merely, the process by which persons are attracted to a place called the city and incorporated into its system of life. It refers also to that cumulative accentuation of the characteristics distinctive of the mode of life which is associated with the growth of cities, and finally to the changes in the direction of modes of life recognized as urban which are apparent among people, wherever they may be, who have come under the spell of the influences which the city exerts by virtue of the power of its institutions and personalities operating through the means of communication and transportation.

The shortcomings which attach to number of inhabitants as a criterion of urbanism apply for the most part to density of population as well. Whether we accept the density of 10,000 persons per square mile as Mark Jefferson[4] proposed, or 1,000 which Willcox[5] preferred to regard as the criterion of urban settlements, it is clear that unless density is correlated with significant social characteristics it can furnish only an arbitrary basis for differentiating urban from rural communities. Since our census enumerates the night rather than the day population of an area, the locale of the most intensive urban life – the city center – generally has low population density, and the industrial and commercial areas of the city, which contain the most characteristic economic activities underlying urban society, would scarcely anywhere be truly urban if density were literally interpreted as a mark of urbanism. Nevertheless, the fact that the urban community is distinguished by a large aggregation and relatively dense concentration of population can scarcely be left out of account in a definition of the city. But these criteria must be seen as relative to the general cultural context in which cities arise and exist and are sociologically relevant only in so far as they operate as conditioning factors in social life.

The same criticisms apply to such criteria as the occupation of the inhabitants, the existence of certain physical facilities, institutions, and forms of political organization. The question is not whether cities in our civilization or in others do exhibit these distinctive traits, but how potent they are in molding the character of social life into its specifically urban form. Nor in formulating a fertile definition can we afford to overlook the great variations between cities. By means of a typology of cities based upon size, location, age, and function, such as we have undertaken to establish in our recent report to the National Resources Committee,[6] we have found it feasible to array and classify urban communities ranging from struggling small towns to thriving world-metropolitan centers; from isolated trading-centers in the midst of agricultural regions to thriving world-ports and commercial and industrial conurbations. Such differences as these appear crucial because the social characteristics and influences of these different "cities" vary widely.

A serviceable definition of urbanism should not only denote the essential characteristics which all cities – at least those in our culture – have in common, but should lend itself to the discovery of their variations. An industrial city will differ significantly in social respects from a commercial, mining, fishing, resort, university, and capital city. A one-industry city will present different sets of social characteristics from a multi-industry city, as will an industrially balanced from an imbalanced city, a suburb from a satellite, a residential suburb from an industrial suburb, a city within a metropolitan region from one lying outside, an old city from a new one, a southern city from a New England, a middle-western from a Pacific Coast city, a growing from a stable and from a dying city.

A sociological definition must obviously be inclusive enough to comprise whatever essential characteristics these different types of cities have in common as social entities, but it obviously cannot be so detailed as to take account of all the variations implicit in the manifold classes sketched above. Presumably some of the characteristics of cities are more significant in conditioning the nature of urban life than others, and we may expect the outstanding features of the urban-social scene to vary in accordance with size, density, and differences in the functional type of cities. Moreover, we may infer that rural life will bear the imprint of urbanism in the measure that through contact and communication it comes under the influence of cities. It may contribute to the clarity of the statements that follow to repeat that while the locus of urbanism as a mode of life is, of course, to be found characteristically in places which fulfil the requirements we shall set up as a definition of the city, urbanism is not confined to such localities but is manifest in varying degrees wherever the influences of the city reach.

While urbanism, or that complex of traits which makes up the characteristic mode of life in cities, and urbanization, which denotes the development and extensions of these factors, are thus not exclusively found in settlements which are cities in the physical and demographic sense, they do, nevertheless, find their most pronounced expression in such areas, especially in metropolitan cities. In formulating a definition of the city it is necessary to exercise caution in order to avoid identifying urbanism as a way of life with any specific locally or historically conditioned cultural influences which, while they may significantly affect the specific character of the community, are not the essential determinants of its character as a city.

It is particularly important to call attention to the danger of confusing urbanism with industrialism and modern capitalism. The rise of cities in the modern world is undoubtedly not independent of the emergence of modern power-driven machine technology, mass production, and capitalistic enterprise. But different as the cities of earlier epochs may have been by virtue of their development in a preindustrial and precapitalistic order from the great cities of today they were, nevertheless, cities.

For sociological purposes a city may be defined as a relatively large, dense, and permanent settlement of socially heterogeneous individuals. On the basis of the postulates which this minimal definition suggests, a theory of urbanism may be formulated in the light of existing knowledge concerning social groups.

III. A Theory of Urbanism

In the rich literature on the city we look in vain for a theory of urbanism presenting in a systematic fashion the available knowledge concerning the city as a social entity. We do indeed have excellent formulations of theories on such special problems as the growth of the city viewed as a historical trend and as a recurrent process,[7] and we have a wealth of literature presenting insights of sociological relevance and empirical studies offering detailed information on a variety of particular aspects of urban life. But despite the multiplication of research and textbooks on the city, we do not as yet have a comprehensive body of compendent hypotheses which may be derived from a set of postulates implicitly contained in a sociological definition of the city, and from our general sociological knowledge which may be substantiated through empirical research. The closest approximations to a systematic theory of urbanism that we have are to be found in a penetrating essay, "Die Stadt," by Max Weber,[8] and a memorable paper by Robert E. Park on "The City: Suggestions for the Investigation of Human Behavior in the Urban Environment."[9] But even these excellent contributions are far from constituting an ordered and coherent framework of theory upon which research might profitably proceed.

In the pages that follow we shall seek to set forth a limited number of identifying characteristics of the city. Given these characteristics we shall then indicate what consequences or further characteristics follow from them in the light of general sociological theory and empirical research. We hope in this manner to arrive at the essential propositions comprising a theory of urbanism. Some of these propositions can be supported by a considerable body of already available research materials; others may be accepted as hypotheses for which a certain amount of presumptive evidence exists, but for which more ample and exact verification would be required. At least such a procedure will, it is hoped, show what in the way of systematic knowledge of the city we now have and what are the crucial and fruitful hypotheses for future research.

The central problem of the sociologist of the city is to discover the forms of social action and organization that typically emerge in relatively permanent, compact settlements of large numbers of heterogeneous individuals. We must also infer that urbanism will assume its most characteristic and extreme form in the measure in which the conditions with which it is congruent are present. Thus the larger, the more densely populated and the more heterogeneous a community, the more accentuated the characteristics associated with urbanism will be. It should be recognized, however, that in the social world institutions and practices may be accepted and continued for reasons other than those that originally brought them into existence, and that accordingly the urban mode of life may be perpetuated under conditions quite foreign to those necessary for its origin.

Some justification may be in order for the choice of the principal terms comprising our definition of the city. The attempt has been made to make it as inclusive and at the same time as denotative as possible without loading it with unnecessary assumptions. To say that large numbers are necessary to constitute a city means, of course, large numbers in relation to a restricted area or high density of settlement. There are, nevertheless, good reasons for treating large numbers and density as separate factors, since each may be connected with significantly different social consequences. Similarly the need for adding heterogeneity to numbers of population as a necessary and distinct criterion of urbanism might be questioned, since we should expect the range of differences to increase with numbers. In defense, it may be said that the city shows a kind and degree of heterogeneity of population which cannot be wholly accounted for by the law of large numbers or adequately represented by means of a normal distribution curve. Since the population of the city does not reproduce itself, it must recruit its migrants from other cities, the countryside, and – in this country until recently – from other countries. The city has thus historically been the melting-pot of races, peoples, and cultures, and a most favorable breeding-ground of new biological and cultural hybrids. It has not only tolerated but rewarded individual differences. It has brought together people from the ends of the earth *because* they are different and thus useful to one another, rather than because they are homogeneous and like-minded.[10]

There are a number of sociological propositions concerning the relationship between (*a*) numbers of population, (*b*) density of settlement, (*c*) heterogeneity of inhabitants and group life, which can be formulated on the basis of observation and research.

Size of the Population Aggregate

Ever since Aristotle's *Politics*,[11] it has been recognized that increasing the number of inhabitants in a settlement beyond a certain limit will affect the relationships between them and the character of the city. Large numbers involve, as has been pointed out, a greater range of individual variation. Furthermore, the greater the number of individuals participating in a process of interaction, the greater is the *potential* differentiation between them. The personal traits, the occupations, the cultural life, and the ideas of the members of an urban community may, therefore, be expected to range between more widely separated poles than those of rural inhabitants.

That such variations should give rise to the spatial segregation of individuals according to color, ethnic heritage, economic and social status, tastes and preferences, may readily be inferred. The bonds of kinship, of neighborliness, and the sentiments arising out of living together for generations under a common folk tradition are likely to be absent or, at best, relatively weak in an aggregate the members of which have such diverse origins and backgrounds. Under such circumstances competition and formal control mechanisms furnish the substitutes for the bonds of solidarity that are relied upon to hold a folk society together.

Increase in the number of inhabitants of a community beyond a few hundred is bound to limit the possibility of each member of the community knowing all the others personally. Max Weber, in recognizing the social significance of this fact, pointed out that from a sociological point of view large numbers of inhabitants and density of settlement mean that the personal mutual acquaintanceship between the inhabitants which ordinarily inheres in a neighborhood is lacking.[12] The increase in numbers thus involves a changed character of the social relationships. As Simmel points out:

> [If] the unceasing external contact of numbers of persons in the city should be met by the same number of inner reactions as in the small town, in which one knows almost every person he meets and to each

of whom he has a positive relationship, one would be completely atomized internally and would fall into an unthinkable mental condition.[13]

The multiplication of persons in a state of interaction under conditions which make their contact as full personalities impossible produces that segmentalization of human relationships which has sometimes been seized upon by students of the mental life of the cities as an explanation for the "schizoid" character of urban personality. This is not to say that the urban inhabitants have fewer acquaintances than rural inhabitants, for the reverse may actually be true; it means rather that in relation to the number of people whom they see and with whom they rub elbows in the course of daily life, they, know a smaller proportion, and of these they have less intensive knowledge.

Characteristically, urbanites meet one another in highly segmental roles. They are, to be sure, dependent upon more people for the satisfactions of their life-needs than are rural people and thus are associated with a greater number of organized groups, but they are less dependent upon particular persons, and their dependence upon others is confined to a highly fractionalized aspect of the other's round of activity. This is essentially what is meant by saying that the city is characterized by secondary rather than primary contacts. The contacts of the city may indeed be face to face, but they are nevertheless impersonal, superficial, transitory, and segmental. The reserve, the indifference, and the blasé outlook which urbanites manifest in their relationships may thus be regarded as devices for immunizing themselves against the personal claims and expectations of others.

The superficiality, the anonymity and the transitory character of urban-social relations make intelligible, also, the sophistication and the rationality generally ascribed to city-dwellers. Our acquaintances tend to stand in a relationship of utility to us in the sense that the role which each one plays in our life is overwhelmingly regarded as a means for the achievement of our own ends. Whereas, therefore, the individual gains, on the one hand, a certain degree of emancipation or freedom from the personal and emotional controls of intimate groups, he loses on the other hand, the spontaneous self-expression, the morale, and the sense of participation that comes with living in an integrated society. This constitutes essentially the state of *anomie* or the social void to which Durkheim alludes in attempting to account for the various forms of social disorganization in technological society.

The segmental character and utilitarian accent of interpersonal relations in the city find their institutional expression in the proliferation of specialized tasks which we see in their most developed form in the professions. The operations of the pecuniary nexus lead to predatory relationships, which tend to obstruct the efficient functioning of the social order unless checked by professional codes and occupational etiquette. The premium put upon utility and efficiency suggests the adaptability of the corporate device for the organization of enterprises in which individuals can engage only in groups. The advantage that the corporation has over the individual entrepreneur and the partnership in the urban-industrial world derives not only from the possibility it affords of centralizing the resources of thousands of individuals or from the legal privilege of limited liability and perpetual succession, but from the fact that the corporation has no soul.

The specialization of individuals, particularly in their occupations, can proceed only, as Adam Smith pointed out, upon the basis of an enlarged market, which in turn accentuates the division of labor. This enlarged market is only in part supplied by the city's hinterland; in large measure it is found among the large numbers that the city itself contains. The dominance of the city over the surrounding hinterland becomes explicable in terms of the division of labor, which urban life occasions and promotes. The extreme degree of interdependence and the unstable equilibrium of urban life are closely associated with the division of labor and the specialization of occupations. This interdependence and instability is increased by the tendency of each city to specialize in those functions in which it has the greatest advantage.

In a community composed of a larger number of individuals than can know one another intimately and can be assembled in one spot, it becomes necessary to communicate through indirect mediums and to articulate individual interests by a process of delegation. Typically in the city, interests are made effective through representation. The individual counts for little, but the voice of the representative is heard with a deference roughly proportional to the numbers for whom he speaks.

While this characterization of urbanism, in so far as it derives from large numbers, does not by any means exhaust the sociological inferences that might be drawn from our knowledge of the relationship of the size of a group to the characteristic behavior of the members, for the sake of brevity the assertions made may serve to exemplify the sort of propositions that might be developed.

Density

As in the case of numbers, so in the case of concentration in limited space, certain consequences of relevance in sociological analysis of the city emerge. Of these only a few can be indicated.

As Darwin pointed out for flora and fauna and as Durkheim[14] noted in the case of human societies, an increase in numbers when area is held constant (i.e., an increase in density) tends to produce differentiation and specialization, since only in this way can the area support increased numbers. Density thus reinforces the effect of numbers in diversifying men and their activities and in increasing the complexity of the social structure.

On the subjective side, as Simmel has suggested, the close physical contact of numerous individuals necessarily produces a shift in the mediums through which we orient ourselves to the urban milieu, especially to our fellow-men. Typically, our physical contacts are close but our social contacts are distant. The urban world puts a premium on visual recognition. We see the uniform which denotes the role of the functionaries and are oblivious to the personal eccentricities that are hidden behind the uniform. We tend to acquire and develop a sensitivity to a world of artefacts and become progressively farther removed from the world of nature.

We are exposed to glaring contrasts between splendor and squalor, between riches and poverty, intelligence and ignorance, order and chaos. The competition for space is great, so that each area generally tends to be put to the use which yields the greatest economic return. Place of work tends to become dissociated from place of residence, for the proximity of industrial and commercial establishments makes an area both economically and socially undesirable for residential purposes.

Density, land values, rentals, accessibility, healthfulness, prestige, aesthetic consideration, absence of nuisances such as noise, smoke, and dirt determine the desirability of various areas of the city as places of settlement for different sections of the population. Place and nature of work, income, racial and ethnic characteristics, social status, custom, habit, taste, preference, and prejudice are among the significant factors in accordance with which the urban population is selected and distributed into more or less distinct settlements. Diverse population elements inhabiting a compact settlement thus tend to become segregated from one another in the degree in which their requirements and modes of life are incompatible with one another and in the measure in which they are antagonistic to one another. Similarly, persons of homogeneous status and needs unwittingly drift into, consciously select, or are forced by circumstances into, the same area. The different parts of the city thus acquire specialized functions. The city consequently tends to resemble a mosaic of social worlds in which the transition from one to the other is abrupt. The juxtaposition of divergent personalities and modes of life tends to produce a relativistic perspective and a sense of toleration of differences which may be regarded as prerequisites for rationality and which lead toward the secularization of life.[15]

The close living together and working together of individuals who have no sentimental and emotional ties foster a spirit of competition, aggrandizement and mutual exploitation. To counteract irresponsibility and potential disorder, formal controls tend to be resorted to. Without rigid adherence to predictable routines a large compact society would scarcely be able to maintain itself. The clock and the traffic signal are symbolic of the basis of our social order in the urban world. Frequent close physical contact, coupled with great social distance, accentuates the reserve of unattached individuals toward one another and, unless compensated for by other opportunities for response, gives rise to loneliness. The necessary frequent movement of great numbers of individuals in a congested habitat gives occasion to friction and irritation. Nervous tensions which derive from such personal frustrations are accentuated by the rapid tempo and the complicated technology under which life in dense areas must be lived.

Heterogeneity

The social interaction among such a variety of personality types in the urban milieu tends to break down the rigidity of caste lines and to complicate the class structure, and thus induces a more ramified and differentiated framework of social stratification than is found in more integrated societies. The heightened mobility of the individual, which brings him within the range of stimulation by a great number of diverse individuals and subjects him to fluctuating status in the differentiated social groups that compose the social structure of the city, tends toward the acceptance of instability and insecurity in the world at large as a norm. This fact helps to account, too, for the sophistication and cosmopolitanism of the urbanite. No single group has the undivided allegiance of the individual. The groups with which he is affiliated do not lend themselves readily to a simple hierarchical arrangement. By virtue of his different interests arising out of different aspects of social life, the individual acquires membership in widely divergent groups, each of which functions only with reference to a single segment of his personality. Nor do these groups easily permit of a concentric arrangement so that the narrower ones fall within the circumference of the more inclusive ones, as is more likely to be the case in the rural community or in primitive societies. Rather the groups with which the person typically is affiliated are tangential to each other or intersect in highly variable fashion.

Partly as a result of the physical footlooseness of the population and partly as a result of their social mobility, the turnover in group membership generally is rapid. Place of residence, place and character of employment, income and interests fluctuate, and the task of holding organizations together and maintaining and promoting intimate and lasting acquaintanceship between the members is difficult. This applies strikingly to the local areas within the city into which persons become segregated more by virtue of differences in race, language, income, and social status, than through choice or positive attraction to people like themselves. Overwhelmingly the city-dweller is not a homeowner, and since a transitory habitat does not generate binding traditions and sentiments, only rarely is he truly a neighbor. There is little opportunity for the individual to obtain a conception of the city as a whole or to survey his place in the total scheme. Consequently he finds it difficult to determine what is to his own "best interests" and to decide between the issues and leaders presented to him by the agencies of mass suggestion. Individuals who are thus detached from the organized bodies which integrate society comprise the fluid masses that make collective behavior in the urban community so unpredictable and hence so problematical.

Although the city, through the recruitment of variant types to perform its diverse tasks and the accentuation of their uniqueness through competition and the premium upon eccentricity, novelty, efficient performance, and inventiveness, produces a highly differentiated population, it also exercises a levelling influence. Wherever large numbers of differently constituted individuals congregate, the process of depersonalization also enters. This leveling tendency inheres in part in the economic basis of the city. The development of large cities, at least in the modern age, was largely dependent upon the concentrative force of steam. The rise of the factory made possible mass production for an impersonal market. The fullest exploitation of the possibilities of the division of labor and mass production, however, is possible only with standardization of processes and products. A money economy goes hand in hand with such a system of production. Progressively as cities have developed upon a background of this system of production, the pecuniary nexus which implies the purchasability of services and things has displaced personal relations as the basis of association. Individuality under these circumstances must be replaced by categories. When large numbers have to make common use of facilities and institutions, an arrangement must be made to adjust the facilities and institutions to the needs of the average person rather than to those of particular individuals. The services of the public utilities, of the recreational, educational, and cultural institutions must be adjusted to mass requirements. Similarly, the cultural institutions, such as the schools, the movies, the radio, and the newspapers, by virtue of their mass clientele, must necessarily operate as leveling influences. The political process as it appears in urban life could not be understood without taking account of the mass appeals made through modern propaganda techniques. If the individual would participate at all in the social, political, and economic life of the city, he must subordinate some of his individuality to the demands of the larger community and in that measure immerse himself in mass movements.

IV. The Relation Between a Theory of Urbanism and Sociological Research

By means of a body of theory such as that illustratively sketched above, the complicated and many-sided phenomena of urbanism may be analyzed in terms of a limited number of basic categories. The sociological approach to the city thus acquires an essential unity and coherence enabling the empirical investigator not merely to focus more distinctly upon the problems and processes that properly fall in his province but also to treat his subject matter in a more integrated and systematic fashion. A few typical findings of empirical research in the field of urbanism, with special reference to the United States, may be indicated to substantiate the theoretical propositions set forth in the preceding pages, and some of the crucial problems for further study may be outlined.

On the basis of the three variables, number, density of settlement, and degree of heterogeneity, of the urban population, it appears possible to explain the characteristics of urban life and to account for the differences between cities of various sizes and types.

Urbanism as a characteristic mode of life may be approached empirically from three interrelated perspectives: (1) as a physical structure comprising a population base, a technology, and an ecological order; (2) as a system of social organization involving a characteristic social structure, a series of social institutions, and a typical pattern of social relationships; and (3) as a set of attitudes and ideas, and a constellation of personalities engaging in typical forms of collective behavior and subject to characteristic mechanisms of social control.

Urbanism in Ecological Perspective

Since in the case of physical structure and ecological processes we are able to operate with fairly objective indices, it becomes possible to arrive at quite precise and generally quantitative results. The dominance of the city over its hinterland becomes explicable through the functional characteristics of the city which derive in large measure from the effect of numbers and density. Many of the technical facilities and the skills and organizations to which urban life gives rise can grow and prosper only in cities where the demand is sufficiently great. The nature and scope of the services rendered by these organizations and institutions and the advantage which they enjoy over the less developed facilities of smaller towns enhances the dominance of the city and the dependence of ever wider regions upon the central metropolis.

The urban-population composition shows the operation of selective and differentiating factors. Cities contain a larger proportion of persons in the prime of life than rural areas which contain more old and very young people. In this, as in so many other respects, the larger the city the more this specific characteristic of urbanism is apparent. With the exception of the largest cities, which have attracted the bulk of the foreign-born males, and a few other special types of cities, women predominate numerically over men. The heterogeneity of the urban population is further indicated along racial and ethnic lines. The foreign born and their children constitute nearly two-thirds of all the inhabitants of cities of one million and over. Their proportion in the urban population declines as the size of the city decreases, until in the rural areas they comprise only about one-sixth of the total population. The larger cities similarly have attracted more Negroes and other racial groups than have the smaller communities. Considering that age, sex, race, and ethnic origin are associated with other factors such as occupation and interest, it becomes clear that one major characteristic of the urban dweller is his dissimilarity from his fellows. Never before have such large masses of people of diverse traits as we find in our cities been thrown together into such close physical contact as in the great cities of America. Cities generally, and American cities in particular, comprise a motley of peoples and cultures, of highly differentiated modes of life between which there often is only the faintest communication, the greatest indifference and the broadest tolerance, occasionally bitter strife, but always the sharpest contrast.

The failure of the urban population to reproduce itself appears to be a biological consequence of a combination of factors in the complex of urban life, and the decline in the birth-rate generally may be regarded as one of the most significant signs of the urbanization of the Western world. While the proportion of deaths in cities is slightly greater than in the country, the outstanding difference between the failure of present-day cities to maintain their population and that of cities of the past is that in former times it was due to the exceedingly high death-rates in cities, whereas today, since cities have become more liveable from a health standpoint, it is due to low birth-rates. These biological characteristics of the urban population are significant sociologically, not merely because they reject the urban mode of existence but also because they condition the growth and future dominance of cities and their basic social organization. Since cities are the consumers rather than the producers of men, the value of human life and the social estimation of the personality will not be unaffected by the balance between births and deaths. The pattern of land use, of land values, rentals, and ownership, the nature and functioning of the physical structures, of housing, of transportation and communication facilities, of public utilities – these and many other phases of the physical mechanism of the city are not isolated phenomena unrelated to the city as a social entity, but are affected by and affect the urban mode of life.

Urbanism as a Form of Social Organization

The distinctive features of the urban mode of life have often been described sociologically as consisting of the substitution of secondary for primary contacts, the weakening of bonds of kinship, and the declining social significance of the family, the disappearance of the neighborhood, and the undermining of the traditional basis of social solidarity. All these phenomena can be substantially verified through objective indices. Thus, for instance, the low and declining urban-reproduction rates suggest that the city is not conducive to the traditional type of family life, including the rearing of children and the maintenance of the home as the locus of a whole round of vital activities. The transfer of industrial, educational, and recreational activities to specialized institutions outside the home has deprived the family of some of its most characteristic historical functions. In cities mothers are more likely to be employed, lodgers are more frequently part of the household, marriage tends to be postponed, and the proportion of single and unattached people is greater. Families are smaller and more frequently without children than in the country. The family as a unit of social life is emancipated from the larger kinship group characteristic of the country, and the individual members pursue their own diverging interests in their vocational, educational, religious, recreational, and political life.

Such functions as the maintenance of health, the methods of alleviating the hardships associated with personal and social insecurity, the provisions for education, recreation, and cultural advancement have given rise to highly specialized institutions on a community-wide, statewide, or even national basis. The same factors which have brought about greater personal insecurity also underlie the wider contrasts between individuals to be found in the urban world. While the city has broken down the rigid caste lines of preindustrial society, it has sharpened and differentiated income and status groups. Generally, a larger proportion of the adult-urban population is gainfully employed than is the case with the adult-rural population. The white-collar class, comprising those employed in trade, in clerical, and in professional work, are proportionately more numerous in large cities and in metropolitan centers and in smaller towns than in the country.

On the whole, the city discourages an economic life in which the individual in time of crisis has a basis of subsistence to fall back upon, and it discourages self-employment. While incomes of city people are on the average higher than those of country people, the cost of living seems to be higher in the larger cities. Home ownership involves greater burdens and is rarer. Rents are higher and absorb a larger proportion of the income. Although the urban dweller has the benefit of many communal services, he spends a large proportion of his income for such items as recreation and advancement and a smaller proportion for food. What the communal services do not furnish the urbanite must purchase, and there is virtually no human need which has remained unexploited by commercialism. Catering to thrills and furnishing means of escape from drudgery, monotony, and routine thus become one of the major functions of urban recreation, which at its best furnishes means for creative self-expression and spontaneous group association, but which more typically in the urban world results in passive spectatorism on the one hand, or sensational record-smashing feats on the other.

Being reduced to a stage of virtual impotence as an individual, the urbanite is bound to exert himself by joining with others of similar interest into organized groups to obtain his ends. This results in the enormous multiplication of voluntary organizations directed toward as great a variety of objectives as there are human needs and interests. While on the one hand the traditional ties of human association are weakened, urban existence involves a much greater degree of interdependence between man and man and a more complicated, fragile, and volatile form of mutual interrelations over many phases of which the individual as such can exert scarcely any control. Frequently there is only the most tenuous relationship between the economic position or other basic factors that determine the individual's existence in the urban world and the voluntary groups with which he is affiliated. While in a primitive and in a rural society it is generally possible to predict on the basis of a few known factors who will belong to what and who will associate with whom in almost every relationship of life, in the city we can only project the general pattern of group formation and affiliation, and this pattern will display many incongruities and contradictions.

Urbanism Personality and Collective Behavior

It is largely through the activities of the voluntary groups, be their objectives economic, political, educational, religious, recreational, or cultural, that the urbanite expresses and develops his personality, acquires status, and is able to carry on the round of activities that constitute his life-career. It may easily be inferred, however, that the organizational framework which these highly differentiated functions call into being does not of itself insure the consistency and integrity of the personalities whose interests it enlists. Personal disorganization, mental breakdown, suicide, delinquency, crime, corruption, and disorder might be expected under these circumstances to be more prevalent in the urban than in the rural community. This has been confirmed in so far as comparable indices are available; but the mechanisms underlying these phenomena require further analysis.

Since for most group purposes it is impossible in the city to appeal individually to the large number of discrete and differentiated individuals, and since it is only through the organizations to which men belong that their interests and resources can be enlisted for a collective cause, it may be inferred that social control in the city should typically proceed through formally organized groups. It follows, too, that the masses of men in the city are subject to manipulation by symbols and stereotypes managed by individuals working from afar or operating invisibly behind the scenes through their control of the instruments of communication. Self-government either in the economic, the political or the cultural realm is under these circumstances reduced to a mere figure of speech or, at best, is subject to the unstable equilibrium of pressure groups. In view of the ineffectiveness of actual kinship ties we create fictional kinship groups. In the face of the disappearance of the territorial unit as a basis of social solidarity we create interest units. Meanwhile the city as a community resolves itself into a series of tenuous segmental relationships superimposed upon a territorial base with a definite center but without a definite periphery and upon a division of labor which far transcends the immediate locality and is worldwide in scope. The larger the number of persons in a state of interaction with one another the lower is the level of communication and the greater is the tendency for communication to proceed on an elementary level, i.e., on the basis of those things which are assumed to be common or to be of interest to all.

It is obviously, therefore, to the emerging trends in the communication system and to the production and distribution technology that has come into existence with modern civilization that we must look for the symptoms which will indicate the probable future development of urbanism as a mode of social life. The direction of the ongoing changes in urbanism will for good or ill transform not only the city but the world. Some of the more basic of these factors and processes and the possibilities of their direction and control invite further detailed study.

It is only in so far as the sociologist has a clear conception of the city as a social entity and a workable theory of urbanism that he can hope to develop a unified body of reliable knowledge, which what passes as "urban sociology" is certainly not at the present time. By taking his point of departure from a theory of urbanism such as that sketched in the foregoing pages to be elaborated, tested, and revised in the light of further analysis and empirical research, it is to be hoped that the criteria of relevance and validity of factual data can be determined. The miscellaneous assortment of disconnected information which has hitherto found its way into sociological treatises on the city may thus be sifted and incorporated into a coherent body of knowledge. Incidentally, only by means of some such theory will the sociologist escape the futile practice of voicing in the name of sociological science a variety of often unsupportable judgments concerning such problems as poverty, housing, city-planning, sanitation, municipal administration, policing, marketing, transportation, and other technical issues. While the sociologist cannot solve any of these practical problems – at least not by himself – he may, if he discovers his proper function, have an important contribution to make to their comprehension and solution. The prospects for doing this are brightest through a general, theoretical, rather than through an *ad hoc* approach.

Notes

1. William Graham Sumner, *Folkways* (Boston, 1906), p. 12.
2. S. V. Pearson, *The Growth and Distribution of Population* (New York, 1935), p. 211.
3. Whereas rural life in the United States has for a long time been a subject of considerable interest on the part of governmental bureaus, the most notable case of a comprehensive report being that submitted by the Country Life Commission to President Theodore Roosevelt in 1909, it is worthy of note that no equally comprehensive official inquiry into urban life was undertaken until the establishment of a Research Committee on Urbanism of the National Resources Committee. (Cf. *Our Cities: Their Role in the National Economy* [Washington: Government Printing Office, 1937].)
4. "The Anthropogeography of Some Great Cities," *Bull. American Geographical Society*, XLI (1909), 537–66.
5. Walter F. Willcox, "A Definition of 'City' in Terms of Density," in E. W. Burgess, *The Urban Community* (Chicago, 1926), p. 119.
6. *Op. cit.*, p. 8.
7. See Robert E. Park, Ernest W. Burgess, *et al.*, *The City* (Chicago, 1925), esp. chaps. ii and iii; Werner Sombart, "Städtische Siedlung, Stadt," *Handwörterbuch der Soziologie*, ed. Alfred Vierkandt (Stuttgart, 1931); see also bibliography.
8. *Wirtschaft und Gesellschaft* (Tübingen, 1925), Part II, chap. viii, pp. 514–601.
9. Park, Burgess, *et al.*, *op. cit.*, chap. i.
10. The justification for including the term "permanent" in the definition may appear necessary. Our failure to give an extensive justification for this qualifying mark of the urban rests on the obvious fact that unless human settlements take a fairly permanent root in a locality the characteristics of urban life cannot arise, and conversely the

living together of large numbers of heterogeneous individuals under dense conditions is not possible without the development of a more or less technological structure.

11. See esp. vii. 4. 4–14. Translated by B. Jowett, from which the following may be quoted:

"To the size of states there is a limit, as there is to other things, plants, animals, implements; for none of these retain their natural power when they are too large or too small, but they either wholly lose their nature, or are spoiled . . . [A] state when composed of too few is not as a state ought to be, self-sufficing; when of too many, though self-sufficing in all mere necessaries, it is a nation and not a state, being almost incapable of constitutional government. For who can be the general of such a vast multitude, or who the herald, unless he have the voice of a Stentor?

"A state then only begins to exist when it has attained a population sufficient for a good life in the political community: it may indeed somewhat exceed this number. But, as I was saying, there must be a limit. What should be the limit will be easily ascertained by experience. For both governors and governed have duties to perform; the special functions of a governor are to command and to judge. But if the citizens of a state are to judge and to distribute offices according to merit, then they must know each other's characters; where they do not possess this knowledge, both the election to offices and the decision of lawsuits will go wrong. When the population is very large they are manifestly settled at haphazard, which clearly ought not to be. Besides, in an overpopulous state foreigners and metics will readily acquire the rights of citizens, for who will find them out? Clearly, then, the best limit of the population of a state is the largest number which suffices for the purposes of life, and can be taken in at a single view. Enough concerning the size of a city."

12. *Op. cit.*, p. 514.

13. Georg Simmel, "Die Grossstädte und das Geistesleben," *Die Grossstadt*, ed. Theodor Petermann (Dresden, 1903), pp. 187–206.

14. E. Durkheim, *De la division du travail social* (Paris, 1932), p. 24.

15. The extent to which the segregation of the population into distinct ecological and cultural areas and the resulting social attitude of tolerance, rationality, and secular mentality are functions of density as distinguished from heterogeneity is difficult to determine. Most likely we are dealing here with phenomena which are consequences of the simultaneous operation of both factors.

24

Sociology as a Religious Movement: Thoughts on its Institutionalization in the United States

Russell R. Dynes

Recently, sociologists have begun to take their own behavior more seriously and the sociology of sociology has become a growth industry. Peek (1971) reports over 250 articles on the sociology of sociologists up to 1967 and the production since that time has probably increased. Several books have appeared since then (Friedrichs, 1970; Tiryakian, 1971; Reynolds and Reynolds, 1970). From one vantage point, it is incredible that one of the smallest occupational groups should command such inordinate attention. It would seem, however, that one area of possible understanding which has not been sufficiently explored would draw on theories of social movements, particularly religious movements. This stream of literature seems particularly cogent since it grapples with the relationship between ideas and structure, particularly with the institutionalization of ideologies. Such an approach may be useful in understanding the past, present, and future of sociology. It may provide some understanding of the ambiguities and contradictions current within the field. One cannot understand what has gone on in sociology within the past several decades unless one understands that most issues within the field have their analogue in religion. In recent years, we have been dealing with issues of orthodoxy and heresy, questions of the relation of the faith to the corrupt world, and discussion of choices in the means of salvation. Future historians may look back on these years as an important period of "theological" ferment. It is also possible, of course, that they may look at these "theological" arguments as having been irrelevant and trivial, much like the issue of the number of angels to be accommodated on a pin. Such arguments are seldom trivial to those involved, since they have at stake their own meaning system. Consequently, passion has infused many issues in recent years – on the nature of reality, on the relation of fact to value, on the role of sociologists, and on the relation of sociology to public policy.

Source: *American Sociologist*, 1974, vol. 9, pp. 169–176.

Some of these current concerns can be illuminated if the sociological tradition is seen to contain many elements which have similarities and identities with other major religious traditions. It is necessary first to identify certain religious themes which have been embedded in the sociological tradition from the very beginning. The conception of religion used here would follow Tillich's idea that it is that which concerns us ultimately. Yinger (1970: 33) has phrased a similar idea in the following terms:

> Where one finds awareness and interest in the continuing, recurrent problems of human existence – the human condition itself . . . where one finds rites and shared beliefs relevant to that awareness, which defines the strategy of an ultimate victory: where one has groups organized to heighten that awareness and maintain those rites and beliefs – there one has religion.

Not only are there similarities to religion in the ideological function of the sociological tradition, but there are also similarities to religious roles in the role of the social scientist. Waldo (1961: 28) has commented that "I believe that there is no denying that the social scientist will exercise the same social role and function as the Roman temple priest who reads the future from the entrails of oxen . . . though the social scientist reads it from graph, from report and from computer." This suggests that, second, it is important to consider the forms of institutionalization of sociology. Over time and in differing social contexts, the institutionalization has incorporated different ideologies and has assumed different structural forms. In the movement's early history, it might best be characterized as a cult, particularly as evidenced by the followers of Saint Simon and Comte. In the United States, it may be more accurate to conceptualize its institutionalization primarily in sectarian terms. Recently, however, some discussion has centered around whether sociology has departed from its traditional sectarian stance and has assumed denominational status or whether it has moved toward an ecclesia. Before commenting on that, it is useful to identify the ways in which sociology can be seen, historically, as one substitute necessitated by the disintegration of traditional religions.

Urbane Renewal in the City of God

Most intellectual historians suggest that sociology emerged in the context of the breakdown of the old regime in France and the spread of the industrial form of production from England (Nisbet, 1966). It is in this context that Raymond Aron (1959) suggests that sociology could be interpreted initially as the consciousness of the modernization of society. Others concluded that 18th century thought got rid of God. Perhaps, but it might be better to suggest that God was sought in other ways. One of God's legacies before He disappeared was that He had ordered the world so that proper inquiry would allow the understanding of it. It was in this context that sociology emerged, addressing itself to the tasks of understanding the structures of the new industrial societies and to consider whether man is to live in it without God.

One way to cope with the loss of God is to create other gods, to develop new means of salvation when older means fail, and to create a massive urbane renewal project which would build the kingdom of man to replace the lost Kingdom of God. In effect, sociology, as it emerged, could be viewed as a new secular religion.

Two themes have been persistent in sociology from the very beginning. First, sociology accepted knowledge as the primary means of salvation. All religions have used some variation on faith, works, or knowledge as the major means of salvation. Sociology, from the very beginning, opted for knowledge. (Although one might suggest that more recently this must be supplemented by works, which is now called graduate education, and by faith which is now the anticipated outcome of professional socialization.) The continuing and continual debates over methods have as their intent the overcoming of sources of error since they were impediments to our apprehension of truth.

Second, in addition to the continuing concern about the means of salvation, sociologists have also had their visions about the City of God. Over time, the layout and the architecture of the new City of God has varied. There have been those visions which are revealed by those who raise the question "knowledge for what" and by those who have the answer. And those who raise the question usually have an answer. The reasons that there has been no uniform vision is that utopias are as difficult to describe as they are to construct.

Sociologists, however, have been more adept in identifying sources of evil in the garden than they have in its planning and maintenance. They have taken a rather consistent position on the location of evil in the world, contending anyone with power must be evil. In sociology's initial stages, those corrupted by the power of the church and the government not only stood in the way of truth but also in the way of renewal. As other sources of worldly power emerged, such as industrial leaders, they also were consigned to the sociologist's hell. Such a posture is not unusual for a sectarian group because it provides a justification for the sect's worldly failure. Such a posture also insures the purity of the sect, since any knowledge accepted by those in power has, by their very acceptance, questionable truth value.

It is difficult to document fully here the themes just indicated within the heterogeneity which is called sociology. As Shils (1970: 760) has suggested, however, sociology is held together by a more or less common tradition linked to common monuments or classical figures or works. Some of the themes can be illustrated by short stops at some of the conventional shrines.

Obviously these themes are best illustrated initially by the Old Testament positivist, Comte. Comte experienced the consequences of the distintegration of the old order and he was driven to end the disorganization of the present and to make peace with the uncertainties of the future. His solution was to adopt the methods of the natural sciences, and he coined the term sociology to represent this means of salvation. Included in his view were two themes that he saw as inseparable. On the one hand, he wanted to establish a program for understanding society and he wished this program to become the basis for society's total reconstruction. Sociology would provide, through its apprehension of the truth, redemption from the chaos of the decaying social order. Arbousse-Bastide (1966) suggested that Comte presented "Not a sociological interpretation of religion, but a religious interpretation of sociology." Comte saw sociology as the hope for arresting the moral ravages of the Enlightenment and moved toward the development of positivism which rested on the base of scientific knowledge and love. Positivism, born of the new scientific temper, would become the new religion for man. Comte also developed a new doctrine of the elect and described in detail the new religion's rituals, symbols, sacraments, and vestments which would be worn by the new priests of Positivism, who were at the same time the scientists. Although we look back at Comte today, it is often with embarassment for his claims mixed with respect for his audacity. At the same time, the duality of Comte still persists within sociology – the emphasis on sociological knowledge as a means of salvation in providing the materials necessary for rebuilding the City of God.

While Comte today may be a prophet without honor within his own discipline, the same themes persist. A New Testament positivist, George Lundberg, made his plea for ritual purity under the title *Can Science Save Us?* At the end of his book, he wrote (1947: 104):

> To those that are skeptical and unimpressed by the promise of social science, we may address this question: What alternatives do you propose that hold greater promise? If we do not place our faith in social science, to what shall we look for social salvation?

Marx, of course, provides additional support for the themes just suggested. Since Marx has attracted so many disciples and his writings have been subject to so much exeigesis, today it is difficult to find the historical Marx. But it is clear that Marx was concerned about knowledge and the sources of error in knowledge. His commitment was clear that scientific knowledge of society was possible even if previous intellectual history was primarily a reflection of class struggle. For many traditional religions had obscured the alienation that man experienced and prevented him from achieving salvation. Both the barriers to knowledge and the barriers to salvation were gone in Marx's new eschatology. The various illusions that men were forced to live with would disappear when man could associate freely in his new City of God. Marx, of course, was confronted by the paradox that the means of salvation – knowledge – could only be perfected after the City of God had already been renewed. In view of the continuing debate since Marx as to whether, where, or if the City of God exists, the possible delays in such renewal has caused some latter-day Marxists to forgo knowledge as the means to salvation and to reemphasize faith and/or works as being more effective. One should also note that, in contrast to Comte, Marx had a different doctrine of the elect, the proletariat, but the proletariat could expect some help from those middle class intellectuals who hoped to enter the Kingdom of God early.

Moving along in the history of sociology, it is necessary to stop for short visits with Durkheim and Weber. They were much more modest theologians than some of their predecessors. Durkheim's initial academic position was predicated on his attempt to develop a secular morality (Clark, 1968). In the context of the anticlericalism of the times in France, a Primary Education Law was passed in 1882 providing for free, obligatory, non-religious education for children from 6 to 13. Substitutes had to be found for nuns and brothers who were the former teachers in religious schools and substitutes had to be found for the Catholic morality which had been at the center of that education. The Director of Higher Education, aware of Durkheim's interest and desire to formulate a secular morality, provided him with a fellowship to Germany and in 1887 appointed him to teach social science and pedagogy at the University of Bordeaux. Durkheim's concerns are interestingly reflected in the original preface to *The Division of Labor in Society*. In it, he says:

> This book is pre-eminently an attempt to treat the facts of moral life according to the methods of the positive science . . .
>
> Although we set out primarily to study reality, it does not follow that we do not wish to improve it; we should judge our researchers to have no worth at all if they were to have only a speculative interest . . . for we shall see that science can help us adjust ourselves, determining the ideal toward which we are heading confusedly . . .
>
> Even on the ultimate question, whether we ought to wish to live, we believe that science is not silent. (1933: 32–35).

Durkheim's view of the world and of the scope and mission of sociology was narrower than Comte and was more clearly this worldly in its orientation. Through the understanding of social facts, salvation could be achieved, since it would move us to our ideals.

Weber was more complex and paradoxical. Weber was critically concerned with the means of salvation – knowledge. But Weber's major contribution was to attack the current images of the City of God, particularly those current in the academy at that time. The use of the term *vocation* in his moving essay "Science as a Vocation" (Gerth and Mills, 1946: 134–6) was deliberate, based on the religious connotation of the term in the sense of calling. He sought to warn those who had accepted the calling of the dangers of idolatry. In the essay, Weber posed Tolstoy's question, "What shall we do, and how shall we arrange our lives?" and he says, ". . . only a prophet or a savior can give the answers.

If there is no such man, or if his message is no longer believed in, then you will not compel him to appear by having thousands of professors, as privileged hirelings of the state, attempt as petty prophets in their lecture rooms to take over his role." He went on to say that "[Some modern intellectuals] . . . play at decorating a sort of domestic chapel with small sacred images from all over the world or they produce surrogates through all sorts of psychic experience to which they ascribe the dignity of mystic holiness, which they peddle on the book market." He added "academic prophecy . . . will create only fanatical sects but never a genuine community."

Weber went on to point out that, since there were always multiple gods and since life cannot be brought to a definite conclusion, man faced a decisive choice. Only one of the choices was science. While everyone should give account of the ultimate meaning of their own conduct, there were choices available other than science. He said, "To the person who cannot bear the fate of the times like a man, one must say, 'May he return silently, without the usual build-up of renegades, but simply and plainly. The arms of the old churches are open widely and compassionately for him . . . In my eyes, such religious return stands higher than the academic prophecy, which does not clearly realize that in the lecture halls of the university no other virtue holds but plain intellectual integrity.'" Weber was saying that there were those around in the academy offering their own utopias, but when one accepts science as a vocation, the security which utopias provide and the seductions they offer fall away, and man is left with his existential choice. It is in this context that Benjamin Nelson (Stammer, 1971: 170) offers an eloquent evaluation of Weber:

> Who indeed has explored the dilemma of action in the twentieth century so deeply and honestly as did Weber. Not Tolstoy, not Freud, not Schweitzer, not Camus or Sartre, not even Kafka – none of the acclaimed moralists of our century – matched Weber in the range of his moral imagination or in his courage to reject simple solutions.

Perhaps what is so paradoxical about Weber is that while he challenged the idolatry of the times, he did not offer the clear substitutes which those before him had. He left existential choice and, as Fromm and others have suggested, this is too great a burden for some to bear, so they must attempt to "escape from freedom." In many ways, Weber is a precursor for the "God is dead" theology. Obviously for many persons currently in sociology, this was not a satisfactory solution.

Most of the sociologists discussed here were not traditionally religious. This is also true of most of their intellectual descendants. Even those who considered religion in their own theoretical orientation generally saw little future for traditional religion. Most were convinced that God had disappeared. But perhaps God has been like the Cheshire Cat in *Alice in Wonderland*, always threatening to disappear but remaining as a disembodied smile throughout the work of most sociologists. Sociologists usually recognize that purposive social action can have unanticipated consequences.

Durkheim and Weber were more modest than Comte and Marx in the scope of their "theological" views. One reason is that both of them were involved with sociology as an academic discipline, not solely as an intellectual discipline. Sociology had moved into the academy in Europe. Its foothold was tenuous. Weber, in particular, was concerned about its institutionalization and the threats to it from outside and from within. The nature and process of institutionalization is obviously important. No religious system is effective unless it is institutionalized. In the process, of course, transformations occur when intellectual passions become committed to social structure. It is to this process in the United States that we turn next.

The Institutionalization of the Faith: Finding Housing for the Chosen People

Sociology has gone through various stages and has experienced the problems attendant in routinizing any "religion." Since certain beliefs are more strategic at one time than another, the members have had, in Weber's terms, an elective affinity toward certain sets of beliefs. As the belief structure changes, the recruitment base for new converts changes and the nature of the problems they face will differ from those of the original set of disciples. The institutionalization process in the United States can only be briefly sketched in here but several good histories of the discipline can provide extended support (Hinkle and Hinkle, 1954; Bernard, 1943; Odum, 1951; Gouldner, 1970).

The initial institutionalization (1883–1917) was characterized by the predominant ideology centering around sociology as "reform." As Protestantism was moving away from traditional notions of individual salvation, sociology offered another alternative base for ethics. As a sect, it was confident in its identification of the sources of evil as well as optimistic about the potential perfectibility of the social order. Many of the early "converts" were those who earlier might have intended to Christianize the whole world, but these motives "became transferred in the men to the more secular and similarly inspiring aims of higher education and the creation of a new science of human behavior" (Faris 1967: 26). As a sectarian movement, sociology established its first foothold in the midwest, primarily in colleges of Protestant origin, and Bernard (1945) has suggested that by 1910 sociology had been introduced into most colleges. The initial foothold was tenuous, however, and the second stage concentrated on a firmer base of institutionalization.

The second stage (1917–1945) was characterized by preoccupation with the role of sociology as an academic discipline within the academy. The humanities, legitimized by tradition, were suspicious of new competitors. On the other hand, the physical and biological sciences had, at that time, been making a successful transition toward academic respectability. It was apparent that the most efficacious ideology was one that defined sociology as a science. During this stage, there was preoccupation with the methods that would guarantee scientific status. The notion of sociology as reform was gradually downplayed. What the first generation wanted to emphasize, the second "generation" wished to forget and to acknowledge reform only as the pre-scientific origin of a now respectable discipline.

The legitimation of sociology as an academic discipline still came easier in the midwest and in the west. In addition, the sources of recruitment stayed essentially the same: the ideal type was a midwestern Protestant whose reform impulses were now channeled into remaking the world through sociology as a science. The City of God could still be built if one could find the appropriate methodological tools.

As a consequence of this period, sociology might more adequately be viewed as having become an "established" sect. It has been accorded status within the structure of colleges and universities, but sociologists were constantly reminded of their sectarian identity by others who based their academic legitimacy on more traditional grounds. Even though established, it should be recalled that sociologists were still a small sect. The membership of the American Sociological Society in 1945 was only 1,651 when sociology moved into its third stage (Hinkle and Hinkle, 1954: 44).

The third stage (1946-) was characterized by a greater diversity in the dominant schools involved in graduate education, in the sources of recruitment, and in methodological and theoretical orientations. To the myth that sociology was a science was added the notion that sociology was value free. But the more important element in the third stage was not ideological change but structural changes which in turn affected the dominant ideological stance. The most unsettling element in this period has been the rapid expansion of sociology. No sectarian group is ever prepared for success. In its past sociology had always had a theodicy of failure, but no sect ever develops an elaborate theodicy of success.

After the initial post-World War II bulge, most American universities settled down to a somewhat static universe. However, during the 1950s, enrollments grew gradually. While in the 1940s, college enrollments reached 2.6 million, by 1963, they had reached almost 4.8 million. Not only were there more students but there was much more money. Excluding capital outlay, expenditures for public higher education increased almost 14 times between 1937-38 and 1961-62 and expenditures for private education increased about eleven times. Since sociology departments were institutionalized by this time, when universities expanded, sociology departments expanded. When new universities were created, new departments of sociology were created. During this time sociology may have expanded more rapidly than most other disciplines. Orlans (1973: 261) reports that the social sciences in the United States increased from 20,700 in 1947 to 81,400 in 1967, fourfold increase. By contrast, in 1950 there were 2,364 members of the A.S.A. and in 1968 there were over 12,000 – a fivefold increase.

Such rapid expansion created an unfamiliar context for sociology and provided the basis for a breakdown in consensus within the field. As a sect, it always had a deviant perspective toward the world. Since this perspective was "true," there was always a normative obligation to convince others of its validity. Sociologists, however, never had much success (outside the educational system) in convincing others. For a sect to sustain motivation in the face of continued "failure," considerable attention must be given to collective self-glorification, detailing the gains that the group makes in spreading the doctrine. Articles are written telling of successful ventures among the multitudes of heathens, while being very careful to document their considerable resistances. Sessions are planned at annual meetings to convince ourselves of our relevance. Such myths sustain motivation so they constitute a large part of the oral and written tradition within the field.

During the early 1960s, many sociologists began to believe their own myths. Sociologists could get jobs. New departments were opening. Graduate support and research money was readily available. These were pure signs of grace, not mere demographic coincidences. But for the sect, success is actually failure. If the doctrine is being accepted, particularly by those with power, this is also an indication that sociology had compromised with the corrupt world. Since success is failure, scapegoats had to be found. There were a number of possibilities for blame. One was the sociological "establishment," who, it was claimed, had been busy patrolling the corridors of power and had themselves been corrupted. Other criticism focused on the prevailing ideology of sociology as value free, which was said to have converted contemporary sociology into an elaborate distortion of the truth and a tool for the establishment. To others, the dominant theoretical orientation was the culprit. Functionalism was seen as a static hell and functionalists seen as conservative fools. Some saw the villain to be the universities, since, having accepted sociology, they too must be corrupt.

There is no doubt that the rapid expansion of sociology was confusing. Many older sectarians, having made vows of poverty when they entered the order, felt guilty about being able to live comfortably doing what they enjoyed. Even some of the elder prophets found that they could do what Jeremiah never could, that is, call for repentance and collect royalties at the same time.

In any case, the period is over simply because the expansion of the university and college system in the United States is at an end – and sociologists can be content with "failure" again. Some intellectual historian will probably look back at the early seventies and identify "The Year That Sociology Demythologized Itself" – when they came to the conclusion that they were not as significant as they had been telling themselves. The historians may also call it "The Year That Sociology Refused to be Saved."

Toward the Future: Learning to Like Inner Worldly Asceticism

It is clear that sociology is now involved in a transition period but it is more popular today to identify "crises" than transition periods. The current "crisis" will be important to the future of sociology. In many ways, the basic problem remains the one that has continually preoccupied sociology. It is the question of how a sectarian group can maintain its version of truth in a basically hostile environment. It is the question of how sociology will survive in a future that will be characterized by a scarcity of resources.

This crisis is particularly cogent since perhaps over 75 percent of the present "converts" to the discipline have not experienced a time when there was any significant scarcity of resources for the field. With only vague remembrances of things past, they may assume that acceptance, support, and all of the necessities of continued institutionalization are automatic. In spite of past accomplishments, one can still argue that the institutional base remains tenuous and that future energy must continue to be expended in dealing with the hostile external world. The immediate past may not provide a valid model for survival. A long time ago, Ruth Benedict (1939) popularized the notion that adaptive skills at one level of development may not be appropriate for the next. Some of the conditions of the last decade encouraged certain tactics and skills that will not be adaptive in the future. Too, the dialectical nature of social life as well as the ambiguities of sectarian existence may require new strategies.

Since it is impossible to draw a conclusion from what is obviously a process, only a final parable is necessary. What may be necessary for the future is a change in the discipline's central-theological position. During the 1960s, sociologists were good Calvinists. Most interpreted the expansion as a clear sign of grace. In the 17th century, there was a reaction to the Calvinist doctrine of unconditional election and irresistable grace when Jacobus Arminius suggested instead that man faced alternatives and was actually free to make choices. Instead of the grim determination of Calvin, he presented a theology of hope, even if grace was not guaranteed. It is that opportunity and those choices that sociologists face in the 1970s. We must use them effectively or else sociology may be remembered in the future as only latter-day versions of the Gnostic or the Albigensian heresies.

References

Arbousse-Bastide, P. 1966 "Auguste Comte et la sociologie religieuse." Archives de Sociologies des Religions 22: 3–57.

Aron, R. 1959 "Societé moderne et sociologie." Transactions of the Fourth World Congress of Sociology 19.

Benedict, R. 1939 "Cultural continuities and discontinuities." Psychiatry 1: 161–167.

Bernard, L. L. 1943 Origins of American Sociology. New York: Thomas Y. Crowell.
Bernard, L. L., and Jessie Bernard 1945 "The teaching of sociology in the United States in the last fifty years." American Journal of Sociology 50(May): 534–548.
Clark, T. 1968 "Emile Durkheim and the institutionalization of sociology in the French university system." Archives Européennes de Sociologie 9, No. 1: 37–71.
Durkheim, Emile 1933 The Division of Labor in Society. New York: Macmillan.
Faris, Robert E. L. 1967 Chicago Sociology 1920–1932. Chicago: University of Chicago Press.
Friedrichs, Robert W. 1970 A Sociology of Sociology. New York: The Free Press.
Gerth, H. H. and C. Wright Mills (Eds). 1946 From Max Weber: Essays in Sociology. New York: Oxford University Press: 134–146.
Gouldner, Alvin 1970 The Coming Crisis of Western Sociology. New York: Basic Books.
Hinkle, Roscoe C. and Gisela J. Hinkle 1954 The Development of Modern Sociology: Its Nature and Growth in the United States. Garden City, New York: Doubleday.
Lundberg, George 1947 Can Science Save Us? New York: Longmans, Green.
Nisbet, Robert A. 1966 The Sociological Tradition. New York: Basic Books.
Odum, Howard W. 1951 American Sociology: The Story of Sociology in the United States – Through 1950. New York: Longmans, Green.
Orlans, Harold 1973 Contracting for Knowledge. San Francisco: Jossey-Bass.
Peek, C. W. 1971 "The sociology of sociologists: a bibliographical evaluation." In The Phenomenon of Sociology: A Reader in the Sociology of Sociology. Edward Tiryakian, ed. New York: Appleton-Century-Crofts.
Reynolds, Larry T., and Janice M. Reynolds 1970 The Sociology of Sociology. New York: David McKay.
Shils, E. 1970 "Tradition, ecology and institution in the history of sociology." Daedalus 99 (Fall): 760–825.
Stammer, Otto (Ed.) 1971 Max Weber and Sociology Today. New York: Harper and Row.
Tiryakian, Edward (Ed.) 1971 The Phenomenon of Sociology: A Reader in the Sociology of Sociology. New York: Appleton-Century-Crofts.
Waldo, D. 1961 "Panel Comments." Pp. 21–29 in Research for Public Policy. Washington: Brookings Institution.
Yinger, J. Milton 1970 The Scientific Study of Religion. New York: Macmillan.

25

Origins of American Sociology: Associationist Social Science

L.L. Bernard and J. Bernard

General Sketch of Associationist Social Science

General Character of Associationism. Although John Adams had spoken of a science of society as early as 1784, the first substantial phase of the Social Science movement in the United States was Associationism, the American counterpart of Fourierism, which flourished in the United States in the eighteen–forties. The followers of Fourier in the United States called themselves Associationists rather than Fourierists for the two following reasons:[1]

> 1st. Charles Fourier often and earnestly protested against giving the name of any individual man to the Social Science, which he humbly believed to be, and reverently taught as a discovery of Eternal Laws of Divine Justice, established and made known by the Creator. 2d. While we honor the magnanimity, consummate ability and devotedness of this good and wise man, and gratefully acknowledge our belief that he has been the means, under Providence, of giving to his fellow men a clue which may lead us out from our actual Scientific and Social labyrinth, yet we do not receive all the parts of his theories, which in the publications of the Fourier school are denominated 'Conjectural' – because Fourier gives them as speculations – because we do not in all respects understand his meaning – and because there are parts which individually we reject; and we hold ourselves not only free, but in duty bound, to seek and obey Truth wherever revealed, in the Word of God, the Reason of Humanity and the Order of Nature.

In many respects Associationism was really tangential to the wider movement as a whole, since the leaders of the later Social Science movement repudiated it entirely. They regarded it as more or less fantastic and even as in some

---

Source: L. L. Bernard and J. Bernard, *Origins of American Sociology, The Social Science Movement in the United States,* (New York: Crowell, 1943).

respects immoral.[2] But since it assumed the sanction and even the title of Social Science it must be considered as belonging legitimately within the sphere of the general movement. As contrasted with the later phases of Social Science, Associationism was romantic, spectacular, demagogic, popular, and Utopistic. It managed to convert to its point of view the Transcendental colony of Brook Farm, with its coterie of brilliant literary, artistic, and more or less philosophic, minds. It stirred people's emotions and made them talk and argue. Numerous articles and books were written about it, both to promote and condemn it. Its humanitarian principles inspired people to action of a concrete and appealing sort. It assumed, in fact, many of the aspects of a craze and its pronouncements and questions were therefore news, whereas the soberer activities of the later Social Scientists lacked the dynamic qualities of the craze and were seldom regarded as news.[3] For these reasons, perhaps, and because it was so symptomatic of its age, historians have given more attention to the early form of Social Science, that is, Associationism, than to the later and more scientific phases of the movement.

Parrington on Associationism. Parrington[4] sees the social Utopianism, of which Associationism was simply a phase, as one of three major strands in the social, literary, and philosophical renaissance which was occurring in New England in the early years of the nineteenth century. This renaissance, according to Parrington, was the counterpart in the intellectual and social realm of the industrial and economic revolution taking place at this same time, a revolution which disintegrated aristocratic ideals and organization and put the middle class into the political saddle. The old aristocratic order of noblesse oblige was being cleared out to make way for the new capitalistic or bourgeois regime then emerging as a result of the industrial revolution. The ethical motivation of this renaissance, says Parrington, was due to its romantic purpose, namely, its aim to humanize the new society then in process of growth. French liberalism, he points out, won its way into New England by round-about and devious paths,[5] and finally emerged in the form of Channing's Unitarianism, an ethical religion with a strongly humanitarian bias. Thus the heretical French philosophy which had entered Virginia in the 1770's as Physiocratic agrarianism, and which had gone west to the frontier to become an indomitable individualism, was finally transferred to New England by Channing and transformed into an anti-Calvinistic religion which preached human perfectibility after the model of the later French Enlightenment and the possibilities of making the sojourn of man on earth something more than a gloomy resting place on the way to judgement day. Unitarianism was thus the vehicle for disseminating eighteenth century French idealism throughout New England, as Jeffersonianism had earlier been the vehicle for spreading those same ideals throughout the South and Southwest.[6] That the New England capitulation to the persuasive French philosophy was so long delayed was due to the tough tenacity of Calvinism which had dominated the New England mind so thoroughly as to have become second nature to it. The battle royal which the humanistic doctrines of Unitarianism had to wage with Calvinism before the former finally won the contest is among the most interesting and significant events in the history of American thought, but its consideration lies outside the scope of the present study. For our purposes it is sufficient to note Parrington's interpretation of Associationism as one of the offshoots of the American version of eighteenth century French liberalism.

Associationism and Science. If it were not for the fact that Associationism claimed for itself the title of science it would have little more place in a history of the Social Science movement than its parent, Unitarianism, or its sibs, Abolitionism, Pacifism, Feminism, or any of the other *isms* of that age. It possessed in common with all of these the traits of an ardent, emotional reform movement, Utopistic or at least millennial in character, which stirred deeply the humanitarian impulses of its followers. All were speculative social philosophies of the time, but Associationism in particular included a considerable number of fantastic and even impossible schemes of social renovation of a speculative character. Associationism, in spite of the fact that its social psychology and economics were not the least dependable, alone of these *isms* insisted upon claiming for itself a scientific status. We must, therefore, tear it from its theological and metaphysical matrix and consider it as a phase of the Social Science movement, for in fact such it earnestly considered itself and persistently sought to be – if indeed it did not regard itself as the characteristic embodiment of this movement.

The insistence of the Associationists that their system constituted a science does not, it need scarcely be noted, mean that it actually was genuinely such a science, nor does its inclusion in the present study indicate that it should be so considered. The important consideration, from our historical viewpoint, as we have indicated in the preceding chapter, is simply that its adherents proudly and piously claimed for it the status of a science.

Science and Scientific Laws. The concept of science itself changes like any other concept from age to age. A century ago, when thought was still so largely under the dominance of theology and the metaphysics of Natural Law, science was conceived in theological and metaphysical terms, as, indeed, it still is even among many social scientists in good standing today. The function of science was conceived, therefore, in that day as that of "discovering" laws already existing in nature or in the mind of God.[7]

None of the adherents and expositors of science had yet attained the point of view made possible and initiated by the epoch-making theory of Comte that scientific laws and principles are not formulated in the mind of a pre-existent Supreme being nor inherent in the very nature and constitution of the universe as a body of Natural Law, but are the intellectual projections of human thinking, the result of an attempt to see all phenomena as functionally related parts of an orderly system. Man is born into chaos, except for the very elementary guidance his inadequate equipment of instincts gives him in making his earliest adjustments to his environment. But he cannot live with any degree of satisfaction in this chaos. Consequently he learns to look meaning into his world, that is, to project order into the chaos of forces, factors, and stimuli which surround and operate upon him. At first he integrates specific perceptions of concrete objects in this environing chaos. Every child of normal intelligence does this, just as the human race as a whole has done it before him. From concrete perceptions he moves forward to abstract conceptions. These are nothing more nor less than the recognition of similarities among a large number of otherwise discrete phenomena which enable the perceiver or conceptualizer to classify perceived phenomena that have acquired similar or related meanings for him under the same general headings and to utilize or manipulate them logically for the same or similar adjustment ends.

Science and Social Laws. Social laws and principles are merely the broader and more stable conceptualizations of phenomena of this type which can be used for guidance in thinking or making practical material adjustments. The essential fact is that all such conceptualizations are not inherent in the human mind or in nature, but are projections of order into the chaos of isolated and undefined perceptions called forth by man's need for a better working adjustment to his social environment. They are in the nature of projective inventions.[8] The Fourierists or Associationists, like their reformistic contemporaries, were metaphysicians primarily, and upon occasion even theologians, in their mode of thinking. They saw social laws as psychic entities emanating from the mind of Divinity or as orderly generalizations (Natural Laws) inherent in the order of Nature. They did not grasp the human experiential and experimental or relativistic character of science and of its principles. They believed that the principles of Associationism, as they understood them, were a part of the personal revelation of God made for man's guidance in a new and complex industrial world, or at least those principles of human nature and of human association inherent in the Natural Order itself (for they believed there was a Natural Order). They believed therefore that these principles were scientifically accurate, definite, incontrovertible, and unchangeable.

Associationism and Religion. So far from being a science, Associationism was in fact a religion, with a theory of history, of society, of human nature, and of a future heaven, just like any other religion. The essentially religious character of Associationist Social Science was not only admitted, but even emphasized and insisted upon by its sponsors, without any sense of inconsistency whatever with their claims for scientific standing. Thus W. H. Channing, at the Associationist Convention of April 4, 1844, says:[9]

> It would be doing injustice to this occasion, not to open our discussions of the Principles of Social Reorganization, by an expression of feelings

with which we have come up, from far and near, to this assembly. It is but giving voice to what is working in the hearts of those now present, and of thousands whose sympathies are at this moment with us over our whole land, to say, this is a Religious Meeting. Our end is to do God's will.

The religious pattern of thought is also revealed in a resolution of a similar convention (February 22–23, 1844) to express their gratitude "for the earnest zeal and efficiency with which they [the advocates of Social Science, particularly the editors of the New York *Tribune*, *The Phalanx*, and *The Present*] devote themselves to the propagation of the truly glad tidings of great joy in relation to the Social Destiny of Man."[10]

We shall find this strongly religious and theological emphasis recurring again and again throughout all phases of the Social Science movement. The reason is not difficult to find. Since most of the scholars and learned men of this country were divines their peculiar bias colored practically all philosophical discussions. They alone had sufficient background in scholarship to react intelligently to Social Science. In the colleges, even those not sectarian in spirit, the courses in which Social Science first appeared, were taught by the presidents, who were almost without exception ministers. As late as 1880, Cliffe Leslie pointed out that even political economy in the United States was strongly theological in viewpoint.[11] This was still more markedly true a third of a century earlier.

As a religion, Associationism was an almost point for point counterpart of Calvinistic Protestantism. Like Unitarianism, it rejected the old Calvinistic ferocities and substituted a more benign view of God and man. But the old framework remained. Associationist Social Science answered the same type of questions as that put by the Scotch catechism, but it answered these questions differently. If Calvinism taught that human nature was depraved and that it must therefore be repressed, Associationism insisted that human nature was good and that it must be followed exclusively in social organization. For the Calvinistic doctrine of predestination, Associationism substituted a glorious social destiny of man, a sort of Utopian Cooperative Commonwealth which later became an essential element in the creed of doctrinaire Socialism. The framework of men's thoughts had been thoroughly set to run in Calvinistic and deterministic channels, and even when men reacted against such doctrines they nevertheless retained the old forms.

Although the new social philosophy of Associationism dispensed with Calvinism – in fact revised its main teaching regarding the original nature of man and his ultimate destiny – it did not do away with determinism. It held as religiously to the eighteenth century doctrine of inevitable progress, so optimistically formulated by Condorcet, as Calvinism had clung to the belief in the ultimate and inevitable damnation of the larger portion of the human race. Like the French philosophers, from whom they had stemmed intellectually, the Associationists believed that human progress was as much a part of the Law of Nature as the Calvinists had thought, and still believed, that eternal damnation was a postulate of the Law of God. Some of the Associationists even went so far as to express the belief that progress was a part of the divine law and connected it up with the New Testament dispensation of the atonement, asserting that the coming of Jesus as an atonement for Adam's sin had reversed the old Calvinistic order in which all men were under the ban and had provided a new constitution of hope and continuous progress for mankind.[12] Thus, like the philosophers of the Enlightenment, they placed the golden age in the future and built around this doctrine a new metaphysical – sometimes even a theological – religion in which their "Social Science" would be the gospel of the new order and regeneration of man. Thus even in revolt they remained true to the old religious frame of reference.[13]

Albert Brisbane. It was through an enthusiastic young journalist, Albert Brisbane (1809–1890),[14] that Fourier's doctrines were transmitted to the United States. Brisbane, the son of a well-to-do New York landowner, had been very deeply impressed by the social philosophy of his tutor in New York, John Monesca, under whom he had studied. This social philosophy stimulated him greatly since, probably because of his Scotch cultural heritage, which was at that time much occupied with cultural history and social philosophy, he had already been thinking on the subject of man's social destiny. As a gentleman of means he went abroad to study, taking work under Cousin and Guizot, among others, but he derived no satisfaction from any of these instructors, whose teaching impressed him as formal and sterile. He therefore went to Germany and studied under Hegel. But here, too, he was disappointed in the intellectual guidance he received and he went off to Constantinople. At the age of twenty-one he returned to Paris, convinced that social evils could be removed only by a fundamental reorganization of society. He rejected Saint-Simonism, in which he had dabbled, but when he came across Fourier's *Traité de l'Association Domestique-Agricole* (1821–1822) he felt that at last he had found what he was looking for, and for two years thereafter he studied under Fourier's personal direction.

Fourier and Brisbane. François Marie Charles Fourier (1772–1837) was a French business man who, quite in the manner of the social philosophers of his day, had developed a most interesting and suggestive philosophy of history and theory of society. The stages of history since the fall of man were, as he conceived them, savagery, patriarchy, barbarism, civilization (i.e., contemporary society), guarantyism, simple association, and composite association or harmony. The last three stages belonged to the future and referred to a system of social organization in which the human passions, instead of being repressed as at present, would be encouraged and used as guides to behavior. The result would be that since God had endowed all men differently, presumably to serve different social functions, each individual in following his native promptings would find himself acting in the best interests not only of himself but of society as a whole. In this future society, social organization would take the form of phalanxes of about 1800 people working together on about 5000 acres of land, under cooperative living and working conditions. And thus, finally, social harmony would be achieved.[15]

To Fourier, engaged in the hum-drum routine of business, this system was no doubt a delightful escape mechanism, and we can imagine what pleasure its elaboration must have given him. To young Brisbane, son of a wealthy land owner, the idyllic and semi-rural life pictured in Fourier's system must have seemed like the real and necessary future of society. His capitulation was complete and he spent years of effort in attempting to convert the world to the new gospel. He returned to the United States in 1834, somewhat broken in health; but as soon as his health permitted – five years later – he began a vigorous propaganda campaign, with what success we shall presently see.

Brisbane's Propaganda Activities. In New York Brisbane organized a Fourier society, gave lectures on the subject of Fourierism, and suggested that similar activities be undertaken by others in different parts of the country.[16] In accordance with this suggestion similar societies did actually spring up throughout the country.[17] Indeed, Brisbane was himself surprised at the interest he evoked. In the meantime he had captured the imagination of Horace Greeley, who offered him the use of his *New York Tribune* as an avenue of publication. Thus Brisbane's paper, *The Future*, which he had been editing for two months, was transferred to the columns of the *Tribune*. This arrangement, however, was by no means satisfactory to the readers of the *Tribune*. Brisbane got no further in his explanations of Fourier's Social Science than the industrial parts when letters of protest began to pour in and he was obliged to discontinue his column.[18] Undaunted, however, he edited the *Chronicle*, wrote twice a week for the *Plebeian*, and finally, in October, 1843, established *The Phalanx, or Journal of Social Science*, "Devoted to the Cause of Association, or a Social Reform and the Elevation of the Human Race."[19]

W. H. Channing and Brook Farm. Unfortunately, from the point of view of Associationism as a secular movement, at about this time (1843) William H. Channing was converted to the new social gospel, and through him, the Brook Farm Colony in the winter of 1843–1844.[20] We say unfortunately, not because Channing and the Brook Farm colonists were not brilliant and outstanding men, for they were; more brilliant, perhaps, than Brisbane and Greeley themselves. But Associationism was not ripe for a practical trial as yet, as Brisbane himself later confessed.[21] And even if it had been, the brilliant, unstable intellectuals of New England, overly sensitive to every Utopistic wind that blew, were not the people to try it. That phalanxes should fail was a foregone conclusion. But inconspicuous phalanxes in the wilds of Ohio or Wisconsin might have failed without discrediting the idea as a whole. Brook Farm was too conspicuous to do anything without widespread publicity.

The Effect of Brook Farm. The conversion of Brook Farm to Associationism was the crucial event in the history of Associationist Social Science. It changed the whole tone and temper of the movement. As Noyes points out,[22] New York had been the center of the movement before this, but now the headquarters were shifted to Massachusetts. Brisbane, Greeley, and Parke Godwin had been the recognized heads of the movement, but now William H. Channing became the real leader.[23] The old New York Conventions were succeeded by a National Union of Socialists, which met at Boston. As long as the movement remained in the hands of the New York journalists it continued to be more or less firmly anchored to its original purpose. When the Massachusetts men came into control, German transcendentalism with a goodly mixture of New England theology gradually transformed it. The Massachusetts mind was sympathetic to the ideals of Associationism, but as Parrington says,[24] collectivism and communism were alien to Yankee individualism. New England, therefore, emphasized the more mystical elements in the system rather than the concrete reform elements, as Brisbane had done. The temperamental differences had their overt expression. Brisbane did not get along well with the Transcendentalists personally.[25] The change produced by the New England group in the Associationist movement is succinctly and tellingly summarized in the subtitle of *The Phalanx*. When Brook Farm took over control of the movement, *The Phalanx, Journal of Social Science* became, significantly, *The Phalanx, Organ of the Doctrine of Association.*

The Phalanx. *The Phalanx* had been originally without doubt an imitation of its European counterparts, the French *Phalange, revue de la science sociale*, published, with interruptions, from 1834 to 1849 in Paris, and the *London Phalanx*, published in England from 1841–1843. The first seven numbers of the American publication had been under the direct management of Brisbane and Osborne Macdaniel.[26] The motto on the title page was the same as that on the title page of Brisbane's *Social Destiny of Man* (1840), viz. "Our Evils are Social, not Political; and a Social Reform Only Can Eradicate Them." The editors state that *The Phalanx* will explain Fourier's system and "enter into a frank and impartial criticism of the present false system of Society, and will expose its evils, and the defects of its leading social Institutions – among other: – its repugnant, ill-requited, and degrading system of industry: – Its system of Free Competition or false rivalry and envious strife and anarchy in Trade and Industry: – Its system of anarchical Commerce: – Its menial system of Hired Labor or labor for Wages: – The unjust and unnatural relation which it establishes between Capital and Labor: – Its defective and partial systems of Education: – Its permanent conflict of the individual with the collective Interest – its system of isolated Households. The Phalanx will discuss political, social and religious questions on the broadest grounds of universality and impartiality, and with reference to their practical bearing upon Social Progress and the Happiness of Mankind. . . ."

The Phalanx contained sixteen very large pages per issue and the subscription price was to be $2.00 the year. The editors had planned to make it a weekly if enough subscriptions could be obtained, otherwise a monthly.

By April, 1844, it became clear that it could not, for the present at least, be a weekly. At that time Channing's *The Present* and Parke Godwin's *The Pathfinder* merged with *The Phalanx* and the plan was to publish it every two weeks until it was possible to make it a weekly.

Editorial Policy. With the shift in leadership from New York to Massachusetts, a change in editorial policy became evident. At the April 4, 1844, General Convention of the Associationists, an Executive Committee had been appointed whose duties included that of editing *The Phalanx*.[27] This editorial Committee consisted of Parke Godwin and W. H. Channing, in addition to the original editors, Brisbane and Macdaniel. Brisbane, however, had gone to Europe to get some manuscript material of Fourier's, with the result that the editorial duties fell upon the other members of the committee. And now the complexion of the journal began to change, but the change was so subtle that it is difficult to formulate it in words. We have already commented on the modification of the sub-title which marked the transition from control by the New York group to that by the Massachusetts group. Copious translations from Fourier, as well as notes on the doings of local phalanxes in various parts of the country continued to be published. But one feels that the more mystical and religious members of the editorial committee were getting increasing control of the journal.

This change in editorial policy had a dampening effect. Being more mystical and theological in their outlook than the publicists and the journalists, who had formerly been responsible for the publication, these men were consequently more sensitive to the criticisms of their heterodox religious opinions which came from their readers. The movement was thus put on the defensive against the attacks of the conservative clergy, and this change was reflected in *The Phalanx*, which now began to give undue emphasis to matters of religious controversy. The earliest members had a more social orientation, were more reformistic, more aggressive. The later ones were more mystical, more theological, more defensive. The leading original articles in the first numbers were by Brisbane and Macdaniel. Those in the later issues were by various writers, and especially by Parke Godwin. In the later numbers fiction was introduced; there was more news of phalanxes; and less emphasis upon theoretical discussion. Articles appeared defending Fourierism against criticisms in the theological quarterlies. These changes did not occur abruptly; and it is impossible to measure them by any specific quantitative criterion. But one feels the transformation in the atmosphere of the pages as he goes through them consecutively. That the new editorial policy was due to the New England influence is unquestionable.[28]

The Triumph of Mysticism. Unfortunately these changes reacted upon Brisbane himself. In December of 1844 he returned from Europe with the Fourier manuscripts he had gone to get and in a letter to the Associationists of the United States announced that "A class will be formed of persons who have time and capacity to prosecute the study of the Mss., and higher parts of Social Science."[29] So far, he says, the practical and industrial aspects of the doctrine have been emphasized, but now "the time has . . . come when it is necessary to make known the higher parts – those parts relating to the theory of the passions and faculties of the soul; the theory of cosmology; of the Immortality of the soul; of the causes of Evil; the material unity of the Globe, and other great questions which are embraced in the science of Universal Unity . . . ." Here we see clearly exhibited the growing mysticism and theological bias of the movement. The "practical and industrial" parts give way to discussions of the soul, cosmology, causes of evil, and the science of universal unity.[30] Other factors than the New England influence may have played a role in this change of emphasis. It may be that the practical impetus had exhausted itself in the establishment of the various associations and phalanxes. Or it might be proper to assume that the practical minded reformers of the movement, like Greeley, for example, were being drained off by other more concrete reforms, leaving the main movement to the more mystically inclined. *The Phalanx* itself continued only until May, 1845, when it became *The Harbinger*, "Devoted to Social and Political Progress, to be published by the Brook Farm Phalanx simultaneously in New York and Boston." It was to be democratic, "devoted to the cause of a radical, organic social reform." It was to discuss and defend Fourier's doctrines.[31] The triumph of the Brook Farm group was now complete.

The Associationist Theory of Social Organization

The Philosophy of History. In the eighteenth century, which was pre-eminently the century of the philosophy of history, the historical approach would undoubtedly have been regarded as the one of chief value for the justification of Associationism, but the psychological interpretation of man and of his institutions was coming to be very influential in the nineteenth century. Begun by Hobbes, Locke, Condillac, and Hume, it had been broadened and strengthened by Hartley, Helvetius, William Godwin and Adam Smith, and by other Scotch philosophers, until it now seemed to many that social organization grew naturally out of the so-called instincts and natural moral propensities of man. But as important as these subjective factors in social behavior and social organization seemed to many, the rival environmentalist theory of social causation, which at that time took the form of the philosophy of history, appeared to many others to be of equal or of even greater importance. As we have already seen, the eighteenth century, with its new perceptions of social phenomena and its sure grasp for the first time in history of the full significance of social organization and social evolution, had matured two modes of explaining and interpreting these important new phases of social consciousness and behavior. These were the theories of human nature, for which the Scotch ethical philosophers were primarily although not exclusively responsible, and the philosophy of history, for which the French naturalistic philosophers were the chief but not the sole sponsors. Fourier and Brisbane had undoubtedly been influenced by the first of these lines of thought here named and they accordingly made it primary in their philosophy of society. However, they were too close to the French Enlightenment – with its strong emphasis upon a pattern of historical progress, now considered as an inevitable postulate of the metaphysical theory of Natural Law – to disregard this aspect of the question of sanctions or justifications for proclaiming the new social order which they regarded not only as an inevitable successor to the present stage of civilization, but in fact as now approximately due.

Brisbane, himself, therefore, as we have seen, presented a philosophy of history as well as a theory of human nature, to function as a basic sanction for his theory of social organization. We shall now return to a consideration of this approach to Associationism from the standpoint of historical philosophy as a preliminary to an analysis of the theory of social organization itself. In the following passage we see how Brisbane used his theory of cultural evolution, as set forth in his philosophy of history, as a sanction to his scheme of social organization:[32]

> Four societies have existed on the earth, the Savage, Patriarchal, Barbarian and Civilized. Under these general heads may be classed the various social forms, through which man has progressed up to the present day. *If four have existed, may not a fifth or even a sixth be discovered and organized?* Common sense would dictate that there could, although the world hitherto has entertained a different opinion.
>
> In our efforts to prove the possibility of a reform in the social organization, no preliminary is more important than that of doing away with the almost universally entertained opinion, that society cannot be changed. It is a prejudice which rises up at every moment, and in the mind of every individual; it repels investigation and all unprejudiced discussion of this important problem. To combat with a chance of success this deeply rooted prepossession, let us enter into an examination of the four periods above mentioned, and by a study of their mechanisms, particularly that of civilization, judge whether other social principles – perhaps more just and equitable in their action – can be established.

He is thus at the outset establishing to his own satisfaction not only the possibility but even the inevitability of social change as the most important prerequisite for accepting the theory of Associationism.

The Four Stages. The main characteristics of the four stages – savage, patriarchal, barbarian, and civilized – are summarily sketched as follows:[33]

The Savage [Stage]

The leading characteristic of the savage state is its refusal or avoidance of industry. . . . So simple is the organization of this period, that it can scarcely be called a society. To the horde belong in common fields, forests and streams. Hunting and fishing form the two sources from which it forms its subsistence, and each of its members takes as a right the spontaneous productions of Nature, wherever he finds them. . . .

The Patriarchal [Stage]

This society . . . is without importance or influence. The first step, however, in social progress, takes place in this period: industry begins to be developed; flocks are reared; a few branches of manufactures are undertaken, and some other of the elements of society are called into existence. Man becomes attached to the soil, and commences its cultivation; he looks to his own industry for subsistence, and does not trust to the precarious mode of existence of the savage, – to hunting and fishing. . . .

The Barbarian [Stage]

A rapid stride in social progress characterizes the third or Barbarian period. Industry receives an important and in some respects a brilliant development; agriculture and manufactures become the occupation of the mass, and the arts and sciences are called into existence. . . . This period must consequently be considered as an important social progress, although accomplished at the expense of the liberty of the mass, and accompanied by the most oppressive tyranny, – the corporal slavery of the producing classes. . . .

Civilization

In this society man accomplishes the task of his social infancy, – the development of the elements of Industry, Art and Science, which are necessary to the founding of Association. . . .

In the first ages of civilization, war is the leading occupation of society; in later ages, commerce and industry take its place. . . .

This last statement, it might be added parenthetically, is curiously like the later theory of Herbert Spencer, in which he implies the tendency for industrialism to supplant militarism.[34]

Having, by means of his theory of history, satisfactorily established the fact of social change, Brisbane is by no means dogmatic with reference to the exact sequence of stages through which cultures develop. The four stages sketched above have not always occurred in just the order stated, owing to various disturbing and interfering factors, but such is the logical order. He says:[35]

> The four societies which have existed on the earth, should, according to the natural course of things, succeed each other with regularity; but various circumstances, – soil, climate, rivers, seas, formation of countries, etc., influence to a greater or less degree their form and character. Some nations develop themselves faster, some more slowly; some pass over entire periods, particularly the Patriarchal, and organize the Barbarian at once; others after passing a short time in Barbarianism enter the first age of Civilization. A nation, after having progressed as far as the second or third age of civilization, may, by the action of disorganizing events – revolutions within or invasions from without – be suddenly arrested in its career and retrograde to the barbarian period.

Brisbane and Cultural Relativity. In this passage Brisbane shows himself to be quite modern in his views as to the relativity with which these stages or forms of culture succeed one another. At a time when many, and perhaps most, ethnologists and archaeologists were reputed still to believe that the succession of cultures followed a fixed and invariable order,[36] and almost a generation before Lewis H. Morgan published his famous work, *Ancient Society*, in which he discussed the development of the forms of civilization, Brisbane saw clearly that there was no inherent metaphysical order in the evolution of culture, but that this evolution took place in close correspondence with the limiting and conditioning factors imposed by the larger physical environment within which culture itself originated and had its growth. It is also worth noting that this insight on the part of Brisbane was manifested fully two generations before it was brought to popular attention by the so-called newer school of cultural anthropologists, who within the last generation have promulgated the principle as one of the major discoveries of "scientific anthropology," and used it as the chief basis of their criticism of classical or comparative anthropology. It is of course true that Brisbane's societies or stages are not at present recognized as the major divisions of cultural development, the patriarchal being now considered as a subdivision of the barbarian culture. Also, the recent anthropologists have directed their criticisms of fixed succession of stages mainly against the so-called economic stages or food economies rather than against the major divisions of culture as such; but the principle of criticism remains the same. It should likewise be observed that Brisbane recognized the validity of a logical order of cultural succession, that is of a predominant cultural succession, while admitting its variability within certain limits. This is undoubtedly scientifically the more justifiable view, since it conforms more closely to the facts of cultural evolution than the rather extreme position of the "scientific" anthropologists of the invidiously critical school.

Civilization. Brisbane believed our society now to be in the fourth stage of development, that is, in the stage of civilization. He proposes to present, "metaphysically speaking, a map of civilization," by the aid of which "we can see what progress this society has made, and in what manner it is destined to terminate," since at the time he wrote, according to Brisbane, "Politicians and Legislators may be compared to travellers, wandering in some strange and uninhabited country, who have neither compass maps, nor other means by which to direct themselves. Like those travellers, they are wandering in the labyrinth of civilization, without a true social science to guide them; legislating for the requirements of the moment without any high object or policy in view."[37]

It is Brisbane's purpose to give to the legislator as well as to the intelligent citizen some insight into the significance of this civilization in which we live. He wishes also to present a plan by which such men may guide themselves and others in achieving the social reforms or improvements which will constitute the essence of Association. It is true, according to Brisbane, that the "instinct for social progress" and other instincts, if untrammelled, should do much to lead mankind out of the blind alleys of which he speaks. But these beneficent forces in the nature of man can find a free opportunity to operate for human welfare and betterment only under the ideal social organization – that is, Association – which he proposes.

The Four Phases of Civilization. Civilization, like society in general, also has four phases or stages, according to Brisbane. "A society," he says, "like an organic body, has its different ages – has its infancy, growth, maturity, decline, and dissolution."[38] In this statement Brisbane does not show himself to be original. He has merely copied the views in this respect which were current in his time.[39] Even Lord Byron had set forth a poetic version of the same theory in his *Childe Harold's Pilgrimage.*

Each of these social periods or ages "commences with some leading principles which distinguish it from the period which precedes it. . . . It then develops the Institutions, Laws, and Customs which are inherent in the principles upon which it is based, and gives to the efforts of the human mind, and to industry, art, and science a character and direction in keeping with those laws and customs."[40] Thus the Infancy of civilization establishes the principles of monogamy and feudalism and recognizes for the first time the principle of civil rights of the wife. Society is ruled by a federation of the great barons, with the aid of the illusion of chivalry; for each age has its characteristic illusion, which gives it moral sanction. The Age of Growth establishes free towns and cities and cultivates the arts and sciences. It recognizes the principle of the enfranchisement of the serfs and laboring classes. Government is nominally through representative systems, sanctioned by the illusion of liberty and democracy. The Age of Decline now sets in under the regime of the commercial and fiscal spirit and establishment of stock companies. The ruling principle is maritime monopoly – we should say modern imperialism – and the ruling power is anarchical commerce; while the sanctioning illusion is that of financial prosperity. The fourth or final age is that of Decrepitude, which is characterized by agricultural loaning companies indicating the decline of individual farm ownership, associated farms, and a "discipline system of cultivation." The reigning principle is that of commercial and industrial feudality. Society is under the control of contractors, of feudal monopoly and an oligarchy of capital. The sanctioning illusion here is that the people have a true form of association.[41]

Meaning of the Analysis. This analysis is, of course, Fourier's, but Brisbane accepts it as the true general law of civilization.[42] It is meant to show that the so-called democratic or representative system that arises during the period of social growth finally develops into a plutocratic social organization in which the average man returns to a new form of feudalism under the illusion of efficient organization. Such a society as described by Fourier and Brisbane might readily be characterized as either Fascism (regimented capitalism) or Communism (the regimented soviet system) by opponents of those systems. As prophets of future economic–social developments, it can scarcely be said that the exponents of Associationism are wholly unjustified by present developments. Brisbane's analysis of the four ages or phases of civilization is of course illustrated from history,[43] but we lack space in which to present this material.

The Decline of Civilization. However, we may properly give some attention to Brisbane's conclusions regarding the decline of civilization preparatory to the coming of the stage of super-civilization, which he denominates Association. He represents the decline of civilization as a perversion of the good aspects of this civilization. Such perversion is indeed recognized as a very frequent method of producing abnormal adjustments, both personal and social. He says, "Civilization in its decline perverts the germs of good, which characterize its maturity, and after carrying out all the consequences of a false application of those germs, brings forth characters, which enable it to pass to the next higher period. Civilization will end with a *Commercial feudality* or a general monopoly of commerce and industry, and replace individual action and free competition by a false system of Association."[44]

He predicts maritime monopoly, or commercial imperialism, which will bring about wars of nations and social decline. "It has been reserved to England to exercise this monopoly," he says. "The maritime monopoly of England is the greatest scourge which the descending movement of civilization has inflicted upon the world."[45] The other great evidence of decline comes from the manipulation of the new science of chemistry, which "becomes in the hands of industry and commerce the means of giving an unlimited extension to fraud and adulteration."[46]

It is, however, from the growth of capitalistic commerce and industry that the greatest impulse to the decline of civilization is to be expected. Indeed, capitalism (the idea, although not the term, is used by Brisbane) will bring us to the final stage of decline and to the dissolution of civilization.[47]

> As industry is becoming the absorbing occupation of society, political tyranny is giving way to the tyranny of capital. . . . The world is tending to a commercial and financial vassalage, at which it is destined to arrive, when Commerce, – not content with the profits which it makes in the exchange of products, will discover the means of becoming possessor of the fundamental capital itself, that is, of the soil. As soon as a third of the landed property passes into the hands of large capitalists, and the system of stock-companies is applied to agriculture, an entrance into the fourth Phasis of civilization will be effected.

The Establishment of a True Society. The only escape from the evils outlined above is for mankind to take its fate in its own hands and to organize a rational or scientific society. We have already described this projected society in its general outline in Chapter IV of the present work. Consequently we shall confine ourselves in the remaining portion of the present chapter to an account of the method by which the new social order was to be brought about. Brisbane recognized the difficulty of inducing mankind to seek its own development. He says, "the human race, to accomplish their Destiny, have to be urged on by force."[48] It required the driving power of capitalism and its political arm, the actual government, to accomplish this. If left to itself this capitalistic trend would ultimately organize the people into an efficient industrial society, which they might take over from the owners of capital and operate themselves, apparently very much in the manner later predicted by Karl Marx as the ultimate revolutionary culmination of socialism. No form of government, not even a representative democracy, could "arrest the social movement which is tending in this country, as it is in Europe, towards a vast combination in industry, commerce, and finance – a combination which we have designated under the name of *Commercial feudality*."[49] This social movement is stronger than any checking political movement could be and cannot be stopped, except by a counter social movement.

Controlled Social Mutation. It is clear that Brisbane and Fourier did not wish to wait for the slow process of evolution through "commercial feudality" or capitalism to work itself over into Association by means of compulsory evolution. Brisbane denied that social changes are necessarily gradual and that "neither human science nor human power can control them, and that man to organize a more perfect system of society must go through a regular series of social transformations."[50] This is Nature's method when men do not cooperate. But Brisbane believed in social mutations (although he did not employ the term) long before DeVries propounded the mutation theory for plants. It is only necessary to discover the social laws by means of which such social mutations might be brought about. Consequently he would not wait for the slow course of natural events or ordinary social evolution to accomplish the social changes he desired, but would hasten them by means of an apt utilization of human intelligence. He says, "If, as we believe, a true system of society remains to be discovered, which will relieve mankind from their present misery, there can be no need of waiting to be forced to it by necessity and suffering; provided the elements, which are necessary to the organization, have been called into existence, and that the laws upon which it is based can be discovered."[51] Brisbane was sure, moreover, that Fourier had discovered these laws of social mutation and he himself was undertaking to make them familiar to the American public. Thus it was that he sought to transform society rationally or by controlled mutation.

Notes

1. *The Phalanx*, April 20, 1844, 103–106. Reproduced in J. R. Commons, *Documentary History of American Industrial Society* (Cleveland, 1910), Vol. VII, p. 198. The rejected elements of Fourier's system no doubt included his criticisms of certain institutions such as marriage which did not fit well into the American *Weltanschauung*.

2. For example, S. G. Howe, one of the early leaders in the eclectic phase of the Social Science movement, had this to say of Fourier's *Théorie de l'Unité Universelle*, in a letter to Charles Sumner, 1847: "It is the work of a great mind, led astray by a false philosophy; the Herculean effort of a blind giant. . . . Among the morals to be drawn from the book is the important one that the clearest heads and the kindest hearts may be cloudened and hardened by a life spent in an immoral and vicious, though ever so refined a community." Reproduced in *The Journals and Letters of Samuel Gridley Howe* (Edited by Laura E. Richards, 1906–1909), pp. 255–256. Reprinted by permission of the publishers, D. Appleton–Century Co.

3. Sometimes, however, the news made by the Associationists was of an unwelcome sort, as was the case in the following instance, cited by F. L. Mott, in his *History of American Magazines*, Vol. II, 1850–1865 (Cambridge, Harvard University Press, 1938): "The free love doctrines of certain communist groups aroused wide popular antagonism and the police raid on Albert Brisbane's Progressive Union Club in New York, after columns of exposé in the newspapers of that city, produced an excitement which *Leslie's* said was 'only equalled by the fall of Sevastopol and the arrival from Arctic regions of Dr. Kane'" (pp. 207–208). Reprinted by permission of the President and Fellows of Harvard College.

4. Vernon Louis Parrington, *Main Currents in American Thought*, II. *The Romantic Revolution in America, 1800–1860* (1927), p. 319.

5. *Ibid.*, pp. vi–vii.

6. *Ibid.*, p. 322.

7. L. L. Bernard, "Scientific Method and Social Progress," *Amer. Jour. Sociol.*, XXXI: 1–18 (July, 1925).

8. L. L. Bernard, "Invention and Social Progress," *Amer. Jour. Sociol.*, XXIX: 1–33 (July, 1923).

9. *The Phalanx*, April 20, 1844. Reproduced in Commons, *op. cit.*, Vol. VII, p. 189.

10. *The Phalanx*, April 1, 1844, p. 98. Reproduced in Commons, *op. cit.*, Vol. VII, p. 246.

11. T. E. Cliffe Leslie, "Political Economy in America," *Fortnightly Review*, XXXIV: 488ff. (Oct., 1880).

12. See Albert Brisbane, *A Concise Exposition of the Doctrine of Association* (New York, 7th Ed., 1844), p. 2; also the writings of the Unitarian theologians of similar date, especially William Ellery Channing, William H. Channing, Ralph Waldo Emerson, Amos Bronson Alcott, Theodore Parker, and Octavius Brooks Frothingham.

13. The old discipline of moral philosophy had had a similar pattern. See, e. g., Gladys Bryson, "The Emergence of the Social Sciences from Moral Philosophy," *Internatl. Jour. Ethics*, XLII: 306 (Apr., 1932).

14. The biographical data on Brisbane are based on the article by W. Randall Waterman in the *Dictionary of American Biography*, III: 52–55, and *Albert Brisbane, A Mental Biography*, by Redelia Brisbane (Arena Pub. Co., Boston, 1893).

15. For an excellent brief analysis of Fourier's theories see Robert Flint, *The Philosophy of History in France and Germany* (1874), pp. 168–170. See also *The Encyclopaedia of the Social Sciences* VI: 402–404.

16. In the *New York Daily Tribune* for July 9, 1842, for example, there appeared a notice to the effect "that the friends of Associationism in the City have founded a Society bearing the above name [Fourier Association of New York], the object of which is to aid the propagation of the principles and doctrines of Association. The Society has a large Lecture Hall in the most central part of the City, capable of containing five or six hundred persons, where Lectures are delivered once or twice a week." The notice further suggests that "Where there are several persons in a place who believe in Association, we would advise them to form a Society in their town or city, and connect it with the Society here; the Societies can then communicate with each other, and carry out measures of general interest with much more promptness and energy than if no regular organizations of the kind existed. If a chain of Societies could be established in some of the towns and cities throughout the country, all connecting closely with the head Society at New York, it would be a powerful means of propagating the Cause." This notice is reproduced in John R. Commons (ed.), *Documentary History of American Industrial Society, VII: Labor Movement, 1840–1860* (1910), p. 185.

17. *The Phalanx*, in February, 1844, for example, describes such a Fourier Club in Southport, Wisconsin, which met once a week for lectures and discussions of the principles of Social Science. *Loc. cit.*, p. 70. Reproduced in Commons, *op. cit.*, pp. 186–187. Similar groups were organized in Rochester, Buffalo, Pittsburgh, and Cincinnati (*The Phalanx*, No. 18).

18. Albert Brisbane, *General Introduction to Social Science* (1876), p. iii.

19. Other journals consecrated to the propagation of Fourier's theories were *The Social Reformer*, published in Boston by John Allen and Joseph A. Whitmarsh, whose object "will be the exposition of the Science of Unity, and the laws of attractive organized industry discovered by Charles Fourier," and William H. Channing's *The Present* (1843–1844), whose aim was "to aid all movements which seem fitted to produce union and growth in religion, science and society . . . . It will seek to reconcile faith and free inquiry, law and liberty, order and progress: to harmonize sectarian and party differences by statements of universal principles, and to animate hopeful efforts on all sides to advance the reign of Heaven on earth." *The Present* was merged with *The Phalanx* in 1844.

20. The details of this process of conversion are presented in the form of original documents by John Humphrey Noyes in his *History of American Socialisms* (1870), Chapter XXXIX.

21. *General Introduction to Social Science* (1876), p. iv.

22. John Humphrey Noyes, *op. cit.*, pp. 529–530.

23. Channing was very much of an orator. "His zeal and eloquence . . . for a short time, well entitled him to the honors of the chief Apostle of Fourierism. In fact he succeeded to the post of Brisbane" (Noyes, *op. cit.*, p. 530).

24. *Op. cit.*, p. 350.

25. *Ibid.*

26. Noyes, in the work cited, pp. 212 ff., gives a list of contributors to *The Phalanx*. Among the names of men who wrote for it are those of Greeley, W. H. Channing, Rev. B. F. Barrett, Fred Grain, Edward Giles, Solymon Brown, P. Maroncelli, E. P. Grant, H. H. Van Amringe, D. H. Barlow, Lydia Maria Child, Mrs. M. S. Gove, and Stephen Pearl Andrews.

27. The other duties of this Executive Committee were "2nd. To receive, record, and diffuse information in regard to existing Associations and others which may be organized within the year. 3rd. To communicate all possible intelligence to those who in any part of the country may wish to unite practically with any Associations. 4th. To arrange a system of concerted action with Associations throughout the United States, for the thorough and systematic diffusion of Social Science, and a knowledge of the practical details of Association . . . ." (*The Phalanx*, Apr. 20, 1844. Reproduced in Commons, *op. cit.*, p. 201).

28. "These manifestations of religious feeling," says Noyes, in the work cited above, "were mainly due to the presence of the Massachusetts men, and especially to the zeal of William H. Channing" (*Op. cit.*, p. 228).

29. *The Phalanx*, No. 21.

30. *Ibid.*

31. Announcement in *The Phalanx*, No. 22.

32. Albert Brisbane, *Social Destiny of Man* (1840), p. 269.

33. *Ibid.*, pp. 270–278

34. Herbert Spencer, *Principles of Sociology: Political Institutions* (1882), pp 659–660.

35. *Social Destiny of Man*, p. 283.

36. See R. H. Lowie, *Primitive Society* (1920), pp. 430 ff., for a criticism of this point of view.

37. *Social Destiny of Man*, p. 286.

38. *Ibid.*, p. 283.

39. See F. W. Coker, *Organismic Theories of the State* (New York, 1910) for a review of such theories.

40. *Social Destiny of Man*, p. 283.

41. *Ibid.*, p. 284

42. *Ibid.*, p. 285.

43. *Ibid.*, pp. 285–330.

44. *Ibid.*, p. 303.

45. *Ibid.*, p. 304.

46. *Ibid.*, p. 305.

47. *Ibid.*, p. 308.

48. *Ibid.*, p. 334.

49. *Ibid.*, p. 331.
50. *Ibid.*,
51. *Ibid.*, pp. 332.

26

The Social Construction of Style: Thorstein Veblen's *The Theory of the Leisure Class* as Contested Text

Gary Alan Fine

> Veblen, a grayfaced shambling man lolling resentful at his desk with his cheek on his hand, in a low sarcastic mumble of intricate phrases subtly paying out the logical inescapable rope of matter-of-fact for a society to hang itself by, dissecting out the century with a scalpel so keen, so comical, so exact that the professors and students nineteenths of the time didn't know it was there, and the magnates and the respected windbags and the applauded loudspeakers never knew it was there. – John Dos Passos, "The Bitter Drink" *The Big Money* (1946, pp. 106–107)

Writing is not only the conduit through which meaning is shared, but it is the meaning (Marcus and Clifford 1986; Becker 1986). As Stanley Fish argues in his *Is There a Text in This Class?*, we must be concerned with the *how* of a text and not only the *what*: the doing of texts. Narratives mean how they are told. Academics rely on fact, logic, metaphor, and story. In this I follow the argument of Bryan Green (1988, p. vii; Overington 1981) who argues that "sociological theory is a form of literary activity which belongs to a ubiquitous social practice: the simultaneous representation and construction of social life in determinate ways of word use." Texts are in Hayden White's (1987, p. 213) terms a form of "meaning production," and as such provide some measure of typicality for understanding the world in which they were both inscribed and read. As scholars we are engaged in "text work," attempting to depict the world in ways that communicate to a community of readers (Van Maanen 1988). Increasingly we experiment with the forms of our discourse, producing documents that would have been roundly scorned a few years ago (Pfohl 1992; Schneider 1991; Richardson and Lockridge 1991), an earlier age in which sociologists seemed to *avoid* style (Mills 1953, p. vii).

Source: *Sociological Quarterly*, 1994, vol. 35, no. 3, pp. 457–472.

Some aesthetic romantics eschew normal science discourse, believing that artistic genres ennoble the social scientist: preferring the book of Revelation to Deuteronomy. Robert Bierstedt (1960, p. 4) proposes that sociology "owns a rightful place in the domain of humane letters and belongs, with literature, history, and philosophy, among the arts that liberate the human mind." Our good neighbor, economist Donald McCloskey (1990, p. 162) addresses his colleagues:

> If even economics can be shown to be fictional and poetical and historical its story will become better. Its experts will stop terrorizing the neighborhood and peddling snake oil. Technically speaking the economist's story will become, as it should, a useful comedy – comprising words of wit, amused tolerance for human folly, stock characters colliding at last in the third act, and, most characteristic of the genre, a universe in equilibrium and a happy ending.

Reading McCloskey, one hears Garrison Keillor and his ruddy, above average Lake Wobegon kin cheering the upbeat denouement. But even if one prefers tragedy or satire, McCloskey's claim of a variety of discourse is compelling.

This stance presumes that style is easily knowable – it's *there* after all. Yet, if all social reality is a social construction, then style is as well. In line with much contemporary literary theory, I recognize that a text is not a finished object, but is continually reconstructed in reading performances (Green 1988, p. 60). The comforting belief that we can easily assess what a style is, and how it is to be judged, is questionable. Readers disagree about texts, and such dissensus does not suggest misreading, but rather is part of the essential and necessary deconstruction of texts (Clough 1992; Atkinson 1992). A simple claim that we need to write *better* is inadequate if one recognizes the diversity of interpretation. Avoiding jargon, verbosity, or obscurity is helpful, but eschewing these sins, does not mean that textual practices are translucent (Green 1988, p. 15). The underlying problem in the sociology of knowledge is to describe how we *know* what a writer *really* means. How do we place a writer in light of the text, and beyond that how do we determine whether a work is "well-written," itself a contested concept. The content of the work, the genre in which the text is placed, the reputation and identity of the author, and conventions of interpretation permit the establishment of consensus, but the definition of style is precarious, subject to dispute.

In this essay, I examine the interpretation of style, using a case study: the writings of the sociologist/economist Thorstein Veblen, emphasizing his "classic" *The Theory of the Leisure Class: An Economic Study of the Evolution of Institutions* (TLC).[1] Veblen's writing itself is a source of dispute, touched on by virtually every critic. My goal is not to treat Veblen's life or theory in detail, but rather I explore how his writings – as stylistic embodiments and discursive practices – have been received by generations of readers.

Ironic Detachment

Sociology, the child of dissenting, Social Gospel ministers, is not, even at its most bracing, a hopeful discipline. We are outsiders. Sociologists proclaim (Mills 1959) that analytic detachment is the *sine qua non* of our collective enterprise. The sociologist is, or should be, the community's marginal man.[2] With one foot inside and one outside the world described, cutting alienation and member's knowledge can meld into a report: if not cynical, contentious, and facetious, at least rigorously suspicious, questioning the taken-for-granted.[3]

In practice, the idea of a lean and hungry sociology is shunted aside by practitioners, intellectually weighty and lazy, living off comfortable social institutions: universities, foundations, granting agencies. A debunking stance, admired and evinced by sociological giants as C. Wright Mills, Erving Goffman, Harold Garfinkel, George Homans, Joseph Gusfield, and Robert Merton, should be our domain.

Irony is the footman/handmaiden of detachment. The sociological imagination is an ironic imagination (Machalek 1979). Irony is parcel of the outsider's dialectic between the incongruous *is* and *ought to be* that detached observation emphasizes (Brown 1983, 1987). By creating alternative worlds as possibilities (Tam 1984) and implying that things are not as they should be (Schneider 1975a), we create the world from our ironic perspective. Writings may induce change in our readers who, confronting the text, see the world through a new lens (Schneider 1975b). The ironic stance withholds consensus (Burns 1953), until one's audience adapts. Beyond irony lies satire, with a blurred boundary[4] – a trope with a demanding moral basis, exposing sins by extending them and mocking them by taking them too seriously, arguing for ought claims held up, not held to.

Detachment, irony, and satire by virtue of their subversive indirection represent archetypal cases in which stylistic devices are potentially (and, sometimes, deliberately) ambiguous. These devices conjure a *mysterious* author, making humor a dangerous and rare technique in scholarly writing. In humorous and metaphorical tropes the author and the authorial persona are *not* identical, in contrast to much social scientific writing where the translucent writer stands as the honest broker; as a consequence, extracting meanings from these texts is especially problematic.

I argue that certain topics are especially likely to produce problematic, detached, ironic, satiric texts because of the ambivalent relationship of writer (and, often, the reader as well) to the theme. These pesky topics force the social scientist to gaze upward in the social structure, confronting the limits of his or her status claim. For instance, the role of elites in bourgeois, capitalist society, is both too close to and too distant from the author and audience, making ambiguous writings and readings particularly likely. One rarely finds ironic or satiric treatments of status inferiors; we use other stylistic tropes – for example, pathos or direct injustice claims – and do not use sly wit.

Thorstein Veblen: Academic Manqué

Thorstein Veblen has settled into the sloganized memory of sociologists, little used in practice (Ryan 1982). His is a known name, an *éminence grise*, not a read presence. Those who refer to the leisure class, conspicuous consumption, or invidious distinctions are legion, greater than those who have actually read *The Theory of the Leisure Class*. John Dewey predicted that Veblen's terminology would outlive him, forever altering academic discourse (Dorfman 1934, pp. 196–197). His defenders are many and enthusiastic. Bernard Rosenberg (1963, p. 3), for instance, described Veblen as "the greatest social scientist America has produced." C. Wright Mills (1953, p. vi) calls Veblen "the best critic of America that America has produced." Yet, David Riesman (1953, p. xi) found him more "interesting than attractive, more pungent than wise." The dispute about Veblen's overall reputation was neatly summarized by John Maurice Clark (1929 in Dorfman 1934, p. 595) in his obituary in the *American Economic Review*:

> He is rated among the great economists of history, or as no economist at all; as a great original pioneer or as a critic and satirist without constructive talent or achievement.

Veblen was born July 30, 1857 on a small Wisconsin farm, a child of the middle border. His parents were industrious, and eventually prosperous, Norwegian immigrants; Thorstein was the sixth of twelve children.[5] When eight his family moved to southern Minnesota, and, in 1880 he graduated from Carleton College. After a term at Johns Hopkins, studying with Charles S. Peirce, Veblen settled at Yale, receiving a Ph.D. in philosophy for a dissertation on Kant's *Critique of Judgement*. After seven years at his family's homestead, he appeared at Cornell to study with the noted economist J. Laurence Laughlin. When Laughlin joined the newly opened, Rockefeller-financed, University of Chicago, he brought his protégé. Veblen joined the faculty, and remained on staff until 1906, when, because of his extra-marital relations and indifferent teaching, he was asked to resign. Mills (1953, p. viii) suggests, admiringly, Veblen was never a "decent man."[6] Moving to Stanford, Veblen was asked to resign three years later for similar reasons. Eventually he found a position at the University of Missouri, and later worked in the U.S. Food Administration, served for a year as an editor of the radical magazine, *The Dial*, and taught at the New School of Social Research from its establishment in 1919 until the mid 1920s. By that time Veblen had become a center of much left/liberal debate – the *Nation/New Republic* axis. Veblen died on August 3, 1929 at his rundown shack in the northern California woods. During his life Veblen published nine books – notably *The Theory of Business Enterprise* (1904), *An Inquiry into the Nature of Peace and the Terms of its Perpetuation* (1917), and *The Higher Learning in America: A Memorandum on the Conduct of Universities by Business Men* (1918), two collections of essays, and a translation of the Icelandic *Laxdaela Saga* (1925).

The social construction of Veblen's biography depicts him as a marginal man through his background, preferences, and his career (Rosenberg 1955; Kazin 1942). He combined shy diffidence with a bitter dyspepsia, a talent for alienating potential supporters with a coterie of devotees, and, according to some (e.g., Riesman 1953), contradictory desires to be accepted and rejected. Veblen was likened to a "Martian professor" (Mumford 1931; Johnson 1941), the outsider looking in.

Disciplinary politics contributed to the creation of Veblen's reputation. Veblen taught economics, edited the *Journal of Political Economy*, is a founder of institutional economics, and was proposed for the presidency of the American Economic Association. His ties to economics appear secure. Yet, some claim that his links to sociology, a discipline with which he had no formal affiliation, were equally real. Several critics, including liberal economist John Kenneth Galbraith, social critic Lewis Mumford (1931), and leftist British sociologist John Hobson (1929) felt that Veblen was a better sociologist than economist. TLC was based on a trio of articles published in the *American Journal of Sociology* in 1898. One bitter contemporary critic of TLC (D. Wells 1899) felt that the work brought sociology into "disrepute," no easy task then as now.

Tracing influences on Veblen's thought is complex; he is a synthetic thinker: the sources of Veblen's thought include German idealism (Kant), British empiricism (Hume), American pragmatism (Peirce, Dewey), European socialism (Marx), evolution (Spencer, Sumner), American socialism (Bellamy), British socialism (Hobson), French utopian socialism (Fourier, St. Simon), Scottish political economy (Rae), Norwegian Lutheranism, Psychology (Loeb, James), and Anthropology (Boas, Tylor) (Edgell and Tilman 1989). Some (Ryan 1982; Diggins 1978, p. vii) believe that Veblen was a proto-feminist; others (Fontana, Tilman, and Roe 1992; Lewis and Smith 1980; Rucker 1969) trace a connection to pragmatism and the Chicago school. This lengthy list suggests, first, many contrary readings of Veblen, and, second, that his thought is not narrowly derivative, but is fundamentally original.

Writing *The Theory of the Leisure Class*

The Theory of the Leisure Class is an autochthonous and subversive contribution: "a stick of dynamite wrapped up ... to look like a stick of candy" (Mumford 1935). Today its originality may be partially overlooked because our post-Goffman age has taken many of Veblen's claims for granted.[7] TLC is now vaguely enshrined as a classic, but contemporaries considered it controversial. Now, as with many "canonized" texts, those who dispute the label keep their thoughts private. Yet, according to Veblen interpreter, Rick Tilman (personal communication 1993), Veblen is "one of America's most difficult-to-interpret writers," and the subject of hearty debate among his readers.

My brief is not to present what Veblen "really" meant, perhaps both an impossible and inappropriate task, yet neither do I hew to relativistic interpretative anarchy. Not all cases are equally easy to make (Fine and Kleinman 1986), and there are themes in TLC on which fair consensus exists. Style is never wholly divorced from content. Although my focus is on Veblen's style, it is useful to remind readers of Veblen's main arguments.

Veblen asserted that the mark of the elite was its choice to use resources without regard to productivity. He damned business leaders, while ennobling the productive worker, enshrining technology and workmanship as core virtues (Bell 1963; Schwartz 1990). Like so many culture critics, Veblen had high standards that society could never meet. In its exploration of status politics as the motivator of human development, TLC stands as the first important American sociological treatise: the only work of Nineteenth Century American sociology still widely referenced.[8] By emphasizing the role of "wasteful" public dress, leisure activities, religion, servants, and ornamental women, Veblen notes that status is linked to non-productive activity. By drawing on anthropological sources, he argues, in a mode now ignored or dismissed by most sociologists, that the development of conspicuous consumption is evolutionary. Veblen's complaint is, in some measure, with the nature of humankind, which often seems to strive not for creature comforts, but, more significantly, for the symbolization of creature comforts, whether or not those artifacts and conveniences actually bring ease. Veblen wishes us to elevate function over form, and it is the prominence of form in so many social arenas that provokes Veblen's ire. Aesthetic concern is for Veblen a *prima facie* indication of injustice. Consider, for instance, the cathedral, for some the zenith of the human aesthetic (Veblen 1934, p. 120:

> ... in all communities, especially in neighborhoods where the standard of pecuniary decency for dwellings is not high, the local sanctuary is more ornate, more conspicuously wasteful in its architecture and decoration, than the dwelling houses of the congregation.

Parks are similarly seen as less worthy than the functional pasture (associated with thrift and usefulness) and female dress less worthy than male dress, for it is further removed from the demands of labor. Likewise, Veblen (1934, pp. 126–128) is expansive on the subject of spoons:

> A hand-wrought silver spoon, of a commercial value of some ten to twenty dollars, is not ordinarily more serviceable . . . than a machine-made spoon of the same material. It may not even be more serviceable than a machine-made spoon of some "base" metal, such as aluminum, the value of which may be no more than ten to twenty cents. The former of the two utensils is, in fact, commonly a less effective contrivance for its ostensible purpose than the latter . . . . The superior gratification derived from the use and contemplation of the costly and supposedly beautiful products is, commonly, in great measure a gratification of our sense of costliness masquerading under the name of beauty.

That cathedrals, parks, gowns, or spoons might have an aesthetic standing that does not deserve scorn is dismissed by Veblen as a function of status politics.

Despite Veblen's scorn for "style," from its publication, style proved crucial to the volume's reception. When Veblen sent his completed manuscript to Macmillan, his eventual publisher, they responded that the major problem was stylistic (Dorfman 1973, p. 9), and Veblen rewrote the manuscript several times, eventually agreeing to a guarantee because of the publisher's uncertainty over sales (Dorfman 1934, p. 174). After being sent a page proof, Veblen requested that Macmillan eliminate "the ornamental rule under the heading, and [I] suggest that everything of an ostensibly decorative character be omitted." (Dorfman 1973, p. 13). While this request was linked to Veblen's financial arrangements (he would have reimbursed Macmillan if sales did not reach a set level), this stylistic choice was congruent with the volume's themes.

The reviews of TLC were decidedly mixed, with some such as William Dean Howells and Lester Frank Ward (the latter in the *American Journal of Sociology*) writing glowing notices, while other reviewers were bitter. Veblen wrote sarcastically to his brother:

> Reviews of the *Leisure Class* are coming in, for the most part quite severe. Opinion seems to be divided as to whether I am a knave or a fool, though there are some who make out that the book is a work of genius – I don't know just how. (Quoted in Dorfman 1973, p. 18)

Whatever the evaluation, few avoided discussing Veblen's distinctive style, rare for a social scientific work. Selecting passages to exemplify the style is difficult, because, as so often the case, passages are written differently, and one might choose different examples, depending on one's emphasis.

In that this essay is primarily about the *interpretation* of Veblen's style, rather than a description of it, I avoid extensive quotations, distracting from the argument of how the work is taken, rather than given. Still, it is desirable to expose the reader to Veblen's "style." But which passage? Each choice is a selection by an author with a argument. Each choice reflects some of Veblen's rhetorical techniques, eclipsing others. At various points in my essay I will present quotations to demonstrate either the wit or cumbrous qualities of the discourse. Here I provide a fairly lengthy selection, from Veblen's final chapter of TLC, which, to me, captures some of the literary, ironic, satiric, inarticulate, and archaic features of Veblen's prose. In this passage, Veblen (1934, pp. 398–400) writes about academic and professional discourse using archaic diction for purposes of displaying status:

> [T]he archaic idiom of the English language is spoken of as "classic" English. Its use is imperative in all speaking and writing upon serious topics, and a facile use of it lends dignity to even the most commonplace

and trivial string of talk.... Elegant diction, whether in writing or speaking, is an effective means of reputability. It is of moment to know with some precision what is the degree of archaism conventionally required in speaking on any given topic.... A discriminate avoidance of neologisms is honorific, not only because it argues that time has been wasted in acquiring the obsolescent habit of speech, but also as showing that the speaker has from infancy habitually associated with persons who have been familiar with the obsolescent idiom. It thereby goes to show his leisure class antecedents.... As felicitous an instance of futile classicism as can well be found, outside of the Far East, in the conventional spelling of the English language. A breach of the proprieties in spelling is extremely annoying and will discredit any writer in the eyes of all persons who are possessed of a developed sense of the true and beautiful. English orthography satisfies all the requirements of the canons of reputability under the law of conspicuous waste. It is archaic, cumbrous, and ineffective; its acquisition consumes much time and effort; failure to acquire it is easy of detection. Therefore it is the first and readiest test of reputability in learning, and conformity to its ritual is indispensable to a blameless scholastic life.... It is contended, in substance, that a punctilious use of ancient and accredited locutions will serve to convey thought more adequately and more precisely than would the straightforward use of the latest form of spoken English; whereas it is notorious that the ideas of to-day are effectively expressed in the slang of to-day.... The advantage of the accredited locutions lies in their respectability; they are reputable because they are cumbrous and out of date, and therefore argue waste of time and exemption from the use and the need of direct and forcible speech.

Reading this passage, and others similar, provokes one to wonder whether Veblen is serious? Is there an ironic stance for one who chooses to write as he condemns? This is Veblen's style, a style that is found, largely, in his other works, and is not a cloak that he dons only in a temporary masquerade. Is this great literature or a royal mess? Who is to know?

Parsing *The Theory of the Leisure Class*

The Theory of the Leisure Class *as Literature*

Throughout the past century, a stream of admirers contend that TLC is a major literary work. When Sinclair Lewis (1920) wishes to demonstrate the alienation of Carol Kennicott from the stolid Minnesotans of Gopher Prairie in *Main Street* he has her read Veblen; Veblen, for his part, refers to Lewis's stultifying Gopher Prairie. Lewis is "dramatized Veblen" (Johnson 1941, p. 122). Some critics believe that "almost any passage of Veblen ... is instantly recognizable" (Riesman 1953, p. 44) and that Veblen was a conscious stylist (Conroy 1968, p. 608).

William Dean Howells (1899) discovered in Veblen the material for novels, and Veblen has been likened to both the "novelists of manners" (Diggins 1978, p. xi) and the *fin de siècle* naturalist writers, including Theodore Dreiser, Jack London, and Frank Norris (Richard Hofstadter, cited in Riesman 1953, p. 7). Veblen's ironical realism led Mills (1953, p. xiii) to contend that Veblen "has made Alices of us all, and dropped us through the looking glass into the fantastic world of social reality." This attitude is bolstered by the use of heroes (faculty members, workers, engineers) and villains (modern businessmen, captains of industry, university presidents and trustees), adding a moral overlay (Riesman 1953, p. 80).

The impression that Veblen was more artist than scientist (Young 1925) is given heft by Veblen's playfulness (Wesley Mitchell, cited in Galbraith 1973, p. v), coupled with his refusal to cite sources or present systematic data. His statements rest on the authority of the man of genius, not the man of research. Veblen put his method thus:

> Partly for reasons of convenience, and partly because there is less chance of misapprehending the sense of phenomena that are familiar to all men, the data employed to illustrate or enforce the argument have by preference been drawn from everyday life, by direct observation or through common notoriety, rather than from more recondite sources at a farther remove. It is hoped that no one will find his sense of literary or scientific fitness offended by this recourse to homely facts, or by what may at times appear to be a callous freedom in handling vulgar phenomena whose intimate place in men's life has sometimes shielded them from the impact of economic discussion (Veblen 1934, p. viii).[9]

It is not from the ordering of phrases alone, but from method – or its absence – that some allege TLC is literature.

The Theory of the Leisure Class as Academic Treatise

While some emphasize the literary qualities of Veblen's writing, others emphasize his dispassionate, academic tone. Whether or not one enjoys Veblen's writing, a word count demonstrates that Veblen wrote lengthy sentences: 39 words on average in TLC (Conroy 1968, p. 609).

Several reviewers felt Veblen was clear, composing readable prose (Daniels 1905). Lester Frank Ward wrote of Veblen in the AJS: "The language is plain and unmistakable, as it should be, but the style is the farthest removed possible from either advocacy or vituperation, and the language, to use the author's own words, is 'morally colorless.'" (Ward 1900 in Dorfman 1973, p. 629). David Riesman (1953, p. xiii) also concluded that "there is not a line of Veblen which cannot be understood by a moderately well-read person." Not all agree.

Underlying this academic style is the belief that Veblen was attempting to be dispassionate, uninvolved, detached, merely parsing the facts, leading William Dean Howells to speak of Veblen's "cold, scientific analysis" (Howells 1899 in Dorfman 1973, p. 630). John Kenneth Galbraith (1973, p. xvi, xviii) explains: "He concedes the rich and the well-to-do nothing; and he would not dream of suggesting that his personal attitudes or passion are in any way involved. The rich are merely anthropological specimens whose behavior the possession of money and property has made more interesting and more visibly ridiculous.... Since he does it in the name of science and with the weapons of science – and since no overt trace of animus or anger is allowed to appear – he does it with near perfect safety."

Yet, recognizing that the book is overtly in the *style* of an academic treatise, doesn't mean that it will necessarily be read as such. For some Veblen's academic indifference (Hazlitt 1929, p. 9) or "deliberate stodginess" (Johnson 1941, p. 122) makes the humor and bite of the work so compelling, for others it is a mark of a turgid mind.

The Theory of the Leisure Class as Comic Masterpiece

Humor is a vast domain: puns, wit, mimicry, parody, irony, satire. Some categories are easier to distinguish than others. TLC carries the weight of irony and satire, leading Mills (1953, p. vi) to puff that Veblen is "the only comic writer among modern social scientists" and Conroy (1968, p. 607) to snort "only a person utterly lacking a sense of humor could possibly miss the ironical outlook which pervades every page." For some critics irony and satire seem undefined, overlapping, and ambiguous; others are more likely to distinguish them, claiming that Veblen was either a satirist or an ironist. In either event, humor refers to discursive practices that depend upon a fundamental incongruity between what is and what ought. By framing the unexpected in incongruous ways, with a moral implication (stronger in the satiric than in the ironic), one demands change to avoid hypocrisy. Satiric and ironic writings have power in changing behavior or definitions of behavior (Schneider 1975b; Machalek 1979).

For many readers, particularly those of a liberal or radical slant, Veblen's account of the upper "leisure" class seems designed to ridicule these worthies, valuing a counterexample, ennobling workers. They believed Veblen should be read on two levels – denotative and connotative. His presumed bitter intent was reminiscent of Shaw (Anonymous 1929), Twain (Riesman 1953), or Swift (*North American Review* 1919 in Dorfman 1973, p. 661). For these readers TLC was brilliant satire (Dorfman 1934, p. 196; Johnson 1941), leading some to describe Veblen as the "Bard of Savagery" (Miller 1954, p. xlix):

In part [Veblen] is the remote scholar, the skeptical scientist subjecting everything to the test of his laboratory apparatus and the tribunal of reason. In part he is a growling and surly old Norwegian uncle whose smelly pipe and acid home-truths we wonder at ourselves for putting up with (Johnson 1941, p. 121).

Some critics, recognizing the satire, felt Veblen went to excess (Hazlitt 1929, p. 9); Galbraith (1973, p. vi), a sympathetic commentator, suggested that when "faced with a choice between accuracy and a formulation that he felt would fill his audience with outrage, [Veblen] rarely hesitated. He opted for the outrage." Kenneth Burke (1950, p. 129), capturing the marriage of the academic and satiric, described Veblen's style as "deadpan satire."

Where some speak of satire, others, emphasizing the incongruous, call Veblen's style ironic (Broyard 1973), leading to continued relevance. Riesman (1953, p. 78) writes: "His cavalier quality, the irony which permits him at once to embrace and to fend off life, these make him 'modern.'" His irony cloaks him in a "sociological imagination" (Walton 1979).

These critics point to techniques that depict society in a fractured manner. Veblen combined items in odd, incongruous, and revealing lists, a technique that is known as "the Swiftian miscellaneous catalogue" (Conroy 1968, pp. 612–613; Toulouse 1985, pp. 263–264). For instance, Veblen (1934, p. 73) writes of conspicuous consumption:

> The quasi-peaceable gentleman of leisure, then, not only consumes of the staff of life beyond the minimum required for subsistence and physical efficiency, but his consumption also undergoes a specialisation as regards the quality of the goods consumed. He consumes freely and of the best, in food, drink, narcotics, shelter, services, ornaments, apparel, weapons and accoutrements, amusements, amulets, and idols or divinities.

Linking narcotics, weapons, and divinities among the "quasi-peaceable" is the technique of the satirist. In addition, Veblen deliberately uses words in perverse ways (as Goffman attempted). He relies on highly pejorative and loaded words, but claims that he disregards their moral moorings. Veblen (p. 26) speaks of the accumulation of wealth as an "invidious distinction," then notes innocently:

> In making use of the term "invidious," it may perhaps be unnecessary to remark, there is no intention to extol or depreciate, or to commend or deplore any of the phenomena which the word is used to characterize. (p. 34)

The reader cannot be moved quite so easily.

Further, Veblen suggests the similarity of delinquents and elites (p. 238) and refers to "inmates" of colleges (cited in Conroy 1968, p. 611), much as Goffman for his part refers to the "campus" of a mental hospital (Goffman 1961; see Fine and Martin 1990). Or Veblen writes gently that "gentle blood is blood which has been ennobled by protracted contact with accumulated wealth or unbroken prerogative" (Johnson 1941, p. 123).

While a consensus exists that TLC is a humorous text, agreement is not complete (Conroy 1968, p. 606): even the presence of wit is a social construction. Russell, for example, could not see the irony (Dorfman 1934, p. 134), and Dorfman, noting the similar goals of Veblen and Herbert Spencer, of whom no one would claim is a satirist, is uncertain of Veblen's intent. Riesman (1953, p. 46), impressed by the irony, the drama, and the dash, adds "we don't know where he stands and hence how literally to take him." The author has become shrouded in mystery – until we put him in his place (White 1987). Veblen himself seemed to wish to deflect claims of his satire: "He was disappointed at the popular view of it as a satire upon the aristocratic classes, although he admitted . . . that the book was not altogether free from satire" (Dorfman 1934, p. 197).

The Theory of the Leisure Class as Meretricious Rot

> In an increasing proportion as time goes on, the anthropomorphic cult, with its code of devout observances, suffers a progressive disintegration through the stress of economic exigencies and the decay of the system of status. As this disintegration proceeds, there come to be associated and blended with the devout attitude certain other motives and impulses that are not always of an anthropomorphic origin, nor traceable to the habit of personal subservience. Not all of these subsidiary impulses that blend with the habit of devoutness in the later devotional life are altogether congruous with the devout attitude or with the anthropomorphic apprehension of the sequence of phenomena. Their origin being not the same, their action upon the scheme of devout life is also not in the same direction. In many ways they traverse the underlying norm of subservience or vicarious life to which the code of devout observances and the ecclesiastical and sacerdotal institutions are to be traced as their substantial basis. Through the presence of these alien motives the social and industrial regime of status gradually disintegrates and the canon of personal subservience loses the support derived from an unbroken tradition. Extraneous habits and proclivities encroach upon the field of action occupied by this canon, and it presently comes about that the ecclesiastical and sacerdotal structures are partially converted to other uses, in some measure alien to the purposes of the scheme of devout life as it stood in the days of the most vigorous and characteristic development of the priesthood. (TLC, pp. 332–33)

After the paeans, it is startling to realize that many not only felt Veblen was wrong, but was an egregiously poor writer (Matthews 1919). One biographer speaks of Veblen's "opaque, convoluted style, marked by polysyllabic neologisms and esoteric terminology" (Diggins 1978, p. 37). Another wonders: "Is it too much to hope that some of his followers will translate this book [*The Place of Science in Modern Cilvilization*] into English readable to economic laymen?" (Anon. 1920, cited in Simich and Tilman 1985, p. 15). Contrary to claims that any literate person could understand Veblen, others claim that few could understand him. The best-known criticism of Veblen was penned by that poisoned master, H. L. Mencken (1919, pp. 59, 64, 69, 70):

> The more I read [Veblen's] columns, in fact, the less I could make of them, and so in the end, growing impatient and impolite, I denounced this Prof. Veblen as a geyser of pishposh . . . . the whole canon of the singularly laborious and muggy, the incomparably tangled and unintelligible works of Prof. Dr. Thorstein Veblen . . . . a cent's worth of information wrapped in a bale of polysyllables. It is as if the practice of that incredibly obscure and malodorous style were a relentless disease, a sort of progressive intellectual diabetes, a leprosy of the horse sense. Words are flung upon words until all recollection that there must be a meaning in them, a ground and excuse for them, is lost. One wanders in a labyrinth of nouns, adjectives, verbs, pronouns, adverbs, prepositions, conjunctions and participles, most of them swollen and nearly all of them unable to work. It is difficult to imagine worse English, within the limits of intelligible grammar. It is clumsy, affected, opaque, bombastic, windy, empty . . . . Worse, there is nothing at the bottom of all this strident wind-music – the ideas it is designed to set forth are, in the overwhelming main, poor ideas, and often they are ideas that are almost idiotic.

Mencken is enjoying himself at Veblen's expense,[10] but, as noted above, Veblen does write long and complex sentences – "forbidding writing" (Chase 1934, p. xii) that some deride as "futile, archaic, and cumbrous" (D. Wells 1899, p. 218).

Alfred Kazin (1942, p. 180–81), praising Veblen's wit and facility as a phrase maker, doubts his ability as a writer and his interest in diction and rhythm:

> he was . . . not a good sentence maker. The peculiar quality of his prose lies . . . in the use he made of a naturally cumbersome and (despite its polysyllabic sophistication) primitive medium . . . . Veblen who mumbled in the classroom those "long spiral sentences, reiterative like the eddas," as John Dos Passos called them, also mumbled in his books.

The criticism of Veblen's style is not limited to his early writing; in a review of his harsh attack on university administrators, *The Higher Learning in*

America, regarded by some as superb satire, Professor Brander Matthews (cited in Galbraith 1973, p. xxiv; Dorfman 1934, p. 409) of the English Department at Columbia University assayed in the *New York Times*:

> His vocabulary is limited and he indulges in a fatiguing repetition of a dozen or a score of adjectives. His grammar is woefully defective.... So frequent and so flagrant are Mr. Veblen's violations of accepted usage that I was moved to look him up in *Who's Who*, and I was astonished to learn ... that he is not only a college graduate but that he is even a doctor of philosophy.

Finally, some, recognizing the satire and irony, suggest that Veblen went to excess. One critic suggests that "the average reader needs a walk in the sun to clear his head of sulphuric acid fumes between every two volumes" (Reynaud 1925 in Simich and Tilman 1985, p. 21). John Cummings (1899, p. 455) in a critical review of TLC in Veblen's own journal, *Journal of Political Economy*, noted:

> If there were less consummate cleverness displayed, one would feel less disposed to criticise. It is the cleverness itself, the sophistry consistently maintained that bears witness to a more or less conscious intent on the part of the author, and itself elicits criticism. The author of the *Theory of The Leisure Class* is clearly a master of sophistical dialectic.

When one reads the critics of Veblen's style one is reminded of the "brilliant" works – *Let Us Now Praise Famous Men* and *Finnegan's Wake* come to mind – that many find unappealing and unreadable.

Situated Style

Symbolic interactionist theory (Fine and Kleinman 1986) and post-modern literary analysis both assume that a text receives meaning from the audience. This meaning involves all facets of the text – "substance" and "style." The whole of interpretation is situated. In analyzing Veblen's *The Theory of the Leisure Class* I argue that the divergent interpretations of the text's style cannot be explained by the text itself, but are social constructions by the readers. In cases – such as Veblen – in which the text may not be translucent, issues of stylistic evaluation are particularly central. Irony and satire depend on a fundamental gap between what is written and what is meant, and is found in certain topical areas more often than others. Veblen's text, dealing as it does with the conflict between class positions and the values associated with them, provides a easy base from which an ironic analysis is possible. In such cases, the objective, denotative reading of a text is not sufficient. The reader *must* contribute to the meaning of the text – to recontextualize it.

As suggested above, some social scientific topics plead for an ironic stance. We have had little in the way of irony aimed at those at the bottom of the social structure. Perhaps their position is so severe that humor at their expense is unworthy, perhaps they are not the audience of the text, and, so, could not be changed, perhaps our political stance places us in sympathy with them and so any attack is "politically incorrect." The upper classes, and bourgeois lifestyles in general, present an inviting target. Thus, Goffman's *Asylums* which deals with the unfortunate mental ill, aims its irony at their keepers (Fine and Martin 1990). Goffman's other work – such as "Symbols of Class Status" (1951) and *The Presentation of Self in Everyday Life* (1959) – targets middle-class life styles (Ditton 1980; Goulder 1970).[11] Mills is at his most ironic in *White Collar* and *The Power Elite*.[12] Even E. Digby Baltzell, surely more sympathetic to those wealthy WASPs he portrays and less a marginal man, cannot resist a few ironic jabs.[13] Those targets with status surpluses are easily hit by indirect attack.

The stylistic analysis of social science texts has only begun, but before it extends too far, we should be wary of perspectives that focus on the text as a discrete object, rather than an interactive nexus. The examination of responses to Veblen reveals the diversity of reactions to a literary text. One cannot say objectively – that *The Theory of the Leisure Class* is well or poorly written, that it is satire or serious; rather, audiences make these decisions from external forces, as well as from the text itself. Even the most scrupulous social scientist is ultimately at the mercy of those who choose to digest the text.

Acknowledgements

I thank Lori Ducharme and Lori Holyfield for their help in the preparation of this article. I appreciate the literate and thoughtful responses of Charles Lemert, Patricia Clough, Andrea Fontana, Rick Tilman and the anonymous reviewers.

Notes

1. As with many classics, out of copyright, numerous editions compete. I cite the Random House Modern Library edition (1934).

2. The phrase "marginal woman" rings wrong. Gender rules prevented women from straddling society, as marginal. Women represented values, while always being outside power. The marginal woman is a harlot.

3. Stephen Tyler suggests that ironic writing is characteristic of modernism, whereas parody is the pomo preference. I have never been comfortable with such sharp decisions, but feel that ironic detachment is characteristic of many who we label post-modern.

4. For a discussion of the links and differences between irony and satire, see Fine and Martin (1990).

5. The most complete biography of Thorstein Veblen is Joseph Dorfman's (1934) encyclopedic *Thorstein Veblen and His America* (also Dorfman 1973). Some critics, including

members of the Veblen family, dispute Dorfman's contention that Veblen could not speak English fluently until matriculating at Carleton, and deny the claim that the Veblens were culturally isolated (Tilman 1992, p. 4). Dorfman's argument underlines Thorstein Veblen's marginality. David Riesman's (1953) *Thorstein Veblen: A Critical Interpretation* assays Veblen's life in a quasi-psychoanalytic mode, emphasizing Veblen's passive aggressiveness, record of failure, and deficiencies in "manly virtues."

6. The sympathy Mills felt for Veblen is unsurprising, as cultural outsiders, academic "failures," and home-grown radicals. When Mills speaks of Veblen by saying "there is no failure in American academic history quite so great as Veblen's," the statement has an autobiographical ring.

7. Goffman, himself, surprisingly does not refer to Veblen either in his Veblenian "Symbols of Class Status," or in *Presentation of Self in Everyday Life*, although he uses the phrase "conspicuous consumption." This is curious since Goffman was a student at Chicago at the time that David Riesman, then Assistant Professor, published his book on Veblen.

8. TLC is cited forty-four times in the 1990 issue of the Social Sciences Citation Index. Not all American sociologists give TLC so much weight. Parsons (Simich and Tilman 1983), for instance, felt that there was little of value in Veblen's theories.

9. Pace Goffman (1974, pp. 14–16).

10. Mencken later, in a 1934 letter, admitted that his conscience bothered him about the article, "it was planned as buffoonery, but it turned out to be rather serious" (Dorfman 1973, p. 21). Mencken should have been sympathetic to Veblen's castigation of the idle rich.

11. Goffman (1951, p. 299) writes: "children may share, in part, the status of their parents not only because the connection is demonstrable but also because the number of children a woman can bear is strictly limited. The family name may then be used as a symbol of status on the assumption that it can be acquired legally only by birth or by the marriage of a woman to a son of the house."

12. Mills (1956, p. 93) writes, for instance, after describing various extravagances of the wealthy: "Here are all the expensive commodities, to which the rich seem appendages. Here is the money talking in its husky, silk voice of cash, power, celebrity."

13. Baltzell (1958, p. 396) concludes his *Philadelphia Gentlemen* by noting: "In this young nation, an ancient mansion of democracy, the stairway of social prestige has been 'forever echoing with the wooden shoe going up, and the polished boot descending.' When the echoes die, however, the ancient mansion will have been deserted."

References

Anon. 1919. Review of *The Higher Learning in America*. *North American Review* 209 (March 19): 417–420.
Anon. 1920. "Mr. Veblen's Economics." *Springfield Republican* (March 18): 539.
Anon. 1929. "Veblen, Noted Economist, Dead." *San Francisco Chronicle* (August 6): 5.
Atkinson, Paul. 1992. *Understanding Ethnographic Texts*. Newbury Park: Sage.
Baltzell, E. Digby. 1958. *Philadelphia Gentlemen*. New York: Free Press.
Becker, Howard S. 1986. *Writing for Social Scientists*. Chicago: University of Chicago Press.
Bell, Daniel. 1963. "Veblen and the New Class." *American Scholar* 32: 616–638.

Bierstedt, Robert. 1960. "Sociology and Humane Learning." *American Sociological Review* 25: 1–4.
Brown, Richard H. 1983. "Dialectical Irony, Literary Form and Sociological Theory." *Poetics Today* 4: 543–564.
Brown, Richard H. 1987. *Society as Text: Essays on Rhetoric, Reason and Reality*. Chicago: University of Chicago Press.
Broyard, Anatole. 1973. "Lumps for the Leisure Class." *New York Times* (April 23): 31.
Burke, Kenneth. 1950. *A Rhetoric of Motives*. New York: Prentice-Hall.
Burns, Thomas. 1953. "Friends, Enemies, and the Polite Fiction." *American Sociological Review* 18: 654–662.
Chase, Stuart. 1934. "Foreword." Pp. xi–xv in *The Theory of the Leisure Class*, by Thorstein Veblen. New York: Modern Library.
Clark, John Maurice. 1929. "Thorstein Bundy [sic] Veblen." *American Economic Review* 19: 742–745.
Clough, Patricia. 1992. *The End(s) of Ethnography*. Newbury Park: Sage.
Conroy, Stephen S. 1968. "Thorstein Veblen's Prose." *American Quarterly* 20: 605–615.
Cummings, John. 1899. Review of *The Theory of the Leisure Class*. *Journal of Political Economy* 7: 425–455.
Daniels, Winthrop M. 1905. Review of *The Theory of Business Enterprise*. *Atlantic Monthly* 95: 557–559.
Diggins, John P. 1978. *The Bard of Savagery*. New York: Seabury Press.
Ditton, Jason, ed. 1980. *The View From Goffman*. New York: St. Martin's.
Dorfman, Joseph. 1934. *Thorstein Veblen and His America*. New York: Viking Press.
Dorfman, Joseph. 1973. "New Light on Veblen." In *Essays, Reviews and Reports* by Thorstein Veblen. Clifton, NJ: Augustus M. Kelley.
Dos Passos, John. 1946/1930. *The Big Money*. Boston: Houghton Mifflin.
Edgell, Stephen and Rick Tilman. 1989. "The Intellectual Antecedents of Thorstein Veblen: A Reappraisal." *Journal of Economic Issues* 23: 1003–1026.
Fine, Gary Alan and Sherryl Kleinman. 1986. "Interpreting the Sociological Classics: Can There Be a "True" Meaning of Mead?" *Symbolic Interaction* 9: 129–146.
Fine, Gary Alan and Daniel D. Martin. 1990. "A Partisan View: Sarcasm, Satire, and Irony as Voices in Erving Goffman's *Asylums*." *Journal of Contemporary Ethnography* 19: 89–115.
Fontana, Andrea, Rick Tilman and Linda Roe. 1992. "Theoretical Parallels in George H. Mead and Thorstein Veblen." *Social Science Journal* 29: 241–257.
Galbraith, John Kenneth. 1973. "Thorstein Veblen and *The Theory of the Leisure Class*." In *The Theory of the Leisure Class* by Thorstein Veblen. Boston: Houghton Mifflin.
Goffman, Erving. 1951. "Symbols of Class Status." *British Journal of Sociology* 2: 294–304.
Goffman, Erving. 1961. *Asylums*. Garden City, NY: Anchor.
Goffman, Erving. 1959. *The Presentation of Self in Everyday Life*. Garden City, NY: Doubleday.
Goffman, Erving. 1974. *Frame Analysis*. Cambridge: Harvard University Press.
Goulder, Alvin. 1970. *The Coming Crisis of Western Sociology*. New York: Avon.
Green, Bryan. 1988. *Literary Methods and Sociological Theory*. Chicago: University of Chicago Press.
Hazlitt, Henry. 1929. "Thorstein Veblen." *Century* 119: 8–10.
Hobson, John A. 1929. "Thorstein Veblen." *Sociological Review* 21: 342–345.
Howells, William Dean. 1899. "An Opportunity for American Fiction." *Literature* n.s. 16 (April 28): 361–362.

Johnson, Edgar. 1941. "Veblen: Man From Mars." *New Republic* 105 (July 28): 121–123.
Kazin, Alfred. 1942. "Veblen as Artist." *Sewanee Review* 50: 174–183.
Lewis, J. David and Richard L. Smith. 1980. *American Sociology and Pragmatism: Mead, Chicago Sociology, and Symbolic Interaction.* Chicago: University of Chicago Press.
Lewis, Sinclair. 1920. *Main Street.* New York: Harcourt, Brace.
Machalek, Richard. 1979. "Thorstein Veblen, Louis Schneider and the Ironic Imagination." *Social Science Quarterly* 60: 460–464.
Marcus, George and James Clifford. 1986. *Writing Culture.* Berkeley: University of California Press.
Mathews, Brander. 1919. "Mr. Veblen's Gas Attack on Our Colleges and Universities." *New York Times* (March 16): 125, 127–128.
McCloskey, Donald N. 1990. *If You're So Smart: The Narrative of Economic Experience.* Chicago: University of Chicago Press.
Mencken, H.L. 1919. *Prejudices, First Series.* New York: Knopf.
Miller, Perry. 1954. "Introduction." In *American Thought: Civil War to World War One.* New York: Harcourt.
Mills, C. Wright. 1953. "Introduction to the Mentor Edition." In *The Theory of the Leisure Class* by Thorstein Veblen. New York: Mentor.
Mills, C. Wright. 1956. *The Power Elite.* New York: Oxford University Press.
Mills, C. Wright. 1959. *The Sociological Imagination.* New York: Oxford University Press.
Mitchell, Wesley C. 1929. "Thorstein Veblen, 1857–1929." *Economic Journal* 39: 646–650.
Mumford, Lewis. 1931. "Thorstein Veblen." *New Republic* 67(August 5): 314–316.
Mumford, Lewis. 1935. "A Stick of Dynamite Wrapped Like Candy." *Saturday Review of Literature* 11 (January 12): 417, 421–422.
Overington, Michael. 1981. "A Rhetorical Appreciation of a Sociological Classic: Durkheim's *Suicide.*" *Canadian Journal of Sociology* 6: 447–461.
Pfohl, Stephen. 1992. *Death at the Parasite Cafe.* New York: St. Martin's.
Riesman, David. 1953. *Thorstein Veblen: A Critical Interpretation.* New York: Scribner's Sons.
Reynaud, H. Review of *Les théories économiques et sociales de Thorstein Veblen* by William Jaffe. *Economic Journal* 35: 446–448.
Richardson, Laurel and Ernest Lockridge. 1991. "The Sea Monster: An Ethnographic Drama." *Symbolic Interaction* 14: 335–340.
Rosenberg, Bernard. 1955. "Thorstein Veblen: Portrait of the Intellectual as a Marginal Man." *Social Problems* 2: 181–187.
Rosenberg, Bernard. 1963. *Thorstein Veblen.* New York: Thomas Y. Crowell.
Rucker, Darnell. 1969. *The Chicago Pragmatists.* Minneapolis: University of Minnesota Press.
Ryan, Barbara E. 1982. "Thorstein Veblen: A New Perspective." *Mid-American Review of Sociology* 2: 29–47.
Schneider, Joseph. 1991. "Trouble With Textual Authority in Sociology." *Symbolic Interaction* 14: 295–319.
Schneider, Louis. 1975a. "Ironic Perspective and Sociological Thought." In *The Idea of Social Structure*, edited by Lewis A. Coser. New York: Harcourt Brace Jovanovich.
Schneider, Louis. 1975b. *The Sociological Way of Looking at the World.* New York: McGraw-Hill.
Schwartz, Jonathan Matthew. 1990. "Tracking Down the Nordic Spirit in Thorstein Veblen's Sociology." *Acta Sociologica* 33: 115–124.
Simich, Jerry L. and Rick Tilman. 1985. *Thorstein Veblen: A Reference Guide.* Boston: G.K. Hall.

Tam, William L. 1984. "The Symbolic Interactionist 'I' as Ironist: Toward Alternative Worlds." *Symbolic Interaction* 7: 175–189.

Tilman, Rick. 1992. *Thorstein Veblen and His Critics, 1891–1963*. Princeton: Princeton University Press.

Toulouse, Teresa. 1985. "Veblen and His Reader: Rhetoric and Intention in *The Theory of the Leisure Class*." *Centennial Review* 29: 249–267.

Tyler, Stephen A. 1987. *The Unspeakable: Discourse, Dialague, and Rhetoric in the Postmodern World*. Madison: University of Wisconsin Press.

Van Maanen, John. 1988. *Tales of the Field*. Chicago: University of Chicago Press.

Veblen, Thorstein. 1934/1899. *The Theory of the Leisure Class*. New York: Modern Library.

Walton, John. 1979. "The Sociological Imagination of Thorstein Veblen." *Social Science Quarterly* 60: 432–438.

Ward, Lester F. 1900. Review of *The Theory of the Leisure Class*. *American Journal of Sociology* 5: 829–837.

Wells, B.W. 1899. Review of *The Theory of the Leisure Class*. *Sewanee Review* 7: 369–374.

Wells, D. Collin. 1899. Review of *The Theory of the Leisure Class*. *Yale Review* 8: 213–218.

White, Hayden. 1987. *The Content of the Form*. Baltimore: Johns Hopkins University Press.

27

Introduction to *Middletown: A Study in Modern American Culture*

Robert S. Lynd and Helen Merrell Lynd

The aim of the field investigation recorded in the following pages was to study synchronously the interwoven trends that are the life of a small American city. A typical city, strictly speaking, does not exist, but the city studied was selected as having many features common to a wide group of communities. Neither field work nor report has attempted to prove any thesis; the aim has been, rather, to record observed phenomena, thereby raising questions and suggesting possible fresh points of departure in the study of group behavior.

The stubborn resistance which "social problems" offer may be related in part to the common habit of piecemeal attack upon them. Students of human behavior are recognizing increasingly, however, that "the different aspects of civilization interlock and intertwine, presenting – in a word – a continuum."[1] The present investigation, accordingly, set out to approach the life of the people in the city selected as a unit complex of interwoven trends of behavior.

Two major difficulties present themselves at the outset of such a total-situation study of a contemporary civilization: *first*, the danger, never wholly avoidable, of not being completely objective in viewing a culture in which one's life is imbedded, of falling into the old error of starting out, despite oneself, with emotionally weighted presuppositions and consequently failing ever to get outside the field one set out so bravely to objectify and study; and, *second*, granted that no one phase of living can be adequately understood without a study of all the rest, how is one to set about the investigation of anything as multifarious as the gross-total thing that is Schenectady, Akron, Dallas, or Keokuk?

A clew to the securing both of the maximum objectivity and of some kind of orderly procedure in such a maze may be found in the approach of the cultural anthropologist. There are, after all, despite infinite variations in detail, not so many major kinds of things that people do. Whether in an Arunta village

Source: Robert S. Lynd and Helen Merrell Lynd, *Middletown: A Study in Modern American Culture* (New York: Harcourt, Brace & World, 1929).

in Central Australia or in our own seemingly intricate institutional life of corporations, dividends, coming-out parties, prayer meetings, freshmen, and Congress, human behavior appears to consist in variations upon a few major lines of activity: getting the material necessities for food, clothing, shelter; mating; initiating the young into the group habits of thought and behavior; and so on. This study, accordingly, proceeds on the assumption that all the things people do in this American city may be viewed as falling under one or another of the following six main-trunk activities:

Getting a living.
Making a home.
Training the young.
Using leisure in various forms of play, art, and so on.
Engaging in religious practices.
Engaging in community activities.

This particular grouping of activities is used with no idea of its exclusive merit but simply as a methodological expedient.[2] By viewing the institutional life of this city as simply the form which human behavior under this particular set of conditions has come to assume, it is hoped that the study has been lifted on to an impersonal plane that will save it from the otherwise inevitable charge at certain points of seeming to deal in personalities or to criticize the local life. For, after all, having one's accustomed ways scrutinized by an outsider may be disconcerting at best. Like Aunt Polly in Donald Ogden Stewart's *Aunt Polly's Story of Mankind*, many of us are prone to view the process of evolution as the ascent from the nasty amoeba to Uncle Frederick triumphantly standing at the top of the long and tortuous course in a Prince Albert with one gloved hand resting upon the First National Bank and the other upon the Presbyterian church. To many of us who might be quite willing to discuss dispassionately the quaintly patterned ways of behaving that make up the customs of uncivilized peoples, it is distinctly distasteful to turn with equal candor to the life of which we are a local ornament. Yet nothing can be more enlightening than to gain precisely that degree of objectivity and perspective with which we view "savage" peoples. Even though such a venture in contemporary anthropology may be somewhat hazy and distorted, the very trial may yield a degree of detachment indispensable for clearer vision.

It is a commonplace to say that an outstanding characteristic of the ways of living of any people at any given time is that they are in process of change, the rate and direction of change depending upon proximity to strong centers of cultural diffusion, the appearance of new inventions, migration, and other factors which alter the process. We are coming to realize, moreover, that we today are probably living in one of the eras of greatest rapidity of change in the history of human institutions. New tools and techniques are being developed with stupendous celerity, while in the wake of these technical developments increasingly frequent and strong culture waves sweep over us from without, drenching us with the material and non-material habits of other centers. In the face of such a situation it would be a serious defect to omit this developmental aspect from a study of contemporary life.[3]

The further device has, therefore, been adopted in this investigation, wherever the data available permitted, of using as a groundwork for the observed behavior of today the reconstructed and in so far as possible equally objectively observed behavior of 1890. The year 1890 was selected as the base-line against which to project the culture of today because of greater availability of data from that year onward and because not until the end of 1886 was natural gas struck in the city under study and the boom begun which was to transform the placid county-seat during the nineties into a manufacturing city. This narrow strip of thirty-five years comprehends for hundreds of American communities the industrial revolution that has descended upon villages and towns, metamorphosing them into a thing of Rotary Clubs, central trade councils, and Chamber of Commerce contests for "bigger and better" cities.

Had time and available funds permitted, it would obviously have been desirable to plot more points in observed trends between 1890 and the present. But the procedure followed enables us to view the city of today against the background of the city of a generation ago out of which it has grown and by which it is conditioned, to see the present situation as the most recent point in a moving trend.

To sum up, then: the following pages aim to present a dynamic, functional[4] study of the contemporary life of this specific American community in the light of the trends of changing behavior observable in it during the last thirty-five years.

So comprehensive an approach necessarily involves the use of data of widely varying degrees of overtness and statistical adequacy. Some types of behavior in the city studied lie open to observation over the whole period since 1890; in other cases only slight wisps of evidence are obtainable. Much folk talk, for instance – the rattle of conversation that goes on around a luncheon table, on street corners, or while waiting for a basket ball game to commence – is here presented, not because it offers scientifically valid evidence, but because it affords indispensable insights into the moods and habits of thought of the city. In the attempt to combine these various types of data into a total-situation picture, omissions and faults in proportion will appear. But two saving facts must be borne in mind: no effort is being made to prove any thesis with the data presented, and every effort is made throughout to warn where the ice is thin.

Since the field work aimed at the integration of diverse regions of behavior rather than at the discovery of new material in a narrowly isolated field, it will be easy to say of much of the specific data presented, "We knew that already." Underlying the study, however, is the assumption that by the presentation of these phenomena, familiar though some of them may be, in their inter-relatedness in a specific situation, fresh light may be thrown upon old problems and so give rise to further investigation.

The City Selected

The city will be called Middletown. A community as small as thirty-odd thousand affords at best about as much privacy as Irvin Cobb's celebrated goldfish enjoyed, and it has not seemed desirable to increase this high visibility in the discussion of local conditions by singling out the city by its actual name.

There were no ulterior motives in the selection of Middletown. It was not consulted about the project, and no organization or person in the city contributed anything to the cost of the investigation. Two main considerations guided the selection of a location for the study: (1) that the city be as representative as possible of contemporary American life, and (2) that it be at the same time compact and homogeneous enough to be manageable in such a total-situation study.

In line with the first of these considerations the following characteristics were considered desirable: (1) A temperate climate.[5] (2) A sufficiently rapid rate of growth to insure the presence of a plentiful assortment of the growing pains accompanying contemporary social change. (3) An industrial culture with modern high-speed machine production. (4) The absence of dominance of the city's industry by a single plant, i.e., not a one-industry town. (5) A substantial local artistic life to balance its industrial activity; also a largely self-contained artistic life, e.g., not that of a college town in which the college imports the community's music and lectures. (6) The absence of any outstanding peculiarities or acute local problems which would mark it off from the mid-channel sort of American community. After further consideration, a seventh qualification was added: the city should, if possible, be in that common-denominator of America, the Middle West.[6] Two streams of colonists met in this middle region of the United States: "The Yankees from New England and New York came by way of the Erie Canal into northern Ohio. . . . The southern stream of colonists, having passed through the Cumberland Gap into Kentucky, went down the Ohio River."[7] With the first of these came also a foreign-born stock, largely from Great Britain, Ireland, and Germany.

In order to secure a certain amount of compactness and homogeneity, the following characteristics were sought: (1) A city of the 25,000–50,000 group. This meant selection from among a possible 143 cities, according to the 1920 Census. A city of this size, it was felt, would be large enough to have put on long trousers and to take itself seriously, and yet small enough to be studied from many aspects as a unit. (2) A city as nearly self-contained as is possible in this era of rapid and pervasive inter-communication, not a satellite city. (3) A small Negro and foreign-born population. In a difficult study of this sort it seemed a distinct advantage to deal with a homogeneous, native-born population, even though such a population is unusual in an American industrial city. Thus, instead of being forced to handle two major variables, racial change and cultural change, the field staff was enabled to concentrate upon cultural change. The study thus became one of the interplay of a relatively constant native American stock and its changing environment. As such it may possibly afford a base-line group against which the process of social change in the type of community that includes different racial backgrounds may be studied by future workers.

Middletown, selected in the light of these considerations from a number of cities visited, is in the East-North-Central group of states that includes Ohio, Indiana, Illinois, Michigan, and Wisconsin. The mean annual temperature is 50.8° F. The highest recorded temperature is 102° F. in July and the lowest –24° F. in January, but such extremes are ordinarily of short duration, and weather below zero is extremely rare. The city was in 1885 an agricultural county-seat of some 6,000 persons; by 1890 the population had passed 11,000, and in 1920 it had topped 35,000. This growth has accompanied its evolution into an aggressive industrial city. There is no single controlling industrial plant; three plants on June 30, 1923, had between 1,000 and 2,000 on the payroll, and eight others from 300 to 1,000; glass, metal, and automobile industries predominate. The census of 1890 showed slightly less than 5 per cent. of the city's population to be foreign-born[8] and less than 4 per cent. Negroes, as against approximately 2 per cent. foreign-born in 1920 and nearly 6 per cent. Negroes; over 81 per cent. of the population in 1890 and nearly 85 per cent. in 1920 was native white of native parentage. In the main this study confines itself to the white population and more particularly to the native whites, who compose 92 per cent. of the total population.

The nearest big city, a city under 350,000, is sixty miles away, nearly a two-hour trip by train, with no through hardsurface road for motoring at the time the study was made. It is a long half-day train trip to a larger city. Since the eighties Middletown has been known all over the state as "a good music town." Its civic and women's clubs are strong, and practically none of the local artistic life was in 1924 in any way traceable to the, until then, weak normal school on the outskirts.

The very middle-of-the-road quality about Middletown would have made it unsuitable for a different kind of investigation. Had this study sought simply to observe the institution of the home under extreme urban conditions, the recreational life of industrial workers, or any one of dozens of other special "social problems," a far more spectacular city than Middletown might readily have been found. But although it was its characteristic rather than its exceptional features which led to the selection of Middletown, no claim is made that it is a "typical" city, and the findings of this study can, naturally, only with caution be applied to other cities or to American life in general.

The Historical Setting

Two major experiences in Middletown antedate 1890, the date taken as the horizon of this study: the pioneer life of the earlier part of the century, and the gas boom of the end of the eighties which ushered in Middletown's industrial revolution. Both are within the memory of men who still walk the streets of the city.

The first permanent settlement in this county occurred in 1820, and county government was granted in 1827. The memory of one of the oldest citizens, a leading local physician throughout the nineties, reaches back to the eighteen-forties. Within the lifetime of this one man local transportation has changed from virtually the "hoof and sail" methods in use in the time of Homer; grain has ceased to be cut in the state by thrusting the sickle into the ripened grain as in the days of Ruth and threshing done by trampling out by horses on the threshing floor or by flail; getting a living and making a home have ceased to be conducted under one roof by the majority of the American people; education has ceased to be a luxury accessible only to the few; in his own field of medicine the X-ray, anaesthetics, asepsis, and other developments have tended to make the healing art a science; electricity, the telephone, telegraph, and radio have appeared; and the theory of evolution has shaken the theological cosmogony that had reigned for centuries.[9]

This local physician whose lifetime so nearly spans that of Middletown, the tenth of a family of eleven, was named, with the characteristic political fervor of the time, General William Harrison K –.[10] The log farmhouse of his father was ceiled inside without plaster, the walls bare save for three prized pictures of Washington, Jackson, and Clay. All meals were cooked before the great kitchen fireplace, corn pones and "cracklings" and bread being baked in the glare of a large curved reflector set before the open fire. At night the rooms were lighted by the open fire and by tallow dips; there was great excitement later when the first candle mold appeared in the neighborhood. Standard time was unknown; few owned watches, and sun time was good enough during the day, while early and late candle lighting served to distinguish the periods at night. When the fire went out on the family hearth the boy ran to a neighbor's to bring home fire between two boards; it was not until later that the first box of little sticks tipped with sulphur startled the neighborhood.

The homely wisdom of pioneer life prescribed that children be passed through a hole in the trunk of a hollow tree to cure "short growth"; hogs must be slaughtered at certain times of the moon or the bacon would shrink; babies must be weaned at certain times of the zodiac; the "madstone," "a small bone from the heart of a deer," was a valuable antidote for hydrophobia or snake-bite; certain persons "blew the fire out of a burn," arrested hemorrhage or cured erysipelas by uttering mysterious charms; a pan of water under the bed was used to check night sweats; bleeding was the sovereign remedy for fits, loss of consciousness, fever, and many other ills; and "in eruptive fevers, especially measles, where the eruption was delayed, a tea made of sheep's dung, popularly known as 'nanny tea,' was a household remedy."

Social calls were unknown, but all-day visits were the rule, a family going to visit either by horseback, the children seated behind the grown-ups, or in chairs set in the springless farm wagon. Social intercourse performed a highly important service; there were no daily papers in the region, and much news traveled by word of mouth. Nobody came to the home around mealtime who was not urged to take his place at the table – preachers being particularly welcome. Men would talk together for hours on the Providential portent of the great Comet of 1843, or of the time ten years before when the "stars fell." Men and women went miles and spent days in order to hear champions argue disputed political or religious points. People "got religion" and were "awakened to sin" at camp meetings under the vivid exhortation of baptizing preachers. The "Word" wove its influence closely about everyday acts.

Forty years later, in 1885, before gas and wealth spouted from the earth, bringing in their wake a helter-skelter industrial development, Middletown, a placid county-seat of some 6,000 souls, still retained some of the simplicity of this early pioneer life. "On the streets . . . on fair days lawyers, doctors, the officials of the county courts, and the merchants walked about in their shirt sleeves. The house painter went along with his ladder on his shoulder. In the stillness there could be heard the hammers of the carpenters building a new house for the son of a merchant who had married the daughter of a blacksmith."[11] Men in their prime who had grown up under pioneer conditions now controlled the affairs of Middletown. They were occupied with such momentous matters as offering "$200 for the scalp or body of any person in the city caught setting fire to the property of another," or passing regulations in response to complaints about neighborhood cows running through the streets and destroying lawns, or with badly bungling the job of laying the first town sewer.

The thin edge of industry was beginning to appear, though few people thought of the place then as anything but an agricultural county-seat: a bagging plant employed from a hundred to a hundred and fifty people, making bags from the flax grown in the surrounding countryside; a clay tile yard employed some fifteen; a roller-skate "company" in an old barn up an alley, perhaps eight; a feather-duster "factory," five or six; a small foundry, half a dozen; and a planing mill and two flour mills, a few more. It was still for Middletown the age of wood, and a new industry meant a hardwood skewer shop, a barrel-heading shop, or a small wooden pump works.

Such modest ventures in manufacturing as the community exhibited were the tentative responses of small local capital to the thing that was happening to the whole Middle West. The Federal Census reveals a steady movement westward of the center of manufacturing; in 1880 it was still in Pennsylvania, but by 1890 it had pushed on until it was eight and one-half miles west of Canton, Ohio. Dry-goods clerks were beginning to spend their evenings perfecting little models of washing-machines, mechanical hair-clippers, can-openers, various powerdriven devices. The proprietor of a small Middletown restaurant who led a town band in the evening and "was always neglecting business to tinker around at things" saw a crude cash-register in a saloon in a neighboring city while on a trip there with his band, conceived the idea of a self-adding register, and set to work in the hope of making his fortune. The annual total of patents registered in Washington, which had remained practically constant during the decade of the seventies, jumped in 1890 to roughly double the 1880 figure.

In the state in which Middletown is located, the number of wage-earners increased from 69,508 in 1880 to 110,590 in 1890, and by 1900 was to total 155,956. The capital invested in manufacturing plants in the state doubled between 1880 and 1890 and was almost to double again by 1900.

The quiet life of the town drowsing about its courthouse square with its wooden pump – and iron dippers, punctually renewed every Fourth of July – was beginning to stir to these outside influences. A small Business and Manufacturing Association was formed about 1886 for "the promotion of any and all undertakings calculated to advance the interests, improvements and general welfare of the city."

And then in the fall of '86 came gas.

In 1876 a company boring for coal twelve miles north of the town had plugged up the hole and abandoned the project after boring 600 feet: all they "struck" was a foul odour and a roaring sound deep in the bowels of the earth, and rumor had it that they had invaded "his Satanic Majesty's domain." Nine years later, when natural gas was discovered at other points in the Middle West, the incident of the plugged-up hole north of town was recalled. In October, 1886, there was great local excitement over the plans "to bore for gas or oil or both." In November we read, "The persons employed to bore for oil have this morning 'struck' gas, and everybody is on the way to see for themselves." The roar of the escaping gas is said to have been audible for two miles and the flame when it was "lit up" could be seen in Middletown a dozen miles away.

The boom was on.

The laying of a pipe line to bring the gas into the county-seat began immediately, and new wells were sunk. By the following April a local well was producing 5,000,000 feet daily. New wells multiplied on every hand. In January, 1891, the local paper exclaimed, "We have a new gas well which really does eclipse all others in the [gas] belt. Daily output is nearly 15,000,000 feet, and they worked over thirty hours trying to anchor the flow." No wonder the little town went wild !

Meanwhile, from the spring of '87 on through '91 and '92 the "boomers" were arriving:

> "Four vestibule, one dining-room and one baggage special train from Buffalo with 134 of its capitalists came in last night to see for themselves what gas can do and are much pleased. . . . Taken in carriages to all the factories and sites. . . . Grand manufacturing exhibition at the Rink, and a beautiful display of four open street cars." "A trainload of 1,200 from Cincinnati." "Quite a number of New York City capitalists and newspaper men came in from the East last night; three and one-half pages

of the – Hotel register were covered with their signatures." "American Association for the Advancement of Science visits the city and witnesses the wonders of natural gas; 300 scientists and men of affairs in the party."

Real estate was being turned over with dizzy rapidity. In 1888 a man tried to buy an eight-acre chunk of farm land on the outskirts of town but, shying at the price of $1,600, took only a sixty-day option. Before the sixty-day option expired the eight acres changed hands five times, the final price being $3,200.

Nothing short of the sky seemed an adequate limit to the citizens of Middletown. A contemporary parody runs –

"Tell me not in mournful numbers
That the town is full of gloom,
For the man's a crank who slumbers
In these bursting days of boom."

Optimists predicted a population of 50,000 in five years and even the pessimists allowed only ten years. The general sentiment was that the gas supply was inexhaustible. Some called it "The City of External Gas." The Introduction to the Middletown City Directory announced confidently, "Every forty acres will supply a gas well, and 576 wells can be drilled within . . . [the] corporate limits and suburbs." "The mathematical deduction would be," chanted a "boom book," "that the continuance of this supply would be, at least, one hundred times as long as at Pittsburgh, which would be 700 years." Great flambeaus burned recklessly day and night in the streets and at the wells. When the pipe lines were laid, consumers were charged by the fixture rather than by any system of exact measurement. It was cheaper to leave the gas on and to throw open doors and windows than to expend a match in relighting it.[12]

With the boomers came new industries lured by free fuel and free building sites. The earlier Business and Manufacturing Association awakened to new life in February, 1887, as the "Board of Trade," and concerted efforts were made to "sell the town" to industrial capital. Glass came first. Next were the iron mills – a bridge company, a nail works. A diary for 1888–9 buzzes with rumors of the coming of these new plants:

"Report that another glass factory is coming immediately." "Work progressing on the pulp mill and rubber factory." "A nail works wants to come here from –." "Considerable talk about a Palace Stock Car Factory." "A boot and shoe factory is coming; building commenced this afternoon."

By the summer of 1890 the local paper speaks of the thriving little "gasopolis" with pardonable pride:

"Two and one-half years ago when natural gas was first discovered [Middletown] was a county-seat of 7,000 inhabitants. . . . It has grown since that time to a busy manufacturing city of 12,000. . . . Over forty factories have located here during that time. . . . There has been $1,500,000 invested in Middletown manufacturing enterprises employing 3,000 men. . . . Over thirty gas wells have been drilled in and around the city, every one of which is good. . . ."[13]

The first boom of '87 and '88 was the spontaneous, unorganized rush to a new El Dorado. When the earlier boom was renewed in '91 it was engineered by the Eastern land syndicate and carried forward by the local boosters' association, the Citizens' Enterprise Company, organized in August, 1891. The last-named organization raised a $200,000 fund to lure new industries with free sites and capital.[14]

Several years later, as abruptly as it had come, the gas departed. By the turn of the century or shortly thereafter, natural gas for manufacturing purposes was virtually a thing of the past in Middletown. But the city had grown by then to 20,000, and, while industry after industry moved away, a substantial foundation had been laid for the industrial life of the city of today.

And yet it is easy, peering back at the little city of 1890 through the spectacles of the present, to see in the dust and clatter of its new industrialism a developed industrial culture that did not exist. Crop reports were still printed on the front page of the leading paper in 1890, and the paper carried a daily column of agricultural suggestions headed "Farm and Garden." Local retail stores were overgrown country stores swaggering under such names as "The Temple of Economy" and "The Beehive Bazaar." The young Goliath, Industry, was still a neighborly sort of fellow. The agricultural predominance in the county-seat was gone, but the diffusion of the new industrial type of culture was as yet largely superficial – only skin-deep.

This, then, suggests the background of the city which is the subject of this field investigation.

Notes

1. A. A. Goldenweiser, *Early Civilization* (New York; Knopf, 1919), p. 31.

2. W. H. R. Rivers in his *Social Organization* (New York; Knopf, 1924) sets forth a sixfold classification of social groupings identical with the six types of activity employed here. Clark Wissler presents a ninefold culture scheme, in *Man and Culture* (New York; Crowell, 1923), Chs. V and XII. Frederick J. Teggart criticizes Wissler's use of a universal culture pattern, but himself implicitly recognizes certain activities as common to men everywhere, in *Theory of History* (New Haven; Yale University Press, 1925), p. 171.

3. Cf. Rivers' closing sentence in *The History of Melanesian Society* (Cambridge; Cambridge University Press, 1914): "It is because we can only hope to understand the present of any society through a knowledge of its past that such historical studies as those

of which this book is an example are necessary steps toward the construction of a science of social psychology."

4. "Function" as here used denotes a major life-activity or something contributing to the performance of a major life-activity.

5. The relation of climate to the elaborate equilibrium of activities that make up living is suggested by the late James J. Hill's motto to which he is said absolutely to have adhered: "You can't interest me in any proposition in any place where it doesn't snow," or, more picturesquely, "No man on whom the snow does not fall ever amounts to a tinker's dam." (Quoted in J. Russell Smith's *North America*, New York; Harcourt, Brace and Company, 1925, p. 8.)

6. "The 'Middle West,' the prairie country, has been the center of active social philanthropies and political progressivism. It has formed the solid element in our diffuse national life and heterogeneous populations. . . . It has been the middle in every sense of the word and in every movement. Like every mean, it has held things together and given unity and stability of movement," John Dewey, "The American Intellectual Frontier" (*The New Republic*, May 10, 1922).

7. Smith, *op. cit.*, pp. 296–7.

8. The census of 1890 shows 62.1 per cent. of the foreign-born in the state to have been of German-speaking stock and 24.5 British and Irish. Belgian glass workers were prominent among Middletown's foreign-born population in the nineties.

9. That this stupendous change within a single lifetime was a phenomenon of the whole country, not merely of a backwoods section, is indicated by the recollections of a man born a year earlier than this physician, under the shadow of Boston State House: Henry Adams writes, "on looking back, fifty years later, at his own figure in 1854, and pondering on the needs of the twentieth century, he wondered whether, on the whole, the boy of 1854 stood nearer to the thought of 1904, or to that of the year 1 . . . – in essentials like religion, ethics, philosophy; in history, literature, art; in the concepts of all science, except perhaps mathematics, the America boy of 1854 stood nearer the year 1 than to the year 1900." *Education of Henry Adams* (Boston; Houghton Mifflin, 1918), p. 53.

10. The boy grew up not in the county in which Middletown is situated but in a nearby county. His boyhood environment described here was not that of the rude pioneer villages of the state but of the open country; but the facts that life in the diminutive Middletown of 1840 did not differ markedly in fundamentals from that of the open country around it and that some people in Middletown today grew up under open country conditions not unlike those described are the reasons for the inclusion of this material here.

11. From Sherwood Anderson's description of the even tenor of life in these Middletowns of the '80's in his *Poor White*.

12. "For the past six months" (the latter half of 1887), according to the State Geologist, "there has been an average waste of about 100,000,000 cubic feet of gas per day in [this state]. This is worth $10,000. . . . The volume of gas wasted in the last six months is . . . worth $1,500,000." (*Sixteenth Annual Report of the [State] Department of Geology and Natural History*: 1888, p. 202.)

The value of the natural gas produced (not including that wasted) in the state in 1886 was $300,000; it doubled in '87 and again in '88; by 1890 it was two and one-third million dollars, in '95 passed five million, and in 1900 reached its high point of seven and one-quarter millions.

13. These figures should all be deflated a little, for among the "over forty factories" were many that were operating on a "shoe-string" or less, and plant after plant failed to weather the first year. The air was full of new inventions, and these infant industries plunged courageously into manufacturing anything and everything for a frequently, as yet, vague market. Thus one local industry manufactured a wooden clothes washing-machine, a fire-kindler proclaimed "surely one of the grandest inventions of the age," and a patent can-opener.

14. Bidding was keen for new industries among cities in the gas belt. In return for specific aid from local capital, the new company would frequently pledge itself to grow at a desirable rate, e.g., a Brass and Novelty Company from Rochester, N. Y., contracted "to employ fifty men the first six months, one hundred at the end of the first year, and 150 at the end of the second year."